Medical Factors and Psychological Disorders

A Handbook for Psychologists

Medical Factors and Psychological Disorders

A Handbook for Psychologists

Edited by
Randall L. Morrison
and
Alan S. Bellack
Medical College of Pennsylvania at EPPI
Philadelphia, Pennsylvania

Plenum Press • New York and London

Library of Congress Cataloging in Publication Data

Medical factors and psychological disorders.

Includes bibliographies and index.
1. Psychological manifestations of general diseases—Handbooks, manuals, etc. 2.
Mental illness—Physiological aspects—Handbooks, manuals, etc. I. Morrison, Randall
L. II. Bellack, Alan S. [DNLM: 1. Mental Disorders—therapy. 2. Psychology, Clinical.
WM 105 M4884]
RC455.4.B5M425   1987   616.89   87-7903
ISBN 0-306-42425-8

© 1987 Plenum Press, New York
A Division of Plenum Publishing Corporation
233 Spring Street, New York, N.Y. 10013

Printed in the United States of America

To
Brenda and Randall, Jr.
Jack and Yetta Bellack

Contributors

FRANK ANDRASIK Pain Therapy Centers, Greenville General Hospital System, 100 Mallard Street, Greenville, South Carolina

MICHAEL A. ANDRYKOWSKI Department of Behavioral Science, University of Kentucky, College of Medicine, Lexington, Kentucky

STEVEN BASKIN New England Center for Headache, 40 East Putnam Avenue, Cos Cob, Connecticut

ALAN S. BELLACK Department of Psychiatry, The Medical College of Pennsylvania at EPPI, Philadelphia, Pennsylvania

JEFFREY M. BRANDSMA Department of Psychiatry and Health Behavior, Medical College of Georgia, School of Medicine, Augusta, Georgia

JOSEPH E. CZEKALA Private practice, 85 Shorham Avenue, Miller Place, New York

C. J. DAVIS Department of Psychology, Louisiana State University, Baton Rouge, Louisiana

BARBARA J. DORIAN Department of Psychiatry, Toronto General Hospital, 101 College Street, Toronto, Ontario, Canada

M. ELIZABETH FRANCIS Department of Psychology, University of Pittsburgh, Clinical Psychology Center, Pittsburgh, Pennsylvania

JERRY M. FRIEDMAN Private practice, Box 456, Stony Brook, New York

PERRY C. GOLDSTEIN Department of Rehabilitation Psychology, University of Miami, Jackson Medical Center, Miami, Florida

ANDREA M. HEGEDUS Department of Psychiatry, Western Psychiatric Institute and Clinic, Pittsburgh, Pennsylvania

DOUGLAS P. HOBSON   Department of Psychiatry and Health Behavior, Medical College of Georgia, School of Medicine, Augusta, Georgia

KEVIN T. LARKIN   Department of Psychology, West Virginia University, Morgantown, West Virginia

DOUGLAS F. LEVINSON   The Medical College of Pennsylvania at EPPI, Philadelphia, Pennsylvania

STEPHEN B. MANUCK   Department of Psychology, University of Pittsburgh, Clinical Psychology Center, Pittsburgh, Pennsylvania

RANDALL L. MORRISON   Department of Psychiatry, The Medical College of Pennsylvania at EPPI, Philadelphia, Pennsylvania

EDMOND H. PI   Department of Psychiatry, University of Southern California, School of Medicine, Los Angeles, California

JOANNA M. POLEFRONE   Department of Psychology, University of Pittsburgh, Clinical Psychology Center, Pittsburgh, Pennsylvania

WILLIAM H. REDD   Memorial Sloan-Kettering Cancer Center, 1275 York Avenue, New York, New York

LAURIE RUGGIERO   Department of Psychology, Louisiana State University, Baton Rouge, Louisiana

GEORGE M. SIMPSON   Department of Psychiatry, The Medical College of Pennsylvania at EPPI, Philadelphia, Pennsylvania

RALPH E. TARTER   Department of Psychiatry, Western Psychiatric Institute and Clinic, Pittsburgh, Pennsylvania

C. BARR TAYLOR   Department of Psychiatry, Stanford University Medical Center, Stanford, California

MICHAEL E. THASE   Department of Psychiatry, Western Psychiatric Institute and Clinic, University of Pittsburgh, School of Medicine, Pittsburgh, Pennsylvania

DONALD A. WILLIAMSON   Department of Psychology, Louisiana State University, Baton Rouge, Louisiana

STEVEN ZLUTNICK   San Francisco Institute of Behavioral Medicine and Therapy, Garden Sullivan Hospital, 2750 Geary Boulevard, San Francisco, and the University of San Francisco, San Francisco, California

Preface

Throughout the last decade, the field of clinical psychology has expanded dramatically. Clinical psychologists are involved in the treatment and research of a wider range of problems and disorders than they have ever been before. Evidence has been rapidly accumulating regarding the role of psychological variables and stress in the etiology and maintenance of a range of medical and psychiatric disorders. New models of psychotherapy have been developed and refined, and the specific efficacy of psychotherapeutic interventions for an increasing number of disorders (or subtypes of disorders) has been documented.

However, concurrent with research that demonstrates the impact of psychosomatic factors in various disorders and the efficacy of psychological or psychosocial interventions, dramatic progress has been made with regard to the investigation of biological factors that may mediate certain disorders. That physical factors may underlie many instances of psychiatric illness has been repeatedly demonstrated. Also, the efficacy of somatic treatments for different disorders, or for subtypes of disorders, has been reported with increasing methodological rigor.

Clearly, a number of psychologists have been involved in recent developments regarding the biology of different illnesses, especially those whose expertise is in neuropsychological or cognitive information-processing assessment techniques. However, there remains a burgeoning collection of information regarding medical factors and psychological disorders to which most clinical psychologists are all too infrequently exposed. Although most graduate curricula in clinical psychology include courses in physiological psychology and/or the biological bases of behavior, there is seldom ample consideration given to specific clinical implications of psychophysiology, or to the role of specific biological anomalies in particular disorders. Also, as psychologists become more involved in health psychology, there is a need for greater knowledge and sophistication regarding pertinent medical factors.

Specific areas of concern include biological markers, laboratory assays, the role of pharmacotherapy, the side effects of pharmacotherapy, and the interaction of psychological and somatic interventions. The nonmedically trained clinician has had no resource from which to obtain a current picture of relevant medical factors for the specific disorders with which he or she may routinely come in contact. The need for such a resource served as the stimulus for this handbook. Our intention is to provide a basic reference source, in which leaders in the field provide up-to-date reviews of assessment and treatment issues that are pertinent to specific disorders. Each chapter is intended to give an overview of the current knowledge of medical factors, as well as an integration of their significance and meaning for the non-M.D. clinician involved in the practice of nonsomatic therapies. We included as our focus the disorders for which psychologists are most likely to play a significant, and unique, role in treatment. Thus, we did not include a chapter on schizophrenia, as the non-M.D. professional is usually involved in the treatment of schizophrenic patients in a highly structured, ancillary capacity.

A project of this magnitude requires tremendous effort from many persons. We would like to thank our contributors for providing a collection of excellent manuscripts. Our special appreciation goes to Florence Levito, whose secretarial and administrative assistance has been invaluable. Finally, our editor and friend Eliot Werner served a central role in this project, from start to finish.

RANDALL L. MORRISON
ALAN S. BELLACK

Contents

PART II   PSYCHIATRIC DISORDERS

6. Somatoform, Dissociative, and Factitious Disorders 115

JEFFREY M. BRANDSMA AND DOUGLAS P. HOBSON

7. Organic Mental Disorders 141

RALPH E. TARTER AND ANDREA M. HEGEDUS

PART III   NONPSYCHIATRIC DISORDERS

8. Low Back Pain 173

STEVEN ZLUTNICK

9. Behavioral Aspects of Arterial Hypertension and Its Treatment 203

JOANNA M. POLEFRONE, STEPHEN B. MANUCK, KEVIN T. LARKIN AND
M. ELIZABETH FRANCIS

10. Neurological Disorders 231

PERRY C. GOLDSTEIN AND DOUGLAS F. LEVINSON

11. Psychosomatic Medicine **267**

BARBARA J. DORIAN AND C. BARR TAYLOR

I

INTRODUCTION

1

Physical and Psychological Dysfunction

An Integrative Perspective

ALAN S. BELLACK

AND

RANDALL L. MORRISON

INTRODUCTION

Every course on the history of psychology makes at least passing reference to the so-called mind–body problem and the philosophical debate that once raged over the interaction of the body and the soul. Dualism and the pseudoscientific notion that the pineal gland was the meeting point of the two separate entities are now viewed with curiosity and humor. It is unlikely that anyone who has had even a high school psychology course would question the fact that the mind is a biological phenomenon associated with chemical and electrical activity in the brain.

Nevertheless, until recently, clinical psychology has been marked by a form of functional dualism. Despite paying lip service to the biological underpinnings of cognition and behavior, clinical psychologists have given minimal attention to biological factors in their theories or practice. Some disorders, such as cancer and diabetes, have been viewed as strictly physical and, therefore, as being outside the purview of psychologists. Such biologically based exclusions have extended to brain-related disorders, such as epilepsy and organic brain syndrome, as well as to disorders affecting other organ systems. Conversely, psychiatric disorders and problems in daily living, such as depression and anxiety, have been viewed as "psychological," and as being somehow removed from the domain of biological etiology or treatment. Moreover, scant attention has typically been paid to the physical condition of the person undergoing treatment for a psychological ailment (Strickland & Kendall, 1983). This can be a serious error, as research indicates that somewhere between 10% and 42% of psychiatric symptoms may be caused by somatic conditions (Koranyi, 1980). In some respects, our models and techniques of psychotherapy have been no less dualistic in conception than pre-Cartesian theology.

Of course, clinical psychology is not unique in operating according to an *ad hoc* dualistic model. In fact, several of our sister disciplines seemingly have an even nar-

ALAN S. BELLACK AND RANDALL L. MORRISON • Department of Psychiatry, The Medical College of Pennsylvania at EPPI, Philadelphia, PA 19129.

rower prespective. Medicine, in particular, has been guilty of adhering to an even more simplistic view of human functioning. For the most part, medicine has used a mechanistic, reductionistic way of thinking, characterized by the biomedical model (Engel, 1977). This approach regards dysfunction or disease as a result of one or a few etiological factors, typically biological in nature. Treatment is, likewise, seen as a biological process. All too often, psychological and environmental factors are ignored or are viewed simply as impediments to treatment. Failure to take psychological and environmental factors into account in diagnosis and treatment is just as serious an error as failure to consider biological factors. As many as 35% of patients in primary medical care may meet criteria for DSM-III disorders (Kessler, Cleary, & Burke, 1985). It is widely accepted that a large, but unknown, percentage of somatic complaints for which people seek medical treatment results from or is maintained by psychological problems.

A number of factors have contributed to the development of these compartmentalized models. The twentieth century has been marked by an increased emphasis on disciplinary training and specialization. There has been an information explosion that has made it impossible for scientists or practitioners to keep abreast of developments even in related fields, let alone in other disciplines. At the same time, the economics of professionalism has increased competition between disciplines and has increased the pressures for disciplines to assert their own unique contributions and areas of expertise. For example, until recently, panic disorder has been viewed as a psychological phenomenon and has been treated by psychotherapy (including behavior therapy). Recent research suggests that panic may be a consequence of a biochemical reaction that can be treated with antidepressants (Zitrin, Klein, Woerner, & Ross, 1983). This has become a highly controversial issue. The debate often seems more polemical than empirical (Matuzas & Glass, 1983). If they were to recognize a possible biological cause and a pharmacological treatment for panic disorder, clinical psychologists could be excluding themselves from a large clientele. Conversely, psychiatrists have much to gain by uncovering a biological basis for the disorder and by developing an effective pharmacological treatment.

Yet another factor that has influenced perspectives is the social value system that underlies the various disciplines. Psychologists have broadly adopted a humanistic value system which emphasizes individual freedom of self-control (Krasner & Houts, 1984). Most psychotherapies attempt to enhance self-determination and freedom of choice. Conversely, the biomedical model, with its emphasis on biological etiology and treatment, implies diminished individual freedom. Emphasis is placed on the physician as scientist-healer. Treatment gains result from surgery and/or medication, rather than from the behavior of the patient. Many mental health professionals and patients view typical medical treatment as a process of surrendering control to "the doctor" and chemical agents.

We do not mean to imply that either psychologists or physicians distort data for economic or philosophical reasons. Rather, such factors simply influence what they read, whose arguments they respect, and the types of questions they raise. Despite arguments to the contrary, science is not value-free (Howard, 1985). Values and expectations play a role in what research is conducted and in where research is published. Moreover, the sheer magnitude of published material has made it increasingly difficult to be conversant with the literatures of other disciplines, and economic and philosophical factors have made it desirable to question the validity of alternative models of treatment.

The Biopsychosocial Perspective

In some cases, these circumscribed, reductionistic models have proved to be quite adequate. For example, the biomedical model has led to the identification and eradication (or control) of many infectious diseases, such as mumps, scarlet fever, and polio. Similarly, strictly psychological models seem to be applicable to the understanding and treatment of existential dilemmas and many problems in daily living, such as marital conflict and unassertiveness. However, as will be seen in subsequent chapters in this book, most medical and psychological problems are complex and multifaceted. They defy simplistic etiological explanations and treatments. It has become increasingly apparent that these compartmentalized, single-faceted models are not tenable. As a result, both medicine and psychology are undergoing a paradigmatic shift from reductionistic models to systems approaches, in which multiple factors are considered (Engel, 1977; Schwartz, 1982).

This new perspective is best characterized by Engel's biopsychosocial model (1977). Human functioning is explicitly seen as an interaction of biological factors, psychological factors, and social factors. Psychological and physical health are intertwined and have a dynamic impact on one another. At the same time, both are significantly affected by the environment. Some disorders, such as cancer or simple phobias, may be more a function of one system than another. However, all disorders are affected by each of the three factors to some extent. For example, lung cancer may be viewed primarily as a biological disease, but its etiology is clearly associated with behavior (cigarette smoking and diet) and environmental factors (contact with carcinogens). Similarly, the primary treatments (radiation, chemotherapy, and surgery) are overtly biological. But recovery is substantially affected by behavior (coping skills and compliance with treatment) and environmental support (see Andrykowski & Redd, Chapter 12). In a parallel fashion, the etiology and treatment of agoraphobia may be primarily psychological. But both may be exacerbated or confounded by physical factors, such as tachycardia and mitral valve prolapse, which accentuate the proprioceptive aspects of anxiety (Goldstein, Gallager, & Bright, 1986; Norton, Harrison, Hauch, & Rhodes 1985).

Treating Chronic Illness

One of the most significant stimuli for the development of the biopsychosocial perspective has been a gradual shift in the makeup of clinical populations over the last 25 years. Medical practice in the first half of the twentieth century was substantially concerned with the treatment of infectious diseases, such as mumps, rubella, scarlet fever, polio, influenza, and tuberculosis. As indicated above, these diseases, have now been substantially eliminated. At the same time, major advances in other medical and surgical procedures have increased our ability to control many diseases that had previously almost always been fatal, such as cancer, artherosclerosis, and renal disease. Unfortunately, "control" does not mean cure. Consequently, medical practice is now much more involved in the management of chronic illness (Blanchard & Andrasik, 1982; Russo, 1985). But the traditional biomedical, infectious disease model is not well suited to the complex nature of chronic illness. Chronicity is a unique phenomenon that involves a host of issues beyond the specific somatic handicap:

> In an era of chronic care medicine, it is significant to note that a major component of chronicity is psychological.... Chronicity sets the occasion for learning. The consistency of the medical care environment, the duration of the disorder, the need for continued and periodic care, and the presence of often painful and overt symptomatology represent antecedent setting events which will influence the behavior of the patients and potentially the course of care or emission and exacerbation of symptomatology.
>
> Viewed as a psychological problem, chronicity also provides a consistent set of consequences. The predictability of the medical reaction to symptom expression, the altered social environment of the patient, painful treatments, and family interaction patterns each represent strong shaping influences of patient behavior. (Russo, 1985, p. 44)

The applicability of the biopsychosocial model to chronic illness is well illustrated in several of the chapters in Part III of this book. Hypertension is a physiological phenomenon, but it is clearly related to life-style and a variety of maladaptive health habits. The treatment of cancer is very much affected by the patient's ability to cope with the highly unpleasant side effects of chemotherapy and radiation. Chronic pain, including lower pain and headache, is often more dependent on coping styles and the reaction of the environment to pain complaints than on neurological factors. Conversely, many cases of eating disorders and so-called psychosomatic ailments (e.g., ulcers and colitis) now appear to have a greater physiological involvement than has previously been acknowledged by psychological models.

This discussion of chronicity is no less applicable to more "psychological" disorders than to the somatic disorders referred to above. Psychoanalytic theory has been the predominant influence on the mental health professions and on psychotherapeutic practices over the last century. Although many of the specific tenets of psychoanalysis have come under increasing fire since the end of World War II, several key assumptions of the analytic approach have continued to influence even antianalytic models. Most notable in the context of this discussion is the tacit acceptance of the infectious disease model, which is a cornerstone of much of Freud's conceptualization.

Most post-Freudian models of psychopathology and psychotherapy have followed Freud's lead in attempting to identify a narrow set of critical etiological forces in the individual's history. The specific nature of these forces has varied considerably, ranging from early childhood conflicts and fixations in psychoanalysis, to learning and conditioning experiences in behavior therapy, and to existential dilemmas and low self-regard in humanistic theories. Yet, these differences are probably less significant than the common attempt to identify the critical factor(s) accounting for diverse behavior patterns. In a similar fashion, each approach has adopted the analytic assumption that psychological disorders can be eliminated by somehow correcting for the maladaptive experiences that led to the problem. Once again, the specific methods vary considerably. Some, like psychoanalysis, attempt to uncover the early childhood experiences, and others, such as behavior therapy, are essentially ahistorical and focus on current experience. But almost all share the assumption that, like antibiotics, an adequate dose of psychotherapy will permanently "cure" the patient.

It has become painfully apparent in the last 5 to 10 years that this latter assumption generally is not valid. Distress tied to specific, transient environmental stressors, such as grief after the death of a spouse, can often be eliminated without residual consequences. But, few disorders that meet DSM-III criteria fall into this category. Some, like schizophrenia, often cannot even be totally controlled, let alone cured. Schizophrenia is characterized by intermittent episodes of intense symptom exacerbation surrounded by long periods of residual handicap and dysfunction. In many respects, it is a prototype of a chronic illness. Affective disorders provide an example of a different type of chronic pattern. Recent research documents that affective disorders frequently are cyclical. Bipolar disorders, by definition, involve alternating episodes of mania and depression. But even nonbipolar cases of major depression are often marked by episodic occurrence. Anxiety disorders do not appear to be characterized by clear-cut episodes. However, the results of long-term treatment follow-up studies indicate that a disappointingly large proportion of patients experience relapses, a fact suggesting a chronic illness pattern. The specific reasons for a chronic course of illness vary across diagnostic groups and pertain to both the limitations of the available treatments and the nature of the disorders. The issue of relevance here is simply that chronic illness requires a different perspective from that required by acute illness. We must be much more attuned to the possibility of multiple, diverse influences on the development and course of illness, including both psychological *and* biological factors. At the same time, we must be much more receptive to comprehensive, multidisciplinary treatment.

New Directions in Psychology Training

Along with the increased recognition that traditional models cannot adequately account for all aspects of chronic disorder has come recognition that traditional definitions of professional competencies and expertise are no longer viable. There has been an increased emphasis on multidisciplinary research and treatment programs, as well as on revised roles and responsibilities for various health care and mental health professions, including clinical psychology. Nowhere is this more apparent than in the meteoric development of behavioral medicine and health psychology. Although definitions vary, both terms refer to an effort to deal with the complexity of chronic illness (Matarazzo & Carmody, 1983).

Health psychology appears to be the most rapidly developing psychological subspeciality. The number of graduate training programs with specializations in the area has increased dramatically since the early 1980s, and there has been a parallel increase in the number of health psychologists working with physicians in hospitals and medical schools (Thompson & Matarazzo, 1984). One of the most notable features of this new speciality is the breadth of training required. Health psychologists must be conversant with the biological underpinnings of disease and with somatic treatment regimens, as well as with the associated psychological mechanisms and strategies for behavior change. Thus, they must study physiology, anatomy, pharmacology, and disease mechanics as well as more traditional fields in clinical psychology (Matarazzo & Carmody, 1983; Russo, 1985).

Health psychology has had an important influence on training in clinical psychology in general, by increasing exposure to physiology and multifaceted models of human behavior and behavior change. Until recently, most clinical psychology graduate students took no more than one course in physiological psychology, and they often approached even that course reluctantly. It now appears that the pattern has changed substantially. Both students and graduate programs have increasingly recognized the need for more extensive training in the biological correlates of behavior, and increasing attention is being paid to the role of biological factors in psychopathology and treatment. The remainder of this chapter, along with Part II of this book, underscores the importance of this new perspective.

BIOLOGICAL PSYCHIATRY

Most psychologists are well versed in the "psychosocial" aspects of the disorders with which they deal. However, relatively few psychologists have had significant training in the "bio" part of the biopsychosocial model. The purpose of this handbook is to review critical biological factors relating to specific disorders, and to discuss the implications of these factors in the practice of clinical psychology vis-à-vis these specific disorders. Biological factors relating to etiology and onset, as well as to somatic therapies, will be discussed. As will be emphasized frequently throughout the book, knowledge regarding these factors and their implications is becoming increasing important in the practice of clinical psychology. With specific regard to psychiatric disorders, it is becoming increasingly important that all mental health clinicians have sufficient knowledge regarding recent developments within biological psychiatry as a treatment approach. This is not to say that somatic therapies are of more importance than other interventions. Rather, it is in keeping with the notion of comprehensive treatment from a biopsychosocial perspective.

Basic Tenets

Psychiatry has adopted an increasingly biological orientation since the mid-1960s, and particularly since the mid-1970s. Before this period, psychiatry was perhaps the least scientific of the branches of medicine and was concerned with investigation and understanding of "the mind." Recently, its focus has become the brain and the central nervous system, as well as biological factors that may contribute to mental illness. Advances in psychiatric practice have been based on expanding knowledge and research in the neurosciences. Indeed, a considerable segment of the recent findings in neuroscience research has been reported by psychiatry researchers.

The first significant milestone that was reached by the biological psychiatry movement was the introduction of neuroleptic medication for the treatment of psychotic disorders. The impact of the widespread use of these drugs was profound. The introduction essentially ushered in community psychiatry and resulted in a progressive decline in the number of psychiatric inpatients. Perhaps equally important, the successful widespread use of these medications provided further impetus for the search for biological abnormalties relating to psychiatric disturbances. Third, psychiatry thus became not only more biological but more *medical*. Specific drugs were identified as the treatment of choice for specific symptom clusters. Indeed, since their introduction, neuroleptics have remained the treatment of choice for schizophrenia. Further development and refinement of neuroleptic medications proceeded hand-in-hand with improvements in diagnostic practice. Clearly, biological psychiatry and its emphasis on the medical model have played a significant role in the development of the DSM-III and the DSM-III-R (DSM-III Revised, 1986). Investigations of biological factors together with behavioral observation and analysis procedures have led to the current conceptualizations regarding the subtyping of schizophrenic disorders. For example, biological abnormalities have been implicated in the differentiation between positive and negative schizophrenia (Andreasen & Olsen, 1982). Admittedly, schizophrenia is unique among the psychiatric disorders in that it is the disorder in which biological factors have been most clearly implicated with regard to etiology. Also, there is widespread acceptance of pharmacotherapy as the primary treatment for schizophrenia.

Nevertheless, the biological model has been applied to, and consequently has implications for, the treatment of a wide variety of psychiatric disorders. As a basic tenet, biological psychiatry holds that mental illnesses are diseases affecting the brain and the central nervous system (Andreasen, 1984). Although interactive models involving both endogenous and environmental factors have been posited to explain the etiology of such autonomic insult, the greatest emphasis has been on the identification of biological factors. Thus, major areas of research effort have been genetic/heredity studies of mental illnesses, as well as neurochemical investigations of disease markers and/or metabolic change. As will be detailed in subsequent chapters, biological psychiatry has primarily addressed the "major" mental illnesses: the affective disorders, schizophrenia, the anxiety disorders, and the dementias. As a result of biologically oriented investigations, we now know that there can be a strong hereditary predisposition relating to the development of these disorders. Concordance rates for dizygotic twins generally range from 5% to 20% for schizophrenia, the affective disorders, and anxiety (Gershon, Nurnberger, Berrettini, & Golding, 1985; Rainer, 1985; Weiner, 1985). Although clinical observations suggest that the dementias may run in some families, few statistical evaluations of concordance rates have been conducted. Thus, although concordance rates clearly do not indicate total genetic control, some degree of hereditary involvement is suggested.

Another major line of investigation within biological psychiatry has been the identification of the neurological factors and structural changes in the major mental disorders. Progress in this area was ushered in with the modern era of psychopharmacology, beginning in the 1950s and 1960s. As drugs were developed that had obvious effects on the brain and on symptoms of mental illness, psychiatrists began to explore how these drugs actually worked. Research with drugs led to various neurochemical hypotheses of illness. The "dopamine hypothesis" of schizophrenia and the "catecholamine hypothesis" and "serotonin hypothesis" of affective disorder are prominent examples. Theories of this sort have served to guide pharmacological treatment investigations, and progress in the development of biological hypotheses and somatic therapies has proceeded hand-in-hand. In addition to neurochemical assays, other novel assessment and evaluation strategies have been used. Response to the lactate infusion test has been used in the assessment of panic disorder (Carr & Sheehan, 1984; Pitts & McClure, 1967). Investigations of cardiovascular functioning have documented abnormally high and significant rates of mitral-valve prolapse among panic disorder patients, with implications for assessment, diagnosis, and treatment (Hartman, Kramer, Brown,

& Devereux, 1982; Klein, 1980). Cortisol, insulin, and other "challenge" tests have
been investigated as subclassification or subdiagnostic aids in the treatment of depression, and they may predict response to specific pharmacological therapies. Furthermore, increasingly sophisticated assessment strategies have been useful in helping to
identify physical disorders that can mimic psychiatric illnesses (e.g., hypothyroidism).
The identification of such disorders obviously has important implications for evaluation
and treatment.

One can easily see, then, that the ramifications of the recent progress in biological
psychiatry are far-reaching. Together with the biological emphasis connected with psychologists' increasing involvement in the area of behavioral medicine, the increasing attention placed on biological factors in psychiatry further mandates greater medical
sophistication for all psychologists involved in clinical care. The remaining chapters in
Part I of this book focus on information that is essential for that sophistication. Practitioners must keep abreast with the increasing knowledge regarding psychological and
biological factors in illness. In addition, there are practical implications for everyday
clinical practice and for the ongoing development of the field, which we will now
discuss.

IMPLICATIONS FOR CLINICAL PSYCHOLOGY

Treatment Planning for Psychiatric Disorders

Perhaps the most critical factor relating to the recent progress in biological psychiatry is the need to recognize that these advances will not lead to a cure for mental illnesses. Although the progress has led to more effective care and treatment, preventive
cures are clearly another matter. Furthermore, advances in biological psychiatry and
psychopharmacology do not lessen the importance of interpersonal relations in the lives
of patients, or of psychotherapy in the treatment of psychiatric disorders. The treatment
of mental illness must continue to address the interaction between genetic-biological
factors and psychosocial factors. Indeed, recent evidence suggests that psychosocial interventions remain a critical component in *preventing* relapse in schizophrenia, one of
the most disabling and chronic of the psychiatric disorders. Equally noteworthy is its
status as one of the most biologically mediated psychiatric disorders (Andreasen, 1984).
In fact, given the impact of biological factors on schizophrenia and the primary role of
somatic therapies in the treatment of acute episodes of the disorder, schizophrenic patients are not typically among the patients for whom psychologists are the primary care
providers. (Our decision not to include schizophrenia among the topics outlined in this
book was based on the fact that the nonmedical mental-health professional is usually involved with the treatment of schizophrenic patients in a highly structured ancillary capacity. Clearly, it is widely recognized that a relapsed schizophrenic patient must be
seen for appropriate neuroleptization as a primary step in treatment.) Although
schizophrenia is thus not a disorder for which a psychologist will orchestrate treatment,
to ignore psychosocial factors in the treatment of schizophrenia could be devastating
(Bellack, 1984).

In this regard, schizophrenia is one of the few disorders—and perhaps the only disorder—where the segregation of responsibility for treatment is so clear-cut. The discovery that certain forms of depression or anxiety have significant biological correlates does not necessarily mean that they are entirely biologically mediated in nature and therefore unrelated to psychological factors. Rather, it suggests that certain individuals who are particularly sensitized by their biological constitutions may react with unusual symptomatic severity to stress that, in another person not so predisposed, would lead to symptoms of smaller, more manageable intensity.

Psychiatric theory and practice can best be enhanced by an integration of biological and psychological concepts. The broader a clinician's conceptual view of the etiology of psychiatric disturbance, the more comprehensive his or her therapeutic approach will be (Nemiah, 1983). Treatment planning is a critical aspect of the treatment process. If a treatment plan is not adequately conceptualized, the patient is unlikely to receive the best possible care, as clinicians may tend to conduct treatment that is limited in focus (Halleck, 1984). The exclusive use of pharmacotherapy, psychotherapy, behavior therapy, family therapy, or group therapy may not be sufficient. With increasing specialization among mental health care providers, combined therapies administered by several providers is becoming more common. The number of treatments used and their sequencing and duration should be based on a rational system of planning. As part of the treatment-planning process, the therapist must be aware of the available interventions. This awareness requires knowledge of the empirical evidence of the usefulness of various treatments, understanding of their mechanisms of action, skill in their use, and/or availability of appropriate referrals for cases requiring treatment that is beyond the therapist's expertise (Halleck, 1984).

Laboratory evaluations are becoming increasingly important components of the treatment-planning process for many patients. Responsible clinical practice requires that full attention be paid to physical factors and illnesses that may be affecting patients who are being treated for psychiatric disorders. It has been repeatedly documented that physical illness must be ruled out when making a psychiatric diagnosis (Gold, Pottash, Estroff, & Extein, 1984). Equally important is the need to identify physical-biological precipitants or ramifications of psychiatric disorders. In a study of 658 psychiatric patients, Hall, Popkin, Deuval, Faillace, and Stickney (1978) found that 9.1% had medical disorders that had produced psychiatric symptoms. A later study by Hall, Gardner, Popkin, Lecann, and Sticknet (1981) indicated that 46 of 100 patients admitted to a state hospital had a previously unrecognized and undiagnosed physical illness that was specifically related to their psychiatric symptoms and that had either caused their symptoms or substantially exacerbated them. Effective treatment of the physical disorder resulted in significant improvement in the majority of these cases. Koranyi (1979) studied 2,090 psychiatric outpatients who had been seen for initial evaluation; 43% suffered from at least one major physical illness, of which 46% were undiagnosed at the time of referral. Over 7% of the sample had a physical illness that had caused the psychiatric symptoms. Although these studies refer only to physical illnesses that presented as psychiatric disorders and that had caused the psychiatric symptoms to some degree, it is also the case that physical and psychiatric diseases may occur concomitantly but may be otherwise unrelated, or psychiatric illnesses may be mistaken for physical illness (Gold et al., 1984).

These findings and the array of possible interrelationships between "physical" and "psychiatric" illnesses highlights the need for psychologists to be aware of medical and biological factors that may relate to adequate patient care. Unfortunately, until recently, the training of most clinical psychologists has been lacking in this area. There has been a relative dearth of course in biological psychology and/or biological factors relating to psychopathology in the curricula at most graduate training programs in clinical psychology. Even the professional research literature to which psychologists are exposed tend to ignore issues relating to biological factors and/or basic psychopharmacology. Pishkin and Sengel (1982) surveyed articles published between 1972 and 1980 in three leading psychological journals involving over 175,000 inpatients, and they observed that only a small percentage report any information about medication that the patients were taking. Further, even when medication is mentioned, such crucial information as dosage regimen is often not reported. Also, some articles do provide such information but involve research methodologies that contradict fundamental principles of pharmacokinetics. It is not uncommon for studies to have used drug treatment phases that are significantly shorter than the time required for the drugs to have a clinically therapeutic effect (Alford, 1983). The impact of such oversights causes a double problem. First, the validity of conclusions based on such oversights is obviously suspect. Second, those who read these investigations remain further uninformed regarding the effectiveness of pharmacotherapy, psychotherapy, and combined interventions in treating various psychiatric disorders.

Essentially, psychiatric treatment may involve either psychotherapy alone, pharmacological therapy alone, or a combined intervention. The available data indicate that different intervention strategies, and combinations of strategies are differentially effective for different disorders. As examples, current data suggest that the treatment of choice for panic attacks is often pharmacological therapy (Nemiah, 1983), whereas behavioral psychotherapy is the treatment of choice for agoraphobia (Marks, Gray, Cohen, Hill, Mawson, Ramin, & Stern, 1983). A combined intervention involving behavioral psychotherapy and pharmacological therapy is the preferred treatment for agoraphobia with panic attacks (Zitrin, 1983). Data suggest that certain other major psychiatric disorders may respond to either pharmacotherapy or psychotherapy individually. Primary in this category is depression, for which cognitive and/or behavioral psychotherapy, social skills training, and antidepressant medication may be equally effective (Bellack, 1986). However, as the chapter on major affective disorders will detail, different subtypes of depression may be differentially responsive to different interventions. As we noted above, combined psychosocial and pharmacological intervention is the treatment of choice for schizophrenia, with each component of treatment aimed at different symptoms. Pharmacotherapy is effective for the control of the psychotic symptoms of the disorder, and psychosocial intervention can effectively deal with the negative symptoms (Andreasen, 1984) and the social dysfunction that characterize the disorder (Morrison & Bellack, 1984).

The increasing complexity of information and factors that govern treatment planning requires increasing sophistication on the part of all mental health professionals. Treatment dispositions require a command of the empirical findings relating to the diagnosis at hand, in addition to the ability to derive adequate diagnoses. It may be necessary to refer the patient for laboratory assays to validate the decision process (Andreasen, 1984). For nonphysicians, this referral may necessitate greater collaboration with psychiatrists, neurologists, internists, and so on to facilitate laboratory evaluation. The demands inherent in treatment planning have evolved from differentiating gross psychopathology to differentiating between the subtypes of a disorder that may require markedly different interventions. A purpose of each of the remaining chapters in this book is to deal at length with pragmatic considerations relating to issues of this nature for specific disorders.

Behavioral Medicine and Health Psychology

Increased awareness of the psychosocial factors in health and disease has led to increased involvement by psychologists in the treatment of traditional medical disorders. The implications of this greater involvement are twofold, and fairly obvious. First, psychologists involved in treating traditional "medical" disorders require sufficient knowledge regarding those disorders to make appropriate treatment decisions. The psychologist should have a complete understanding of the disorder that he or she is treating—its course, prognosis, and possible complications—as well as the role of behavioral-psychosocial factors in the disorder. This understanding requires mastery of two knowledge bases: traditional medical knowledge about the disorder and recent literature and findings regarding behavioral approaches to its treatment, as well as the expected outcomes of these approaches. Second, psychologists involved in treating "medical" disorders must work closely with a physician. Such a relationship facilitates referrals to the psychologist, as it is physicians who are still most likely to have initial contact with patients with "medical" disorders, be these disorders amenable to behavioral approaches or not. Also, psychologists working in this area require periodic medical consultations for patients, as well as referral sources for physical and laboratory evaluations of patients and somatic therapies, as necessary. Establishing such close professional relationships typically requires considerable effort. It is most important that a psychologist who is attempting to establish himself or herself in clinical practice in behavioral medicine be able to demonstrate considerable expertise to his or her medical collaborators.

Unfortunately, the translation of research findings into practical clinical expertise often breaks down. Clinicians often fail to keep in touch with research findings to the extent that they should. Conversely, the pragmatic implications of research results are often not made sufficiently clear by investigators. Kaplan (1984) listed several rather humorous examples of what can happen as the result of poor communication between clinicians and researchers. One such example involved a psychologist attempting to recruit referrals by proclaiming that diabetes could be cured through stress inoculation training; another referred to an advertisement placed by a psychologist stating that genital herpes could be controlled through psychotherapy.

Clearly, health psychology has made—and will continue to make—a tremendous impact on the role of psychologists. As suggested by Kaplan (1984), appraisal of psychologists' contributions to health care and the treatment of medical disorders "requires an identification of our objectives, the integration of psychological and biomedical research, and the willingness to collaborate" (p. 763). Our hope is that this book will assist psychologists to practice in these areas by providing up-to-date, pragmatic discussions of research findings, as well as implications for clinical practice and collaboration for a variety of specific disorders.

Neuropsychology and Behavioral Psychopharmacology

In addition to clinical psychopathology and behavioral medicine, other areas in which psychologists are becoming increasingly involved with medical-biological factors are neuropsychology and behavioral psychopharmacology. Clinical neuropsychology is primarily concerned with the assessment of the behavioral expression of brain dysfunction (Lezak, 1983). The results of neuropsychological assessments are the most informative and economical measures of the effect of medications on a patient's cognitive and psychomotor performance. Data from successive neuropsychological examinations repeated at regular intervals can provide reliable information about whether a neurological condition is changing, and, if so, in what ways and how rapidly. Repeated testing can also be used to assess the effects of surgical procedures or other medical treatment (e.g., Tarter & Edwards, 1986). Obviously, considerable knowledge of brain and nervous system structure and function is required in order for the clinical neuropsychologist to practice in these areas.

Behavioral psychopharmacology is the study of interactions of drugs and behavior. Often, studies in this area are concerned with changes in the rate of behavioral responding that occur as the result of some change in, or initiation of, a drug regimen. Psychologists have been involved in behavioral pharmacology research based on expertise in the area of the assessment of behavioral responding, including the effects of environmental (nonsomatic) contingencies on response rates. Frequently at issue is the interaction of medication effects with these environmental contingencies. Although much of the research in this area has been based on animal models of behavior, there have been recent clinical investigations relating to behavioral pharmacology. As an example, tobacco and nicotine dose manipulations have been studied in terms of their effects on subsequent cigarette consumption (Henningfield, 1984). Examples of greater relevance to clinical psychopathology involve investigations of the effects of neuroleptic drugs on the learning and performance of the mentally retarded (e.g., Wysocki *et al.*, 1981) or the psychomotor effects of the benzodiazepines (Pomara, Stanley, Block, Guido, Russ, Berchou, Stanley, Greenblatt, Newton, & Gershon, 1984).

Neuropsychological measures have comprised significant portions of the assessment procedures that have been used in behavioral pharmacology studies (e.g., Pomara *et al.*, 1984). The role of psychologists will continue to expand in these areas, requiring increasing sophistication with regard to the principles and the mechanisms of drug action.

SUMMARY

Clinical psychology is becoming increasingly concerned with biological phenomena, as the knowledge base regarding psychiatric disorders indicates that biological factors may play a significant role in the etiology and treatment of a number of these disorders, and as the impact of psychosocial factors on various medical disorders becomes more apparent. This biological emphasis requires increasing sophistication on the part of psychologists with regard to the role of medical and biological factors. It is no longer appropriate for the psychologist to be concerned only with psychological therapies. Rather, he or she must understand diagnoses based on the medical model, biological or laboratory assessment strategies, and the somatic therapies. Furthermore, this understanding must directly impact on the psychologist's clinical practice. That is, the individual must use his or her knowledge regarding biological factors to help determine when to refer patients to a psychiatrist or neurologist or other physician for evaluation or treatment, and also when to accept referrals from medical practitioners. Unfortunately, there are precious few sources that provide psychologists with such clinically relevant information. We hope that the following chapters regarding specific psychiatric disorders and treatment strategies, as well as disorders that fall under the rubric of behavioral medicine, will be helpful to practicing clinicians and students.

REFERENCES

Alford, G. S. (1983). Pharmacotherapy. In M. Hersen, A. E. Kazdin, & A. S. Bellack (Eds.), *The clinical psychology handbook*. New York: Pergamon Press.

American Psychiatric Association. (1986). *Diagnostic and statistical manual of mental disorders* (3rd ed., revised). Washington, DC: Author. (Original work published 1980)

Andreasen, N. C. (1984). *The broken brain*. New York: Harper & Row.

Andreasen, N. C., R. Olsen, S. (1982). Negative vs. positive schizophrenia. *Archives of General Psychiatry, 39*, 789–794.

Bellack, A. S. (Ed.). (1984). *Schizophrenia: Treatment management and rehabilitation*. Orlando, FL: Grune & Stratton.

Bellack, A. S. (1986). Psychotherapy research in depression. In E. E. Beckham & W. R. Lefer (Eds.), *Depression: Treatment, assessment and research*. Homewood, IL: Dorsey Press.

Blanchard, E. B., & Andrasik, F. (1982). Psychological assessment and treatment of headache: Recent developments and emerging issues. *Journal of Consulting and Clinical Psychology, 50*, 859–879.

Carr, D. B., & Sheehan, D. V. (1984). Panic anxiety: A new biological model. *Journal of Clinical Psychiatry, 45*, 323–330.

Engel, G. L. (1977). The need for a new medical model: A challenge for biomedicine. *Science, 196*, 129–136.

Gershon, E. S., Nurnberger, J. I., Jr., Berrettini, W. H., & Goldin, L. R. (1985). Affective disorders: Genetics. In H. I. Kaplan & B. J. Sadock (Eds.), *Comprehensive textbook of psychiatry, IV* (Vol. 1). Baltimore: Williams & Wilkins.

Gold, M. S., Pottash, A. L. C., Estroff, T. W., & Extein, I. (1984). Laboratory evaluation in treatment planning. In T. B. Karasu (Ed.), *The psychiatric therapies*. Washington, DC: American Psychiatric Association.

Goldstein, A. J., Gallager, R., & Bright, P. (1986). Integrating behavior therapy and psychotherapy in the treatment of agoraphobia. *Psychotherapy*.

Hall, R. C. W., Popkin, M. K., Deuval, R. A., Faillace, L. A., & Stickney, S. K. (1978). Physical illness presenting as psychiatric disease. *Archives of General Psychiatry, 35*, 1315–1320.

Hall, R. C. W., Gardner, E. R., Popkin, M. K., Lecann, A. F., & Sticknet, S. K. (1981). Unrecognized physical illness prompting psychiatric admission: A prospective study. *American Journal of Psychology, 138*, 629–635.

Halleck, S. L. (1984). Treatment planning. In J. B. Karasu (Ed.), *The psychiatric therapies*. Washington, DC: American Psychiatric Association.

Hartman, N., Kramer, R., Brown, W. T., & Devereux, R. B. (1982). Panic disorder in patients with mitral valve prolapse. *American Journal of Psychiatry, 139,* 669–670.

Henningfield, J. E., (1984). Behavioral pharmacology of cigarette smoking. In T. Thompson, P. B. Dews, J. E. Barrett (Eds.), *Advances in behavioral pharmacology.* Orlando, FL: Academic Press.

Howard, S. G. (1985). The role of values in the science of psychology. *American Psychologist, 40,* 255–265.

Kaplan, R. M. (1984). The connection between clinical health promotion and health status. *American Psychologist, 39,* 755–765.

Kessler, L. G., Cleary, P. D., & Burke, J. D. (1985). Psychiatric disorders in primary care: Results of a follow-up study. *Archives of General Psychiatry, 42,* 583–587.

Klein, D. F. (1980). Importance of psychiatric diagnosis in prediction of clinical drug effects. *Archives of General Psychiatry, 37,* 63–72.

Koranyi, E. K. (1979). Morbidity and rate of undiagnosed physical illness in a psychiatric clinic population. *Archives of General Psychiatry, 36,* 414–419.

Koranyi, E. K. (1980). Somatic illness in psychiatric patients. *Psychosomatics, 21,* 887–891.

Krasner, L., & Houts, A. C. (1984). A study of the "value" systems of behavioral scientists. *American Psychologist, 39,* 840–850.

Lezak, M. D. (1983). *Neuropsychological assessment* (2nd ed.). New York: Oxford University Press.

Marks, I. M., Gray, S., Cohen, S. D., Hill, R., Mawson, D., Ramin, L., & Stern, R. S. (1983). Imipramine and brief therapist aided exposure in agoraphobics having self-exposure homework: A controlled trial. *Archives of General Psychiatry, 40,* 153–162.

Matarazzo, J. D., & Carmody, T. P. (1983). Health psychology. In M. Hersen, A. E. Kazdin, & A. S. Bellack (Eds.), *The clinical psychology handbook.* New York: Pergamon Press.

Matuzas, W., & Glass, M. (1983). Treatment of agoraphobia and panic attacks. *Archives of General Psychiatry, 40,* 220–222.

Morrison, R. L., & Bellack, A. S. (1984). Social skills training. In A. S. Bellack (Ed.), *Schizophrenia: Treatment, management, and rehabilitation.* New York: Grune & Stratton.

Nemiah, J. C. (1983). Forward. In M. H. Greenhill & A. Granlick (Eds.), *Psychopharmacology and psychotherapy.* New York: Free Press.

Norton, G. R., Harrison, B., Hauch, J., & Rhodes, L. (1985). Characteristics of people with infrequent panic attacks. *Journal of Abnormal Psychology, 94,* 216–221.

Pishkin, V., & Sengel, R. A. (1982). Research in psychopathology, 1972–1980: Unreporting of medication and other relevant demographic data. *The Clinical Psychologist, 35,* 13–14.

Pitts, F. M., & McClure, J. N. (1967). Lactate metabolism in anxiety neurosis. *New England Journal of Medicine, 227,* 1329–1336.

Pomara, N., Stanley, B., Block, R., Guido, J., Russ, D., Berchou, R., Stanley, M., Greenblatt, D. J., Newton, R. E., & Gershon, S. (1984). Adverse effects of single therapeutic doses of diazepam on performance in normal geriatric subjects: Relationship to plasma concentrations. *Psychopharmacology, 84,* 342–346.

Rainer, J. D. (1985). Genetics and psychiatry. In H. I. Kaplan & B. J. Sadock (Eds.), *Comprehensive textbook of psychiatry, IV* (Vol. 1). Baltimore: Williams & Wilkins.

Russo, D. C. (1985). Clinical training in behavioral health psychology. *The Behavior Therapist, 8,* 43–46.

Schwartz, G. E. (1982). Testing the biopsychosocial model: The ultimate challenge facing behavioral medicine? *Journal of Consulting and Clinical Psychology, 50,* 1040–1053.

Strickland, B. R., & Kendall, K. E. (1983). Psychologic symptoms: The importance of assessing health status. *Clinical Psychology Review, 3,* 179–200.

Tarter, R. E., & Edwards, K. (1986). Neuropsychological batteries. In T. Incagnoli, G. Goldstein, & C. Golden (Eds.), *Clinical application of neuropsychological test batteries.* New York: Plenum Press.

Thompson, R. J., & Matarazzo, J. D. (1984). Psychology in United States medical schools: 1983. *American Psychologist, 39,* 988–995.

Weiner, H. (1985). Schizophrenia: Etiology. In H. I. Kaplan & B. J. Sadock (Eds.), *Comprehensive textbook of psychiatry, IV* (Vol. 1). Baltimore: Williams & Wilkins.

Wysocki, T., Fuqua, W., Davis, V., & Breuning, S. E. (1981). Effects of thioridazine (Mellaril) on titrating delayed matching-to-sample performance of mentally retarded adults. *American Journal of Mental Deficiency, 85,* 539–547.

Zitrin, C. M. (1983). Differential treatment of phobias: Use of imipramine for panic attacks. *Journal of Behavior Therapy and Experimental Psychiatry, 14*, 11–18.

Zitrin, C. M., Klein, D. F., Woerner, M. G., & Ross, D. C. (1983). Treatment of phobias. *Archives of General Psychiatry, 40*, 125–138.

2

Issues in Pharmacological Treatment

GEORGE M. SIMPSON

AND

EDMOND H. PI

INTRODUCTION

The history of psychopharmacology is only three and a half decades old, dating back to the discovery of the first neuroleptic (chlorpromazine) in the early 1950s. This discovery may be considered one of the major advances in twentieth-century medicine. Like most advances, the introduction of chlorpromazine led to a period of rapidly expanding use, if not overuse, followed by a more gradual delineation of the specific areas of the drug's usefulness.

There is now abundant evidence of the therapeutic efficacy of a variety of psychoactive drugs: neuroleptics for schizophrenia, antidepressants for many depressive disorders, lithium salts for mania, and anxiolytics for anxiety disorders. There are reasonably specific indications for prescribing psychotropic agents, and these indications are, in general, tied to diagnostic criteria. As an example, a diagnosis in the third edition of the *Diagnostic and Statistical Manual* (American Psychiatric Association, 1980) of major affective disorder not only operationally defines the condition but predicts a good outcome with the use of antidepressants whether there are major "precipitants" or not. Psychopharmacology is moving in the direction of more specific treatment for specific diagnosis or symptom clusters—a step in the direction of the "right" drug for the "right" patient. Careful diagnosis is essential to the prediction of the outcome of the treatment.

The impact of psychopharmacology is illustrated by the progressive decline in the number of psychiatric inpatients since 1956, the first year of the widespread use of neuroleptics. This use made outpatient and community-oriented treatment programs possible for patients who suffer from major psychiatric disorders. Furthermore, psychopharmacology has immensely accelerated progress in biological psychiatry and understanding of the neurosciences, which, in turn, have provided hypotheses regarding the etiology and a possible explanation for certain psychiatric conditions.

This chapter discusses general issues regarding the mechanisms of drug action, pharmacokinetics, pharmacodynamics, the route of administration, dosage schedules, and the

GEORGE M. SIMPSON • Department of Psychiatry, The Medical College of Pennsylvania at EPPI, Philadelphia, PA 19129.   EDMOND H. PI • Department of Psychiatry, University of Southern California, School of Medicine, Los Angeles, CA 90033.

19

common major side effects of the following major classes of psychotropic agents: (1) the neuroleptics, (2) the antidepressants, (3) lithium salts, and (4) the anxiolytics (antianxiety agents). It also briefly mentions the combination of these agents with psychotherapy.

BASIC CONCEPTS

Neurotransmitters

Chemical substances that are released between nerves and that transmit impulses across these nerve terminals (synapses) in the central nervous system (CNS) are called *neurotransmitters*. These chemical substances function as messengers that diffuse from the presynaptic site across the synaptic cleft, to the specific postsynaptic site on the cell membrane referred to as a *receptor*. This series of events causes the neuron to alter its resting electrical charge, and the result is either excitation or inhibition. Such agents are central to the theories of the mode of action of psychotropic agents (Axelrod, 1976). The major relevant neurotransmitters are

1. Catecholamines: norepinephrine (NE), dopamine (DA)
2. Indoleamines: 5-hydroxytryptamine (5HT), also known as serotonin
3. Others: acetylcholine (Ach), gamma-aminobutyric acid (GABA)

Pharmacokinetics

The development of technology for measuring the minute amount of psychotropic agents circulating in the blood led to pharmacokinetic studies that are, in effect, studies of the absorption, distribution, metabolism, and excretion of these agents expressed mathematically. Frequently, these levels are present in the nanogram/milliliter level, that is, levels of one millionth of a gram per milliliter in plasma. Pharmacodynamics is the actual drug effect at the target site including clinical efficacy and adverse effects, that is, the total effect on the organism.

Absorption refers to the process by which a drug is made available for distribution in the body fluids, and it depends on the route of administration. If the administration is oral, the absorption will be affected by acidity, the motility of the gastrointestinal tract, and the solubility of the drug. This absorption can be measured by obtaining levels that show the time of peak plasma concentration and disappearance. A curve can thus be constructed that describes the blood's absorption and elimination of the drug.

In general, psychotropic agents are well absorbed from the gastrointestinal tract. Parenteral administration usually achieves higher plasma levels and availability than oral administration. These statements may not hold for certain drugs; for example, chlordiazepoxide (Librium) is poorly absorbed when given intramuscularly, and oral chlorpromazine (Thorazine) may be poorly absorbed in some subjects.

In order to reach the site of action, psychotropic agents must pass various barriers throughout the body, including the blood–brain barrier. Distribution is affected by the ability of the drug to bind to protein because the plasma protein-bound fraction of a drug does not enter the central nervous system and is inactive until it becomes "free" (often as much as 95% is bound to plasma protein). Therefore, variations in protein binding among individuals are important factors in the distribution of drugs; for example, the elderly have fewer protein-binding sites and therefore require, in general, lower dosages of psychotropic drugs than young, healthy people.

The metabolism or breakdown of psychotropic agents occurs mainly in the liver and involves several enzyme systems. Therefore, any chemical agent that affects enzymatic activity in the liver can alter the rate of metabolism of the psychotropic agent. The breakdown during absorption and passage through the liver—the so-called first-pass effect—can produce major effects on some drugs; for example, up to 80% of the dose may be lost as active and/or inactive metabolites are produced.

The most important route of excretion for psychotropic agents is the kidney. The elimination half-life is the time required for half of the drug to be excreted from the body. Related to this half-life is the concept of the *steady state* (SS), which occurs at roughly five half-lives after starting the drug and is the time when no further concentration or accumulation of the drug takes place; thus, ingestion of the drug is equal to excretion of the drug. Psychotropic agents (e.g., neuroleptics, tricyclic antidepressants, chlordiazepoxide, and diazepam) have long elimination half-lives. If given in multiple (divided) doses, they may cause accumulation of the parent and/or active metabolites over the first week or two; that is, it takes this length of time to reach SS. By the same token, a once-a-day dosage at bedtime can be prescribed after the SS plasma level is achieved, thereby minimizing unwanted effects during the daytime because peak levels take place before or during sleep. In addition, such simplified regimens improve patient compliance. However, psychotropic agents with short elimination half-lives need to be prescribed in multiple (divided) dose regimens to be effective, for example, lorazepam (Ativan) or oxazepam (Serax) for anxiety.

A knowledge of pharmacokinetics enables clinicians to monitor the plasma levels of these agents not only for compliance but also to improve treatment. However, establishing a meaningful relationship between the plasma levels of psychotropic agents and clinical efficacy or side effects is complicated for many reasons (Simpson & Pi, 1981; Simpson & Yadalam, 1985). Nevertheless, it is now possible to measure all psychotropic agents, and such measurements are helpful to the clinician, particularly in dealing with difficult cases, unwanted side effects, the elderly, and so on.

NEUROLEPTICS

The term *neuroleptic* denotes the integrating neurological effects of these drugs in the brain. The term antipsychotic refers to the principle therapeutic action of the drugs. Nevertheless, these two terms are commonly used interchangeably in the literature. The term *major tranquilizer* is an erroneous and obsolete term because it reflects only one specific aspect of the pharmacological properties of the drugs: sedation.

Three decades after the introduction of chlorpromazine (Thorazine), the first effective neuroleptic, these agents had superseded all other biologic treatments for schizophrenic disorders. Since the early 1950s many different chemical classes of neuroleptics have become available for psychiatric practice (Table 1). The primary chemical class is the phenothiazines, to which chlorpromazine belongs.

Neuroleptics were initially used to treat nausea, vomiting, allergies, hyperthermia, anxiety, insomnia, and so on. Chlorpromazine is beneficial in all of these conditions, but its unwanted effects (a better term than *side effects)* and the availability of other drugs

Table 1. Chemical Classification of
Commonly Used Antipsychotics

Phenothiazines

Aliphatic group
   Chlorpromazine (Thorazine)
   Promazine (Sparine)

Piperidine group
   Thioridazine (Mellaril)
   Mesoridazine (Serentil)

Piperazine group
   Fluphenazine (Prolixin)
   Long-acting (depot) forms: decanoate/enanthate
   Trifluoperazine (Stelazine)
   Perphenazine (Trilafon)
   Prochlorperazine (Compazine)

Thioxanthenes
   Chlorprothixene (Taractan)
   Thiothixene (Navane)

Butyrophenones
   Haloperidol (Haldol)

Dibenzoxazepines
   Loxapine (Loxitane)

Dihydroindolones
   Molindone (Moban)

Rauwolfia
   Reserpine

that are more effective for treating these conditions (i.e., more efficiently and with less risk) have gradually restricted the use of chlorpromazine to the psychotic disorders. Neuroleptics are the key treatment in schizophrenia and are helpful in acute mania and certain depressive disorders such as psychotic depression (Glassman, Kantor, & Shostake, 1975). They are also helpful in the treatment of psychoses in the elderly, or of psychoses associated with mental retardation or organic mental disorders. The mode of action of neuroleptics is thought to be their blockade of postsynaptic dopaminergic sites with consequent reduction of access of the neurotransmitter dopamine to the receptors in the central nervous system. There are several dopaminergic systems, two of which are of interest to the practicing clinician. The mesolimbic system integrates various portions of the limbic system and projects to the frontal cortex. The nigrostriatal system projects the substantia nigra to the basal ganglia. Blocking the mesolimbic system is thought to be the mechanism for reducing schizophrenic systems, and blocking the nigrostriatal system produces the unwanted extrapyramidal symptoms (Niemegeers & Janssen, 1979).

The pharmacokinetic and pharmacodynamic studies of neuroleptics are complicated by both technical (laboratory problems) and patient-related problems, which include diagnosis, stage of illness, and quantification of psychopathology. The laboratory problems are further complicated by the metabolic complexity of many neuroleptics. For example, more than 150 theoretically possible metabolites of chlorpromazine exist, some of which also possess active antipsychotic effects.

Recent efforts and advances in technology have made it possible to measure the more potent neuroleptics, such as haloperidol and fluphenazine. Haloperidol has a less complicated and simpler metabolic pathway than chlorpromazine and, therefore, has an advantage from the point of view of monitoring progress via plasma determination of the active treatment compounds. Methods exist for measuring all neuroleptics.

The methods involved vary widely. Initially, simple chemical methods using spectrofluorometry were used. Gas chromatography and high-performance liquid chromatography (HPLC) are some of the methods used today that are time-consuming and that involve complicated chemical extractions. Radioimmunoassay antigens, when suitable, can be prepared and may be a very sensitive method. However, there is often cross-reactivity with other drugs, and therefore, in some cases, this method cannot be used, particularly if a patient is on a combination of medications. This problem should not arise, as there is little or no clinical indication or rationale for prescribing two drugs with similar pharmacological activity (Tywer, 1978; Yosselson-Superstein, Sternik, & Liebanzon, 1979). One neuroleptic is adequate to remove psychotic symptoms if an adequate dose is prescribed. However, even if only one neuroleptic is used, there may be cross-reactivity with metabolities, or with an antidepressant if prescribed concurrently.

The development of radioreceptor assays appeared to be a way out of the problem of multiple metabolites or multiple drugs. This assay measures the displacement of a known radioactive dopamine-blocking agent from tissue dopamine receptors. Because the mode of action of antipsychotic agents is thought to be the blockage of dopamine receptors, this method should measure the total antipsychotic activity of the sample. This method works well for some drugs but, unfortunately not for all. So, most laboratories use one or several of the above methods for monitoring neuroleptics.

The route of administration influences the bioavailability and the pharmacokinetics of neuroleptics. Intramuscular administration almost always provides a faster onset of action and greater availability of the drug than oral administration, which may be complicated by erratic absorption in the gastrointestinal tract and metabolism in the gut and the liver before actually reaching the blood for distribution throughout the body (Hansen, Christiansen, Elley, Hansen, Kragh-Sorensen, Larsen, Nestoft, & Hvidberg 1976; Loo, Midha, & McGilvery, 1980). The pharmaceutical preparation, (e.g., tablet vs. liquid) can also alter the rate of absorption (Hollister, Curry, Derr, & Kantor, 1970). Divided doses of neuroleptics are often prescribed in the early course of treatment to permit greater flexibility in dosing. Parenteral administration is preferred over oral administration in acute or emergency situations because it achieves adequate and prompt therapeutic effects. In some cases, particularly in acute, severe psychotic states, rapid neuroleptization has been used (Mason & Granacher, 1976). This regimen involves prescribing high-potency neuroleptics (e.g., haloperidol or prolixin) rapidly and frequently (i.e., hourly) until control of acute psychotic states is attained. The total dose used per day tends to be higher than conventional doses. The real advantage of prescribing such a regimen has been questioned (Donlon, Meadow, Tupin, & Wahba, 1978), but it may be of use in highly excited states.

Neuroleptics are considered long-acting drugs because their elimination half-life ranges from 8 to 35 h (Hollister, 1983). Therefore, a once-daily dose schedule is possible after SS plasma concentration of the neuroleptic is attained, usually from 5 to 7 days after starting neuroleptic treatment. Prescribing a single bedtime or evening dose, or a major portion of the total dosage required in a 24-h period, may help the patient fall asleep and may prevent the experience of unpleasant side effects related to the peak plasma concentrations of neuroleptics. It may, thus, prevent daytime sedation and, because of the simplicity of the regimen, may improve compliance.

Long-acting (depot form) neuroleptics such as fluphenazine decanoate have a useful place in psychiatric practice. The major advantage of such a prescription is that the medication need be given only every 2 to 4 weeks for maintenance treatment of patients with chronic schizophrenia and, in addition, eliminates any problem with compliance or absorption.

Numerous studies have demonstrated wide interindividual differences in SS plasma concentrations of neuroleptics (Cooper, Simpson, & Lee, 1976). This difference results from genetic factors as well as from other environmental factors, including diet, cigarette smoking, and the chronic use of alcohol or barbiturates, that alter the hepatic microsomal enzyme systems. Autoinduction of hepatic enzymes, which results in increased metabolism and a decrease of plasma levels of neuroleptics, may explain why some chronic patients who receive prolonged administration of neuroleptics tend to be refractory to treatment and to have lower plasma levels than newly admitted patients (Cooper, Simpson, Haher, & Bergner, 1975).

Much study has taken place in an attempt to correlate plasma concentrations of neuroleptics and clinical efficacy. So far, such relationships as exist are weak and explain only a small part of the variance. Thus, there is little need for routine measurements in clinical practice. However, there is some evidence that upper and lower therapeutic limits may exist for certain neuroleptics such as chlorpromazine (Rivera-Calimlim, Castaneda, & Lasagna, 1973; Wode-Helgodt, Borg, Fyro, & Sedvall, 1978) and haloperidol (Magliozzi, Hollister, Arnold, & Earle, 1981). Measuring plasma levels of neuroleptics is certainly indicated when things are not going right, that is, when the patient fails to respond to orthodox dosages, or when side effects are present at suborthodox dosages (Simpson & Yadalam, 1985).

Side Effects

Neuroleptics produce a wide range of unwanted effects in many organ systems (Simpson, Pi, & Sramek, 1981, 1984). These range from mild drowsiness to occasional serious and irreversible effects. In general, low-potency neuroleptics (e.g., chlorpromazine and thioridazine) tend to cause more sedation, cardiovascular changes, and anticholinergic effects, such as dry mouth, blurred vision, or constipation. High-potency neuroleptics (e.g., haloperidol and fluphenazine) tend to cause more extrapyramidal side effects, such as muscle spasm, restlessness, and parkinsonian symptoms.

Sedation is the most common unwanted CNS effect of neuroleptics. It is dose-related and usually disappears within 1 to 2 weeks after the start of treatment when "tolerance" to this effect develops. Acute exacerbation of psychoses and catatonialike states associated with neuroleptics have been reported but are rare. Decreasing or discontinuing neuroleptic treatment usually helps, and sometimes prescribing anticholinergic agents relieves these unwanted effects.

The neuroleptic malignant syndrome has gained attention recently. It is characterized by muscular rigidity, hyperthermia, autonomic dysfunction, and altered consciousness (Caroff, 1980). There is disagreement about the boundaries of this disorder because all of these effects can occur on their own (Levinson & Simpson, 1986). However, it is important to know that hyperpyrexia with or without the neuroleptic malignant syndrome, if not diagnosed and treated promptly, may progress to coma and death. Thus, it is imperative that rigidity produced by neuroleptics should be recognized and treated promptly.

Neuroleptics produce parkinsonian and other extrapyramidal side effects. These were observed before the importance of dopamine in idiopathic parkinsonism or the effect of neuroleptics on dopamine was known. Acute dystonia is characterized by dramatic, bizarre muscle spasms mainly involving the eyes, the head, the neck, the tongue, the mouth, the extremities, and the back. This reaction tends to occur in the early stage of neuroleptic treatment (95% in the first 72 h) and to affect the young more than the old, and males more than females. Antiparkinsonian (anticholinergic) agents provide prompt and effective relief of dystonic reactions.

Akathisia is characterized by manifestations of fidgetiness, pacing, intolerance to inactivity, and rocking and shifting of the legs while sitting or standing. The onset usually occurs within the first week but can also occur later in neuroleptic treatment. Akathisia is often mistaken for anxiety or worsening of the psychotic state, which could result in an increase of the neuroleptic dose, which, in turn, could worsen the condition. There is a driven quality about akathisia that the patient may be able to describe. A subjective feeling of anxiety may be present. Antiparkinsonian agents or benzodiazepines may help, and/or a reduction of the neuroleptics may be necessary.

Pseudoparkinsonism consists of akinesia (loss or diminution of spontaneous movements and inability to initiate movement), resting tremor, and rigidity. In more severe cases, excessive salivation, slow monotonous speech, stooped posture, depression like manner, and dysphoria can also be observed. The onset usually occurs within a few weeks of treatment. Diminished swing of the arms while walking or loss of facial expression is the earliest sign. Reducing the dosage of neuroleptics or prescribing anti-Parkinson agents alleviates the symptoms significanty.

Tardive dyskinesia is a serious side effect of neuroleptic treatment that, as its name implies, is a late-onset neurological condition. It consists of spontaneous irregular movements (nonrhythmical) mainly affecting the mouth and tongue, the fingers, and the arms and legs. Thus, constant chewing movement, facial grimacing, pouting, puffing of the lips and cheeks, tongue protrusion, and abnormal movements of the trunk and rocking movements of the pelvis may also be observed (Simpson, Pi, & Sramek, 1982). In most cases, the symptoms of tardive dyskinesia worsen or appear for the first time when the dosage of the neuroleptic is reduced or is discontinued (withdrawal tardive dyskinesia). There has been increased optimism regarding the reversibility of tardive dyskinesia although this reversibility is impossible to predict, (Wegner & Kane, 1982). Considerable efforts have been made to identify predisposing factors. So far, the two most consistent factors are age and sex; that is, elderly females are more at risk of developing tardive dyskinesia than young or elderly males. Other possible predisposing factors include the use of estrogen, anti-Parkinson agents, and alcohol; the duration and dosage of neuroleptic treatment; organicity; the affective disorders; and, perhaps most of all, individual susceptibility.

No consistent and successful treatment for tardive dyskinesia is available at present. Therefore, prevention must be the major aim. Prevention measurements include the following: The indications for neuroleptic treatment should be carefully evaluated. The dose should be titrated to the lowest possible dose and should be prescribed for the shortest period of time. And periodic assessment for signs of tardive dyskinesia should be carried out (Pi & Simpson, in press).

Postural hypotension and electrocardiographic (EKG) changes are the major cardiovascular side effects of the neuroleptics. The low-potency neuroleptics (e.g., chlorpromazine) possess higher risks than high-potency neuroleptics, particularly for the elderly and when given parenterally.

Phenothiazine-induced sudden death has been reported, but no definite etiological factor has been identified. This is a rare event and is complicated by the knowledge that stress results in an increase in sudden death in a "normal" population. So, although it is possible for the neuroleptics to produce sudden death, it is also likely that they reduce sudden death by reducing agitation.

Often, extrapyramidal side effects (particularly dystonic reactions) are confused with allergic reactions by the patients. The common forms of true allergic reactions to the neuroleptics are skin reactions, mostly a very mild form of rash. More serious types of skin reactions include photosensitivity and exfoliative dermatitis. Rarely, suppression of the hematological systems, causing pancytopenia and agranulocytosis has been reported. These conditions require immediate medical attention.

High doses of thioridazine (Mellaril) have been associated with changes in the retina that can cause visual disturbance. For this reason, the upper dose of thioridazine is limited to 800 mg per day. Sexual dysfunctions, including diminished libido, erectile failure, and retrograde ejaculation, have been reported as side effects of the low-potency neuroleptics. Neuroleptics may cause weight gain, amenorrhea, lactation, hirsutism, engorged breasts, and false-positive pregnancy test. Again, low-potency neuroleptics have a greater likelihood of producing such disturbances.

Although controlled studies have not demonstrated a significant danger of dysmorphogenic effects related to the neuroleptics, caution must be exercised when neuroleptics are administered during pregnancy, especially in the first trimester, when rapid development takes place. The risk of the illness versus the risk of the drug needs to be weighed.

In conclusion, the neuroleptics cause a wide range of unwanted effects that when listed as shown, could make one wonder why anyone would use such agents. However, the serious side effects, with the exception of tardive dyskinesia, are rare, and as there is no other proven treatment for schizophrenia, the neuroleptics will continue to be widely used in the foreseeable future.

ANTIDEPRESSANTS

Since the introduction of the monomine oxidase inhibitors (MAOIs) and tricyclic antidepressants (TCAs) in the 1950s, these drugs have been used with great success for a broad range of depressive disorders. Recent advances in psychiatric diagnosis allow clinicians to predict the outcome of pharmacotherapy at a satisfactory level. Thus, diagnosis of major depression, irrespective of the antecedents or the psychosocial stressors, predicts improvement in symptoms in 70% to 80% of patients receiving antidepressants. This improvement in diagnostic technique is important because patients who may appear to have "obvious reasons to be depressed" (e.g., the recent loss of a spouse or recent serious physical illness, heart attack, or development of a cancer) are often deprived of a treatment that would improve their depression (and that therefore would improve their coping) merely because their physicians or therapists feel that they have "an understandable depression." Table 2 lists the commonly available antidepressants, including a few of the "new" ones.

The proposed modes of action of tricyclic antidepressants are (1) inhibiting the reuptake of norepinephrine or serotonin at presynaptic sites; (2) down-regulating the inhibitory feedback of alpha$_2$ presynaptic receptors; and (3) reducing the sensitivity to norepinephrine at brain noradrenergic beta receptors (Sulser, 1983). The mode of action of monoamine oxidase inhibitors is thought to be an inhibition of monoamine oxidase, an enzyme in many sites in the body, including the brain, that breaks down catecholamine neurotransmitters. This action would produce effects compatible with all of the above-proposed modes of action of TCAs.

There are marked interindividual differences (i.e., 5- to 30-fold) in steady-state plasma concentrations of TCAs in similar subjects receiving similar doses (Burrows, Davies, & Scoggio, 1972). The large range of levels is related to individual biological differences in breaking down or metabolizing drugs that are mainly due to genetic and environmental factors. It has been shown that identical twins metabolize antidepressants identically and, therefore, have plasma concentrations of drugs that are equal, whereas ordinary siblings vary in their individual metabolisms and have different steady-state plasma con-

Table 2. Classification of Common Antidepressants

Tricyclics

Tertiary amines
  Amitriptyline (Elavil, Endep)
  Imipramine (Tofranil)
  Trimipramine (Surmontil)
  Doxepin (Sinequan, Adapin)
Secondary amines
  Protriptyline (Vivactil)
  Desipramine (Norpramin, Pertofrane)
  Nortriptyline (Aventyl, Pamelor)

Tetracyclics
  Maprotiline (Ludiomil)[a]

Dibenzoxapine
  Amoxapine (Asendin)[a]

Triazolopyridine
  Trazodone (Desyrel)[a]

Monoamine oxidase inhibitors (MAOIs)
  Phenelzine (Nardil)
  Tranylcypromine (Parnate)
  Isocarboxazide (Marplan)

[a]Newly marketed antidepressants in the United States.

centrations. Arising from these differences is a further refinement in treatment: rather than prescribing an average or routine dose of a drug, one can attempt to titrate to an individual dosage that produces the desired therapeutic blood level. Such practice should reduce the treatment failure rate in depressive patients.

Misdiagnosis of depression, the use of improper medications, subtherapeutic dosages, and insufficient duration of antidepressant treatment are common in clinical practice (Kline, 1974; Kotin, Poser, & Goodwin, 1973). With the exception of nortriptyline (Aventyl, Pamelor), which has a defined therapeutic window, upper limits are defined by side effects rather than by blood levels. Therefore, once an antidepressant is prescribed, the highest possible tolerated dose should be continued for at least four weeks before the patient is considered a treatment failure. It has been reported that the intravenous administration of antidepressants produces higher plasma concentration and more rapid and effective amelioration of depressive symptoms—even with refractory patients—than oral administration (Beckman, 1981; Kielholz, 1981). This is not a widespread treatment at this time. Some of the newer antidepressants, such as Ludiomil and Asendin, are claimed to have faster onset of action than the tricyclic antidepressants, but this claim still remains to be confirmed.

Most of the available antidepressants have a long elimination half-life, ranging from 8 to 198 h (Hollister, 1983), and thus can be prescribed as a single daily dose in the evening or at bedtime. This regimen may also be beneficial to the depressed patient suffering from initial insomnia, particularly if the more sedating antidepressants (e.g., amitriptyline or trazodone) are used. In contrast, some MAOIs have a short elimination half-life and may need to be prescribed in divided doses (Robinson, Nies, & Corcella, 1981).

As it is impossible to predict which depressive patient will respond favorably to a specific antidepressant, physicians usually select an antidepressant based on the side effect profile of each drug. Recently, greater efforts have been made to develop ''ideal'' antidepressants, in an attempt to eliminate some of the troublesome side effects caused by conventional antidepressants; for example, the dietary restrictions of MAOIs are a nuisance because of the potential danger of developing a hypertensive crisis from interaction with tyramine present in food such as aged cheese and red wine. Safer MAOIs are currently under study that could potentially eliminate this danger. Cardiovascular side effects, including orthostatic hypotension or conduction disturbances, can be particularly troublesome for the elderly population and for patients with preexisting heart conditions. Although there exists an array of drugs that vary in their propensity to produce these side effects, the search is for a new drug that will produce few or none, and here, too, there is good reason to be optimistic. Anticholinergic side effects, including blurred vision, dry mouth, constipation, urinary retention, erectile failure, and exacerbation of glaucoma by the increase of intraocular pressure, are produced by many antidepressants. Tricyclic antidepressants possess potential hazardous risks of successful suicide by overdose and may trigger manic episodes in bipolar-affective-disorder patients.

However, the new antidepressants are not free of side effects (Pi & Simpson, 1985). Sedation is a common side effect of all antidepressants, particularly the tricyclic tertiary amines and trazodone. This side effect can be minimized or may even become a therapeutic advantage when a single bedtime dose is prescribed. Maprotiline causes a higher incidence of rashes and may be associated with an increase of seizures. Amoxapine is an analogue of the neuroleptic loxapine and inhibits dopamine reuptake in the central nervous system. Thus, it may produce extrapyramidal side effects and dyskinetic movements.

Trazodone possesses no anticholinergic effects but causes gastric distress, headache, and priapism.

The relationship between plasma concentrations of antidepressants and their clinical efficacy or side effects has been extensively studied since the mid-1960s. The results remain inconclusive with the possible exception of those on nortriptyline, which has a therapeutic range of 50–140 ng/ml. Other antidepressants have a less definitive range of plasma levels. Thus, there remains little indication for routine measurement of plasma concentrations except in unusual situations (Simpson, Pi, & White, 1983).

LITHIUM

The antimanic effect of lithium was first reported in 1949 by the Australian psychiatrist John F. J. Cade. Unfortunately, around that time, lithium had produced a number of severe toxic reactions, including death, when used as a substitute for table salt in the United States. The serious complications were in subjects who suffered from renal and cardiac failure, which were later found to be the only absolute contraindications for lithium.

The first controlled study of the antimanic property of lithium was conducted by Schou, Juel-Nielsen, Stromgren, and Voldby in Denmark (1954). Since then, despite the "dark era" of lithium from the 1950s to 1970s in the United States, the therapeutic and prophylactic effects of lithium salts on major affective disorders have been firmly proved and represent a remarkable advance in psychiatric practice. The mechanism of action of lithium has not been clearly delineated, but several hypotheses have been proposed. Lithium affects most neurotransmitters. Serotonin is increased in the brain. Choline transportation across the blood–brain barrier is decreased, but the conversion to acetylcholine is increased, an effect possibly leading to restoration of balance of neurotransmitters in mania.

Lithium salts are absorbed fairly completely (i.e., 99%) and rapidly. Parenteral administration of lithium salts failed to show significant advantage over oral administration (Rimon & Rakkolainen, 1968). The salt preparation used, whether carbonate, citrate, acetate, chloride, or sulfate, does not alter the therapeutic effect of lithium. The carbonate is the salt most frequently used, and peak levels occur 1–3 h after oral ingestion. Slow-release forms of lithium produce lower serum lithium peaks than regular lithium salt preparations (Cooper & Simpson, 1976). Thus, slow-release lithium reduces the frequency of dosing and diminishes the side effects related to peak plasma concentrations, as well as improves compliance.

The distribution of lithium is also very quick, particularly to the kidneys, but it is distributed more slowly into the muscle, bone, liver, and central nervous system (Schou, 1958). Blood samples for measuring plasma lithium levels should be obtained 8–12 h after the last dose in order to monitor the stable dynamics of lithium distribution.

Lithium is not metabolized in the body. The main organ of elimination for lithium salts is the kidney: 95% is excreted in the urine. The elimination half-life of lithium is about 24 h; chronic administration of lithium could increase the half-life (Goodnick, Fieve, Meltzer, & Dunner, 1981).

Lithium salts are prescribed in divided doses because a single large dose would produce a high peak plasma level, which, in turn, could produce side effects. It usually takes from 5 to 7 days to build up therapeutic levels of plasma lithium concentration, which range from 1.0 to 1.5 mEq/L for the acute manic episode of 0.5 to 1.2 mEq/L for maintenance treatment. The amount of lithium necessary to produce these levels varies considerably between individuals. Techniques have been established that permit rapid determination of the dosage required to produce therapeutic levels and to reach a therapeutic range rapidly (Cooper & Simpson, 1976).

The ability to monitor lithium and to keep the levels within a range that will produce therapeutic effect with a minimal number of side effects is undoubtedly a considerable advance in therapeutics. However, it still remains difficult to predict the response to lithium treatment (Taylor & Abrams, 1981). Furthermore, reliable criteria regarding how long to give maintenance lithium treatment are not yet available.

Parallel to the increased clinical application of lithium treatment come reports of a variety of early and late side effects, including neurotoxicity. Lithium side effects in general correlate with serum lithium levels. Most patients who start taking lithium experience some of the early side effects, including gastrointestinal discomfort, nausea, gastric irritation, sometimes diarrhea, thirstiness, frequent urination, and even muscular weakness and sleepiness. These side effects tend to subside after a few weeks of treatment. The late side effects include hand tremor, which does not respond to anti-Parkinsonian drugs; weight gain; polyuria; polydipsia; diabetes insipidus-like syndrome; and hypothyroidism (Reisberg & Gershon, 1979). Neurotoxicity (i.e, cognitive impairment, somnolence, or even convulsions) is usually associated with serum lithium levels exceeding 1.5 mEq/1, but on occasion, neurotixicity may be associated with therapeutic serum lithium levels. The treatment for lithium neurotoxicity is mainly symptomatic (i.e., stop lithium and push fluids). Infusion of sodium lactate alkalyzes the urine and thus promotes lithium excretion by the kidneys. In severe cases of lithium overdose, dialysis may be indicated.

Recently, kidney biopsy samples obtained from patients who received prolonged lithium treatment showed some morphological changes. This finding raises the question of how long lithium treatment should be continued. Many chronic manic patients relapse without lithium treatment, and the evidence for renal damage is slight but is part of the risk-to-benefit ratio considered before making a decision to continue lithium. In order for side effects to be detected early in treatment and thus for the benefit of the treatment to be increased, patients in long-term treatment require regular visits to a psychiatrist for psychiatric and medical evaluations.

ANTIANXIETY AGENTS

In dealing with the pharmacotherapy for anxiety disorders, a precise delineation of the "right" drug for the "right" disorder cannot be made, with the exception of the use of antidepressants for panic attacks. Antianxiety agents have been found to be very useful in treating anxiety symptoms, but because of the potential of abuse and the widespread publicity given to it, their therapeutic effects are perhaps hampered. However, some data suggest that antianxiety agents are actually underused in a psychiatrically distressed patient population, and it is thought that dependency and abuse may be less a problem than the widespread use of antianxiety agents might suggest (Rickels, 1981). Such a trend of underuse may deprive patients who could benefit from the therapeutic effects of the drugs and may increase the risk of abuse of alcohol, illegal drugs, or over-the-counter medication.

Since the discovery of the first benzodiazepine-chlordiazepoxide (Librium) in the late 1950s, this group of antianxiety agents has supplanted almost all other antianxiety agents for the alleviation of the debilitating effects of anxiety, mainly because of several favorable attributes, such as safety and an insignificant degree of hepatic enzyme induction. These same attributes are, to an extent, responsible for the concern about the overuse, misuse, and abuse of these agents. There is little doubt that some physicians incorrectly prescribe antianxiety agents, but by no means does this probability justify statements that the drugs are "not good," that they are "only crutches," that they interfere with the "treatment," that they lead to abuse, and that "you need to get to the root of your problem"—statements that are invalid and that have no data to support them.

In 1977, two independent research groups discovered specific receptors for benzodiazepines in the brain of various mammals, including humans (Mahler & Okada, 1977; Squires & Braestrup, 1977). Thus, in different areas of the brain, there are sites that selectively attach to the benzodiazepines. Benzodiazepine receptors are chemically linked to receptors for gamma-aminobutyric acid (GABA) and to a chloride channel. Benzodiazepines increase the inhibitory action of GABA (Tallman, Paul, Skolnick, & Gallagher, 1980). The existence of benzodiazepine receptors leads to speculation that people who have constant high levels of anxiety (trait anxiety) may have a deficiency in the receptor-endogenous ligand system. It has been shown that animals with differing numbers of benzodiazepine receptors behave very differently in stressful situations, a finding that, to an extent, supports a possible genetic factor for trait anxiety. This theory and, indeed, the presence of the benzodiazepine receptor suggest that the organism must produce its own benzodiazepine, but as yet no such substance (ligand) has been identified. Benzodiazepines are conveniently divided into two groups according to their pharmacokinetic profile: long-acting and short-acting. Long-acting benzodiazepines have relatively long elimination half-lives and produce active metabolites, whereas short-acting benzodiazepines have relatively short elimination half-lives and produce no active metabolites (Table 3).

Multiple (divided) doses of long-acting benzodiazepines that are metabolized in the liver may cause an accumulation of both the parent and the metabolic compounds over a period of days or even weeks. Therefore, they may not be a good choice for treating the elderly or people with liver disease. Short-acting benzodiazepines may be used in these situations because they do not possess the above properties.

Table 3. Benzodiazepines

Short-acting	Long-acting
Temazepam (Restoril)	Chlordiazepoxide (Librium)
Alprazolam (Xanax)	Diazepam (Valium)
Lorezepam (Ativan)	Prazepam (Centrax)
Triazolam (Halcion)	Chorazepate (Tranxene)
Oxazepam (Serax)	Halazepam (Paxipam)
	Flurazepam (Dalmane)

Short-acting benzodiazepines need to be prescribed in divided doses and usually reach steady state in 2 to 3 days. Long-acting ones can be prescribed as a single bedtime dose after a steady state has been reached, usually 5 to 7 days after treatment is started.

The time of peak concentration of benzodiazepines may be important. For the treatment of acute anxiety, the important factor may be how soon there will be relief. Agents that are more rapidly absorbed (e.g., diazepam) may be the treatment of choice despite their long activity. Intramuscular injection of chlordiazepoxide and diazepam should be avoided because absorption is slow and unreliable. Lorazepam (Ativan) is much more rapidly absorbed. The use of more than one benzodiazepine in a combination treatment should be avoided because there is little or no rationale for the combination, which is more complicated and expensive than the use of a single drug. An exception would be the use of long-acting drugs (e.g., diazepam) in the withdrawal treatment of people addicted to short-acting drugs.

The most common side effect of benzodiazepines is sedation, which usually disappears over a period of days when tolerance develops. Combined with alcohol, these relatively safe agents can become lethal by producing respiratory depression and coma. Withdrawal symptoms are a source of concern in benzodiazepine treatment, particularly if the patient has been on high doses for a long time; these symptoms include lethargy, tremulousness, anxiety, gastrointestinal withdrawal symptoms, insomnia, acute organic brain symdrome, and grand mal seizures. The withdrawal of benzodiazepines must be done gradually in order to prevent the severe withdrawal symptoms that can be caused by an abrupt discontinuation.

Alprazolam is a relatively new benzodiazepine that is chemically and pharmacologically distinct from the earlier ones. It is short-acting and has been shown to possess antipanic properties (Sheenan, 1982) and possible antidepressive properties (Fabre & McLendon, 1980).

DRUG INTERACTIONS

Benzodiazepines potentiate alcohol and barbiturates and increase phenytoin plasma levels. Such interactions may be clinically important whereas others (e.g., antacids decrease absorption of the benzodiazepines) may be of less importance. Cimetidine (Tagamet) increases plasma levels of long-acting but not of short-acting benzodiazepines, and this interaction could be clinically significant.

COMBINING PHARMACOTHERAPY AND PSYCHOTHERAPY

The landmark study by May in 1968 used a stratified random-assignment method of 228 first-admission male and female schizophrenic patients and divided them as follows: 46 with psychotherapy alone, 48 with drug alone, 44 with psychotherapy plus drug, 47 with electroconvulsive therapy (ECT) and 43 with milieu. Outcome criteria included length of stay, relapse rate, nurses' assessment, and assessments by independent raters and independent psychiatrists. ECT was slightly less beneficial than drug treatment, and psychotherapy (dynamic) and milieu therapy were the least effective. Critics of this study pointed out that the psychodynamic therapy was given by residents (they were supervised by experienced analysts). No mention was made of the fact that similar supervision was available for the pharmacotherapy groups. Because, at that time, there were no experts in this area, little teaching or training was available on this subject. Later studies using more structured directive approaches confirmed these findings. For examples, Hogarty, Goldberg, and Schooler (1974) suggested that major role therapy, as delivered by social workers, appeared to have a slight additive effect if combined with appropriate antipsychotic medication. Whereas if given alone, it had, if anything, a negative effect. Goldstein, Rodnick, and Evans (1978) also showed that six sessions of family therapy, combined with an adequate amount of antipsychotic medication, appeared to have a synergistic or additive effect, whereas, if given to similar subjects who received a subtherapeutic amount of antipsychotic agent, the family therapy had no effect and was less effective than adequate amounts of antipsychotic agents alone. Studies by Falloon and colleagues in the United States (Falloon, Boyd, & McGill, 1982) and workers in England (Leff, Kuipers, & Berkowitz, 1983) have also shown a positive effect of behavioral family therapy in high-risk schizophrenic patients who were receiving antipsychotic agents.

Reviews of the literature in the early 1970s revealed no acceptable data regarding the efficacy of psychotherapy for the treatment of depression—a position which has since changed (Liberman & Eckman, 1981; Luborsky, Singer, & Luborsky, 1975).

Since the early 1960s there was abundant evidence for the efficacy of tricyclic antidepressants in the treatment of acute depression, as well as data on the efficacy of antidepressants in maintenance treatment. Several studies, particularly those of Weissman (1978), clearly showed that psychotherapy had no effect on preventing recurrences of depression but that, in subjects who did not relapse, there was improvement in social functioning. In effect, these studies showed that psychotherapy was beneficial for patients who were symptom-free and that drugs had a positive effect, in that the symptom relief produced more readily by drugs rendered the patient more accessible to psychotherapy. There was no evidence that drugs had a negative effect, nor did they make patients less interested in psychotherapy. This finding has been confirmed in other studies (Beck, Hollon, Young, Bedrosian, & Budenz, 1985). With the possible exception of stimulants compared to behavior therapy for weight reduction no negative interactions have been shown for the combined use of drugs and psychotherapy in any DSM-III condition.

CONCLUSION

The introduction of psychotropic drugs to psychiatry in the 1950s represents a remarkable advance in therapeutics. In a few short years, new agents were discovered that, for the first time, showed a significant beneficial effect for all major illnesses. Rigorous clinical trials demonstrated that lithium was beneficial for acute and/or maintenance treatment of mania as well as for prophylaxis.

Tricyclic antidepressants and neuroleptics had similar beneficial effects on unipolar depression and schizophrenia. Newer and more specific antianxiety agents (benzodiazepines) were discovered and were shown to be effective in treating generalized anxiety disorder. The initial concerns about the usefulness of these agents, as well as concern that they might interfere with other treatmeants, have been shown to be spurious. The appropriateness of prescribing psychotropic medication for the above disorders is no longer a scientific issue. The ideological arguments regarding the value of psychotherapy have now given way to questions of how to combine such treatments. From a pharmacological point of view, indications for the appropriate use of these agents are now well delineated. Thus, the neuroleptics are the only proven treatment for florid schizophrenia. Although they reduce or remove psychotic symptoms, this effect does not ensure adequate social functioning or rehabilitation. For such results, combinations of medication with other psychosocial interventions are indicated. To a lesser extent, the same is true for lithium in the treatment of mania. Again, it has to be emphasized that the pharmacological treatment is the primary treatment in these conditions, as it is for severe depressions where antidepressants or ECT are the treatment of choice. An array of best treatments now exists, and the future will bring improvement, including the appropriate best combination treatment for patients suffering from major psychiatric disorders. The combined use of these agents has revealed much about their distribution in the body and the pharmacological effects in different areas of the brain. These findings, in turn, have led to many theories about the etiology of psychiatric disorders and have provided much research. Biological theories concerning the etiology of the major mental illnesses, as well as of panic disorders and anxiety states, now exists, to a large extent, related to these innovative treatments.

Many of these treatments also have potent and sometimes serious side effects, which raise issues of reevaluating the existing agents. This reevaluation has resulted in the production of an array of new pharmacotherapeutic agents that have fewer side effects, at least in the case of the antidepressants. Unfortunately, antipsychotic agents lacking potential serious side effects such as tardive dyskinesia have not yet materialized. Newer and safer antianxiety agents that cause less sedation and that do not interact with alcohol are currently undergoing clinical trials.

Despite the problems with psychotropic agents, when pharmacotherapy is clearly indicated the therapist who fails to prescribe or who intentionally denies the patient such a treatment may be perceived as unethical or even negligent. Thus, it is important for all involved in the treatment of the mentally ill, especially nonphysicians, to be knowledgeable about the indications for various treatment modalities. In general, a DSM-III Axis 1 diagnosis suggests the need for some type of somatic intervention. This diagnosis does not imply that somatic intervention is the only treatment, but therapists should be aware of the indications for specific treatments and the need to make referrals. In a minority of Axis 1 diagnoses (e.g., dysthymic disorder, obsessive-compulsive disorder, or even some types of generalized anxiety disorders), pharmacotherapy may not be the primary therapy, and in many cases, combination therapy is needed. Thus, psychologists should be experienced in obtaining consultation from psychiatrists, and vice versa.

REFERENCES

American Psychiatric Association. (1980). *Diagnostic and statistical manual of mental disorders* (3rd ed.). Washington, DC: Author.

Axelrod, J. (1976). Neurotransmitters. In R. E. Thompson (Ed.), *Progress in psychology*. San Francisco: Freeman.

Beck, A. T., Hollon, S. D., Young, J. E., Bedrosian, R. C., & Budenz, D. (1985). Treatment of depression with cognitive therapy and amitriptyline. *Archives of General Psychiatry, 42,* 142–148.

Beckman, H. (1981). Drug therapy of depression. *Nervenarzt, 52,* 135–146.

Burrows, G. D., Davies, B., & Scoggio, B. A. (1972). Plasma concentration of nortriptyline and clinical response in depressive illness. *Lancet, 2,* 619–623.

Cade, J. F. J. (1949). Lithium salts in the treatment of psychotic excitement. *Medical Journal of Australia, 36,* 349–352.

Caroff, S. N. (1980). The neuroleptic malignant syndrome. *Journal of Clinical Psychiatry, 41,* 79–83.

Cooper, T. B., & Simpson, G. M. (1976). The 24-hour lithium level as a prognostic indicator of dosage requirements: A 2-year follow-up study. *American Journal of Psychiatry, 133,* 440–443.

Cooper, T. B., Simpson, G. M., Haher, E. J., & Bergner, P. E. (1975). Butaperazine pharmakinetics: Effect of dosage regimen in steady state blood levels. *Archives of General Psychiatry, 32,* 903–905.

Cooper, T. B., Simpson, G. M., & Lee J. H. (1976). Thymoleptic and neuroleptic drug plasma levels in psychiatry: Current status. *International Review of Neurobiology, 19,* 297–298.

Donlon, P. T., Meadow, A., Tupin, J. P., & Wahba, M. (1978). High vs standard dosage fluphenazine HCI in acute schizophrenia. *Journal of Clinical Psychology, 39,* 800–804.

Fabre, L. F., & McLendon, D. M. (1980). A double-blind study comparing the efficacy and safety of alprazolam with imipramine and placebo in primary depression. *Current Therapeutic Research, 27,* 474–482.

Falloon, I. R. H., Boyd, J. L., McGill, C. W., Ranzani, J., Moss, H. B., & Gilderman, A. M. (1982). Family management in the prevention of exacerbations of schizophrenia. *New England Journal of Medicine, 306,* 1437–1444.

Glassman, A. H., Kantor, S. J., & Shostake, M. (1975). Depression, delusions and drug response. *American Journal of Psychiatry, 132,* 716–719.

Goldstein, M. J., Rodnick, E. H., & Evans, J. R. (1978). Drug and family therapy in the aftercare of acute schizophrenics. *Archives of General Psychiatry, 35,* 1169–1177.

Goodnick, P. J., Fieve, R. R., Meltzer, H. L., & Dunner, D. L. (1981). Lithium elimination half-life and duration of therapy. *Clinical Pharmacology and Therapeutics, 29,* 47–50.

Hansen, C. E., Christiansen, T. R., Elley, J., Hansen, L. B., Kragh-Sorensen, P., Larsen, N. E., Nestoft, J., & Hvidberg, E. F. (1976). Clinical pharmacokinetic studies of perphenazine. *British Journal of Clinical Pharmacology, 3,* 915–923.

Hogarty, G. E., Goldberg, S. C., & Schooler, N. R. (1974). Drug and sociotherapy in the aftercare of schizophrenic patients: III. Adjustment of non-relapsed patients. *Archives of General Psychiatry 31,* 609–618.

Hollister, L. E. (1983). *Clinical pharmacology of psychotherapeutic drugs.* New York: Churchill Livingstone.

Hollister, L. E., Curry, S. H., Derr, J. E., & Kantor, S. L. (1970). Studies of delayed action medication vs. plasma levels and urinary excretion of four different dosage forms of chlorpromazine. *Clinical Pharmacology and Therapeutics, 11,* 49–59.

Kielholz, P. (1981, June). *Comparison of oral and intravenous treatment in therpay-refractory repression.* Paper presented at Third World Congress of Biological Psychiatry, Stockholm.

Kline, N. S. (1974). Antidepressant medications: A more effective use by general practitioners, family physicians, internists and others. *Journal of American Medical Association, 227,* 1158–1160.

Kotin, J., Post, R. M., & Goodwin, F. K. (1973). Drug treatment of depressed patients referred for hospitalization. *American Journal of Psychiatry, 130,* 1139–1141.

Leff, J. P., Kuipers, L., & Berkowitz, R. (1983). In W. R. McFarlane (Ed.), *Family therapy in schizophrenia.* New York: Guilford Press.

Levinson, D. F., & Simpson, G. M. (1986). Neuroleptic induced EPS with fever: Heterogeneity of the "neuroleptic malignant syndrome." *Archives of General Psychiatry, 43,* 839–848.

Liberman, R. P., & Eckman, T. (1981). Behavior therapy vs. insight-oriented therapy for repeated suicide attemptors. *Archives of General Psychiatry, 38,* 1126–1130.

Loo, J. C. K., Midha, K. K., & McGilveray, I. J. (1980). Pharmacokinetics of chlorpromazine in normal volunteers. *Community Psychopharmacology, 4,* 121–129.

Luborsky, L., Singer, B., & Luborsky, L. (1975). Comparative studies of psychotherapies. *Archives of General Psychiatry, 32,* 995–1008.

Magliozzi, J. R., Hollister, L. E., Arnold, K. V., & Earle, G. M. (1981). Relationship of serum haloperidol levels to clinical response in schizophrenic patients. *American Journal of Psychiatry, 138*, 365–367.

Mason, A. S., & Granacher, R. P. (1976). Basic principles of rapid neuroleptization. *Disease of the Nervous System, 37*, 547–551.

May, R. (1968). *Treatment of schizophrenia: A comparative study of five treatment methods.* New York: Science House.

Mahler, H., & Okada, T. (1977). Benzodiazepine receptors: Demonstration in the central nervous system. *Science, 198*, 849–851.

Niemegeers, C. J. E., & Janssen, P. A. J. (1979). A systematic study of the pharmacological activities of dopamine antagonists. *Life Science, 24*, 2201–2216.

Pi, E. H., & Simpson, G. M. (1985). New antidepressants: A review. *Hospital Formulary, 20*, 580–588.

Pi, E. H., & Simpson, G. M. (in press). Prevention of tardive dyskinesia. In N. S. Shah & A. G. Donald (Eds.), *Neurobehavioral dysfunction induced by psychotherapeutic agents: Neurophysiological, neuropharmacological bases and clinical management,* New York: Plenum Press.

Reisberg, B., & Gershon, S. (1979). Side effects associated with lithium therapy. *Archives of General Psychiatry, 36*, 879–887.

Rickels, K. (1981). Are benzodiazepines overused and abused? *Journal of Clinical Pharmacology, 11*, 71–83.

Rimon, R., & Rakkolainan, V. (1968). Lithium iodide in the treatment of confusional states. *British Journal of Psychology, 114*, 109–110.

Rivera-Calimlim, L., Castaneda, L., & Lasagna, L. (1973). Effects of mode of management on plasma chlorpromazine in psychiatric patients. *Clinical Pharmacology Therapy, 14*, 978–986.

Robinson, D., Nies, A., Corcella, J., & Cooper. T. (1981). Phenelzine plasma levels, pharmacokinetics and clinical outcome. *Psychopharmacology Bulletin, 17*, 154–157.

Schou, M. (1958). Lithium studies 3: Distribution between serum and tissues. *Acta Pharmacologica et Toxicologica, 15*, 115–124.

Schou, M., Juel-Nielsen, N., Stromgren, E., & Voldby, H. (1954). The treatment of manic psychoses by the administration of lithium salts. *Journal of Neurology, 17*, 250–260.

Sheenan, D. V. (1982). Current perspectives in the treatment of panic and phobic disorders. *Drug Therapy, 12*, 173–193.

Simpson, G. M., & Pi, E. H. (1981). Pharmacokinetics of antipsychotic agents. In B. Angrist (Ed.), *Recent advances in neuropsychopharmacology.* New York: Oxford.

Simpson, G. M., & Yadalam K. (1977). Blood levels of neuroleptics: State of the art. *Journal of Clinical Psychiatry, 46*, 22–28.

Simpson, G. M., Pi., E. H., & Sramek, J. J. (1981). Adverse effects of antipsychotic agents. *Drugs, 21*, 138–151.

Simpson, G. M., Pi, E. H., & Sramek, J. J. (1982). Management of tardive dyskinesia: Current update. *Drugs, 23*, 381–383.

Simpson, G. M., Pi, E. H., & White, K. L. (1983). Plasma drug levels and clinical response to antidepressants. *Journal of Clinical Psychiatry, 44*, 27–34.

Simpson, G. M., Pi, E. H., & Sramek, J. J. (1984). Neuroleptics and antipsychotics. In M. N. G. Dukes (Ed.), *Meyler's side effects of drugs* (10th ed.). Amsterdam: Elsevier Science Publishing.

Squires, R. F., & Braestrup, C. (1977). Benzodiazepine receptors in rat brain. *Nature, 266*, 732–734.

Stone, A. (1983). The new paradox of psychiatric malpractice. *New England Journal of Medicine, 311*, 1384–1387.

Sulser, F. (1983). Mode of action of antidepressant drugs. *Journal of Clinical Psychiatry, 44*, 14–20.

Tallman, J. F., Paul, S. M., Skolnick, P., & Gallagher, D. W. (1980). Receptors for the age of anxiety: Pharmacology of the benzodiazepines. *Science, 207*, 274–281.

Taylor, M. A., & Abrams, R. (1981). Prediction of treatment response in mania. *Archives of General Psychiatry, 38*, 800–803.

Tyrer, P. (1978). Drug treatment of psychiatric patients in general practice. *British Medical Journal, 2*, 1008–1010.

Wegner, J. T., & Kane, J. M. (1982). Follow-up study on the reversibility of tardive dyskinesia. *American Journal of Psychiatry, 139*, 308–372.

Weissman, M. M. (1978). Psychotherapy and its relevance to the pharmacotherapy of affective disorders:

From ideology to evidence. In M. A. Lipton, A. Dimascio, & K. F. Killom (Eds.), *Psychopharmacology: A generation of progress.* New York: Raven Press.

Wode-Helgodt, B., Borg, S. Fyro, B., & Sedvall, G. (1978). Clinical effects and drug concentrations in plasma and cerebrospinal fluid in psychotic patients treated with doses of chlorpromazine. *Acta Psychiatrica Scandinavica, 58,* 149–173.

Yosselson-Superstein, S., Sternik, D., & Liebanzon, D. (1979). Prescribing patterns in psychiatric hospitals in Israel. *Acta Psychiatrica Scandinavica 60,* 477–482.

II

PSYCHIATRIC DISORDERS

3

Anxiety Disorders

EDMOND H. PI

AND

GEORGE M. SIMPSON

INTRODUCTION

Today, because of the rapid changes, competition, and constant demands for higher achievement of contemporary society, it is inevitable that people will experience different degrees of anxiety. Indeed, anxiety is now the most prevalent psychological symptom. In general, *anxiety* refers to a subjective state of inner distress, such as apprehension, nervousness, or uneasiness related to threats that are vague, internal, and unknown. In contrast, *fear* refers to a response related to threats that are specific, external, and known real-life circumstances. Both anxiety and fear can be manifested in similar somatic symptoms or in signs of hyperactivity of the autonomic nervous system.

It is known that the relationship between arousal, or anxiety, and performance is an inverted U-shaped function (Duffy, 1957). That is, in order to improve one's performance, a certain level of anxiety is needed; however, when anxiety exceeds the individual's level of tolerance, performance begins to decline. Furthermore, anxiety can be manifested in many different constellations. Therefore, it becomes necessary for us to differentiate between the levels and meanings of types of anxiety: (1) "normal" anxiety as a part of life experience, which is an adaptive reaction for everyone and (2) "pathological" anxiety, which is grossly out of proportion to one's adaptive reaction and is part of anxiety disorders. Nevertheless, *anxiety disorder* should not be used as a synonym for *nervousness, anxiousness, worry,* or *anxiety* that is a symptom rather than a psychopathological syndrome or a clinical diagnostic entity.

This chapter focuses on the issues regarding the anxiety disorders, not "normal" anxiety, which is most likely to be self-limited and to be resolved by changing and modifying environmental factors, or simply by ventilation and/or reassurance. The chapter also presents the recent advances in knowledge about the biology and the pharmacotherapy of anxiety.

EDMOND H. PI • Department of Psychiatry, University of Southern California, School of Medicine, Los Angeles, CA 90033.   **GEORGE M. SIMPSON** • Department of Psychiatry, The Medical College of Pennsylvania at EPPI, Philadelphia, PA 19129.

THE DIAGNOSIS AND CLASSIFICATION OF ANXIETY DISORDERS

As early as 1869, the American physician G. M. Beard described anxiety disorders and introduced the term *neurasthenia*. A few years later, DaCosta (1871) and Freud (1894/1960) coined the terms *irritable heart* and *anxiety neurosis*, respectively. Since then, the disorders have been described under many different names (Cohen & White, 1950). In 1871, Westphal described "agoraphobia," but the disorder failed to generate much interest until recently. In the last few decades, numerous classification systems have been proposed regarding anxiety disorders. Some clinicians differentiate *trait anxiety* from *state anxiety*; the former refers to a persistent and chronic experience of prevailing anxiousness; the latter refers to a brief experience of anxiousness that is situational.

The third edition of the *Diagnostic and Statistical Manual of Mental Disorders* (American Psychiatric Association, 1980) lists three major categories of anxiety disorders: (1) phobic disorders, (2) anxiety states, and (3) posttraumatic stress disorder. These categories comprise a total of 10 specifically defined subtypes of the disorders (Table 1). It is estimated that from 2% to 5% of the general population at one time suffers from some type of anxiety disorder (Cohen & White, 1950; Marks & Lader, 1973). A recent study suggests an even higher incidence of the disorder than had been previously reported (Noyes, Clancy, Hoenk, & Slymen, 1980).

Phobic Disorders

It is estimated that from 19% to 44% of the general population suffers from some phobic symptoms (Goodwin & Guze, 1984a). The prevalence rate of phobic disorders has been reported as ranging from 1.4% to 3.5% of the general population (Uhlenhuth, Balter, Mellinger, Cisin, & Clinthorne, 1983; Weissman, Myers, & Harding, 1978).

The essential feature of phobic disorders is persistent, unreasonable dread or fear of

Table 1. DSM-III Classification of Anxiety Disorders

Phobic disorders
  Agoraphobia with panic attacks
  Agoraphobia without panic attacks
  Social phobia
  Simple phobia

Anxiety states
  Panic disorders
  Generalized anxiety disorder
  Obsessive-compulsive disorder

Posttraumatic stress disorder
  Acute
  Chronic or delayed

Atypical anxiety disorder

Note. From *Diagnostic and Statistical Manual of Mental Disorders* (3rd ed.) (pp. 225–228, 230–235, 239). Copyright 1980 by the American Psychiatric Association. Reprinted by permission.

Table 2. Diagnostic Criteria for Simple Phobia

A. A persistent, irrational fear of and compelling desire to avoid an object or a situation, other than being alone or in public places away from home (agoraphobia), or other than fear of humiliation or embarrassment in certain social situations (social phobia). Phobic objects are often animals, and phobic situations frequently involve heights or closed spaces.

B. Significant distress from the disturbance and recognition by the individual that his or her fear is excessive or unreasonable.

C. Not due to another mental disorder, such as schizophrenia or obsessive-compulsive disorder.

Note. From *Diagnostic and Statistical Manual of Mental Disorders* (3rd ed.) (pp. 229–230). Copyright 1980 by the American Psychiatric Association. Reprinted by permission.

specific objects, activities, or situations that result in compelling desires to avoid the phobic stimulus, as well as avoidance behavior that interferes with usual social functioning. The phobic disorders are subdivided into three types in the DSM-III:

1. *Simple phobia* (Table 2) is an isolated fear of a single object or situation (e.g., a needle, flying in an airplane, animals, and heights) and is the most common phobia in the general population. It affects women more often than men. Age at onset is variable. When a simple phobia occurs in childhood, it usually decreases or even disappears spontaneously. However, if it persists into adulthood, it may not remit without treatment. The amount of impairment produced by simple phobias varies, depending on one's social role and the specific phobia. In noncomplicated cases, people seldom seek psychiatric help.

2. *Social phobia* (Table 3) usually starts in late childhood or early adolescence and affects both sexes equally. It may progress to a chronic condition, with the addition of avoidance behavior (e.g., avoidance of travel or public lavatories). Such patients are subject to periods of self-medication, using alcohol and antianxiety agents.

3. *Agoraphobia* (Table 4) is an excessive fear of being alone, away from home, or in public places. Such patients often do not go out unless accompanied by a relative or a friend. Avoidance behavior commonly increases, and the person may become housebound and socially incapacitated. Women develop the disorder more often than men. Onset is typically in early adulthood; however, it can also be in late adulthood. Depression, anxiety, rituals, minor compulsions, and rumination frequently develop as associated features.

Table 3. Diagnostic Criteria for Social Phobia

A. A persistent, irrational fear of and a compelling desire to avoid a situation in which the individual is exposed to possible scrutiny by others, as well as fears that he or she may act in a way that will be humiliating or embarrassing.

B. Significant distress because of the disturbance and recognition by the individual that his or her fear is excessive or unreasonable.

C. Not due to another mental disorder, such as major depression or avoidant personality disorder.

Note. From *Diagnostic and Statistical Manual of Mental Disorders* (3rd ed.) (p. 228). Copyright 1980 by the American Psychiatric Association. Reprinted by permission.

Table 4. Diagnostic Criteria for Agoraphobia

A. The individual has marked fear and thus avoids being alone or in public places from which escape might be difficult or help not available in case of sudden incapacitation (e.g., crowds, tunnels, bridges, public transportation).

B. There is increasing constriction of normal activities until the fears and avoidance behavior dominate the individual's life.

C. Not due to a major depressive episode, obsessive-compulsive disorder, paranoid personality disorders, or schizophrenia.

Note. From *Diagnostic and Statistical Manual of Mental Disorders* (3rd ed.) (p. 227). Copyright 1980 by the American Psychiatric Association. Reprinted by permission.

Drug dependency can become a complication if the individual tries to self-medicate by taking alcohol or anxiolytics. If panic attacks are present, the diagnosis is agoraphobia with panic attacks. Otherwise, a diagnosis of agoraphobia without panic attack is made.

Anxiety States

The anxiety states are subdivided into three types in the DSM-III:

1. *Generalized anxiety disorder (GAD)* (Table 5). This diagnostic category describes the clinical entity reported as anxiety neurosis in the earlier literature. The diagnosis is made when there is generalized, persistent anxiety of at least one month's duration without the presence of panic disorder, phobic disorders, or obsessive-compulsive disorder. The diagnosis of "adjustment disorder with anxious mood," in which the occurrence of anxiety symptoms is related to a clearly identifiable psychosocial stressor, needs to be ruled out before making the diagnosis of GAD. No data regarding age at onset, prevalence, sex

Table 5. Diagnostic Criteria for Generalized Anxiety Disorder

A. Generalized, persistent anxiety is manifested by symptoms from three of the following four categories:

1. *motor tension*: shakiness, jitteriness, jumpiness, trembling, tension, muscle aches, fatigability, inability to relax, eyelid twitch, furrowed brow, strained face, fidgeting, restlessness, easy startle
2. *autonomic hyperactivity*: sweating; heart pounding or racing; cold, clammy hands; dry mouth; dizziness; light-headedness; paresthesia (tingling in hands or feet); upset stomach; hot or cold spells; frequent urination; diarrhea; discomfort in the pit of the stomach; lump in the throat; flushing; pallor; high resting pulse and respiration rate
3. *apprehensive expectation*: anxiety, worry, fear, rumination, and anticipation of misfortune to self or others
4. *vigilance and scanning*: hyperattentiveness resulting in distractibility, difficulty in concentrating, insomnia, feeling "on edge," irritability, impatience

B. The anxious mood has been continuous for at least one month.

C. Not due to another mental disorder, such as a depressive disorder or schizophrenia.

D. Subject is at least 18 years of age.

Note. From *Diagnostic and Statistical Manual of Mental Disorders* (3rd ed.) (p. 233). Copyright 1980 by the American Psychiatric Association. Reprinted by permission.

ratio, familial pattern, or predisposing factors for this disorder are available at present. Depressive symptoms, alcohol abuse, and abuse of antianxiety agents have frequently been associated with GAD.

2. *Obsessive-compulsive disorder (OCD)* (Table 6). Obsessions are recurrent ego-dystonic thoughts that are usually unpleasant. The most common obsessions are repetitive thoughts of violence, contamination, and doubt. Compulsions are repetitive and seemingly purposeful behaviors performed according to certain rules and in a stereotyped fashion. The most common compulsive rituals are hand washing, counting, checking, and touching. The prevalence rate of OCD in the general population is unknown. The disorder afflicts both sexes equally and usually begins in adolescence or early adulthood. The average age of onset is around 20, and the average age at first hospitalization is the early or mid-30s. There is a suggestion that individuals suffering from OCD have a higher educational level and come from a higher socioeconomic class (Goodwin & Guze, 1984b). The clinical course is usually chronic, with exacerbation and remission of symptoms, secondary depression, anxiety, and phobic avoidance of situations as common complications.

3. *Panic disorder* (Table 7). The separate diagnostic entity of panic disorder results from the observations and work of Klein (1964). He demonstrated significant improvement in mixed panic disorder and agoraphobia when they were treated with the antidepressant imipramine. It is also reported that panic attacks precede the agoraphobia, which is considered a complication of panic attacks.

Panic disorder is characterized by recurrent spontaneous sudden attacks of panic (anxiety) that terminate without intervention. The discrete attacks are accompanied by symptoms of autonomic nervous system hyperactivity, with cardiovascular symptoms being the most frequent. Some people also report experiences of depersonalization and dereali-

---

Table 6. Diagnostic Criteria for Obsessive-Compulsive Disorder

---

A. Either obsessions or compulsions:

Obsessions: recurrent, persistent ideas, thoughts, images, or impulses that are ego-dystonic; i.e., they are not experienced as voluntarily produced, but rather as thoughts that invade consciousness and are experienced as senseless or repugnant. Attempts are made to ignore or suppress them.

Compulsions: repetitive and seemingly purposeful behaviors that are performed according to certain rules or in a stereotyped fashion. The behavior is not an end in itself but is designed to produce or prevent some future event or situation. However, either the activity is not connected in a realistic way with what it is designed to produce or prevent or it may be clearly excessive. The act is performed with a sense of subjective compulsion coupled with a desire to resist the compulsion (at least initially). The individual generally recognizes the senselessness of the behavior (this may not be true for young children) and does not derive pleasure from carrying out the activity, although it provides a release of tension.

B. The obsessions or compulsions are a significant source of distress to the individual or interfere with social or role functioning.

C. Not due to another mental disorder, such as Tourette's disorder, schizophrenia, major depression, or organic mental disorder.

Note. From *Diagnostic and Statistical Manual of Mental Disorders* (3rd ed.) (p. 235). Copyright 1980 by the American Psychiatric Association. Reprinted by permission.

Table 7. Diagnostic Criteria for Panic Disorder

A. At least three panic attacks within a three-week period in circumstances other than during marked physical exertion or in a life-threatening situation. The attacks are not precipitated only by exposure to a circumscribed phobic stimulus.

B. Panic attacks are manifested by discrete periods of apprehension or fear, and at least four of the following symptoms appear during each attack:

1. dyspnea
2. palpitations
3. chest pain or discomfort
4. choking or smothering sensations
5. dizziness, vertigo, or unsteady feelings
6. feelings of unreality
7. paresthesia (tingling in hands or feet)
8. hot and cold flashes
9. sweating
10. faintness
11. trembling or shaking
12. fear of dying, going crazy, or doing something uncontrolled during an attack

C. Not due to physical disorder or another mental disorder, such as major depression, somatization disorder, or schizophrenia.

D. The disorder is not associated with agoraphobia.

Note. From *Diagnostic and Statistical Manual of Mental Disorders* (3rd ed.) (pp. 231–232). Copyright 1980 by the American Psychiatric Association. Reprinted by permission.

zation. The attacks vary in frequency and intensity, ranging from a few per week to a few per year. The attacks last for several minutes to several hours, commonly from 10 to 30 min. Women are more vulnerable to the disorder. The sex ratio is approximately 2:1. Age at onset is most frequently late adolescence or early adulthood, but onset in midadult life is not uncommon. Separation anxiety in childhood and sudden object loss may predispose a person to the development of panic disorder in adulthood (Klein, 1980). The main complication of this disorder is agoraphobia and abuse of alcohol and antianxiety medications.

Some individuals who experience "hyperventilation syndrome" (HVS) may not meet the criteria for panic disorder. Whether or not HVS exists as a distinctive entity of anxiety disorders is not clear.

Posttraumatic Stress Disorder

How each individual reacts to psychologically traumatic events may depend on her or his premorbid personality and "ego" strength, but when a stressor, whether natural or created, surpasses the range of usual human experience, no one is immune to the development of the characteristic symptoms of the posttraumatic stress disorder (PTSD) as described in the DSM-III (See Table 8).

The symptoms of PTSD may develop immediately or shortly after the traumatic event although in some cases a latency period of months or even years after the trauma has been observed. The disorder is categorized into three subtypes: (1) the acute type has an on-

Table 8. Diagnostic Criteria for Posttraumatic Stress Disorder

A. Existence of a recognizable stressor that would evoke significant symptoms of distress in almost everyone.

B. Reexperiencing of the trauma as evidenced by at least one of the following:

   1. recurrent and intrusive recollections of the event
   2. recurrent dreams of the event
   3. sudden acting or feeling as if the traumatic event were recurring, because of an association with an environmental or ideational stimulus

C. Numbing of responsiveness to or reduced involvement with the external world, beginning some time after the trauma, as shown by at least one of the following:

   1. markedly diminished interest in one or more significant activities
   2. feeling of detachment or estrangement from others
   3. constricted affect

D. At least two of the following symptoms that were not present before the trauma:

   1. hyperalertness or exaggerated startle response
   2. sleep disturbance
   3. guilt about surviving when others have not, or about behavior required for survival
   4. memory impairment or trouble concentrating
   5. avoidance of activities that arouse recollection of the traumatic event
   6. intensification of symptoms by exposure to events that symbolize or resemble the traumatic event

Note. From *Diagnostic and Statistical Manual of Mental Disorders* (3rd ed.) (p. 238). Copyright 1980 by the American Psychiatric Association. Reprinted by permission.

set of symptoms within six months of the trauma and duration of symptoms lasts less than six months; (2) the delayed type has an onset of symptoms six months after the trauma; and (3) the chronic type has a duration of symptoms of six months or more.

PTSD is different from adjustment disorder, in which the stress is less severe and is within the range of usual human experience, and in which the characteristic symptoms of PTSD are absent.

Another Diagnostic System

Sheehan (1982a) has proposed a new diagnostic system to aid research and the development of a logical management strategy for anxiety disorders. The presence or absence of spontaneous panic attacks is identified as the single most important discriminating item between (1) "endogenous anxiety" (e.g., panic disorder) and (2) "exogenous anxiety" (e.g., adjustment disorder with anxious mood). Recent research data appear to support such a distinction. Endogenous anxiety is regarded as being of metabolic origin, a biological phenomenon in which there is genetic vulnerability to anxiety. It has a distinctive familial trend and characteristic sex distribution, and the usual time of onset is around age 24. It may also begin in childhood, but rarely after age 40. The age of onset for endogenous anxiety compares with the fairly uniform distribution of age of onset for exogenous anxiety. Endogenous anxiety responds poorly to behavioral or other therapy alone until the spontaneous panic attacks have been successful suppressed with antidepressant treatment (Carr & Sheehan, 1984).

DIFFERENTIAL DIAGNOSIS

Anxiety is a universal phenomenon as well as the most common psychological complaint. Anxiety disorders represent a spectrum of subjective feelings, such as anxiousness and nervousness, and objective somatic symptoms related to the hyperactivity of the autonomic nervous system (Table 9). Often, individuals with anxiety disorders are misdiagnosed as suffering from physical conditions and may undergo numerous unnecessary medical evaluations and treatments. Alternately, anxiety symptoms are known to occur in a variety of psychiatric and medical disorders that mimic anxiety disorders (Table 10). Therefore, once "pathological" anxiety is recognized, it is critically important to differentiate the source of anxiety (Rakeli, 1981). Is it a primary anxiety disorder not related to other psychiatric or medical disorders, or is it a secondary anxiety disorder associated with a variety of possible clinical conditions other than anxiety disorder? In order that medically or surgically treatable disorders, especially life-threatening conditions such as a myocardial infarction not be overlooked, it is recommended that patients suffering from "pathological" anxiety have a physical examination and that clinically appropriate laboratory tests be done (e.g., thyroid function tests and electrocardiograms) before the individual is labeled with the diagnosis of primary anxiety disorder.

There has been an increased interest in the possible association between mitral valve prolapse syndrome (MVPS) of the heart and panic disorders. MVPS occurs in 5% of the general population and is usually an asymptomatic condition. Abnormal electrocardiogram (EKG) findings are usually present, a cardiac auscultation reveals a systolic click and late systolic murmur. Diagnosis can be confirmed by means of an echocardiogram.

Approximately one third of patients with panic disorders and agoraphobia have the MVPS (Hartman, Kramer, Brown, & Devereux, 1982; Klein, 1980). However, the reported prevalence rate and the clinical significance of such an association have been questioned and still remain unclear (Kane, Woerner, Zeldis, Kramer, & Saravey, 1981). Also, the MVPS had no influence in precipitating panic attacks by infusion of sodium lactate (Gorman, Fryer, Gliklich, King, & Klein, 1981), and no difference was reported in the antipanic effect of imipramine between the two groups (with and without MVPS) (Klein, 1980).

Anxiety and depression are frequently reported as associated symptoms. Separation of primary anxiety disorder from primary depressive disorder is not always easy, especially in cases of "anxious" depression. Depressive disorder is predominantly manifested by dysphoric mood accompanied by vegetative symptoms of depression, such as change in appetite, sleep disturbance, loss or decrease of interest or pleasure in usual activities, loss of energy, and inability to concentrate. Persistent anxiety and somatic symptoms of a hyperactive autonomic nervous system are presented infrequently. A study of anxiety symptoms in patients suffering from major depressive disorder found that both psychic and somatic symptoms of anxiety appeared to be common in this group of patients. Some subjects also reported phobia, obsessions and/or compulsions, and panic attacks. This study (Sheehan, 1982b) suggested that anxiety is common in major depressive disorders and that these patients often experience significant anxiety symptoms or even panic attacks before the development of symptoms of major depression.

The relationship between these two disorders, whether distinct or continuous, remains obscure and controversial. It has been speculated that anxiety disorders may be an atyp-

Table 9. Somatic Symptoms of Anxiety

Cardiovascular system (most common)
Palpitation
Chest pain or discomfort
Heart pounding or racing
Facial flushing
Pallor
High resting pulse
Transient elevated blood pressure
Hot and cold flashes
Sweating
Cold, clammy hands

Respiratory system
Dyspnea
Choking or smothering sensations
Lump in the throat
Transient increased respiratory rate
Hyperventilation

Genitourinary system
Frequent urination
Inhibited sexual desire,
    and/or excitement
Inhibited orgasm
Premature ejaculation
Amenorrhea
Menstrual disturbance

Gastrointestinal system
Indigestion
Nausea and vomiting
Constipation
Diarrhea
Epigastric distress
Stomachache or discomfort in the stomach
Anorexia
Compulsive eating

Neuromuscular system
Paresthesia (tingling sensation in hands or feet)
Light-headedness and headaches
Dizziness and faintness
Vertigo
Unsteady feelings
Shakiness
Trembling
Strain in face
Furrowed brow
Fatigue and weakness
Body aches and pains
Nightmares and sleep disturbance
Goose bumps

Table 10. Common Medical Conditions Mimicking Anxiety Disorders

Cardiovascular system
  Congestive heart failure
  Angina pectoris
  Essential hypertension
  Dysrhythmia, especially paroxysmal atrial tachycardia
  Costal chondritis
  Mitral valve prolapse syndrome
    (systolic-click–murmur syndrome)
  Myocardial infarction (heart attack)

Respiratory system
  Hypoxic conditions
  Chronic obstructive pulmonary disease

Metabolic and endocrine system
  Hypoglycemia
  Hyper- or hypothyroidism
  Hyper- or hypoadrenalism (Cushing's or Addison's disease)
Diabetes mellitus

Neurological system
  Brain tumor
  Migraine headache
  Seizure disorders
  Multiple sclerosis
  Other organic brain syndromes
    (e.g., parkinsonism, encephalopathy)

Hematologic system
  Anemia

Neoplasma
  Pheochromocytoma
  Carcinoid tumor

Drug-related conditions
  Withdrawal reaction of addictive drugs
    (e.g., alcohol, barbiturates, benzodiazepines)
  Caffeinism
  Tobacco
  Central nervous system stimulants
    (e.g., amphetamine, cocaine)
  Central nervous system depressants
    (e.g., neuroleptic-induced side effects [akathisia])

ical manifestation and a variant of affective disorder. This hypothesis appears to be supported by pharmacological and family studies (Leckman, Weissman, Merikangas, Pauls, & Prusoff, 1983). Some subtypes of anxiety disorders, particularly panic disorder, agoraphobia, and obsessive-compulsive disorder, have been successfully treated with certain antidepressants (Matuzas & Glass, 1983; Yaryura-Tobia, Nezirogul, & Bergman, 1976). However, other studies do not support such a hypothesis. Depressive symptoms had no predictive value for drug treatment in anxiety disorders (Sheehan, Ballenger, & Jacobson, 1980; Zitrin, Klein, & Woerner, 1980).

Some studies have reported an increased risk of major affective disorder in the relatives of patients with anxiety disorders (Leckman *et al.*, 1983; Munjack & Moss, 1981). In contrast, other studies have found no such increase in the rate of affective disorders in the relatives of patients with anxiety disorders compared with a control group (Harris, Noyes, Crowe, & Chaudry, 1983; Roth, Mountjoy, & Caetano, 1982). In one study, it was found that depressed women with panic attacks were less likely to have depressed parents (VanValkenburg, Winokur, Behar, & Lowry, 1984). Furthermore, patients with panic disorder showed normal dexamethasone suppression test (DST) results. The test is claimed to be a biological marker for major depression. These results support the hypothesis that these disorders are distinct (Curtis, Cameron, & Neese, 1982). In contrast, abnormalities in DST results were found to be characteristic of panic disorders as well as some forms of affective disorder (Bueno, Sabanes, Gascon, Casto, & Salamero, 1984). The effectiveness of the DST in diagnosing panic disorder is uncertain and unproved at this time.

GENETIC AND FAMILY STUDIES

The question of why certain people seem more vulnerable to anxiety disorders remains unanswered. There are many different schools of thought, including Freudian psychoanalytical theory, behavioral theory originating from Pavlov's conditioning theory, and biological theory originating from Cannon's "flight or fight" response. None of these hypotheses provides a satisfactory explanation for this complicated condition. However, a few genetic and family studies suggest that panic disorders, agoraphobia, and obsessive-compulsive disorders are more common among family members of the patients than in the general population (Crowe, Noyes, Pual, & Slymen, 1983; Noyes, Clancy, Crowe, Hoenk, & Slymen, 1978; Pauls, Paucher, Crowe, & Noyes, 1980; Raymond, Pauls, Slymen, & Noyes, 1980). In twin studies of anxiety disorders, a higher concordance rate was shown among monozygotic twins than among dizygotic twins (Inouye, 1965; McGuffin & Mawson, 1980; Slater & Shields, 1969).

BIOLOGY OF ANXIETY

Adrenergic Pathways in the Central Nervous System

Catecholamines such as epinephrine and norepinephrine are one group of neurotransmitters involved in the transmission of nerve impulses between neurons and involve receptor sites at the synapse. The adrenergic receptors were classified by Ahlquist (1948) as alpha (α) and beta (β) types. These are further subdivided into α_1 and α_2 and β_1 and β_2. When α receptors are stimulated, the effects include vasoconstriction; pupillary dilation; contraction of the smooth muscles of the bowel, the sphincters of the urinary bladder, and the stomach and splenic capsule; secretory activity of the sweat glands; and constriction of the ducts of the salivary glands. When β receptors are stimulated, some of the effects are vasodilation in skeletal muscles; relaxation of the bronchi; increased heart rate, increased conduction, velocity, and contractility of heart; and alterations in carbohydrate and fat metabolism.

The association of increases in systemic catecholamines with stress and anxiety is well documented. Plasma epinephrine and norepinephrine concentrations are both elevated in patients with anxiety disorders, (Mathew, Ho, Kralik, Taylor, Semchuk, Weiman, & Cloghorn, 1980). In animal models, anxiety can be induced by stimulating the nucleus locus ceruleus, which mainly consists of adrenergic neurons and is a component of the brain information system (Foote, Bloom, & Aston-Jones, 1983). Anxiety can be diminished by inhibiting this nucleus (Redmond & Huang, 1979). The α_2-adrenergic receptor is considered important to the pathophysiology of anxiety. But, recently, β-receptor overactivity due to increased receptor sensitivity (Charney, Heninger, & Breier, 1984) or increased stimulation of the system (Neese, Cameron, Curtis, McCann, & Humber-Smith, 1984) has also been implicated.

Gamma-Amino-Butyric-Acid-(GABA)-Ergic Pathways and Benzodiazine Receptors in the Central Nervous System

GABA is an inhibitory transmitter in the central nervous system. In 1977, two independent research groups discovered the high-affinity receptors in the CNS of reptiles and mammals for benzodiazepines, the most commonly used antianxiety agents (e.g., diazepam [Valium]). In the mammalian CNS, they are highly concentrated in the limbic system (Mohler & Okada, 1977; Squires & Braestrup, 1977). Later, the benzodiazepine receptor was found to be closely associated with GABA receptors (Hoehn-Saric, 1982). Through this GABAergic receptor, the antianxiety effects of benzodiazepines are mediated (Tallman, Paul, Skolnick, & Gallager, 1980). These discoveries have created much of our understanding of the biological basis of anxiety and provide further evidence to explain and perhaps distinguish differences between "endogenous" and "exogenous," or "trait" and "state," anxiety disorders.

On the basis of the above-mentioned neurotransmitter pathways, Insel, Ninan, Aloi, Jimerson, Skolnick, and Paul (1984) suggested two different neuropharmacological models of anxiety (i.e., the noradrenergic and the benzodiazepine receptor models), which represent two very different clinical phenomena. The noradrenergic activation corresponds to "alarm"; the benzodiazepine system corresponds more to "fear or conflict." Most likely, neither of these systems is the specific or exclusive mediator of anxiety disorders. Rather, both system are probably involved.

Sodium Lactate Infusion Test

Blood lactate levels after exercise were found to be higher in individuals susceptible to anxiety attacks than in normal individuals (Linko, 1950). Pitts and McClure (1967) reported that anxiety attacks could be provoked by infusing lactate solution into susceptible individuals. Since this experiment, this test has been used as a chemical diagnostic tool for investigating panic attacks. Sodium lactate, when administered intravenously 10 ml/kg body weight of a 0.5 molar solution over 20 min, provokes panic attacks in vulnerable individuals, whereas normal individuals do not experience panic attacks. This finding further supports the distinction of endogenous and exogeous anxiety. The exact mechanism of aciton is unknown, but it is possible that it is due to the rise in the lactate–pyruvate ratio, lowering the level of ionized calcium, and the concomitant fall of intraneuronal pH in the chemoreceptor (Carr & Sheehan, 1984). Lactate-induced panic attacks can be prevented by pharmacotherapy with either tricyclic antidepressants (e.g., imipramine) or monoamine oxidase inhibitors (e.g., phenelzine) (Kelly, Mitchell-Heggs, & Sherman, 1971; Rifkin, Klein, Dillon, & Levitt, 1981), but not by benzodiazepine or β-adrenergic blockers (e.g., propranolol) (Kathol, Noyes, Slymen, Crowe, Clancy, & Kerber, 1980). Liebowitz, Fryer, Gorman, Dillon, Appleby, Levy, Anderson, Levitt, Palij, Davies, and Klein (1984) found that the proportion of patients with panic disorder or agoraphobia with panic attacks during lactate infusion was approximately equal. This finding suggests that these disorders share a core vulnerability; that is, panic attacks are not just another symptom of agoraphobia.

Other Physiological Measurements

Some studies report physiological differences between people with anxiety disorder and normal individuals. Anxiety disorder individuals tended to be more responsive to painful stimuli of various types and had low exercise tolerance and spontaneous fluctuations of galvanic skin response (Lader, Gelden, & Marks, 1967). They also showed increased resting forearm blood flow (Kelly & Walter, 1968), brisker deep tendon reflexes, and elevated resting pulse-rate (Claycomb, 1983).

In summary, major advances in biological research on anxiety disorders suggest that specific treatment and new information regarding the etiology of certain subtypes of anxiety disorder may become available in the near future (Braestrup & Nielsen, 1982).

PHARMACOTHERAPY AND PREDICTION

The treatment modalities for anxiety disorders include (1) simple reassurance, training in coping techniques, and modification of environmental factors; (2) behavioral therapy in the form of desensitization, exposure *in vivo*, or flooding for phobic avoidance behavior; (3) psychotherapy of various types to help the individual understand the conscious and unconscious factors that may provoke anxiety; and (4) pharmacotherapy for generalized debilitating anxiety symptoms, as well as for the more specific disorders such as panic attacks. Most frequently, treatment involves a multimodal approach given sequentially or simultaneously.

In treating anxiety disorders, pharmacotherapy is a proven effective treatment modality, but anxiolytics should be avoided unless the anxiety impairs the individual's ability to function or the symptom cluster meets the criteria of a "disorder" (Pi & Simpson, 1982). The available medications for the treatment of anxiety disorders are listed in Table 11. Since the introduction of the benzodiazepines in the late 1950s, this class of anxiolytics has replaced all the other groups of anxiolytics (e.g., the barbiturates). That the benzodiazepines are the drugs of choice can be attributed to their efficacy and safety, compared to other agents. The benzodiazepines create less probability of dependency, fewer withdrawal symptoms, and less addiction than the barbiturates. They also have a wide safety margin. It is virtually impossible to commit suicide by overdose of the drug alone; however, if combined with alcohol, they can be lethal.

Benzodiazepines are particularly effective in treating "anticipatory" or "free-floating" anxiety, and maximal therapeutic effects may be attained if the drugs are combined with behavior therapy, psychotherapy, or both in the treatment of generalized anxi-

Table 11. Anxiolytics (Antianxiety Agents)

Generic name	Trade name	Usually daily dose[a]
A. Benzodiazepines (the drug of choice)		
Short-acting		
Lorazepam	Ativan	2–6 mg
Oxazepam	Serax	30–120 mg
Alprazolam	Xanax	0.5–4 mg
Long-acting		
Chlordiazepoxide	Librium	15–100 mg
Diazepam	Valium	5–40 mg
Prazepam	Centrax	20–60 mg
Clorazepate	Tranxene	10–60 mg
Halazepam	Paxipam	20–160 mg
B. Barbiturates		
Long-acting (more than 6h)		
Phenobarbital	Luminal	60–300 mg
Mephobarbital	Mebaral	
Intermediate acting (3–6 h)		
Amobarbital	Amytal	50–250 mg
Butabarbital	Butisol	50–100 mg
Vinbarbital	Delvinal	
Short-acting (3 h)		
Secobarbital	Seconal	50–200 mg
Pentobarbital	Nembutal	50–200 mg
Ultra-short-acting (minutes) (only used as IV anesthetics)		
Methohexital	Brevital	
Thiopental	Pentothal	
Thiamyltal	Surital	
Hexobarbital	Sombulex	
C. Antihistamines		
Hydroxyzine	Vistaril, Atarax	50–100 mg
Diphenhydramine	Benadryl	25–100 mg
Promethazine	Phenergan	50–200 mg
D. Propanediols		
Meprobamate	Miltown, Equanil	1.0 gm
Tybamate	Solacen, Tybatran	750 mg–2.0 gm
E. Beta-adrenegic blockers		
Propranolol	Inderal	30–120 mg
F. Antidepressants (block spontaneous panic attacks)[b]		
Imipramine	Tofranil	25–300 mg
Phenelzine	Nardil	15–90 mg
G. Neuroleptics (not for routine use)		
H. Alcohol (not recommended)		

[a]Usual daily doses must be titrated individually.
[b]May have therapeutic effects on obsessive-compulsive disorders and agoraphobia.

ety disorder, agoraphobia, simple or social phobia, obsessive-compulsive disorder, and posttraumatic stress disorder. Rickels (1978) reported that individuals with high levels of anxiety and somatic complaints without obsessive-compulsive symptoms, interpersonal difficulties, or depressive symptoms showed the best response to benzodiazepines. Other favorable predictors are good response to benzodiazepines in the past, evidence of some sedative effects within the first two weeks of treatment, a stress-related disorder, an expectation of receiving pharmacotherapy with a positive view toward pharmacotherapy, and the physicians' psychological support. Response to treatment is often rapid, often within one or two days, but if there is no improvement after two to four weeks on adequate amounts of benzodiazepine, then the diagnoses must be reconsidered. The individual may be suffering from another psychiatric disorder, particularly depression. Unlike other benzodiazepines, alprazolam, a relatively new benzodiazepine, in addition to its anxiolytic effects, is also claimed to block panic attacks in panic disorder and agoraphobia with panic attacks (Sheehan, 1982a).

The barbiturates were widely prescribed for anxiety before 1960. However, because of the risk of fatal overdose, the serious withdrawal symptoms (Wikler, 1968), and significant induction of live microsomal enzymatic activities, their clinical use declined dramatically in the 1970s and has been supplanted by use of the benzodiazepines.

Antihistamines such as diphenhydramine (Benzdryl) may not be as effective as the benzodiazepines, but they are of value in treating anxious individuals, particularly those with allergic and dermatologic disorders or those who may be addiction prone. Caution should be exercised when these drugs are prescribed for the elderly because they possess anticholinergic side effects that can cause negative effects on cognitive function as well as on physical condition, such as heart disease or narrow-angle glaucoma.

Propranediol derivatives such as meprobamate (Miltown) are seldom prescribed for anxiety because they have most of the same disadvantages as the barbiturates. Also their clinical efficacy is claimed to be inconsistent (Greenblatt & Shader, 1971).

Beta-adrenergic blockers are helpful in alleviating symptoms of hyperactive adrenergic discharge, such as tachycardia, tremor, palpitation, and sweating. They do not help the psychic symptoms of anxiety, but as they produce little or no sedation, they may be useful in alleviating "situational" stress or anxiety, such as public-speaking or performance anxiety, when combined with behavioral techniques. Propranolol does not appear to block panic attacks (Heiser & Defrancisco, 1976).

The neuroleptics are not recommended for use in the treatment of anxiety disorders. There is little or no advantage in prescribing neuroleptics, and there is a risk of developing tardive dyskinesia.

Alcohol is the most commonly self-prescribed anxiolytic, but its side effects and potential abuse outweigh its possible therapeutic merit.

Recently, there has been much interest in the use of antidepressants for the treatment of anxiety disorders. The tricyclic antidepressant imipramine, as well as newer antidepressants such as maprotiline and trazodone, and monoamine oxidase inhibitors such as phenelzine, have been found to be effective in controlling panic attacks and some phobic behavior (Klein, 1980).

Pharmacotherapy for obsessive-compulsive disorders includes a variety of antidepressants (Marks, Stern, & Mawson, 1980). However, most of the research has been on clomipramine, a tricyclic antidepressant not yet available in the United States. It is claimed that clomipramine is associated with significant improvement in measures of obsessions, anxiety, and depression (Thoren, Asberg, Cronholm, Jornestedt, & Traskman, 1980). In a recent study, (Insel, Murphy, Cohen, & Alterman, 1983), it was found that clomipramine was effective in the treatment of obsessions and that the antiobsessional response was not dependent on the presence of depression. This finding does not support the notion that it is necessary to have depressive symptoms in order to obtain a response to clomipramine. Improvement was correlated with plasma concentrations of clomipramine. Patients with obsessive-compulsive disorders tended to relapse when the clomipramine was withdrawn (Yaryura-Tobias et al., 1976). There are also anecdotal reports that monoamine oxidase inhibitors, including phenelzine and tranylcypromine, are effective for obsessive-compulsive disorder. This possibility requires more rigorous study.

Pharmacotherapy may not be indicated for PTSD because medication may mask the victim's coping mechanism and may thus delay the adaptation process. However, if the subject experiences overwhelming psychological and physiological reactions that may be harmful, then a small dose of a short-acting benzodiazepine for a few days may be useful. Insomnia associated with nightmares is a common complaint among people suffering from posttraumatic stress syndrome. Benzodiazepines for a short period of time may be helpful, but the therapeutic effects must be reevaluated periodically in order to minimize the risk of drug misuse and abuse. Nightmares, flashbacks, and the clinical syndrome of depression may be treated with antidepressants (Burstein, 1984). Neuroleptics may be prescribed under close psychiatric supervision for people who exhibit clear psychotic symptoms, but other concomitant or primary psychiatric disorders should be ruled out.

COMPLICATIONS AND PROGNOSIS

Depression has been found to be the most common complication secondary to anxiety disorders (Clancy, Noyes, Hoenk, & Slymen, 1978). Although suicide has appeared infrequently, recent studies have found a higher rate of suicide among patients who fulfilled DSM-III criteria for panic disorder than in a group of depressed patients (Coryell, Noyes, & Clancy, 1982). It was also found that there was an increase in secondary depression and mortality from cardiovascular diseases in a male patient population (Coryell, 1981; Coryell et al., 1982). Other significant complications are self-medication with alcohol and misuse of sedative-hypnotics (Quitkin, Rifkin, Kaplan, & Klein, 1972).

Claycomb (1983) studied 57 patients seeking treatment for anxiety and phobic symptoms who met the criteria for endogenous anxiety. Of these patients, 70% had seen at least 10 medical consultants before coming to a specialized anxiety-disorder clinic, and 94% had received anxiolytics, some for more than 10 years. High (up to 70%) relapse rates were also reported, and a late-onset group had a 30% to 40% relapse rate. This study supports the previously reported findings that a mean age of 30 or older at the time of seeking psychiatric help for the first time is associated with poor outcome (Noyes & Clancy, 1976). Furthermore, Sheehan (1982a) proposed a natural course of endogenous anxiety. If untreated or partially treated, the disorder evolves from subpanic symptoms to polysymptomatic panic attacks, to hypochondriasis, to social phobia, to polyphobic and agoraphobic behavior, and finally to depression (demoralization). Outcome studies showed that, for panic disorder, less than 25% of patients achieve complete recovery (Marks & Lader, 1973; Schapira, Roth, Kerr, & Gurney, 1972). In a long-term follow-up study of anxiety disorder, about 50% of patients had recovered or were much improved. About 15% of patients continued to have significant disability (Wheeler, White, Reid, & Cohen, 1950). It is therefore important that patients with anxiety disorders be carefully evaluated and receive definite and, as far as possible, specific treatment in order to prevent the development of a chronic debilitating condition that may be refractory to all treatment. When any anxiety condition does not respond to psychotherapeutic or other treatment given for a reasonable period of time, the diagnosis should be reconsidered.

In the treatment of the posttraumatic stress syndrome, we still do not know whether the premorbid personality profile (Helzer, Robins, & Wish, 1979) or the severity of the traumatic stress (Ursano, 1981) is the best predictor of psychiatric status at follow-up. Complications of the post-Vietnam syndrome include difficulty in social adjustment; problems with family life, marriage, and vocational accomplishments; drug and alcohol use; and poor impulse control, with criminal activity; in the extreme, the syndrome may manifest as a paranoid disorder (Friedman, 1981). However, some patients with PTSD who are in treatment have coexisting psychiatric disorders, including affective disorders, anxiety states, substance abuse, and personality disorders (Sierles, Chen, McFarland, & Taylor, 1983; Van Putten & Yager, 1984). It is important to note that early detection and early application of appropriate treatment will best help patients with PTSD to cope with everyday stressors.

CONCLUSION

Marked advances in the treatment of anxiety have taken place since the mid-1960s. Biological factors have been discovered and have helped to create experimental models of anxiety. Pharmacotherapy has advanced dramatically and has resulted in specific treatments for disorders associated with panic. Differential responsiveness to chemical agents suggests an approach to classification that may in the future have etiological significance. A variety of treatments have been identified, and it seems reasonable to predict that more rapid, more specific, and safer treatments will appear by the mid-1990s. As always, those dealing with anxiety disorders have to pay careful attention to diagnosis, which should, in time, predict outcome.

REFERENCES

Ahlquist, R. P. (1948). A study of the adrenotropic receptors. *American Journal of Physiology, 153,* 586.

American Psychiatric Association. (1980). *Diagnostic and Statistical Manual of Mental Disorders* (3rd ed.). Washington, DC: Author.

Beard, G. M. (1869). Neurasthenia or nervous exhaustion. *Boston Medical and Surgical Journal, 3,* 217–225.

Braestrup, C., & Nielsen, M. (1982). Anxiety. *Lancet, 2,* 1030–1034.

Bueno, J. A., Sabanes, F., Gascon, J., Casto, C., & Salamero, M. (1984). Dexamethasone suppression test in patients with panic disorder and secondary depression. *Archives of General Psychiatry, 41,* 723–724.

Burstein, A. (1984). Treatment of post-traumatic stress disorder with imipramine. *Psychosomatics, 25,* 681–688.

Carr, D. B., & Sheehan, D. V. (1984). Panic anxiety: A new biological model. *Journal of Clinical Psychiatry, 45,* 323–330.

Charney, D. S., Heninger, G. R., & Breier, A. (1984). Noradrenergic function in panic anxiety: Effects of Yohimbine in healthy subjects and patients with agoraphobic and panic disorders. *Archives of General Psychiatry 41,* 751–763.

Clancy, J., Noyes, R., Hoenck, P. R., & Sylmen, D. J. (1978). Secondary depression in anxiety neurosis. *Journal of Nervous and Mental Disease, 166,* 846–850.

Claycomb, J. B. (1983). Endogenous anxiety: Implications for nosology and treatment. *Journal of Clinical Psychiatry, 44(8 sec. 2),* 19–22.

Cohen, M. E., & White, P. D. (1950). Life situations, emotions and neurocirculatory asthenia (anxiety neurosis, neuroasthenia, effort syndrome). *Association for Research and Mental Disease, 29,* 832–869.

Coryell, W. (1981). Obsessive-compulsive disorder and primary unipolar depression: Comparisons of background, family history, course and mortality. *Journal of Nervous and Mental Disease, 169,* 220–224.

Coryell, W., Noyes, R., & Clancy, N. (1982). Excess mortality in panic disorder. *Archives of General Psychiatry, 39,* 701–703.

Crowe, R. R., Noyes, R., Paul, D. L., & Sylmen, D. (1983). A family study of panic disorder. *Archives of General Psychiatry, 40,* 1065–1069.

Curtis, G. C., Cameron, O. G., & Neese, R. M. (1982). The dexamethasone suppression test in panic disorder and agoraphobia. *American Journal of Psychiatry, 139,* 1043–1046.

DaCosta, J. M. (1871). On irritable heart, a clinic form of functional cardiac disorder and its consequences. *American Journal of Medical Sciences, 61,* 17.

Duffy, E. (1957). The psychological significance of the concept of "arousal" or "activation." *Psychological Review, 64,* 844–914.

Foote, S. L., Bloom, F. E., & Aston-Jones, G. (1983). Nucleus locus ceruleus: New evidence of anatomical and physiological specificity. *Physiological Review, 63,* 844–914.

Freud, S. (1960). The justification for detaching from neurasthenia a particular syndrome: The anxiety-neurosis. In E. Jones (Ed.), *Sigmund Freud: Collected Papers* (Vol. 1). New York: Basic Books. (Original work published 1894).

Friedman, M. J. (1981). Post-Vietnam syndrome: Recognition and management. *Psychosomatics, 22,* 931–943.

Goodwin, D. W., & Guze, S. B. (1984a). Phobic disorder. In D. W. Goodwin & S. B. Guze, (Eds.), *Psychiatric disorders.* New York: Oxford University Press.

Goodwin, D. W., & Guze, S. B. (1984b). Obsessive-compulsive disorder. In D. W. Goodwin & S. B. Guze, (Eds.), *Psychiatric disorders.* New York: Oxford University Press.

Gorman, J. M., Fryer, A. F., Gliklich, J., King, D., & Klein, D. F. (1981). Effect of sodium lactate on patients with panic disorder and mitral valve prolapse. *American Journal of Psychiatry, 138,* 247–249.

Greenblatt, D., & Shader, R. I. (1971). Meprobamate, a study of irrational drug use. *American Journal of Psychiatry, 127,* 1297.

Harris, E. I., Noyes, R., Crowe, R. R., & Chaudhry, R. (1983). A family study of agoraphobia: Report of a pilot study. *Archives of General Psychiatry, 40,* 1051–1064.

Hartman, N., Kramer, R., Brown, W. T., & Devereux, R. B. (1982). Panic disorder in patients with mitral valve prolapse. *American Journal of Psychiatry, 139,* 669–670.

Heiser, J. F., & Defrancisco, D. (1976). The treatment of pathological panic states with propranolol. *American Journal of Psychiatry, 133,* 1389–1394.

Helzer, J. E., Robins, L. N., & Wish, E. (1979). Depression in Vietnam veterans and civilian controls. *American Journal of Psychiatry, 136,* 526–529.

Hoehn-Saric, R. (1982). Neurotransmitters in anxiety. *Archives of General Psychiatry, 39,* 735–742.

Inouye, E. (1965). Similar and dissimilar manifestations of obsessive-compulsive neurosis in monozygotic twins. *American Journal of Psychiatry, 121,* 1171–1175.

Insel, T. R., Murphy, D. L., Cohen, R. M., Alterman, I., Kilts, C., & Linnoila, M. (1983). Obsessive-compulsive disorder: A double blind trial of clomipramine and cloryline. *Archives of General Psychiatry, 40,* 605–612.

Insel, T. R., Ninan, P. T., Aloi, J., Jimerson, D. C., Skolnick, P., & Paul, S. M. (1984). A benzodiazepine receptor-mediated model of anxiety: Studies in non-human primates and clinical implications. *Archives of General Psychiatry, 41,* 741–750.

Kane, J. M., Woerner, M., Zeldis S., Kramer, R., & Saravey, S. (1981). Panic and phobic disorders in patients with mitral valve prolapse. In D. F. Klein & J. Rabkin (Eds.), *Anxiety: New research and changing concepts*. New York: Raven Press.

Kathol, R. G., Noyes, R., Slymen, P. J., Crowe, R. R., Clancy, J., & Kerber, R. E. (1980). Propranolol in chronic anxiety disorders. *Archives of General Psychiatry, 27,* 1361–1365.

Kelly, D. H. W., & Walter, C. J. S. (1968). The relationship between clinical diagnosis and anxiety assessed by forearm blood flow and other measurements. *British Journal of Psychiatry, 114,* 611–626.

Kelly, D. H. W., Mitchell-Heggs, N., & Sherman, D. (1971). Anxiety and the effects of sodium lactate assessed clinically and physiologically. *British Journal of Psychiatry, 119,* 129–141.

Klein, D. F. (1964). Delineation of two drug-responsive anxiety syndromes. *Psychopharmacologia* (Berlin), *5,* 397–408.

Klein, D. F. (1980). Importance of psychiatric diagnosis in prediction of clinical drug effects. *Archives of General Psychiatry, 17,* 63–72.

Lader, M. H., Gelder, M. G., & Marks, I. M. (1967). Palmar skin-conductance measures as predictors of response to desensitization. *Journal of Psychosomatic Research,* 11, 283–290.

Leckman, J. F., Weissman, M. M., Merikangas, R., Pauls, D. L., & Prusoff, B. A. (1983). Panic disorder and depression: Increased risk of depression alcoholism, panic and phobia disorders in families of depressed probands with panic disorders. *Archives of General Psychiatry, 40,* 1055–1060.

Liebowitz, M. R., Fryer, A. J., Gorman, J. M., Dillon, D., Appleby, I. L., Levy, G., Anderson, S., Levitt, M., Palij, M., Davies, S. O., & Klein, N. F. (1984). Lactate provocation of panic attacks: I. Clinical and behavioral findings. *Archives of General Psychiatry, 41,* 764–770.

Linko, E. (1950). Lactic acid response to muscular exercise in neurocirculatory asthenia. *Annales Medicinae Internae Fenniae, 39,* 161–176.

Marks, I., Lader, M. (1973). Anxiety states (anxiety neurosis): A review. *Journal of Nervous and Mental Disease, 156,* 3–18.

Marks, I. M., Stern, R. S., & Mewson, D. (1980). Clomipramine and exposure for obsessive-compulsive rituals: I and II. *British Journal of Psychiatry, 136,* 1–25, 161–166.

Mathew, R. J., Ho, B. T., Kralik, P., Taylor, D., Semchuck, K., Weiman, M., & Cloghorn, J. L. (1980). Catechol-o-methyltransference and catecholamines in anxiety and relaxation. *Psychiatry Research, 3,* 85–91.

Matuzas, W., & Glass, R. M. (1983). Treatment of agoraphobia and panic attacks. *Archives of General Psychiatry, 40,* 220–222.

McGuffin, P., & Mawson, D. (1980). Obsessive-compulsive neurosis: Two identical twin pairs. *British Journal of Psychiatry, 137,* 285–287.

Mohler, H., & Okada, T. (1977). Benzodiazepine receptor: Demonstration in the central nervous system. *Science, 198,* 849–851.

Munjack, D. J., & Moss, H. B. (1981). Affective disorders and alcoholism in families of agoraphobia. *Archives of General Psychiatry, 38,* 869–874.

Neese, R. M., Cameron, O. G., Curtis G. C., McCann, D. S., & Humber-Smith, M. J. (1984). Adrenergic function in patients with panic anxiety. *Archives of General Psychiatry, 41,* 771–776.

Noyes, R., & Clancy, J. (1976). Anxiety Neurosis: A 5-year follow-up. *Journal of Nervous and Mental Disease, 162,* 200–205.

Noyes, R., Clancy, J., Crowe, R., Hoenk, P. R., & Slymen, D. J. (1978). The familial prevalence of anxiety neurosis. *Archives of General Psychiatry, 35,* 1957–1059.

Noyes, R., Jr., Clancy, J., Hoenk, P. R., & Slymen, D. J. (1980). The prognosis of anxiety neurosis. *Archives of General Psychiatry, 37,* 173–178.

Pauls, D. L., Paucher, K. D., Crowe, R. R., & Noyes, R. (1980). A genetic study of panic disorder pedigrees. *American Journal of Human Genetics, 32,* 639–644.

Pi, E. H., & Simpson G. M. (1982). The use and misuse of benzodiazepines: An update. *The Journal of Continuing Education for the Family Physician, 16,* 102–106.

Pitts, F. N., & McClure, J. N. (1967). Lactate metabolism in anxiety neurosis. *New England Journal of Medicine, 227,* 1329–1336.

Quitkin, F. M., Rifkin, A., Kaplan, J., & Klein, D. F. (1972). Phobic anxiety syndrome complicated by drug dependence and addiction. *Archives of General Psychiatry, 27,* 159–162.

Rakel, R. E. (1981). Differential diagnosis of anxiety. *Psychiatric Annals, 11*(supplement), 11–14.

Raymond, R. C., Pauls, D. L. Slymen, D. J., & Noyes, R. (1980). A family study of anxiety neurosis. *Archives of General Psychiatry, 37,* 77–79.

Redmond, D. E., Jr., Huang, Y. H. (1979). New evidence for a locus coeruleus-norepinephrine connection with anxiety. *Life Sciences, 25,* 2149-2162.

Rickels, K. (1978). Use of antianxiety agents in anxious outpatients. *Psychopharmacology, 58,* 1-18.

Rifkin, A., Klein, D. F., Dillon, D., & Levitt, M. (1981). Blockage by imipramine or desipramine of panic induced by sodium lactate. *American Journal of Psychiatry, 138,* 676-677.

Roth, M., Mountjoy, C., & Caetano, D. (1982). Further investigations into the relationship between depressive disorders and anxiety states. *Pharmacopsychiatria, 15(4),* 135-141.

Schapira, K., Roth, M., Kerr, T. A., & Gurney, C. (1972). The prognosis of affective disorders: The differentiation of anxiety states from depressive illnesses. *British Journal of Psychiatry, 121,* 175-181.

Sheenan, D. V. (1982a). Current perspectives in the treatment of panic and phobic disorders. *Drug Therapy, 12,* 49-63.

Sheenan, D. V. (1982b). Panic attacks and phobias. *New England Journal of Medicine, 307,* 156-158.

Sheenan, D. V., Ballenger, J., & Jacobson, G. (1980). Treatment of endogenous anxiety with phobic, hysterical and hypochondriacal symptoms. *Archives of General Psychiatry, 37,* 51-59.

Sierles, F. S., Chen, J. J., McFarland, R. E., & Taylor, M. A. (1983). Post-traumatic stress disorder and concurrent psychiatric illness: A preliminary report. *American Journal of Psychiatry, 140,* 1177-1179.

Slater, E., & Shields, J. (1964). Genetical aspects of anxiety. In M. H. Loder (Ed.), *Studies of anxiety.* Ashford Kent: Headley.

Squires, R. F., & Braestrup, C. (1977). Benzodiazepine receptors in rat brain, *Nature, 266,* 732-734.

Tallman, J. F., Paul, S. M., Skolnick, P., & Gallager, D. W. (1980). Receptors for the age of anxiety: Pharmacology of the benzodiazepines. *Science, 207,* 274-281.

Thoren, P., Asberg, M., Cronholm, B., Jornestedt, L., & Traskman, L. (1980). Clomipramine treatment of obsessive-compulsive disorder: A controlled clinical trial. *Archives of General Psychiatry, 37,* 1281-1289.

Uhlenhuth, E. H., Balter, M. B., Mellinger, G. D., Cisin, I. H., & Clinthorne, J. (1983). Symptom checklist syndrome in the general population. *Archives of General Psychiatry, 40,* 1167-1173.

Ursano, R. J. (1981). The Vietnam era prisoners of war: Precaptivity personality and the development of psychiatric illness. *American Journal of Psychiatry, 138,* 315-318.

Van Putten, T., & Yager, J. (1984). Post-traumatic stress disorders. Emerging from the rhetoric. *Archives of General Psychiatry, 41,* 411-413.

VanValkenburg, C., Winokur, G., Behar, D., & Lowry, M. (1984). Depressed women with panic attacks. *Journal of Clinical Psychiatry, 45,* 367-369.

Weissman, M. M., Myers, J. K., & Harding, P. S. (1978). Psychiatric disorders in a U.S. urban community. *American Journal of Psychiatry, 135,* 459-462.

Westphal, C. (1871). Die Agoraphobie: Eine neuropathische Erscheinung. *Archives für Psychiatrie und Nervenkrankheiten, 3,* 138-171.

Wheeler, E. D., White P. D., Reid, E. W., & Cohen, M. E. (1950). Neurocirculatory asthenia (anxiety neurosis, effort syndrome, neuroasthenia). *Journal of the American Medical Association, 142,* 878-889.

Wikler, A. (1968). Diagnosis and treatment of drug dependence of the barbiturate type. *American Journal of Psychiatry, 125,* 758-765.

Yaryura-Tobias, J. A., Nezirogul, F., & Bergman, L. (1976). Chlorimipramine in obsessive-compulsive neurosis: An organic approach. *Current Therapeutic Research, 20,* 541-548.

Zitrin, C. M., Klein, D. F., & Woerner, M. G. (1980). Treatment of agoraphobic with group exposure in vivo and imipramine. *Archives of General Psychiatry, 37,* 63-72.

4

Affective Disorders

MICHAEL E. THASE

INTRODUCTION

The term *affective disorders* encompasses a variety of conditions in which the principal disturbance involves mood and affect. They include disorders commonly referred to as *clinical depressions*, as well as manic and hypomanic states. It is now recognized that the affective disorders constitute the most common set of emotional conditions for which individuals seek consultation from mental health providers or general medical practitioners. A number of recent epidemiological surveys confirm that affective disorders are also common among the general population: approximately 5% are depressed at any given time, and as much as 20% of the total population experiences a clinical depression at some point during the life-span (see Boyd & Weissman, 1981). Thus, knowledge of methods for the assessment and treatment of affective disorders is essential for all mental health practitioners.

This chapter provides an overview of the current biomedical approach to affective disorders. Since the mid-1960s, research concerning the classification, assessment, basic biological mechanisms, and pharmacological treatment of affective disorders has proceeded at a rapid pace. It is therefore timely to integrate these findings as they relate to contemporary clinical practice. We will focus on four main areas: (1) classification and differential diagnosis; (2) the incidence and significance of biological abnormalities in manic and depressive disorders; (3) the efficacy and side effects of medical therapies; and (4) indications for the selection of medical and psychosocial therapies.

CLASSIFICATION AND DIFFERENTIAL DIAGNOSIS

The third edition of the American Psychiatric Association's *Diagnostic and Statistical Manual* (DSM-III) was published in 1980. The DSM-III represents a significant departure from the previous two editions. Stereotypical descriptions of diagnostic groupings have been replaced by operationalized criteria and hierarchical decision rules. Diagnostic formulations based on unvalidated theoretical considerations (e.g., involutional melancholia or depressive neurosis) have been discarded in favor of atheoretical categories for the affective disorders that had been empirically established for research purposes (Feighner, Robins, Guze, Woodruff, Winokur, & Munoz, 1972; Spitzer, Endicott, & Robins,

MICHAEL E. THASE • Department of Psychiatry, Western Psychiatric Institute and Clinic, University of Pittsburgh, School of Medicine, Pittsburgh, PA 15213.

1978). Despite criticism regarding the arbitrary and rigid nature of this approach (it has jokingly been referred to as a Chinese-menu system), it has succeeded with respect to achieving acceptable levels of interrater reliability for the major psychiatric syndromes. Needless to say, poor reliability of diagnoses has been a longstanding limitation of the medical approach to problems in human behavior (Mischel, 1968).

Overview of DSM-III Diagnosis

The system used for diagnosis of the affective disorders in the DSM-III follows the tradition of Kraepelin's classic descriptions. As illustrated in Figures 1 and 2, affective syndromes are initially subdivided on the basis of whether a full syndrome is present (major affective disorders) or a less severe (minor), subsyndromal condition is present. A residual category of atypical affective disorder is included for the classification of conditions that defy the major–minor dichotomy. Next, each category may be further divided on the basis of the history of a manic episode. Conditions marked by a history of manic episodes are termed *bipolar*. Bipolar disorders are subdivided further by the nature of the current episode: depressed, manic, or mixed. Subsyndromal bipolar disorders are classified as cyclothymia.

Nonbipolar major depressions are subdivided into single-episode or recurrent (unipolar) types. Chronic (i.e., of more than two years, duration) subsyndromal depressions are termed *dysthymic disorders*. Individuals with such conditions frequently develop episodes of major depression superimposed on a more chronic course (Keller, Lavori, Endicott, Coryell, & Klerman, 1983). Each of the major affective disorders may also be classified as psychotic if delusions and/or hallucinations are present. Finally, major depressions characterized by pervasive anhedonia, loss of mood reactivity, and at least three associated neurovegetative features are termed *melancholic*. As will be discussed later, melancholia corresponds to depressions previously referred to as *endogenous* or *vital*.

Specific Diagnostic Categories

Manic Disorders. The diagnostic criteria for a manic episode are summarized in Table 1. Approximately 10% to 20% of individuals with a major affective disorder are ultimately classified as bipolar (Akiskal, 1983a; Klerman, 1984). Early age of onset, greater number of episodes of illness, a similar incidence in men and women, response to lithium treatment, and family history data have traditionally been used to validate the bipolar–nonbipolar (unipolar) dichotomy (Akiskal, 1983a). A history of at least three episodes of depression without a manic episode conveys a 90% certainty that the disorder is unipolar (recurrent) depression, not bipolar disorder (Akiskal, 1983a). Nevertheless, individuals with apparently unipolar depressive conditions may develop a manic episode at any point in the life span.

Mania is a pervasive condition, encompassing changes in mood (euphoria, elation, or irritability), cognition, and behavior. Impulsivity, poor judgment, and overvalued ideas can lead to disastrous economic and interpersonal consequences. Moreover, manic individuals frequently are noncompliant with treatment because of a loss of insight and an inflated sense of well-being.

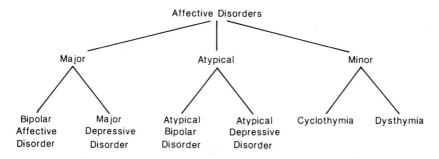

Figure 1. Schematic overview of the DSM-III classification of affective disorders.

A significant minority of manic patients exhibit psychotic features. In addition to mood-congruent delusions, as many as 20% of severely disturbed manic patients experience formal thought disorder, paranoid delusions, Schneiderian first-rank symptoms, and/or catatonic features (Pope & Lipinski, 1978). Before the introduction of operationalized diagnostic criteria, American psychiatrists tended to overdiagnose schizophrenia in such cases (Cooper, Kendell, Gurland, Sharpe, Copeland, & Simon, 1972).

Less severe episodes of mania are referred to as *hypomania*. Such episodes commonly occur over the longitudinal course of bipolar disorder, as well as in some "nonbipolar" patients during pharmacological treatment or following recovery. Individuals with ma-

Table 1. Diagnostic Criteria for a Manic Episode

A. One or more distinct periods in which mood is elevated, expansive, or irritable.[a]

B. At least three of the following symptoms have persisted to a significant degree for at least one week (four symptoms are required if the mood is only irritable):

    1. increased social, vocational, and/or sexual activity
    2. more talkative than usual; pressured speech
    3. racing thoughts; flight of ideas
    4. grandiosity; inflated self-esteem
    5. reduced need for sleep
    6. distractibility
    7. poor judgment, as reflected by involvement in activities that are likely to have adverse consequences, for example, spending sprees, sexual promiscuity, or risky business investments

C. Neither of the following are prominent when the affective syndrome is remitted:

    1. mood-incongruent delusions or hallucinations
    2. bizarre behavior

D. Not superimposed on a nonaffective psychotic disorder (i.e., schizophrenic, schizophreniform, or paranoid disorders).

E. Not due to an organic mental disorder, including intoxication with psychostimulants.

Note. Adapted from *Diagnostic and Statistical Manual* (3rd ed.), American Psychiatric Association (1980).
[a]Items A through E must be met for a definite diagnosis of a manic episode.

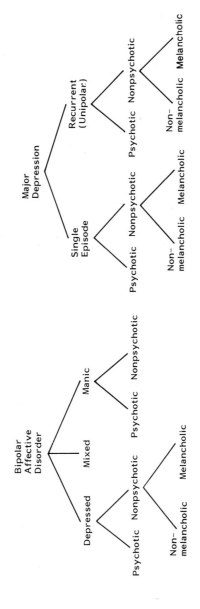

Figure 2. DSM-III subtypes of bipolar and nonbipolar major affective disorders.

jor depression who have occasionally experienced periods of hypomania are referred to as having *atypical bipolar disorder* in the DSM-III or bipolar II in the Research Diagnostic Criteria (RDC; Spitzer *et al.*, 1978).

The term *mixed state* refers to an episode in which both manic and depressive features are present. Mixed states may develop spontaneously or, perhaps more commonly, reflect the deleterious effects of intercurrent abuse of alcohol or sedatives on mood (Himmelhoch, 1979).

Major Depression. The diagnostic criteria for major depression are summarized in Table 2. These criteria apply to classification of both bipolar and nonbipolar depressions. A diagnosis of major depression depends on the presence of depressed mood and/or anhedonia, an associated syndromal cluster of symptoms (at least four of the items described in Table 2), and persistence (i.e., symptoms present nearly every day for at least two weeks).

Perhaps the most serious aspect of major depression is the risk of suicide. Although suicidal ideation is not specific to depression, longitudinal studies indicate that as many as 15% of individuals with major affective disorders die by suicide (Clayton, 1983). Assessment of suicidal ideation is an essential part of the evaluation of all depressed individuals.

The available evidence indicates that depressive disorders in childhood and adolescence have symptomatology similar to adult forms. Accordingly, the DSM-III does not include a specific diagnostic category for childhood depression.

Table 2. Diagnostic Criteria for a Major Depressive Episode

A. Sad, down, or irritable mood or loss of interest or pleasure (if dysphoria is masked). These affective disturbances must be prominent and relatively persistent.[a]

B. An accompanying syndrome including at least four of the following symptoms (which have been present nearly every day for at least two weeks):

   1. poor appetite/weight loss or increased appetite/weight gain
   2. insomnia or hypersomnia
   3. psychomotor agitation or retardation
   4. decreased interest, pleasure, or libido
   5. fatigue/decreased energy
   6. feelings of worthlessness or guilt
   7. poor concentration; diminished ability to think clearly
   8. thoughts of death or suicidal behavior/ideation

C. Neither of the following are prominent when the affective syndrome is remitted:

   1. mood-incongruent delusions or hallucinations
   2. bizarre behavior

D. Not superimposed on a nonaffective psychotic disorder (i.e., schizophrenic, schizophreniform, or paranoid disorders).

E. Not due to a recent bereavement or to a physical illness (e.g., hypothyroidism) known to cause an organic effective syndrome.

Note. Adapted from *Diagnostic and Statistical Manual* (3rd ed.), American Psychiatric Association (1980).
[a]Items A through E must be met for a definite diagnosis of major depression.

Review of the symptomatic criteria for major depression illustrates the variability of the syndrome. Either decreased appetite and weight loss or increased appetite and weight gain, insomnia or hypersomnia, and agitation or motor retardation may be present. The most common clinical presentation of nonbipolar major depression includes insomnia, decreased appetite, and anxiety and/or agitation. Weight gain, hypersomnia, and "leaden" anergia are more characteristic of bipolar depressions or nonbipolar depressions that have been linked to the bipolar spectrum (Akiskal, 1983a; Davidson, Miller, Turnbull, & Sullivan, 1982).

Some investigators argue that the diagnostic criteria for major depression are not stringent enough, permitting inclusion of individuals with mild dysphorias associated with demoralization or long-standing characterological disturbances (Akiskal, 1983a; Nelson & Charney, 1981). Such a position is strengthened by the relatively low predictive validity for drug response of a number of DSM-III criteria for major depression and a higher incidence of personality disorders and maladaptive personality traits in individuals with nonmelancholic major depressions (Charney, Nelson, & Quinlan, 1981; Nelson & Charney, 1981). The DSM-III criteria for the melancholic subtype appear to meet these objections (Nelson & Charney, 1981). It remains to be seen if these arguments will lead to the adoption of more stringent diagnostic criteria for major depression.

The diagnostic criteria for melancholia are summarized in Table 3. These criteria are more exacting than the RDC criteria for definite endogenous depression: both pervasive anhedonia *and* lack of mood reactivity are required to be present. *Mood reactivity* refers to the ability of an individual to show at least a transient lift in mood if something positive happens. Pervasive anhedonia and lack of reactivity have been shown to predict the need for somatic treatment in hospitalized depressed individuals (Nelson & Charney, 1981). Other criteria for melancholia include guilt, early-morning awakening, weight loss, diurnal mood variation, and psychomotor disturbances. These features are generally associated with high ratings of global severity.

It remains a point of controversy whether melancholia represents a distinct subtype of major depression or, conversely, simply the most extreme end of a continuum (Kendell, 1976; Klerman, 1984). Research using biological parameters (see Carroll, 1982; Thase, Frank, & Kupfer, 1985) and family history data (Leckman, Weissman, Prusoff, Caruso, Marikangas, Pauls, & Kidd, 1984) tend to support the validity of melancholia as a distinct subtype.

Approximately 5% to 10% of major depressions are characterized by the presence of delusions or hallucinations (Klerman, 1984). Depressive delusions are frequently mood-congruent; that is, they involve themes of guilt, sin, poverty, illness, or nihilism. Psychotic depressions are often associated with marked severity, psychomotor disturbances, and poor response to treatment with tricyclic antidepressants (Charney & Nelson, 1981; Coryell, Pfohl, & Zimmerman, 1984).

Chronic Depressions. Chronic depressions may be categorized in the DSM-III as major depression or dysthymia, depending on whether or not a full syndrome is present. Although major depression is generally thought of as an episodic condition, roughly 15% of such disorders may persist for more than two years (Klerman, 1984). Chronicity may be related to advancing age, chaotic interpersonal affairs, intercurrent substance or alcohol abuse, coexisting medical conditions, and/or inadequate treatment (Akiskal, 1983a; Thase & Kupfer, in press).

Table 3. Diagnostic Criteria for a Melancholia

A. Loss of pleasure in all or almost all activities *and* lack of mood reactivity to usually pleasurable activities.[a]

B. A syndrome including at least three of the following symptoms:

1. distinct mood quality (i.e., the depressed mood is distinctly different from "normal" sadness or grief)
2. diurnal variation of mood (i.e., mood worse in the morning)
3. early morning awakening (greater than two hours earlier than usual)
4. marked psychomotor disturbance (retardation or agitation)
5. significantly decreased appetite and/or weight loss
6. pathological guilt (i.e., excessive or inappropriate to the situation)

Note. Adapted from *Diagnostic and Statistical Manual* (3rd ed.), American Psychiatric Association (1980).
[a]Both items A and B must be met, in addition to all criteria for major depression, for a diagnosis of melancholia.

The DSM-III diagnosis of dysthymic disorder describes a heterogeneous group of individuals. Akiskal (1983b) has extensively studied a large sample of chronically depressed individuals. Drawing on clinical phenomenology, longitudinal course, family history, treatment response, and electroencephalographic (EEG) sleep studies, he concluded that chronic depressions could be subdivided into cases with either late-onset, unremitted major depressions, lifelong patterns of maladjustment and dysphoria, or early-onset forms of primary affective disorders.

Other Related Conditions. Three DSM-III conditions that are not classified as affective disorders merit brief discussion. First, a depressive syndrome associated with bereavement is not routinely classified as a mental disorder in the DSM-III because the normal grieving process usually resolves without specific treatment or sequelae (Clayton, 1982). If, however, a bereaved individual should develop a more prolonged and severe syndrome, particularly if characterized by marked psychomotor disturbances or guilt, a major depressive disorder should be diagnosed.

Second, mildly dysphoric reactions to clearly upsetting life events are termed *adjustment disorders with depressed mood*. This diagnosis should not be used if the individual has a full major depressive syndrome, even if there is an apparent relationship between the onset of the episode and a stressful life event.

Finally, the term *schizoaffective disorder* is included in the DSM-III as a residual category without operationalized criteria. This condition was previously grouped among the schizophrenic disorders. Recognition of psychotic forms of mania and depression have reduced the need for a schizoaffective classification, and numerous studies have documented a close association with bipolar affective disorder (see Taylor, 1984). It may be prudent to reserve the diagnosis of schizoaffective disorder for individuals who show acute psychotic features, clear-cut mood swings, a chronic longitudinal course, and the presence of residual thought disorder even during periods of remission.

Organic Affective Disorders. This term refers to a broad group of conditions in which the affective syndrome is known to be caused by a medical condition. Although medical conditions are most commonly associated with depression, secondary manic syndromes have also been described (Krauthammer & Klerman, 1978). Organic affective syndromes may be indistinguishable from major affective disorders on the basis of clinical examinations.

Lists of the various conditions and medications known to cause organic affective syndromes are provided in Tables 4 and 5. The exact incidence of organic affective syndromes is not known. However, both hypothyroidism and antihypertensive treatment are known to convey a high risk for development of depression. Initial assessment of all depressed persons should include careful ascertainment of medical history and medication usage patterns. A physical examination and appropriate laboratory studies are indicated for most adults. The emergence of an affective syndrome following the initiation of a medication or during the course of a severe medical illness should provide a red flag for recognition of an organic affective syndrome.

One commonly overlooked form of organic affective syndrome follows detoxification from long-standing alcoholism. A number of surveys indicate that as many as 50% of recently detoxified alcoholics manifest a depressive syndrome (see Klerman, 1984). However, a majority of such cases remit spontaneously after a 2- to 4-week period of abstinence from alcohol, proper nutrition, and supportive care.

Differential Diagnosis

Use of the standardized criteria provided in the DSM-III lessens but does not eliminate diagnostic problems that arise in clinical settings. The concept of differential diagnosis is applicable in such ambiguous cases. A list of possible diagnoses is formed and rank-ordered, on the basis of the available information, from most probable to least likely. This process is facilitated by collection of the most complete database possible. An initial interview lasting from one to two hours, past medical and psychiatric records, and collateral contact with a significant other provide an ideal starting point. Contact with family members is especially important in detecting a history of hypomanic mood swings or alcohol and substance use patterns, as these tend to be underreported in standard clinical interviews. In more severe and complicated cases, an inpatient evaluation with an extended alcohol and drug-free observation period are particularly useful.

The standards used to validate medical diagnoses also facilitate differential diagnosis. These standards include (1) clinical phenomenology, (2) family history, (3) longitudinal course, (4) treatment response, and (5) laboratory studies (Goodwin & Guze, 1979). In cases with ambiguous clinical features, detection of a family history of affective disorder or suicide, a clinical course marked by episodes of mental disorder and periods of full remission, or a past positive response to treatment with lithium, tricyclics, or electroconvulsive therapy (ECT) would raise the probability of an affective disorder diagnosis. Finally, although routine application of tests for various biological distrubances in depression and mania is still premature, both EEG sleep studies (Kupfer & Thase, 1983) and the dexamethasone suppression test (DST; Carroll, 1982) are now used in selected cases to confirm an affective disorder diagnosis. Some common differential diagnostic problems are described below.

Psychotic States. Individuals with a complex intermingling of psychotic and affective features present a rather frequent differential-diagnostic problem, particularly when it is a first episode of mental disorder. A tentative diagnosis of atypical psychosis or schizophreniform disorder is often assigned. A significant proportion of such cases subsequently show a clinical course consistent with major affective disorder, although others

Table 4. Medical Conditions Associated with Organic Affective Syndromes

Endocrine causes
  Acromegaly
  Hypoadrenalism
  Hyperparathyroidism
  Hypoparathyroidism
  Hypopituitarism
  Hyperthyroidism
  Hypothyroidism

Vitamin and mineral disorders
  Beri-beri (vitamin B1 deficiency)
  Hypervitaminosis A
  Hypomagnesemia
  Pellagra (nicotinic acid deficiency)
  Pernicious anemia (vitamin B12 deficiency)
  Wernicke's encephalopathy

Neurological disorders
  Multiple sclerosis
  Tuberous sclerosis
  Wilson's disease
  Dementia Alzheimer's type
  Stroke
  Huntington's disease

Infections
  Encephalitis
  Hepatitis
  Influenza
  Malaria
  Mononucleosis
  Pneumonia
  Syphilis
  Tuberculosis

Collagen disorders
  Systematic lupus erythematosus
  Polyarteritis nodosa

Cardiovascular disease
  Cardiomyopathy
  Congestive heart failure
  Myocardial infarction

Malignancy
  Carcinoid
  Pancreatic carcinoma
  Pheochromocytoma

Metabolic
  Porphyria
  Intoxication states

Note. Adapted from Klerman (1984).

Table 5. Medications Associated with Organic Affective Syndromes

	Generic names	Selected trade names
Antihypertensive	Reserpine	Serpasil, Sandril
	Methyldopa	Aldomet
	Propranolol hydrochloride	Inderal
	Guanethidine sulfate	Ismelin sulfate
	Hydralazine hydrochloride	Apresoline hydrochloride
	Clonidine hydrochloride	Catapres
Antiparkinsonian	Levodopa	Dopar, Larodopa
	Levodopa, carbidopa	Sinemet
	Amantadine hydrochloride	Symmetrel
Hormones	Estrogen	Estrace, Menrium, Premarin
	Progesterone	Progestasert
Corticosteriod	Cortisone acetate	Cortone acetate
Antituberculosis	Cycloserine	Seromycin
Anticancer	Vincristine sulfate	Oncovin
	Vinblastine sulfate	Velban
Antiulcer	Cimetidine	Tagamet

Note. Adapted from Klerman (1984).

develop a schizophrenic disorder (Taylor, 1984). In many cases, monitoring of response to mood-altering treatments (i.e., lithium or tricyclics) and careful long-term follow-up are necessary to clarify the diagnosis.

Anxiety Disorders. The overlap between anxiety and depression disorders has long been troublesome to clinicians and clearly points to the lack of specificity of selected clinical symptoms (e.g., insomnia, tension, fatigue, or appetite changes). Extensive investigations using psychometric techniques, such as factor or cluster analysis, as well as longitudinal follow-up and pharmacological studies, have been used to validate the distinction between anxiety and depressive disorders (see Roth & Mountjoy, 1982).

There are several salient areas of overlap between anxiety and depressive disorders with direct clinical implications. First, a relatively large number (perhaps up to 50%) of individuals with clear-cut cases of panic disorder, generalized anxiety, agoraphobia, or obsessive-compulsive disorder subsequently develop an episode of major depression (Grunhaus & Birmaher, 1985). In the DSM-III, both the "primary" anxiety disorder and the "secondary" major depression would be diagnosed.

Second, as many as 10% to 20% of individuals with clear-cut depressive episodes experience panic attacks (Grunhaus & Birmaher, 1985). Differentiation of a primary diagnosis of panic disorder from a diagnosis of depression would depend on obtaining a history of the temporal relationship between the onset of each of the symptoms. The current convention is that the onset of panic disorder must precede the development of a depressive syndrome if both conditions are to be diagnosed.

The distinction between anxiety and depressive disorders may be blurred further by the fact that both monoamine oxidase inhibitors and tricyclic antidepressants have some utility in treating panic disorder, obsessive-compulsive disorder, and agoraphobia (Grunhaus & Birmaher, 1985; Klein, Gittelman, Quitkin, & Rifkin, 1980). Similarly, recent family studies support a genetic link between depression and selected DSM-III anxiety disorders (Leckman, Weissman, Merikangas, Kidd, Pauls, & Prusoff, 1983; Weissman, Leckman, Merikangas, Gammon, & Prusoff, 1984).

One practical implication of these findings is to recognize the coexistence of anxiety and depressive disorders in some individuals, rather than resolutely trying to identify the "pure" condition. The persistence, frequency, and nature of the anxiety-related complaints may also impact on the course of the depressive disorder: the presence of panic attacks may predict a favorable response to selected antidepressant agents, whereas more enduring generalized anxiety or a primary panic disorder may forbode a poorer clinical outcome (Grunhaus & Birmaher, 1985; Thase & Kupfer, in press).

*Dementia.*Depressive disorders and dementia occur with a similar prevalence in the elderly (Blazer, 1983). Moreover, apathy, dysphoria, and concentration difficulties typically accompany both conditions. Cognitive impairments may be so striking in some depressed elders that a diagnosis of dementia is suspected. This condition has been referred to as *pseudodementia* (Wells, 1979). A past history of affective disorder, psychomotor changes, a negative neurological work-up, and the use of "I don't know" responses are considered suggestive of pseudodementia rather than a true dementia (Wells, 1979). However, clinical differentiation is often difficult, and antidepressant treatment is indicated if the depressive features are prominent. Pseudodementia has also been described in mania (Thase & Reynolds, 1984).

BIOLOGICAL ABNORMALTIES

Several lines of indirect evidence point to the role of biological factors in affective disorders. These observations include episodicity of the clinical course, a dramatic shift from depression to mania, a profile of neurovegetative symptoms seen in severe (melancholic) depressions, and a high familial incidence of mood disorders (Baldessarini, 1983; Thase et al., 1985). The tendency for selected antihypertensive drugs to cause clinical depressions and the antidepressant effects of "somatic treatments" (ECT, tricyclics, and monoamine oxidase inhibitors) may also be added to this list (Baldessarini, 1983; Thase et al., 1985). Appropriate experimental methods to directly study complex neurochemical, endocrine, and neurophysiological processes have been available only since the mid-1960s. Research methods in these areas are being refined constantly, the result being improved precision of measurement, a lessening of the effects of experimental artifact, and further advances in understanding normal physiological mechanisms.

Before turning to evidence regarding biological abnormalities in affective disorders, a brief summary of some conceptual issues related to such studies may be helpful. First, as major depression is a syndrome and not a distinct illness, there is no reason to expect to find a single biological disturbance underlying all forms of the disorder. Second, study of grouped biological data may obscure the detection of distinct biological subtypes that are present in only a minority of patients (Thase et al., 1985). Third, it is expected that some individuals (particularly those with a single episode of nonmelancholic major depression) will show little evidence of biological dysfunction. Fourth, detection of a physiological abnormality does not guarantee biological causality. The abnormality may reflect an artifact or an epiphenomenon of the clinical state (i.e., sleep loss, altered activity level, or weight change), hospitalization, or drug treatment. Methodological factors requiring attention include the use of a drug-free "washout" period, a standardization of the experimental conditions (i.e., time of day and diet), and comparisons against both normal controls and nonaffective patient samples. Fifth, abnormalities may be present only during periods of acute symptomatology (state markers) or may persist during periods of remission (trait markers) (Kupfer, 1982). Longitudinal studies are needed to address this distinction. With these issues in mind, the incidence and significance of various biological abnormalities are next reviewed.

Neurochemical Abnormalities

Monoamines. Early biological hypotheses of depression focused on possible disturbances of catecholamines, such as norepinephrine (NE) and dopamine (DA), and the indoleamine serotonin (5HT) (Bunney & Davis, 1965; Glassman, 1969; Schildkraut, 1965). These hypotheses are collectively referred to as the *monoamine* (MA) *hypotheses.* The MA hypotheses were guided by the observations that many antidepressants produce increased levels of MA in the neuronal synapse and that MAs are important neurotransmitters in the regulation of sleep, appetite, and emotional processes (Bunney & Davis, 1965; Glassman, 1969). It was predicted that depressions would be found to be associated with decreased MA activity (either through decreased synthesis, increased degradation, or altered synaptic function), and that mania might involve increased NE or DA activity (Bunney & Davis, 1965; Schildkraut, 1965).

Nearly 20 years of research has been devoted to the MA hypotheses, with frankly equivocal results (Baldessarini, 1983; Zis & Goodwin, 1982). It should be noted that despite the development of precise methods of measuring MAs and their metabolites, brain neurochemistry may not be reflected by studies of plasma, urine, or even cerebrospinal fluid specimens (Zis & Goodwin, 1982). Moreover, even assays of brain tissue from suicide victims are subject to methodological artifacts (i.e., correct diagnosis, drug treatment effects, or specimen preparation).

The most widely studied index of NE activity is 3-methoxy-4-hydroxy-phenylglycol (MHPG), a key metabolite of NE in the brain. A number of studies indicate that some depressed patients show reduced levels of 24-h excretion of urinary MHPG (see Schildkraut, 1982; Thase et al., 1985). It has been proposed that individuals with low MHPG levels have a deficiency of NE, and that the remainder of patients who show normal or high urinary MHPG levels having depressions related to 5HT or other abnormalities (Baldessarini, 1983; Schildkraut, 1982). This hypothesis is supported by several studies reporting favorable response to noradrenergic antidepressants in patients with low MHPG levels (see Schildkraut, 1982). However, conflicting reports regarding the utility of MHPG levels in predicting drug response, as well as technical and methodological issues, have clouded the significance of this parameter (Baldessarini, 1983; Kelwala, Jones, & Sitaram, 1983). It is of interest that low urinary MHPG is commonly seen in bipolar depression, and that switches into mania are accompanied by increased levels of urinary MHPG (Schildkraut, 1982). Thus, it is conceivable that low urinary MHPG levels reflect a clinical state common in bipolar disorder (low activity level, relative absence of anxiety, and psychomotor retardation), which, in turn, is associated with response to tricyclics such as imipramine (Thase et al., 1985).

Other investigations of NE activity in depressed individuals, including studies of the brains of suicide victims, have failed to yield definitive evidence of either an NE deficiency state in major depression or an excess in mania (Rotman, 1983; Zis & Goodwin, 1982). Several studies document increased NE activity in some depressed individuals (Koslow, Maas, Bowden, Davis, Hanin, & Javaid, 1983; Linnoila, Karoum, & Potter, 1982). Other studies have focused on measurement of the activity of the enzyme monoamine oxidase (MAO) in blood platelets. Low levels of MAO activity have been reported in bipolar depression, whereas high levels tend to be found in individuals with depressions characterized by anxious features (Rotman, 1983).

There is even less evidence of DA disturbance in affective disorders (Thase et al., 1985; Zis & Goodwin, 1982). One possible exception is in psychotic depression, where increased levels of homovanillic acid (HVA, a DA metabolite) and decreased dopamine beta-hydroxylase (a degradative enzyme) have been reported (Meltzer, Cho, Carroll, & Russo, 1976). Similarly, dopaminergic overactivity may be inferred from EEG sleep and neuroendocrine studies in psychotic depression (Thase, Kupfer, & Ulrich, 1986). Other investigations that report decreased levels of HVA in depression and increased levels in mania suggest a relationship with psychomotor activity levels (Linnoila, Karoum, & Potter, 1983; van Praag, 1980b).

Also, few firm conclusions can be reached with respect to 5HT activity in depression and mania. Several groups have reported a subgroup of depressed patients with low levels of 5-hydroxyindoleacetic acid (5HIAA, the principal 5HT metabolite) in the cerebrospinal fluid (see van Praag, 1980a). Low 5HIAA levels may predict response to both the serotonergic antidepressant amitriptyline in nonbipolar depression (Maas, Koslow, Katz, Gibbons, Bowden, Robins, & Davis, 1984) and response to supplemental treatment with precursors of 5HT synthesis (van Praag, 1980a). Low 5HIAA levels have also been associated with violent suicidal behavior (Asberg & Traskman, 1981; Brown, Ebert, Goyer, Jimerson, Klein, Bunney, & Goodwin, 1982). However, other groups have failed to confirm the existence of a distinct group of depressed individuals with low 5HIAA (Koslow et al., 1983). As was the case with urinary MHPG, it appears that some depressed patients show decreased levels of 5HT, and such an abnormality may have predictive validity for treatment response. Nevertheless, the clinical utility of such findings remains very limited at this time.

Results from several groups indicate that a subgroup of unmedicated depressed patients (perhaps 40%–50%) manifest reduced levels of serotonin receptor sites, as measured by the binding of radioactively labeled [³H]-imipramine (Paul, Rehavi, Skolnick, Ballenger, & Goodwin, 1981) or uptake of [¹⁴C]-serotonin (Meltzer, Arora, Tricou, & Fang, 1983). Sherman and Petty (1984) demonstrated a similar reduction in [³H]-imipramine binding in rats following a learned-helplessness procedure. A reduced number of serotonin receptor sites does not appear to be related to clinical subtypes of major depression but may aggregate in families of depressed persons (Meltzer et al., 1983).

Other Neurochemical Studies. A possible relationship between depression and increased activity of another key neurotransmitter, acetylcholine (ACH), has also received investigation (Janowsky, Risch, & Gillin, 1983). It may be further argued that mania is associated with decreased ACH activity. Although direct support of these hypotheses is lacking, studies of the effects of cholinergic agents on mood, EEG sleep, and neuroendocrine parameters are suggestive (Janowsky et al., 1983; Sitaram, Nurnberger, Gershon, & Gillin, 1982). Lack of antidepressant efficacy of agents with purely anticholinergic properties weighs against this hypothesis. Moreover, the physiological "balancing" role of ACH versus NE and 5HT in brain neurochemistry would suggest that a primary deficiency of NE or 5HT could produce an apparent excess of ACH (McCarley, 1982).

Other groups have studied trace biogenic amines, neuropeptides, salt and mineral regulation, prostaglandins, cyclic nucleotides, and membrane transport mechanisms in affective disorders (see Post & Ballenger, 1984). Although there are several promising leads, findings in these areas are still preliminary, and more definitive research is under way.

Receptor Changes. It was noted previously that the effects of antidepressant medications at the synapse appear to support MA theories of depression. However, although such MA-enhancing effects are apparent within hours, clinical antidepressant effects take 3 to 6 weeks to emerge (Baldessarini, 1983). Further, amphetamine and cocaine have potent MA-enhancing effects (and produce transient euphoria in normal individuals) but do not have durable antidepressant effects (Zis & Goodwin, 1982). By contrast, chronic treatment with a variety of antidepressant agents produces changes in both presynaptic and postsynaptic neurotransmitter receptors over a time course that corresponds more closely with clinical response (Charney, Menkes, & Heninger, 1981). It remains to be seen if alterations in specific subtypes of adrenergic or serotonergic receptors are present in depressed persons before treatment.

A summary of neurochemical findings in affective disorders is provided in Table 6.

Table 6. Summary of Neurochemical Abnormalities in Affective Disorders

1. Reduced 24-h urinary excretion of norepinephrine metabolite MHPG in a subset of depressions (bipolar); low levels predict positive response to imipramine.

2. Elevated plasma levels of norepinephrine and its metabolites in a subset of depressions, associated with panic–anxiety and agitation.

3. Possible increased dopaminergic activity in psychotic depressions and mania, probably associated with agitation and/or activity level.

4. Low CSF levels of serotonin metabolite 5HIAA in a subgroup of melancholic depressions; low 5HIAA may predict response to amitriptyline and is associated with violent suicidal behavior.

5. Reduced serotonin receptor binding in 40%–50% of depressed patients.

6. Increased cholinergic activity in depressions inferred from pharmacological studies on mood and neuroendocrine and sleep physiology parameters.

Neurophysiological Abnormalities

Electroencephalographic Sleep Changes. Clinical reports of sleep disturbances in manic and depressed individuals have been quantified by the use of all-night EEG recordings. A typical sleep profile of a depressed individual is presented in Figure 3. This profile illustrates the four types of EEG sleep abnormalities commonly seen in depression: impaired sleep continuity (i.e., frequent awakenings and early-morning awakening), diminished deep slow-wave sleep (i.e., reduced percentage of Stage 3 and Stage 4 sleep time), shortened latency to the onset of the first episode of rapid-eye-movement (REM) sleep, and shifting of REM sleep activity into the first few hours of sleep (Gillin, 1983; Kupfer & Thase, 1983).

Both sleep continuity disturbances and diminished slow-wave sleep are nonspecific findings; they are observed in a variety of nonaffective psychiatric conditions and medical disorders (Gillin, 1983; Kupfer & Thase, 1983). By contrast, shortened REM latency is more specific to depression. Mean REM-latency values in major depressions generally range from 45 to 60 min, that is, values much lower than those seen in normal populations (90 $\pm$ 20 min) (Kupfer & Thase, 1983).

Shortened REM latency in depression is present in 60% to 90% of depressed individuals, as compared to 15% to 30% of control populations (see Kupfer & Thase, 1983). A majority of individuals with each of the DSM-III subtypes of major affective disorder—bipolar, recurrent (unipolar), melancholic, and psychotic depressions—have shortened REM latency: (Kupfer & Thase, 1983). Shortened REM latency is also seen in roughly one half of cases of atypical depression and dysthymic disorder; in such instances, it may suggest a subsyndromal form of primary affective disorder (Akiskal, 1983a). Moreover, other conditions in which shortened REM latency is observed have been linked to the affective disorders, including alcoholism, anorexia nervosa, schizoaffective disorder, borderline personality disorder, and obsessive-compulsive disorder (Gillin, 1983; Kupfer & Thase, 1983). Less extensive data are available regarding EEG sleep changes in mania. It appears that sleep-continuity changes and decreased slow-wave sleep are common, and some manic individuals also show shortened REM latency (Gillin, 1983).

Shortened REM latency is found in some patients with depressions developing "secondary" to other nonaffective psychiatric conditions (Thase, Kupfer, & Spiker, 1984). By contrast, more transient blue moods in normal individuals generally do not appear to affect REM latency (Cohen, 1979). However, Cartwright (1983) found shortened REM latency in a nonpatient sample of women who were experiencing significant depressive symptomatology while in the process of divorce. This finding indicates that a well-described "biological" sign of depression may develop following a clearly situational onset of an affective syndrome.

It is not clear if EEG sleep disturbances are entirely state-dependent or if some features may persist as traits markers (Kupfer, 1982). For example, although REM latency values tend to return to nearly normal values in drug-free individuals following recovery (Kupfer, 1982), pharmacological challenges with cholinergic agents may elicit shortened REM latency months after clinical remission (Sitaram et al., 1982). We are currently studying whether shortened REM latency may predict vulnerability to relapse in recovered, medication-free individuals.

Other Neurophysiological Disturbances. Comparisons of waking EEG rhythms in depression and mania fail to reveal any characteristic abnormalities. However, routine waking-EEG studies may be of considerable value in the assessment of individuals with complicated or atypical affective states, where temporal lobe epilepsy or other cerebral dysrhythmias may be recognized.

Application of more sophisticated approaches, such as spectral analyses of EEG rhythms or average evoked potentials, suggests several possible disturbances in depression (see Thase et al., 1985). These findings include reduced frequency and amplitude of EEG waves (Shagass, Roemer, & Straumanis, 1982) and abnormal lateralization of EEG rhythms (Flor-Henry, 1984). Investigations using motoric activity monitoring (see Greden & Carroll, 1981) or EEG average evoked-potential patterns (Buchsbaum, 1975) tend to support the validity of subgrouping depressions into hypoactive (bipolar) and agitated (unipolar) forms. Other studies of neurophysiological parameters in depression suggest reduced electrodermal activity (Iacono, Lyken, Peloquin, Lumry, Valentine, & Tuason, 1983; Ward, Doerr, & Storrie, 1983) or hypoactive colonic motility (Lechin, Van der Dijs, Acosta, Gomez, Lechin & Arocha, 1983). It should be noted, however, that such observations may reflect neurophysiological correlates of psychomotor retardation rather than specific pathophysiological abnormalities (Thase et al., 1985).

Neurophysiological abnormalities in depression and mania are summarized in Table 7.

Neuroendocrine Abnormalities

Diseases of endocrine glands, such as Cushing's syndrome (hypercortisolism) and hypothyroidism, are well-known causes of organic affective states. Considerable attention has been given to changes in endocrine function in persons with affective syndromes. Such changes are of particular interest because the neurotransmitters implicated in affective disorders (i.e., norepinephrine, dopamine, serotonin, and acetylcholine) also are involved in the regulation of endocrine processes (Brown & Seggie, 1980). The following sections summarize the evidence of disturbances of the hypothalamic-pituitary-adrenal cortex (HYPAC) function, thyroid regulation, and other endocrine systems in affective disorders.

HYPAC Disturbances. Increased secretion of cortisol by the adrenal cortex is a normal physiological response to a variety of psychological and physical stressors. However,

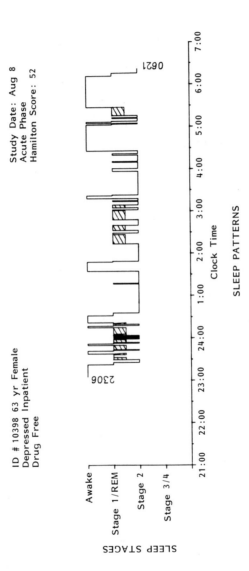

Figure 3. EEG sleep recording in an individual with melancholic major depression, illustrating (1) sleep continuity disturbance; (2) absence of slow-wave (Stages 3 and 4) sleep; (3) shortened REM latency; and (4) increased REM time during the first hours of sleep.

Table 7. Summary of Neurophysiological Abnormalities in Affective Disorders

1. All-night sleep EEG studies document both specific (shortened REM latency and altered REM distribution) and nonspecific (sleep continuity disturbances) abnormalities in a majority of depressives; such findings may also be present in mania.

2. Waking-EEG studies indicate an "augmenting" evoked-potential response in bipolar depressions and a "reducing" amplitude response in nonbipoilar depressions.

3. Possible reduced mean frequency and amplitude of waking EEG in depressions but not mania; findings may be related to level of psychomotor retardation or agitation.

4. Possible abnormal lateralization of cerebral function in depressions, with relatively increased nondominant activity.

5. Possible reduced electrodermal activity in depression (linked to psychomotor retardation).

6. Possible reduced colonic motility in depression (linked to psychomotor retardation).

research since the early 1970s suggests that the HYPAC disturbances in affective states represent more than a nonspecific stress response. Common HYPAC disturbances in depression include elevated plasma concentrations of cortisol, increased urinary excretion of cortisol and its metabolites, blunted circadian cortisol rhythm, altered feedback inhibition, and possible elevations of adrenocorticotrophic hormone (ACTH) (Carroll, 1982; Sachar, 1982; Thase *et al.*, 1985).

Numerous investigators have studied the dexamethasone suppression test (DST) as an index of HYPAC activity (see Carroll, 1982). The DST assesses the integrity of the feedback inhibition system that controls HYPAC functioning. A bedtime dose of 1.0 and 2.0 mg of dexamethasone, a potent synthetic corticosteroid, normally shuts off HYPAC activity for over 24 h. However, in a significant proportion of depressed patients, plasma cortisol levels either remain high for at least 24 h following dexamethasone administration or escape from initial suppression during the afternoon or evening of the following day. Such reactions thus mimic the DST pattern seen in Cushing's syndrome.

Studies at the University of Michigan (see Carroll, 1982) suggested that DST nonsuppression identified melancholia with 67% sensitivity and 95% specificity. These results compared favorably with those of many standard diagnostic tests used in medical practice. Other investigators have failed to fully replicate the high levels of sensitivity and specificity initially reported by Carroll (1982). For example, DST nonsuppression rates of only 15% to 30% are reported in several outpatient studies (see Thase *et al.*, 1985), and two investigations found false-positive rates of greater than 30% (Meltzer, Fang, Tricou, Robertson, & Piyaka, 1982; Stokes, Stoll, Koslow, Maas, Davis, Swann, & Robins, 1984). Such observations illustrate the profound impact of assessment and setting variables on the performance of the DST as a diagnostic test. For example, the diagnosis of melancholia used by Carroll group is not synonymous with DSM-III major depression or RDC endogenous depression. Furthermore, factors such as patient age, weight loss, recent drug or alcohol abuse, medication use (including certain antihypertensives and contraceptives), and the presence of intercurrent medical illnesses (including relatively "minor" allergic or respiratory conditions) may alter DST results (Carroll, 1982; Stokes *et al.*, 1984).

If we put aside the limitations of the DST as a diagnostic test, a significant number of depressed individuals show abnormal results when compared with normal controls. As was the case with shortened REM latency, abnormal findings are most likely to occur in individuals with severe and pervasive depressive syndromes. High rates of DST non-suppression also are seen in conditions linked to the affective spectrum, such as obsessive-compulsive disorder, schizoaffective disorder, borderline personality disorder, alcoholism, and anorexia nervosa (see Carroll, 1982; Thase et al., 1985). Several groups have reported high rates of DST nonsuppression in mania as well (Graham, Booth, Boranga, Galhenage, Myers, Teoh, & Cox, 1982; Stokes et al., 1984).

The available evidence indicates that DST nonsuppression is a state marker for depression (Carroll, 1982). Indeed, DST results may normalize days or even several weeks before clinical recovery. Persistently abnormal DSTs generally correspond to either nonresponse or a high risk of relapse (Greden, Gardner, King, Grunhaus, Carroll, & Kronfol, 1983).

Several groups have studied the concordance of the DST and REM latency (see Thase et al., 1985). Most patients with DST nonsuppression also have shortened REM latency. An additional 20% to 30% of depressed patients with normal DSTs have shortened REM latency (Rush, Schlesser, Roffwarg, Giles, Orsulak, & Fairchild, 1983).

Thyroid Axis Disturbances. As previously noted, a small percentage of depressed individuals have an organic affective disorder caused by hypothyroidism. Conversely, a larger percentage of manic and depressed persons show transiently elevated thyroid hormone levels (Whybrow & Prange, 1981). It has been suggested that increased thyroid function may represent either a type of stress response or possibly a compensatory adaptation to blunted adrenergic receptor activity (Whybrow & Prange, 1981).

The integrity of thyroid regulation can be directly tested by the injection of thyrotropin-releasing hormone (TRH), a hypothalamic peptide that stimulates the pituitary release of thyroid-stimulating hormone (TSH). Administration of TRH produces an exaggerated release of TSH in hypothyroid individuals (Gold & Pottash, 1983). On the other hand, a significant minority (i.e., 25%–40%) of depressives show a *blunted* TSH response to TRH stimulation (i.e., ≤ 5-unit rise in TSH over 60 min) (Kirkegaard, 1981; Targum, 1983). Most normal controls and a majority (i.e., > 60%) of individuals with depression show an intermediate (normal) TSH response.

The low incidence of a blunted TSH response in depression limits the routine use of the TRH stimulation test as a diagnostic test for depression. Nevertheless, several interesting results of the TRH stimulation merit further discussion. First, TSH responses appear to be similarly blunted in mania (Extein, Pottash, Gold, & Martin, 1980). Second, there is little overlap between the results of TRH tests and the DST (Rush et al., 1983). Thus, the two abnormalities do not appear to be caused by the same mechanism(s). However, most depressed individuals with blunted TRH tests also have shortened REM latency (Rush et al., 1983). Unfortunately, studies attempting to relate blunted TRH tests to neurochemical measurements have yielded conflicting results (see Thase et al., 1985).

Other neuroendocrine studies of depression have evaluated possible disturbances of growth hormone (GH) regulation, insulin–glucose metabolism, and prolactin secretion (see Thase et al., 1985). Research in these areas is complicated by numerous methodological pitfalls, and it would be premature to draw firm conclusions. For example, apparent abnormalities of insulin and/or glucose metabolism may be secondary to hypercortisolemia

(Koslow, Stokes, Mendels, Ramsey, & Casper, 1982). Similarily, postmenopausal status may alter GH response to pharmacological challenges (Halbreich, Sachar, Asnis, Quitkin, Nathan, Halpern, & Klein, 1982). Despite such problems, studies of possible alterations in GH release remain of interest because of an association with noradrenergic mechanisms (Brown & Seggie, 1980). Possible abnormalities of prolactin secretion in agitated and/or psychotic depressions warrant further study because of dopamine's role in inhibiting prolactin secretion (Thase *et al.*, 1985). (Neuroendocrine findings in affective disorders are summarized in Table 8.)

SOMATIC TREATMENT

Four types of somatic therapy currently are widely used for treatment of affective disorders: antidepressant medications, lithium, neuroleptics (antipsychotics), and electroconvulsive therapy (ECT). In the next sections, the clinical use, efficacy, and side-effects of each of these modalities are considered.

Antidepressant Medications

Antidepressant medications include three main types of drugs: tricyclics (TCAs), monoamine oxidase inhibitors (MAOIs), and the newer, "second-generation," antidepressants. Several common principles apply to all forms of antidepressant pharmacotherapy; these principles are summarized before the review of specific types of drugs.

First, treatment with any form of medication involves an assessment of potential benefits and risks. In this particular case, the affective syndrome should be of sufficient severity to warrant daily ingestion of medication and the possibility of side effects. Second, antidepressants need to be taken regularly (i.e., daily) in order to achieve a therapeutic response. Third, there is a lag of up to six weeks between initiation of treatment

Table 8. Summary of Neuroendocrine Abnormalities in Affective Disorders

1. Hypothalamic-pituitary-adrenal cortex (HYPAC) disturbances:
   a. Hypercortisolemia
   b. Blunting of diurnal cortisol rhythm
   c. Dexamethasone nonsuppression
   d. Probable elevation of ACTH levels
   e. May be present in depressions and mania

2. Hypothalamic-pituitary-thyroid distrubances:
   a. Transient elevation of circulating thyroid hormones (probably stress-related)
   b. Altered TSH response to TRH stimulation:
      i. Blunted response in depression and mania
      ii. Heightened response in depressions related to hypothyroidism

3. Altered growth hormone (GH) regulation in depression:
   a. Blunted GH response to insulin-induced hypoglycemia (probably secondary to hypercortisolemia)
   b. Blunted GH response to noradrenergic agents (possibly related to menopausal status)

4. Possible alterations of prolactin secretion.

and therapeutic response. Titration of dosage upward to a standard level should normally proceed as rapidly as possible during the first several weeks of treatment. Much support and encouragement may be needed in order for a depressed individual to continue to take a medication that does not produce immediate positive effects. Fourth, the correct dosage of antidepressant medication for a given individual may vary as much as 10-fold. Body weight, smoking habits, and individual metabolism affect dosage requirements (Klein *et al.*, 1980). Fifth, all available antidepressants have a limited margin of safety. This means that the ingestion of more than one week's supply of antidepressant may have serious, or even fatal, consequences. Caution is necessary in prescribing large amounts of medication to any depressed individual, particularly one who is suicidal. Finally, antidepressant medications are generally not abruptly terminated as soon as a depressed person has recovered. Most practitioners provide at least several months of continuation therapy after recovery to minimize the probability of relapse. In individuals who have had multiple bouts of depression, long-term maintenance medication may be of use to prevent a recurrence of subsequent episodes (Klein *et al.*, 1980).

Tricyclic Antidepressants. Tricyclic antidepressants (TCAs) have been used for over 25 years. Seven members of the TCA family are available for prescription (see Table 9). Although these drugs vary in chemical structure and, to a lesser extent, in side-effect profiles, they appear to be equally effective (Klein *et al.*, 1980). Therefore, the choice of a particular TCA may be based on past response, potential concerns about side effects, or, more simply, familiarity with a given agent.

Tricyclic antidepressants are generally started at a low dosage (i.e., 50 mg of imipramine each day) and are adjusted upward, as tolerated, over several weeks to the "usual" dosage range (see Table 9). Such a titration strategy enhances tolerance to side effects, which generally emerge long before the therapeutic effects are apparent. Most TCAs have some sedative properties, and hence, a full dosage can be beneficially given at bedtime in patients with sleep difficulties. Tricyclics have long pharmacological half-lives (i.e., the time necessary to eliminate one half of a dosage from the body), which also facilitate use of a once-a-day dosage strategy (Klein *et al.*, 1980).

A number of exhaustive reviews of the efficacy of TCAs have been published (e.g., Klein *et al.*, 1980; Morris & Beck, 1974). Across a wide range of settings and samples, it can be concluded that about 60% to 70% of patients who receive a "standard" 4- to 6-week trial of a TCA (i.e., dosage of 150–200 mg/day of imipramine or its equivalent) show a favorable response to treatment. This rate may be contrasted to response rates produced by placebo, which range from 0% to 50% under controlled conditions (Klein *et al.*, 1980; Morris & Beck, 1974).

More recently, these novel antidepressants were proved for use in the United States: amoxapine, maprotiline, and trazodone. These agents appear to be about as effective as TCAs (Baldessarini, 1983; Cole & Schatzburg, 1983). Preliminary data indicating that these novel antidepressants may produce more rapid antidepressant response than TCAs have not been confirmed by subsequent studies (Baldessarini, 1983). Moreover, the newer antidepressants have been most widely studied in outpatient samples, and hence, TCAs remain the preferred agents for more severely depressed individuals.

Clinical studies indicate that certain features of the depressive syndrome predict the response to TCAs. The correlates of a positive response include psychomotor retardation, early-morning awakening, and weight loss (Bielksi & Friedel, 1976; Nelson & Char-

Table 9. Tricyclic and Heterocyclic Antidepressants Currently Approved for Use in the United States

Generic name	Brand name(s)	Daily dosage (mg) Range[a]	Usual[b]
Amitriptyline	Elavil, Endep	25–300	150–200
Desipramine	Norpramin, Pertofrane	25–300	100–200
Doxepin	Adapin, Sinequan	25–300	150–200
Imipramine	Janimine, SK-Pramine, Tofranil	25–300	150–200
Nortriptyline	Aventyl, Pamelor	20–200	50–150
Protriptyline	Vivactil	10–60	20–40
Trimipramine	Surmontil	25–300	150–200
Amoxapine	Asendin	50–600	200–400
Maprotiline	Ludiomil	25–400	100–120
Trazodone	Desyrel	50–600	150–300

Note. Adapted from Baldessarini (1983) and Cole and Schatzburg (1983).
[a]Minimum dosages generally apply to debilitated or geriatric populations; dosages higher than the listed maximum are sometimes used for individuals who are not responding to treatment.
[b]The usual dosage values are the daily amount needed to achieve a therapeutic response in a majority of individuals.

ney, 1981). Poor response to TCAs is associated with the presence of delusions, generalized anxiety, chronicity, or "neurotic" features (e.g., hypochondriasis) (Bielksi & Friedel, 1976; Nelson & Charney, 1981). Global severity may show an inverted-U relationship to response, with the best outcome rates being associated with moderate levels of severity (Thase & Kupfer, in press).

Plasma levels of TCAs also may be associated with response. Generally, low plasma levels are associated with poor response (i.e., not greater than placebo), whereas moderate levels are predictive of a positive drug response (Perel, 1983). Low plasma levels during treatment with an "adequate" dosage generally indicate poor absorption, rapid metabolism, or noncompliance. Increasing drug dosage for nonresponders with low plasma levels often increases response rates (Nelson, Jatlow, Quinlan, & Bowers, 1982). However, very high plasma levels seldom correspond with improved response rates and, in the specific case of nortriptyline, may actually be associated with poorer outcome (Perel, 1983).

Many of the side effects of antidepressants are related to the drugs' action on multiple neurotransmitter systems. For example, dry mouth, urinary hesitancy, blurry vision, and constipation are often caused by anticholinergic effects. Excessive sedation and weight gain are probably related to antihistaminic properties. Changes in blood pressure control may be related to a blockade of adrenergic receptors. Development of severe lightheadedness due to orthostatic hypotension is one of the major causes of intolerance to treatment with TCAs (Klein et al., 1980). TCAs also affect the cardiovascular system by causing increased pulse rates (tachycardia) and changes in cardiac conduction patterns. A pretreatment electrocardiogram (ECG) is indicated for all patients over age 40. Most severe cardiac-conduction disturbances are relative contraindications for TCA treatment. Patients with less pronounced cardiac-conduction disturbances should be monitored with serial ECGs.

The novel antidepressants generally have favorable side-effect profiles when compared to the TCAs (Cole & Schatzburg, 1983). This is particularly true of trazodone and nomifensine, which have few anticholinergic effects. Nevertheless, as more is learned about the second-generation antidepressants, some specific hazards are noted. For example, maprotiline is now known to increase the risk of seizures, and amoxapine, by virtue of its dopamine-blocking properties, may convey the risk of tardive dyskinesia with long-term treatment (Cole & Schatzburg, 1983).

The emergence of distressing side effects is generally managed by lowering the drug dosage. Perhaps 10% to 20% of individuals cannot tolerate a given antidepressant because of its side effects; the substitution of an unrelated TCA or a novel antidepressant is often useful in such cases (Klein *et al.*, 1980).

Monoamine Oxidase Inhibitors. Monoamine oxidase inhibitors (MAOIs) are summarized in Table 10. Although this class of antidepressants has been in use as long as the TCAs, the MAOIs fell out of favor in the late 1960s and early 1970s because of concerns about their therapeutic efficacy and their apparently high toxicity. However, subsequent research has established that the MAOIs are effective antidepressants when used in sufficiently high dosages, and that proper clinical management reduces the risk of toxic reactions to an acceptable level (Klein *et al.*, 1980).

The available evidence from placebo-controlled trials and comparative studies suggests that phenelzine (45–90 mg/day), isocarboxazid (20–60 mg/day), and tranylcypromine (30–60 mg1/day) are as affective as conventional TCAs (see Davidson, 1983; Klein *et al.*, 1980). Possible differences in clinical response profiles between MAOIs and TCAs are of continuing interest. For example, it has been suggested that phenelzine has superior clinical efficacy in depressions characterized by anxious or phobic features (Nies & Robinson, 1982). MAOIs may also be particularly effective for individuals with other "atypical" features of depression, such as hypersomnia, weight gain, or panic attacks (Davidson, 1983; Nies & Robinson, 1982). The results of one investigation support such opinions: phenelzine was significantly more effective than both imipramine and placebo in a sample with atypical, nonendogenous depressions, and such effects were most pronounced in patients with panic attacks (Liebowitz, Quitkin, Stewart, McGrath, Harrison, Rabkin, Tricamo, Markowitz, & Klein, 1984).

The response to phenelzine treatment is also related to the degree of inhibition of platelet MAO activity, with levels of greater than 80% MAO inhibition associated with a positive clinical response (Davidson, 1983; Nies & Robinson, 1982). However, such findings may not apply to treatment with other MAOIs.

The most notorious side effect of MAOI treatment is the hypertensive crisis. This potentially fatal reaction is caused by an interaction between MAOIs and certain drugs or foodstuffs rich in tyramine, which normally are metabolized by MAO in the intestinal tract. Medications that may provoke hypertensive reactions include stimulants, diet pills, and most decongestants. Foods rich in tyramine include cheeses, sour cream, liver, and broad beans. Recognition of these interactions has led to use of an "MAOI diet" (see Nies & Robinson, 1982). Careful adherance to this diet virtually eliminates the risk of hypertensive crises during MAOI treatment. Nevertheless, MAOI drugs should be preferentially prescribed to responsible individuals who understand and will comply with these dietary restrictions.

Table 10. Monoamine Oxidase Inhibiting Antidepressants
Currently Approved for Use in the United States

Generic name	Brand name	Daily dosage (mg)	
		Range[a]	Usual[b]
Isocarboxazid	Marplan	10–60	20–40
Phenelzine	Nardil	15–90	30–75
Tranylcypromine	Parnate	10–60	20–40

Note. Adapted from Baldessarini (1983) and Cole and Schatzburg (1983).
[a]Minimum dosages generally apply to debilitated or geriatric populations; dosages higher than the listed maximum are sometimes used for individuals who are not responding to treatment.
[b]The usual dosage values are the daily amounts needed to achieve a therapeutic response in a majority of individuals.

Other side effects of MAOI treatment include insomnia, weight gain, dry mouth, anorgasmia, afternoon sleepiness, and lightheadedness due to postural hypotension (see Nies & Robinson, 1982). Because MAOIs generally lack an initial sedative effect, they often are prescribed in daytime dosages. In most cases, side effects can be managed by dosage reduction or modification of the dosage schedule.

Lithium. Lithium is a metallic element that exerts pronounced antimanic effects. It is usually administered as a salt, such as lithium carbonate (Li_2CO_3) or lithium citrate. Numerous controlled clinical trials have established that lithium salts are superior to placebo, and that they are as effective as (if not more effective than) neuroleptics for the treatment of acute mania. Acute response rates of 70% are generally seen, and the poorest response is observed in individuals with a rapid-cycling pattern of illness (i.e., more than four episodes per year) (Klein *et al.*, 1980). Long-term lithium treatment also has well-established prophylactic effects in preventing both manic and depressive relapses (see Coppen, Metcalfe, & Wood, 1982). Despite such clear-cut treatment efficacy, the exact mode of action of lithium is not yet known.

Lithium treatment is usually initiated in doses of 600–900 mg/day. Lower initial dosages are chosen for frail or elderly individuals. The dosage is titrated to achieve acute plasma levels of 0.6–1.2 mEq/L. Lithium levels are checked at least weekly during acute treatment and should be followed regularly (e.g., monthly) during long-term maintenance therapy. Generally, antimanic effects are apparent over 1–3 weeks of treatment. Adjunctive treatment with neuroleptics or sedatives is often required to achieve more rapid behavioral control of hyperactivity, irritability, or psychotic features.

The acute antidepressant effects of lithium salts are somewhat less robust than the antimanic efficacy (Klein *et al.*, 1980). The use of lithium as an antidepressant may be most productive in individuals with mild recurrent depressions or in bipolar disorder (Coppen *et al.*, 1982). Lithium may also have a role as an adjunctive agent in depressions that are only partially responsive to MAOIs or TCAs (deMontigney, Cournoyer, Morissette, Langlois, & Caille, 1983).

The side effects of acute lithium treatment include excessive thirst, polyuria, tremor, diarrhea, skin eruptions, and upset stomach (Klein *et al.*, 1980). As with the TCAs, lithium treatment has a low index of safety: plasma levels greater than 1.5 mEq/L are associated with an increased risk of side effects, and serious toxicity may develop at plasma levels greater than 2.0 mEq/L. Thus, a dosage only two to four times the usual therapeutic amount may produce severe side effects. Weight gain is the most common long-term side effect of lithium treatment. Lithium may also exert negative effects on both renal and thyroid functioning during long-term treatment (Coppen *et al.*, 1982). It is suggested that laboratory tests of thyroid and kidney functioning be obtained at six-month intervals during long-term treatment to monitor for possible changes. Decreased thyroid function during lithium treatment is corrected easily by the prescription of supplemental thyroid hormone; no lasting damage is done. It is not clear at this time if prolonged lithium treatment (e.g., 10 years) can produce clinically significant changes in the kidneys.

Neuroleptics

Antipsychotic medications play a secondary role in the treatment of affective disorders. As previously noted, adjunctive treatment with neuroleptics is commonplace in acute mania. However, lithium is preferred as a long-term treatment because neuroleptic medications convey the risk of tardive dyskinesia, a potentially irreversible movement disorder.

Neuroleptics are also useful as adjuncts to tricyclic antidepressants in psychotic depressions (Charney & Nelson, 1981; Spiker, Weiss, Dealy, Griffin, Hanin, Neil, Perel, Rossi, & Soloff, 1985). It is not clear if concurrent neuroleptic treatment makes its effect on delusional depression by increasing plasma TCA levels or by some other mechanism (Spiker *et al.*, 1985). Neuroleptics generally are not useful as primary agents in major depression (Klein *et al.*, 1980). Moreover, the spectre of tardive dyskinesia again should limit the use of neuroleptics for the treatment of nonpsychotic individuals. Acute treatment with neuroleptics also conveys a high likelihood of extrapyramidal side effects (tremor, salivation, restlessness, and bradykinesia), as well as many of the side effects noted for the TCAs.

Electroconvulsive Therapy

Electroconvulsive therapy (ECT) is the most controversial treatment used in current psychiatric practice. Such notoriety is unfortunate, for ECT is a safe and extremely effective treatment that may be life-saving for individuals with severe manic and depressive states that have not responded to pharmacotherapy.

ECT has been used as a psychiatric treatment since the 1940s. The CNS seizures induced during ECT appear to be a crucial ingredient in its efficacy. However, neither motoric convulsions nor use of electrical current are essential components of ECT; forms of convulsive therapy using various epileptigenic chemical agents are also effective, and a modified ECT procedure including muscle paralysis is now widely practiced (American Psychiatric Association, 1978).

A therapeutic course of ECT generally includes 6 to 15 treatments, administered every other day. The use of anesthesia, oxygen, and muscle relaxants produces a more humane and better-tolerated treatment. Seizures may be administered by either unilateral (nondominant) or bilateral electrode placement. Unilateral ECT definitely results in less confusion and memory impairment, but bilateral ECT may be slightly more effective (American Psychiatric Association, 1978; Kiloh, 1982).

Comparative clinical trials have consistently shown ECT to be superior to various no-treatment control conditions and to be either equivalent or superior to treatment with TCAs; response rates range from 70% to 90% (American Psychiatric Association, 1978; Janicak, Davis, Gibbons, Ericksen, Chang, & Gallagher, 1985; Kiloh, 1982). Studies of clinical predictors of ECT response reveal favorable response in individuals with melancholic depressions, and features such as guilt, psychomotor retardation, weight loss, and early-morning awakening are associated with a positive response (Kiloh, 1982). As in the responses to TCAs, anxious, hypochondriacal, and "neurotic" features are associated with a poor response to ECT (American Psychiatric Association, 1978; Kiloh, 1982). However, unlike tricyclics, ECT may also be quite effective in delusional or psychotic depressions (Kiloh, 1982). Because ECT confers no prophylactic antidepressant effects, maintenance pharmacotherapy is often needed to prevent relapse after successful treatment (see Kiloh, 1982).

The major side effect of ECT is a *transient and temporary* loss of memory. Extensive research on memory disturbances following ECT indicates that retrograde and anterograde memory disturbances generally disappear over the first several months after treatment (see American Psychiatric Association, 1978). As previously mentioned, unilateral electrode placement lessens, but does not prevent, such memory disturbances.

Other complications of ECT treatment include transient confusional states, cardiac arrhythmias during a seizure episode, and bone fractures secondary to convulsions (Kiloh, 1982). The use of muscle relaxants and anesthesia has greatly reduced the risk of fractures during ECT. Perhaps the only clear medical contraindication to ECT treatment is the presence of a brain tumor or other type of intracranial mass (American Psychiatric Association, 1978).

The debate still continues about whether repeated treatment with ECT can cause more enduring brain disturbances. Several studies documenting brain damage in animals following electric shock are not entirely relevant because these investigations used procedures that are not typical of ECT, such as the administration of higher levels of current or prolonged exposure to electrical stimuli. At this time, there is no firm evidence that ECT, as currently practiced, produces irreversible structural changes in the brain (American Psychiatric Association, 1978).

Other studies emphasize the safety of ECT. Reviews by Kiloh (1982) and the American Psychiatric Association (1978) indicate a mortality rate of only 0.03% in patients receiving ECT. This rate is roughly equivalent to the risk of general anesthesia for any minor surgical procedure. A longitudinal study by Avery and Winokur (1976) indirectly supports the safety and efficacy of ECT: mortality rates following ECT treatment of depression were less than one half the rates observed in similar depressed patients treated with either TCAs or psychosocial modalities.

Debates over the ethical issues surrounding ECT have led to the establishment of certain standards and legal guidelines (see Winsdale, Liston, Ross, & Weber, 1984). In most states, these include explicit informed-consent procedures. Before an unwilling individual can receive ECT, competency proceedings, guardianship, and independent second opinions are often required, and it should be established that the clinical state is life-threatening (American Psychiatric Association, 1978). Such cases include severe psychotic depressions, stuporous or catatonic states, and delirious manic states. Finally, ECT should not be given for punitive reasons under any circumstances.

Other Somatic Treatments. In addition to the four classes of treatment reviewed above, a variety of other agents have been tested on individuals with affective disorders. These include monoamine precursors (e.g., L-tryptophan and L-dopa), benzodiazepines (e.g., diazepam and alprazolam), anticonvulsants, and psychostimulants (e.g., amphetamine). Klein *et al.* (1980) provided useful reviews of the largely negative results obtained with these agents. The antidepressant efficacy of alprazolam is currently under investigation. This agent differs from other benzodiazepines in its effects on EEG sleep and, in one large multicenter study, was found to be superior to placebo and somewhat more effective than low-dose imipramine in outpatients with mild to moderately severe depressions (Feighner, Aden, Fabre, Rickels, & Smith, 1983). The anticonvulsant carbamazepine (Tegretol) may represent another exception. Recent studies (see Post & Uhde, 1983) indicate that carbamazepine is useful in bipolar affective disorder as an adjunct or as an alternative to treatment with lithium and neuroleptics. However, antidepressant effects of carbamazepine in nonbipolar major depressions are not well established. Moreover, the potential toxicity and side effects of carbamazepine (which include the suppression of white-blood-cell production) may limit its use to severe, treatment-resistant cases.

Antidepressant–Psychotherapy Combinations

Many individuals with affective disorders receive a combination of medication and psychosocial therapy. There are several reasons for this practice: (1) Psychosocial and pharmacological treatments may act via different mechanisms and, hence, may have additive or complementary effects. (2) Adjunctive psychosocial treatment may improve medication compliance. And (3) affectively disordered patients may have an increased incidence of maladaptive interpersonal skills or coping styles that are not fully corrected by treatment with medication (Klerman & Schechter, 1982; Thase, 1983). Unfortunately, useful guidelines for determining when an individual should receive such combination treatment have not yet been empirically derived. Several intuitively useful clinical indications for combining treatments include chronicity, ongoing interpersonal distress (e.g., lack of social support and/or marital discord), medication noncompliance, and apparent maladaptive personality traits or social skill deficits. In the case of the latter factors, however, it should be recognized that clinical depressions may adversely color assessments of enduring personality disturbance or skill-based problems (Akiskal, Hirschfeld, & Yerevanian, 1983). Conversely, medication management alone may be most appropriate for an individual with an uncomplicated affective disorder characterized by an acute onset, good social support, and/or relatively normal premorbid functioning.

The question might also be asked: When is a psychosocial therapy indicated instead of a somatic treatment? This question is most relevant to the choice of treatments for outpatients with nonbipolar major depressions, as increasing evidence suggests that short-term, problem-oriented psychosocial therapies may match, or even exceed, the effectiveness of TCAs in such patients (see Kovacs, 1983; Thase, 1983). Again, firm empirical guidelines are lacking, although the clinical features of melancholia (such as pervasive anhedonia, marked sleep and appetite disturbances, or psychomotor changes) may indicate the need for somatic treatment instead of, or in addition to, psychotherapy (Rush, 1983). It will be of interest to see if some of the biological disturbances discussed earlier in the chapter, such as DST nonsuppression and/or shortened REM latency, prove useful as indicators of the need for somatic therapies (Thase, 1983). With respect to other types of affective disorder, including psychotic depression and bipolar states, there are virtually no data to support the use of psychosocial modalities as a sole treatment approach (Rush, 1983; Thase, 1983). Thus, a psychotherapy-alone strategy probably should be restricted to individuals with nonbipolar, nonmelancholic depressions.

CONCLUSION

Extensive research efforts over the past several decades have led to numerous advances in the biomedical approach to affective disorders. Such advances include the development of more reliable and valid diagnostic approaches, greater knowledge of neurobiological disturbances, and the application of efficacious treatment strategies. The biomedical approach certainly is best suited to individuals suffering from the more severe and incapacitating forms of affective disorder. One area of interest over the next decade will be to further define the applications and limitations of this approach to the less severe forms of mood disorder. Patients with conditions such as dysthymic disorder, adjustment disorder with depressed mood, and nonmelancholic, nonbipolar major depression frequently receive care by nonmedical mental-health practitioners and the findings described in this chapter may, or may not, be relevant to the assessment and treatment of their problems (Thase et al., 1985). Another major area for further investigation relates to the role of psychosocial factors in the course of more clearly biological forms of affective disorder. Integration of the biomedical model with investigations of the impact of life events, personality traits, social support, and cognitive and coping styles will lead to a fuller understanding of the psychobiology of affective disorders.

REFERENCES

Akiskal, H. S. (1983a). The bipolar spectrum: New concepts in classification and diagnosis. In L. Grinspoon (Ed.), Psychiatry update (Vol. 2). Washington, DC: American Psychiatric Association.

Akiskal, H. S. (1983b). Dysthymic disorder: Psychopathology of proposed chronic depressive subtypes. American Journal of Psychiatry, 140, 11–20.

Akiskal, H. S., Hirschfeld, R. M. A., & Yerevanian, B. I. (1983). The relationship of personality to affective disorders. Archives of General Psychiatry, 40, 801–810.

American Psychiatric Association. (1978). Electronconvulsive therapy: Task force report 14. Washington, DC: Author.

American Psychiatric Association. (1980). Diagnostic and statistical manual of mental disorders (3rd ed.). Washington, DC: Author.

Asberg, M., & Traskman, L. (1981). Studies of CSF 5-HIAA in depression and suicidal behavior. Advances in Experimental Medicine and Biology, 133, 739–752.

Avery, D., & Winokur, G. (1976). Mortality in depressed patients treated with electroconvulsive therapy and antidepressants. Archives of General Psychiatry, 33, 1029–1037.

Baldessarini, R. J. (1983). Biomedical aspects of depression. Washington, DC: American Psychiatric Association.

Bielski, R. J., & Friedel, R. O. (1976). Prediction of tricyclic antidepressant response. Archives of General Psychiatry, 33, 1479–1489.

Blazer, D. (1983). The epidemiology of psychiatric disorder in the elderly population. In L. Grinspoon (Ed.), Psychiatry undate (Vol. 2). Washington, DC: American Psychiatric Association.

Boyd, J. H., & Weissman, M. M. (1981). Epidemiology of affective disorders: A reexamination and future directions. *Archives of General Psychiatry, 38,* 1039–1046.

Brown, G. L., Ebert, M. H., Goyer, P. F., Jimerson, D. C., Klein, W. J., Bunney, W. E., Jr., & Goodwin, F. K. (1982). Aggression, suicide, and serotonin: Relationship to CSF amine metabolites. *American Journal of Psychiatry, 139,* 741–746.

Brown, G. M., & Seggie, J. (1980). Neuroendocrine mechanisms and their implications for psychiatric research. *Psychiatric Clinics of North America, 3,* 205–221.

Buchsbaum, M. S. (1975). Average evoked response augmenting/reducing in schizophrenia and affective disorders. In D. X. Freedman (Ed.), *The biology of major psychoses: A comparative analysis.* New York: Raven Press.

Bunney, W. E., Jr., & Davis, J. M. (1965). Norepinephrine in depressive reactions: A review. *Archives of General Psychiatry, 13,* 483–494.

Carroll, B. J. (1982). The dexamethasone suppression test for melancholia. *British Journal of Psychiatry, 140,* 292–304.

Cartwright, R. D. (1983). Rapid eye movement sleep characteristics during and after mood-disturbing events. *Archives of General Psychiatry, 40,* 197–201.

Charney, D. S., & Nelson, J. C. (1981). Delusional and nondelusional unipolar depression. *American Journal of Psychiatry, 138,* 328–333.

Charney, D. S., Menkes, D. B., & Heninger, G. R. (1981). Receptor sensitivity and the mechanism of action of antidepressant treatment. *Archives of General Psychiatry, 38,* 1160–1180.

Charney, D. S., Nelson, J. C. & Quinlan, D. M. (1981). Personality traits and disorder in depression. *American Journal of Psychiatry, 138,* 1601–1604.

Clayton, P. J. (1982). Bereavement. In E. S. Paykel (Ed.), *Handbook of affective disorders.* New York: Guilford Press.

Clayton, P. J. (1983). Epidemiologic and risk factors in suicide. In L. Grinspoon (Ed.), *Psychiatry update* (Vol. 2). Washington, DC: American Psychiatric Association.

Cohen, D. B. (1979). Dysphoric affect and REM sleep. *Journal of Abnormal Psychology, 88,* 73–77.

Cole, J. O., & Schatzburg, A. F. (1983). Antidepressant drug therapy. In L. Grinspoon (Ed.), *Psychiatry update* (Vol. 2). Washington, DC: American Psychiatric Association.

Cooper, J. E., Kendeell, R. E., Gurland, B. J., Sharpe, L., Copeland, J. R. M., & Simon, R. (1972). *Psychiatric diagnosis in New York and London: A comparative study of mental hospital admissions.* London: Oxford University Press.

Coppen, A., Metcalfe, M., & Wood, K. (1982). Lithium. In E. S. Paykel (Ed.), *Handbook of affective disorders.* New York: Guilford Press.

Coryell, W., Pfohl, B., & Zimmerman, M. (1984). The clinical and neuroendocrine features of psychotic depression. *Journal of Nervous and Mental Disease, 172,* 521–528.

Davidson, J. (1983). MAO inhibitors: What have we learned? In F. J. Ayd, I. J. Taylor, & B. T. Taylor (Eds.), *Affective disorders reassessed: 1983.* Baltimore: Ayd Medical Communications.

Davidson, J. R. T., Miller, R. D., Turnbull, C. D., & Sullivan, J. L. (1982). Atypical depression. *Archives of General Psychiatry, 39,* 527–534.

deMontigney, C., Cournoyer, G., Mortissette, R., Langlois, R., & Caille, G. (1983). Lithium carbonate addition in tricyclic antidepressant-resistant unipolar depression. *Archives of General Psychiatry, 40,* 1327–1334.

Extein, I., Pottash, A. L. C., Gold, M. C., & Martin, D. M. (1980). Differentiating mania from schizophrenia by the TRH-test. *American Journal of Psychiatry, 137,* 981–982.

Feighner, J. P., Robins, E., Guze, S. B., Woodruff, R. A., Winokur, G., & Munoz, R. (1972). Diagnostic criteria for use in psychiatric research. *Archives of General Psychiatry, 26,* 57–63.

Feighner, J. P., Aden, G. C., Fabre, L. F., Rickels, K., & Smith, W. T. (1983). Comparison of alprazolam, imipramine, and placebo in the treatment of depression. *Journal of the American Medical Association, 249,* 3057–3064.

Flor-Henry, P. (1984). Hemispheric laterality and disorders of affect. In R. M. Post & J. C. Ballenger (Eds.), *Neurobiology of mood disorders.* Baltimore: Williams & Wilkins.

Gillin, J. C. (1983). Sleep studies in affective illness: Diagnostic, therapeutic, and pathophysiological implications. *Psychiatric Annals, 13,* 367–384.

Glassman, A. (1969). Inodoleamines and affective disorders. *Psychosomatic Medicine, 31,* 107–114.

Gold, M. D. & Pottash, A. L. C. (1983). Thyroid dysfunction or depression? In F. J. Ayd, I. J., Taylor, & B. T. Taylor (Eds.), *Affective disorders reassessed: 1983*. Baltimore: Ayd Medical Communications.

Goodwin, D. W., & Guze, S. B. (1979). *Psychiatric diagnosis*. New York: Oxford University Press.

Graham, P. M., Booth, J., Boranga, G., Galhenage, S., Myers, C. M., Teoh, C. L., & Cox, L. S. (1982). The dexamethasone suppression test in mania. *Journal of Affective Disorders, 4*, 201–211.

Greden, J. F., & Carroll, B. J. (1981). Psychomotor function in affective disorders: An overview of new monitoring techniques. *American Journal of Psychiatry, 11*, 1441–1448.

Greden, J. F., Gardner, R., King, D., Grunhaus, L., Carroll, B. J., & Kronfol, Z. (1983). Dexamethasone suppression test in antidepressant treatment of melancholia. *Archives of General Psychiatry, 40*, 493–500.

Grunhaus, L., & Birmaher, B. (1985). The clinical spectrum of panic attacks. *Journal of Clinical Psychopharmacology, 5*, 93–99.

Halbreich, U., Sachar, E. J., Asnis, G., Quitkin, F., Nathan, R. S., Halpern, F. S., & Klein, D. F. (1982). Growth hormone response to dextroamphetamine in depressed patients and normal subjects. *Archives of General Psychiatry, 39*, 189–192.

Himmelhoch, J. M. (1979). Mixed states, manic-depressive illness, and the nature of mood. *Psychiatric Clinics of North America, 2*, 449–459.

Iacono, W. G., Lykken, D. T., Peloquin, L.J., Lumry, A. E., Valentine, R. H., & Tuason, V. B. (1983). Electrodermal activity in euthymic unipolar and bipolar affective disorders: A possible marker for depression. *Archives of General Psychiatry, 40*, 557–565.

Janicak, P. G., Davis, J. M., Gibbons, R. D., Ericksen, S., Chang, S., & Gallagher, P. (1985). Efficacy of ECT: A meta-analysis. *Journal of Psychiatry, 142*, 297–302.

Janowsky, D. S., Risch, S. C., & Gillin, J. C. (1983). Adrenergic-cholinergic balance and the treatment of affective disorders. *Progress in Neuropsychopharmacology and Biological Psychiatry, 7*, 297–307.

Keller, M. B., Lavori, P. W., Endicott, J., Coryell, W., & Klerman, G. L. (1983). "Double-depression": Two-year follow-up. *American Journal of Psychiatry, 140*, 689–694.

Kelwala, S., Jones, D., & Sitaram, N. (1983). Monoamine metabolites as predictors of antidepressant response: A critique. *Progress in Neuropsychopharmacology and Biological Psychiatry, 7*, 229–240.

Kendell, R. E. (1976). The classification of depressions: A review of temporary confusion. *British Journal of Psychiatry, 129*, 15–28.

Kiloh, L. G. (1982). Electroconvulsive therapy. In E. S. Paykel (Ed.), *Handbook of affective disorders*. New York: Guilford Press.

Kirkegaard, C. (1981). The thyrotropin response to thyrotropin-releasing hormone in endogenous depression. *Psychoneuroendocrinology, 6*, 189–212.

Klein, D. F., Gittelman, R., Quitkin, F., & Rifkin, A. (1980). *Diagnosis and drug treatment of psychiatric disorders: Adults and children* (2nd ed.). Baltimore: Williams & Wilkins.

Klerman, G. L. (1984). History and development of modern concepts of affective illness. In R. M. Post & J. C. Ballenger (Eds.), *Neurobiology of mood disorders*. Baltimore: Williams & Wilkins.

Klerman, G. L., & Schechter, G. (1982). Drugs and psychotherpay. In E. S. Paykel (Ed.), *Handbook of affective disorders*. New York: Guilford Press.

Koslow, S. H., Stokes, P. E., Mendels, J., Ramsey, A., & Casper, R. (1982). Insulin tolerance test: Human growth hormone response and insulin resistance in primary unipolar depressed, bipolar depressed and control subjects. *Psychological Medicine, 12*, 45–55.

Koslow, S. H., Maas, J. W., Bowden, C. L., Davis, J. M., Hanin, I., & Javaid, J. (1983). CSF and urinary biogenic amines and metabolites in depression and mania. *Archives of General Psychiatry, 40*, 999–1010.

Kovacs, M. (1983). Psychotherapies for depression. in L. Grinspoon (Ed.), *Psychiatry update* (Vol. 2). Washington, DC: American Psychiatric Association.

Krauthammer, C., & Klerman, G. L., (1978). Secondary mania. *Archives of General Psychiatry, 35*, 1333–1339.

Kupfer, D. J. (1982). EEG sleep as biological markers in depression. In I. Hanin & Usdin (Eds.), *Biological markers in psychiatry and neurology*. New York: Pergamon Press.

Kupfer, D. J., & Thase, M. E. (1983). The use of the sleep laboratory in the diagnosis of affective disorders. *Psychiatric Clinics of North America, 6*, 3–25.

Lechin, F., Van der Dijs, B., Acosta, E., Gomez, F., Lechin, E., & Arocha, L. (1983). Distal colon motility and clinical parameters in depression. *Journal of Affective Disorders, 5*, 19–26.

Leckman, J. F., Weissman, M. M., merikangas, K. R., Pauls, D. L., & Prusoff, B. A. (1983). Panic disorder and major depression: Increased risk of depression, alcoholism, panic and phobic disorders in families of depressed probands with panic disorder. *Archives of General Psychiatry, 40,* 1055–1060.

Leckman, J. F., Weissman, M. M., Prusoff, B. A., Caruso, K. A., Merikangas, K. R., Pauls, D. L., & Kidd, K. K. (1984). Subtypes of depression: Family study perspective. *Archives of General Psychiatry, 41,* 833–838.

Liebowitz, W. M., Quitkin, F. M., Stewart, J. W., McGrath, P. J., Harrison, W., Rabkin, J., Tricamo, E., Markowitz, J. S., & Klein, D. F. (1984). Phenelzine *v* imipramine in atypical depression. *Archives of General Psychiatry, 41,* 669–677.

Linnoila, M., Karoum, F., & Potter, W. Z. (1982). High correlation of norepinephrine and its major metabolite excretion rates. *Archives of General Psychiatry, 39,* 521–523.

Linnoila, M., Karoum, F., & Potter, W. Z. (1983). Effects of antidepressant treatments on dopamine turnover in depressed patients. *Archives of General Psychiatry, 40,* 1015–1017.

Maas, J. W., Koslow, S. H., Katz, M. M., Gibbons, R. L., Bowden, C. L., Robins, E., & Davis, J. M. (1984). Pretreatment neurotransmitter metabolites and tricyclic antidepressant drug response. *American Journal of Psychiatry, 141,* 1159–1171.

McCarley, R. W. (1982). REM sleep and depression: Common neurobiological control mechanisms. *American Journal of Psychiatry, 139,* 565–570.

Meltzer, H. Y., Cho, H. W., Carroll, B. J., & Russo, P. (1976). Serum dopamine-beta-hydroxylase activity in affective psychosis and schizophrenia. *Archives of General Psychiatry, 33,* 585–591.

Meltzer, H. Y., Fang, V. S., Tricou, B. J., Robertson, A., & Piyaka, S. K. (1982). Effect of dexamethasone on plasma prolactin and cortisol levels in psychiatric patients. *American Journal of Psychiatry, 139,* 763–768.

Meltzer, H. Y., Arora, R. C., Tricou, B. J., & Fang, V. S. (1983). Serotonin uptake in blood platelets and the dexamethasone suppression test in depressed patients. *Psychiatry Research, 8,* 41–47.

Mischel, W. (1968). *Personality and assessment.* New York: Wiley.

Morris, J. B., & Beck, A. T. (1974). The efficacy of antidepressant drugs. *Archives of General Psychiatry, 30,* 667–674.

Nelson, J. C., & Charney, D. S. (1981). The symptoms of major depressive illness. *American Journal of Psychiatry, 138,* 1–13.

Nelson, J. C., Jatlow, P., Quinlan, D. M., & Bowers, M. B. (1982). Desipramine plasma concentration and antidepressant response. *Archives of General Psychiatry, 39,* 1419–1422.

Nies, A., & Robinson, D. S. (1982). Monoamine oxidase inhibitors. In E. S. Paykel (Ed.), *Handbook of affective disorders.* New York: Guilford Press.

Paul, S. M., Rehavi, M., Skolnick, P., Ballenger, J. C., & Goodwin, F. K. (1981). Depressed patients have decreased binding of tritiated imipramine to platelet serotonin "transporter." *Archives of General Psychiatry, 38,* 1315–1317.

Perel, J. C. (1983). Tricyclic antidepressant plasma levels, pharmacokinetics, and clinical outcome. In L. Grinspoon (Ed.), *Psychiatry, update* (Vol. 2). Washington, DC: American Psychiatric Association.

Pope, H. G., Jr., & Lipinski, J. F., Jr. (1978). Diagnosis in schizophrenia and manic-depressive illness. *Archives of General Psychiatry, 35,* 811–828.

Post, R. M., & Ballenger, J. C. (1984). *Neurobiology of mood disorders.* Baltimore: Williams & Wilkins.

Post, R. M., & Uhde, T. W. (1983). Alternatives to lithium: A focus on carbamazepine. In F. J. Ayd, I. J. Taylor, & B. T. Taylor (Eds.), *Affective disorders reassessed: 1983.* Baltimore: Ayd Medical Communications.

Roth, M., & Mountjoy, C. Q. (1982). The distinction between anxiety states and depressive disorders. In E. S. Paykel (Ed.), *Handbook of affective disorders.* New York: Guilford Press.

Rotman, A. (1983). Blood platelets in psychopharmacological research. *Progress in Neuro-Psychopharmacology and Biological Psychiatry, 7,* 135–151.

Rush, A. J. (1983). Cognitive therapy of depression: Rationale, techniques, and efficacy. *Psychiatric Clinics of North America, 6,* 105–127.

Rush, A. J., Schlesser, M. A., Roffwarg, H. P., Giles, D. E., Orsulak, P. J., & Fairchild, C. (1983). Relationships among the TRH, REM latency, and dexamethasone suppression tests: Preliminary findings, *Journal of Cinical Psychiatry, 448* (Sec. 2) 23–29.

Sachar, E. J. (1982). Endocrine abnormalities in depression. In E. S. Paykel (Ed.), *Handbook of affective disorders.* New York: Guilford Press.

Schildkraut, J. J. (1965). The catecholamine hypothesis of affective disorder: A review of supporting evidence. *American Journal of Psychiatry, 122,* 509–522.

Schildkraut, J. J. (1982). The biochemical discrimination of subtypes of depressive disorders: An outline of our studies on norepinephrine metabolism and psychoactive drugs in the endogenous depressions since 1967, *Pharmakopsychiatry, 15,* 121–127.

Shagass, C., Roemer, R. A., & Straumanis, J. J. (1982). Relationship between psychiatric diagnosis and some quantitative EEG variables. *Archives of General Psychiatry, 39,* 1423–1435.

Sherman, A. D., & Petty, F. (1984). Learned helplessness decreases 3H imipramine binding in rat cortex. *Journal of Affective Disorders, 6,* 25–32.

Sitaram, N., Nurnberger, J. I., Gershon, E. S., & Gillin, J. C. (1982). Cholinergic regulation of mood and REM sleep: Potential model and marker of vulnerability to affective disorders. *American Journal of Psychiatry, 139,* 571–576.

Spiker, D. G., Weiss, J. C., Dealy, R. S., Griffin, S. J., Hanin, I., Neil, J. F., Perel, J. M., Rossi, A. J., & Soloff, P. H. (1985). The pharmacological treatment of delusional depression. *American Journal of Psychiatry, 142,* 430–436.

Spitzer, R., Endicott, J., & Robins, E. (1978). Research Diagnostic Criteria. *Archives of General Psychiatry, 34,* 773–782.

Stokes, P. E., Stoll, P. M., Koslow, S. H., Maas, J. W., Davis, J. M., Swann, A. C., & Robins, E. (1984). Pretreatment DST and hypothalamic-pituitary-adrenocortical function in depressed patients and comparison groups. *Archives of General Psychiatry, 41,* 257–267.

Targum, S. D. (1983). Neuroendocrine challenge studies in clincial psychiatry. *Psychiatric Annals, 13,* 385–395.

Taylor, M. A. (1984). Schizoaffective and allied disorders. In R. M. Post, & J. C. Ballenger (Eds.), *Neurobiology of mood disorders.* Baltimore: Williams & Wilkins.

Thase, M. E. (1983). Cognitive and behavioral treatments for depression: A review of recent developments. In F. J. Ayd, I. J. Taylor, & B. T. Taylor (Eds.), *Affective disorders reassessed: 1983.* Baltimore: Ayd Medical Communications.

Thase, M. E., & Kupfer, D. J. (in press). Characteristics of treatment resistant depression. In J. Zohar & R. H. Belmaker (Eds.), *Special treatments for resistant depression.* New York: Spectrum.

Thase, M. E., & Reynolds, C. F. (1984). Manic pseudodementia. *Psychosomatics, 25,* 256–260.

Thase, M. E., Kupfer, D. J., & Spiker, D. G. (1984). EEG sleep secondary depression: A revisit. *Biological Psychiatry, 19,* 805–814.

Thase, M. E., Frank, E., & Kupfer, D. J. (1985). Biological processes in major depression. In E. E. Beckham & W. R. Leber (Eds.), *Depression: Basic mechanisms, diagnosis, and treatment.* New York: Dow Jones/Irwin.

Thase, M. E., Kupfer, D. J., & Ulrich, R. F. (1986). EEG sleep in psychotic depression—"A valid subtype?" *Archives of General Psychiatry, 43,* 886–893.

van Praag, H. M. (1980a). Central monoamine metabolism in depressions: I. Serotonin and related compounds. *Comprehensive Psychiatry, 21,* 30–43.

van Praag, H. M. (1980b). Central monoamine metabolism in depressions: II. Catecholamines and related compounds. *Comprehensive Psychiatry, 21,* 44–54.

Ward, N. G., Doerr, H. O., & Storrie, M. C. (1983). Skin conductance: A potentially sensitive test for depression. *Psychiatry Research, 10,* 295–302.

Weissman, M. M., Leckman, J. F., Merikangas, K. R., Gammon, G. D., & Prusoff, B. A. (1984). Depression and anxiety disorders in parents and children. *Archives of General Psychiatry, 41,* 845–852.

Wells, C. E. (1979). Pseudodementia. *American Journal of Psychiatry, 136,* 895–890.

Whybrow, P. C., & Prange, A. J. (1981). A hypothesis of thyroid catecholamine-receptor interaction. *Archives of General Psychiatry, 38,* 106–113.

Winsdale, W. J., Liston, E. H., Ross, J. W., & Weber, K. D. (1984). Medical judicial, and statutory regulation of ECT in the United States. *American Journal of Psychiatry, 141,* 1349–1355.

Zis, A. P., & Goodwin, F. K. (1982). The amine hypothesis. In E. S. Paykel (Ed.), *Handbook of affective disorders.* New York: Guilford Press

5

Psychosexual Disorders

JERRY M. FRIEDMAN

AND

JOSEPH E. CZEKALA

The third edition of the *Diagnostic and Statistical Manual of Mental Disorders* (DSM-III) of the American Psychiatric Association (APA, 1980) represents a major step forward in the definition and organization of problems of sexual functioning. There are separate diagnoses for each of the major sexual dysfunctions, something that was not true of the DSM-II, and such imprecise terms as *impotence* and *sexual deviation* are not used at all. The DSM-III subdivides the psychosexual disorders into four groups: (1) gender identity disorders; (2) the paraphilias; (3) psychosexual dysfunctions; and (4) other psychosexual disorders (p. 261). The authors make it clear that the use of this diagnostic class is restricted to disorders that are caused, at least in part, by psychological factors. Disorders of sexual functioning that are caused exclusively by organic factors, even though they may have psychological consequences, are not to be listed in this classification. For example, erectile dysfunction due to spinal cord injury is to be coded on Axis III as a physical disorder, with the psychological reaction to that condition coded as an adjustment disorder on Axis I. As will become clear below, it is often very difficult to know if a particular psychosexual disorder is caused exclusively by organic factors. Particularly in sexual dysfunction, even when organic components are present, significant psychological factors may contribute to the disorder.

The presentation of psychological treatments for the various psychosexual disorders is beyond the scope of this chapter. For a summary of psychotherapy strategies see Friedman, Wyler, LoPiccolo, and Hogan (1982); Friedman and Hogan (1985); and Langevin (1983).

GENDER IDENTITY DISORDERS

Transsexualism (302.5x); Gender Identity Disorder of Childhood (302.60); and Atypical Gender-Identity Disorder (302.85)

The DSM-III diagnostic criteria for transsexualism include a sense of discomfort and inappropriateness about one's anatomic sex; wishing to be rid of one's own genitals and

JERRY M. FRIEDMAN • Private practice, Box 456, Stony Brook, NY 11790. JOSEPH E. CZEKALA • Private practice, 85 Shorham Avenue, Miller Place, NY 11784.

to live as a member of the other sex; the disturbance has been continuous (not limited to periods of stress) for at least two years (APA, 1980). The last character of the code (x) is used to indicate asexual, homosexual, heterosexual, or unspecified sexual object choice.

The criterion for gender identity disorder of childhood for females is a strong and persistent desire to be a boy or a belief that she is a boy. There is also a repudiation of female anatomy. The disturbance has onset prior to puberty. For males, the criterion is a desire to be a girl, or a belief that he is a girl. Also involved is a repudiation of male anatomy or a preoccupation with activity that may be considered stereotypically female. Again onset is before puberty (APA, 1980).

Atypical gender-identity disorder is a residual category for gender disorders not classifiable in the above categories. For example, if most of the criteria for transsexualism are met except that the condition has not been continuous for at least two years, the diagnosis would be atypical gender-identity disorder.

The gender dysphoria described usually begins in early childhood and may lead to a request for sex reassignment surgery in adulthood. There have been over 4,000 sex change operations in the United States since 1966, when the first gender-identity clinic was established at the Johns Hopkins Medical Center. More recently, such clinics, including the one at Johns Hopkins, have closed, and sex reassignment surgery is becoming less popular (Geer, Heiman, & Leitenberg, 1984). This result has come out of a growing suspicion that the entire transsexual phenomenon is based on a sexist and homophobic foundation, and on some evidence that when transsexuals who have had surgery are compared to those who have not, there is no significant difference on measures of adjustment (Meyer & Reter, 1979). Therapists have also demonstrated more success in treating transsexuals psychologically (Barlow, Reynolds, & Agras, 1973).

Although most transsexuals report that they always believed they were of the opposite sex (Green, 1974), there is little solid evidence of any history of chromosomal abnormality, anatomic abnormality, or hormonal abnormality. However, although the cause is unknown, the fact that self-perception as being of the opposite gender often stems from earliest childhood suggests that transsexualism depends on some biologic substratum. Hoenig and Kenna (1974) reviewed studies on electroencephalogram abnormalities in transsexuals and found some general suggestion that temporal lobe or general dysfunction of the brain is related to transsexualism. However, the authors pointed out some confounding factors, such as lack of a control group and lack of screening for drugs that may have been administered. Because many transsexuals take opposite-sex hormones, it is not clear how their EEG recordings were influenced.

Many transsexuals enter treatment to get physician-prescribed hormones and possibly to get support and help in seeking reassignment therapy. For the male transsexual, taking estrogen results not only in skin texture changes, redistribution of subcutaneous fat, and breast growth, but also in a marked decrease in sexual desire. Testosterone in the female transsexual may have the opposite effect. Many transsexuals seek hormones through nonprescription means, and male transsexuals often take birth control pills to gain access to some female hormones. The therapist should work closely with an endocrinologist and should be aware of the medical and behavioral side effects that may occur form hormone therapy.

PARAPHILIAS

The paraphilias are usually referred to as *sexual deviations, sexual variants,* or *perversions.* These include fetishism, transvestism, zoophilia, pedophilia, exhibitionism, voyeurism, sexual masochism, and sexual sadism. The DSM-III restricts the use of the term *paraphilia* to conditions in which there is persistent and repetitive or exclusive sexual arousal to unusual stimuli associated with either non-human objects; with humans involving humiliation or suffering, real or simulated; sexual acts with nonconsenting partners; or subjective distress around any stimuli leading to sexual arousal. DSM-III only labels deviations from "standard" sexuality a disorder when the individual is impaired in the ability to be aroused with a partner or acknowledges subjective distress about the source of his or her sexual arousal (APA, 1980, see pp. 266–268).

Fetishism (302.81) refers to the use of objects as the preferred or exclusive method of achieving sexual excitement (APA, 1980). There has been some suggestion that fetishism reflects a problem in the "sex centers" of the brain. Epstein (1975) proposed that brain pathology alters the neural system in a way that makes an individual more vulnerable to fetishistic behavior. He made an analogy between the reflexive discharge of epilepsy and the stereotypical discharge that a fetish object evokes. Blumer (1970) and Koralsky, Freund, Machek, and Polak (1967) have suggested that sexual behavior, aggressive behavior, and the motor behavior of epileptic seizures are all related.

Transvestism (302.30) refers to persistent and recurrent cross-dressing for sexual arousal by a male who is heterosexual. Such a person experiences recurrent frustration from interference with the cross-dressing (APA, 1980). There are few studies that have examined organic and genetic factors in transvestism, and these few have been criticized on methodological grounds (Langevin, 1983). Cross-dressing has been related to the onset of temporal lobe dysfunction (Ball, 1968; Blumer, 1970), and possibly to limbic or hypothalamic dysfunction (Langevin, 1983). In reporting the results of studies on 26 patients whom he labeled transvestites, Walinder (1965) found that 38% of their EEGs were abnormal, and that 60% of the EEGs involved disorders of the temporal lobes. In a review of earlier case studies of biological factors in transvestism, Housden (1965) found that most of the subjects were biologically normal males with normal male sex organs, endocrine functions, and chromosomes. Based on the existing evidence, the presence of organic and constitutional factors appears unlikely.

Zoophilia (302.10) is sexual activity or the fantasy of such activity with animals as a repeatedly preferred or exclusive method of achieving sexual excitement (APA, 1980). It is also referred to as *bestiality.* There is no significant literature pointing to the presence of biological factors in this disorder, probably partly because of the rarity of the disorder (Snyder, 1980) and the difficulty in finding subjects, rather than because of the exclusive absence of biological factors.

Pedophilia involves the act or fantasy of engaging in sexual activity with prepubertal children as a repeatedly preferred or exclusive method of achieving sexual excitement. Some theorists have suggested that a disease process such as senility or mental retardation is operative in pedophilia. Others (Langevin, Paitich, Freeman, Mann, & Handy, 1978; Mohr, Turner, & Jerry, 1964) suggest that the pedophile is unlikely to be retarded or senile, and that their lower IQ scores reflect their poorer educational achievements.

As with several sexual anomalies, it has been hypothesized that brain pathology is associated with pedophilia. The evidence is not convincing because brain pathology related to the frontal and temporal lobes is often related to a wide range of bizarre behavior, and little systematic work in pedophiles has been done. A causal relationship between organic factors and pedophilia has yet to be demonstrated (Langevin, 1983).

Exhibitionism (302.40) involves exposing the genitals to strangers for the purpose of achieving sexual excitement. There is usually no attempt at further sexual activity with the stranger (APA, 1980). It has been hypothesized that exhibitionists have excessive levels of testosterone in their blood stream. Langevin, Paitich, Freeman, Mann, and Handy (1979) compared normals and exhibitionists on serum testosterone levels and penile volume output. No significant differences were found in testosterone level or penile volume output; however, testosterone and the output measure were weakly related. More work needs to be done to test this hypothesis.

A voyeur (302.82) is an individual who observes unsuspecting people while they are naked, undressing, or engaging in sexual activity. No sexual activity with those being observed is sought (APA, 1980). No biological factors have been implicated in this disorder.

Sexual masochism (302.83) and sexual sadism (302.84) are conditions in which sexual pleasure is associated with humiliation, domination, and even physical pain. In sexual masochism, sexual excitement is achieved by being humiliated, bound, beaten, or made to suffer in other ways (APA, 1980). In sexual sadism the individual intentionally inflicts psychological or physical suffering on a nonconsenting partner in order to produce sexual excitement (APA, 1980). There are no existing biological studies on sadism or masochism. A positive association of serum testosterone levels and aggression has been found in criminals, particularly in rapists, but not necessarily in sexual sadists. Studies of brain pathology in sadomasochism have yet to be done (Langevin, 1983).

PSYCHOSEXUAL DYSFUNCTIONS

Until recently, there has been a lack of consensus and precision in the terminology and classification of sexual dysfunctions. Problems of overlapping definitions and lack of consensus among clinicians have contributed to confusion and imprecision. For example, the term *impotence* has been used to describe almost any male sexual dysfunction, including difficulties with erection, orgasm, and sexual interest. Likewise, the term *frigidity* had been used to describe almost any female sexual dysfunction. Kaplan (1974) made a strong argument for the elimination of the term *impotence*, not only because of its lack of descriptive utility, but because it may also imply pejorative personality attributes. Masters and Johnson (1970) rejected the term *frigidity* as "poor slang" and made an attempt to add more precision to the definition of sexual dysfunctions by outlining several male and female dysfunctions.

Kaplan (1974) introduced a classification system that attempted to organize and classify dysfunctions according to a biphasic description of the sexual response cycle that allowed parallel diagnoses for males and females. The dysfunctions were divided into disorders of excitement and disorders of orgasm. In 1979, Kaplan expanded her system into a triphasic system that added disorders of desire as a third category. The DSM-III classification of sexual dysfunction is based on Kaplan's work and therefore includes diagnoses for inhibited sexual desire (302.71), inhibited sexual excitement (302.72), and three diagnoses for inhibited sexual orgasm: inhibited female orgasm (302.73), inhibited male orgasm (302.74), and premature ejaculation (302.75). In addition, there are three other diagnoses: functional dyspareunia (302.76), functional vaginismus (306.51), and atypical psychosexual dysfunction (302.70).

Inhibited Sexual Desire (302.71)

The DSM-III criteria for a diagnosis of inhibited sexual desire involves a persistent, global inhibition of sexual desire. When making the diagnosis, the clinician is cautioned to take into account such factors as age, sex, health, intensity, and frequency of sexual desire and the context of the individual's life. It is further stated that this diagnosis is rarely used unless the lack of desire is a source of distress to th ʾ individual or his or her partner. The second diagnostic criterion is that this disorder is not caused exclusively by organic factors such as a physical disorder or medication and is not due to another Axis I disorder (APA, 1980).

One of the most striking changes in the nature of the problems observed by clinicians working in the field of sexual dysfunction is a marked increase in the number of cases presenting with low sexual desire both alone and in conjunction with other sexual dysfunctions (Friedman & Hogan, 1985). Kaplan (1979) indicated that the prognosis for cases in which disorders of desire are present are substantially poorer than those in which excitement or orgasm dysfunction are present alone. Even when low desire is successfully treated, the course of treatment tends to be longer and more complex. Although low sexual desire is a topic of current concern, there seems to be little agreement about what this syndrome actually is, and particularly about how to define it operationally. As is clear from the DSM-III diagnostic criteria, what is normal or abnormal is difficult to define, and the definition can be only a subjective one.

Inhibited sexual desire has achieved the status of a mental disorder as a result of its inclusion in the DSM-III. This problem was not listed at all in the DSM-II. Clinical reality, however, necessitates that low sexual desire be defined within the context of a particular relationship. Clinical experience has shown that the low-desire individual is often perfectly content with his or own level of desire and often presents for therapy because of pressure from his or her partner. Zilbergeld and Ellison (1980) took the view that the therapist should think in terms of a desire discrepancy within the couple rather than diagnosing low desire in one partner. However, in some cases, the identified low-desire patient does appear to have a pathologically low desire, rather than one that is simply discrepant from that of his or her partner. In many cases, the subject actively avoids sex and appears to have more an aversion to sex than low desire. In a study by Frank, Anderson, and Rubenstein (1978), 100 predominantly white, middle-class, nonclinical couples showed a surprisingly high incidence of problems relating to low sexual desire. Of those interviewed, 35% of the women and 16% of the men complained of lack of interest in sex, and 28% of the women and 10% of the men experienced being "turned off" to sex. This finding indicates that the incidence of lack of interest in and a distaste for sex in a nonclinical population may be higher than had previously been assumed.

Kaplan (1979) discriminated between hypoactive sexual desire and inhibition of sexual desire. The term *hypoactive sexual desire* is used to describe physiologically based low desire, whereas *inhibited sexual desire* is used if it is has been determined that the low desire is due to psychological factors. However, Kaplan did not say how one makes this determination with any degree of assurance. The most common physiological factors associated with hypoactive sexual desire, according to Kaplan, are depression, stress, drugs, hormonal abnormality, and medical illness. Although medical illness can interfere with sexual desire for organic reasons, psychological and interpersonal factors often play at least some role in both causing and maintaining the dysfunction. Although sexual desire may diminish or cease because of such organic factors as pain, immobility, or changes in body function, concomitant factors, disfigurement, fear of death, preoccupation with body integrity, suppression of feelings, anxiety, and depression over the illness can also interfere with sexual desire in both men and women. Anxiety arising from physical illness often leads to a concern about sexual functioning and a loss of desire. A person's partner may react to illness with withdrawal or anger or fear that sex will be harmful.

Chronic stress and anxiety have been linked to low sexual desire, as has abstinence from sex for a prolonged period, which may produce a suppression of the sexual impulse. Depression has long been linked with low desire in both men and women.

The association of the hormone testosterone with changes in sexual desire in males has been well documented. The evidence is clear that castrated men have lower sexual motivation, fewer fantasies, and less arousal and erection that intact men (Comhaire & Vermeulen, 1975; Money, Wiedeking, Walker, Migeon, Meyer, & Borgaonkar, 1975). Some studies have shown that administration of testosterone does restore sexual desire to such men (Davidson & Levine, 1972). Similarly, administration of androgen has been shown to significantly raise sexual desire in women who are sexually dysfunctional (Bancroft, 1977), and the effects of androgen on increasing sexual desire in nondysfunctional women receiving testosterone for medical therapeutic reasons has long been known (Greenblatt, Mortara, & Torpin, 1942). Similarly, it is well known that removal of endogenous androgen by adrenalectomy markedly reduces or even eliminates sexual arousal and responses (Winokur, 1963). Thus, the necessity of some threshold level of testosterone as a necessary condition for sexual arousal and response seems relatively well established. It seems to be the case, however, that once testosterone levels are above some threshold level, any behavioral response is possible, including no sexual desire at all.

Other hormones that may be implicated in low sexual desire include luteinizing hormone (LH), prolactin, and estradiol. LH stimulates testosterone production. Hyperprolactinemia has been associated with hypogonadism and galactorrhea in both males and females. Males with hyperplolactinemia have been reported to have sexual disorders, including low sexual desire (Thorner, Edwards, Hanker, Abraham, & Besser, 1977; Thorner, McNeilly, Hagan, & Besser, 1974). High levels of estrogen in men has been shown to result in lower sexual desire (Bancroft, 1984). Some women using oral contraceptives have also complained of low desire (LaFerla, 1984).

Disease or the fear of disease can affect the sexual desire of both men and women, just as it would tend to reduce their desire to engage in other forms of physical exertion.

For example, most postmyocardial infarction (heart attack) patients can return to sexual activity within several weeks after discharge from the hospital. However, without adequate medical and psychological advice, fear of a reinfarct may reduce the desire to do so. Patients who suffer from angina may often benefit from the prophylactic use of nitroglycerin. Untreated chronic renal failure also can produce major changes in sexual desire. As many as 90% of men with uremia and 80% of uremic women reported a decrease in desire compared to preillness levels (Kolodney, Masters, & Johnson, 1979). Although the disease itself may account for some of this change, the psychological reaction to chronic illness often plays a major role.

Thus, in evaluating patients with low sexual desire, in addition to the usual evaluation of personal and interpersonal characteristics, several other factors should be evaluated as well. In both males and females, level of stress and the presence of Type A personality characteristics should be assessed. Clinical depression, as well as subclinical levels of depression, should be assessed. A complete medical history should be taken, including the presence of disease states, general feeling of well-being, and both prescription and street drug use. We suggest a complete medical checkup for all patients presenting with low sexual desire. Hormonal assays should be ordered, particularly testosterone (including free testosterone) and proclactin for men. If the male patient has testosterone levels abnormally low or even in the low normal range, a course of exogenous testosterone administration may be tried if there are no medical contraindications. In women, there is no evidence that such administration will help except in virilizing doses (La Ferla, 1984). Where disease states exist, it is important for the therapist to work with the primary physician to reduce the impact of organic factors while treating the psychological response to the illness.

Inhibited Sexual Excitement (302.72)

Males. The DSM-III diagnostic criteria for inhibited sexual excitement call for a persistent and recurrent inhibition of excitement while engaging in sexual activity, with partial or complete inability to get or maintain an erection until the sexual act is completed. The clinician must judge that the man is engaging in sexual activity of sufficient intensity and duration and also that the problem is not caused exclusively by organic factors (physical disorder or medication) and is not due to another Axis I disorder (APA, 1980). Note that to receive this diagnosis, difficulty with erections is not sufficient if the male is not engaging in activity that would reasonably lead to an erection.

More research has been carried out on erectile dysfunction than on any other sexual problem. Much of this research has focused on ways to make a differential diagnosis between organic and psychogenic dysfunction. A variety of medical and physiological advances have been made in the recent past that have greatly improved the ability of clinicians to assess the physical component of erection problems. Masters and Johnson (1970) claimed that 95% of men with erectile dysfunction had exclusively psychogenic etiology, but more recently, Spark, White, and Connolly (1980) claimed that over 50% of men with this dysfunction had organic etiology. Traditionally, investigators have made the conceptual error of attempting to classify cases dichotomously, that is, as having either psychogenic or organic etiology. It is our belief that organicity and psychogenicity should be conceptualized as two dimensions, rather than as categories or end points of a single dimension. Thus, organic and psychogenic variables may be involved in both the etiology and the maintenance of the dysfunction, and a high degree of one in no way implies a low degree of the other. Organic and psychogenic variables often interact to produce erectile problems.

It is widely agreed that adequate medical evaluation of erectile dysfunction requires evaluation of vascular, hormonal, and neurological systems, as well as the general health systems that underlie the erectile response (Krauss, 1983; Melman & Leiter, 1982). For the nonmedical therapist (as well as for some medical therapists), the assumption is that referral from a medical source means that medical factors have been ruled out. This may not be the case. Medical assessment of erectile functioning has been developing and changing so rapidly that, frequently, only urologists who subspecialize in sexual dysfunction are aware of the more subtle assessments. Moreover, some of the techniques (such as nocturnal-penile-tumescence studies and some radiographic studies) are not readily available in all areas. Below is a review of some of the assessment strategies for evaluating organic involvement in erectile dysfunction.

Erection is a complex event involving poorly understood neurological, hemodynamic, and hormonal substrates (Krauss, 1983). Reviews of vascular disorders as causes of erectile functioning have been provided by Wagner and Metz (1980), Malloy and Wein (1983), and Wagner (1981). These authors have stressed that there are many vascular mechanisms that can interfere with erection, including failure of arteriovenous shunts, abnormal fistulae between the penile chambers, and defective venous valves that cause excessive rapid drainage of the blood in the penis. Although there are still some unknowns in our understanding of the mechanism of erection, the vascular network is an important object of assessment for organic factors in erectile dysfunction.

The simplest and first step in a vascular evaluation is palpation of the pulse in the penile arteries (Jevtich, 1983). Abnormal pulses serve as a first clue to the possibility of vascular involvement. Another noninvasive assessment is the monitoring of penile blood pressure and arterial flow (Melman & Leiter, 1982; Zorngniotti, Rossi, Padula, & Makovsky, 1980). The accepted procedure for assessing arterial flow is to use a Doppler flow meter (Abelson, 1975). With this devise, blood flow is measured by the Doppler frequency shift of back-scattered ultrasound directed into the penile body. The Doppler flow meter, along with a cuff originally designed to take an infant's blood pressure, is often used to take penile blood pressure. It has been proposed that a simple measure of normal penile blood pressure is comparing it to brachial (arm) pressure. Taking penile blood pressure takes considerable time and skill on the part of the examiner, as it is often difficult to find the deep penile arteries.

Another method of assessing vascular problems is to measure reactive hyperemia, described by Kempczinski (1979). This measure is obtained by inflating a pneumatic cuff around the penis to a pressure of 50 mm of mercury above brachial systolic pressure for 5 min. The cuff is then deflated, and the penile-volume waveform is recorded with the Doppler probe. Increases in amplitude of less than 10% indicate abnormally low reactive hyperemia and thus possible vascular problems. Michal, Kramer, and Pospichal (1978) proposed a procedure that consists of recording penile blood pressure and flow with the Doppler probe both before and after the patient engages in knee bends, leg lifts, or other exercise that uses the large muscle masses in the lower body. An "external iliac steal syndrome" leading to defects in penile erection has been documented in some men with previously undiagnosed coronary insufficiency.

There are a variety of other examinations, many of them invasive, that can be done to identify possible vascular involvement in erectile dysfunction (Jevtich & Maxwell, 1983). For example, a corpora cavernosogram can be performed in which a radiopaque contrast medium is injected directly into the penis allowing the visualization of the superficial dorsal and deep dorsal veins which drain into the pelvic plexuses. Similarly, other arteriographic procedures are available. Most recently, the drug papaverine, a muscle relaxant that causes erection when directly injected into the cavernosa tissue, has been used to assess vascular involvement as well as to treat erectile dysfunction (Abber, Lue, McClure, & Williams, 1985; Lue, Hricak, Schmidt, & Tanagho, 1985).

In reviewing the literature on the effects of sex hormones on erectile dysfunction, not very much can be said with certainty. Although it is agreed that hormonal abnormalities can indeed interfere with erection, it is not clear what levels of which hormones are necessary and sufficient for erection to occur (Pirke & Kockett, 1982; Schiavi & White, 1976). Spark *et al.* (1980) concluded that 35% of "impotent" patients had abnormally low testosterone or abnormally high prolactin levels. However, another study by Seagraves, Schoenberg, and Ivonoff (1983) found only 15% of patients to have abnormal levels of testosterone or prolactin. Furthermore, it has been reported that many men who have actually been castrated continue sexual activity with no erectile dysfunction (Roen, 1965 ; Schiavi & White, 1976). It has also been shown that other hypogonadal patients may maintain sexual activity, including erectile function, at unchanged levels (Money & Ehrhardt, 1973). Bancroft (1984) reported that, although androgens are necessary for normal sexual appetite and for ejaculation, erectile mechanisms (providing appropriate erotic stimuli are present) are probably not androgen-dependent. In the case of men with testosterone levels in the normal range, there is virtually no evidence that administration of androgens has any effect. Yet, these are frequently administered. For men with abnormally low testosterone, and when not medically contraindicated, it may be valuable to try hormone therapy, as the evidence in these cases is less clear-cut.

The neurology of erection involves both peripheral and central innervation (Krauss, 1983). Within the penis itself, significant sympathetic nervous system activity is involved in erection (Melman & Henry, 1979). Important neurological factors may be involved in the organic etiology of some erectile dysfunction. A variety of diseases known to produce neurological pathology are associated with high rates of erectile dysfunction (Krauss, 1983; Melman & Leiter, 1982). Specifically, multiple sclerosis, spinal cord injury, lower motor neuron injuries, diabetes mellitus, and alcohol abuse are all associated with erectile failure. (Of course, a hormonal component may contribute in some of these conditions.) A complete examination would include the evaluation of the cremasteric reflex, bulbocavernosus reflex, and anal sphincter tone as well as assessment of intactness of peripheral sensation. This assessment is usually done by testing for discrimination between blunt and sharp pressure on the perineal and penile skin and intactness of perception of the difference between simple pressure and vibration in the same areas. Patients who obtain any abnormal results on the screening for pelvic reflexes should be referred to a neurologist for a more sophisticated exam.

A good history and blood chemistry, as well as a physical exam, should be part of the medical assessment of erectile dysfunction and should include (1) overall appearance, including recent changes in weight, central versus peripheral obesity, skin striae, and limb wasting suggesting endocrine, renal, or vascular disease; (2) posture and gait for signs of spinal cord or other neurological illness; (3) blood pressure, as hypertension suggests possible small-vessell atherosclerosis; (4) arrhythmias as a possible indication of cardio-vascular disease and possible peripheral vascular disease; (5) retinopathy; (6) gynecomastia as evidence of endocrine disease or a drug effect; (7) abdominal examination checking for liver disease, venacaval occlusion, or obstruction of the femoral vessels; (8) penile examination, particularly of the corporal bodies and the urethra for plaques of Peyronie's disease or other trauma, and for hypospadias; (9) testes examination for symmetry, size, texture, and possible endocrine active tumors; (10) rectal examination including sphinc-ter reflexes and abnormalities of the prostate; (11) lower limb check of deep tendon reflexes, check of pressure and flow in the femoral and other arteries and check of loss of hair or change in skin texture or color in feet or toes as indicative of peripheral vas-cular disease. As part of the general physical exam, fasting blood sugar should be checked, as it has been reported that, in many diabetic men, erectile dysfunction is the first symp-tom of the disease (Kolodney et al., 1979).

In addition, the therapist should be aware of any drugs the patient is taking. Many prescription drugs have reported side effects that include erectile dysfunction. This is es-pecially true of many antihypertensive medications. Erectile dysfunction has also been reported in men taking antipsychotic drugs, anticholinergic drugs, and, less frequently, lithium carbonate or cardiac drugs such as digitalis (Kolodny et al., 1979; Wagner & Green, 1981).

A noninvasive, but expensive and not readily available test for organic erectile dys-function is the nocturnal penile tumescence (NPT) study. Penile erection during sleep was first described by Ohlmeyer, Brilmayer, and Hullstrung in 1944. It was later noted that the occurrence of these periods of penile erection corresponded with rapid-eye-movement (REM) or dream sleep (Aserinsky & Kleitman, 1955). The use of NPT to differentiate psychogenic from organic erectile dysfunction was proposed by Karacan in 1970. It seemed that, at last, a reliable and valid measure had been found to make a differential diagnosis. Many studies found that nocturnal erection was a purely physiological response not related to dream content; that individuals showed little or no variation in degree of erection or time of erection from night to night; and that there are clear nonoverlapping patterns of erectile response between groups of men who are sexually functional and others with known organic impairment. More recently, some investigators have questioned whether an abnormal NPT pattern can truly always be associated with organicity. Was-serman, Pollak, Spielman, and Weitzman (1980), as well as Schiavi and Fisher (1982), have noted that, on at least some occasions for some men who are fully sexually func-tional, their NPT will be markedly abnormal, even during normal sleep with normal du-ration of REM stage sleep. The causes of these variations are unclear. It does seem that anxiety may be a factor, as well as depression. Karacan, Goodenough, Shapiro, and Star-ker (1966) and Fisher (1966) have presented evidence that dreams with anxiety content suppress NPT. Procci, Moss, Boyd, and Barron (1983) found that, in approximately 21% of their subjects, one night's recording could be classified as markedly abnormal and a second night's recording could be classified as completely normal.

Another problem with NPT is that, in recording, mercury strain gauges are placed around the base and tip of the penis, and the measured change is in circumference of the penis. However, it is possible to have large circumference changes without any concur-rent increase in rigidity or turgidity of the penis (Ek, Bradley, & Krane, 1983; Metz & Wagner, 1981). This finding may mean that, unless rigidity is carefully checked, men with normal NPT responses may not have sufficient rigidity to effect vaginal penetration.

In spite of some shortcomings, NPT monitoring is still a very useful test. Although there may be false negatives, normal NPT records (with an additional check for rigidity) can be accepted as evidence of organic intactness. Unfortunately, many profiles indicate some erectile response, but not of sufficient duration or intensity to be considered normal. In addition, the presence of false negatives is troublesome because major treatment decisions are often made on the basis of these results.

There have been other attempts to measure nocturnal tumescence without the expense of a sleep laboratory. One such technique, reported by Barry, Blank, and Boileau (1980), uses a ring of common postage stamps around the penis. The stamp ring is overlapped and the ends glued together. If the man has normal erection during the night, the increase in penile circumference, it is posited, will tear the perforations between the individual stamps in the ring. The problem with this technique is that it is simply a measure of degree of maximum erection during the night. There is no measure of number of erections or of duration or pattern of full versus partial erections. Thus, a man with one brief erection would apparently break the perforations. Once it has been accepted that the presence of a full erection under some circumstances does not necessarily mean organic intactness, the usefulness of this test is seen to be quite limited.

Similar to the stamp test, but somewhat more sophisticated, is the use of a plastic strain gauge marketed by the Dacomed Corporation (Ek *et al.*, 1983). This device may be very useful in measuring the rigidity of the penis as well as the duration of erections.

In summary, there is an array of medical assessment tools ranging from simple and inexpensive to costly. Although in many cases it is possible to document organic etiology or to rule it out, in many other cases this is not possible. It is important not to assume that, if a patient can have full erections some of the time, he is organically intact. We may be dealing with a "threshold" effect: organic involvement may raise the "threshold" of stimulus conditions, making it more difficult, but not impossible, for erection to occur.

When treating men with erectile dysfunction, it is important to entertain the hypothesis that, unless there is clear evidence to the contrary, the problem may be caused by some combination of organic and psychogenic elements. It is also important to remember that the problems could be caused by one thing and maintained by another. In one case, erectile dysfunction was clearly caused by fatigue and malaise associated with undiagnosed diabetes. The problem brought to the surface many issues of anger in the marriage, and the wife put a good deal of pressure on her husband to perform. After the diabetes was brought under control and general health improved, erectile dysfunction was maintained primarily by performance pressures.

Our treatment strategy is to begin with the least invasive intervention. The first step is a complete workup of the vascular, neurological, and endocrine systems as described above. If the workup produces evidence of organicity that can be treated, medical treatment is carried out. If there is no such evidence or if there is simply suspicion of organic involvement, we suggest a course of sex therapy to deal with the psychogenic components and to help the individual get over any "threshold" that may be making it more difficult to function. If there are not satisfactory improvements, more invasive medical tests can be initiated.

One medical treatment for erectile dysfunction is the use of one of the several penile implants available. This is an essentially irreversible surgical procedure and should not be undertaken until it can be determined with certainty that there is genuine organic impairment of sufficient degree to make normal functioning impossible. It is precisely because NPT studies are often the basis for decisions to perform such surgery that the concern over false negatives on this test is so great. Recently, another medical treatment has been used: the administration of a chemical prosthesis. Men are taught to inject intracavernous drugs used to increase blood flow to the penis and to bring about erection. The usual drug is papaverine HCL, and reports of its success are starting to appear in the literature (Zorgniotti & Lefleur, 1985).

Females. In women, inhibited sexual excitement is defined as "the partial or complete failure to attain and/or maintain the lubrication-swelling response until the completion of the sexual act" (APA, 1980). The physiology of excitement involves the diffuse dilation of blood vessels in the labia and around the vagina, which produces genital swelling and vaginal lubrication. Its symptoms are, in most cases, vaginal dryness accompanied by painful coitus (Kaplan, 1985).

There are fewer organic factors that may contribute to excitement phase disorders for women than for men. The most prominent involve estrogen deficiencies resulting either from menopause or the surgical removal of adrenals, ovaries, or pituitary for the treatment of estrogen-sensitive breast cancer. This surgery may result in diminished lubrication. Other organic factors include neurogenic disorders affecting the sex centers of the brain (e.g., hypothalamic lesions and psychomotor epilepsy) or those affecting the lower neural structures that serve the genital reflexes (e.g., spinal cord injury, alcoholic neuropathy, diabetes mellitus, and surgical or traumatic injuries). Vascular disorders (e.g., leukemia), may also affect the ability to become sexually aroused and the consequent lack of lubrication. With respect to specific genital disorders, in atrophic vaginitis lubrication is reduced or absent (Kaplan, 1979).

Inhibited Female Orgasm (302.73)

Inhibited female orgasm is defined in the DSM-III as the persistent and recurrent inhibition of orgasm following "normal" sexual excitement which is adequate in focus, intensity, and duration as judged by the clinician (APA, 1980). Orgasm can be either delayed or totally absent in this dysfunction. Many women who are inorgasmic are nevertheless sexually responsive and report that they enjoy sexual activity despite the lack of orgasm (Nadelson & Marcotte, 1983). Some women have never consciously experienced orgasm by any means. Others have experienced orgasm in the past but are currently unable to do so or can only do so in some situations such as with self-stimulation or with a vibrator. Because many women do not experience coital orgasms, most therapists do not consider this a dysfunction if the woman is orgasmic through other means with a partner. Anorgasmia is considered the most common female complaint (Kaplan, 1974), and in most cases, it does not have an organic basis (LaFerla, 1984; Nadelson & Marcotte, 1983).

Organic factors that may contribute to orgasmic dysfunction in a minority of cases include conditions that affect the nerve supply to the pelvis (e.g., spinal chord tumors or multiple sclerosis) or conditions that impair the vascular supply to the pelvis; endocrine disorders (diabetes or hypothyroidism); and gynecological factors (extensive surgical procedures, chronic vaginal infections, or congenital anomalies) (Kolodney *et al.*, 1979).

Although diabetes is associated with erection difficulties in men, in women it tends to interfere with the ability to have orgasms. The correlation between orgasmic dysfunction and the duration of diabetes suggests that either neuropathic or microvascular changes may be implicated. As in men, we may be dealing with a "threshold effect." Perhaps these women do not lose their ability to have orgasm but require higher levels of stimulation. Renal failure, often associated with decreased desire in women, can also affect their orgasmic responses (Kolodney et al., 1979).

Pregnancy can affect orgasmic responsiveness. During the first trimester, most women experience nausea and decreased energy. During the second trimester, there seems to be a facilitation of sexual responsiveness, and finally, during the third trimester, sexual responsiveness often declines because of an increased concern with the well-being of the infant and with getting through the experience of labor and delivery (LaFerla, 1984).

Commonly prescribed drugs can result in sexual dysfunction. However, the literature related to men is much greater than that about women. For some women, the use of oral contraceptive agents can result in decreased libido and, indirectly, in anorgasmia. If this occurs, another method or a change in the type of drug prescribed is recommended. Tricyclic antidepressants, MAO inhibitors, and antipsychotic medications can also cause anorgasmia. The administration of bethanechol has been found to be helpful in alleviating these side effects (Gross, 1982). It is important to take a careful drug history because patients do not often see the possible connection between sexual dysfunction and the use of various medications (LaFerla, 1984).

For most women, behavioral and/or relationship or individual psychotherapy will result in an ability to become orgasmic. Where medical conditions do exist, the therapist should work with the physician to minimize the contribution of psychological factors. Where orgasm is impossible or unlikely because of such conditions, therapy should focus on the process of sexual enjoyment rather than the goal of having an orgasm to help reduce expectations and consequent disappointment.

A surgical technique that has occasionally been advocated to enhance orgasm, particularly if adhesions are present, is "female circumcision," or excision of the clitoral hood. This surgery involves the resection of a wedge-shaped portion of the clitoral hood. Opposition to the technique stems from the fact that the clitoral hood serves both as a means of indirect stimulation and as a protection to the clitoris during coitus. Many women who undergo this operation report a transient increase in sensitivity, which then returns to preoperative conditions (Morningstar, Scibetta, & LaFerla, unpublished data, 1977). Although the operation is simple to perform, these results do not justify the means. Sexual counseling, which is a much less radical procedure, may be equally effective (LaFerla, 1984).

Inhibited Male Orgasm (302.74)

The DSM-III diagnostic criteria for inhibited male orgasm is persistent and recurrent inhibition of the orgasm following adequate sexual excitement. Orgasm can be either delayed or absent in this condition. The clinician judges that the problem is not caused exclusively by organic factors (e.g., physical disorder or medication) and is not due to another Axis I disorder (APA, 1980).

Inhibited male orgasm has been known by several other terms, including *inhibited ejaculation, ejaculatory incompetence,* and *retarded ejaculation.* It is also the rarest of male dysfunctions (Masters & Johnson, 1970). It is rare for men with this dysfunciton to have erectile difficulties. Functionally, this problem can be viewed as the opposite of premature ejaculation. The most common form of this dysfunction is the inability to ejaculate intravaginally. Some men may have difficulty ejaculating through any means in the presence of a partner, but they are usually able to ejaculate through self-stimulation. Most rarely, some men are unable to ejaculate by any means. This latter group are those most likely to have an organic basis for the problem. Those with situational inability will most often respond to traditional behavioral treatments (Masters & Johnson, 1970; McCarthy, 1981).

When a patient presents with global inhibited orgasm, a complete medical and drug history should be taken. (If indeed the problem can be attributed exclusively to organic causes, this diagnosis is not used.) The most common organic causes of inhibited male orgasm are drug-induced. Some antihypertensive drugs in high doses, such as alpha blockers and some antiadrenergic drugs, result in this dysfunction. Estrogen (given to men being treated for prostrate cancer) has resulted in orgasmic dysfunction, as have some phenothiazines, tricyclic antidepressants (rare), and MAO inhibitors (not so rare). Heroin use has also led to this orgasm dysfunction (Kolodney *et al.*, 1979). Some congenital anatomic lesions of the genitourinary system, spinal cord lesions, and lower extremity surgery of the abdominal aorta have all been implicated in this disorder (Kolodney *et al.*, 1979). Of course, when a medical etiology is determined, the therapist must work with the physician to see if there is any medical remediation, such as changing drug therapies. If not, the same goals apply as with organically induced female dysfunction, namely, to help the patient adjust to what is available.

Premature Ejaculation (302.75)

The DSM-III diagnostic criterion for premature ejaculation is ejaculation occurring before the male wishes it, because of recurrent and persistent inability to exercise reasonable voluntary control during sexual activity. The judgement of reasonable control is made by the clinician. Such factors such as age, novelty of the sexual partner, and the frequency and duration of coitus are taken into account. The problem should not be due to another Axis I disorder (APA, 1980). Premature ejaculation has been one of the most difficult dysfunctions to define. Masters and Johnson (1970) originally defined it in terms of the partner's ability to reach orgasm. Others have defined it in terms of the number of minutes to orgasm. The concept of voluntary control used in the DSM-III derives from the definition proposed by Helen Kaplan (1974) and seems to be the most sensible. The behavioral treatment of premature ejaculation has one of the highest success rates of all treatments for sexual dysfunction. This dysfunction almost never has medical involvement. Latency to orgasm does tend to increase with age, and many premature ejaculators are "cured" simply by growing older. In assessing this dysfunction, it is important to question the patient thoroughly. Some men complain of erectile dysfunction when, on further questioning, it is found that they really are ejaculating prematurely and subsequently losing their erection.

Functional Dyspareunia (302.76)

The DSM-III defines dyspareunia as the presence of recurrent and persistent genital pain during intercourse (APA, 1980). The term derives from the Greek and translates as "bad or difficult mating." Although the dysfunction can be present in men or women, it generally refers to the occurrence of vaginal pain in women from penile penetration or thrusting. The pain is experienced as tearing, burning, aching, or feelings of pressure, and it typically occurs during or just after intercourse (Geer *et al.*, 1984). Next to anorgasmia, it is the most common female sexual dysfunction. Many women experience vaginal pain at some time. Dyspareunia refers to pain that is persistent and severe. It is usually a disabling dysfunction, and therefore, the motives for seeking therapy are compelling (Fordney, 1978).

Dyspareunia can be subclassified as either primary versus secondary or complete versus situational. *Primary* refers to the presence of symptoms throughout the person's sexual lifetime, whereas *secondary* indicates that there has been a significant period without the symptom. *Complete* means that the symptom is present under all circumstances and *situational* indicates that it occurs in selective situations, such as with particular partners or type of stimulation. Dyspareunia can also be classified as either superficial (i.e., occurring at the introitus or vaginal barrel) or deep i.e., occurring at the cervix. (Fordney, 1978).

In 30% to 40% of cases, organic causes for female dyspareunia can be demonstrated. For the remaining 60% to 70% of women with long-standing dyspareunia, it is tempting to assume that the problem stems exclusively from psychological causes. However, there are specific organic pathologies that are difficult to detect and to diagnose. Thus, as in erectile failure, it may be that undiagnosed organic conditions are responsible for this problem. However, the presence of some organic conditions does not negate the role of psychological factors. Even though the initiating factor may indeed have been medical, psychological conditioning factors may be operant. Women with and without causal physical factors demonstrate a conditioned response to repetitive painful coitus that leads to fear and avoidance of sexual contacts. The subtle interplay of the psychic and the somatic is evident in the problem of inadequate lubrication, one of the most common causes of dyspareunia. Lubrication depends on arousal, and arousal depends on a psychological and physical process.

Are there any specific differences between women who have a physical component to dyspareunia and those who do not? Fordney (1978) offered the following clinical impressions based on 225 women evaluated for dyspareunia. Women without organic involvement are more likely to have secondary rather than primary dyspareunia, to be anorgasmic, to have both superficial- and deep-thrust combined pain, and to have sexually dysfunctional partners. They are less likely to have had a history of gynecologic disease and are unlikely to be able to specifically localize or describe the character of their pain. Palpation usually fails to reproduce the pain and instead produces a generalized discomfort. The discomfort of an examinaiton is not quite the same as or seems less severe than coital thrusting pain.

Many women with dyspareunia are also anorgasmic. Either dyspareunia precedes anorgasmia or the presence of anorgasmia may be important in the development of dyspareunia (Fordney, 1978). Masters and Johnson (1970) pointed out that the complaints of women with dyspareunia of psychic origin are usually vague.

Physical factors that can cause dyspareunia include most pelvic disease, chronic pelvic infection, endometriosis, advanced pelvic carcinoma, extensive prolapse, mediolateral episiotomy, overzealous posterior repairs, acute vulvovaginitis, cystitis, and introital, vaginal, and cervical scarring or mass-occupying lesions. Other prominent causes of dyspareunia include estrogen deprivation, spermicidal jelly or douches, sympathomimetic drugs, amphetamines, and cocaine use.

In some cases, it is easy to miss subtle underlying physical factors because these factors are considered gynecologically normal. The importance of careful examination to exclude these factors before psychological therapy cannot be overstated. A gynecologist who is alert to subtle pathology that may be affecting the sexual response should be consulted. These subtle medical factors fall into three groups: subacute vaginitis, pain in association with scars, and uterine or adnexal factors. The diagnosis of subacute vaginitis usually requires careful and multiple culturing techniques. Its symptoms consist of introital pain, not infrequently accompanied by vaginal pain or burning with coitus, which is increased at ejaculation and is followed by persistent burning immediately after sexual contact. Two of three patients presenting with superficial pain have identifiable subacute vaginitis. Subacute vaginitis can stem from allergic or chemical irritation; infectious agents such as candida albicans; and enteric organisms such as *Haemophilis vaginalis*, enterococci, or trichomonads such as chlamydic and mycoplasmic organisms.

Small scars stemming from laceration during childbirth, introital injury or episiotomy complications, pelvic surgery, or gynecologic disease may also lead to dyspareunia. These scars are usually small in size and are judged insignificant or are missed in a routine examination. Evidence that the scar is a contributing factor comes from the patient's ability to specifically localize the pain and accurately date its onset, and from the examiner's ability to reproduce the pain during examination by applying pressure at the site.

The last group of subtle factors easily missed are seen in patients with deep-thrust pain and consist of uterine or adnexal factors, such as ovarian fixation at or near the vault or cervix, small endometrial implants in the uterosacral ligaments, and uterine descensus (Fordney, 1978).

Other medical factors include those contributing to vaginal barrel pain, utrethral syndrome, and vaginal apex dyspareunia. Causes of introital or vaginal barrel pain include an increased sensitivity of vaginal introital tissues, which is part of the sexual response. This takes the form of burning or itching that is exacerbated by intercourse. Bartholin's gland cyst can also swell to painful proportions under the influence of sex arousal. Usually, there is a long history of chronic intermittent vulvitis with a developing focus of tenderness. Vaginal barrel discomfort may also stem from deficiencies in vaginal lubrication, from vaginal inflammatory conditions, from frictional dyspareunia, and from subclinical vaginitis. The urethral syndrome is a combination of urinary frequency, urgency, and dysuria, which occurs in the absence of documented bacteriuria. It may be the result of undiagnosed bacterial growth or of a combination of psychological and psychophysiological factors. It seems to be maintained by some degree of vaginismus. Vaginal apex dyspareunia or deep dyspareunia is pain that is experienced on deep vaginal penetration and is often seen as a symptom of an organic disease. Organic factors contributing to this condition include vaginitis, chronic cervicitis, and intrapelvic disease, such as endometriosis. Basically, it involves anything that limits the elevation of the uterus and the expansion of the upper end of the vagina, or that makes these tissues more sensitive. Deep dyspareunia, also termed *pelvic congestion syndrome* or *Duncan and Taylor syndrome* is diagnosed by laparoscopic evidence of distention of the pelvic veins (Steege, 1984).

Although less frequent, dyspareunia also occurs in males. As in dyspareunia in females, pain resulting from intercourse or sexual activity can lead to loss of desire and/or sexual avoidance. Organic causes include genital muscle spasms; infections and irritations of the penile skin (e.g., herpes genitalis and dermatitis); cancer of the penis; disorders that disturb the penile anatomy (e.g., Peyronie's disease and penile fracture); prostate infections and prostate enlargement; infections of the seminal vesicles; testicular disease; torsion of the spermatic cord (e.g., hernia); musculoskeletal disorders of the pelvis and lower back (e.g., low back pain and arthritis); cardiovascular and respiratory disorders; and postejaculatory headache (Kaplan, 1979).

In treating female dyspareunia, if physical factors are present it is first necessary to treat these conditions either medically or surgically. In most cases, surgery is not required and may even aggravate the condition. If after appropriate medical treatment dyspareunia still persists, sex therapy techniques are required to help alleviate the guarding and lack of relaxation that are associated with the inhibition of sexual pleasure and the resultant lack of lubrication. In the treatment of pelvic congestion syndrome, moderate salt restriction, knee–chest exercises, and counseling concerning avoiding deep vaginal penetration until sufficient levels of sexual arousal are reached are recommended (Steege, 1984).

The therapist's attitude when treating dyspareunia is very important. If doubt exists regarding the interaction of organic factors, it is most important that the therapist express acceptance that the pain is real and show empathy for the patient's situation as well as patience and understanding (Fink, 1972). Part of the therapy then becomes pain management, that is, trying to help the patient get the most out of her sex life in spite of the pain.

Functional Vaginismus (306.51)

The DSM-III defines vaginismus as a condition in which there is an involuntary spasm of the musculature of the outer third of the vagina interfering with coitus persistently and recurrently (APA, 1980). This reflex contraction is triggered by imagined or anticipated attempts at penetration during intromission or the act of coitus (Lamont, 1978). The spectrum of symptoms that accompanies vaginismus may range from severe debilitating pain that prevents intercourse altogether to varying degress of sexual inhibition due to dyspareunia. On physical examination, women with vaginismus appear tense and fearful. Touching induces fear and withdrawal behavior, and palpation of the perineum usually leads to a marked contraction of the pubococcygeus muscle. The patient seems unable either to relax or to recognize the contraction (Fordney, 1978). At times, vaginismus can be both frightening and humiliating. Not infrequently, male partners develop secondary impotence and feel angry, frustrated, and rejected because they believe that the symptom is voluntary (Nadelson & Marcotte, 1983). Among women with vaginismus, there is a high association of sexual dysfunction in male partners, which usually, but not necessarily occurs after onset. Despite vaginismus, many women are still orgasmic to fantasy and to nongenital and genital stimulation (Fordney, 1978).

Although vaginismus is one of the most disabling sexual dysfunctions, it is also one of the least frequently seen (Fertel, 1977; Kaplan, 1974; Masters & Johnson, 1970). Because vaginismus is often overlooked as the cause of dyspareunia (Lamont, 1978), it is advisable that a careful assessment be made. The usual subclassifications of sexual dysfunction also apply to vaginismus: primary versus secondary, and situational versus complete. Perhaps, the most comprehensive classificatory system for types of patients presenting with vaginismus and degree of symptomatology was presented by Lamont (1978). He classified patients with vaginismus into five categories: (1) unconsummated relationship; (2) successful and comfortable coitus before the onset of presenting symptoms but no coitus since; (3) pain with each attempt since first coitus; (4) comfortable coitus initially, followed by onset of pain with each subsequent attempt; and (5) primary vaginismus. He classified the presenting symptomatology according to four degrees of vaginismus based on the intensity and degree of involvement of the associated muscles (perineal, levator, and gluteus maximus) in the vaginal spasm. A fifth category was added for those who refused examination.

Again, some attempts (Harlow & McCluskey, 1972; Novak, 1948) have been made in the past to dichotomize organic and psychogenic causes, with dyspareunia being used to describe coital pain with organic cause and vaginismus encompassing all painful coitus without organic cause (Lamont, 1978). Masters and Johnson (1970) saw both factors as playing an integral part in the disorder and viewed it as the "classic example of a psychosomatic illness." Outside their specific etiological origins, vaginismus and dyspareunia are linked. There is a cycle of fear that inhibits sexual response. Repeated dyspareunia leads to increasing fear of pain and anxiety, which, in turn, produces vaginismus, and vaginismus, in turn, may be the causal factor in dyspareunia (Lamont, 1978).

In understanding how medical and psychological factors interact, it is helpful to think of vaginismus as a combination of the problem itself and the physiological finding that causes it (Fordney, 1978). Vaginismus is a psychophysiological syndrome. Traditionally, it is diagnosed only when the spasm is sufficient to prevent vaginal penetration (Steege, 1984). The vaginal spasm is an involuntary conditioned response resulting from the association of painful coital attempts or even imagined attempts at vaginal penetration. The original stimulus may have been either physical pain resulting from an organic problem or psychological distress. However, once a conditioned reflex is established, the resolution of the original condition alone may not result in the extinction of the vaginal response. In addition to the vaginal spasm, most women with vaginismus usually have a phobia of penetration that makes attempts at coitus frustrating and painful (Kaplan, 1974). Women seem caught in the dilemma of wanting to be helped, while being frightened of the cure (Fertel, 1977).

Frequently, women suffering from psychogenic vaginismus are reticent to discuss their sexual problems. The presenting complaint is often quite apart from vaginismus and may involve difficulty in breathing, abdominal pain, and so on (Ellison, 1972). Masters and Johnson (1970) insisted that diagnosis not be made without a pelvic examination so as to eliminate the possibility of simple phobic avoidance or physical conditions that may be obstructing vaginal entry.

Specific organic factors that have been implicated in the etiology of vaginismus include a rigid hymen, endometriosis, pelvic inflammatory disease, tumors, vaginitis, constipation, retroversion, pelvic congestion, and injuries related to obstetrical trauma (Lamont, 1978; Nadelson, 1983). In general, any disorder of the pelvic organs that makes penile entry painful or difficult may be implicated. Kegel (1952) associated vaginismus with weak and tender pubococcygeal muscles, the spasm being seen as a defense against pain where these muscles are located.

Treatment for vaginismus ranges from surgery to muscle-strengthening exercises to various psychotherapeutic interventions. The most important considerations seem to be the patient's understanding of the reflexive nature of the vaginal spasm and the therapist's flexibility of approach (Fertel, 1977). Of course, the first priority is to treat any existing organic pathology. In most cases, therapy is straightforward and involves the progressive use of vaginal dilators or fingers to help alleviate the patient's avoidance of vaginal penetration. Muscle-strengthening exercises devised by Kegel (1952) are used as an adjunct to help the patient achieve greater voluntary control over vaginal contraction.

OTHER PSYCHOSEXUAL DISORDERS

Ego-Dystonic Homosexuality (302.00)

The DSM-III diagnosis is used when the individual complains about absent or weak heterosexual arousal that significantly interferes with desired heterosexual relationships. There should be a sustained pattern of unwanted homosexual response that the individual explicitly states has been a persistent source of distress (APA, 1980).

It is important to note that homosexuality itself has been eliminated as a mental disorder in the DSM-III. This diagnosis is for those whose sexual preference is causing distress; therefore, it would not be appropriate to discuss psychological or biological theories of homosexuality. Clearly, there are no medical issues associated with the above diagnostic category.

Psychosexual Disorder Not Elsewhere Classified (302.89)

This is a residual category whose chief manifestations are psychological disturbances related to sexuality not covered by any of the other categories. These might include feelings of inadequacy about one's sex organs or distress over a pattern of repeated sexual conquests or confusion about sexual orientation. In practice, this category is rarely used, and there are no significant medical issues involved. Of course, any patient report that may imply some medical problem should be immediately evaluated.

SUMMARY

There are many disease states and other organic factors that can affect sexual functioning. Most important, there is frequently an interaction between organic and psychological factors, and careful attention to both is necessary in treating sexual dysfunction. For the most part, the paraphilias and gender disorders do not have any significant underlying organic factors. Therapists, however, should be aware of the behavioral effects of any drugs or hormones that such patients may be using. With increasing medical advances, we are learning more about biological influences on behavior, and these need to be increasingly integrated into a psychological treatment strategy.

REFERENCES

Abben, J. G., Lue, T. F., McClure, R. D., & Williams, R. D. (1985). Diagnostic tests for impotence. *Journal of Urology, 133 (4)*, 188A.

Abelson, D. (1975). Diagnostic value of the penile pulse and blood pressure: A Doppler study of impotence in diabetes. *Journal of Urology, 133*, 636.

American Psychiatric Association. (1980). *Diagnostic and statistical manual of mental disorders* (3rd ed.). Washington, DC: Author.

Aserinsky, E., & Kleitman, N. (1955). A motility cycle in sleeping infants as manifested by ocular and gross bodily activity. *Journal of Applied Psychology, 8,* 11–18.

Ball, J. R. (1986). A case of hair fetishism, transvestism and organic cerebral disorder. *Acta Psychiatrica Scandinavica, 44,* 249–254.

Bancroft, J. (1977). Hormones and sexual behavior. *Psychological Medicine, 7,* 553–556.

Bancroft, J. (1984). Hormones and human sexual behavior. *Journal of Sex and Marital Therapy, 10,* 1.

Barlow, D. H., Reynolds, E. J., & Agras, W. S. (1973). Gender identity change in a transsexual. *Archives of General Psychiatry, 28,* 569.

Barry, J. M., Blank, B., & Boileau, M. (1980). Nocturnal penile tumescence monitoring with stamps. *Urology, 15,* 171–172.

Blumer, D. (1970). Changes of sexual behavior related to temporal lobe disorders in man. *Journal of Sex Research, 6,* 1173–1180.

Comhaire, P., & Vermeulen, A. (1975). Plasma testosterone in patients with varicocele and sexual inadequacy. *Journal of Clinical Endocrinology and Metabolism, 40,* 824–829.

Davidson, J. M., & Levine, S. (1972). Endocrine regulation of behavior. *Annual Review of Physiology, 34,* 375–408.

Ek, A., Bradley, W., & Krane, R. J. (1983). Nocturnal penile rigidity measured by the snap gauge band. *Urology, 129,* 964–966.

Ellison, C. (1972). Vaginismus. *Medical Aspects of Human Sexuality, 8,* 34.

Epstein, A. W. (1975). The fetish object: Phylogenetic considerations. *Archives of Sexual Behavior, 4,* 303–308.

Fertel, N. S. (1977). Vaginismus: A review. *Journal of Sex and Marital Therapy, 3,* 113–121.

Fink, P. J. (1972). Dyspareunia: Current concepts. *Medical Aspects of Human Sexuality, 6,* 28–46.

Fisher, C. (1966). Dreaming and sexuality. In R. M. Loewenstein, L. M. Newman, & M. Schur (Eds.), *Psychoanalysis—A general psychology: Essays in honor of Heinz Hartman.* New York: International Universities Press.

Fordney, D. S. (1978). Dyspareunia and vaginismus. *Clinical Obstetrics and Gynecology, 21,* 205–221.

Frank, E., Anderson, C., & Rubinstein, D. (1978). Frequency of sexual dysfunction in "normal" couples. *New England Journal of Medicine, 299,* 111–115.

Friedman, J. M., & Hogan, D. (1985). Treatment of low sexual desire. In D. H. Barlow (Ed.), *Treatment of adult disorders.* New York: Guilford Press.

Friedman, J. M., Weiler, S. J., LoPiccolo, J., & Hogan, D. (1984). Sexual dysfunctions and their treatment: Current status. In A. Bellack, M. Hersen, & A. Kazdin (Eds.), *International handbook of behavior modification and therapy.* New York: Plenum Press.

Greer, J., Heiman, J., & Leitenberg, H. (1984). *Human sexuality.* Englewood Cliffs, NJ: Prentice-Hall.

Green, R. (1974). *Sexual identity conflict in children and adults.* Baltimore: Penguin Books.

Greenblatt, R. B., Mortara, F., & Torpin, R. (1942). Sexual libido in the female. *American Journal of Obstetrics and Gynecology, 44,* 658–663.

Gross, M. (1982). Reversal by bethanechol of sexual dysfunction caused by anticholinergic antidepressants. *American Journal of Psychiatry, 139,* 1193.

Harlow, R. A., & McCluskey, C. J. (1972). Introital dyspareunia. *Clinical Medicine, 27,* 25–27.

Hoenig, J., & Kenna, J. C. (1979). EEG abnormalities and transsexualism. *British Journal of Psychiatry, 3,* 293–300.

Housden, J. (1965). An examination of the biologic etiology of transvestism. *International Journal of Social Psychiatry, 11,* 301–305.

Jevtich, M. J. (1983). Vascular noninvasive diagnostic techniques. In R. I. Krane, M. B. Siroky, & I. Goldstein (Eds.), *Male sexual dysfunction.* Boston: Little, Brown.

Jevtich, M. J., & Maxwell, D. D. (1983). Invasive vascular procedures. In R. J. Krane, M. B. Siroky, & I. Goldstein (Eds.), *Male sexual dysfunction.* Boston: Little, Brown.

Kaplan, H. S. (1974). *The new sex therapy.* New York: Brunner/Mazel.

Kaplan, H. S. (1979). *Disorders of sexual desire.* New York Brunner/Mazel.

Kaplan, H. S. (1985). *Comprehensive evaluation of disorders of sexual desire.* New York: American Psychiatric Press.

Karacan, I. (1970). Clinical value of nocturnal erection in the prognosis and diagnosis of impotence. *Medical Aspects of Human Sexuality, 4*, 27–34.

Karacan, I., Goodenough, D. R., Shapiro, A., & Starker, S. (1966). Erection cycle during sleep in relation to dream anxiety. *Archives of General Psychiatry, 15*, 183–189.

Kegel, A. H. (1952). Sexual functions of the pubococcygeus muscle. *Western Journal of Surgical Obstetrics and Gynecology, 60*, 521.

Kempczinski, R. F. (1979). Role of the vascular diagnostic laboratory in the evaluation of male impotence. *American Journal of Surgery, 138*, 278–282.

Kolarsky, A., Freund, K., Machek, J., & Polak, O. (1967). Male sexual deviations association with early temporal lobe damage. *Archives of General Psychiatry, 17*, 735–743.

Kolodny, R. C., Masters, W. H., & Johnson, V. E. (1979). Female sexual dysfunction. In *Textbook of Sexual Medicine*. Boston: Little, Brown.

Krauss, D. (1983). The physiologic basis of male sexual dysfunction. *Hospital Practice, 2*, 193–222.

LaFerla, J. J. (1984). Inhibited sexual desire and orgasmic dysfunction in women. *Clinical Obstetrics and Gynecology, 27(3)*, 738–479.

Lamont, J. A. (1978). Vaginismus. *American Journal of Obstetrics and Gynecology, 131*, 632–636.

Langevin, R. (1983). *Sexual strands: Understanding and treating sexual anomalies in men*. Hillsdale, NJ: Lawrence Erlbaum.

Langevin, R., Paitich, D., Freeman, R., Mann, K., & Handy, L. (1978). Personality characteristics and sexual anomalies in males. *Canadian Journal of Behavioral Science, 10*, 222–236.

Langevin, R., Paitich, D., Ramsay, G., Anderson, C., Kamrad, J., Pope, S., Geller, G., & Newman, S. (1979). Experimental studies in the etiology of genital exhibitionism. *Archives of General Psychiatry, 8*, 307–331.

Lue, T. F., Hricak, H., Schmidt, R. A., & Tanagho, E. A. (1985). Functional evaluation of penile arterial flow during erection. *Journal of Urology, 133(4)*, 218A.

Malloy, T. R., & Wein, A. J. (1983). Penile flacidity due to vascular insufficiency. *Medical Aspects of Human Sexuality, 17*, 211–220.

Masters, W. H., & Johnson, V. E. (1970). *Human sexual inadequacy*. Boston: Little, Brown.

McCarthy, B. W. (1981). Strategies and techniques for the treatment of ejaculatory inhibition. *Journal of Sexual Education and Therapy, 7(2)*, 21.

Melman, A., & Henry, D. P. (1979). The possible role of the catecholamines of the corpora in penile erection. *Journal of Urology, 121*, 419–423.

Melman, A., & Leiter, E. (1982). The urologic evaluation of impotence. In H. Kaplan (ED.), *The assessment of sexual disorders*, New York: Brunner/Mazel.

Metz, P., & Wagner, G. (1981). Penile circumference and erection. *Urology, 18*, 268–270.

Meyer, J. K., & Reter, D. J. (1979). Sex reassignment: Follow-up. *Archives of General Psychiatry, 36*, 1910.

Michal, V., Kramer, R., & Pospichal, J. (1978). External iliac "steal syndrome." *Journal of Cardiovascular Surgery, 19*, 255–257.

Mohr, J., Turner, R. E., & Jerry, M. (1964). *Pedophilia and exhibitionism*. Toronto: University of Toronto Press.

Money, J., & Ehrhardt, A. A. (1973). *Man & woman, boy & girl*. Baltimore: Johns Hopkins Press.

Money, J. Wiedeking, C., Walker, P., Migeon, C., Meyer, W., & Borgaonkar, D. (1975). 47 XYY 46 XY males with antisocial and/or sex-offending behavior: Antiandrogen therapy plus counseling. *Psychoneuroendocrinology, 1*, 165–180.

Nadelson, C. C., & Marcotte, D. B. (1983). Problems in sexual functioning. In C. Nadelson & D. Marcotte (Eds.), *Treatment interventions in human sexuality*. New York: Plenum Press.

Novak, J. (1948). Nature and treatment of vaginismus. *Urology Cutaneous Review, 52*, 128.

Ohlmeyer, P., Brilmayer, H., & Hullstrung, H. (1944). Periodishe Vorgange im Schlap. *Pflugers Archives, 248*, 559–560.

Pirke, K. M., & Kockett, G. (1982). Endocrinology of sexual dysfunction. In J. Bancroft (Ed.), *Diseases of sex and sexuality: Clinics in endocrinology and metabolism, 2(3)*, 625–638.

Procci, W. R., Moss, H. G., Boyd, J. L., & Barron, D. A. (1983). Consecutive night reliability of portable nocturnal penile tumescence monitor. *Archives of Sexual Behavior, 12(4)*, 307–316.

Roen, P. R. (1965). Impotence: A concise review. *New York Journal of Medicine*, 2576–2582.

Schiavi, R., & Fisher, S. (1982). Measurement of nocturnal erections. In J. Bancroft (Ed.), *Disease of sex and sexuality: Clinics in endocrinology and metabolism, 2(3)*, 769–784.

Schiavi, R. C., & White, D. (1976). Androgens and male sexual function. *Journal of Sex and Marital Therapy, 2*, 214–228.

Seagraves, R. T., Schoenberg, H. W., & Ivonoff, J. (1983). Serum testosterone and prolactin levels in erectile dysfunction. *Journal of Sex and Marital Therapy, 9(1)*, 19.

Snyder, S. H. (1980). *Biological aspects of mental disorder*. New York: Oxford University Press.

Spark, R. F., White, R. A., & Connolly, P. B. (1980). Impotence is not always psychogenic: Newer insights into hypothalamic-pituitary-gonadal dysfunction. *Journal of the American Medical Association, 243*, 750–755.

Steege, J. F. (1984). Dyspareunia and vaginismus. *Clinical Obstetrics and Gynecology, 3*, 750–759.

Thorner, M. O., McNeilly, A. S., Hagan, C., & Besser, G. M. (1974). Long-term treatment of galactorrhea and hypogonadism with bromoscriptine. *British Medical Journal, 2*, 419–422.

Thorner, M. O., Edwards, C. R. W., Hanker, J. P., Abraham, G., & Besser, G. M. (1977). Prolactin and gonadotropin interaction in the male. In P. Troen & H. Rankin (Eds.), *The testis in normal and infertile men*. New York: Raven Press.

Wagner, G. (1981). Erection: Physiology and endocrinology. In G. Wagner & R. Green (Eds.), *Impotence: Physiological, psychological, surgical diagnosis and treatment*. New York: Plenum Press.

Wagner, G., & Green, R. (1981). *Impotence: Physiological, psychological, surgical diagnosis and treatment*. New York: Plenum Press.

Wagner, G., & Metz, P. (1980). Impotence due to vascular disorders. *Journal of Sex and Marital Therapy, 6(4)*, 223–233.

Walinder, J. (1965). Transvestism, definition and evidence in favor of occasional derivation from cerebral dysfunction. *International Journal of Neuropsychiatry, 1*, 567–573.

Wasserman, M. D., Pollak, C. P., Spielman, A. J., & Weitzman, E. D. (1980). Theoretical and technical problems in the measurement of nocturnal penile tumescence for the differential diagnosis of importence. *Psychosomatic Medicine, 42*, 575–585.

Winokur, G. (1963). *Determinants of human sexual behavior*. Springfield, IL: Charles C Thomas.

Zilbergeld, B., & Ellison, C. R. (1980). Desire discrepancies and arousal problems in sex therapy. In S. Leiblum & L. A. Pervin (Eds.), *Principles and practice of sex therapy*. New York: Guilford Press.

Zorgniotti, A. W., & Lefleur, R. S. (1985). Auto-injection of the corpus cavernosum with a vasoactive drug combination for vasculogenic importence. *Journal of Urology, 133(1)*, 39–41.

Zorngniotti, A. W., Rossi, G., Padula, G., & Makovsky, R. D. (1980). Diagnosis and therapy of vasculogenic impotence. *The Journal of Urology, 123*, 674–677.

6

Somatoform, Dissociative, and Factitious Disorders

JEFFREY M. BRANDSMA AND DOUGLAS P. HOBSON

The fully functioning human brain is remarkable in its level of complexity and organization, although this fact is usually taken for granted. When difficulties arise or it suffers insult, we notice many symptom patterns, and it is difficult to attribute causality at times because of the brain's capability of mimicking various disease states. The hypnotic literature reminds us that consciousness is not a strong or unitary gestalt, and this fact is especially striking in the area of the dissociative disorders (Fromm & Shor, 1979). But the mind–body problem and the difficulties in attributing the causality of symptoms are evident throughout this chapter.

In the past few decades, great advances in diagnostic technology (for example, the CAT and MRI scanners) and in the understanding of brain functioning (neuropsychology) have been helping professionals to more deeply respect both sides of the psychological-biological equation of human functioning. There have been solid advances in the fields of the epilepsies (Aird, Masland, & Woodburg, 1984; Blumer, 1984; Reynolds & Trimble, 1981); multiple personality disorder (MPD) (Kluft, 1985a); and neuropsychology; and in the diagnostic clarity represented in the multiaxial system of the third edition of the American Psychiatric Association's *Diagnostic and Statistical Manual* (DSM-III; APA, 1980). Psychologists of various stripes continue to contribute to these advances. The usual role of a clinical psychologist has been to remind her or his medical colleagues of the importance and sometimes the critical place of behavioral or psychological factors in the expression of illnesses. This chapter requires a different and reverse mind set; that is, given an acceptance of psychological factors and explanations, we must be aware of what biological-medical factors psychologists must concomitantly consider to better treat the patient. Following the DSM-III format, we will begin with somatoform disorders and then cover dissociative and, finally, factitious disorders.

SOMATOFORM DISORDERS

Background

Somatoform disorders are without question the nosological brier patch of psychiatric classification. The colorful and varied history of hysteria (Veith, 1965) reflects the many

JEFFREY M. BRANDSMA AND DOUGLAS P. HOBSON • Department of Psychiatry and Health Behavior, Medical College of Georgia, School of Medicine, Augusta, GA, 30912.

pendular swings in the philosophy of psychiatric thinking, so much so that the term *hysteria* seems to have lost much of its clinical utility (Van Dyke, 1983). Although it is true that the diagnosis of hysteria "tends to outlive its obituarists" (Lewis, 1975, p. 12), there has been an increasing trend among mental health epidemiologists to further refine the diagnostic criteria for these diagnostic chameleons.

Chodoff and Lyons (1958) argued that "hysterical" conversion disorders did not occur solely in patients exhibiting hysterical personality disorder, that no single personality type was characteristically encountered among this group. Furthermore, with apparent prescience of things to come, they declared that even the so-called hysterical personality was dubious because it had the earmarks of the male caricature of femininity. Others carried the torch for a greater specification of the different uses of the term *hysteria* (Chodoff, 1974; Gatfield & Guze, 1962; Hyler & Spitzer, 1978), with intimations that these might be discrete entities with separate prognoses and treatments. This history has led to the current DSM-III grouping of somatoform disorders, consisting of (1) somatization disorder; (2) conversion disorder (or hysterical neurosis, conversion type); (3) psychogenic pain disorder; (4) hypochondriasis (or hypochondriacal neurosis); and (5) atypical somatoform disorder.

Somatization Disorders

The patient with somatization disorder (see Table 1) typically responds to the clinician's review of systems with an affirmation of virtually all afflictions known to each organ. In whatever systematic fashion the clinician inquires about the individual's health, a sickly note is likely to be struck. Indeed, it is about this aspect that Stoudemire (1984) wrote, "Probably no other general category of patients causes as much confusion, frustration, and exasperation. . .as this group of patients who often present with a seemingly endless litany of complaints" (p. 593). A good analogue would be a Chinese menu of symptoms from which the patient orders at least one from each category. Of course, confounding the already murky picture provided by self-report is the possibility of a latent organic malady that is overlooked amidst the ever-present "cries of wolf." Lipowski (1975) cautioned us that there is no sharp boundary between organic and so-called functional psychiatric disorders. With sage advice, he reminded us, "The criterion of demonstrability of cerebral pathology reflects no more than the limitations of our knowledge and diagnostic techniques" (p. 116). Even the DSM-III lists in the differential diagnoses for this disorder such protean disorders as multiple sclerosis, porphyria, hyperparathyroidism, and systemic lupus erythematosis.

Equally sobering to the clinician is the study by Hall, Popkin, De Vaul, Faillace, and Stickney (1978) of over 600 psychiatric outpatients, in which 9.1% of the entire population studied had medical disorders productive of psychiatric symptoms. Among the more common medical pathologies accounting for this group were infectious blood, liver, and CNS diseases. In terms of psychiatric symptoms caused by medical diseases, it was found that depression, confusion, anxiety, and speech and memory disorders headed the list. The study concluded that a detailed physical examination and laboratory screening should be routine in the initial evaluation of psychiatric patients, with great importance being placed on a review of systems. Although the interpretation of such a review of systems is perhaps best left to the internist or neurologist, the clinical psychologist could easily perform a perfunctory screening of various organ functions by asking about such symp-

Table 1. DSM-III Diagnostic Criteria for Somatization Disorder

---

A. A history of physical symptoms of several years' duration, beginning before the age of 30.

B. Complaints of at least 14 symptoms for women and 12 for men from the 37 symptoms listed below. To count a symptom as present the individual must report that the symptom caused him or her to take medicine (other than aspirin), alter his or her life pattern, or see a physician. The symptoms, in the judgment of the clinician, are not adequately explained by physical disorder or physical injury and are not side effects of medication, drugs or alcohol. The clinician need not be convinced that the symptom was actually present, e. g., that the individual actually vomited throughout her entire pregnancy; report of the symptom by the individual is sufficient.

Sickly: Believes that he or she has been sickly for a good part of his or her life.

Conversion or pseudoneurological symptoms: Difficulty swallowing, loss of voice, deafness, double vision, blurred vision, blindness, fainting or loss of consciousness, memory loss, seizures or convulsions, trouble walking, paralysis or muscle weakness, urinary retention or difficulty urinating.

Gastrointestinal symptoms: Abdominal pain, nausea, vomiting spells (other than during pregnancy), bloating (gassy), intolerance (e.g., gets sick) of a variety of foods, diarrhea.

Female reproductive symptoms: Judged by the individual as occurring more frequently or severely than in most women: painful menstruation, menstrual irregularity, excessive bleeding, severe vomiting throughout pregnancy or causing hospitalization during pregnancy.

Psychosexual symptoms: For the major part of the individual's life after opportunities for sexual activity: sexual indifference, lack of pleasure during intercourse, pain during intercourse.

Pain: Pain in back, joints, extremities, genital area (other than during intercourse); pain on urination; other pain (other than headaches).

Cardiopulmonary symptoms: Shortness of breath, palpitations, chest pain, dizziness.

Note. From *Diagnostic and Statistical Manual of Mental Disorders* (3rd ed.) (p. 243). Copyright 1980 by the American Psychiatric Association. Reprinted by permission.

toms as shortness of breath, insomnia, anorexia, abdominal cramps, and so on. From such a review, it could be determined if a more extensive consultation and workup are warranted.

Particularly germane would be a routine inquiry into common neurovegetative signs of an affective disorder, such as changes in appetite, weight gain or loss, changes in sleep pattern (either insomnia or hypersonmia), psychomotor retardation or activation, and changes in energy level. Katon, Reis, and Kleinman (1984), although using criteria different than those of the DSM-III, found a significant association of somatization with depression. With depression being one of the more successfully treated psychological conditions, it behooves the clinician to be aware of both the possibility of a treatable depression masquerading as somatization disorder and the possibility of a pernicious physical malady for which a medical workup is in order.

Nevertheless, the hallmark of somatization disorder remains the production of a stream of somatic symptoms for which organic etiologies cannot be found. The diagnosis should be made after genuine pursuit of some of the more common illnesses that can take on multiorgan manifestations, a search best conducted by an empathic internist willing to be a team player in the investigation. Essential to such an investigation is the medical history and the physical examination, on which the majority of clinical diagnoses still rest.

For somatoform disorders such as somatization disorder and hypochondriasis, the search may have a tendency to lead the physician in several directions simultaneously. If, as an example to show complexity, the chief complaint ran along the lines of joint or musculoskeletal pain, the focus of the workup would center on (but would not restrict itself to) diseases of a rheumatologic nature or of connective tissue and immunoreactive disorders. Depending on the "fit" of the patient's presenting complaints to a recognizable disorder, the corroborative laboratory tests ordered may vary from one patient to the next. In the case of symptomatology suggestive of connective tissue pathology, the tests may include such items as rheumatoid factor, antinuclear antibody titer, and lupus erythematosis preparation. This line of inquiry would, on the other hand, be rather out of place if the predominant complaints were gastrointestinal.

The clinical dilemma is how far to proceed with the ancillary laboratory testing. Although certain laboratory testing has become nearly routine—for example, complete blood count (CBC), electrolytes (sodium, potassium, chlorine, and carbon dioxide), automated chemistry profile (blood urea nitrogen, calcium, phosphorus, creatinine, phosphokinase, etc.), urinalysis, electrocardiogram (EKG), and tests for syphilis—other testing, usually comparatively more expensive or complicated, is not indicated unless the severity of the symptoms suggests such procedures to the physician.

Exhausting the possible pathologies in this way for all of the symptoms that present in somatization disorder could easily lead to exorbitant expense, not to mention the ever-cumulative risk of introducing genuine iatrogenic problems. The astute and experienced clinician therefore needs to make rational judgments on such investigative endeavors, knowing when to vigorously pursue the trail of symptoms, and when to leave well enough alone. Good clinicians seem to base such judgments on the predominance and severity of the individual complaint, the gestalt of all the symptoms, and his or her clinical experience and intuition. Unfortunately, the chronic somatoform-disorder patient often makes this an exceedingly challenging task.

As Nemiah (1980 b) aptly noted "in the absence of any systematic studies of the treatment of somatization disorder, it is not possible to speak about definitive therapeutic treatment" (p. 1527). Except for uncovering a clinical depression presenting with multitudinous somatic symptoms, the prognosis and treatment outlook is probably bleak. It may be, however, that in the repetitive, warm interaction of a supportive psychotherapy, the patient's conflictual material may be expressed verbally rather than somatically, and better strategies of coping may be developed.

Conversion Disorders

As noted earlier, the DSM-III has sought to further refine the phenomenological entities that had previously been lumped together as hysteria. Conversion disorders are those afflictions in which an individual unconsciously loses control over some usually volitional aspect of his or her body, yet without recognizable lesions to account for such inabilities. An essential feature distinguishing conversion disorder (see Table 2) from factitious illnesses is that the person is not *consciously* aware that he or she influences the production of the symptoms. Traditionally, this *lack of conscious awareness* has been explained within the framework of psychodynamic understandings of the human being, based originally on the work of Breuer and Freud (1895). This view held that energy from repressed

*Table 2. DSM-III Diagnostic Criteria for Conversion
Disorder (or Hysterical Neurosis, Conversion Type)*

A. The predominant disturbance is a loss of or alteration in physical functioning suggesting a physical disorder.

B. Psychological factors are judged to be etiologically involved in the symptom, as evidenced by one of the following:
   1. there is a temporal relationship between an environmental stimulus that is apparently related to a psychological conflict or need and the initiation or exacerbation of the symptom
   2. the symptom enables the individual to avoid some activity that is noxious to him or her
   3. the symptom enables the individual to get support from the environment that otherwise might not be forthcoming

C. It has been determined that the symptom is *not* under voluntary control.

D. The symptom cannot, after appropriate investigation, be explained by a known physical disorder or pathophysiological mechanism.

E. The symptom is not limited to pain or to a disturbance in sexual functioning.

F. Not due to somatization disorder or schizophrenia.

Note. From *Diagnostic and Statistical Manual of Mental Disorders* (3rd ed.) (p. 247). Copyright 1980 by the American Psychiatric Association. Reprinted by permission.

sexual conflicts is converted and discharged through somatic symptomatology, which confers a protective shield from the distress that would otherwise attend the conflict. Frequently in this view, the afflicted body part was thought to have special symbolic significance with regard to the neurotic psychopathology.

More contemporary students have looked to other etiologic explanations (cf. DeVaul, 1980; Ford, 1983), including neurophysiological paradigms. After reviewing recent neuropsychological studies, Flor-Henry (1983) concluded that "hysterics are characterized by bilateral frontal dysfunction and nondominant hemispheric dysfunction, with a gradient of dysfunction which is greater in the anterior than in the posterior cerebral regions." (p. 283). Moreover, on intense scrutiny of the case report of Anna 0., a historic cornerstone for the Freudian hermeneutics of hysteria, Flor-Henry reasoned that she probably "suffered from limbic encephalitis of the dominant hemisphere with nonconvulsive seizures." (p. 272).

Others have emphasized the aspects of secondary gain as important factors to consider in conversion disorders (Ziegler & Imboden, 1962). Inspection of the DSM-III diagnostic criteria for conversion disorder reveals that it is required that psychological factors be etiologically involved, as judged by the clinician. Indeed, it is such a requirement of *positive* criteria that prevents the diagnosis from slipping into an exclusionary "garbage bag" nosology in which the diagnosis is made only after the latest technology has failed to reveal a medical explanation. Identifying positive psychological criteria (for example, symptoms enabling the individual to avoid noxious activities) rather than a simple grouping of all unexplained illnesses into one medical maelstrom would seem to help purify this pathology phenomenologically. At the same time, Van Dyke (1983) reminded us that *"all illnesses have secondary gain, and this fact is not synonymous with etiology"* (p. 193; italics in the original).

Theoretical issues notwithstanding, the incidence of this disorder is inherently difficult to establish with any certainty. Although the near-thespian presentations that characterized the conversion disorders of Charcot's day seem to have abated, it may very well be that, rather than decreasing in frequency, the manifestations of conversion have merely changed (Weintraub, 1983). It is now better appreciated, for instance, that populations other than neurotic nineteenth-century Viennese women suffer with conversion disorder, and that it is not exclusively associated with histrionic personality disorder. It appears to be not uncommon in children (Maloney, 1980; Rada, Meyer, & Kellner, 1978; Weintraub, 1983), but here, it generally remits within a relatively brief period. In adolescent females, there is a high correlation with incest (Goodwin, Simms, & Bergman, 1979; Gross, 1979), and here, it responds well to therapeutic and social interventions.

Psychological testing is helpful as a diagnostic tool in the workup of patients suspected of having no organic pathology to explain their deficits. Known to most psychologists is the "Conversion V" found on Scales 1-2-3 of the MMPI. It is not pathognomonic in itself for DSM-III conversion disorder, however, and needs to be balanced with the rest of the clinical exam (Duerksen & Smith, 1982).

A thorough physical examination, including rigorous neurological testing, is mandatory for the proper diagnosis of conversion disorder. In fact, it is the marked complexity of human neuroanatomy and neurophysiology that aids the astute clinician in detecting conversion symptomatology. For the layperson it would seem counterintuitive that certain neurological deficits would spare certain areas or would produce a gradient of sensory loss (e.g., pain, then temperature, then touch) rather than a well-delineated loss of function (which tends to be a common presentation of conversion). It is these neuroanatomical inconsistencies that usually ensnare the patient. Weintraub (1983) produced a splendid compendium of illustrated techniques for diagnosing these frequently baffling disorders by sophisticated physical examination. However, at times, even the most advanced technology and physical examinations fail to uncover an inconsistency in the symptomatology, and some investigators have found amytal interviews to be helpful at this point in corroborating the criteria for conversion disorder (Ford, 1983; Kwentus, 1984).

There is a double-edged diagnostic sword that ought to be wielded with Solomonesque wisdom: Even in the presence of a justifiably diagnosed conversion disorder, there may concomitantly and coincidentally exist a genuine physical disease to which attention is not given because it is assumed to be psychological. As one adage has it, "Even 'crocks' die sometime." Therefore, one needs to be concerned not only about coexisting, authentic physical illness, but also about certain slippery diagnostic dilemmas, such as multiple sclerosis (Wells & Duncan, 1980), that have a propensity to present as hysterical disease. It goes without further explanation, therefore, that the diagnosis of conversion disorder is best handled in an interdisciplinary effort among internists, neurologists, and medically cognizant psychologists.

There are some items that should raise the index of suspicion for the clinical psychologist that conversion symptomatology may be playing a part in the clinical picture and that consultation with a neurologist is in order (Hier, 1978). These would include a previous history of conversion reactions as well as a history of psychosomatic symptoms, such as hyperventilation, headaches, dizziness, vomiting, and ill-defined abdominal complaints. Also, a history of "psychoneurotic" symptoms—depression, phobia, anxiety, or obsessiveness—may also raise a flag of caution. A demonstration that the deficits are modified by suggestion or placebo responses may also be a clinical clue. The clinical main-stays, however, remain the inconsistencies in the physical examination, in combination with apparent psychological factors (Hobson, 1985). In the case of hysterical paralysis, it rarely involves alterations of muscle tone or reflexes. In the situation of hysterical anesthesias, the distribution of the alleged sensory deficit rarely follows the rather com-plicated neuroanatomical dermatomes; rather, the deficit is usually more sharply defined (and anatomically inaccurate). Pseudoseizures have a proclivity for wild flailing, often without the loss of consciousness, urinary incontinence, and tongue biting that are fre-quent accompaniments of genuine seizure disorders (cf. Gross, 1983; Riley & Roy, 1982).

In contrast to some of the more recalcitrant somatoform disorders and factitious ill-nesses, conversion disorders appear to have a moderately hopeful outcome. A variety of apparently inefficacious "treatments" have been found to alleviate a number of conver-sion deficits, often without symptom substitution (Hafeiz, 1980). The explanation is that the patient requires some credible, "face-saving" technique(s) that will allow, with proper encouraging suggestion by the clinician, the symptoms to be removed. It is generally recommended that a supportive psychotherapeutic relationship be established with either the psychologist, the psychiatrist, or the primary-care physician, depending on the needs and allowance of the patient for psychotherapeutic intervention. During the course of such psychotherapy, some degree of somatization may be expected to surface with increased awareness of conflicts or in the problems of the transference relationship in psychother-apy (Rodin, 1984). Nevertheless, outcomes are far less disparaging in this group than in many of the other somatoform and psychosomatic disorders.

Psychogenic Pain Disorders

The diagnosis of psychogenic pain disorder (see Table 3) is a new classification with the advent of the DSM-III, but a clinical phenomenon long recognized. It shares many characteristics with conversion disorder; for example, psychological factors are judged to be etiologically involved in the pain. Unlike conversion symptomatology, however, the dysfunction here is restricted to pain inconsistent with organic pathology or is grossly in excess of what one would ordinarily anticipate given the physical findings. Again, by DSM-III criteria, it is not simply the absence of explanatory physical deficits but also relies on an identifiable psychogenic contribution.

Although the location of the pain can be anywhere in the body, some of the more common psychogenic pain disorders involve chronic back pain, pelvic pain, phantom limb pain, facial pain, and headaches. Because the symptom list is restricted to pain, it does not in any way lessen the complexity of understanding or treatment of psychogenic pain disorders. Behavioristic psychologists, with their emphasis on specificity, now believe that each type of pain ought to be approached on its own terms. Indeed, with respect to headaches alone, the task is so demanding that Wells and Duncan (1980) declared that the occurrence of headaches requires a high level of neurological and medical sophisti-cation on the part of the clinician. As in conversion disorder, the workup is most effi-ciently and accurately performed in a well-organized interdisciplinary fashion between psychologist, psychiatrist, neurologist, and internist.

It has been suggested, however, that the association between psychogenic pain dis-order and depression is so high that a routine psychological evaluation for the presence

Table 3. DSM-III Diagnostic Criteria for Psychogenic Pain Disorder

A. Severe and prolonged pain is the predominant disturbance.

B. The pain presented as a symptom is inconsistent with the anatomic distribution of the nervous system; after extensive evaluation, no organic pathology or pathophysiological mechanism can be found to account for the pain; or, when there is some related organic pathology, the complaint of pain is grossly in excess of what would be expected from the physical findings.

C. Psychological factors are judged to be etiologically involved in the pain, as evidenced by at least one of the following:

1. a temporal relationship between an environmental stimulus that is apparently related to a psychological conflict or need and the initiation or exacerbation of the pain
2. the pain enables the individual to avoid some activity that is noxious to him or her
3. the pain enables the individual to get support from the environment that otherwise might not be forthcoming

D. Not due to another mental disorder.

Note. From *Diagnostic and Statistical Manual of Mental Disorders* (3rd ed.) (p. 249). Copyright 1980 by the American Psychiatric Association. Reprinted by permission.

of potentially etiological dysphoria is warranted (Hier, 1978). Such a close connection has been discovered, in fact, that researchers now explore psychobiological markers in an effort to further understand their connection as, for example, in the case of urinary 3-methoxy-4-hydroxypheneylethylene glycol (MHPG) and the severity of pain in depressed patients (Ward, Bloom, Dworkin, Fawcett, Narasimhachari, & Friedel, 1982); however, such biologic variables have yet to reach the level of clinical utility. Among the classic contributions to the psychological understanding of psychogenic pain is the article by Engel (1959) that discusses the attributes of the ''pain-prone patient.'' Key ingredients to be examined are the presence of guilt for which the pain functions as explanation and punishment, a personal history filled with unhappiness and rejection, and exposure to a parent or close relative who was noted to be a chronic sufferer.

Thus, although the definitive diagnosis of psychogenic pain disorder requires input from different specialists, the psychological clinician would be well served by routinely screening for the usual symptoms of depression, as well as for the special features of the personality style that may be ''pain-prone.'' The treatment of psychogenic pain disorder is similarly enhanced by a multimodel, interdisciplinary effort, frequently involving a variety of somatic (Hackett, 1978; Stimmel, 1983) as well as nonsomatic (behavioral and psychotherapeutic) therapies (Ford, 1983; Turk, Meichenbaum, & Genest, 1983). Successful treatment is likely to depend, in part, on the chronicity of the symptoms and the degree to which the pain is determined by the many possible variables in the psychic equation.

Hypochondriasis

Although less flamboyant and colorful in its presentation than hysterical conversion disorders or certain psychogenic pain disorders, the diagnosis of hypochondriasis (see Table 4) nevertheless enjoys equally ancient roots in medicine (cf. Ford, 1983; Murray,

Table 4. DSM-III Diagnostic Criteria for Hypochondriasis

A. The predominant disturbance is an unrealistic interpretation of physical signs or sensations as abnormal, leading to preoccupation with the fear or belief of having a serious disease.

B. Thorough physical evaluation does not support the diagnosis of any physical disorder that can account for the physical signs or sensations or for the individual's unrealistic interpretation of them.

C. The unrealistic fear or belief of having a disease persists despite medical reassurance and causes impairment in social or occupational functioning.

D. Not due to any other mental disorder such as schizophrenia, affective disorder, or somatization disorder.

Note. From *Diagnostic and Statistical Manual of Mental Disorders* (3rd ed.) (p. 251). Copyright 1980 by the American Psychiatric Association. Reprinted by permission.

1979; Nemiah, 1980b) with comparable conceptual controversy. As Van Dyke (1983) intimated, there are considerable similarities between somatization disorder and hypochondriasis, with somatization disorder having a greater number and diversity of somatic complaints. The essential characteristics of DSM-III hypochondriasis are the unrealistic interpretation of physical signs and the unrealistic fear of having a disease despite reassurance that, in fact, there is no medical evidence of pathology. Pilowsky (1970) made the distinction between "primary hypochondriasis" and "secondary hypochondriasis" in an effort to further subtype this heterogeneous group for the purposes of diagnosis, prognosis, and treatment. "Primary hypochondriasis" was diagnosed when the morbid preoccupation with health was the only feature of the illness and where it was unlikely that another diagnosis would be made. "Secondary hypochondriasis," on the other hand, was the label when the symptoms were accompanied by anxiety and depression or were a reflection of some other psychiatric disease or a prior history of psychopathology. Based on epidemiological and outcome studies, Pilowsky concluded that "secondary hypochondriasis" comprises depressive and anxiety syndromes, whereas "primary hypochondriasis" does not.

Although this intriguing and potentially clinically useful differentiation has yet to be officially recognized in the diagnostic nomenclature, there are other considerations of hypochondriacal symptomatology that are useful to keep in mind. Murray (1979) has appropriately reminded us that hypochondriasis remains a *syndrome,* that is, a number of symptoms linked in some unknown way. The distinctions engineered by clinical theoreticians are applaudable but have yet to be shown to be clearly useful (i.e., related to different treatments, outcomes, and so on). Moreover, a recent review by Barsky and Klerman (1983) brilliantly demonstrated the gaping holes in the etiologic understanding of this somatoform disorder.

In terms of diagnostic and clinical clues, hypochondriacal features tend to be obvious even to the layperson. The astute clinician is quickly able to pick up on the droning details that the patients are apt to produce. They may exhibit some hostility intermingled with their uninformative histories (Murray, 1979), and many essential features of hypochondriasis tend to unfold in the course of the development of the doctor–patient relationship (Pilowsky, 1983); these lead the clinician to feel inadequate, helpless, guilty, frustrated, and angry, with misperceptions by both the patient and the clinician about how the workup is proceeding (Hobson & Mabe unpublished data, 1986). Other tip-offs for the clinician are the vague and nebulous quality of many of the bodily complaints of the patient and the often hostile response from the patient when the clinician begins to probe.

Again, because of the disguised way in which certain neurological and metabolic-endocrine disturbances may present themselves, it is prudent to require a thoroughgoing physical examination and routine laboratory tests before ascribing these complaints to hypochondriacal disorders, lest an authentic medical disorder be treated as a "functional" hypochondriacal complaint. In the differential diagnosis, it would be mandatory to rule out other psychiatric conditions that have hypochondriacal features attending the primary disorder, for example, schizophrenia, obsessive-compulsive disorder, depression, post-concussive syndrome, conversion disorder, and malingering (Murray, 1979).

Psychotherapy of a supportive nature is frequently recommended, but often with medi-ocre results. The defense mechanisms of somatization have usually been relatively effective in keeping conflicts less bothersome. Indeed, in many cases (as judged by results), it may be contraindicated to discuss the many contributing aspects of the conflicts that for so long had been more-or-less dealt with by the defenses involving somatization. Clearly, each treatment needs to be tailored to the needs of the patient and his or her ability to adapt to alternate methods of coping.

DISSOCIATIVE DISORDERS

Amnesia

Amnesia has basically one criterion in the DSM-III (see Table 5), and it is descrip-tive: "a sudden inability to recall important personal information that is too extensive to be explained by ordinary forgetfulness" (p. 255). The second and secondary criterion suggests ruling out organic factors. Although these criteria are limited, they are neces-sarily so, and the description surrounding them is good. These two criteria together are important in implication; that is, amnesia is a symptom of many diverse disorders, in-cluding a wide variety of organic problems. Organization and access of the brain's mem-ory systems can be affected by drugs, "functional" mental illness, trauma (head injury), psychological stress, and finally, simulation, to name the main categories. Of late, the iteration of posttraumatic stress disorder (PTSD) has provided another category under which the symptoms of amnesia may be considered. Thus, amnesia, in its several forms, is usually a symptom of something else, and one must understand its causal matrix in order to treat it.

The description of psychogenic amnesia caused by psychosocial stress is important because the description distinguishes this amnesia from its organically caused cousins. This is particularly important when the stressor is intrapsychic (usually guilt or an unac-ceptable impulse) and is thus not as easily identifiable. More specifically, the psychological phenomena of dissociation are escape-oriented and arbitrarily selective; the patient re-tains complete intellectual capacity; the symptoms often last longer than seven days; and the patient has a sudden and complete recovery (cf. Nemiah, 1980a). Going further descriptively, the DSM III lists four types having to do with extensivity: circumscribed, selective (the two most common), generalized, and continuous. The latter two are more likely to be related to organic causes, for organic amnesia is not as selective.

Table 5. DSM-III Diagnostic Criteria for Psychogenic Amnesia

A. Sudden inability to recall important personal information that is too extensive to be explained by ordinary forgetfulness.

B. The disturbance is not due to an organic mental disorder (e.g., blackouts during alcohol intoxication).

Note. From *Diagnostic and Statistical Manual of Mental Disorders* (3rd ed.) (p. 255). Copyright 1980 by the American Psychiatric Association. Reprinted by permission.

In contrast to a psychological phenomenon, a concussive amnesia usually lasts only a week, and function returns slowly. Other organic difficulties are marked by more extensive *recent* memory loss rather than the loss of *remote* memory. Epilepsy can frequently be distinguished by EEG and other motor abnormalities. Malingering (simulation) presents a difficult dilemma of diagnosis in a sophisticated client. Most often, the only way to ascertain the difference is for the diagnostician to be more sophisticated. A complete understanding of the psychosocial context and the patient's response to an amytal interview or hypnosis can usually discriminate the two. That is to say, a true psychogenic amnesiac will recover at least some memory under hypnosis or amytal procedure.

Treatments of amnesia are obviously different depending on the putative cause, and they are reasonably effective. In the case of psychogenic amnesia, careful psychotherapeutic interviewing, hypnosis, or an amytal procedure(s) usually produces significant results in one to two weeks, if not sooner. If not, a differential diagnostic rundown of organic possibilities, logically with neuropsychological consultation and quantification, would best be considered.

Fugue

Psychogenic fugue (see Table 6) is different from the confused wandering found in amnesia in that it is more purposeful and better organized; hence, it is labeled "travel" and has the assumption of a different identity along with it. These criteria are in the historical mainstream of how fugue has been considered. When one adds the rest of the description from the DSM-III (i.e., inability to recall former identity, severe stress, briefness, amnesia after recovery, and no recurrence), one has a more narrow and specific definition than has ever before been used. Venn (1984) reviewed the 78 cases reported in the literature since 1890 by seven authors and found that only 4 would meet all these criteria. Thus, "true fugue" is likely to be found only rarely, if only because of its more narrow

Table 6. DSM-III Diagnostic Criteria for Psychogenic Fugue

A. Sudden unexpected travel away from one's home or customary place of work, with inability to recall one's past.

B. Assumption of a new identity (partial or complete).

C. The disturbance is not due to an organic mental disorder.

Note. From *Diagnostic and Statistical Manual of Mental Disorders* (3rd ed.) (p. 257). Copyright 1980 by the American Psychiatric Association. Reprinted by permission.

definition in the DSM-III. Yet, the problem of "runaways," particularly among adolescents, continues apace, and one wonders about the extent of dissociation in these episodes. One can usually only speculate because, methodologically, fugue is very hard to study, for obvious reasons, during the phenomenon, and because of the amnesia that occurs post-recovery. Nevertheless, it is likely that family dynamics play a large role psychologically in its instigation.

Somnambulism used to be thought of as a type of fugue, but sleep research and its biological orientation have tended to swing the pendulum more recently toward the extreme of rarely considering a dissociative disorder. Especially in children, sleepwalking is classified as a sleep disorder thought to result from a physiological immaturity in various inhibition centers of the brain. It generally arises from Stage 3 or 4 sleep, is not associated with REM sleep, and is awkward and nonpurposive (Hartmann, 1980). The careful clinician, however, will inquire, especially of adults, about the length of time that these episodes last, their degree of purposefulness, and possible symbolic meanings in order to consider the possibilities of a fugue. Consciousness is usually more clouded during somnambulism in contrast to a fugue, in which a more clear identity and state of consciousness is maintained; fugues last hours or days, are highly purposeful, and are often symbolic.

Other organic etiologies for fugue are similar to those described for amnesia. One in particular needs further treatment here, and that is temporal lobe epilepsy (TLE), also labeled *complex partial seizures*. Part of the presentation of TLE can involve fairly complex automatisms (for example, brushing the hair and rubbing the hands) but without awareness. TLE can also exhibit symptoms of fear, problems in concentrating, and the several kinds of hallucinations, which, when acted upon, may resemble a dissociative state short of a fugue. On investigation, however, TLE often has a history of aura, exhibits a loss of reality contact, and usually has no psychological provocation. As a last diagnostic resort, it is noted that TLE responds to antiseizure medication, and dissociative disorders do not. The appropriate EEG is often quite determinative, as 90% of TLE cases exhibit a focal abnormality, and although 15% of hysterical patients have abnormal EEGs, they are usually not epileptiform (Aird *et al.*, 1984). However, one must not make the mistake of equating EEG, especially with surface electrodes, to a complex clinical entity (Corcores, Bender, & McBride, 1984; Murray, 1981; Spencer, Spencer, Williamson, & Mattson, 1982).

Mesulam (1981) noted that the temporal lobe is involved in the integration of sensory, thought, and affective processes. Thus, he suggested that different TLE foci can produce sensory symptoms (hallucinations) or affective symptoms (dread, panic, sadness, and so on) or, in combination, can produce *déjà vu, jamais vu,* or depersonalization. He described 12 cases in which both TLE and dissociative states (including Multiple Personality Disorder—MPD) were related. Schenk and Bear (1981) studied 40 cases of confirmed TLE and found that 13 had later developed striking, recurrent dissociative phenomena. Some reported amnesia, others did not. Schenk and Bear proposed that these dissociative phenomena are related to an interictal (between-seizures) behavioral syndrome in which the limbic epilepsy tends to intensify and deepen emotional responsiveness. (This syndrome is not found in other neurological groups.) The dissociation, then, is not a seizure phenomenon but a psychological response or defense used to control the intense affect probably produced by the limbic epileptic focus. Papers by Mesulam and Schenk and

Bear suggest that dissociation is more likely when the epileptogenic focus is in the nondominant temporal lobe, perhaps because these foci tend to produce more ego-alien experiences. Others propose that the dissociation and other interictal affective and behavioral disturbances are caused by subclinical limbic dysfunction (Engel, Lieb, Rausch, Kuhl, & Crandall, 1980; Gloor, Olivier, Quesney, Andermann, & Horowitz, 1982; Kiloh, 1980; Sherwin, 1980). Thus, complex partial seizures and dissociative phenomena are related in complex ways, and the possibility of TLE or limbic epilepsy should be kept in mind. Taylor (1977) summarized the similarities and contrasts between TLE and schizophrenia.

Depersonalization Disorder

This diagnosis (see Table7) is reserved in the DSM-III for only those cases in which, on the one hand, there is no relationship to other syndromes, such as anxiety disorders, schizophrenia, or depression, and, on the other hand, these feelings of unreality in the experiencing of the self are so intense that social or occupational impairment is noted. This is a disorder in the experience of oneself to be contrasted with derealization, in which the sense of reality of the external world is lost. If derealization only is present (which is unusual), it is classified as an atypical dissociative disorder. But the fact that the two disorders are separable indicates the possibility that different brain systems are involved. *Jamais vu* is similar: a failure to recognize well-known people or places as being familiar. *Déjà vu* is related, but it is an obverse phenomenon in the reversal between the familiar and the strange (i.e., in this disorder the strange is experienced as familiar).

Like amnesia, depersonalization is often a symptom of other illnesses, and we have already mentioned the anxiety, depressive, and schizophrenic categories. One must always consider drugs when presented with this symptom: it is more common among those who use (abuse) LSD, mescaline, and PCP, as well as other hallucinogens, and some opiates have hallucinogenic metabolites or may themselves be psychotomimetic; it can be a part of alcohol withdrawal; and it is often integral to a "marijuana high." Beyond drugs, an environmental condition that can cause this symptom is sensory deprivation in its various forms. If these possibilities are unlikely, one must rule out a brain tumor (especially if the onset is in middle age) or epilepsy. Tumors are usually temporal or parietal and are best documented by CAT scan and/or neuropsychological testing (cf. Lezack, 1983; Lishman, 1978; Smith & Craft, 1984; Strub & Black 1981), in combination with a thorough neurological exam. Neuropsychological testing is superior for small, subcortical tumors and usually involves tests of memory and drawing tasks. If epilepsy is involved, it is likely to be idopathic, localized, and documentable by the appropriate EEG. As a

Table 7. DSM-III Diagnostic Criteria for Depersonalization Disorder

A. One or more episodes of depersonalization sufficient to produce significant impairment in social or occupational functioning.

B. The symptom is not due to any other disorder, such as schizophrenia, affective disorder, organic mental disorder, anxiety disorder, or epilepsy.

Note. From *Diagnostic and Statistical Manual of Mental Disorders* (3rd ed.) (p. 260). Copyright 1980 by the American Psychiatric Association. Reprinted by permission.

final caveat, it should be noted that depersonalization has been associated with TLE, encephalitis, basilar migraine, and lupus (Freeman, 1980).

Multiple Personality Disorder

Multiple personality disorder (MPD) is the chameleon *par excellence* of the dissociative disorders; it can mimic many neurological, gastrointestinal, or cardiac conditions. Medical confirmation is usually not forthcoming, however, and/or "full syndromal criteria are rarely met" (Putnam, Lowenstein, Silberman, & Post, 1984). Thus, the category of MPD is a more inclusive, superordinate category (involving memory and identity disturbances) that subsumes and organizes symptoms, usually providing the diagnostician with a quantum leap of insight, allowing clarity and understanding of what was previously a confusing array of unrelated symptoms (cf. Kluft, 1987). That being stated, one must not overlook the possibility that some of the medical conditions indicated do have an organic basis and should be treated. The possibility of MPD in children should definitely *not* be overlooked (Fagan & McMahon, 1984; Kluft, 1985).

MPD provides unique diagnostic problems when there are personality-specific physiological changes or symptoms, such as allergies or differential response to medications. In these cases where the symptoms do not affect the whole system, the symptoms should be left untreated while psychotherapeutic work proceeds. In what follows we will iterate how to differentiate medical symptoms from MPD where possible.

The DSM-III has made several strides in the classification of MPD (see Table 8), not the least of which is to separate it from hysterical personality disorder. The criteria, as can be seen, are very general, and several authorities believe that a specification of several syndromes will occur over the next decade (e.g., Greaves *et al.*, unpublished manuscript, 1987). Prevalence is traditionally assumed to be rare, but recent studies have suggested that true MPD is more common than is realized, and that this is especially true of the spectrum of dissociative disorders. Thus, it is likely that the category of atypical dissociative disorder will grow in sophistication and specification in the next decade.

For complex MPD (four or more personalities) in general, we shall deal with five major areas of diagnostic concern:

1. *Headache.* A key diagnostic indicator of MPD is headaches preceding and relating to the transition states between personalities. These have a quick onset, can be relieved hypnotically, and are related to switching before treatment and to the emergence of painful affects during treatment. However, persons with MPD also experience several other kinds of headache, including muscular-tension and flu-related headaches. These are general across personalities, although with various degrees of attenuation or dramatization, depending on the needs and organization of the given personality fragment.

2. *Mood changes.* MPD is characterized by marked changes in mood and behavior, which often look like or may be related to a bipolar depressive disorder. It is difficult to distinguish MPD from bipolar illness before the completion of successful, integrative treatment because many of these symptoms attenuate in the treatment process. Diagnostically, at the outset, one must be aware of the possibility of a rapid-cycling manic disorder. Aside from the hallmark of identity disturbance, MPD is more rapid than a mood disorder in its changes and is less cyclic; that is, its shifts are less time-related and are more related to psychological stressors that can be identified. It is generally better not

Table 8. DSM-III Diagnostic Criteria for Multiple Personality Disorder

---

A. The existence within the individual of two or more distinct personalities, each of which is dominant at a particular time.

B. The personality that is dominant at any particular time determines the individual's behavior.

C. Each individual personality is complex and integrated with its own unique behavior patterns and social relationships.

Note. From *Diagnostic and Statistical Manual of Mental Disorders* (3rd ed.) (p. 259). Copyright 1980 by the American Psychiatric Association. Reprinted by permission.

to treat bipolar symptomatology with drugs during integrative therapy, but this caveat will probably necessitate an inpatient context for control.

3. *Schizophrenia.* The general schizophrenic syndrome provides some differentiation from MPD. Although MPD can, in various personality states, exhibit confusion, blocking, neologisms, disorientation, and differences in being very concrete (regressed) or abstract, the symptoms do not persist when the personalities switch (Bliss, 1980) or are abreacted appropriately. The "thought disorder" in MPD is less disconnected, fragmented, and disorganized. MPD does not usually exhibit a flatness of affect nor a consistent delusional system across all personalities. Perhaps most telling, there is no loss of interpersonal relatedness in MPD as is often found in schizophrenia; indeed, the reverse is often notable. When catatonic stupors occur, they are short-lived and self-limiting in MPD. Some multiples have one personality that is more disorganized (Brandsma & Ludwig, 1974) than the others, but the designation of schizophrenia does not fit the system as a whole. Auditory hallucinations are found in one third of MPD cases (Bliss, 1980; Putnam, Post, Guroff, Silberman, & Barban, 1983), but these are usually different from those of schizophrenia in that they are experienced within the head and are not projected onto the external world. Multiples often experience several different voices within their heads (with different gender, types, and so on), whereas schizophrenics more often experience only one voice (for example, "the voice of God"). Command hallucinations and complex visual hallucinations are more bizarre when caused by alcohol withdrawal or other toxic delirium states.

4. *Amnesia.* As mentioned, amnesia can be a part of many disorders. In MPD, it is associated with the related shifts in identity as well as with the problems with memory. Some multiples in some personality states are aware of the original personality, something not true in amnesia. In amnesia, the complex activities and relationships are not present, as is true in MPD.

5. *Anxiety.* In the more traditional anxiety disorders, although the onset may be rapid, the termination is more gradual than in MPD. In MPD, the rapid fluctuations and change to a flat affect are more pronounced and noticeable than in anxiety disorders *per se*.

6. *Other.* There are many other symptoms that are mimicked or engaged in in MPD: paralysis, parkinsonism, anorexia–bulimia, somatization disorder, and psychophysiological bowel disease. Again, the full syndrome will not be present, and the symptoms usually respond to abreactive-integrative treatment. If the patient exhibits a full physical syndrome in its own right with a documentable organic basis, expressed across personalities, of

course, it deserves to be treated. It is to be hoped that the treatment will not interfere with the psychotherapeutic work necessary for the treatment of MPD (Braun, 1986).

Atypical Dissociative Disorder

"This is a residual category to be used for individuals that appear to have a dissociative disorder but do not satisfy the criteria for a specific dissociative disorder" (APA, 1980, p. 260). This category includes trance states, derealization without depersonalization, and the aftermath of "brainwashing" or other coercive-persuasive techniques (Krystal, 1971). As mentioned earlier, this category needs to be made more specific, for there are many diverse phenomena experienced by persons with high trance capacity. As a way of organizing thinking for the dissociative spectrum, let us present a continuum of dissociative phenomena that will alert the clinician to the various degrees of severity possible with dissociative disorders (see Table 9).

Another discrimination from those who have been brainwashed has to do with a personality style rather than a dissociative aftermath. This is what Nemiah (1978) has elaborated as "alexithymia" (Sifneos, 1972). It describes an inability to label and discuss affective states, an absence of fantasy (impoverished inner life), and a stiff woodenness during an interview. These traits are quite generalized having the extensivity of a personality style, whereas when dissociative, they are selective and are related to conflicts or symptoms.

FACTITIOUS DISORDERS

Factitious disorders are among the most frustrating encountered by the clinician. Luckily they are rare and are even more rarely seen by psychologists. The patient's history is riddled with deceit, and the behavior is generally impervious to treatment. Charac-

Table 9. Continuum of Dissociative States (Read Left to Right)

Normal waking attention	Selective inattention	Altered states of consciousness	Loss of consciousness
Generalized reality orientation[a]	Absent-mindedness Parapraxis	"Road hypnosis" Reverie states Partial amnesia Experience of psychic phenomena	Blackouts "Seizures" "Fits"

Major dissociative states	Personality fragments		Multiple personality
Fugue Automatic writing Psychogenic amnesia Automatisms	Repeated fugue Elements with low level of functional organization Organized elements accessible by trance only		Elements with high level of functional organization Elements with independent functioning Irrepressible rotating

[a]After Shor (1959). The generalized reality orientation may be defined as the organization of consciousness or the structural hierarchy of information processing that allows a person to be relatively stable in terms of perception and cognitive responding, that is, to maintain a stable frame of reference.

terized by the repeated willful simulation of a physical or mental illness, these patients falsify their presenting illness and previous medical history for no apparent reason other than obtaining medical attention and care. To corroborate their claims, these patients may artificially create the illusion of a disorder, such as contaminating specimen collections of urine or sputum with blood, or injecting fecal material intravenously to produce an infection. Unlike other disorders, in which the secondary gain may be clear, these illnesses appear to have as their sole objective the assuming of the role of patient, its identity and attention presumably being the reinforcements. The DSM-III recognizes three subtypes of factitious disorder: (1) chronic factitious illness with physical symptoms; (2) factitious illness with psychological symptoms; and (3) atypical factitious illness with physical symptoms. Of these, the greatest attention has been focused on patients with chronic factitious illness with physical symptoms, the most well-recognized version being the Munchausen syndrome.

Chronic Factitious Disorder with Physical Symptoms

Although descriptions of feigned medical illnesses exist from antiquity, it was not until the twentieth century that they received more intense scrutiny. Karl Menninger (1934) examined those patients who managed to have repeated unnecessary operations performed on them—a polysurgical addiction. The most popular account, however, is to be found in Asher's paper (1951), in which he christened this disorder the "Munchausen syndrome." The name was derived from the stories of Karl Friedrich Hieronymous, Freiherr von Munchausen, a retired German cavalry officer who was undeservedly (Jurgen & Mann, 1983) noted for extensive traveling and telling tall tales. With this eponym, Asher hoped to capture the essence of patients who traveled great distances, from one hospital to the next, with a "tall tale" regarding their physical illness. Often using aliases and concocting fanciful complaints, these patients gain admission to a hospital and, when confronted by the medical staff about their stories, stormily discharge themselves from the hospital and wander to the next receptive hospital.

These patients often develop a familiarity with medical jargon and usually have had some exposure to hospital and/or medical surroundings. Generally, the patient is facile in articulating a plausible (albeit false) medical history and, depending on the chronicity of the disorder, may have suffered genuine injuries iatrogenically during the course of previous medical workups. Ironically, it is often these "bona fide" injuries that abet the story and enable the patient to gain yet another hospitalization.

Diagnostic criteria in the DSM-III (see Table 10) require that the disorder be under voluntary control. This is usually inferred, however, because these patients are unlikely to concede to the manufacturing of an illness. Yet, they easily assume the role of impostor and are prone to pseudologica fantastica, the practice of habitual lying to intrigue the listener. The patient's behavior, particularly after admission to a medical or surgical inpatient unit, is likely to be demanding and manipulative, though sometimes with a paradoxical affability (perhaps because the stories they tell truly do capture the initial interest of the staff). One patient, for example, claimed to hail from Hawaii and to be a former drummer for a nationally known rock group, and he gave an initially credible, although vague, history of a motor vehicle accident with resultant neurological injuries and fever. Aroused by the inconsistencies in the story, an atypical fever pattern, and the patient's

Table 10. Diagnostic Criteria for Chronic Factitious Disorder with Physical Symptoms

A. Plausible presentation of physical symptoms that are apparently under the individual's voluntary control to such a degree that there are multiple hospitalizations.

B. The individual's goal is apparently to assume the "patient" role and is not otherwise understandable in light of the individual's environmental circumstances (as in the case of malingering).

Note. From *Diagnostic and Statistical Manual of Mental Disorders* (3rd ed.) (p. 290). Copyright 1980 by the American Psychiatric Association. Reprinted by permission.

adamant insistence on keeping the door to his room shut at all times, an enterprising intern perched himself in an adjacent wing of the hospital and, with adroit reconnaissance, peered into the patient's room through an outside window—only to find the patient waving a cigarette lighter under the thermometer. Other inquiries failed to confirm his medical history. When confronted and offered the opportunity to be treated by psychotherapy, the patient became instantly irate and declared his intention to leave town the next morning. This is the typical though unfortunate outcome, usually to be repeated in a different hospital in the near future.

An even more disturbing variation that has received recent attention is the so-called Munchausen by proxy, in which a parent, usually the mother, feigns illness in an offspring. Since the original report by Meadow (1977), subsequent reports have come to our attention of this distressing, if bizarre, form of battered-child syndrome (Vaisurb, 1978).

Generally, patients with chronic factitious illness have evidence of previous treatment at other hospitals. Academic teaching hospitals are indeed often a favorite target of these disturbed patients (Jacoby & Stern, 1984; Reich & Gottfried, 1983) probably because the staff in these esteemed institutions have a propensity to rule out rare clinical entities, and because these institutions frequently do get peculiar and atypical presentations of some of the most rare diseases.

Some clues that should raise one's index of suspicion regarding the possibility of a factitious disorder are inappropriate anger and demandingness by the patient, a history of illicit drug use, and inconsistencies in the medical history. Psychologists are usually not well trained in systematic history taking, so what they note is anger and haughtiness on the part of the patient when attempts are made to discuss possible psychological contributions. An attendant quick willingness to check out of the hospital against medical advice may confirm both frustration and diagnosis.

Etiologic explanations for the development of such a strange condition abound, ranging from psychodynamic to organic. Spiro (1968) drew attention to the masochistic elements of the syndrome, with the hospital serving a dual role of providing for dependency needs while simultaneously representing a place of fear and pain, perhaps similar to the patient's childhood situation, in which parental figures gave attention to illness, but in a larger context of emotional deprivation. Cramer, Gershberg, and Stern (1971) emphasized prior relationships with doctors in these patients, with physicians being selected as objects with whom love and anger are acted out. Ford (1983) most reasonably suggested that, for any particular patient, there may be a number of different motivations that have changed from time to time. He went on to suggest that a number of these patients could properly be understood as borderline personalities, exhibiting weak ego strength and primitive defenses.

A study by Reich and Gotfried (1983) challenged some of the time-honored beliefs concerning factitious disorders. They investigated 41 cases seen over a 10-year period at a teaching hospital in Boston. Of this group, however, it should be noted that only 3 had a history that could be construed as fitting the full prototypical pattern of the Munchausen syndrome. Most patients were immature, passive, and hypochondriacal, and many exhibited personality disorders. The researchers did *not* find, however, the intense anger, impulsivity, identity disturbances, or instability of interpersonal relationships associated with borderline personality disorder (suggested by Ford, 1983). Furthermore, although only 13 patients acknowledged causing their disorders, most improved after confrontation by the medical personnel. The conclusions drawn were that factitious disorders are motivated by deeply ingrained hypochondriacal beliefs and fears, along with wishes for the attention given in medical care.

Although detection of theses cases is difficult even in the best of diagnostic centers, the demanding individual with a very sketchy medical history, pleomorphic over the course of time, whose database simply does not fit, should stimulate thoughts of factitious illness in the clinician. The most efficient use of time at this point would be making several calls to prior treaters to see if the medical history can, indeed, be corroborated.

In most cases, the suspicion of a factitious disorder has already been entertained by the medical or surgical staff who have been unable to uncover any reasonable organic cause. By the time the psychologist is consulted, the therapeutic ambience has often been dealt a severe blow by feelings of anger and counteraccusations on both the physicians' part and the patient's. A consensus is nonexistent regarding how to deal with the patient at this precarious crossroad, though a good argument is made for having the referring physician make the initial confrontation, as outlined by Hollender and Hersh (1970). This approach allows the psychologist to get off to a better start in a very difficult contest.

It must be conceded, however, that many a valiant and sincere effort has been for naught in the treatment of these usually refractory cases. With a few isolated exceptions, the treatment track record is dismal, and the scarce number of successes have generally had brief follow-up periods. Nevertheless, it may be that certain subtypes of factitious disorders have a better prognosis, as suggested in the study of Reich and Gottfried (1983). One recent treatment technique for chronic factitious illness has emphasized a behavioral approach, coordinated by a team of therapists (Klonoff, Younger, Moore & Hershey, 1983). In this single case report, an array of behavioral approaches by cotherapists was used in combination with biofeedback to help reduce stress, which induced a factitious episode of "seizures." This team proffered the idea that this combined behavioral approach promoted the patient's sense of control and positive self-esteem, permitting contact with medical instrumentation without its physically invasive and destructive aspects. A 6 month follow-up in their patients demonstrated not a cure, but a decreased number of hospitalized days, with work and social functioning improved. It should be pointed out that even such partial successes are so noteworthy and uncommon that they are still regarded as appropriately publishable case reports.

Thus, a glimmer of optimism remains for this pathology, though, in general, the prognosis is abysmally poor. It may be that, as we further sharpen the distinctions of the variety of factitious disorders, a better outcome study may help us distinguish which cases are more likely to be psychotherapeutically and behaviorally salvageable. The prototypical Munchausen syndrome is unlikely to be one of these hopeful diagnostic groups, because of their notorious noncompliance and wandering lifestyle.

Factitious Disorder with Psychological Symptoms

Although there remain differences of opinion over the proper nosological distinctions of factitious illness (Eisendrath, 1984), the DSM-III distinguishes a separate group of factitious disorders with prominence of *psychological* symptoms feigned for the apparent purpose of assuming the "patient" role (see Table 11). In contrast to malingering, where the motivation and the secondary gain are often obvious, there does not seem to be any payoff to the patient other than obtaining medical or psychiatric attention. One example of this pathology would be Ganser's syndrome, named for the German psychiatrist (Ganser, 1898) who called this a "peculiar hysterical state" in which patients "pass by" *(Vorbeigehen)* the correct answer when queried by the examiner. His patients were noted to give absurd answers to obvious questions, often giving "approximate" answers that would seem to indicate that the patient understood the query and domain of the inquiry but was apparently unable to give the proper reply. Because of the appearance of a fluctuating level of consciousness with defects of memory, Ganser proposed that this was an example of an acute hysterical mental state—a twilight state. More recently, it has been suggested that the strong association between approximate answers and amnesia argues for the classification of this disorder as a dissociative state (Cocores, Santa, & Patel, 1984). The disorder appears to be one of the rarer psychopathologies and, in severe cases, stands out noticeably on even the most cursory of interviews. Because of the generally uncommon and transient characteristics of the syndrome, its etiology and treatment(s) remain in the realm of conjecture.

A contemporary and potentially more important example of factitious disorder with psychological symptoms has been discovered by Lynn and Belza (1984), who gave several case studies of war veterans claiming to suffer symptoms of posttraumatic stress disorder due to combat in Vietnam. Not only had none of these "victims" been in combat, some had never been in Vietnam. A variety of psychodynamic explanations could explain such phenomena, ranging from forms of survival guilt to unconscious feelings of entitlement from being in such a war. The permutations of this theme are endless, demonstrating that, among other things, simply because we have subdivided factitious disorders into those with physical symptoms and those with psychological symptoms, we are not necessarily closer to having a leash on these clinical beasts.

Table 11. Diagnostic Criteria for Factitious Disorder with Psychological Symptoms

---

A. The production of psychological symptoms is apparently under the individual's voluntary control.

B. The symptoms produced are not explained by any other mental disorder (although they may be superimposed on one).

C. The individual's goal is apparently to assume the "patient" role and is not otherwise understandable in light of the individual's environmental circumstances (as is the case in malingering).

Note. From *Diagnostic and Statistical Manual of Mental Disorders* (3rd ed.) (p. 287). Copyright 1980 by the American Psychiatric Association. Reprinted by permission.

Table 12. DSM-III Diagnostic Description for Characteristics of Malingering

The essential feature is the voluntary production and presentation of false or grossly exaggerated physical or psychological symptoms. The symptoms are produced in pursuit of a goal that is obviously recognizable with an understanding of the individual's circumstances rather than of his or her individual psychology. Examples of such obviously understandable goals include to avoid military conscription or duty, to avoid work, to obtain financial compensation, to evade criminal prosecution, or to obtain drugs.

Note. From *Diagnostic and Statistical Manual of Mental Disorders* (3rd ed.) (p. 331). Copyright 1980 by the American Psychiatric Association. Reprinted by permission.

Finally, it should be clear from this discussion that, although the boundaries blur with aggravating frequency, the distinction between factitious disorders and malingering is primarily one of being able to recognize avoidance behavior in malingering (see Table 12). Both disorders, by inference at least, are voluntary and conscious; however, the person with factitious disorder has as his or her main objective entering into the role of patient; that is, the reinforcements are internal. The treatment for malingering is usually best approached in a problem-solving fashion to deal with the external problem. If an alliance can be formed here, perhaps some exploration of the aspects of motivation can proceed.

CONCLUSION

Thus we have covered some very interesting and difficult interactions between psychic and physical pathology (see Table 13). In certain areas, some, depending on their specialization, will think our coverage cursory, in others, obsessive. Be that as it may, these disorders have always been on the interface of body and mind, an area that finds increasing understanding, but where more needs to be done. The promise of the future beckons us all to be more competent and informed clinicians in these areas.

Table 13. Differentiations in Diagnoses Suggesting Physical Illness [a]

Classification	Physical mechanism explains the symptom	Symptoms are linked to psychological factors	Symptom initiation is under voluntary control	Obvious, recognizable environmental goal
Somatoform disorders	No[b]	Yes[d]	No	Variable
Factitious disorders	Variable[c]	Yes[e]	Yes	No
Malingering	Variable[c]	Variable	Yes	Yes
Undiagnosed physical illness	Variable	Variable	No	No

[a]Adapted from Hyler and Spitzer (1978), p. 1501.
[b]No, but a genuine medical disorder not associated with the symptom may coexist.
[c]Variable, but usually *not* explanatory.
[d]Yes, but presumably unconscious.
[e]Yes, but presumably conscious.

REFERENCES

Aird, R. B., Masland, R. L., & Woodburg, D. M. (1984). *The epilepsies: A critical review.* New York: Raven Press.

American Psychiatric Association. (1980). *Diagnostic and statistical manual of mental disorders* (3rd ed.). Washington, DC: Author.

Asher, R. (1951). Munchausen's syndrome. *Lancet, 1,* 339–341.

Barsky, A. J., & Klerman, G. L. (1983). Overview: Hypochondriasis, bodily complaints, and somatic styles. *American Journal of Psychiatry, 140,* 273–283.

Bliss, E. L. (1980). Multiple personalities: A report of 14 cases with implications for schizophrenia and hysteria. *Archives of General Psychiatry, 37,* 1388–1397.

Blumer, D. (Ed.). (1984). *Psychiatric aspects of epilepsy.* Washington, DC: American Psychiatric Press.

Brandsma, J., & Ludwig, A. (1974). A case of multiple personality: Diagnosis and therapy. *International Journal of Clinical and Experimental Hypnosis, 22(3),* 216–233.

Braun, B. G. (Ed.). (1986). *The Treatment of Multiple Personality.* Washington, DC: American Psychiatric Press.

Breuer, J., & Freud, S. (1895). Studies on hysteria. *Standard Edition* (Vol. 2). London: Hogarth Press.

Chodoff, P. (1974). The diagnosis of hysteria: An overview. *American Journal of Psychiatry, 131,* 1073–1078.

Chodoff, P., & Lyons, H. (1958). Hysteria: The hysterical personality and "hysterical" conversion. *American Journal of Psychiatry, 114,* 734–740.

Cocores, J., Bener, A., & McBride, E. (1984). Multiple personality, seizure disorders, and the electroencephalogram. *Journal of Nervous and Mental Diseases, 172,* 436–438.

Cocores, J., Santa, W. G., & Patel, M.D. (1984). The Ganser syndrome: Evidence suggesting its classification as a dissociative disorder. *International Journal of Psychiatry in Medicine, 14,* 47–56.

Cramer, B., Gershberg, M. E., & Stern, M. (1971). Munchausen syndrome: Its relationship to malingering, hysteria and the physician–patient relationship. *Archives of General Psychiatry, 24,* 573–578.

DeVaul, R. A. (1980). Hysterical symptoms. In R. C. W. Hall (Ed.), *Psychiatric presentations of medical illness.* New York: Spectrum Publications.

Duerksen, D. L., & Smith, W. L. (1982). Differential diagnosis in clinical neuropsychology. In W. L. Smith, M. H. Hitchcock, & L. G. Best (Eds.), *Neurological evaluation of the psychogenic patient.* New York: Spectrum.

Eisendrath, S. J. (1984). Factitious illness: A clarification. *Psychosomatics, 25,* 110–113, 116–117.

Engel, G. L. (1959). Psychogenic pain and the pain-prone patient. *American Journal of Medicine, 26,* 899–918.

Engel, J., Lieb, J. P., Rausch, R., Kuhl, D. E., & Crandall, P. H. (1980). Interictal and ictal abnormalities of the temporal lobe in patients with partial complex epilepsy. In M. Girgis & L. G. Kiloh (Eds.), *Limbic epilepsy and the dyscontrol syndrome.* Amsterdam: Elsevier/North-Holland Biomedical Press.

Fagan, J., & McMahon, P. P. (1984). Incipient multiple personality in children: Four cases. *Journal of Nervous and Mental Disease, 172,* 26–36.

Flor-Henry, P. (1983). *Cerebral basis of psychopathology.* Boston: John Wright/PSG.

Ford, C. V. (1983). *The somatizing disorders.* New York: Elsevier/North-Holland Biomedical Press.

Freeman, A. M. (1980). Delusions, depersonalization, unusual psychopathological systems. In R. C. Hall, (Ed.), *Psychiatric presentations of medical illness: Somatopsychic disorders.* New York: Spectrum.

Fromm, E., & Shor, R. (Eds.), (1979). *Hypnosis: Developments in research and new perspectives* (2nd ed.). Hawthorne, NY: Aldine.

Ganser, S. (1974). A peculiar hysterical state. In S. R. Hirsh & M. Shepherd (Eds.), *Themes and variations in European psychiatry: An anthology.* Charlottesville: University Press of Virginia. (Original work published 1898)

Gatfield, P. D., & Guze, S. B. (1962). Prognosis and differential diagnosis of conversion reactions. *Diseases of the Nervous System, 23,* 623–631.

Gloor, P., Olivier, A., Quensey, L. F., Andermann, F., & Horowitz, S. (1982). The role of the limbic system in experiential phenomena of temporal lobe epilepsy. *Annals of Neurology, 12,* 129–144.

Goodwin, J., Simms, M., & Bergman, R. (1979). Hysterical seizures: A sequel to incest. *American Journal of Orthopsychiatry, 49,* 698–703.

Greaves, G., Brandsma, J., Burns, J., & Damgaard, J. (1987). The etiology, phenomonology, morphology, and dynamics of complex multiple personality. Unpublished manuscript.

Gross, M. (1979). Incestuous rape: A cause for hysterical seizures in four adolescent girls. *American Journal of Orthopsychiatry, 49,* 704–708.

Gross, M. (Ed.), (1983). *Pseudoepilepsy.* Lexington, MA: Lexington Books.

Hackett, T. P. (1978). The pain patient. In T. P. Hackett & N. H. Cassem (Eds.), *Massachusetts General Hospital handbook of general hospital psychiatry.* St. Louis: C. V. Mosby.

Hafeiz, H. B. (1980). Hysterical conversion: A prognostic study. *British Journal of Psychiatry, 136,* 548–551.

Hall, R. C. W., Popkin M. K., DeVaul R. A., Faillace, L. A., & Stickney, S. K. (1978). Physical illness presenting as psychiatric disease. *Archives of General Psychiatry, 35,* 1315–1320.

Hartmann, E. L. (1980). Sleep disorders. In H. Kaplan, A. Freedman, & B. Sadock (Eds.), *Comprehensive textbook of psychiatry* (Vol. 2, 3rd ed.). Baltimore: Williams & Wilkins.

Hier, D. B. (1978). Neuropsychiatric disorders. In M. A. Samuels (Ed.), *Manual of neurologic therapeutics.* Boston: Little, Brown.

Hobson, D. P. (1985). The "psychogenic" component of psychosomatic illness. *Atlanta Medicine, 59,* 37–40.

Hollender, M. H., & Hersh, S. P. (1970). Impossible consultation made possible. *Archives of General Psychiatry, 23,* 343–345.

Hyler, S. E. & Spitzer, R. L. (1978). Hysteria split asunder. *American Journal of Psychiatry, 135,* 1500–1504.

Jacoby, G. A., Jr., & Stern, T. A. (1984). Case records of the Massachusetts General Hospital: A 30-year-old man with gas in the soft tissues of the left forearm. *New England Journal of Medicine, 311,* 108–115.

Jurgen, L., & Mann, R. J. (1983). Munchhausen versus Munchausen. *Mayo Clinic Proceedings, 58,* 767–769.

Katon, W., Ries, R. K., & Kleinman, A. (1984). A prospective DSM-III study of 100 consecutive somatization patients. *Comprehensive Psychiatry, 25,* 305–314.

Kiloh, L. G. (1980). Psychiatric disorders and the limbic system. In M. Girgis & L. G. Kiloh (Eds.), *Limbic epilepsy and the dyscontrol syndrome.* Amsterdam: Elsevier/North-Holland Biomedical Press.

Klonoff, E. A., Younger, S. J., Moore, D. J., & Hershey, L. A. (1983). Chronic factitious illness: A behavioral approach. *International Journal of Psychiatry in Medicine, 13,* 173–183.

Kluft, R. P. (1985). *Childhood antecedents of multiple personality.* Washington, DC: American Psychiatric Press.

Kluft, R. P. (1987). An update on multiple personality disorder. *Hospital and Community Psychiatry 38(4),* 363–373.

Krystal, H. (1971). trauma: Considerations of its intensity and chronicity. In H. Krystal & W. G. Niederland (Eds.), *Psychic traumatization.* Boston: Little, Brown.

Kwentus, J. A. (1984). The drug-assisted interview. In F. G. Guggenheim & M. F. Weiner (Eds.), *Manual of psychiatric consultation and emergency care.* New York: Jason Aronson.

Lewis, A. (1975). The survival of hysteria. *Psychological Medicine, 5,* 9–12.

Lezack, M. (1983). *Neuropsychological assessment* (2nd ed.). New York: Oxford University Press.

Lipowski, Z. J. (1975). Psychiatry of somatic diseases: Epidemiology, pathogenesis, classification. *Comprehensive Psychiatry, 16,* 105–124.

Lishman, W. A. (1978). *Organic psychiatry.* Oxford: Blackwell Press.

Lynn, E. J. & Belza, M. (1984). Factitious posttraumatic stress disorder: The veteran who never got to Vietnam. *Hospital and Community Psychiatry, 35,* 697–701.

Maloney, M. J. (1980). Diagnosing hysterical conversion reactions in children. *Journal of Pediatrics, 97,* 1016–1020.

Meadow, R. (1977). Munchausen syndrome by proxy. *Lancet, 2,* 343–345.

Menninger, K. A. (1934). Polysurgery and polysurgical addiction. *Psychoanalytic Quarterly, 3,* 173–199.

Mesulam, M. (1981). Dissociative states with abnormal temporal lobe electroencephalogram. *Archives of Neurology, 38,* 176–181.

Murray, G. B. (1979). Hypochondriasis. In T. C. Manchreck (Ed.), *Psychiatric medicine update: Massachusetts General Hospital reviews for physicians, 1979.* New York: Elsevier.

Murray, G. B. (1981). Complex partial seizures. In T. C. Manschreck (Ed.), *Psychiatric medicine update: Massachusetts General Hospital reviews for physicians, 1981.* New York: Elsevier.

Nemiah, J. (1978). Alexithyma and psychosomatic illness. *Journal of Continuing Education of Psychiatry, 39*, 25–37.

Nemiah, J. C. (1980a). Dissociative disorders (hysterical neuroses, dissociative type). In H. I. Kaplan, A. M. Freedman, & B. J. Sadock (Eds.), *Comprehensive textbook of psychiatry* (Vol. 2, 3rd ed.). Baltimore: Williams & Wilkins.

Nemiah, J. C. (1980b). Somatoform disorders. In H. I. Kaplan, A. M. Freedman, & B. J. Sadock (Eds.), *Comprehensive textbook of psychiatry* (Vol. 2, 3rd ed.). Baltimore: Williams & Wilkins.

Pilowsky, I. (1970). Primary and secondary hypochondriasis. *Acta Psychiatrica Scandinavica, 46*, 273–285.

Pilowsky, I. (1983). Hypochondriasis. In G. F. M. Russell & L. Hersov (Eds.), *The neurosis and personality disorders*. In M. Shepherd (Gen. Ed.), *Handbook of psychiatry* (Vol. 4). Cambridge: Cambridge University Press.

Putnam, F. W., Post, R. M., Guroff, J. J., Silberman, E. A., & Barban, L. (1983). *One hundred cases of multiple personality disorders*. Paper presented at American Psychiatric Association meeting, New Research Abstract No. 77, New York.

Putnam, F. W., Loenwenstein, R. J., Silberman, E. A., & Post, R. M. (1984). Multiple personality disorders in a hospital setting. *Journal of Clinical Psychiatry, 45*, 172–175.

Rada, R. T., Meyer, G. G., & Kellner, R. (1978). Visual conversion reaction in children and adults. *Journal of Nervous and Mental Diseases, 166*, 580–587.

Reich, P., & Gotfried, L. A. (1983). Factitious disorders in a teaching hospital. *Annals of Internal Medicine, 99*, 240–247.

Reynolds, E. H., & Trimble, M. R. (Eds.). (1981). *Epilepsy and psychiatry*. Edinburgh: Churchill Livingstone.

Riley, T. L., & Roy, A. (Eds.). (1982). *Pseudoseizures*. Baltimore: Williams & Wilkins.

Rodin, G. (1984). Somatization and the self: Psychotherapeutic issues. *American Journal of Psychotherapy, 38*, 257–263.

Schenk, L., & Bear, D. (1981). Multiple personality and related dissociative phenomena in patients with temporal lobe epilepsy. *American Journal of Psychiatry, 138*, (*10*), 1311–1315.

Sherwin, I. (1980). Specificity of psychopathy in epilepsy, significance of lesion laterality. In M. Girgis & L. G. Kiloh (Eds.), *Limbic epilepsy and the dyscontrol syndrome*. Amsterdam: Elsevier/North-Holland Biomedical Press.

Shor, R. E. (1959). Hypnosis and the concept of the generalized reality orientation. *American Journal of Psychotherapy, 13*, 582.

Sifneos, P. E. (1972). *Short-term psychotherapy and emotional crisis*. Cambridge: Harvard University Press.

Smith, D. B., & Craft, R. B. (1984). Sudden behavioral change: Guide to initial evaluation. *Neurologic Clinics, 2(1)*, 3–22.

Spencer, S. S., Spencer, D. D., Williamson, P. D., & Mattson, R. H. (1982). The localizing value of depth electroencephalography in thirty-two patients with refractory epilepsy. *Annals of Neurology, 12*, 248–253.

Spiro, H. R. (1968). Chronic factitious illness. *Archives of General Psychiatry, 18*, 569–579.

Stimmel, B. (1983). *Pain, analgesia, and addiction: The pharmacologic treatment of pain*. New York: Raven Press.

Stoudemire, A. (1984). Differential diagnosis and management of the chronically somatizing patient. *Journal of Medical Association of Georgia, 73*, 593–597.

Strub, R., & Black, F. (1981). *Organic brain syndromes: An introduction to neurobehavioral disorders*. Philadelphia: Davis.

Taylor, D. C. (1977). Epileptic experience, schizophrenia, and the temporal lobe. In D. Blumer & K. Levin (Eds.), *Psychiatric complications in the epilepsies: Current research and treatment*. Boston: McLean Hospital Journal.

Turk, D. C., Meichenbaum, D., & Genest, M. (1983). *Pain and behavioral medicine: A cognitive-behavioral perspective*. New York: Guilford Press.

Vaisurb, S. (1978). Baron Munchausen and the abused child. *Journal of the American Medical Association, 239*, 752.

Van Dyke, C. (1983). Hysteria and hypochondriasis. In H. Leigh (Ed.), *Psychiatry in the practice of medicine*. Menlo Park, CA: Addison-Wesley.

Veith, I. (1965). *Hysteria: The history of a disease*. Chicago: University of Chicago Press.

Venn, J. (1984, September). *Evolving concepts of fugue: A historical review and illustrative case*. Paper presented at First International Conference on Multiple Personality/Dissociative Disorders, Chicago.

Ward, N. G., Bloom, V. L., Dworkin, S, Fawcett, J., Narasimhachari, N., & Friedel, R. (1982). Psychobiological markers in coexisting pain and depression: Toward a unified theory. *Journal of Clinical Psychiatry, 43*, 32–39.

Weintraub, M. I. (1983). *Hysterical conversion reactions*. New York: Spectrum.

Wells, C. E., & Duncan, G. W. (1980). *Neurology for psychiatrists*. Philadelphia: F. A. Davis.

Ziegler, F. J., & Imboden, J. (1962). Contemporary conversion reactions: II. A conceptual model. *Archives of General Psychiatry, 6*, 279–287.

7

Organic Mental Disorders

RALPH E. TARTER AND ANDREA M. HEGEDUS

The initial classification of organic mental disorders in the first edition of the American Psychiatric Association's *Diagnostic and Statistical Manual* (DSM-I; APA, 1952) consisted of an acute (reversible) and chronic (unreversible) dichotomy. This classification was improved in DSM-II (APA, 1968) by subdividing the disorders into psychotic and nonpsychotic states, and by substituting the word *syndrome* for the word *disorder*. The DSM-II also retained the subdivision of acute and chronic. However, there were several flaws in this classification system. First, the DSM-II classification of organic mental disorders was thought to be too narrow and restricted in definition. It included only those cerebral disorders that featured global cognitive impairment. Second, subdivisions into psychotic versus nonpsychotic and acute versus chronic provided little clinical information or diagnostic assistance. The distinction between psychotic and nonpsychotic was thought to be ill defined and tended to stigmatize the patient with a label. The latter dichotomy was often based on a prognostic judgment that could not be confirmed without long-term follow-up and that might result in a failure to detect a treatable condition. Reversibility of cognitive dysfunction must be thought of as a continuum from partial to total recovery, rather than as an all-or-none dichotomy.

Several key changes were instituted within the DSM-III (APA, 1980) to overcome these serious flaws. First, the concept of organicity was expanded to include a variety of psychiatric disorders whose psychological and behavioral abnormalities are associated with transient or permanent brain dysfunction. Within this definition, no one psychopathological symptom or syndrome is indicative of all organic psychiatric disorders; rather, a multifactorial process is recognized. Second, the overlap between organic and nonorganic (functional) disorders is less defined. Under the new categorization, any disorder whose etiology can be demonstrated or inferred to be organic can be included. Organic mental disorders encompass psychiatric disorders resulting from physical illness, focal brain lesions, or intoxication. In addition, the subdivisions between psychotic and nonpsychotic and between acute and chronic have been eliminated.

To recognize the heterogeneity of these types of disorders, the DSM-III has been expanded to include 10 broad categories of organic brain syndromes. These diagnostic cat-

Various DSM-III criteria from *Diagnostic and Statistical Manual of Mental Disorders* (3rd ed.). Copyright 1980 by the American Psychiatric Association. Reprinted by permission.

RALPH E. TARTER AND ANDREA M. HEGEDUS • Department of Psychiatry, Western Psychiatric Institute and Clinic, Pittsburgh, PA 15213.   The research of this chapter was supported by grants NIH 1RO1 AM 32556-02 and NIAAA 1RO1 AA06601-01.

egories include delirium, dementia, amnestic syndrome, delusional syndrome, hallucinosis, affective syndrome, personality syndrome, intoxication, withdrawal, and a residual category of atypical or mixed organic brain syndrome. These neurological syndromes are descriptive categories that use psychological or behavioral criteria for diagnosis.

Where the etiology of a disorder is verifiable or is presumed to have a specific organic basis, the manifest condition is referred to as an *organic mental disorder*. Therefore, within each of the organic brain syndromes, there can be from one to several organic mental disorders. For example, delirium can be the result of such organic mental disorders as metabolic disruption, endocrine disturbance, avitaminosis, and drug or alcohol abuse. As will be seen in this chapter, the organic mental disorders that are most commonly found in psychiatric settings differ sharply with respect to age and mode of onset, progression, prognosis, and underlying pathophysiological process. Yet, they all share a critical feature: by encompassing brain structure and functional integrity, they militate against optimal behavioral efficiency and social adjustment.

There also are several additional reasons that these conditions are important to the practice of psychology. First, the clinical presentation of the organic mental disorders is, to a large extent, influenced by the person's premorbid characteristics and psychosocial context (Lipowski, 1984). Second, these disorders are typically associated with disturbances of affect and behavior, similar in nature to functional psychiatric disorders. Third, psychological assessment, particuarly where neuropsychological procedures are used, may constitute the most powerful diagnostic tools for determining whether a manifest disorder is "organic" or "functional" in nature. Neuropsychological tests are more sensitive indicators of brain pathology than the EEG, the X ray, or the clinical neurological examination (Filskov & Goldstein, 1974) and may also be more useful in detecting early cerebral atrophy before evidence is visible on the CT scan. Fourth, in cases where the disorder is irreversible (i.e., either static or progressive), psychological techniques can be effectively used to objectively monitor clinical status. And fifth, inasmuch as these disorders often occur in the elderly and, in almost all cases, affect cognitive functioning, efficient and effective interventions are most likely to have a circumscribed, problem-oriented focus. These intervention strategies, involving specific programs for either cognitive or behavioral rehabilitation, are most skillfully used by psychologists.

Although psychologists are important in the diagnosis and treatment of the organic mental disorders, it can be argued that, by training and experience, they are relatively unfamiliar with these various conditions. Therefore, the following discussion reviews the clinical characteristics, the differential diagnoses, and the treatment interventions for the organic mental disorders. Where possible, special consideration is given to elaborating on the underlying neuropathological mechanisms and their relation to the nature of the overt disorder.

DEMENTIA

According to the DSM-III (p. 107), dementia is diagnosed if all of the following conditions are met:

1. There is an intellectual deterioration so that social and occupational functioning is impaired.

2. Memory is impaired.
3. Deficits are present either in abstraction, judgment, or higher cortical functions (language, gnostic, or praxic functions), or a personality disturbance is present.
4. Consciousness is clear.
5. An organic process can be implicated or presumed from the physical examination, history, or laboratory tests.

For a diagnosis of dementia to be made, a number of other conditions must be ruled out, including schizophrenia, depression, and factitious disorder. Also, as a pathological process, dementia must be distinguished from changes due to normal aging.

Dementia, though emanating from disrupted brain functioning, is, in effect, a psychological construct because it denotes disturbances of intellect, personality, and cognition. Depending on the context, the term has been used in at least two different ways (Lishman, 1978). It has been used to describe a number of disease entities originating in middle to late life in which the onset is insidious and the course progressive and irreversible. An expanded inclusionary criterion is used in the DSM-III. In this context, dementia can be diagnosed if any neurological condition results in overt changes, so that the above five criteria are met. Hence, although neurologists and pathologists have tended to use the term *dementia* in a rather restrictive fashion to describe such disorders as Alzheimer's disease, Huntington's chorea, and multi-infarct disease, psychiatrists and psychologists have applied the term more loosely so as to include virtually any organic cause of cognitive deterioration. Thus, it is apparent that, apart from describing a change in intellectual and adaptive capacity, the term, as commonly used in the DSM-III, has little, if any, explanatory value. Bearing this vagueness of usage in mind, the following discussion examines the most frequently occurring conditions for which dementia is a sequela.

Alcoholism

Dementia associated with alcoholism in the DSM-III is differentiated from alcohol amnestic disorder. It is characterized by a substance-(alcohol)-specific dementia that persists for at least three weeks beyond the termination of drinking. Three grades of severity are identified: mild, in which there is only slight disruption of social and occupational functioning; moderate, in which the social and occupational incapacity is more marked; and severe, in which there is a pronounced personality disturbance and an inability to function independently.

Inasmuch as alcoholism is a multisystem disorder, it is likely that the manifest dementia has a multifactorial etiology (Tarter & Alterman, 1984). In addition to the direct effects of ethanol neurotoxicity, hepatic disease, pancreatitis, cardiovascular, and metabolic and endocrine changes also influence the development of a dementia. Indeed, significant, although not complete, recovery from dementia occurs with extended sobriety (Parsons & Farr, 1981). Thus, reestablishing adequate nutritional intake, combined with restitution of normal biologic functioning, can substantially facilitate recovery from dementia. Moreover, it has recently been shown that the administration of lactulose, a disaccharide shown to be effective in treating hepatic encephalopathy, also promotes cognitive recovery in alcoholics with advanced liver disease (McClain, Porter, Krombout, & Zieve, 1984).

Although alcoholic dementia is a common sequela of chronic and excessive alcohol-beverage consumption, it is noteworthy that a significant proportion of alcoholics do not present evidence of either cognitive deterioration or an organic personality disturbance. In one study, approximately 25% of hospitalized alcoholics were found to be unimpaired on a battery of intellectual and cognitive tests (Goldstein & Shelly, 1980). When group comparisons are made (i.e., contrasting alcoholics and normals), it is typically found that a variety of deficits are exhibited by alcoholics on tests of memory, abstraction, and visuospatial and psychomotor capacity (Tarter, 1975). Overall, these impairments are in the moderate ranges of severity. The extent to which these manifest deficits militate against social and occupational functioning, however, is not known.

There are definitive neuropathological changes associated with chronic alcoholism. At autopsy, diffuse cerebral atrophy is evident (Courville, 1955). Quantified CT scan indices of atrophy also reveal rather widespread cortical and subcortical atrophy (Wilkinson & Carlen, 1980a). The etiology of the atrophying process, as noted above, is probably multifactorial. For example, in one study, cerebral atrophy was found to covary with the severity of liver disease (Acker, Majumdar, Shaw, & Thomson, 1982), a finding suggesting that the neuropathological manifestations, to some extent, may be the result of chronic hepatic encephalopathy.

Even though a specific causal factor responsible for the dementia in alcoholism may not be possible to determine, the diagnosis itself is rather simple to establish. Standard neuropsychological testing is usually sufficient. In this regard, the Halstead–Reitan battery has been most frequently used to demonstrate cognitive deterioration. This battery, even if used along with the Wechsler Adult Intelligence Scale (WAIS), does not quite yield sufficient information to implicate alcohol dementia, as a memory impairment has to be observed to quality the person for this diagnosis. Because standard tests of memory have yielded equivocal results (Tarter, 1975), it is recommended that more rigorous, laboratory-based memory measures be used, as they have been found to reliably elicit an impairment in alcoholics (Ryan & Butters, 1980). Hence, for routine assessment purposes, alcoholic dementia can be easily diagnosed by use of the WAIS, the Halstead–Reitan battery (or other comprehensive battery), and a test of memory capacity.

Other neurological conditions resulting in dementia need to be ruled out, however, in order to make an accurate differential diagnosis. For example, alcoholism dementia is usually first recognizable during the person's fifth or sixth decade of life. At this time, other dementing conditions that could underlie the manifest intellectual cognitive deterioration need to be ruled out. Although this cannot be accomplished with certainty because other conditions (e.g., Alzheimer's disease) could be concurrent, the documentation of an alcoholism history, particularly from an informant, will facilitate a valid differential diagnosis. Other dementing neurological conditions, such as tumors, arteriosclerosis, and general paresis, can be ruled out by laboratory data and neuroradiological examination.

In summary, dementia associated with alcoholism is a multisystem disease that produces neurological pathology from numerous potential sources, including ethanol neurotoxicity, hepatic pathology, nutritional deficiency, and cerebrovascular disruption. It is differentiable from the alcoholic amnestic (Korsakoff) syndrome by virtue of its being a more generalized form of cognitive deterioration and a more pronounced cortical atrophy relative to subcortical atrophy (Wilkinson & Carlen, 1980b). Also, by definition, it is differentiable from other organic mental disorders that are alcohol-specific, such as intoxication and withdrawal, inasmuch as the manifest symptoms are evident and persist after long-term abstinence from alcohol. Diagnosis is rather simple, being based on a history of alcohol abuse and the pattern of neuropsychological deficit and, if necessary, confirmed by computerized tomography. There is no known effective treatment for alcoholism dementia.

Alzheimer's Disease

This disorder typically has a presenile onset and occurs in conjunction with delirium, delusions, or depression. Differential diagnosis may be difficult at first because it is not always possible on clinical grounds to rule out other etiologic variables, such as major depression. Neurological disorders that need to be excluded include normal pressure hydrocephalus, hematoma, nutritional deficiency, Parkinson's disease, and multi-infarct dementia. These latter conditions are discussed later.

There are two diagnostic criteria, in addition to the five general criteria for dementia, that must be met for the diagnosis of Alzheimer's disease:

1. The onset is insidious and the clinical course is progressive.
2. All other potential causes of the dementia can be excluded on the basis of history, laboratory tests, and physical examination.

Alzheimer's disease, initially described in the first decade of this century, is among the most prevalent of the presenile dementias. There is evidence of a genetic influence, but as yet, the mode of inheritance is not understood (Lishman, 1978). The clinical presentation is usually first noted between the ages of 40 and 60. Often, the symptoms remain relatively benign, and then, following some stressor such as an unrelated medical illness or hospital admission, a rapid deterioration takes place.

Lishman (1978) identified three stages of the illness. Initially, memory problems, confusion in performing everyday routines, and disorientation in space and time are evident. Agitation, restlessness, and other mood disturbances may also be detected. In the second phase of the illness, beginning after approximately three years, focal neurological symptoms can be observed in conjunction with general personality and intellectual deterioration. Impairments in posture, gait, and muscle tone implicate an extrapyramidal motor-system dysfunction, and dyspraxia, dysphasia, and agnosia point to widespread cortical pathology. In the final stage, delusional and hallucinatory symptoms may occur, which are accompanied by advanced neurological deterioration. Seizures, spastic hemiparesis, rigidity, increased sucking reflexes, and tremor are common. Ultimately, in the terminal stage of the illness, the patient is bedridden, and with time, death occurs.

The most significant pathognomonic sign of early-stage Alzheimer's disease is failing memory. This may be noted by a family member or may represent a complaint by the patient. Invariably, the memory impairment precedes the changes in mood and behavior (Sim, Turner, & Smith, 1966), and for this reason should be viewed as a critical factor, based on history and psychometric measurement, in making the diagnosis.

Cerebral biopsy, revealing the presence of neurofibrillary tangles and plaques, is necessary for an unequivocal diagnosis, although this may not be warranted given adequate clinical documentation of onset and clinical course. The CT scan may reveal generalized atrophy, depending on the stage of the illness, and also assists in the diagnostic formulation. Overall, however, astute clinical observation and monitoring of the patient's cognitive progress over time are sufficient for making a valid diagnosis.

Parkinson's Disease

Traditionally, Parkinson's disease has been considered a disorder of the extrapyramidal motor system. Consequently, the emphasis in syndrome analysis has been on the motor disturbances, which are typically very pronounced and are manifest in the form of impaired posture, rigidity, and hypokinesis. The most common form is idiopathic; that is, neither examination nor history reveals evidence of an etiologic basis of the symptoms. The disorder appears to have a genetic influence and typically is first manifest in the presenium, that is, before age 65.

A variety of factors can produce parkinsonian symptoms. Features of akinesia and rigidity can be induced by certain drugs (e.g., reserpine or the phenothiazines), which ameliorate within several weeks after discontinuation of drug use. Repeated brain trauma (as found in boxers), anoxia, poisoning, and syphilis can also produce parkinsonian symptoms. Lesions in the basal ganglion and the substantia nigra are most prominent; however, brain lesions also are found scattered elsewhere in the cerebrum. Cortical atrophy of a diffuse nature is common, is particularly marked in the frontal regions (Alvord, 1971), and is undoubtedly a factor responsible for the widespread cognitive impairments found in persons suffering from Parkinson's disease. The biochemical basis for this disease appears to involve the pigmented neurons in the brain stem (e.g., the substantia nigra) that manufacture the neurotransmitters dopamine and noradrenaline (Parkes & Marsden, 1973). Dopamine is found in high concentrations in the tract connecting the substantia nigra and the globus pallidus and is substantially reduced in persons suffering from Parkinson's disease.

The treatment of Parkinson's disease is primarily pharmacological. In mild cases, it has been reported that anticholinergic drugs are effective. Medications of this type include Artane (benzhexol) and Cogentin (benztropine). Levodopa, the precursor of dopamine, has been found to have great therapeutic value in more severe cases and is generally acknowledged as the treatment of choice. However, it is far from being a "miracle drug"; only 10% of patients show complete symptom reversal, although about two thirds of all patients show significant improvement in clinical status (Parkes & Marsden, 1973). Side effects, such as nausea, vomiting, hypertension, and appetitive disturbances, have been observed in patients on a levodopa regimen, which can be attenuated if this drug is used in conjunction with a decarboxylase inhibitor, such as Sinemet.

Although medication is the treatment of choice, stereotaxic surgery is still occasionally performed in the most intractible cases. Selective lesioning of various nuclei in the extrapyramidal system has been conducted. The effectiveness of this procedure is disputed, and there is no consensus regarding the optimal site of surgery.

The clinical presentation is marked by interindividual variability. Intellectual and cognitive deterioration is evident in a sizable portion of patients (Boller, Mizutani, Roessmann, & Gambetti, 1980). Suspiciousness, paranoia, emotional lability, and even frank psychotic symptoms are not uncommon. Depressive symptoms, often to a very severe degree, are also common (Lishman, 1978) and may compound the cognitive deficits. It also is noteworthy that the psychiatric symptoms may be induced or exacerbated by pharmacological treatment, such as levodopa. Thus, in arriving at a differential diagnosis, one must be cognizant of the multifactorial etiology of this condition, the interindividual variation in clinical presentation, and the complexity of the interacting factors that influence the expression of the cognitive and psychiatric disturbances.

Huntington's Chorea

This disease is an insidious dementing condition that is accompanied by a pronounced choreiform movement disorder. The etiology is traceable to a single autosomal gene that, if present, invariably results in the overt disorder. There is some variability, however, in age of onset, ranging from the third to the fifth decade of life. There is no cure or method of controlling the progressive degenerative process.

Usually, the chorea antedates the dementia, a factor that is of major importance for diagnostic purposes. Dementia without chorea, nonetheless, has been reported. The neurological symptoms are first expressed as awkwardness or clumsiness. At the onset, the chorea may be subtle and may be expressed simply as facial or finger twitching. As the disease progresses, the movement disturbances become more obvious and are reflected in jerky, uncoordinated, and rapid twitchings. Unsteadiness and compensatory walking with a wide gait develop. As the range of muscle groups affected expands, the disease is overtly expressed as motor disturbances throughout the body.

The psychiatric symptoms are generally thought to precede the neurological manifestations. Lability, irritability, suspiciousness, apathy, and anger are common early signs. There is some suggestion that a schizophrenic illness may precede the overt expression of the neurological symptoms by several years (Lishman, 1978); hence, the determination of a family history of Huntington's disease and a systematic neuropsychiatric examination, with particular attention given to motor signs, need to be obtained in cases of an atypical schizophrenic presentation.

Examination for dementia may, surprisingly, reveal intact memory, a factor that can help to discriminate this disorder from other dementing conditions. Typically, these individuals are also aware of their condition long into the deteriorating stages of the illness. Eventually, global intellectual deterioration ensues, but without evidence of focal symptoms (Aminoff, Marshall, Smith, & Wyke, 1975). Even after productive employment must be terminated, about half of all patients maintain spatiotemporal orientation to the environment. There is, however, an apparent lessening of inhibitory mechanisms, which is manifested cognitively as inattentiveness, behaviorally as restlessness and even violent behavior, and affectively as irritability, heightened excitement, and volatility.

Pick's Disease

This degenerative disease usually first becomes overtly evident between the fifth and sixth decades of life. Differential diagnosis must distinguish this condition from Alzheimer's disease. Generally, the onset age is slightly later, and the course of the illness is slower.

The clinical presentation of Pick's disease stems from lesions in the anterior frontal cerebrum. Disinhibition, ranging from tactlessness to sexual inappropriateness, may be evident. Also, there is a lack of conformity to well-established norms of conduct, a neglect of daily routines, and a tendency toward impulsivity and impaired insight and judgment. These symptoms commonly precede the cognitive impairments. The dementia is slow but insidious in progression. Memory impairment, dysphasia, speech perseveration, and intellectual deterioration invariably occur. Typically, the person succumbs within 10 years of the onset of the disease.

Differentiating this condition from Alzheimer's disease is difficult and usually can be accomplished with certitude only at autopsy. The clinical diagnosis is most likely to be valid if made in the very early phases of the illness, when the overt signs are more-or-less limited to frontal lobe pathology. Hence, unlike Alzheimer's disease, where memory impairments are first noted, Pick's disease is initially marked by behavioral and motivational disturbances (Lishman, 1978). Also, in the early stages of Pick's disease, the patient often presents a picture of restlessness, euphoria, and disinhibition that is not characteristic of the Alzheimer's patient. As the deterioration progresses and the clinical picture becomes more enveloping, differentiation between Pick's disease and Alzheimer's disease becomes increasingly difficult. At autopsy, a differential diagnosis can be advanced based on the fact that, unlike in Alzheimer's disease, neurofibrillary tangles and senile plaques are absent in Pick's disease.

Senile Dementia

This disorder has a late-life onset, beginning in the seventh or eighth decade. Often, the triggering event is some stressor in the person's life during which the insidious deterioration begins. Both cognitive and personality changes are noted in the early stages, with the former being manifest as forgetfulness and confusion, and the latter as suspiciousness, stubbornness, and angry outbursts. Dysphasia, agnosia, and dyspraxia have been observed as specific deficits in the degenerative process. As the disease progresses, confusion and even delirium become pronounced to the point where the person is spatially and temporally disoriented.

There is no effective treatment for the condition. Death typically results within two years (Shah, Banks, & Merskey, 1969). A differential diagnosis is somewhat difficult but can usually be made on the basis of onset age and early clinical presentation. A point to be underscored is that senile dementia is not merely the consequence of the normal aging process; rather, it is a pathological disorder (or group of disorders) that begins in the senium, that is, after age 65.

Creutzfeld-Jakob Disease

This rapid, dementing, late-life disease is associated with severe neurological disturbance. It is though to be virally transmitted, but no specific agent has yet been identified. This inference is based on the observation that the injection of brain homogenate of a patient who succumbed to this disease into a chimpanzee produced neurological symptoms similar to those found in humans (Beck, Daniel, Mathews, Stevens, Alpers, Asher, Gajduski, & Gibbs, 1969).

Initially, symptoms take the form of anxiety, depression, dullness, and sleep disturbances. Weakness, gait unsteadiness, and memory problems also develop relatively early in the clinical course. Subsequently, widespread neurological disturbances are evident, including sensory and motor impairments, dysarthria, dysphasia, and dyspraxia. Substantial interindividual variation in symptom expression is characteristic of the dementing process, but as the person deteriorates, intellectual capacities are virtually lost as the patient progresses to a state of delirium and spastic paralysis. Finally, the patient lapses into coma, from which death ensues.

Differential diagnosis is accomplished on careful clinical examination. The combined presentation of cognitive, motoric, affective, and neurological symptoms, when viewed *in toto*, are distinct from those found in the other degenerative dementias. There is no effective treatment, and death invariably occurs within one to two years after onset.

Multiple Sclerosis

This demyelinating disease usually begins between the third and fifth decade of life. In the early stage of the illness, when "hard" neurological signs may be equivocal, there is often the suspicion of a conversion hysteria. Over the course of the illness, interspersed with varying intervals of symptom remission, the differential diagnosis can be validly established. Tremor, nystagmus, abnormal tendon and abdominal reflexes, abnormal position and vibratory sense, ataxia, and dysarthria are typically present.

The dementia is most pronounced on abstracting ability and memory capacity for remote events. Only a small minority of patients exhibit a generalized dementia. The psychiatric symptoms are rather benign, with reactive depression, emotional blunting, and anxiety being among the most common sequelae.

Although multiple sclerosis is a degenerative condition, its progression is substantially slower than that of the dementias discussed above. Based on onset, history, course, and clinical presentation, a differential diagnosis with respect to other dementias is easy to make. The more difficult discrimination is between multiple sclerosis and conversion hysteria. In the former disorder, the ataxia, paresis, and somesthetic symptoms may be mistakenly ascribed to a conversion disorder. In the absence of other neurological symptoms or laboratory test data, it is important to obtain comprehensive information about cognitive status, personality disposition, and psychopathology. Such information can substantially facilitate the determination of whether the manifest symptoms have an "organic" or a "functional" basis.

Normal Pressure Hydrocephalus

There are two distinct processes by which the brain ventricles can become enlarged, with resulting hydrocephalus. In the first type, there is an obstruction that limits or stops the flow of cerebrospinal fluid (CSF); in the second type, atrophy of the periventricular brain mass produces enlarged ventricles, or *hydrocephalus ex vacuo*.

It is a variant of the first type of hydrocephalus that is pertinent to the present discussion. The obstruction, typically located in the basal cisterns of the brain, reduces the flow of CSF to the sagittal sinus for reabsorption. Hence, the CSF cannot communicate between the ventricles and the subarachnoid space; however, pressure within the ventricles, not uncommonly, is normal.

Generally, the condition has its onset between the seventh and eighth decades of life. Early in the disease, the person experiences forgetfulness, which progressively worsens.

Unlike in senile dementia, social behavior is appropriate, whereas emotions are more blunted. There is a general reduction of activity and psychomotor efficiency. Global cognitive deterioration inevitably results and is marked by severe memory deficits, agnosia, dyspraxia, and dysphasia. Gait disturbance, manifested as a broad-based slow shuffle, has particular pathognomonic value for differential diagnosis.

The only treatment, having only modest effectiveness, is to implant a ventricular-caval shunt; that is, to insert a catheter into one of the lateral ventricles, which, through a one-way valve, allows the CSF an egress to the superior vena cava (Ojemann, Fisher, Adams, Sercet, & Neiv, 1969).

General Paresis

This affliction usually begins between the fourth and sixth decade of life. The etiology is specific and is traceable to syphilis. Initially, personality alterations are observed, which are followed by cognitive disturbances, lability, angry outbursts, apathy, and forgetfulness. Insight and mental efficiency are also reduced. Affective symptoms are expressed as either depression or grandiose and expansive euphoria. In its simplest manifestation, the symptom picture in general paresis is one of apathy, superficiality, and lassitude. Neurological signs and symptoms include optic atrophy, tremor, dysarthia, abnormal pupillary reactions, spasticity, and exaggerated reflexes and ataxia.

With respect to a differential diagnosis, the abnormal pupillary reflexes are of particular pathognomonic importance, because they are not characteristic of other dementias. Testing for syphilis is obviously an essential requirement for arriving at an unequivocal diagnosis.

Insofar as treatment is concerned, it has been suggested (Lishman, 1978) that penicillin can eliminate the syphilitic brain infection in the majority of sufferers. In a study of over a thousand cases, Hahn, Webster, Weikhardt, Thomas, Timberlake, Solomon, Stokes, Moore, Heyman, Gammon, Gleeson, Curtis, and Cutler, (1959) reported that penicillin was effective in 80% of early or mild cases. These investigators also claimed that penicillin treatment was also partially effective in about one third of advanced cases. Thus, depending on the time of treatment and the severity of the condition, the dementing process may be arrested, more or less, by penicillin.

Multi-Infarct Dementia

This dementing disease takes a stepwise, rather than a uniformly progressive, deteriorating course. As implied by the term, it is a cerebrovascular disease and, consequently, is categorized separately from the primary degenerative dementias, which stem directly from pathology to the nervous tissue itself. It is also sometimes referred to as *arteriosclerotic dementia*. The disease usually has its onset during the seventh or eighth decade of life; however, it has also been found, in some cases, to begin at an appreciably earlier age.

An important differentiating feature of multi-infarct dementia is its uneven clinical course. The clinical presentation in the early stage is variable and is marked by periods of exacerbation and remission. This fluctuating pattern, often evidenced as well by nocturnal consciousness-clouding and even delirium, distinguishes multi-infarct dementia from the other dementing conditions. Consequently, the course of the illness is much longer than that of the other irreversible dementias and may endure for as long as 10 years before the person succumbs. With respect to clinical diagnosis, it is generally not possible to unequivocally implicate multi-infarct dementia without temporal monitoring of the clinical signs and symptoms.

As the disease progresses, the cognitive deficits become more severe but are not as encompassing as in the other dementias. Visceral problems, dysphasia, dyspraxis, and hemiparesis are not uncommon and emerge according to the particular episode in which an infarct occurred. Although restitution occurs, in whole or in part, after each episode, the cumulative episodes eventually produce an irreversible dementia. Until late in the disease process, judgment and insight are preserved; they, in turn, through self-appraisal of one's circumstances, can produce a reactive depression.

The affective changes take the form of emotional liability and a general propensity to be easily aroused to anger, tears, or laughter. The person's personality is not substantially impaired. This factor may also help in arriving at a differential diagnosis. No effective treatment is now known, nor is there any way to retard or stop the accumulation of the infarcts that underlie the disease process (Hachinski, Lassen, & Marshall, 1974).

Commentary

The above discussion reviews the differential diagnosis and the clinical presentation of the dementias that have a progressive course. It is noteworthy that the DSM-III divides these conditions into two primary categories: primary degenerative, in which the pathology is specific to nervous tissue and the course is uniformly progressive (e.g., Alzheimer's disease), and multi-infarct dementia, in which the pathology is cerebrovascular and the course is a stepwise deterioration.

It is important to note that the various dementias, even those that are obviously degenerative, are not necessarily so classified. For example, Parkinson's disease, being a dopaminergic disorder of the extrapyramidal motor system, is not always associated with a dementing course; hence, its occurrence is more likely to be diagnosed as an "atypical organic brain syndrome" for the Axis I diagnosis and as Parkinson's disease for the Axis III diagnosis. The same principle would hold for other neurological disorders that do not invariably have a dementing course (e.g., multiple sclerosis), but that need to document this course when it is present. Also, other dementing conditions that have their etiologic basis extrinsic to the brain (e.g., alcoholism, general paresis, and normal pressure hydrocephalus) do not qualify for a diagnosis of primary degenerative dementia. Thus, it is important to be aware that the DSM-III does not recognize those conditions that have an infectious, toxic, or cerebrovascular etiology as primary degenerative diseases, even though these disorders may have a progressive course.

It is also noteworthy that a dementia, as defined by the DSM-III and described in the opening section of this discussion, need not necessarily have a deteriorating course. Brain trauma, space-occupying lesions (e.g., tumor, and subdural hematoma), anoxia (e.g., cardiac arrest and carbon monoxide poisoning), and certain forms of epilepsy can all meet the criteria for a dementia. However, these conditions are not *necessarily* progressive, as in the primary degenerative or multi-infarct types; rather, they may reach a static level of impairment from premorbid levels. Moreover, other disorders characterized by a dementia may be reversible; chronic nutritional deficiency, hypoglycemia, encephalitis, hypo- and hyperthyroidism, Addison's disease, uremia, and hepatic encephalopathy are examples. These dementias can be of either an acute or a chronic nature and, as noted, can originate from a disruption of a variety of organs and biological systems. However, they all fall outside the primary degenerative and multi-infarct categories; rather, these dementias can be classified best as atypical organic brain syndromes as the Axis I diagnosis (clinical syndrome), and the disease entity can be specified Axis III (physical disorder).

Based on the above discussion, it is apparent that there is no uniform clinical presentation in persons who qualify for a dementia diagnosis. The patient may not even present obvious emotional, behavioral, or cognitive disorders, and without a comprehensive psychological and neurological evaluation, a diagnosis may not be possible. The cardinal feature that could facilitate the diagnostic process is the detection or documentation of a deterioration in psychological status. This being the case, psychologists are likely to encounter persons who present a dementing condition in nearly any clinical setting, especially any in which there is a high prevalence of aging individuals. Under these circumstances, psychologists play an integral role in the diagnostic process and in quantifying changes in functional capacity during the natural course of the disease.

Recently, cognitive rehabilitation techniques have also been applied to patients with certain types of dementia (e.g., alcoholism and stroke); however, the value of these procedures still remains uncertain. These new procedures seem promising, particularly those involving computer interaction methods, but substantial research is required to establish their efficacy.

Thus, *dementia* is a concept that is applied very broadly. It is a psychological construct, describing an attenuation of intellectual and cognitive abilities, where there is evidence to implicate disturbed neurological functioning or neuropathology. The term *dementia*, by itself, conveys little information. Information pertinent to treatment or patient management and prognosis, however, is communicated if the underlying pathology is specified (e.g., primary degenerative or multi-infarct) and the physical basis is established (e.g., Parkinson's disease, postnecrotic cirrhosis, or hyperthyroidism).

DELIRIUM

This condition denotes a heightened state of organismic activation or excitement so that consciousness is impaired with respect to clarity and perceptual integrity. The DSM-III (p. 107) requires that five criteria be met for a diagnosis of delirium:

1. Clouding of consciousness resulting in reduced capacity to attend to the environment.
2. Disorientation and memory impairment.
3. At least two of the following symptoms:
   a. perceptual dysfunction (e.g., hallucinations or illusions)
   b. incoherant speech
   c. disruption of sleep–wakefulness cycle
   d. increased or reduced psychomotor activity
4. Rapid onset and fluctuating clinical status.
5. Evidence of an organic basis obtained from either a physical examination, laboratory test data, or a history.

The most common and representative of these conditions is delirium tremens following the abrupt cessation of a bout of heavy alcohol consumption. This disorder, however, is treated in the DSM-III as a special condition and is discussed under "Withdrawal—Substance-Specific"; thus, it will not be addressed in this section.

Delirium is often, but not always, associated with an acute organic brain disorder involving a disruption of biochemical and metabolic processes. The manifest psychological disturbances range along a continuum from confusion to impending coma. Therefore, the validity of a psychometric evaluation or, for that matter, a clinical interview depends to a large extent on the patient's status.

The impairment in consciousness is global. Unlike in the dementias, where the cognitive disturbance takes the form of a *deficit*, the cardinal characteristic of delirium is *distortion*. Indeed, in the delirious state, the person may have a very full mental life, but characterized by hallucinatory, illusionary, or otherwise misrepresentative content. In the dementias, such distortions are rare, although they can appear as secondary disturbances, as in the case of multi-infarct dementia.

It is important to note that delirium is not one disease condition but may be the culmination of a variety of disorders, including metabolic, toxic, and endocrine disturbances. For example, it can occur as the result of a thiamine deficiency, producing Wernicke's encephalopathy. It can also be the product of hepatocellular failure and portacaval shunting, leading to a hepatic encephalopathy. Acute infections and fever often result in delirium. Thus, although a clinical diagnosis may be readily obtained, effective intervention requires an understanding of the particular etiology. Finally, although delirium is reversible (by the reestablishment of biochemical homeostasis), repeated occurrences may cause permanent neurological pathology in certain disorders. Hence, the causes and the prior number of delirium episodes need to be ascertained when assessing these neurological disturbances.

The common feature of delirium is a disturbance in consciousness. Consequently, judgment, awareness of surroundings, and orientation to time, place, and person may be more or less disturbed. Overtly, the person may appear either mildly confused but otherwise complacent, or vociferous and aggressive. No single dispositional state characterizes a delirious condition. However, being an acute disorder for the most part, it is likely to be encountered in emergency rooms, on wards that treat various medical conditions (e.g., endocrine, metabolic, and toxic), and on admission to psychiatric hospitals. Not uncommonly, persons in delirium are inappropriately arrested for disorderly conduct and incarcerated (usually temporarily). The psychologist, faced with diagnosis, is in a position to objectively and quantitatively assess clarity of consciousness, orientation, and overall functional capacity.

AMNESTIC SYNDROME

Three criteria must be satisfied to fulfill a DSM-III diagnosis (p. 113) of amnestic syndrome:

1. Anterograde amnesia, or inability to learn new information, and retrograde amnesia, or incapacity to recall remote information.
2. Clear conscious state and reduction of "major" intellectual abilities.

3. Evidence from either history, examination, or laboratory test data that implicates an organic basis for the amnesia.

Unlike any of the organic mental disorders discussed up to this point, the chronic amnestic syndrome is the product of a focal neurological pathology confined essentially to the hippocampus and the diencephalon (Talland, 1965). When the memory disturbances are found in conjunction with diffuse cerebral lesions (e.g., in Alzheimer's disease), there are other salient intellectual and cognitive impairments so that the memory problems are not preeminent. Hence, they do not qualify for a primary diagnosis of amnestic syndrome.

Korsakoff psychosis, without doubt, is the most prevalent amnestic syndrome. For reasons that are not yet understood, a minority of alcoholics develop this syndrome, usually after a Wernicke's encephalopathy. However, whereas Wernicke's encephalopathy is a potentially reversible biochemical condition (the result of a thiamine deficiency) and could occur independently of a history of alcohol abuse, the Korsakoff syndrome is irreversible, is not linked directly to nutritional factors, and is invariably the result of chronic alcoholism.

The predominant feature of the Korsakoff psychosis is a memory deficit of debilitating proportions. Typically, the anterograde amnesia is so severe as to prevent the encoding of information and its retention in long-term memory (Butters & Cermak, 1980). The inability to sustain an orderly temporal record of experience results in disorientation and confabulation. The appearance of confabulation is an important pathognomonic sign, as it reflects a fundamental attempt by the person to reconstruct experience by accessing fragments of the past, although superficially and inaccurately. Thus, although at first glance a coherent verbal response is demonstrated, subsequent inquiry by the clinician readily reveals that the patient is interrelating elements of past experience that are disconnected in time and place.

The etiology of the Korsakoff psychosis is linked to lesions primarily in the hippocampus and the mamillary bodies (Victor, Adams, & Collins, 1971). Surgical resection of this brain tissue, performed for the treatment of epilepsy, also produces an amnestic syndrome (Milner, Corkin, & Teuber, 1968), implicating, quite unequivocally, the importance of these limbic-system structures in memory functioning. It also is noteworthy that an alcohol amnestic syndrome, which is less severe than Korsakoff's syndrome, has recently been described that is characterized by relatively greater subcortical than cortical pathology (Wilkinson & Carlen, 1980b). This amnestic disorder is marked by memory impairment in the context of normal intellectual functioning.

A number of conditions need to be recognized that can result in a misdiagnosis. First, the possibility of a transient global amnesia needs to be ruled out. This disorder is marked by a circumscribed anterograde amnesia; however, remote or long-term memories are not as impaired as in the amnestic syndrome. Also, as the term transient denotes, this is a temporary condition that is reversible after an amnesia attack of several hours or days. Thus, based on clinical observation and monitoring, it is possible to differentiate an amnestic syndrome from transient global amnesia.

It is also always important, when a memory impairment is reported by a patient, that the clinician suspect the presence of a factitious disorder, particularly when litigation is involved. A differential diagnosis, however, can readily be obtained in most situations by psychometric testing and after a thorough interview.

More difficult is the distinction between amnestic syndrome and functional disorders of memory. These disorders include dissociative reactions, fugue states, and other alterations in the modulation of conscious experience. The differential diagnosis, however, can usually be accomplished because of the absence of personality disturbance in the amnestic syndrome in comparison to multiple episodes of somatic reactions, anxiety, and interpersonal problems in the functional disorders. Also, psychometric testing invariably reveals that individuals with a functional amnesia can learn new information. Moreover, the information that is ostensibly lost in the functional disorders tends to be restricted to a particular segment of the person's life and is often related to a personal stressor.

Amnestic disorders are rather uncommon. The profundity of the impairment almost invariably leads to hospitalization on a neurological or psychiatric word. Amnestic disturbances are also readily found in chronic-care facilities required for the elderly. Frequently, amnestic conditions are discovered in patients admitted to specialized alcoholism treatment programs or facilities. Apart from the memory impairment, which is not necessarily obvious in casual conversation, the amnestic person does not usually exhibit a gross behavioral disorder. Indeed, the patient more typically presents as affable and cooperative, seemingly without emotional distress or concern about his or her condition. Only in comprehensive neuropsychological evaluation is the severity of the cognitive deficit revealed.

There is no effective treatment for the amnestic syndrome. It is possible that cognitive rehabilitation may be therapeutic, although the value of the available techniques has yet to be proved.

ORGANIC DELUSIONAL SYNDROME

This DSM-III diagnosis (p. 115) requires that three criteria be met:

1. The predominant feature of the disorder is in the form of delusions.
2. Consciousness is clear; there is no dementia; hallucinations are not evidenced; and there are no signs of delirium.
3. Findings from laboratory testing, history, or physical examination implicate an organic basis for the disorder.

The first criterion is the critical defining variable and, in effect, represents the judgment of the clinician in ranking the salience of the various signs and symptoms presented. Delusions do not occur in the organic disorders as an isolated phenomenon. Therefore, advancing this diagnosis depends on the impressions of the examiner regarding the relative importance of delusions with respect to the spectrum of cognitive and emotional manifestations.

Delusions are a common accompaniment to a variety of neurological conditions, including tumors, head injury, general paresis, delirium, and dementia. The delusional content is typically not a crystallized thought disorder; rather, it takes on the appearance of general suspiciousness, grandiosity, or jealousy. As a result of being easily threatened, it is not uncommon for such patients to react inordinately, even to mild provocation.

One particular form of delusional disturbance, which apparently has a neurological basis, is the Capgras syndrome. This condition takes various forms, but the defining feature is that the person believes that well-known friends and relatives have been replaced by doubles. This disorder superficially presents as paranoid schizophrenia; however, comprehensive neuropsychological examination reveals, among other cognitive deficits, a disorder in face recognition (Morrison & Tarter, 1984).

ORGANIC HALLUCINOSIS

Hallucinations may be the predominant feature of acute, as well as chronic, organic conditions. They are most common, however, in the acute conditions consequent to metabolic disruption. To qualify for a DSM-III diagnosis of organic hallucinations, three criteria (p. 116) must be satisfied:

1. The predominant clinical feature must be either persistent or recurrent hallucinations.
2. Consciousness must be clear.
3. Evidence obtained from history, physical examination, or laboratory tests points to an organic etiology.

It is noteworthy that the differential diagnosis precludes hallucinosis due to delirium, in which, by definition, consciousness is clouded. In the "functional" psychoses, no organic factor can be implicated. The key factors in advancing a differential diagnosis are that the hallucinations are the most salient clinical feature in an otherwise clear sensorium and that intellectual deficits are absent.

The hallucinations may be highly variable, ranging from a misperception of simple objects and shapes to highly complex mental distortions. Also, the hallucinations may occur in any modality. With respect to drug-induced hallucinations, alcohol most typically causes auditory hallucinations, whereas hallucinogenic drugs generally induce visual hallucinations.

Hallucinations are also common sequelae of tumors and seizure disorders. The modality of expression is typically predicted from the location of the lesion (e.g., occipital lobe lesions cause visual hallucinations, whereas temporal lobe lesions are associated with auditory hallucinations). Hallucinations also are not uncommon in migraine headaches.

The course and treatment of organic hallucinosis depend on the underlying etiology. In some disorders, such as alcoholic hallucinosis, the symptoms will remit spontaneously, although they may persist for several years. When hallucinations are the product of metabolic disruption, medication is usually sufficient to reverse the condition. Under certain circumstances, the hallucinations may not be treatable, as for example, in cases of sensory deprivation due to deafness or blindness.

ORGANIC AFFECTIVE SYNDROME

This disorder, along with the previously discussed organic delusional syndrome, most closely resembles schizophrenia and the affective spectrum disorders. To meet DSM-III criteria (p. 116), an organic affective syndrome must consist of:

1. A predominant disturbance of mood accompanied by at least two symptoms found in either manic or major depressive disorders.
2. Clear consciousness without global intellectual impairment and significant signs of hallucinations or delusions.
3. Evidence, from physical examination, history, or laboratory tests, that implicates an organic factor.

Affective disturbances can occur as a consequence of a number of different neurological disorders, including tumors, migraines, multiple sclerosis, and epilepsy. Most commonly, however, this disorder is the result of metabolic or toxic disturbances. The most pronounced conditions are associated with such disorders as hypothyroidism, hyperthyroidism, hypoadrenocorticalism, and hyperadrenocorticalism. Medications, including methyldopa and reserpine, also have been known to induce an organic affective reaction.

Clinically, the person presents a mood disturbance that is very similar to that seen in patients who are in a depressive or manic episode. To rule out these latter two possibilities in arriving at a differential diagnosis, it is imperative that the clinician implicate an organic factor underlying the clinical phenomenology. Once the organic etiology is identified, targeted treatment may be implemented.

ORGANIC PERSONALITY SYNDROME

A great variety of neurological conditions have been found to be associated with personality changes. Mass lesions, trauma, Parkinson's disease, cerebrovascular accidents, degenerative conditions, and temporal lobe epilepsy are among the most common causes. For a DSM-III diagnosis (pp. 119–120) of organic personality syndrome, three basic conditions must be met:

1. A change in behavior or personality is reflected in at least one of the following ways:
   a. emotional lability
   b. deficient impulse control
   c. apathy
   d. suspiciousness or paranoia
2. Clear consciousness with no global intellectual impairment, significant affective disturbance, delusional disorder, or hallucinosis.
3. Evidence from laboratory, physical examination, or history that implicates an organic basis.

The manifestations of the particular personality change depends, to some extent, on the location of the lesion. Frontal lobe lesions tend to be reflected in lability, disinhibition, poor goal persistence, and apathy (Damasio, 1979), whereas temporal lobe lesions are more likely to result in personality changes of either a depressive or an aggressive nature (Gainotti, 1979). Not uncommonly, personality changes are the harbinger of a progressive cognitive disorder, such as dementia.

The clinical course and the severity of the disorder vary among individuals and types of neurological condition. Treatment, where it is available, is targeted to the etiology of the disorder.

Organic personality disorders, along with organic delusional and affective disorders, as well as hallucinosis, are most likely to be observed in hospital admitting settings or in psychiatric services. Occasionally, patients in medical services may present with these types of conditions, either as a result of systemic illness or as a consequence of treatment. The predominant features are behavioral; thus, persons with these conditions are initially routed to psychiatric facilities, where the organic basis of the condition is usually established. The clinical presentations are not unlike those of patients with "functional" psychiatric disorders; indeed, it is usually the task of psychologists to assist in the differential diagnosis vis-à-vis the determination of the etiologic basis of the manifest symptomatology.

INTOXICATION

This organic brain syndrome encompasses a number of acute substance-specific mental disorders. The clinical presentation is contingent on the specific substance consumed; however, several shared general disturbances are induced by all psychoactive agents used at high dosage levels. These include disturbances in psychomotor efficiency, in emotional control, in cognitive proficiency, and in consciousness.

Three DSM-III criteria must be met for a diagnosis (p. 122) of intoxication:

1. Recent ingestion and presence in the body of an exogenous substance;
2. Maladaptive waking-state behavior as a consequence of the CNS effects of the substance (e.g., impaired judgment and aggression).
3. The clinical syndrome cannot be subsumed within other organic brain syndromes as discussed in the previous sections of this chapter.

It is important to note that the DSM-III distinguishes intoxication from the physiological and psychological alterations associated with the social and recreational use of substances. Only where social behavior, judgment, or job responsibilities are compromised can the diagnosis of intoxication be legitimately applied.

In addition to the type of substance used, the clinical presentation also depends on the drug dosage, the social context, and the premorbid personality. There are no effective antidotes; the passage of time, allowing for the metabolism of the substance and amelioration of the symptoms, is the best treatment. In cases of overdose, emergency medical-surgical care may be needed. Diagnosis is usually simple and can be accomplished from blood or urine assays, smelling the patient's breath, and observation of behavior, as well as from the person's self-report.

Discussed below are the common organic mental disorders associated with intoxication.

Alcohol Intoxication

Without doubt, alcohol intoxication is the most common organic mental disorder. The diagnostic criteria (DMS-III, p. 131) consist of:

1. Recent ingestion of alcohol.
2. Maladaptive behavior that impairs social and occupational functioning.
3. At least one of:
   a. slurred speech
   b. incoordination
   c. unsteady gait
   d. nystagmus
   e. flushed face
4. At least one of:
   a. mood change
   b. irritability
   c. loquacity
   d. attentional impairments

Acute intoxication must be differentiated from cerebellar ataxia, which is limited to unsteadiness in gait and in stationary standing. There is also a certain degree of overlap between the signs and symptoms of alcohol intoxication and multiple sclerosis; however, these resemblances are superficial. Testing for blood or breath alcohol concentration definitively produces a valid differential diagnosis when doubt exists concerning the presence of either multiple sclerosis or cerebellar ataxia.

The overt presentation depends on a number of factors. The blood-alcohol concentration is unquestionably an important factor, but other variables, such as the situational context, the individual's cognitive appraisal of his or her state and circumstances, and whether the person is in the absorption or elimination phase of alcohol metabolism, also determine the behavioral and affective manifestations of acute intoxication.

There is no treatment or cure for acute alcohol intoxication despite many myths and the availability of folk medicines purporting to have sobering properties. Alcohol is metabolized at a more-or-less constant rate of 5 to 10 ml/h, and only the passage of time will reinstate sobriety.

Alcohol Idiosyncratic Intoxication. Some individuals, for reasons that are entirely unknown, exhibit an inordinately deviant response to alcohol at levels of intoxication that are not usually found in conjunction with aberrant behavior. In this state, sometimes referred to as *pathological intoxication*, the behavioral presentation is usually marked by a propensity for violence. Although this disorder has been attributed to a low tolerance for alcohol and a preexisting neurological dysfunction, its etiology is unknown.

There is little documentation of this condition. No information about its prevalence is available. Nor are the premorbid characteristics understood, except that the manifestations of violent or assaultive behavior, found after the consumption of even modest amounts of alcohol, are not dispositional features of the person in a sober state.

Barbiturate Intoxication

This class of organic mental disorders includes barbiturates and other similarly acting sedatives and hypnotics. The diagnostic criteria (DSM-III, p. 140) are

1. Recent ingestion of the substance.
2. One of:
   a. mood lability
   b. disinhibition of sexual and aggressive impulses
   c. irritability
   d. loquacity
3. One of:
   a. slurred speech
   b. incoordination
   c. unsteady gait
   d. attention or memory impairments
4. Maladaptive behavioral changes involving judgment, social interaction, or occupational functioning.

The differential diagnosis can be readily obtained from blood or urine analysis. Because of the similarity to alcohol intoxication in clinical presentation, laboratory assessment is necessary to establish a valid diagnosis if a recent history is not possible to obtain or is unavailable because of the individual's nondisclosure or incapacity.

Opioid Intoxication

These organic mental disorders result from the use of natural opioids, such as heroin and morphine, as well as from the nonmedical use of synthetic opioids, such as methadone. The diagnostic criteria (DSM-III, p. 143) are

1. Recent use of an opioid.
2. Pupillary constriction.
3. At least one of:
   a. euphoria
   b. dysphoria
   c. apathy
   d. psychomotor retardation
4. At least one of:
   a. drowsiness
   b. slurred speech
   c. attention or memory impairment
5. Behavioral maladaptation reflected in judgment, occupational functioning, or social interaction.

Opioid overdose can lead to shock and coma, and in more severe cases, respiratory arrest may occur, raising the specter of death. In such cases, intravenous injection of a narcotic antagonist (e.g., nalaxone) can reverse the process. However, treatment must be expeditious because anoxia will produce irreversible brain damage within 6 minutes after cardiac arrest.

Cocaine Intoxication

Cocaine intoxication is short-lived, and reversibility takes place within several hours. Large doses, however, can produce seizures, syncope, chest pains, and even respiratory paralysis. Also, very high doses may cause stereotyped movements, suspiciousness, ideas of reverence, increased libido, tinnitus, and somesthetic distortions. Typically, cocaine intoxication is associated with an increased feeling of well-being and alertness. The specific diagnostic criteria (DSM-III, pp. 146–147) are

1. Recent cocaine use.
2. At least two of the following symptoms occurring within 2 hours of use:
   a. psychomotor agitation
   b. elation
   c. grandiosity
   d. loquacity
   e. hypervigilance
3. At least two of the following occurring within one hour after use:
   a. tachycardia

  b. pupillary dilation
  c. increased blood pressure
  d. chills or perspiration
  e. nausea and vomiting
4. Maladaptive behavioral consequences.

The presence of cocaine in plasma or of cocaine metabolites in the urine firmly establishes the diagnosis. Because a certain degree of similarity exists between hypomania and cocaine intoxication, laboratory testing may be desirable if a diagnosis must be made rapidly. If time constraints are not an issue, the passage of time will differentiate hypomania from cocaine intoxication because of the rapid metabolism of this drug.

Amphetamine Intoxication

The clinical expression is very similar to that found in cocaine intoxication. The only clinical distinction is that, in amphetamine intoxication, the thought disorder and hallucinations may persist beyond the period of acute intoxication. The following DSM-III criteria must be met for a diagnosis (p. 148) of amphetamine intoxication:

1. Recent use of amphetamines or other sympathomimetic drugs.
2. At least two of the following symptoms occurring within 1 hour of use:
   a. psychomotor agitation
   b. elation
   c. grandiosity
   d. loquacity
   e. hypervigilance
3. At least two of the following symptoms occurring within 1 hour of use:
   a. tachycardia
   b. pupillary dilation
   c. increased blood pressure
   d. perspiration or chills
   e. nausea of vomiting
4. Maladaptive behavior, such as impaired judgment, fighting, social disruption, and impaired occupational functioning.

Phencyclidine (PCP) Intoxication

A number of neurological, physiological, and psychological characteristics accompany PCP intoxication. The following features comprise the diagnostic criteria (DSM-III, pp. 151–152):

1. Recent PCP use.
2. Two or more of the following symptoms emerging within 1 hour after use:
   a. vertical and horizontal nystagmus
   b. increased blood pressure and heart rate
   c. numbness or reduced pain response
   d. ataxia
   e. dysarthria

3. Two or more of the following symptoms occurring within 1 hour:
   a. euphoria
   b. psychomotor agitation
   c. anxiety
   d. emotional lability
   e. grandiosity
   f. synesthesia
   g. sensation of slowing of time
4. Maladaptive behavior.

Violent, unpredictable, and suicidal behavior are not uncommon following PCP use. Detoxification can take up to 6 hours, after which depression, irritability, and anxiety may be present. Differential diagnosis can be most accurately accomplished by laboratory testing for PCP in urine or blood.

Hallucinogen Intoxication

Hallucinosis is the characteristic response to hallucinogen intoxication. The course is relatively brief and, depending on the particular drug, ranges from a few hours to a few days. The diagnostic criteria (DSM-III, 154–155) are

1. Recent hallucinogen ingestion.
2. Perceptual alterations during the waking state.
3. At least two of the following:
   a. pupillary dilation
   b. tachycardia
   c. palpitations
   d. blurring of vision
   e. tremors
   f. incoordination
4. Maladaptive behavior, including paranoia, depression, anxiety, fear, impaired judgment, disrupted social interaction and impaired occupational functioning.

A predominant clinical feature in many cases is the presence of religious ideation or experience. Disturbed thought processes may result in rash and unpredictable behavior. There also may be a feeling of euphoria and deep insight into philosophical issues.

Occasionally, hallucinations persist or recur long after the period of intoxication has ended. These are sometimes referred to as *flashbacks*. They are not a universal phenomenon, but when present, they can have a very distressing impact on the individual. Diagnosis is unequivocally established by laboratory assay of metabolites in the blood or urine.

Cannabis Intoxication

Next to alcohol intoxication, this is probably the most common organic mental disorder. The time course is quite rapid, intoxication beginning within minutes of inhalation, and persisting for up to 3 hours. There are five basic diagnostic criteria (DSM-III, p. 158):

1. Recent cannabis use.
2. Tachycardia.
3. At least one of the following within 2 hours after use:
   a. euphoria
   b. subjective intensification of experience
   c. perception of slowing of time
   d. apathy
4. At least one of the following within 2 hours after use:
   a. conjunctival injection
   b. increased appetite
   c. dry mouth
5. Maladaptive behavior, including suspiciousness, anxiety, ideas of reverence, impaired judgment, and disrupted social and occupational functioning.

The euphoria is a highly reinforcing state that may be experienced as a heightened sense of well-being and tranquillity. A dysphoric reaction may also occur, accompanied by a fear of loss of mental control and impaired reality-testing and paranoia. Under very high doses, hallucinations may occur, although they are rare.

Caffeine Intoxication

This psychoactive substance is found in proprietary analgesics, coffee, tea, and other over-the-counter stimulant preparations. The diagnostic criteria (DSM-III, p. 161) for caffeine intoxication are

1. Recent caffeine consumption.
2. At least five of the following:
   a. restlessness
   b. nervousness
   c. excitement
   d. insomnia
   e. flushed face
   f. diuresis
   g. gastrointestinal complaints
   h. muscle twitching
   i. rambling thoughts or speech
   j. cardiac arrhythmia
   k. periods of inexhaustibility
   l. psychomotor agitation

The diagnosis is usually established on clinical grounds, that is, ascertainment that the symptoms are temporally linked to caffeine ingestion. At very high doses—say, in the range of 1 g per day—the above symptoms are commonly manifest. A dose of caffeine exceeding 10 g can produce generalized seizures, respiratory failure, and even death. As a cup of coffee contains between 100 and 150 mg of caffeine, it can be concluded that caffeine's potential effects, in cumulative doses, are not innocuous.

WITHDRAWAL SYNDROMES

The last major cateogry of brain syndromes to be discussed is the organic mental disorders that accompany substance withdrawal. Withdrawal syndromes are manifest after either the sudden cessation or the sharp reduction of substance consumption after a period of continual use. Discussed below are the withdrawal syndromes specific to the regular consumption and termination of the various substances.

Alcohol Withdrawal Syndrome

Alcohol withdrawal syndrome is a time-limited phenomenon, usually decreasing between 5 and 7 days after cessation of drinking. It is usually a benign process, although generalized seizures, especially in persons with preexisting epilepsy, are not uncommon. Delirium during withdrawal is a frequent feature and may be the most profound clinical presentation. In such cases, clouding of consciousness, autonomic hyperactivity, hallucinations, delusions, and agitation are usually manifest. Alcohol withdrawal delirium, or "delirium tremens," may or may not be present during alcohol withdrawal.

When hallucinations are the most salient feature during withdrawal, a diagnosis of alcohol hallucinosis may be advanced. Usually, a person in this condition hears voices, often of a threatening nature; however, unlike in withdrawal delirium, there is no clouding of consciousness. This particular disorder of alcohol withdrawal is rare and is typically exhibited by individuals who are physically dependent on alcohol.

A diagnosis of alcohol withdrawal, without delirium or hallucinosis, requires the following criteria according to the DSM-III (pp. 133–134):

1. Cessation or reduction of heavy prolonged alcohol consumption after which there is gross motor tremor.
2. At least one of:
   a. nausea and vomiting
   b. malaise and weakness
   c. autonomic hyperactivity
   d. anxiety
   e. depressed mood or irritability
   f. orthostatic hypotension

The differential diagnosis can easily be made if a valid history is obtained. This is especially necessary for barbiturate withdrawal, as the symptoms and signs of this organic mental disorder are virtually identical to those of alcohol withdrawal. There is also some similarity in symptom expression between this latter disorder and acute hypoglycemia, diabetic ketoacidosis, and essential tremor. The differential diagnosis, however, can be readily established by means of appropriate laboratory tests and from the history.

Barbiturate Withdrawal Syndrome

The clinical manifestations are essentially the same as for alcohol withdrawal. Consequently, a valid differential diagnosis depends on information obtained from the patient

or an informant regarding recent substance abuse. Delirium occasionally occurs after barbiturate cessation, and here, too, the clinical presentation closely resembles that of alcohol withdrawal delirium.

Opioid Withdrawal Syndrome

Symptoms and signs of opioid withdrawal are typically seen within 6 to 8 h after the
last dose and may persist for up to 1 week. The opioid withdrawal syndrome occurs in
individuals who are physically dependent on opioids and is rare in persons who have
received these drugs for medical-surgical reasons. The diagnostic criteria (DSM-III, p.
145) are

1. Prolonged, heavy use of opioids followed by cessation of use.
2. At least four of the following:
   a. lacrimation
   b. rhinorrhea
   c. pupillary dilation
   d. piloerection
   e. diarrhea
   f. yawning
   g. mild hypertension
   h. tachycardia
   i. fever
   j. insomnia

A history taken from the patient or an informant is usually sufficient for arriving at
a valid diagnosis. Laboratory analysis of blood and urine may also be useful in the early
stages of withdrawal. Opioid withdrawal is distinct from other substance withdrawal syndromes and can be discriminated from these on the basis of the overt clinical presentation. It is of interest, however, that the signs and symptoms of influenza greatly resemble those of opioid withdrawal.

Amphetamine Withdrawal Syndrome

Amphetamine withdrawal generally begins about 3 days after the last usage of the
drug. The following DSM III criteria (p. 150) must be met for a diagnosis:

1. Prolonged heavy use of amphetamine or other sympathomimetic; and
2. At least two of the following after reduction or cessation of drug use:
   a. fatigue
   b. disturbed sleep
   c. increased dreaming

It is noteworthy that the affective symptoms may persist for several months. Agitation and suicidal ideation may be additional accompanying features. The differential diagnosis can be easily established upon history-taking from the patient or from an informant.

Tobacco Withdrawal Syndrome

This organic mental disorder occurs in an undetermined proportion of moderate and heavy tobacco consumers. Characteristically, the withdrawal symptoms emerge about two hours after the last cigarette. Within approximately one day the symptoms are most florid, and they eventually subside after a few days or within a week.

The DSM-III diagnostic criteria (pp. 159–160) are

1. At least 10 cigarettes a day for several weeks.
2. Sudden cessation of use followed by at least four of the following symptoms within 24 h:
   a. craving for tobacco
   b. irritability
   c. anxiety
   d. difficulty concentrating
   e. restlessness
   f. headaches
   g. drowsiness
   h. gastrointestinal distress

The differential diagnosis can be readily established in the course of history taking. However, the symptom expression is not typically severe, and individuals undergoing tobacco withdrawal usually do not come to the attention of physicians or other health professionals.

ATYPICAL OR MIXED ORGANIC BRAIN SYNDROME

This category is used for those conditions in which there are concurrent elements of two or more syndromes. For example, an individual who presents features of both an amnestic and a dementia syndrome, a common occurrence in alcoholism, may be classified as having a mixed organic brain syndrome.

Moreover, atypical disorders encompass those conditions that are not ordinarily classified within any of the above nine categories of brain syndrome. For instance, metabolic, endocrine, or toxic disorders that are secondary to medical conditions may also be assigned to this category.

The diagnostic criteria are twofold:

1. The disturbance occurs during the waking state and does not meet the criteria for any of the other organic brain syndromes.
2. Evidence obtained from either the history, a physical examination, or laboratory tests implicates an organic basis.

Given the marked individual variation in the expression of neurological conditions, it is to be expected that using the DSM-III criteria will sometimes result in a person's being diagnosed according to one of the above nine organic brain syndromes, whereas other individuals may be classified as suffering from an atypical organic brain syndrome. To illustrate this point simply, depending on the configuration of signs and symptoms and the stage of illness, a person suffering from Huntington's chorea may be diagnosed as having either a dementia or an atypical organic brain syndrome. Thus, the label or diagnostic category, being based on clinical phenomenology, may result in different diagnoses for the same pathological process.

COMMENT

This chapter has outlined the characteristics and the diagnostic criteria for the 10 categories of organic brain syndrome. These neurological conditions are defined primarily by behavioral or psychological signs and symptoms. They are descriptive categories. Theoretically, at least, they are mutually exclusive clinical entities; however, it is quite apparent, on inspection of the clinical phenomenology and the criteria, that the various organic brain syndromes share numerous features.

When the etiology of an organic brain syndrome is either known or can be presumed, an organic mental disorder is implicated. Within each of the syndromes, the most prevalent or commonly encountered organic mental disorders were described. The criteria for differential diagnosis and treatment interventions, where applicable, were discussed. The underlying pathophysiological process, the onset factors, the reversibility potential, and the progress vary among the different organic mental disorders.

The management of the organic brain syndromes or the organic mental disorders falls primarily under the purview of the specialties of psychiatry and neurology. Psychologists, however, can play an important role in the assessment process by providing objective and quantified data in the form of a neuropsychological evaluation. In addition, these measures are useful for monitoring the course of the disorder. For example, neuropsychological tests are more sensitive indicators of brain dysfunction than either the EEG or neurological examination (Filskov & Goldstein, 1974). Hence, they are particularly valuable in the detection of pathology that is beyond the reach of these latter techniques, and they may be used to track treatment effects to the stage of recovery or to some optimal level. Two illustrations include the evaluation of the efficacy of thiamine therapy in Wernicke's encephalopathy and lactulose treatment for portal-systemic encephalopathy. Moreover, neuropsychological testing can identify subclinical variants of an organic mental disorder, such as amnestic alcoholism (Wilkinson & Carlen, 1980a) or latent hepatic encephalopathy (Tarter, Hegedus, Van Thiel, Schade, Gavaler, & Starzl, 1984). Thus, psychologists can perform an important diagnostic function by drawing on their expertise in psychometric evaluation.

SUMMARY

Numerous organic mental disorders are covered by the general descriptive categories of the organic brain syndromes. These disorders are diverse with respect to etiology, natural history, prognosis, and the underlying pathophysiological processes. This chapter has reviewed the disorders that are most frequently encountered in psychiatric settings. The emphasis was on diagnostic criteria because, at this stage of understanding, treatment procedures are either limited or nonexistent for most of these disorders.

In attempting to marshal this vast and disparate multidisciplinary literature, the authors pursued two major objectives: (1) discussing the various organic mental disorders in such a fashion that they may be readily compared with each other; and (2) presenting the material so that its relevance to psychological practice may be readily appreciated. Consequently, rather than dwelling on the details of any one disorder or group of disorders with respect to a critical appraisal of current research findings, it was deemed more useful to address this topic from a clinical standpoint. With increasing attention being given by psychologists to the biological basis of behavior, this chapter has attempted to convey to the reader the complexity of etiologic determinants and the diversity of clinical presentation of the various organic mental disorders.

REFERENCES

Acker, W., Majumdar, S., Shaw, G., & Thomson, A. (1982). The relationship between brain and liver damage in chronic alcoholic patients. *Journal of Neurology, Neurosurgery and Psychiatry, 45*, 984–987.

Alvord, E. (1971). The pathology of parkinsonism: II. An interpretation with special reference to other changes in the aging brain. In F. McDowell & C. Markham (Eds.), *Recent advances in Parkinson's disease*. Oxford: Blackwell Scientific.

Aminoff, M., Marshall, J., Smith, E., & Wyke, M. (1975). Pattern of intellectual impairment in Huntington's chorea. *Psychological Medicine, 5*, 169–172.

Beck, E., Daniel, P., Mathews, W., Stevens, D., Alpers, M., Asher, D., Gajduski, E., & Gibbs, C. (1969). Creutzfeldt-Jakob disease: The neuropathology of a transmission experiment. *Brain, 90*, 699–716.

Boller, F. Mizutani, T., Roessmann, U., & Gambetti, P. (1980). Parkinson disease, dementia and Alzheimer's disease: Clinical pathological correlations. *Annuals of Neurology, 7*, 329–335.

Butters, N., & Cermak, L. (1980). *Alcoholic Korsakoff's syndrome: An information processing approach to amnesia*. New York: Academic Press.

Courville, C. (1955). *Effects of alcohol on the nervous system of man*. Los Angeles: San Lucas Press.

Damasio, A. (1979). The frontal lobes. In K. Heilman & E. Valenstein (Eds.), *Clinical neuropsychology*. New York: Oxford University Press.

Filskov, S., & Goldstein, S. (1974). Diagnostic validity of the Halstead-Reitan Neuropsychological Battery. *Journal of Consulting and Clinical Psychology, 42*, 328–388.

Gainotti, G. (1979). The relationship between emotions and cerebral dominance: A review of clinical and experimental evidence. In J. Gruzelier & P. FlorHenry (Eds.), *Hemispheric asymmetries of function in psychopathology*. New York: Elsevier.

Goldstein, G., & Shelly, C. (1980). Neuropsychological investigation of brain lesion localization in alcoholism. In H. Begleiter (Ed.), *Biological effects of alcohol*. New York: Plenum Press.

Hachinski, V., Lassen, N., & Marshall, J. (1974). Multi-infarct dementia: A cause of mental deterioration in the elderly. *Lancet, 2*, 207–210.

Hahn, R., Webster, B., Weikhardt, G., Thomas, E., Timberlake, W., Solomon, H., Stokes, J., Moore, J., Heyman, A., Gammon, G., Gleeson, G., Curtis, A., & Cutler, J. (1959). Penicillen treatment of general paresis (dementia paralytica). *Archives of Neurology and Psychiatry, 81*, 557–590.

Lishman, W. (1978). *Organic psychiatry: The psychological consequences of cerebral disorder*. London: Blackwell Scientific.

McClain, C., Potter, T., Krombout, T., & Zieve, T. (1984). The effect of lactulose on psychomotor performance in alcoholic cirrhotics without overt hepatic encephalopathy. *Journal of Clinical Gastroenterology, 6*, 325–329.

Milner, B., Corkin, S., & Teuber, H. (1968). Further analysis of the hippocampal amnestic syndrome: 14-year follow-up of H.M. *Neuropsychologica, 6*, 215–234.

Morrison, R., & Tarter, R. (1984). Neuropsychological findings relating to Capgras syndrome. *Biological Psychiatry, 19*, 1119–1128.

Ojemann, R., Fisher, C., Adams, R., Sercet, W., & Neiv, P. (1969). Further experience with the syndrome of "normal" pressure hydrocephalus. *Journal of Neurosurgery, 31,* 279–294.

Parkes, J., & Marsden, C. (1973). The treatment of Parkinson's disease. *British Journal of Hospital Medicine, 10,* 284–294.

Parsons, O., & Farr, S. (1981). The neuropsychology of alcohol and drug use. In S. Filskov & T. Boll (Eds.), *Handbook of clinical neuropsychology.* New York: Wiley.

Ryan, C., & Butters, N. (1980). Learning and memory impairments in young and old alcoholics: Evidence for the premature-aging hypothesis. *Alcoholism: Clinical and Experimental Research, 4,* 288–293.

Shah, K., Banks, G., & Merskey, H. (1969). Survival in atherosclerotic and senile dementia. *British Journal of Psychiatry, 115,* 1283–1286.

Sim, M., Turner, E., & Smith, W. (1966). Cerebral biopsy in the investigation of presenile dementia: I. Clinical aspects. *British Journal of Psychiatry, 112,* 119–125.

Talland, G. (1965). *Deranged memory.* New York: Academic Press.

Tarter, R. (1975). Psychological deficit in chronic alcoholics: A review. *International Journal of the Addictions, 10,* 327–368.

Tarter, R., & Alterman, A. (1984). Neuropsychological deficits in alcoholics: Etiological considerations. *Journal of Studies on Alcohol, 45,* 1–9.

Tarter, R., Hegedus, A., Van Thiel, D., Schade, R., Gavaler, J., & Starzl, T. (1984). Nonalcoholic cirrhosis associated with neuropsychological dysfunction in the absence of overt evidence of hepatic encephalopathy. *Gastroenterology, 86,* 1421–1427.

Victor, M., Adams, R., & Collins, G. (1971). *The Wernicke-Korsakoff syndrome.* Philadelphia: F. A. Davis.

Wilkinson, D., & Carlen, P. (1980a) Chronic organic brain syndromes associated with alcoholism: Neuropsychological and other aspects. In Y. Israel, F. Glaser, H. Kalant, R. Popham, W. Schmidt, & R. Smart (Eds.), *Research advances in alcohol and drug problems* (Vol. 6). New York: Plenum Press.

Wilkinson, D., & Carlen, P. (1980b). Chronic organic brain syndromes associated with alcoholism: Discrimination between groups of alcoholics. *Journal of Alcoholism, 41,* 129–139.

III

NONPSYCHIATRIC DISORDERS

8

Low Back Pain

STEVEN ZLUTNICK

Chronic pain problems are a major source of referrals for psychologists and other mental-health professionals in medical settings. Whether as a member of a liaison–consultation team, a pain clinic staff, or as a private consultant to a physician, the psychologist's role vis-à-vis medicine has changed markedly in the past decade. Although the *psychological* aspects of disease and illness have been acknowledged for centuries, the role of the psychologist in the treatment process has only recently emerged. With the application of behavioral technology, often developed by psychologists, to clinical medicine (Doleys, Meredith, & Ciminero, 1982; Ferguson & Taylor, 1981; Katz & Zlutnick, 1975), psychologists now find themselves in a major consulting position on the health care team in an environment brimming with vague terminology, muliple (often conflicting) diagnoses, and a plethora of treatment modalities, ranging from simple bed rest to life-threatening surgical procedures.

In this chapter, an attempt is made to review a number of issues with which psychologists must grapple, and that they must eventually master, in order to enhance their effectiveness in the assessment and/or management of patients who have chronic pain. These issues include (1) the role of the psychologist in the treatment of pain; (2) the skills necessary for successful entrée into the patient management routine; (3) familiarization with pertinent aspects of the medical chart; (4) an understanding of the differential diagnoses of low back pain; (5) the traditional treatment modalities for back pain, and (6) iatrogenic issues in the treatment of low back pain.

Low back pain has been selected as the illustrative kind of pain for a number of reasons. First, it is the most frequent pain problem encountered by pain and behavioral medicine services. Second, its treatment usually involves a number of diverse practitioners; thus, it serves as an excellent model for interdisciplinary collaboration. Third, with only a few exceptions (e.g., the ergotamines in the treatment of migraine), the medication regimens presented here are similar to those used for most pain problems. Finally, organic etiology and subsequent medical treatment are most commonly identified in low-back-pain patients compared to other kinds of pain patients.

Psychologists who are interested in other kinds of pain, such as abdominal, arthritic, and cancer pains, should educate themselves along similar dimensions presented here. This can be done by consulting with appropriate medical specialists, making use of medical libraries, and attending lectures and grand rounds at one's own academic-medical institution.

STEVEN ZLUTNICK • San Francisco Institute of Behavioral Medicine and Therapy, Garden Sullivan Hospital, 2750 Geary Boulevard, San Francisco, CA 94118, and the University of San Francisco, San Francisco, CA 94117.

THE ROLE OF THE PSYCHOLOGIST IN THE TREATMENT OF PAIN

Historically, psychologists have functioned as auxiliary health-care professionals, usually, though not always, under the supervision of a psychiatrist or a department of psychiatry. Although this arrangement remains the rule, the exceptions are growing, particularly in the area of chronic pain. With *multidisciplinary* as the catch word, chronic pain programs have proliferated, with treatment teams headed by a variety of health-care professionals, such as psychologists and members of other disciplines as well.

In spite of (or perhaps because of) this new state of affairs, psychologists, as well as those around them, are often unsure about the specifics of their role definition. The physician's role is clear: he or she makes *medical* decisions, that is, writes medical orders, chooses treatment modalities, and so on. The nursing role, though also changing, is similarly rather clear, including direct patient care and major responsibility to see that the medical decisions are implemented.

Although the emerging roll of the psychologist has yet to be clearly defined, what follows are some guidelines concerning professional activities that pertain primarily to the assessment and treatment of chronic pain patients.

The Psychologist as Therapist or Psychometrician

Although many psychologists practicing as clinicians see psychometrics as only a small part of their repertoire, the fact that many are still primarily involved with it has reinforced the notion of the psychologist as a psychometrician in the eyes of our medical colleagues. Thus, psychologists need to decide before entering the medical setting how they wish to be viewed. Although the utility of psychometrics in the assessment of chronic pain is debatable (see below), it is also difficult for one to push for therapeutic leadership when one's role is defined basically as being a psychometrician.

More important to the issue of role, however, is the nature of the pain phenomenon itself. For pain, regardless of its etiology, its neurochemical basis, and so on, is basically and foremost a *behavioral* phenomenon. Thus it is a uniquely *psychological* issue, one that the psychologist is *the most appropriately trained professional to manage.* Convincing other health-care professionals of the validity of this claim is another matter, of course. But it will never be addressed or accepted if psychologists as a group fail to articulate it to themselves and (tactfully) to others, first. If pain is seen primarily as *behavior* that needs to be modified, then the psychologist's role as *primary* care specialist begins to emerge. Psychologists have frequently abrogated their authority and their potential ability to lead and produce change in chronic pain populations by failing to assert their knowledge and expertise to medical colleagues. (See the section on psychological skills that follows.)

The Psychologist as Advocate

Although the fact is seldom mentioned, much of the chronic pain syndrome is iatrogenic (see "Iatrogenic Issues," below). The fact is that pain is the result of a complex interaction between individuals frequently under stress and a system that is frequently health-endangering (Shealy, 1976b). For a more extensive exposition of the issue of iatrogenics in medicine (see, for example, Illich, 1976). Much of the pain, depression, and anger seen in these patients is either caused or exacerbated by some combination of prolonged medication use, personal stress factors, lack of communication among treating professionals, repeated surgery in the absence of positive findings, and so on. Therefore, a major role for the psychologist—and, indeed, for the treatment team—is to serve as an *advocate* for patients and to help them deal more effectively with the system. To do so requires the ability to desensitize the patient to the often threatening notion of stress and its exacerbating effect on pain; to explain the mood-depressing and pain-enhancing effects of medications, as well as the frequent lack of agreement on diagnosis among physicians, and to convince the patient of the poor likelihood of success of repeated surgical procedures. However, if psychologists are to be successful in these endeavors, they must more clearly understand the criteria for the diagnosis of disease and, subsequently, for surgery; the *behavioral* effects of medications; and in general, the iatrogenic nature of chronic pain.

PSYCHOLOGICAL SKILLS REQUIRED FOR SYSTEM ENTRY

A number of specific skills are required if the psychologist is to successfully enter the complex medical system of the chronic pain patient. First and foremost among them is *assertion*. Particularly in light of the issue of advocacy, the psychologist must be assertive at a number of levels: to physicians, in general, who will question his or her ability or expertise in what is seen as the traditional purview of those who practice medicine; to psychiatrists, who frequently have defined the psychological aspects of disease as *their* area of expertise; to nonmedical personnel, who don't know whom to believe; and to patients and family, who will see the psychologist as just another doctor (the worst kind) who thinks they are "crazy."

A number of examples from this author's experience come to mind, from the seemingly innocuous and petty ones, such as having to instruct the switchboard operator to page the psychologist on the team as *Dr.* Smith instead of John Smith (in reality a subtle undermining of authority), to confronting physicians who have, with the best of intentions, prescribed narcotics to patients who were being *withdrawn* from medications as a part of their treatment.

As important as assertive skills is *a clear understanding of the basic principles of learning*. Nowhere in the area of clinical medicine are the principles of shaping, fading, discrimination, extinction, and so on more critical than in the rehabilitation of the chronic pain patient. Whether by not realizing that increased pain complaints during detoxification are an extinction "burst" (see Taylor, Zlutnick, Corley, & Flora, 1980; Zlutnick & Taylor, 1982), or by not knowing that the age-old physical-therapy strategy of "work till it hurts" is in reality a punishment paradigm (Fordyce, Fowler, & Lehmann, 1973), the psychologist who is ignorant of basic principles of learning compromises his or her effectivenesss in major ways. The rehabilitation process is clearly one of relearning. As the above examples illustrate, however, traditional treatment modalities for chronic pain are either poor approximations to or outright violations of basic learning principles.

Another important skill required for successful entry into the medical milieu is perhaps best described as *sociability*. Although terms like *multidisciplinary* are bandied about routinely in chronic pain settings, the fact is that if the psychologist accepts the role of therapist-advocate, he or she must deal effectively with a variety of health-care professionals, including physicians; nurses; physical, occupational, and activity therapists; ward clerks; pharmacists; and clergy. To accomplish this, one must be able to communicate effectively on a personal as well as a professional level with a large number of people with different goals, skills, and status. This requires a certain ease of sociability that, unfortunately, is not intrinsic to graduate training.

Last, but certainly not least, is *the ability to ask questions* (the corollary to this skill is *the ability to say "I don't know"*). There must be a critical balance between asserting one's abilities and knowing when to ask questions. In the long run, lack of information will decrease the psychologist's personal effectiveness and impede patient progress (the chronic pain patient thrives on mixed messages given in answer to unanswerable questions). Psychologists should never hesitate to pursue issues that they do not understand. Many professionals in the system will gladly share their knowledge. They should be identified early as resources and should be used regularly.

MEDICAL SYSTEM–HOSPITAL MECHANICS

When entering the hospital environment, the psychologist will encounter a number of levels of structure that must be understood and used appropriately. They include (1) admission–discharge and patient-care procedures and responsibilities; (2) the "pecking order" of personnel; and (3) the medical chart and how it functions.

Patient Responsibility

The ultimate responsibility for patient care rests with the physician. The psychologist may in many instances (depending on state law) *share* some portion of it. The fact remains that the major responsibility for care (and errors in care) rests with the physician. This fact permeates the atmosphere of the medical setting and will be felt at many levels by the psychologist. Rank does indeed have its privileges, and one of the privileges for bearing responsibility is power. Only when psychologists begin to experience this themselves will they understand the power (and limitations on it) of physicians. It is easy to give advice, but it is harder to take it when you alone bear the ultimate responsibility if something goes wrong. Psychologists should keep this in mind when advising their physician colleagues.

Similarly, a decision by psychologists to admit or discharge a patient (if they are in a position to affect these decisions) must again be borne by the attending physician. For all of these reasons, the psychologist must have a close working relationship with this physician (i.e., the physician who bears ultimate responsibility for the patient's care). Even in a multidisciplinary team involving many physicians, generally only one assumes primary responsibility.

Status

Although the physician assumes primary responsibility for the patient, *all personnel* are critical in the management of the chronic pain patient. To forget this fact is an error with frequently irreversible consequences. The management of a staff of varied health-care professionals is no different from other management situations. If the group is not cohesive, and if all individuals in the group are not attended to, the product or goal (patient improvement) will not be realized. For example, trying to treat a pain patient without the cooperation of nursing is like trying to get through graduate shcool without knowing the secretary. (It is possible, but not without enormous difficulty.) The same applies to the clerk who answers the phone, finds doctors, arranges transportation, takes care of paperwork, and so on, as well as to all other ancillary personnel. In short, although status may be of sociological as well as personal interest, there is no level that the psychologist can afford to ignore without serious consequences to the treatment plan.

The Medical Chart

The medical chart is the place where treatment is coordinated as well as documented. It is ironic that psychologists, who staunchly espouse data and their importance, are often the ones most ignorant of the medical chart and how it is used. Although the order frequently varies, most charts contain the following sections of special interest in the management of pain patients:

History and Physical. This is usually completed by the attending physician (or her or his *house officer,* i.e., intern or resident) and includes presenting complaints, history of medical problems, some social context, diagnosis, review of systems (and findings), and impressions. From the psychologist's perspective, the most important aspects of this document are the *diagnosis* and the *clinical impressions.* The diagnosis is critical because the patient is, in all probability, expecting one. As the advocate, the psychologist will often be called on to deal with the patient concerning the diagnosis (either what it means or why there isn't one). In any event, the patient will, in all probability, receive some input from the physician, and the psychologist needs to be prepared to discuss it. At this point, it is imperative to note that no clinician should *ever* see a patient without first reviewing the chart and talking with staff. Walking in ''blind'' to visit a pain patient invites ambiguity of communication resulting in loss of effectiveness in his or her management (Corley & Zlutnick, 1981).

The *review of systems* will often provide the psychologist with additional information on the diagnostic process, discussed at length below. Similarly, under clinical impressions, the physicians will often share their views on the problem, including psychological bias or misunderstandings, which, inevitably, are communicated to the patient. Examples include statements like ''I do not believe that this is real pain'', or ''The complaints were out of proportion to the findings.'' Conversely, diagnostic ''red flags'' may also be raised, such as ''I think the possibility of malignancy has been overlooked'' or ''I find no evidence of myelogram, which should be routine in a case of this kind.''

Progress Notes. The manner in which progress notes are arranged varies greatly but usually includes sections for doctors' progress, nursing progress, consultants, and some combination or permutation of them all. In some very progressive institutions, all progress notes are combined in problem-oriented record (POR) fashion (Katz & Wooley, 1975; Weed, 1969). In this author's experience, however, a truly integrated POR (i.e., including all notes in the same section) is rare.

The most common errors made in reviewing these notes are either (1) not reading them at all or (2) reading only the doctor's progress and the consultant notes (usually from other physicians). The most serious consequence of this error is missing out on the wealth of excellent behavioral observations usually to be found in nursing progress notes. In our own experience, few clinicians at any level match experienced rehabilitation nurses for completeness, clarity, and precision of charting.

Medical Orders. Usually in the front of the chart, these orders document all current medications and procedures. From this portion of the chart, it is possible to tell the kinds of medications that have been and are being tried, as well as diagnostic procedures under consideration. In some institutions, separate records are kept for the administration of narcotics, and the clinician should become familiar with the institution's procedures.

Previous Records. No amount of history taking can fully account for all information needed for an accurate assessment of chronic pain patients. The psychologist needs to read *all* previous records and also ascertain whether previous records have even been collected. Critical information for reliability as well as for proper diagnosis is often buried in these records. Institutions vary as to whether this information is placed in the current chart, kept at the nurses' station, or stored in the medical records department.

DIFFERENTIAL DIAGNOSIS OF BACK PAIN (PSYCHOLOGICAL)

Theoretically, the psychologist will be asked to intervene in the care of a patient at a number of points in treatment: (1) shortly after an appropriate interval of time, during which an injury would be expected to heal; (2) before major invasive procedures such as surgery; and (3) when the condition is chronic, and all avenues of treatment have failed.

In the first instance (e.g., 12 weeks after a lumbosacral strain), psychologists (or any mental-health practitioners) are rarely consulted, except by physicians who routinely refer and have a history of successful collaboration. If the patient is seen this early in the pain process (i.e., if the patient is *not yet chronic*), psychological intervention in the form of self-control procedures such as relaxation, biofeedback, and the like, coupled with problem solving around stress issues, is usually quite successful.

In the second category of intervention, however, psychologists continue in the role of the psychometrician, in an effort to predict successful outcome of surgical procedures. The continued attempt by psychologists to offer psychological testing as a solution to the very important question of patient selection and treatment, despite lack of clear empirical support (see, for example, Pheasant, Gilbert, & Goldfarb, 1979) remains an enigma. In fact, successful outcome in surgery can already be predicted rather accurately and will be discussed at length later in this chapter. In addition, those psychological factors that may add to prediction of outcome, such as compensation, reinforcement for ''sick'' role behavior, and avoidance of unpleasant issues and activities, are unlikely to be illuminated by current testing methods. For example, the administration of the Minnesota Multiphasic Personality Inventory (MMPI) typically elicits the classic elevated triad of hypochondriasis, depression, and hysteria. Do we really need to accrue the added expense of psychological testing in order to discover that pain patients are depressed and suggestible and that they somaticize their complaints? It is far more likely that a thorough interview and behavioral assessment (Barlow, 1981) with corroboration from a family member would more accurately assess these issues.

Other variables that have recently been studied, but that are generally ignored in presurgical pain populations, include information and modeling. Kolouch (1974), for example, found that knowing the name of one's surgeon, coupled with information about expected postsurgical symptoms, greatly reduced both requests for pain-reducing medications and length of stay postsurgically. These findings were, in many ways, precursors of the more experimentally controlled findings of Melamed, Robbins, and Fernandez (1982) and of Melamed, Robbins, and Graves (1982), who demonstrated the utility of coping models in postsurgical adjustment.

It is in the last category, however, that psychologists are most frequently consulted, namely, for chronic pain that has been treated extensively to no avail. At this point, a number of diagnostic issues present themselves. First is the definition of chronic pain. Zlutnick and Taylor (1982) have defined chronic pain according to the following criteria:

1. Pain for at least 6 months or longer
2. Pain is out of proportion to physical (organic) findings, or physical findings are absent (static)
3. The patient is dependent on analgesic or hypnosedative medications
4. Depression
5. Dramatic reduction in activities
6. Polysurgical (numerous surgeries, such as laminectomies)
7. Polyphysician (has seen numerous physicians over time)
8. Sleep disorder
9. Anger directed at physicians and often returned by them

Most professionals who have encountered these patients have little difficulty in accepting the above criteria; the problem seems to be the other issues that frequently arise in conceptualizing the case: malingering, the diagnosis of "psychogenic pain" (somatoform disorder), and theoretically biased notions such as conversion. However, unless one can prove a history of lying or can produce continued contradictory somatic complaints, the issue of malingering is seldom viable. Similarly, compensation factors, although often present, have seldom been demonstrated *empirically*. It is easy to assume that, because a patient is receiving disability, he or she is being reinforced for remaining ill. Our experience, however, has shown that, although this may be true in some instances, in general, maintaining the lifestyle of a chronic pain patient for disability payments is hard, grueling work; most patients, when presented with viable alternatives (*after* the successful completion of a pain program), are quite open to them. Finally, Zlutnick and Taylor (1982) previously addressed the difficulties with the somatoform diagnosis, including the difficulty in determining empirical relationships between psychological factors and the occurrence of pain problems.

Ultimately, diagnosis is supposed to facilitate treatment; unfortunately, in the current health system, it usually encourages pejorative views of patients and a cumbersome relabeling process, often in psychological, as well as medical, terms. What needs to be assessed, however, are the following categories of patient characteristics, some of which may be incompatible with successful outcome:

1. Serious psychological disturbance, such as schizophrenia or manic-depressive illness, with incidental pain complaints (Zlutnick & Taylor, 1982). Unless the pain

clinic or consultation service functions in conjunction with inpatient psychiatry, appropriate management of these patients is unlikely.

2. Chronic organic brain syndromes, especially those associated with the elderly, as well as elderly patients *per se*. Organicity that is not solely a function of over-medication will seriously interfere with a successful (psychological) rehabilitation process. Further, although there is a paucity of cost-effectiveness and outcome data in chronic pain treatment, current studies (Patterson, 1983) indicate that elderly patients (over 60 years old) fare less well than their younger counterparts in pain clinic treatment.

3. Patients with antisocial personality disorders who have discovered "pain" as a legitimate source of drugs. For obvious reasons, this group is unlikely to cooperate or to fare well in treatment.

4. Current (or multiple past) litigation around disability. Although this may not automatically rule out treatment of disability cases, patients seeking to increase benefits or settlements seldom make good candidates for treatment.

5. Multiple sites of pain. The more numerous the sites of pain, particularly when they do not follow an expected neurological distribution, the less likely patients are to experience improvement (Patterson, 1983).

6. Unwillingness of the patient and/or his or her physician to acknowledge the necessity for detoxification from all analgesic and hypnosedative medications. There has been virtually unanimous consensus among researchers and clinicians that improvement is highly unlikely without the elimination of medications.

7. Work skills and level of job satisfaction with work before disability. Common sense, as well as clinical experience, dictates that dissatisfied and unhappy workers are less likely to return to work.

8. The extent to which the patient possesses a repertoire for beginning a new career if unable to return to her or his preinjury occupation (i.e., education, experience, resources, and problem-solving abilities).

9. Early onset of full-time employment responsibilities (often in teen-age years) often resulting in a 15- to 30-year work history at the time of injury. Many injured workers who show such histories often have the conviction that they have more than earned their "retirement."

10. Knowledge of workers' compensation laws (if applicable), including the difference between disability and handicap. Many patients confuse their unwillingness to return to work with disability.

11. Knowledge about the relevant disease and the criteria for surgery. Patients must be educated about these issues if we are to expect them to withdraw themselves from the medical system.

12. Attitude toward stress (awareness of their own stressors) and its relationship to illness. Patients need to be properly educated in this area if they are to accept psychologically based interventions (i.e., the pain clinic approach).

13. Areas of stress that exacerbate pain complaints, such as marital difficulties and social isolation. The standard assessment of behavior for the purpose of developing a treatment plan includes an assessment of the patient's support system (family, friends, and so on).

In summary, for psychologists to be effective in terms of treatment, they must address assessment of those variables that are related to the syndrome. Because many contemporary psychological testing and diagnostic procedures fail to do this, they serve little purpose in effecting therapeutic change.

DIFFERENTIAL DIAGNOSIS OF BACK PAIN (PHYSIOLOGICAL)

In order to better understand the problems that chronic-back-pain patients encounter, and to enhance the understanding of the diagnosis of back disease, a brief review of the anatomy of the back is in order. Although it is in no way intended as a complete review, it should aid in understanding the medical diagnostic process. (See especially Finneson, 1980; Smith, Murphy, Blair, & Lowe, 1983.)

The vertebral column is formed by a series of 33 vertebrae: from top to bottom, there are 7 cervical (Cl–C7), 12 thoracic (Tl–T12), 5 lumbar (Ll–L5), 5 sacral (Sl–S5), and 4 coccygeal vertebrae. The cervical, thoracic, and lumbar are all distinct and separate and are considered the "true" vertebrae. The adult sacral and coccygeal vertebrae are fused with each other to form two bones, the sacrum and the coccyx.

A lateral view of the column would reveal three "curves," which are identified by the predominant region in which they occur: the cervical curve (Cl–T2), the thoracic curve (T2–T12) and the lumbar curve (T12 to the lumbosacral articulation). The pelvic curve begins at the lumbosacral joint and terminates at the end of the coccyx.

The *intervertebral disc* is a type of cartilaginous joint that connects one vertebra to another. These discs contribute one third of the overall length to the lumbar spine (i.e., L1–L5), and in the remainder of the entire vertebral column, make up just a bit more than one fifth of the overall length. They are commonly referred to as the *shock absorbers* of the spine.

The lumbar vertebrae are heavier than the other vertebrae, and their primary purpose is *weight-bearing*. They also make up a disproportionate 25% of the total length of the spine. Because of their anatomical design, the lower (e.g., L4, L5, and Sl) nerve roots are more vulnerable to compression from a protruding or ruptured disc. It is this primary weight-bearing role of the lumbar spine, coupled with its striking difference in bone-to-disc ratio, that accounts for the unique characteristics of lumbar disc disease. These "diseases," *whose etiology is frequently unknown* (Finneson, 1980), are described below in somewhat ascending order of severity.

Acute Lumbosacral Strain

This is frequently referred to as a *wastebasket diagnosis* because of its lack of diagnostic meaning without other clinical or laboratory findings. It may be a precursor to disc disease (or its identification), nerve root irritation, malignancies, and so on.

Signs and Symptoms. This syndrome usually presents as mildly irritating rather than disabling. It is often described as stiffness of the low back, usually worse on one side, with localized pain. Muscle spasms are frequently reported. However, as most patients tend to attempt routine activities, which, in turn, greatly exacerbate muscle spasm, many soon present as completely incapacitated.

Etiology. The cause of this problem is usually an injury resulting from heavy lifting (often from an anatomically poor position); trauma, such as a blow to the back; or falls, in which the lower back musculature is strained.

Laboratory Findings. X rays are usually normal. Other diagnostic tests (e.g., electromyelograms, discography) are not routine at this time.

Differential Diagnosis. Patients with lumbosacral strain sometimes complain of a radiating pain that is often confused with sciatic pain, falsely indicating disc disease (see later). Other issues need to be ruled out over time, as well, including spinal tuberculosis, metabolic bone disease, and spinal tumors.

Prognosis. Barring additional injury or trauma, and given responsiveness to conservative care (see below), improvement should be expected in 2 to 12 weeks.

Chronic Lumbosacral Strain

This disorder retains the reputation as a wastebasket diagnosis, perhaps even more because symptoms of the acute phase have persisted. It is frequently referred to as the most common low back problem encountered in medical practice (Finneson, 1980).

Signs and Symptoms. The symptoms of this disorder vary greatly. By the chronic phase, the pattern is frequently one of long intervals of mild discomfort marked by severe exacerbation of pain. In addition to pain, patients generally complain of fatigue, despite adequate sleep. A "tired feeling" is sometimes described in lieu of pain. Muscle spasm is often noted on examination, but reflex, sensation, and straight-leg-raising tests are usually normal.

Etiology. The cause of this condition is uncertain. Although a history of a fall or trauma may be elicited at examination, some history of discomfort usually precedes it. This is somewhat paradoxical, as many chronic-low-back patients with a diagnosis of chronic lumbosacral strain attribute their continued problems to some initial trauma. This subgroup of patients are frequently receiving benefits from workers' compensation, and this fact should be noted during assessment.

This population is often over 35 years old and overweight. Posture is often poor, and musculature is atonic and flabby. Not surprisingly, this condition is often referred to as the *Flabby Back Syndrome* (Wilkinson, 1983).

Laboratory Findings. Laboratory findings remain negative for this syndrome. Routine procedures include standard laboratory studies, and X rays of the lumbar and thoracic spine.

Differential Diagnosis. At this stage, a number of diseases must be ruled out, including rectal or pelvic disease, osteoarthritis, spondylolisthesis, inflammatory spondylitis, inflammatory and degenerative arthritis, and malignancy.

Prognosis. Because of the relatively few physical findings in clinical or laboratory workups, psychological factors are a key issue in prognosis. Motivation to engage in appropriate exercise, weight loss, and general reconditioning is frequently low. Stress factors are usually present and need to be carefully assessed. This population is highly at risk for the chronic pain syndrome, and early intervention with a multidisciplinary approach to treatment is required (Fordyce, 1976; Zlutnick & Taylor, 1982).

Lumbar Disc Disease

As the overwhelming majority of low-back-pain patients are diagnosed as having involvement at the lumbar levels of the spine, other categories such as cervical disc disease are not included here. The reader is referred to the literature in this and other areas. Further, although other disc diseases are mentioned under "Differential Diagnosis," it is the problem of herniation, or bulging, that is, in the majority of cases, at issue in chronic-low-back patients seen on consultation or in the pain clinic.

Herniation (Rupture) or Protrusion. In the treatment of chronic pain patients, the issue, or in many cases the specter, of disc disease is raised continually. In fact, the overwhelming majority of chronic-back-pain patients have sustained at least one major surgical procedure for the disc disease by the time they are seen in a pain clinic (Shealy, 1976b). What strikes the psychologist most clearly is that most of these procedures are tried as amelioration of either corroborated or suspected disc disease. Because of this fact, some understanding of the diagnostic criteria not only for the diagnosis, but for *the decision-making process leading to surgical intervention*, is critical when one attempts to decipher the (often) inevitable course of the chronic-low-back patient. As noted earlier, the information to follow is meant only to attempt to clarify procedures, and should in no way be construed as a definitive review of diagnosis in orthopedics.

Disc disease essentially entails *nerve root compression*, either by *disc rupture* (or protrusion) or *nerve root entrapment* (spinal stenosis). By far, the most common form of disc disease under consideration is the chronic-low-back-pain patient is rupture or protrusion, and these will therefore be the primary focus of discussion here. As noted, there are two kinds of disc pathology: *protrusions* and *herniations*. In a protrusion, the nucleus pulposus, or the material in the core of the disc, protrudes (frequently described as *bulging*) through the annulus, a dense fibrocartilaginous ring or envelope for the nucleus pulposus. In some cases, the annulus may actually break or tear (rupture), and the nucleus material may actually extrude into the spinal canal. In either case, a nerve root, because of its proximity, may become compressed, with subsequent signs ranging from irritation to loss of function (McLaughlin, 1982).

Signs and Symptoms. Foremost in the class of patients with lumbar disc disease is a preexisting history of low back pain. Interestingly, this fact is often overlooked, as most of these patients attribute the problem to trauma (see "Etiology," following). One of the most characteristic aspects of this group is the *intermittent* nature of pain episodes. Even more significant is the presence of *sciatica*, experienced as severe pain in the leg along the sciatic nerve felt at the back of the thigh and running down the inside of the leg (Finneson, 1980; Thomas, 1983). Other frequently reported symptoms include *paresthesia* of the leg or foot (a sensation of numbness, prickling, or tingling), muscle spasm, leg buckling because of pain and/or weakness, and increased pain with standing or walking, sitting, bending, and stooping (Finneson, 1980). The low back pain may be a sharp or dull ache, and the radiating (i.e., sciatic) pain may be electrical or shocklike in nature. Further, the radicular pain (i.e., nerve root pain, though to be caused by nerve root compression in a ruptured or protruding disc) of acute disc herniation is markedly exacerbated by movement that increases abdominal pressure, such as coughing, sneezing, and straining during bowel movements (Whitehill, 1982).

A number of maneuvers by the examining physician are designed to elicit the above symptoms and appear frequently in medical reports:

1. The *straight-leg-raising test*, where the leg is actively or passively raised with the knee extended. With nerve root tension, radicular pain is elicited.
2. *Lasègue's maneuver*, in which the thigh is flexed on the trunk with the knee bent. The knee is then extended up. With nerve root tension, this movement produces radicular pain.
3. The *head-lift test* (Kernig's sign), where the head is raised with the leg at the top of a straight leg raise. With nerve root tension, this movement produces radicular pain.
4. The *foot flex*, where flexion of the foot with the leg at the extreme of straight-leg raising produces radicular pain.

Straight-leg raising and Lasègue maneuver are considered positive for nerve root entrapment (disc disease) only if they produce radicular pain. If radicular pain is elicited by either of these maneuvers, it should be aggravated by either the foot-flex or the head-lift movement. With the knees bent, foot flexion should not produce pain, even with nerve root entrapment (Finneson, 1980; Whitehill, 1982).

Etiology. It is perhaps in discussion of the etiology of lumbar disc disease that much of the difficulty surrounding diagnosis in general and workers' compensation in particular arises. It is frequently assumed that a herniated disc is caused by trauma. Yet, on review of the contemporary literature on low back pain, one cannot help but be struck by the fact that many clinicians (e.g., Finneson, 1980; Spengler, 1982) seriously doubt, if not outright reject, this hypothesis. As Finneson (1980) noted:

> On the basis of our present understanding of the pathophysiology of lumbar disc disease, a single episode of trauma may be a precipitating, but rarely a causative factor. Augmenting this reasoning, if sufficient stress is applied to the spine, a fracture of the bony elements will occur before any damage is done to the disc. Furthermore, it is often minor episodes of trauma, such as picking a light object up off the floor or bending forward over a sink to wash one's face, that often precipitate a severe attack. (p. 209)

Interestingly enough, of 1,000 consecutive cases analyzed by Finneson (1980), 764 alleged that trauma was the direct cause of, or played a significant role in, the development of their symptom. Of these, 343 were involved in some form of compensation situation. Of these 343, *100%* gave a history of trauma as the precipitating event in their "disc disease."

Whatever the cause, the two most commonly encountered sites of lumbar disc disease are at the L5–S1 and L4–L5 levels (Finneson, 1980). In the classic paper by Mixter and Barr (1934), the basic pathophysiology of lumbar disc disease was described as protrusions or rupture of the protective envelope of the disc nucleus (i.e., the annulus). Nonetheless, the specific reasons for protrusion or herniation of the annulus of the disc remain speculative at this time.

Laboratory Findings. In addition to the presence of sciatica, the other variables required for a formal diagnosis of this disorder are as follows: (1) positive findings on the EMG, or electromyogram, which is the graphic record of the contraction of a muscle as a result of electrical stimulation; this is often combined with the electrical measurement of motor and sensory nerve conduction velocity; and (2) confirmation of clinical and EMG findings by any one of a number of roentgenographic procedures (Green, 1980), including myelogram, computerized body tomography (referred to alternately as CBT, CAT, or CT scan), and nuclear magnetic resonance (NMR) imaging. These procedures involve the injection of some type of matter that reveals abnormalities via contrast on the X ray. The CT scan, now that its cost has been brought into line with roentgenographic techniques, has revolutionized diagnosis with its often superior accuracy and noninvasiveness, particularly in light of the false positives in myelography, which have been reported to be at 25% to 35% (Finneson, 1980; Shealy, 1976b). Myelography is an invasive procedure, whose most common side effect is headache, often severe, which may occur within hours or even days of the procedure. These tests essentially confirm the clinical impression of nerve root compression.

Anesthetic Blocks—Diagnostic. Although anesthetic blocks are used extensively for therapeutic purposes, relatively few of the procedures are used diagnostically. Experience shows, however, that the distinction between the diagnostic and the therapeutic use of these blocks is often retrospective. Essentially, diagnostic decisions are based on the pain-relieving effects of analgesic agents injected into a variety of sites. These sites are frequently categorized as the *trigger point* (or local tender areas), the *facet nerve*, the *differential spinal*, and the *differential epidural*. The agents used most commonly are lidocaine (Xylocaine), bupivacaine (Marcaine), mepivacaine (Carbocaine), and procaine (Novocaine), used individually and in combination.

Anesthetic injections into local tender areas are used to determine the presence of trigger points (or areas of focal, extreme tenderness, usually located at the sites of ligamentous attachments to bones) and fasciitis (areas of focal tenderness in the lumbar or gluteal regions). They are also useful in diagnosing other focal pain problems such as ischiogluteal bursitis ("pain in the arse"—see Swarthout & Compere, 1974), painful neuromas (tumors composed of nerve cells), and coccygodynia (pain in the coccygeal region).

Anesthetic injections into facet nerves and joints aid in the diagnosis of the facet syndrome. The facet joints permit gliding movements in the spine. When these joints are put under abnormal strain (e.g., because of disc rupture or degeneration), their normal angle of movement is changed, and the result is the painful condition of facet syndrome. Facet injections may also be useful in documenting fusion-related causes of low back pain.

The most common diagnostic use of these anesthetic blocks, however, is in the *differential spinal blockade* (Winnie, 1978). This procedure is designed to sequentially block nerves of increasingly larger-sized nerve fibers, because pain sensitivity has been conclusively linked to this variable (Gasser & Erlanger, 1929). Basically, this procedure involves the use of four or five separate consecutive injections with increased amounts of anesthetic agent administered in each injection. Patients are questioned about the amount and location of their pain before, during, and after each injection. The first injection is placebo (10 ml of normal saline); since 30% of patients are placebo responders (Spengler, 1982). If most or all of the pain disappears after this injection, the patient is considered a placebo responder, and the test is aborted. Because of the high percentage of placebo reaction in all patients, this is the least useful response that can be obtained diagnostically.

The second injection is comprised of 5 ml of 0.25% level procaine and 5 ml of normal saline. Relief at this level indicates sympathetic causes and predicts positive effects of the treatment of causalgias (reflex sympathetic dystrophy).

The third injection contains 5 ml of 0.50% procaine and 5 ml of normal saline. Relief at this level (sensory) may indicate that the mechanism is still considered somatic, with an elevated sensory threshold.

The fourth injection contains 5 ml of 1% procaine with 5 ml of saline and involves blockade at all levels (i.e., sympathetic, sensory, and motor) and should, if the mechanism of pain is somatic, produce near or total relief. Failure to provide relief at this level is indicative of a lesion higher in the central nervous system than the level of spinal anesthesia (unlikely), psychogenic pain, or malingering.

Although the accuracy of all four levels is somewhat in question, in general, failure to report pain relief by the fourth injection is considered grounds for serious consideration of lack of physiological basis for pain.

Differential epidural blocks are virtually identical to differential spinals, except that the drugs are injected sequentially into the epidural space. This procedure is used when the spinal block is contraindicated. However, because of the slower onset of effect from injection into the epidural space, this procedure is significantly longer and less preferred.

Differential Diagnosis. Essential to differential diagnosis in this instance are the relatively fixed and rigid requirements for *acceptance* of the diagnosis. These are clearly specified in the diagnostic literature, and few exceptions are ever noted (Carron, 1982; Finneson, 1980; Whitehill, 1982; Wilkinson, 1983). They include:

1. The presence of sciatic pain, usually more severe than low back pain
2. Abnormal EMG findings
3. Positive Lasègue's sign
4. Neurological deficits (paresthesia, etc.)
5. Pain reduced by immobilization (e.g., traction or body cast)
6. Clear confirmation of the above by myelogram, CT scan, or NMR

Similarly, negative factors, or those that tend to preclude the diagnosis of disc disease, include:

1. Back pain as the primary complaint
2. Gross obesity (flabby back syndrome)
3. Nonorganic signs and symptoms (the entire leg is numb, etc.)
4. History of previous or concurrent litigation
5. Poor psychological functioning

Other issues to be considered in differential diagnosis include misdiagnosed neoplasms, "flabby back syndrome" (chronic lumbosacral strain), arthritic conditions, and spondylitic syndromes. However, what cannot be stressed too strongly, particlarly in regard to surgical intervention (see below), are the requirements listed above for acceptance of the diagnosis.

Prognosis. It is probably the prognosis of disc disease that again seems to confound and greatly affect the care of chronic low-back-pain patients. These patients, and frequently their neuro- or orthopedic surgeons, are convinced that (1) they have disc disease, and (2) that it automatically follows that surgery is the solution. As noted above, the "true" diagnosis of disc disease is often lacking in these patients, and this fact coupled with other issues (compensation and psychological factors) clearly militate against surgical intervention. Further, as will be seen below, surgery is often contraindicated *even in the presence of all necessary diagnostic criteria.* The best discussion of prognosis, however, requires an understanding of the evolving treatment strategies for suspected or diagnosed disease. These strategies are described below.

TREATMENT OF CHRONIC LOW BACK PAIN

The treatment of chronic low back pain from a medical perspective involves a regimen that, freely translated, retains the Hippocratic caution to "Above all, do no harm." Treatment begins conservatively and progresses up to a continuum of modalities (e.g., bed rest, heat and cold, traction, massage, exercise, orthosis, biofeedback or relaxation, medication, anesthetic blocks, and surgery). It should be remembered that, in terms of the chronic low-back-pain patient with multiple surgeries, more than 90% of all patients who complain of low back pain with or without sciatica improve without surgical intervention (Spengler, 1982). Thus, a compendium of procedures antecedent to surgery is presented here. Although some attempt has been made at temporal estimates of adequate clinical trials, basically the use of all the following methods is determined by clinical judgment and patient responsiveness.

Regulated Inactivity

Rest. Without question, the simplest treatment for low-back-pain complaints is reduced activity. This ranges typically from a reduced work and/or activity schedule to complete bed rest. Although activity in the form of exercise is also frequently prescribed, many practitioners believe bed rest to be superior early in treatment. Obvious activities such as heavy lifting and prolonged bending, stooping, sitting, and standing are severely curtailed. Walking and climbing stairs are likewise prohibited. If such a reduction in activity does not provide relief of symptoms, bed rest is usually prescribed for a period of 10 days to 2 weeks.

Bed rest is usually accomplished at home, although on rare occasions, or at later stages of treatment, in the hospital (along with traction; see the following). Generally, the flat supine position is less effective in providing relief than is a position of slight lumbar flexion, sometimes referred to as the *semi-Fowler's position*. If bed rest is used in the hospital setting, the use of bed pans are usually discouraged because it aggravates low back strain. Bed rest is most helpful in patients with low back pain but may help to alleviate leg pain as well.

A variable of some significance is the mattress to be used. A sagging or soft mattress does not permit proper alignment of the back and can cause tension and possibly spasm. A firm mattress is required, or boards may be inserted under the mattress to increase firmness.

A number of limitations and contraindications are associated with prolonged bed rest. They include the potential for muscle atrophy, circulatory complications, lack of motivation, and reinforcement of the sick role. Thus, although bed rest frequently alleviates back pain in acute cases, it is contraindicated in cases of chronic low back pain, as a variety of factors mitigate its success. These include chronicity, muscle atrophy, and medication effects.

Traction. The precise reasons that traction is useful in the treatment of low back pain are conjectural at best, and many writers have essentially dismissed it as a major therapeutic technique (Finneson, 1980; McLaughlin, 1982). Nonetheless, two types of traction are frequently used in the management of low back pain: *pelvic traction* and *hanging traction*, either upright or inverted. Many clinicians seem to feel that traction is most useful in enforcing bed rest in otherwise noncompliant patients, thus establishing a usefulness independent of the original intent. More detailed explanations of traction may be found in other sources (e.g., Wilkinson, 1983).

Again the use of traction is indicated in the acute phase of pain management, and even then, its effectiveness is questionable. In cases of chronic pain, traction is seldom, if ever, considered.

Limitations and contraindications for traction include the fact that, in some patients, the procedure consistently exacerbates the pain. Leg traction in particular may prove to be a problem because it is more likely to cause sciatic stretching, therefore aggravating sciatic pain and potentially causing damage to nerves. The chance of venous thromboembolism is also increased with leg traction.

Regulated Activity

Orthosis. Orthotic devices for low back pain include primarily the use of back supports, corsets, or braces, although in the case of legs of unequal length, the shoe lift is occasionally prescribed. In general, the utility of back braces has been questioned, because most do not immobilize any segment of the spine, including, most significantly, the lumbar spine (McLaughlin, 1982; Norton &Brown, 1957). Nonetheless, symptomatic relief has been reported, partly because the braces remind patients to limit their activity (Wilkinson, 1983). Corsets and girdles provide more back support than lumbar or lumbosacral belts.

Back supports, like the other previously described methods, are most useful in patients with acute pain presentation. Further, these supports (as well as, on rarer occasions, the use of body casts) are often used *diagnostically* to reinforce the contention that pain relief by this means is predictive of relief through spinal fusion (see below).

Limitations and contraindications for these devices, particularly with prolonged use, include progressive muscle weakness and potential aggravation of arthritic stiffness, as well as dependency on devices of questionable utility.

Exercise—General

Most clinicians are in agreement that exercise is useful for individuals with low back pain, particularly after a sufficient trial of bed rest and/or reduced activity. Surprisingly, most sports are possible for patients with low back pain, although a few are clearly more therapeutic and less apt to exacerbate symptoms, such as swimming and bicycling. Swimming has been proved extremely effective because most movement in water is therapeutic, as is immersion in general. Bicycling is also tolerated well by most patients. Although exercise frequently follows a trial of bed rest, it is often also recommended early in the acute phase. Although seemingly contradictory to the notion of bed rest, the choice of exercise seems more embedded in the physician's clinical judgment of the patient.

Exercise—Therapeutic

Although activity in general is useful and adaptive, a specific program of back limbering and strengthening exercise is critical in the rehabilitation of both acute and chronic conditions. Although the specifics of these exercises vary from therapist to therapist and from center to center, the way in which they are performed and maintained is far more important to outcome than subtle variations in form.

It is with the chronic-low-back-pain patient, however, that exercise becomes most critical in rehabilitation. Because many of these patients have been told that they will have pain for the rest of their lives and have likewise been cautioned against too much activity (during the acute phase), they become progressively nonfunctional. Slowly deteriorating both psychologically as well as physically, over months and often years, they present with decreased muscle strength and tone, decreased range of motion, considerable weight gain, and poor posture—precisely the conditions under which most activity becomes painful. At this point, it becomes difficult to evaluate their abilities objectively and to separate physical from motivational impediments. Thus, a program of both general and therapeutic exercise is the *sine qua non* of chronic pain rehabilitation.

Topical and Transcutaneous Therapy

A number of noninvasive therapies are applied cutaneously (to the skin) and include thermal or radiant energy (heat), cryotherapy (cold), and massage. Heat, in whatever form, is usually used for analgesic and muscle-relaxing purposes. Thus, it also may be helpful with muscle spasm. Heat may be provided by a number of modalities, including ultrasound and diathermy, radiant energy (chronic phases) for deep muscle penetration, whirlpool baths (acute phase) for relaxation, and hydrocollator packs, a method of conductive heat. Infrared heating, using an incandescent bulb with a reflector, is another form of heat therapy. In the home setting, topical heat application can be provided by a heating pad or by hot baths, although dry heat does not appear to have the penetrating ability of moist heat. Cautions or contraindications to heat usually apply to overuse, with resultant cutaneous burns.

Although most of the topical procedures are effective in reducing pain complaints (i.e., they produce analgesia) for acute episodes, the heat procedures in particular are also useful adjuncts to the withdrawal procedures during detoxification. This is probably due to their somewhat sedative effects, and should be considered for this reason when treating chronic pain patients.

Therapeutic cold seems to have a strong therapeutic effect in acute low back pain. Because it produces vasoconstriction, it appears to penetrate tissue deeper than heat, producing various degrees of analgesia. It is also helpful, of course, in swelling and muscle spasm. There are a variety of methods of application, including immersion, cold packs, ice massage, and fluoromethane spray. Contraindications include use with arthritic patients, and caution must be used to avoid tissue damage and, in some rare cases with chemical sprays, frostbite.

Massage is a centuries-old remedy for many complaints, and its usefulness, like that of some forms of heat, is often seen as deriving from its sedative effects. In addition to massage professionals and physical therapists, almost anyone in the patient's environment can be used as a therapeutic agent. Frequently used methods include stroking (effleurage), kneading (pétrissage), friction (grottement), and percussion (tapotement), where the area is tapped, clapped, or beaten (McLaughlin, 1982). Caution must be used with any method of this sort, and overall increased pain complaints generally lead to termination.

Transcutaneous electrical nerve stimulation (TNS or TENS) involves passing a small electric current thorough the skin at an intensity that elicits a tingling or buzzing sensation. It should be noted that it's specific mode of action is not understood, although current explanations include Melzack and Wall's (1965) gate-control hypothesis and endorphin stimulation. Nonetheless, its noninvasive aspect, coupled with its ease of portability, has made it a useful and common adjunct in pain management. As with most therapies described to this point, however, its effectiveness appears best with acute pain and diminishes over time and application with chronic pain patients. Thus, it is not uncommon in a chronic pain setting to interview a patient with his or her TENS unit turned to its maximum setting with little or no relief.

Acupuncture, both in classic and electrical forms, appears to produce analgesia in similar, if not identical, ways as TENS. Patients who respond to one technique are likely to respond to the other (Wilkinson, 1983). There is additionally some evidence to suggest that the best responders to TENS and acupuncture are those patients who are strongly suggestible (Edelist, Gross, & Langer, 1976).

The major disadvantage of acupuncture is its invasive nature (i.e., it entails penetration of the skin). TENS, although noninvasive, can produce skin irritation from electrode placement, though, in general, it appears to be relatively safe.

Pharmacological Therapy

Few areas of treatment in chronic pain are more controversial and central than the issue of medication. This section attempts to integrate information about medications at a number of levels. First, there is a description of the *kinds* of drugs prescribed in a somewhat ascending order of potency. Secondly, a description of their pharmacological action, as well as their *behaviorial* actions, is presented—effects that frequently work at cross-purposes. For the psychologist in medical settings in general, and in pain management in particular, familiarity with medications is absolutely necessary, not only to communicate with medical colleagues, but also to better understand the pain process. A variety of means of accomplishing this familiarity are readily available, including general reference books on medications and their use (Gilman, Goodman, & Gilman, 1980; *Physician's Desk Reference*, 1985) and repeated interaction with medical and pharmaceutical colleagues. The last are particularly useful and underutilized. Clinical pharmacists and pharmacologists are only beginning to emerge as critical members of the health-care team. Their knowledge of drug effects and interactions is indispensable in the care of chronic pain patients, many of whom take numerous medications for relief.

Anti-Inflammatory Drugs. Aspirin (acetyl-salicylic acid) remains the most widely used as well as one of the more effective anti-inflammatory drugs on the market today. Analgesic dosages of 300 to 600 mg every 2 to 4 h are often effective for mild to moderate back pain. For anti-inflammatory use, doses are substantially higher and may reach 900 to 1200 mg every 4 h.

The most common limitation on the use of aspirin is its gastrointestinal side effects, especially gastric upset or irritation. A more serious complication is gastric bleeding. Some allergic reactions also occur. Other reactions with toxicity include tinnitus, partial deafness, vertigo, nausea, vomiting, and diarrhea (Finneson, 1980; Wilkinson, 1983).

Of the nonsteroidal anti-inflammatory drugs, phenylbutazone (Butazolidin) and indomethacin (Indocin) have been used the longest. Because of repeated incidents of reported bone-marrow depressions, Butazolidin is used infrequently. Both medications can produce gastric upset, as does aspirin, but have proved successful with some low back pain, primarily *in the absence of sciatica*. Indocin has also been related to severe headaches, peptic ulcers, rashes, and vertigo (Finneson, 1980).

Among the newer anti-inflammatory drugs in use are ibuprofen (Motrin), naproxen (Naprosyn), fenoprofen calcium (Nalfon), tolmetin (Tolectin), sulindac (Clinoril), and piroxicam (Feldene). All of these are thought to be less likely to produce gastrointestinal upset and bleeding; however, all are also poorly tolerated by some patients. The benefit of these medications in low back pain, however, is probably related more to their analgesic than to their anti-inflammatory properties. In general, trials of 4 to 6 weeks are recommended (Wilkinson, 1983). Most of the anti-inflammatory drugs described elsewhere in the chapter have been used with some success in the treatment of sciatic and radicular pain.

Adrenal corticosteroids remain the most potent of the anti-inflammatory agents known. The most commonly prescribed are prednisone, dexamethasone (Decadron), and methylprednisolone (Medrol). Infrequently, these drugs are used in the management of isolated, acute episodes of low back pain and are frequently given in an injectable form such as triamcinolone acetonide (Kenalog). Their limited use in acute episodes (and seldom, if ever, with chronic low back pain) is due primarily to their potency and to the dramatic side effects associated with long-term use. These include Cushing's syndrome, disturbance of other hormonal systems, fluid retention, myopathic weakness, osteoporosis, and psychiatric disturbances, including hallucinations.

Antineuralgia Medications. Three kinds of drugs have been used in dealing with sciatica or radicular pain of a burning nature. They are anticonvulsants, anti-inflammatories, and psychotropics. Among the anticonvulsants, phenytoin (Dilantin) and carbamazepine (Tegretol) are the most widely used. The effectiveness of both of these drugs has long been known in the treatment of tic douloureux and pain associated with multiple sclerosis, but their use with sciatic and radicular pain has been noted. Side effects include allergic skin rashes or ataxia with Dilantin and nausea, dizziness, and leukopenia (abnormal decrease of white blood corpuscles) with Tegretol.

Amitriptyline (Elavil) is the tricyclic antidepressant most commonly prescribed for chronic pain patients. Whether the effectiveness of such medication is due to its action on a (hypothesized) underlying depression, or to its strong sedative rather than antidepressant effect is open to question, although some reports (e.g., Aronoff, 1981) indicate improvement within days of first administration, somewhat supporting the sedative effect of the drug. One confounding variable is the fact that pain patients are frequently on a nighttime dose of 50 mg, which is sufficient for sedation, but insufficient as a therapeutic dose for depression (150–200 mg per day).

Cyclobenzaprine hydrochloride (Flexeril) is a tricyclic amine salt that is frequently used as an antispasmodic agent. It is prescribed in 10-mg doses three times a day.

Muscle-Relaxing Drugs (Minor Tranquilizers). The muscle relaxants (*benzodiazepines*) are also called *sedatives, minor tranquilizers, antianxiety agents,* and *hypnotics.* However, they are used with pain patients primarily as muscle relaxants for spasm and, less frequently, pain relief. They are also used on occasion for insomnia associated with chronic pain.

Diazepam (Valium) continues to be widely used for relief of muscle spasm. It is usually prescribed in either 5- or 10-mg doses every 4 h. Other benzodiazapines frequently prescribed include clorazepate dipotassium (Tranxene), lorazepam (Ativan), oxazepam (Serax), and alprazolam (Xanax).

Two other benzodiazapines are used commonly for relief of insomnia due to pain. They are flurazepam (Dalmane) and temazepan (Restoril). Both are prescribed at doses of 15 to 30 mg by mouth at bedtime, although Dalmane is used more frequently. A third, triazolam (Halcion), is gaining in popularity because it is less dependency-producing and does not remain in the body as long as other benzodiazapines.

Although these drugs are certainly effective for spasm, anxiety, and sleep disturbance, they are also notorious for their side effects. These include physical and psychological dependence, production and/or exacerbation of depression, drowsiness, ataxia, confusion, and irritability. Regarding the treatment of insomnia, it has been estimated that 20% of cases of insomnia are secondary to hypnotic drug dependency (Pirodsky, 1981). Many of these side effects are particularly significant in the chronic pain syndrome. For example, some authors (Zlutnick & Taylor, 1982) have suggested that, rather than causing pain, depression is an iatrogenic effect of overprescribing (see "Chronic Pain and Iatrogenesis," following).

Hydroxyzine (Vistaril or Atarax) is another muscle relaxant in use, though it is unrelated to the benzodiazepines. Often described as an antihistamine, it also has analgesic properties. Its potentiating effect on narcotics and barbiturates makes it a useful adjunct in the detoxification process. In doses of 50 to 100 mg, it can be used for the management of both pain and anxiety.

Nonnarcotic Analgesics. Again, salicylates (aspirin) remain the most commonly used and effective nonnarcotic analgesics, or "pain killers." A few of the anti-inflammatory drugs have also been noted for their analgesic effects, especially Motrin. When analgesia is the goal of treatment, acetaminophen (Tylenol) is equally effective, without the undesirable gastrointestinal effects of aspirin. It does not, however, share aspirin's anti-inflammatory effectiveness. Tylenol's major limitation, however, is its potential for liver damage, and this is sometimes seen in chronic pain patients with extended use of Tylenol and codeine (see later). Similar concerns have been expressed about phenacetin (acetophenetidin), which is usually administered in combination with aspirin and caffeine ("APC" compound); it has, however, been removed from Excedrin and APC compound.

At this point, a departure will be made from traditional classification of medications. Clinical medicine frequently distinguishes *physical* from *psychological* dependency-producing drugs but often fails to recognize the seriousness of the latter. However, it should also be noted that the difference between *psychological* and *physical* dependence is frequently moot. In general, physical dependence refers to a *physiological* dependence producing *tolerance* and physical *withdrawal*.

Tolerance refers to a gradual increase in dose of a substance concomitant with a decrease in effect. *Withdrawal* of some substances produces physical symptoms, such as sweating, chills, nausea, and vomiting, and the withdrawal of others produces predominantly psychological symptoms, such as anxiety and agitation. In clinical practice, however, the distinction (other than for medical management) is moot, because the end result is a great deal of behavior generated by the patient in order to receive more medications (usually seen in the pain patient as severely increased pain complaints).

There is also some evidence to suggest that many medications *reinforce* pain complaints because of either their pharmacological or their behavioral effects, or both (Iverson & Iverson, 1981; Wikler, 1980; Zlutnick & Taylor, 1982). Thus, the addition of the term *dependency-producing* under the heading of nonnarcotic analgesics. The difficulties associated with the relationship between pain and medications are discussed in the section on iatrogenic issues.

Nonnarcotic, Dependency-Producing Analgesics. Of all the nonnarcotic analgesics in use, those that are *routinely dependency producing*, yet of less concern to physicians than narcotics, are propoxyphene (Darvon, Darvon-N) and its compounds; with aspirin (Darvon-N with ASA) and with acetaminophen (Darvocet-N); ethoheptazine citrate (Zactane); methotrimeprazine (Levoprome); pentazocine (Talwin); and mefenamic acid (Ponstel). The most commonly prescribed are Darvon and its compounds, and Talwin. Darvon is taken orally, and considerable controversy exists concerning its effectiveness. Many studies have apparently questioned whether it is even as effective as aspirin (Halpern, 1974). This fact, combined with its extremely dangerous interactive effects with alcohol or barbiturates (CNS depression and, in some cases, death), makes it a poor drug of choice. However, it remains widely prescribed among pain patients.

Talwin, although often described as a nonnarcotic analgesic, is nonetheless often described as addicting and as being comparable to morphine in its potency (Finneson, 1980). Side effects include nausea, vertigo, dizziness, vomiting, and euphoria. It is available in injectable as well as oral form, and its reputation for "nonaddicting" properties, combined with its euphoric effects, make it a frequently abused drug, particularly among health-care professionals.

Synthetic Addicting Analgesics. These synthetic compounds were developed as substitutes for morphine and its derivatives, with the hope that they would have the same analgesic, but not addicting, properties. Unfortunately, this has not proved to be the case. Among the more commonly prescribed drugs in this group are (in increasing order of potency) *codeine* (oral) and its synthetic derivatives hydrocodone and dihydrocodeine compounds (Synalgos and Vicodin); oxycodone with aspirin (Percodan) or acetaminophen (Percocet); meperidine (Demerol); and methadone (Dolophine). Codeine is lowest in potency only when administered orally, usually with Tylenol, in 1/4, 1/2, and full-grain tablets (i.e., numbers 2, 3, and 4, respectively). In its injectable form, it is closer to Demerol in its effect. For short-term use, aspirin is frequently more effective than an ordinary dose of 32 mg of codeine, although the two combined seem to significantly potentiate the analgesic effect. One of the major side effects of codeine is constipation. Consequently, diarrhea is a common withdrawal symptom.

Percodan and Percocet are extremely effective oral analgesics, but very dependency-producing. Their euphoric effects are attested to by the fact that this is one of the most popular drugs on the illicit street market. In addition, Percocet because of the acetaminophen, may produce liver damage with long-term use.

Demerol, although available orally, is most commonly used in injectable form because of its potency and rapid action. Injectable Demerol is the drug of choice of both patients and physicians for emergency room visits for acute pain episodes. Side effects include lightheadedness, dizziness, nausea, vomiting, sweating, respiratory depression, and convulsions. Demerol interacts poorly with MAO inhibitors and may also produce hypotension.

Dolophine, called most commonly by its genetic name, *methadone*, is known primarily for its use in the treatment of heroin addiction. More recently, because its withdrawal symptoms are purported to be less severe than those of other narcotics analgesics, it has been used in detoxification programs. (However, lack of severity remains to be demonstrated experimentally.) When used in comparable doses, however, it is as toxic as morphine. It is usually administered orally, in doses of 2.5 to 10 mg every 4 h.

Morphine and its Semisynthetic Derivatives. The most potent of all narcotic analgesics, morphine, is the drug against which all other analgesics are measured. However, because of its severely addicting nature (i.e., physical dependency) and its potential for causing respiratory depression, it and its derivatives are seldom used for other than extremely acute situations and terminal disease with associated chronic pain. Their action is to relieve pain and induce sleep (the actual meaning of the word *narcotic*). Additionally, they produce euphoria, one of the primary factors of dependence. The most commonly used morphine derivatives are *hydromorphone* (Dilaudid) and *levorphanol tartrate* (Levo-Dromoran). Although all are available in oral form, injection is routine and more potent. Morphine is used in 10-mg doses every 4 h. Dilaudid is 5 to 10 times as potent as morphine, but its duration of effect is less, as are its euphoric properties. It is thus usually prescribed in smaller doses of 2 to 4 mg for acute pain of short duration. Levo-Dromoran is somewhat longer-acting than morphine and is less likely to cause constipation, an occasional side effect of morphine. It is usually administered in doses of 2 to 3 mg. All of these drugs produce extreme physical dependency and are seldom seen in use with chronic-low-back-pain patients.

In general, with the exception of aspirin and some of the antiarthritic medications, *hypnosedatives and most analgesics are clearly contraindicated for chronic low back pain.* In spite of this fact, which receives almost unanimous endorsement among writers in the field of chronic pain, over 50% of all chronic pain patients are dependent on them (Aronoff, 1981).

Anesthetic Blocks—Treatment. Anesthetic blocks are used in the treatment of chronic low back pain under three primary conditions: (1) when roentgenographic studies are normal; (2) as an auxiliary treatment to physical therapy; and (3) in backs that fail to improve within 18 months of surgery. The techniques for the interruption of radicular pain include paravertebral, epidural, and subarachnoid blocks (Carron, 1975).

In general, the psychologist encounters a mind-boggling array of anesthetic procedures used for the management of low-back-pain complaints. Although many patients report relief, they are rarely the ones encountered in chronic pain clinics, or in consultation for chronic pain. By this time, therapeutic blocks are usually discouraged, because they have already been empirically shown to be of little value. Additionally, they are *invasive* procedures and may produce a variety of side effects, including convulsions, cardiorespiratory collapse, hypotension, nerve damage, increased pain, and paralysis. The reader is referred to the anesthesiology literature for a thorough discussion of these techniques. Many of the diagnostic blocks described earlier are identical to those used as treatment.

Surgical Procedures in Diagnosis and Treatment

It will be remembered from the anatomy of the intervertebral disc that bulging or herniation of the disc produces nerve root entrapment. Surgical procedures are designed (1) to free the nerve root in one way or another by the excision of material from the nucleus pulposus (laminectomy) and (2), either immediately or sometime following this procedure, to join permanently the two vertebrae between which the disc has been removed (spinal fusion). To be more precise, *discectomy* refers to the actual excision of disc material, and *laminectomy* to the means by which access to the disc space is attained. By far the more common of the terms used in reports is *laminectomy*.

For surgery to be considered, the following criteria, discussed earlier, are followed:

1. Low back pain and/or sciatic pain are both present
2. Sciatica is often more severe than back pain
3. Positive neurological examination (may include positive findings on EMG)
4. Positive straight-leg-raising test
5. Positive Lasègue's maneuver
6. Herniation or protrusion
7. Roentgenographic or CT corroboration of neurological findings, (i.e., definite nerve-root impingement by the disc material)

The success rates of first-time laminectomies vary from study to study, with a range of 40 to 80% reported. *The single most important factor in the success of this surgical procedure is selection of patients by the above criteria.* Likewise, the most significant factor in poor outcome of back surgery is improper patient selection. For example, in a study of 300 failures of back surgery by review of the original operative notes, definitive reports of disc herniation were found in only six (Shealy, 1982). Similarly, in a study of 94 unsuccessful back surgeries, Wilkinson (1983) concluded that the original surgery was unnecessary in 76 (81%) of them.

Spinal fusions are performed to stabilize the affected lumbar levels and to prevent stress and subsequent damage to the adjacent discs. Once removal of the disc material is complete, bone "plugs" are inserted into the intervertebral space and are "fused" with bone grafts. Occasionally, metal rods and screws are used (Brown, 1980; Lin, 1982).

According to Shealy (1982), the necessity for fusion has never been fully established, and the results show no statistically significant improvement in the original condition. He recommended fusion only in cases of fracture or advanced spondylolisthesis, or when removal of disc material is extensive.

By far, surgical procedures carry the greatest risk of side effects and exacerbation of pain. For example, Wilkinson (1983) suggested that 1% or 2% of all laminectomies result in a *worsening* of the patient's condition. However, Fager and Freidberg (1980) reported that 10% of all cases they treated were rendered significantly worse.

Complications caused by these surgical procedures include hematoma (a swelling or mass of blood caused by a break in a blood vessel in 5% to 10% of cases); arachnoiditis (inflammation of the arachnoid membrane) in 25% of cases; dysesthesia (sensations as of the pricks of pins and needles, or of crawling) in 10% to 20% of cases; and infection in less than 5% of cases (Shealy, 1982). Similarly, Wilkinson (1983) described injury to nerve roots, including avulsion (tearing of a body part or structure), laceration of the dura meningitis as a result of tearing of the arachnoid, and of particular interest, epidural adhesions, which, combined with anachroiditis, are considered by many almost exclusively iatrogenic, being caused by surgical intervention.

Chemonucleolysis (Chymopapain) Chemonucleolysis refers to procedures for chemical dissolution of the nucleus pulposus by injection of compounds into the disc space. Chymopapain is the major component of crude papain, an enzyme obtained from the fruit of the papaya. Although its mechanism is obscure, its action is to dissolve the nucleus pulposus with virtually no effect on the annulus fibrosus. This procedure is recommended for patients who have failed to respond to conservative management and to meet all diagnostic criteria for surgery (i.e., disc disease). In one major study (Sutten, 1983), satisfactory results were obtained in 77% of cases seen between 1973 and 1980, with an 88% figure from 1975 to 1980 (excluding failed backs and workmen's compensation cases). Sutton (1983) and Watts (1977) reported few actual side effects other than potential ones from improper needle placement. Nonetheless, this procedure has not received universal acceptance, partly because of the lack of data from controlled experiemental research (Shealy, 1982).

Sensory Rhizotomy. This procedure involves cutting the dorsal sensory nerve roots of the lumbar or sacral nerves. It is a procedure usually performed on patients with failed back syndrome (i.e., a history of unsuccessful surgery), or, infrequently, on patients with unilateral sciatica with relatively little back pain. A diagnostic nerve block is routine as a predictor of success. Patients with bilateral sciatica or significant back pain rarely obtain relief from this procedure. Published results of success vary from 25% to 80% (Wilkinson, 1983), although Shealy (1982) reported no more than 30% success across studies.

Limitations and precautions for this procedure include the low probability of success and possible improper needle placement, which can result in extremity weakness and incontinence. Other complications include the possibility of trophic ulceration.

Facet Rhizotomy. Facet rhizotomy entails the cutting of articular nerves (i.e., nerves in the facet joints) and is usually performed on patients complaining of referred pain, muscle spasm, limitation of trunk flexion and straight-leg raising, and subjective sensory loss or motor weakness due to pain. According to Shealy (1982), who perfected this technique using radio frequency lesions rather than a scalpel, as many as 79% of back pain patients present with tender facet joints. The facet syndrome is thought to be due to a degenerated, but not necessarily herniated, disc (Shealy, 1976a). As with sensory rhizotomy, a diagnostic nerve block is usually performed as a predictor of responsivity. The results of this procedure range from 55% to 80% on unoperated back patients, 17% on postlaminectomy patients, and 11% to 30% in postfusion patients (Pawl, 1974; Shealy, 1974, 1976a).

Cordotomy. This is a radical procedure involving cutting of the spinal cord to relieve pain. It is performed both unilaterally and bilaterally at different levels of the spinal cord. Because of the dramatic nature of side effects and its irreversibility, this procedure is reserved for terminally ill patients with short life expectancy. In intractable malignant pain in the lower half of the body, cordotomy produces relief of pain for up to six months in 70% to 80% of patients. Side effects, however, include the loss of tickle, itch, and temperature sensations within the zone of analgesia. Some degree of impotence is noted in virtually all patients, both male and female (arousal and erection difficulties in men and orgasmic dysfunction in women). Transitory paralysis is common, and muscular weakness persists permanently in 10% of patients. In addition, respiratory paralysis may occur. Bladder deficit has also been reported in 78% of men and 40% of women (Shealy, 1982). Failure of the procedure is also marked by the eventual return of pain in up to 44% of patients (White & Sweet, 1969). And finally, the mortality rates for this surgery have been reported at 1% to 5% (Shealy, 1982).

Neurostimulator Implantation (Dorsal Column Stimulations). Transcutaneous neurostimulation (TENS) was discussed earlier as a noninvasive method of pain control. Dorsal column stimulation (DCS) involves the implantation of dorsal-column-stimulating electrodes based on the same notion of gate control theory originally proposed by Melzack and Wall (1965). DCS affects pathways of *touch* rather than *pain* input in the spine. Implantation of electrodes allows long-term stimulation with the frequent application and reapplication of surface electrodes. Originally, TENS was developed to predict responsiveness to DCS and remains a good predictor of success. Criteria for its use include chronic intractable pain that has proved unresponsive to traditional methods, including laminectomy, TENS, pharmacological therapy, and behavior modification and other forms of psychotherapy (Shealy, 1982). Further criteria for *exclusion* include narcotic addiciton or dependence and neurosis, as defined by elevations or depressions of two or more standard deviations in four or more scales of the MMPI (Finneson, 1980).

Although a variety of claims have been made for its use (Nielson, Adams, & Hosobuchi, 1975; Shealy, 1982), the overall utility of DCS simply does not outweigh its potent side effects, including cerebrospinal fluid leaks, paralysis of the legs, bladder and bowel incontinence, and infection (Shealy, 1982).

In summary, a number of points should be reiterated concerning the use of surgical procedures:

1. Surgery for disc disease is recommended only in the presence of strict diagnostic criteria, and after extended trials of conservative management. Estimates vary, but almost all studies of failed surgical procedures for disc disease indicate that the overwhelming majority of them were performed on the basis of insufficient criteria (Wilkinson 1983).

2. Each repeated surgery has a reduced likelihood of success.

3. Surgical procedures are invasive and carry with them the potential for worsening the symptoms, as well as iatrogenic side effects that also tend to exacerbate discomfort, and that produce additional symptoms that contribute to the poor physical status of these patients.

In summary, even with all diagnostic criteria in evidence, many authors recommend surgery with great caution. Some (e.g., Shealy, 1982) go so far as to suggest that, with an overall 30% to 40% success rate in laminectomies, it may be the case that this procedure is, in fact, successful only with herniation of the disc, rather than rupture. Because it is usually impossible to determine *a priori* which is producing the symptoms, Shealy suggested avoiding surgery whenever possible and resorting to structured conservative therapy (via pain clinics) instead. Although this may be a minority view among surgeons, it is worth serious consideration.

In order to put all of the foregoing into proper perspective for the treatment of chronic back pain, it is necessary to briefly reconceptualize chronic pain as a combination of patient attributes and iatrogenic factors.

CHRONIC PAIN AND IATROGENESIS

Thomas (1983) defined an iatrogenic disorder as:

> Any adverse mental or physical condition induced in a patient by a physician or surgeon. [The] term implies that such effects could have been avoided by proper and judicious care on the part of the physician. (p. 703)

With this perspective in mind, a number of characteristics pejoratively attributed to the chronic pain patient need to be reassessed in terms of iatrogenic variables.

Doctor shopping, for example, often occurs because we have taught patients both explicitly as well as implicitly that pain without disease is not valid. Thus, what appears to be perseveration on obtaining a diagnosis is a quite logical position on the part of individuals trying to be taken seriously.

Denial and lack of psychology-mindedness are also frequently mentioned as characteristics of this population. These terms refer to the unwillingness of these patients to accept the fact that there is relatively little wrong with them physiologically, and that psychological or psychiatric intervention is in order. Patients immediately interpret such suggestions to mean that their pain is not real or legitimate, and that they are mentally ill. This interpretation is reinforced in part, by health-care professionals, who tend themselves to view organic pain as "real" and stress-related pain as "not real" (psychological). This common misunderstanding about the nature and validity of pain, regardless of its etiology, is largely responsible for the avoidance of psychology and psychiatry by these patients. To them, acknowledging that their pain is related to psychological rather than physiological variables is tantamount to an admission that the pain is not real (and, by implication, that they are malingering).

Dependence on medications is also commonly noted in these patients, who honestly believe that without drugs they will be unable to tolerate their pain. This belief is reinforced during withdrawal (or extinction, if medications are viewed as reinforcers), because the only way to control the *increased* pain experienced during this process is to reintroduce the medications (See Wikler, 1980). Pain patients are often unfairly and incorrectly referred to as sociopathic or as substance abusers, whereas experience has shown that the overwhelming majority of these patients do *not* request narcotic analgesic or hypnosedative medications after completing a comprehensive program of detoxification, training in self-control and problem solving, physical and occupational therapy, and so on (Taylor *et al.*, 1980). Further, these patients have, for the most part, become gradually dependent on medications *prescribed by their physician*. This statement is meant not to criticize physicians, but to provide an awareness that dependence is a complex phenomenon involving patients *and* physicians who are unable (or unwilling) to refuse to prescribe medications, who are unfamiliar with alternative approaches to pain management, and who are unaware of the reinforcing effects of medication on pain.

Depression, although capable of producing somatic problems, is also reactive to the discomfort and disability associated with chronic pain. Further, many of the medications used in treatment produce central nervous system depression, most notably the benzodiazapines such as Valium (Pirodsky, 1981; Zlutnick & Taylor, 1982). Although the use of antidepressants frequently produces some relief, their effects may be due to their sedative rather than to their antidepressant properties. There is also evidence that detoxification, combined with self-control procedures, produces significant changes in mood as well as pain (Taylor *et al.*, 1980). With these points in mind, we must be cautious in our use of depression as a *causative* factor in chronic pain. Statements to this effect divert practitioners from a behavioral analysis of pain as well as of depression. In this context, pain and depression are viewed as behaviors that are a function of medications, loss of reinforcement, and so forth (e.g., job, provider status, and activities; see Moss & Boren, 1972).

Lack of motivation to improve is another characteristic frequently attributed to this population. The use of motivation in this sense, however, is circular: rather than referring to a means of changing behavior, it serves to explain the failure of patients to engage in therapy. Other variables are thus ignored, including medications that reinforce pain complaints, deteriorated physical abilities and stamina resulting from inactivity over long periods of time, lack of the skills necessary to meet new job requirements (because heavy lifting is required for so many jobs for which the patient previously was qualified), and superstition, in the classic behavioral context. This last refers to the fact that these patients soon "learn" that the most effective way to avoid exacerbation of pain is to do nothing. Although obviously dysfunctional from society's point of view, this greatly reduced activity is quite logical to the patient.

The last characteristic of chronic pain patients to be discussed is their alleged propensity to undergo surgery, often repeatedly, without success. Frequently, this is attributed to unconscious needs (e.g., to be punished or mutilated) or to sociopathic tendencies (malingering). Again, although certainly tenable at a theoretical level, these kinds of hypotheses divert practitioners from analyzing a system that somehow allows these patients to receive repeated surgeries in spite of poor results and frequent lack of diagnostic criteria for surgery. For example, the fact that back surgeries performed in the United States far exceed the number performed proportionately in other countries has been documented repeatedly in the literature (Shealy, 1976b; Wilkinson, 1983). We must therefore begin to study the mechanics of a system that allows such excessive variance in procedures, as well as to educate patients to question the viability of surgery.

Thus, although there is little question that, at some level, we must study those who fail to improve, far too little attention has been paid to iatrogenic issues. Among the many variables that seem to contribute to the pain syndrome are improper diagnosis, unnecessary surgeries (with their iatrogenic effects), prolonged use of dependency-producing medications, poor education of the public about the role of stress and illness (exacerbated by outdated notions of psychosomatic problems), and the tacit cooperation of mental-health professionals who aid the system in relabeling its failures. If psychologists as a profession are to be of help in treating these patients, they must educate themselves in the iatrogenic aspects of health care in general and in the treatment of pain in specific, reevaluate the role of psychometrics and relabeling, and assume the position of therapist and advocate. As a result, psychology will attain a primary, functional role in the treatment of chronic pain.

In summary, psychologists need to be aware of the progressively invasive nature of the treatment process, and of how each level of this process carries with it an increased risk of iatrogenic difficulties (psychological as well as physical). Their role should thus entail the use of procedures and techniques designed to:

1. Aid medical colleagues in successful management of the syndrome.
2. Educate patients, as well as health-care colleagues, about the issues described above.
3. Evaluate and identify those patients most "at risk" to interact poorly with the medical system.
4. Facilitate the empirical evaluation of assessment and treatment procedures.

The Association for the Advancement of Behavior Therapy has targeted the 1980s as the Decade of the Empirical Clinician. In no area is this need more critical, nor the consequences more dire, than in the treatment of chronic pain.

Acknowledgments

The author wishes to thank Roger Katz, Ph.D., Neal Birnbaum, M.D. and S. Malvern Dorinson, M.D. for their careful editorial assistance.

REFERENCES

Aronoff, G. (1981). A holistic approach to pain rehabilitation: The Boston pain unit. In L. K. Y. Ng (Ed.), *New approaches to treatment of chronic pain.* (National Institute on Drug Abuse; Research Monograph No. 36). Washington, DC: U.S. Government Printing Office.

Barlow, D. (1981). *Behavioral assessment of adult disorders.* New York: Guilford Press.

Brown, M. D. (1980). Lumbar spine fusion. In B. E. Finneson (Ed.), *Low back pain* (2nd ed.). Philadelphia: J.' B. Lippincott.

Carron, H. (1975). Management of common pain problems. In S. G. Hersey (Ed.), *Refresher courses in anesthesiology* (Vol. 3). Philadelphia: J. B. Lippincott.

Carron, H. (1982). Anatomy of the lumbo sacral spine. In H. Carron & R. E. McLaughlin (Eds.), *Management of low back pain.* Boston: John Wright.

Corley, M. J., & Zlutnick, S. (1981). A model for inpatient liaison-consultation with chronic pain patients. In J. M. Ferguson & C. B. Taylor (Eds.), *The comprehensive handbook of behavioral medicine* (Vol. 2) New York: Spectrum.

Doleys, D. M., Meredith, R. L., & Ciminero, A. R. (1982). *Behavioral medicine: Assessment and treatment strategies.* New York: Plenum Press.

Edelist, G., Gross, A. E., & Langer, F. (1976). Treatment of low back pain with acupuncture. *Canadian Anesthesiology Society Journal, 23,* 303–306.

Fager, C. A., & Freidberg, S. R. (1980). Analysis of failures of lumbar spine surgery. *Spine, 5,* 89–94.

Ferguson, J., & Taylor, C. B. (1981). *The comprehensive handbook of behavioral medicine.* New York: Spectrum.

Finneson, B. (Ed.). (1980). *Low back pain* (2nd ed.) Philadelphia: J. B. Lippincott.

Fordyce, W. H. (1976). *Behavioral methods for chronic pain and illness.* St. Louis: C. V. Mosby.

Fordyce, W. E., Fowler, R. S., & Lehmann, J. F. (1973). Operant conditioning in the treatment of chronic pain. *Archives of Physical Medicine and Rehabilitation, 54,* 399–408.

Gasser, H. S., & Erlanger, J. (1929). Role of fiber size in establishment of nerve block by pressure or cocaine. *American Journal of Physiology, 88,* 581–591.

Gilman, A. G., Goodman, L. S., & Gilman, A. (Eds.). (1980). *Goodman & Gilman's the pharmacological basis of therapeutics* (6th ed). New York: Macmillan.

Green, L. (1980). Electrodiagnostic studies in low back pain. In B. Finneson (Ed.), *Low back pain* (2nd ed.). Philadelphia: J. B. Lippincott.

Halpern, L. M. (1974). Psychotropic drugs and the management of chronic pain. In J. J. Bonica (Ed.), *Advances in neurology: International symposium on pain.* New York: Raven Press.

Illich, I. (1976). *Medical nemesis.* Toronto: Bantam Books.

Iverson, S. D., & Iverson, L. L (1981). *Behavioral pharmacology* (2nd ed.) New York: Oxford University Press.

Katz, R. C., & Wooley, F. R. (1975). Improving patient records through problem orientation. *Behavior Therapy, 6,* 119–124.

Katz, R. C., & Zlutnick, S. (Eds.). (1975). *Behavior therapy and health care: Principles and applications.* New York: Pergamon Press.

Kolouch, F. T. (1974). *Predictions of positive surgical outcome.* Unpublished manuscript, University of Utah College of Medicine.

Lin, P. (Ed.). (1982). *Posterior lumbar interbody fusion.* Springfield, IL: Charles C Thomas.

McLaughlin, R. E. (1982). Anatomy of the lumbo sacral spine. In H. Carron & R. E. McLaughlin (Eds.), *Management of low back pain.* Boston: John Wright.

Melamed, B. G., Robbins, R. L., & Fernandez, J. (1982). Factors to be considered in psychological preparation for surgery. In D. Routh & M. Wolraich (Eds.), *Advances in behavioral pediatrics.* New York: JAI Press.

Melamed, B. G., Robbins, R. L., & Graves. S. (1982). Preparation for surgery and medical procedures. In D. Russo & J. Varni (Eds.), *Behavioral pediatrics: Research and practice.* New York: Plenum Press.

Melzack, R., & Wall, P. D. (1965). Pain mechanisms: A new theory. *Science, 150,* 971–979.

Mixter, W. J., & Barr, J. S. (1934). Rupture of the intervertebral disc with the involvement of the spinal canal. *New England Journal of Medicine, 211,* 210–215.

Moss, R. M., & Boren, J. H. (1972). Depression as a model for behavioral analysis. *Comprehensive Psychiatry, 13,* 581–590.

Nielson, K. D., Adams, J. E., & Hosobuchi, Y. (1975). Experience with dorsal column stimulation for relief of chronic intractable pain: 1968–1973. *Surgical Neurology, 4,* 148–152.

Norton, P. L., & Brown, T. (1957). The immobilizing efficiency of back braces. *Journal of Bone Joint Surgery, 1,* 39–50.

Patterson, T. (1983). *Cost benefit analysis as an outcome measure in the treatment of chronic pain.* Doctoral dissertation, University of San Francisco.

Pawl, R. (1974). Results in the treatment of low back syndrome from sensory neurolysis of the lumbar facets (facet rhizotomy) by thermal coagulation. *Proceedings of the Institute of Medicine, Chicago, 30,* 150–151.

Pheasant, H. C., Gilbert, D., & Goldfarb, T. (1979). The MMPI as a predictor of outcome in low back surgery. *Spine, 4,* 78–84.

Physician's desk reference. (1985). Rutherford, NJ: Medical Economics.

Pirodsky, D. M. (1981). *Primer of clinical psychopharmacology: A practical guide.* Garden City, NY: Medical Examination Publishing.

Shealy, C. N. (1974). Facets in back and sciatic pain. *Minnesota Medicine, 57,* 199–203.

Shealy, N. C. (1976a). Facet denervation in the management of back and sciatic pain. *Clinical Orthopedics, 115,* 157–164.

Shealy, C. N. (1976b). *The pain game.* Millbrae, CA: Celestial Arts.

Shealy, C. N. (1982). A surgeon's approach to the problem. In H. Carron & R. E. McLaughlin (Eds.), *Management of low back pain.* Boston: John Wright.

Smith, J. W., Murphy, T. R., Blair, J. S. G., & Lowe, K. G. (1983). *Regional anatomy illustrated.* New York: Churchill Livingstone.

Spengler, D. M. (1982). *Low back pain: Assessment and management.* New York: Grune & Stratton.

Sutten, J. C. (1983). Chemonucleosis. In J. Chauthen (Ed.), *Lumbar spine surgery: Indications, techniques, failures and alternatives.* Baltimore: Williams & Wilkins.

Swarthout, R., & Compere, E. L. (1974). Ischiogluteal bursitis: The pain in the arse. *Journal of American Medical Association, 227,* 551–552.

Taylor, C. B., Zlutnick, S., Corley, M. J., & Flora, J. (1980). The effects of detoxification, relaxation, and brief supportive therapy on chronic pain. *Pain, 8,* 319–329.

Thomas, C. L. (Ed.), (1983). *Tabor's cyclopedic medical dictionary.* Philadelphia: F. A. Davis.

Watts, C. (1977). Complications of chemonucleosis for lumbar disc disease. *Neurosurgery, 1,* 2–5.

Weed, L. L. (1969). *Medical records, medical education, and patient care.* Cleveland: Press of Case Western Reserve University.

White, J. C., & Sweet, W. H. (1969). *Pain and the neurosurgeon.* Springfield, IL: Charles C Thomas.

Whitehill, R. (1982). The differential diagnosis of low back pain. In H. Carron & R. E. McLaughlin (Eds.), *Management of low back pain.* Boston: John Wright.

Wikler, A. (1980). *Opiod dependence: Mechanisms and treatment.* New York: Plenum Press.

Wilkinson, H. A. (1983). *The failed back syndrome: Etiology and therapy.* Cambridge: Harper & Row.

Winnie, A. P. (1978). Differential diagnosis of pain mechanisms. In S. G. Hersey (Ed.), *Refresher courses in anesthesiology* (Vol. 6). Philadelphia: J. B. Lippincott.

Zlutnick, S., & Taylor, C. B. (1982). Chronic pain. In D. M. Doleys, R. L. Meredith, & A. R. Ciminero (Eds.), *Behavioral medicine: Assessment and treatment strategies.* New York: Plenum Press.

9

Behavioral Aspects of Arterial Hypertension and Its Treatment

JOANNA M. POLEFRONE, STEPHEN B. MANUCK,
KEVIN T. LARKIN, AND M. ELIZABETH FRANCIS

Diseases of the heart and the vasculature account for more than half of all deaths occurring annually in the United States. Among the disorders contributing to this statistic, coronary heart disease and stroke are by far the most significant. These clinical manifestations often result from a lifelong accumulation of fatty lesions (atherosclerosis) in the intima, or inner layer, of arteries carrying blood to the heart muscle and the brain. Atherosclerosis produces no symptoms in its early stages of development, but after decades of continued growth and complication, such lesions begin to encroach on the interior of arteries. Ultimately, such obstructions can compromise blood flow to tissues supplied by the affected vessels. A complete blockage of the arterial blood flow, often associated with sudden formation of a clot (or thrombus) within the artery, results in death or degeneration of the distal tissue; this damage is referred to as *infarction* and has ominous consequences when affecting either the heart (heart attack) or the brain (stroke). It is also possible to experience either heart attack or stroke in the absence of appreciable atherosclerosis, due, respectively, to spasm of the coronary arteries and to embolism or hemorrhaging of the cerebral blood vessels.

Many variables have now been identified that contribute to these clinical events, including elevated lipid concentration in the blood, cigarette smoking, elevated blood pressure, and family history of cardiovascular disease. In turn, each of these "risk factors" has been the subject of extensive epidemiological and laboratory investigation, as have processes involved in the clinical expression of coronary heart disease and stroke. Much has also been written regarding recovery and rehabilitation following the occurrence of nonfatal coronary and cerebrovascular events. Unfortunately, more than a cursory consideration of the many topics pertinent to psychological aspects of cardiovascular disease is not feasible in the scope of a single chapter; hence, we will not attempt to review here the entire domain of cardiovascular behavioral medicine. Rather, our purpose in the present chapter is to provide an overview of behavioral factors that are involved in one con-

JOANNA M. POLEFRONE, STEPHEN B. MANUCK, AND M. ELIZABETH FRANCIS • Department of Psychology, University of Pittsburgh, Clinical Psychology Center, Pittsburgh, PA 15260. KEVIN T. LARKIN • Department of Psychology, West Virginia University, Morgantown, WV 26506. Preparation of this manuscript was supported, in part, by HL 29028.

dition that both is a primary risk factor for catastrophic heart disease and is itself the most prevalent of all cardiovascular disorders: arterial hypertension.

Because of the high prevalence of hypertension in the general population, it is likely that clinical psychologists will frequently encounter hypertensive individuals in their professional work. It is important, therefore, that the clinician be aware of the basic pathophysiology and behavioral dimensions of this disorder. In the latter regard, psychological factors have been implicated in hypertension in at least four ways. First, it is a long-standing psychosomatic hypothesis that behavioral characteristics of the individual, especially those relating to the expression of anger, are of etiologic importance among some hypertensive patients. Second, research of the past several years suggests that hypertensive individuals exhibit a variety of psychomotor, cognitive, and perceptual deficits. Such deficits may represent behavioral consequences of an elevated blood pressure, as there is evidence of restoration of function following effective treatment. A third behavioral aspect of hypertension is the many potential side effects of antihypertensive medications, which range from simple fatigue to depression and sexual dysfunction. The matter of side effects—as well as nonadherence to prescribed medical regimens—has assumed increasing importance with recent advocacy of more aggressive treatment of hypertension by the medical community. Finally, the past 10 years have seen a development of several behavioral interventions aimed specifically at the reduction of elevated blood pressure. With the advent of such interventions, clinical psychologists are increasingly becoming direct partners in the treatment of this pervasive cardiovascular disorder.

DEFINITION AND EPIDEMIOLOGY

Arterial blood pressure varies throughout the cardiac cycle. The maximum pressure—systolic blood pressure—is associated with ventricular contraction and ejection of blood into the circulation. Diastolic blood pressure is the minimum pressure of blood in the arteries at the time that the heart is at rest (i.e., during ventricular relaxation). Systolic and diastolic values of 120 and 80 millimeters of mercury (mm Hg), respectively, are frequently cited as indicative of a "normal" blood pressure. Hypertension is an elevation in systolic and/or diastolic blood pressure that exceeds a diagnostic criterion adopted by consensus of the medical community. Individuals who exhibit systolic/diastolic blood pressures greater than 160/95 mm Hg are said to have established, or sustained, hypertension. A second diagnostic category, borderline hypertension, is typically defined as a blood pressure elevation in the range of 140–160/90–95 mm Hg; there is some extension of these limits with advancing age (Julius & Hansson, 1983). A final category, labile hypertension, is sometimes used to describe the individual whose blood pressure rises above the conventional criteria for hypertension on some occasions, yet at other times falls within normotensive limits.

Prevalence rates for all types of hypertension range from 15% to 24% of the total U.S. population (Lew, 1973; Rowland & Roberts, 1982) and may be as high as 38% and 52%, respectively, among white and black males between the ages of 50 and 59 (Stamler, Stamler, Reidlinger, Algera, & Roberts, 1976). Blood pressure tends to be lower in women than in men until about age 55, after which the blood pressures of women exceed those of males (Rowland & Roberts, 1982; Stamler *et al.*, 1976). The prevalence of hypertension in women is also lower than among men until around 65 years of age. As implied, above, blacks develop hypertension more frequently than do whites, though interestingly, it is only among whites that the prevalence of hypertension differs significantly between males and females (Rowland & Roberts, 1982).

Both systolic and diastolic blood pressures increase with age, as does the prevalence of hypertension. Other risk factors for hypertension include obesity, family history of hypertension, and excessive sodium and alcohol intake (Page, 1983). Primary preventive measures for hypertension are targeted, of course, at those risk factors that seem most amenable to change. Yet, the relative influences of these factors remain controversial. The relationship of intake of sodium and other electrolytes to hypertension is obscured, for example, by confounding variables such as body weight and cultural differences among populations that vary in dietary habits. It is also unclear exactly how these risk factors affect the development of hypertension, though the proposed mechanisms responsible for elevations in blood pressure are discussed in the following section on etiology and pathophysiology.

As indicated earlier, hypertension is itself a significant risk factor for coronary heart disease and stroke; it is also associated with an increased risk of congestive heart failure. Overall, the presence of hypertension raises the risk of coronary heart disease by a factor of 3, of stroke by a factor of 7, and of congestive heart failure by a factor of 4 (Page, 1983). Although risk of cardiovascular morbidity and mortality is increased most substantially above pressures of 140/90 mm Hg, it is misleading to think that increased risk resides only where blood pressure exceeds this criterion. In fact, the relationship between blood pressure and major cardiovascular disease holds even for relative differences among normotensive values. For each increase of 10 mm Hg in blood pressure, for example, there is a 30% increment in risk of serious cardiovascular disease (Page, 1983). Thus, decreasing the blood pressures of persons who do not exceed the threshold of hypertensive diagnosis can be beneficial, even though a more pronounced benefit would be derived from reduction of pressures in the borderline and established ranges of hypertension.

The risks associated with hypertension are particularly evident when the disorder is left untreated and is permitted to advance through increasing levels of severity. When blood pressure elevations are first detected in the third or fourth decade of life and are not brought under effective control, for example, serious complications may emerge before the age of 60 (Epstein & Oster, 1984). A small proportion of patients with uncontrolled hypertension develop malignant hypertension or hypertensive crises, both characterized by severely elevated blood pressure and acute end-organ dysfunction. In addition, a high proportion of patients with malignant hypertension die within a very few years. The various complications and forms of end-organ damage associated with advanced stages of hypertension are described in the later section on the symptoms of hypertension.

ETIOLOGY AND PATHOPHYSIOLOGY

Diagnostic categories of hypertension include primary, or essential, hypertension and secondary hypertension. Essential hypertension denotes an elevated blood pressure of unknown origin and accounts for fully 90% to 95% of all hypertensive cases (Julius & Hansson, 1983). When patients' blood pressure elevations can be traced to specific and identifiable causes, the term *secondary hypertension* is used. Before considering the pathophysiological processes involved in both essential and secondary forms of hypertension, it may first be useful to describe in general terms the physiological mechanisms responsible for normal regulation of arterial pressure.

Blood pressure varies largely as a function of the volume of blood present in the arteries. This volume is affected both by the quantity of blood entering the arteries through the pumping action of the heart (the cardiac output) and by forces impeding the flow of blood out of the arterial system (the total peripheral resistance). An increase in either cardiac output or total peripheral resistance produces a corresponding rise in blood pressure. Cardiac output is itself determined by two factors: the rate at which the heart beats (heart rate) and the volume of blood ejected with each cardiac cycle (stroke volume). Total peripheral resistance reflects the extent of flow restriction, or vasoconstriction, in resistance vessels (arterioles) throughout the peripheral circulation. All factors influencing blood pressure must therefore exert their effects through changes in cardiac output, in total peripheral resistance, or in both of these parameters. It is also the case that blood pressure may remain constant in the face of an altered cardiac output and peripheral resistance, if these hemodynamic changes are directionally opposed (i.e., if an increased cardiac output is offset by a decrease in the peripheral resistance).

Blood pressure control is achieved by a variety of regulatory systems. One of these is the autonomic nervous system, which affects peripheral resistance by altering the caliber of blood vessels and affects the cardiac output through its influences on the pumping action of the heart. Stimulation of the parasympathetic branch of the autonomic nervous system results in deceleration of heart rate, whereas sympathetic activation increases both the rate and the force of ventricular contraction. Sympathetic stimulation also influences the peripheral vasculature; these effects, which involve both the constriction and the dilation of blood vessels, vary across the different vascular beds (e.g., skeletal muscle and viscera). Autonomic control of the hemodynamic parameters that govern blood pressure can be initiated, in turn, by reflexes of the so-called baroreceptor system. Baroreceptor cells are specialized "stretch" receptors that line portions of the walls of the aorta and the carotid arteries. These cells are sensitive to moment-to-moment deviations in blood flow, and they change in firing rate when blood pressure rises or falls. Afferent impulses arising from the baroreceptors project to cardiovascular control centers in the medulla, which orchestrate the efferent arm of the reflex arc. Faced with an acute increase in blood pressure, for instance, the baroreceptor reflex acts to lower arterial pressure through compensating heart-rate deceleration and reduction in vasoconstrictor tone.

Another blood-pressure control-mechanism is termed *intrinsic autoregulation*. This process involves localized changes in blood vessels whereby arterioles constrict in response to the presence of an excess of blood flow. A third homeostatic mechanism is the renin-angiotensin–aldosterone system. The effects of this system on blood pressure are mediated, in part, through changes in blood volume and the cardiac output. In normal functioning, the hormone renin is secreted by the kidneys in response to a variety of stimuli, including decreased renal perfusion, input from the sympathetic nervous system, and various circulating endocrine substances. Renin stimulates the production of angiotensin and aldosterone. Aldosterone causes a retention of sodium and water, which, in turn, increases body fluid volume; blood pressure is then elevated by the increased cardiac output associated with an expanded blood volume. Angiotensin, on the other hand, is a potent vasoconstrictor (Laragh, 1983), as are other humoral substances like vasopressin and the catecholamines.

It is generally believed that long-term regulation of blood pressure depends primarily on the kidneys' overall control of body fluid volume (Guyton, 1977). Homeostasis is achieved through maintenance of a delicate balance between the intake and the excretion of fluid. The normal kidney's response to an elevation in blood pressure is to increase rates of sodium and fluid excretion. When excretion exceeds the intake of fluid, the body's total fluid volume (which, again, includes blood volume) decreases. The result is a lowered cardiac output and a reduction in blood pressure. Conversely, lowered arterial pressure promotes a decrease in urine output, with corresponding increases in fluid volume, cardiac output, and blood pressure.

It should be emphasized that, in this brief outline, we have greatly oversimplified the complex regulatory processes involved in normal blood-pressure control. These mechanisms do not act autonomously; they form a highly integrated system. The categorization of regulatory mechanisms as neural, endocrine, and renal, however, is helpful for understanding the pathophysiological processes involved in the various forms of hypertension. Some of the specific ways in which dysfunction of these regulatory systems may promote high blood pressure are discussed below.

Secondary Hypertension

Alterations in neural, renal, and endocrine function associated with known sources of pathology may produce the various forms of secondary hypertension listed in Table 1. Inability of the kidney to adequately control body fluid volume, for instance, can result from a variety of conditions affecting renal function. Examples of types of secondary hypertension that arise from endocrine disturbances include pheochromocytoma, primary aldosteronism, and Cushing's syndrome. These disorders result from excessive secretion of catecholamines, aldosterone, and cortisol, respectively, due to tumors of the adrenal gland. Neurogenic causes of secondary hypertension include brain tumors, encephalitis, or any condition that increases intracranial pressure.

An interference with blood flow, such as that resulting from atherosclerosis of the aorta or the renal artery, can also produce an elevation in blood pressure. In addition, hypertension may be secondary to the effects of exogenous substances, such as oral contraceptives, licorice, lead, and various pharmacological agents. Two other forms of secondary hypertension are preeclampsia–eclampsia of pregnancy and hypertension associated with complications of diabetes.

Table 1. Sources of Secondary Hypertension

Renal	Endocrine	Neurogenic	Vascular	Exogenous
Renal parenchymal disease	Primary aldosteronism	Brain tumor	Coarctation of the aorta	Monoamine oxidase inhibitors
Renal tumors	Pheochromocytoma	Encephalitis	Renal artery stenosis	Amphetamines
Arteritis	Cushing's syndrome	Guillain-Barré syndrome		Oral contraceptives
	Adrenogenital syndromes			Licorice
	Hyperthroidism			Lead

Essential Hypertension

Although the exact causes of essential hypertension remain undetermined, a variety of etiologic hypotheses have been proposed. In general, current views of essential hypertension emphasize the heterogeneity of this disorder and point to the probable multifactorial nature of its pathogenesis. For a detailed explanation of the roles of various blood-pressure control-systems in the development of essential hypertension, the reader is referred to an excellent view by Weiner (1979). Discussion here is limited to a brief survey of the major etiologic hypotheses.

Guyton (1979) proposed that the kidneys play a primary role in all forms of hypertension, although renal mechanisms may interact with the actions of the other regulatory systems. In this view, kidney function in essential hypertension is considered "abnormal" simply because it fails to maintain normal blood pressure. It is presumed that a significant retention of sodium and water occurs, although for unknown reasons, and that this retention promotes an increase in blood volume; such retention is associated with increased cardiac output and higher blood pressure. It is proposed that the total peripheral resistance may also rise later as a result of autoregulatory processes, which serve to stem an overperfusion of body tissues resulting from the volume-dependent increase in cardiac output. In any case, it is thought that the kidneys' control of pressure via regulation of body fluid volume is impaired in hypertension and becomes reset at an elevated baseline blood pressure.

A related hypothesis is that excessive salt intake contributes to an inability of the kidneys to adequately regulate fluid volume. There is some evidence that excessive sodium intake is implicated in the development of hypertension in animal models, and levels of sodium intake are correlated with the incidence of hypertension in some cross-cultural epidemiological investigations. The human data are confounded, however, by cultural differences on a variety of other potentially influential factors, such as societal structures, obesity, and physical activity (Dustan, 1983; Sokolow & McIlroy, 1981). Nevertheless, there is some evidence that impairment of sodium transport across cell membranes may be associated with an inherited susceptibility to hypertension (Kaplan, 1982).

It has been proposed that the renin–angiotensin–aldosterone system is also disrupted in essential hypertension (Laragh, 1983), at least among hypertensive individuals who exhibit an increased plasma renin activity. It is suggested that among these patients (possibly 20% of essential hypertensives), the normal homeostatic response to elevations in blood pressure (i.e., decreased renin production) has failed, and consequently, plasma renin activity remains inappropriately high relative to prevailing blood-pressure levels. Because renin production is stimulated, in part, by sympathetic nervous activity, some investigators have proposed that elevated plasma renin is indicative of autonomic nervous system involvement in essential hypertension. Support for this hypothesis derives from studies showing high resting concentrations of plasma norepinephrine and normalization of blood pressure following autonomic blockade among "high-renin" hypertensive subjects (Esler, Julius, Zweifler, Randall, Harburg, Gardiner, & DeQuattro, 1977); not all studies, however, have demonstrated similar associations (e.g., Morganti, Pickering, Lopez-Ouejero, & Laragh, 1980).

At the other end of the distribution of renin values are hypertensive patients who exhibit low plasma-renin activity, relative to other hypertensives. Here, it is thought that the renin–angiotensin–aldosterone system is actually functioning normally and that low renin activity in these individuals reflects the appropriate response of this system to an expanded fluid volume (Laragh, 1983). Although it is thus inferred that "low"-renin hypertension is due to increased blood volume, this inference remains controversial (Sokolow & McIlroy, 1981).

Dysfunction of the baroreceptor reflex system has also been proposed as an etiologic factor in essential hypertension, based on animal studies in which denervation of the baroreceptors produced elevations in blood pressure (Ferarrio & Takishita, 1983). Additionally, there is evidence for a resetting of the baroreceptors in human hypertension, so that previously "elevated" pressures cease to trigger compensatory cardiac responses. However, alteration of baroreceptor function appears to follow the development of hypertension, and the hypothesis that baroreceptor dysfunction causes essential hypertension has generally been dismissed (Dustan, 1983; Soklow & McIlroy, 1981). Nevertheless, the resetting of baroreceptors to tolerate higher pressures may play a significant role in the maintenance of hypertension.

Other investigators have emphasized to a greater extent the potential role of the autonomic nervous system in the development of essential hypertension. There is good evidence that autonomic mechanisms do play an important role in maintaining an elevated arterial pressure in many cases of borderline essential hypertension. A particularly interesting feature of borderline hypertension, moreover, is the observation that about 30% of such patients exhibit a significantly elevated cardiac output that stems from autonomic influences (Julius & Esler, 1975). Autonomic involvement is indicated by the fact that heart rate and stroke volume, as well as blood pressure, are normalized following pharmacological blockade of the sympathetic and parasympathetic innervations. Also, circulating catecholamines appear to be elevated in a large proportion of borderline cases, although this relationship has not been observed in all investigations (Goldstein, 1983; Kuchel, 1977).

Despite apparent autonomic involvement in the borderline condition, there is some controversy regarding the overall prognostic significance of early neurogenic hypertension. Indeed, in most cases of borderline hypertension, the blood pressure elevation does not persist over time but returns eventually to normotensive values. This finding suggests that the borderline condition may have limited importance in an understanding of the origins of established essential hypertension. Yet, even though most borderline patients do not experience a progressive rise in blood pressure, prospective studies do show that, as a group, borderline hypertensives are at substantially increased risk for subsequent sustained hypertension (as well as for the development of clinical coronary heart disease) (Julius, 1977; Julius, Weder, & Egan, 1983).

Borderline essential hypertension has also attracted the interest of many behavioral researchers because of well-established associations between psychosocial factors and activities of the autonomic nervous system (Weiner, 1979). In this regard, a frequent finding in psychophysiological studies of hypertension is that hypertensive individuals—especially borderline hypertensives—exhibit exaggerated heart rate and/or blood pressure and catecholamine reactions to common laboratory stressors, when compared to normotensive controls (Steptoe, Melville, & Ross, 1982). Importantly, the normotensive offspring of hypertensive parents also show a heightened cardiovascular reactivity to behavioral stimuli, when contrasted with persons having only normotensive parents (Matthews &

Rakaczky, 1986). Because individuals with a family history of hypertension are at increased risk of developing essential hypertension, such results have encouraged speculation that a cardiovascular hyperresponsivity to stress may be implicated in the etiology of this condition. Although discussed frequently in the psychosomatic literature, this hypothesis is viewed skeptically by many hypertension researchers; in addition, the "reactivity" hypothesis has still received little support from longitudinal studies following prehypertensive individuals through the borderline and established phases of hypertension (Krantz & Manuck, 1984).

One notable exception is a 47-year prospective investigation of initially normotensive individuals who showed, at intake, either exaggerated or normal blood-pressure reactions to a cold pressor test (immersion of a limb in cold water) (Wood, Sheps, Elveback, & Schirger, 1984). On follow-up, the hyperresponsive subjects exhibited hypertensive blood pressure elevations, in both the borderline and established ranges, more frequently than did individuals who had shown a less pronounced blood-pressure response to the same experimental stressor. Much additional evidence is needed, however, before the hypothesized relationship between individual differences in acute psychophysiological reactivity and subsequent development of hypertension may be considered adequately established. A more detailed discussion of this literature and of the proposed mechanisms linking transient cardiovascular responses (as occur under stress) with the chronic blood-pressure elevations of established hypertension may be found in a review article by Krantz and Manuck (1984).

Personality factors have also been implicated in the etiology of hypertension. Despite years of investigation, however, no clear behavioral precursor of essential hypertension has yet been documented. On the other hand, there is much suggestive evidence that some hypertensive patients experience difficulties in the expression of feelings, particularly anger and hostility (Manuck, Morrison, Bellack, & Polefrone, 1985). In a classic statement of this hypothesis, Alexander (1939) proposed that hypertensive individuals experience conflict between their strong dependency needs and their hostile impulses; this conflict is said to result in states of "suppressed hostility." Other investigators have also sought links between elevated blood pressure and aggression-related constructs, the latter being described variously as "inhibited aggressive impulses," "inwardly directed anger," and "inhibited power motivation." Significant associations have now been reported in numerous cross-sectional studies using diverse subject populations (e.g., young adults, middle-aged adults, and patient samples) and in two prospective investigations (e.g., Gentry, Chesney, Gary, Hall, & Harburg, 1982; Harburg, Erfurt, Havenstein, Chape, Schull, & Schork, 1963; Kahn, Medalie, Neufeld, Riss, & Goldbourt, 1972; Light & Obrist, 1983; McClelland, 1979). In several early studies involving direct observations of subjects' behaviors during role-played interpersonal encounters, moreover, hypertensive individuals were also described as reacting in an excessively deferential, submissive, and inhibited manner (e.g., Gressel, Shobe, Saslow, DuBois, & Schroeder, 1949; Harris, Sokolow, Carpenter, Freedman, & Hunt, 1953).

Yet, other investigators have failed to replicate these associations, and in some studies, hypertensives have been found either to behave more aggressively or to report experiencing greater hostility than normotensive controls. In part, inconsistencies in this literature may be due to numerous methodological faults, including (1) nonrepresentative patient sampling and selection of inappropriate comparison groups; (2) failure to control for obvious confounding variables (e.g., body mass and age); (3) reliance on subjective behavioral judgments vulnerable to observer bias; and (4) the use of psychometric instruments that have limited reliability and questionable or unknown external validity (Manuck *et al.*, 1985). It is also likely that true behavioral associations are obscured by the heterogeneity of hypertension itself. If it is presumed that psychological variables influence the development of hypertension largely through autonomic mechanisms, reliable associations between behavioral factors and hypertension should emerge only where the autonomic nervous system is responsible for maintaining patients' elevated blood pressures. Underscoring this point are several studies showing behavioral characteristics to be associated with hypertension only in patients exhibiting high plasma-renin activity (Esler *et al.*, 1977; Perini, Amann, Bolli, & Buhler, 1982). As noted earlier, high plasma renin may represent a "marker" for sympathetic nervous system involvement in mild essential hypertension.

A final consideration is that problems of anger and assertive expression may characterize many hypertensive individuals; yet, the exact nature of these difficulties may differ among patients. Recall that although many studies support the notion that hypertensives suppress hostile feelings or lack appropriate assertiveness, others have found hypertensives to be more hostile or aggressive than normotensive controls. Indeed, Harburg, Blakelock, and Roeper (1979) reported finding an elevated blood pressure associated with "inappropriate submissiveness" in some individuals and with "inappropriate assertiveness" in others. In a similar vein, Morrison, Bellack, and Manuck (1985) described the behavioral performances of borderline essential hypertensives and of normotensive controls during standard role-play tests of assertiveness. Although these investigators found significant assertion-related difficulties among hypertensive patients (as reflected in the subjects' expressive mannerisms and verbalizations), these difficulties were of two kinds: heightened hostility in one subset of hypertensive subjects and greater submissiveness in another. In addition, these two behavioral characteristics were accompanied by distinct patterns of cardiovascular response: the former was associated with exaggerated systolic blood pressure reactions and the latter with marked elevations in diastolic blood pressure. Whether this behavioral variability is also related to corresponding differences in the mechanisms underlying hypertension—or is even a precursor of essential hypertension—awaits further clinical and prospective epidemiological investigation. Hence, currently, the role of psychological or personality characteristics in hypertension must be considered equivocal. Also, because of the retrospective nature of nearly all the available studies, significant associations should currently be viewed as correlates, rather than as causes, of essential hypertension.

SYMPTOMS AND DIAGNOSES

Secondary Hypertension

Some forms of secondary hypertension that have notable symptoms in addition to elevated blood pressure are those hypertensions caused by endocrine dysfunctions, namely, pheochromocytoma, primary aldosteronism, and Cushing's syndrome. The elevated concentrations of catecholamines characteristic of pheochromocytoma commonly produce the symptoms of rapid heart beat, palpitations, headache, excessive sweating, tremor, flushing, tightness of the throat, and feelings of anxiety. Most of these symptoms occur paroxysmally and are transient. Symptoms of primary aldosteronism include headache, muscle weakness, frequent urination, paresthesia, and transient paralysis. Psychiatric disturbances ranging from decreased energy to severe depression occur occasionally in primary aldosteronism but are more common in Cushing's syndrome. The physical signs associated with Cushing's syndrome also include osteoporosis (weakening of bone tissue), glucose intolerance, skin discolorations, weight gain, sluggishness, and menstrual irregularities.

Essential Hypertension

A diagnosis of essential hypertension depends primarily on establishing the presence of a sustained elevation in blood pressure through repeated measurements obtained over a period of at least several weeks. Because blood pressure can be extremely variable across successive measurements, there is currently some interest in the use of ambulatory blood-pressure-monitoring techniques to aid in establishing patients' typical ranges of blood pressure during ordinary daily activities. Because of their high cost in time, equipment, and energy, however, ambulatory measurements are not yet used commonly in clinical practice.

For purposes of the following discussion, the various physical and psychological disruptions associated with essential hypertension are categorized as symptoms, consequences, and correlates. The term *symptom* is used here to denote a physiological sign of disease that is experienced subjectively by the hypertensive individual. The physiological abnormalities, or end-organ damage, that result from hypertension are considered *consequences*. Thus, the consequences of hypertension represent underlying pathology that may or may not be experienced subjectively via related symptoms. A third category of associated features is termed *correlates* of hypertension; this class of variables subsumes cognitive, perceptual, psychomotor, and other behavioral manifestations that may accompany hypertension. The first two categories, symptoms and consequences, reflect the aspects of hypertension that are of most immediate concern to medical practitioners, and they are discussed first.

Symptoms. Uncomplicated essential hypertension is generally viewed either as being asymptomatic or as being characterized by vague symptoms that are not pathognomic of hypertension. Reported symptoms in cases of mild to moderate essential hypertension include nonspecific headache, dizziness, fatigue, pounding of the heart, nosebleeds, insommia, snycope, and sweating (Berkow, 1982; Hoffman, Kolar, Reisenauer, & Matousek, 1973). It remains unclear, however, whether these symptoms actually occur more frequently in hypertensives, than in normotensive individuals. Indeed, two epidemiological surveys found either little or no relationship between such subjective physical complaints and levels of blood pressure: Among a large sample of young adults in Finland, Kottke, Tuomilehto, Puska, and Salonen (1979) found no correlation between blood pressure and the prevalence of 13 physical symptoms. Van Reek, Dierderiks, Philipsen, van Zutphen, and Seelen (1982) similarly reported finding no association between blood pressure and frequency of physical complaints (except for dizziness) in a comparison of untreated male hypertensives with matched normotensive controls. When all subjects were stratified by level of blood pressure, however, a curvilinear relationship was observed: complaints of dizziness, headache, and sleepiness were reported most frequently by individuals falling within both the lowest and the highest ranges of blood pressure.

In sum, reports of increased physical symptoms among mild to moderate essential hypertensives do not appear to reflect a robust phenomenon. Positive associations in earlier studies may also have been confounded by factors such as the patients' knowledge of their hypertensive diagnoses and their associated perceptions of ill health. Of perhaps greater importance, moreover, are iatrogenic symptoms associated with antihypertensive drug treatment itself; these symptoms are discussed below in the section on treatment of hypertension.

In severe or complicated hypertension, there do exist some clear symptoms and consequences that result either from the presence of extremely high levels of blood pressure or from end-organ damage. For example, headaches are often found in severe hypertension; these may be migrainous or localized in the occipital region and are typically worse in the morning. Other symptoms of severe hypertension include visual disturbances and transient neurological aberrations, such as mental confusion or convulsions (Sandok & Whisnant, 1983).

Consequences. The consequences of chronic hypertension involve damaging effects on the retina, the kidneys, the heart and the vascular system, and the brain—many of which can be life-threatening. Retinopathy is damage to the vascular system of the retina and may accompany even mild hypertension. Effects on the kidney, which stem primarily from associated arteriosclerosis, may result in significant renal impairment and, ultimately, kidney failure. As noted earlier, hypertension may lead, in the cerebral vasculature, to thrombosis and hemorrhage, as well as to embolization, resulting in stroke. Finally, chronic effects of hypertension on the heart itself include enlargement of the left ventricle (hypertrophy), heart failure, and myocardial infarction.

Correlates. It has been suggested that hypertension is sometimes accompanied by psychological symptoms, such as anxiety and depression, although evidence of such an association remains equivocal. A high prevalence of depressive symptoms is often reported among hypertensive patients, relative to the general population (Huapaya & Ananth, 1980). In comparing the prevalence of depression as a clinical syndrome between psychiatric patients with and without hypertension, Rabkin, Charles, and Kass (1983) found that a larger proportion of the hypertensive had been diagnosed as suffering from major depression. Levitan (1983) also reported that suicidal attempts and ideation were more prevalent among hypertensive patients than among normotensive controls. Similarly, prevalence of anxiety symptoms is reported to be high among hypertensive patients, when compared to the general population (Wheatley, Balter, Levine, Lipman, Bauer, & Bonato, 1975).

Yet, several other studies have indicated that hypertensives do not differ from normotensive controls on indices of psychiatric morbidity. In the study by Wheatley *et al.* (1975), for example, hypertensives showed no greater incidence of anxiety, depression, or hostility than a comparison group of normotensive medical patients matched for age and sex. Similarly, Foster and Bell (1983) reported that symptoms of anxiety did not differ between hypertensive patients and their spouses. Scores on the Zung Self-Rating Depression Scale also did not differentiate medical outpatients having normal and elevated blood pressures (Friedman & Bennett, 1977). And finally, in one investigation that did reveal higher scores among hypertensive subjects on self-report measures of depression and anxiety compared to normotensive controls, the "elevated" scores of the hypertensive group were still within the normal range (Wood, Elias, Schultz, & Pentz, 1979).

One factor that may be related to the incidence of psychiatric symptoms among hypertensive individuals is the patient's knowledge of his or her diagnosis and the awareness of having a chronic medical disorder. In a study reported by Cochrane (1979), for example, hypertensive patients who were aware of their diagnosis had more neurotic symptoms than normotensive individuals, whereas hypertensives identified through screening and unaware of their high blood pressure did not differ from controls. But not all investigators have observed a relationship between diagnostic knowledge and psychiatric symptoms. In a large-scale investigation of the effects of diagnosis and treatment of hypertension on psychological functioning, for instance, Mann (1984) reported no association between hypertension and psychiatric morbidity, irrespective of the patients' awareness of their diagnosis.

In conclusion, it remains uncertain whether psychiatric symptoms are common correlates of hypertension. It has been suggested, moreover, that depression is an unlikely result of the physiological changes associated with hypertension (Huapaya & Ananth, 1980), and that a high incidence of depression among hypertensives may be coincidental with the increased incidence of both disorders in the second half of life (Burch, 1983). Psychiatric concomitants of hypertension may also depend on the severity of the disorder and on the presence of other health-related consequences. In the investigation described by Mann (1984), for instance, the subjects had only moderately elevated blood pressures and, therefore, may not yet have suffered any serious effects of the disorder. The more frequent attempts at suicide among hypertensives described by Levitan (1983), on the other hand, occurred in hospitalized patients, whose hypertension was presumably of greater severity.

Other correlates of hypertension that are of potential interest to psychologists involve more subtle aspects of behavioral performance, such as memory function, intellectual performance, sensory-perceptual processes, and psychomotor skills. Generally, neuropsychological tests are of value in detecting impairments in cognitive and psychomotor processes that would not be manifested as gross neurological disturbance. Measures of "response slowing" on psychomotor tests (e.g., reaction time and finger tapping) or tasks with cognitive and perceptual-motor components (Tactual Performance Test and Trail-Making), for example, are sensitive to subclinical deficits and reflect skills that may be important in everyday activities (Light, 1980b).

In a review of studies of "response slowing," Light (1980b) concluded that hypertension is associated with delayed responding on both simple and complex perceptual-motor tasks. Measures on which hypertensive subjects exhibited such slowing include the Digit-Symbol subtest of the Wechsler Adult Intelligence Scale (WAIS), the Trail-Making test of the Halstead–Reitan Battery, reaction time tasks, and finger-tapping speed (Light, 1980b; Shapiro, Miller, King, Ginchereau, & Fitzgibbon, 1982). It should be noted, however, that these deficits were apparent only by statistical comparison with the performance of normotensive controls and do not denote impairment sufficient to interfere with ordinary functioning.

Related observations from studies using the Halstead–Reitan Battery include relative deficits on both the categories test and the memory tests (Goldman, Kleinman, Show, Bidus, & Korol, 1975; Wood & Elias, 1980). Poor performance among hypertensives on other measures of memory functions have been observed as well, and they indicate deficits in both long- and short-term memory (Wilkie & Eisdorfer, 1980). However, hypertensives have not been shown to perform differently from normotensive controls on tests of memory for designs (Shapiro et al., 1982), long-term verbal memory, or short-term visual memory (Franeschi, Tancredi, Smirna, Mercinelli, & Canal, 1982).

Studies contrasting the performances of hypertensive and normotensive subjects on the WAIS have produced variable results. Whereas some investigators have demonstrated lower scores among hypertensive individuals, particularly in younger subjects, on both verbal and performance subscales (Schultz & Elias, 1980), others have found no deficits among hypertensives on either the full scale, the verbal and performance subscales, or selected subtests (Boller, Vrtunski, Mack & Kim, 1977; Franeschi et al., 1982). Among other findings, hypertensives have been found to perform more poorly than normotensive subjects on tests of visuospatial recognition (Franeschi et al., 1982; Shapiro et al., 1982) and time estimation (Shapiro et al., 1982), but not on measures of attention, concentration, or abstract thinking (Franeschi et al., 1982).

In conclusion, decrements in several areas of behavioral performance have been found among hypertensive patients, though admittedly, such findings have not emerged in all studies. Perhaps the most consistent observation is that hypertensives exhibit relative deficits on tasks requiring either psychomotor or visuospatial skills. Although some aspects of memory and intellectual functioning also appear to be affected by hypertension, there is little evidence of impaired performance on tests of verbal and abstract reasoning. We should reiterate also that, where behavioral impairments have been observed among hypertensive patients, these effects still reflect only relative deficits and, in general, are not of a severity sufficient to disrupt usual functioning. In fact, in some studies, the "impaired" performance of hypertensive subjects is well within normal limits, even when statistically different from the performance of normotensive controls.

Finally, of considerable importance to the interpretation of these relationships are findings reported by Shapiro and colleagues (Miller, Shapiro, King, Ginchereau, & Hosutt, 1984). These investigators described 15-month follow-up data on hypertensive subjects who either did or did not receive treatment for their elevated blood pressures. Those patients whose hypertension was effectively controlled by antihypertensive medications exhibited significant restoration of function on a variety of sensory-perceptual, psychomotor, and cognitive tests, whereas untreated hypertensives continued to show performance decrements relative to normotensive controls. These findings suggest that behavioral deficits in hypertension are a result of the patients' increased blood pressure and are not a precursor of the hypertensive condition.

Differential Diagnosis

Problems of differential diagnosis in hypertension involve, primarily, the discrimination between essential and secondary forms of hypertension. However, some diagnostic issues are particularly relevant to the psychological correlates of high blood pressure. As noted above, the endocrine disturbances involved in some secondary hypertensions may produce associated psychiatric symptoms, such as depression and anxiety. Pheochromocytoma patients, for instance, may present with symptoms that overlap with those of panic disorder (e.g., episodic feelings of anxiety, choking sensations, palpitations, sweating, or tremor). In such cases, the presence of an adrenal tumor responsible for both the elevated blood pressure and the psychiatric symptoms may be detected through determination of the 24-h urinary catecholamine excretion (Jacob & Rapport, 1984). On the other hand, the relationship of essential hypertension to various other symptoms commonly reported by psychiatric patients (e.g., frequent headaches, fatigue, or dizziness) is more tenuous, and in such cases, a diagnosis of hypertension should not be viewed as precluding other causes of the presenting symptoms.

TREATMENT

The treatment of essential hypertension includes pharmacological therapy, dietary changes to reduce sodium intake, weight loss, exercise, and a variety of behavioral interventions aimed specifically at the reduction of blood pressure (e.g., biofeedback and relaxation). In cases of secondary hypertension, treatment often involves surgery, as for the excision of adrenal tumors, removal of a kidney, or repair of arterial stenosis to kidneys. When surgery is not appropriate or feasible, however, even secondary forms of hypertension are treated pharmacologically. In this section, therefore, actions of the various antihypertensive medications are outlined, and the behavioral implications of pharmacological treatments are described. This discussion is followed by consideration of behavioral interventions and their efficacy in the control of high blood pressure.

Pharmacological Treatment

The modern era of pharmacological therapy for hypertension began with the use of reserpine in the early 1950s which was soon followed by the introduction of diuretics. Since that time, several new classes of antihypertensive medications have been developed, and as a result, the pharmacological treatment of hypertension is now widespread. The current array of antihypertensive drugs falls into four major categories: (1) diuretics, (2) adrenergic inhibitors, (3) vasodilators, and (4) other specific agents. Examples of some common antihypertensive agents and their trade names are listed in Table 2.

The diuretics include three main groups, thiazides, loop diuretics, and potassium-sparing agents. These drugs all act by blocking sodium reabsorption at various sites in the kidney and, hence, increase the urinary excretion of sodium and water. In the short run, blood pressure is reduced by a lowering of a body fluid volume and cardiac output, though it is thought that the long-term effects of diuretics also involve a reduction of the peripheral resistance. Treatment with diuretics can reduce blood pressure by 5 to 20 mm Hg and is effective in controlling blood pressure in about half of mildly hypertensive patients (Kaplan, 1980). Among the three groups of diuretic medications, loop diuretics have more potent effects on diuresis than do thiazides. Potassium-sparing drugs cause fewer side effects associated with potassium depletion (hypokalemia) than are typically seen with use of thiazides but are also weaker antihypertensives.

The adrenergic inhibitors include four classes of drugs that have the effects of lowering cardiac output and peripheral resistance through a reduction in either central or peripheral sympathetic-nervous-system activity. Peripheral sympathetic-blocking agents, such as reserpine and guanethidine, deplete norepinephrine at peripheral nerve endings. Agents

Table 2. Common Antihypertensive Medications

Diuretics	Beta blockers	Vasodilators	Central adrenergic inhibitors	Alpha blockers	Peripheral adrenergic inhibitors
Thiazides (Diuril) [a] (HydroDIURIL)	Propranolol (Inderal)	Hydralazine (Apresoline)	Methyldopa (Aldomet)	Prazosin (Minipress)	Guanethidine (Ismelin)
Chlorthalidone (Hygroton)	Metroprolol (Lopressor)	Minoxidil (Loniten)	Clonidine (Catapres)		Reserpine (Serpasil)
Furosemide (Lasix)	Nadolol (Corgard)				
Spironolactone (Aldactone)	Atenolol (Tenormin)				

[a]Parentheses indicate trade names.

with central effects, such as methyldopa and clonidine, on the other hand, reduce sympathetic activity from the brain centers that regulate blood pressure. Drugs that block receptors of the peripheral sympathetic nervous system act on both beta receptors (e.g., propranolol) and alpha receptors (e.g., prazosin). Beta blockers are thought to affect blood pressure primarily by reducing cardiac output, though it has been suggested that some may also affect peripheral resistance and renin release by the kidney (Kaplan, 1980; Prichard & Owens, 1983). Alpha blockers lower arterial pressure by a reduction in the total peripheral resistance, which is achieved through their vasodilatory effects on blood vessels.

Vasodilators are administered orally, in most cases, or intravenously during hypertensive crises. These drugs cause direct smooth-muscle dilation or counteract circulating humoral vasoconstrictive substances. However, the actions of vasodilators can stimulate counterregulatory mechanisms serving to raise blood pressure, and for this reason, these drugs are ordinarily used in conjunction with other classes of antihypertensive medication. Finally, other recently developed antihypertensives include drugs that affect calcium transport across cell membranes, such as nifedipine, and those that completely block the production of angiotensin II, like Saralasin and Captopril.

The typical approach to pharmacological treatment of hypertension involves a so-called stepped care program, in which various agents are added, as needed, to bring blood pressure under control. The first step ordinarily consists of the administration of a diuretic, usually a thiazide. If this is not sufficient, drugs from Step 2 are added; these include the alpha blockers, the beta blockers, clonidine, methyldopa, and reserpine. More recently, beta-blocking agents have also been considered appropriate Step 1 medications. The third step is to add a vasodilator, and in the fourth step, guanethidine is either added or substituted for other drugs. The efficacy of this type of pharmacological treatment in reducing both blood pressure and subsequent cardiovascular disease (e.g., myocardial infarction) has been established in several large-scale clinical trials, most notably in the Hypertension Detection and Follow-Up Program (1979). In this investigation, lowering blood pressure via antihypertensive medications was shown to reduce hypertension-related cardiovascular morbidity and mortality even among patients having only mildly elevated blood pressures. An additional consideration relevant to pharmacological treatment is that the different classes of medication appear to affect blood pressure differently in blacks and whites; in particular, beta blockers are more effective among whites, whereas diuretics have greater utility in the treatment of hypertension in blacks (Seedat, 1980; Weber, Priest, Ricci, Eltora, & Brewer, 1980).

Side Effects

The pharmacological treatment of hypertension is often complicated by the presence of significant side effects. Prominent adverse reactions associated with common antihypertensive medications are listed in Table 3. The most common of these symptoms are fatigue and sedation, dry mouth, nightmares, dizziness, tachycardia, palpitations, gastrointestinal symptoms, headache, depression, cognitive impairment, and sexual dysfunction. However, the frequency and nature of such reactions vary across the different classes of medication and are often nonspecific. Interestingly, two of the more common side effects, dizziness and headache, are also among those symptoms thought to be associated with hypertension itself. Dizziness that is definitely due to antihypertensive treatment, though, typically takes the form of postural or exercise hypotension (i.e., it is more appropriately described as lightheadedness and is associated with standing or exertion). Overall, beta blockers, diuretics, and calcium blockers have the least frequent and the least serious side effects, whereas drugs affecting the central nervous system or substantially altering catecholamine levels (e.g., clonidine, reserpine, methyldopa, and guanethidine) tend to produce more severe reactions.

Serious side effects that are of particular interest from a behavioral standpoint include depression, sexual dysfunction, and cognitive, psychomotor, and perceptual impairments. The first of these reactions, depression, is most commonly reported among patients prescribed reserpine (10%–25% of cases), but it has also been associated with the use of clonidine, methyldopa, and prazosin (McMahon, 1978; Prichard & Owens, 1983). Although severe depression and even suicidal attempts have been observed in patients treated with reserpine (Quetsch, Achor, Litin, & Faucett, 1959), such responses are less frequent now than in the past because of a reduction in the prescribed dosage. It is generally thought that the depressive effects of reserpine are related to a depletion of the central monoamines: norepinephrine, dopamine, and serotonin. That depressive symptoms are reported as well among patients administered clonidine and methyldopa is consistent with this hypothesis, as these drugs also reduce central norepinephrine activity.

Whether antihypertensive medications actually produce clinical depression remains controversial. It is argued, for example, that reserpine induces a state of sedation and psychomotor retardation, but one lacking in many of the affective and cognitive components of a "true" depression (Pottash, Black, & Gold, 1981). In addition, depressive symptoms have not been related to the use of several other antihypertensive agents, including the diuretics and guanethidine (Bant, 1978; Bulpitt & Dollery, 1973; DeMuth & Ackerman, 1983; Mann, 1984). In this regard, Rabkin *et al.* (1983) examined the DSM-III diagnosis of depression and medication use among hypertensives belonging to an outpatient psychiatric population. These investigators found that the depressed and nondepressed hypertensive groups contained comparable proportions of treated and untreated hypertensive

Table 3. Side Effects of Antihypertensive Medications

Frequency	Diuretics	Clonidine	Methyldopa	Reserpine
Frequent	Fatigue/sedation	Fatigue/sedation Dry mouth Dizziness Cognitive impairment	Fatigue/sedation Dry mouth Dizziness Increased appetite	Drowsiness/sedation Nasal congestion Nightmares Depression
Occasional	Gastrointestinal symptoms Headache Neurological disturbances Impotence Menstrual dysfunction	Edema Headache Weight gain Impotence Nightmares Insomnia Anxiety	Edema Diarrhea Weight gain Impotence Retrograde ejaculation Sleep disturbances Paresthesias Depression	Edema Headache Gastrointestinal symptoms Impotence Decreased libido Dizziness Nightmares Fainting Palpitations Cardiac arrhythmia Anxiety

Frequency	Guanethidine	Propranolol	Hydralazine	Prazosin
Frequent	Impotence Retrograde ejaculation Dizziness Diarrhea	Nightmares Aggravation of asthma Heart failure[a]	Tachycardia Palpitations Aggravation of angina Headache Gastrointestinal symptoms Fatigue	Dizziness
Occasional	Dry mouth	Fatigue Sedation Anorexia Nausea	Dizziness Paresthesias Tremors Anxiety Sleep disturbance	Tachycardia Headache Gastrointestinal symptoms Dry mouth Impotence Depression

[a]Only among patients with preexisting heart disease.

patients, and that, among treated hypertensives, the presence of depression was unrelated to the type of medication.

It should be noted, however, that most studies of depression as a side effect of antihypertensive medication have been plagued by important methodological faults, including (1) inadequate assessment and diagnosis of depression; (2) a failure to account for patients' previous psychiatric histories; (3) the use of inappropriate control conditions; and (4) a failure to distinguish between depression as a symptom or mood state and as a clinical syndrome (Burch, 1983; Pottash *et al.*, 1981; Rabkin *et al.*, 1983). Because of these limitations, it has been difficult to determine whether depression, when occurring among treated hypertensives, is due to the medications prescribed, is a response to the presence of a chronic medical condition, or is unrelated to the patients' hypertension.

Still, the physician or psychologist treating a hypertensive patient should be alert to depression as a potential side effect of antihypertensive therapy. Additionally, individuals having a previous history of depression may be more susceptible to the depressive side effects of such medications (Bant, 1978; Pottash *et al.*, 1981), and possible interactions between antidepressant and antihypertensive agents should be considered (Burch, 1983).

Sexual dysfunction has been reported to occur with the administration of several antihypertensive drugs. Impotence in men is associated with most classes of antihypertensives, and ejaculatory disturbances, such as retrograde ejaculation, are frequently reported among men prescribed clonidine, guanethidine, methyldopa, and reserpine. Loss of libido has been reported also in both men and women taking diuretics, guanethidine, methyldopa, propranolol, and reserpine. Although sexual dysfunction may be less evident in women, reduction of vaginal lubrication and menstrual abnormalities have been related to the use of diuretics (Epstein & Oster, 1984). In addition, orgasmic capacity may be impaired among some women prescribed centrally acting antihypertensives.

In a study of patients following a variety of drug regimens, Watts (1981) found that hypertensives reported significantly impaired sexual desire, orgasm, and sexual satisfaction, but not lower arousal, compared to medical patient controls. Of the various complaints cited, erectile failure was the most common. Estimates of the prevalence of sexual dysfunction have ranged from 14% to 36% for methyldopa, 0% to 24% for clonidine, 54% to 60% for guanethidine, and 1% to 3% for the beta blockers (Bulpitt & Dollery, 1973; Reichgott, 1979). The mechanisms by which antihypertensive agents produce these symptoms relate to their diminishment of the sympathetic nervous system component of the male sexual response, which is involved in orgasm and is necessary to prevent retrograde ejaculation. It is not clear how the thiazides affect sexual function (Reichgott, 1979); however, their mode of action is not thought to involve a significant alteration of sympathetic activity.

Cognitive, psychomotor, and perceptual impairments are a third category of side effects that are of interest from a behavioral perspective. An example of research in this area is a recent study of memory deficits among groups of hypertensive patients receiving diuretic treatment only, diuretics plus methyldopa, or diuretics plus propranolol (Solomon, Hotchkiss, Saraway, Bayer, Ramsey, & Blum, 1983). The results indicated that hypertensives taking propranolol or methyldopa performed more poorly than subjects receiving diuretics alone on the verbal, but not the visual, memory scales of the Wechsler Memory Test. Unfortunately, no comparison was made with untreated hypertensives, and the test was administered with the experimenter's awareness of the subjects' diagnostic status and type of treatment.

Regarding psychomotor performance, Light (1980a) reported that subjects administered reserpine and methyldopa responded poorly in standard reaction time and hand-eye coordination tasks. Fewer behavioral disruptions have been found among patients receiving beta blockers, and in fact, studies have shown no impairment of function related to the use of beta blockers on measures of reaction time, simulated car driving, and other perceptual-motor skills. Similarly, Shapiro and Miller (1985) observed that hypertensives treated with beta-blocking medications performed significantly better on rate of tapping (a psychomotor task), visual recognition time (a sensory-perceptual task), a cognitively challenging video game, and the Digit-Symbol Substitution Test of the WAIS, than patients prescribed either thiazides alone or thiazides in conjunction with vasodilators or centrally acting antihypertensives.

Behavioral Factors in the Treatment of Hypertension

Compliance with Pharmacological Treatment. Although pharmacological treatment is clearly beneficial in the control of high blood pressure, patient compliance remains a major problem in the management of hypertension. Noncompliance occurs at various stages in the medical management of hypertension and can take several forms, including failure to follow through on referral recommendations, to keep appointments, or to take medications as prescribed (Haynes, 1974). Such problems are perhaps not surprising, given the nature of the adverse reactions to the various antihypertensive agents, the need to take such drugs over long periods of time, and the usual absence of notable symptoms when early hypertension is left untreated. McMahon (1978) estimated that 7% to 20% of patients on antihypertensive medications discontinue treatment because of the side effects. Bulpitt and Dollery (1973) reported, similarly, that, in their sample, 5% of patients taking diuretics and 16% to 22% of hypertensives on other medications were not fully compliant. More recently, it has been estimated that up to 50% of patients discontinue treatment within one year, and that 30% do not take the prescribed dosages (Haynes, Taylor, & Sackett, 1983). However, it cannot be assumed that failure to comply is determined solely by the presence of unpleasant side effects. In a study of sexual functioning among hypertensives described earlier, for example, Watts (1981) found no relationship between sexual dysfunction and medication compliance (i.e., similar rates of medication use were reported by patients having good and poor sexual functioning). Other important factors determining compliance with medical regimens that may be relevant to hypertension include the complexity of the regimen itself and the degree of behavioral change required to achieve full compliance (Haynes, 1974).

From their research on adherence to antihypertensive treatment, Haynes and Sackett offered the following conclusions (Haynes *et al.*, 1983). First, the traditional methods used by physicians in detecting and reducing noncompliance, such as clinical judgment and patient education regarding the benefits of treatment, are insufficient to achieve control of blood pressure. More effective strategies for improving compliance include increased supervision through more frequent appointments, routine self-monitoring of blood pressure, recalling of treatment dropouts, use of home or work-site visits, use of reinforcement contingencies, the tailoring of treatment to daily habits, and self-management techniques.

Regarding the assessment of compliance, unfortunately, there are few techniques that are both sensitive and practical for clinical use. Existing measures include monitoring of blood pressure, questioning the patient about difficulties in following the regimen, pill counts, and biochemical assays. Obviously, to the extent that the clinician can employ the latter two of these strategies, a more accurate evaluation of patients' compliance may be expected.

Behavioral Treatments. In the past several years, direct behavioral interventions have been developed as adjunctive or alternative therapies for hypertension. The primary behavioral treatments involve various forms of relaxation, meditation, and biofeedback. Although other psychological interventions have been advocated, such as psychotherapy, hypnosis, and stress reduction, these latter approaches have not been studied extensively and are not discussed here.

Meditation and relaxation techniques include training in Jacobsen's progressive muscle relaxation, hatha yoga, autogenic training, transcendental meditation, Benson's "relaxation response,'' and various biofeedback-assisted relaxation techniques. The use of bio-feedback as an adjunct to relaxation training typically involves feedback of either elec-trodermal or electromyographic activity, or both, and is based on the presumption that these physiological variables reflect the prevailing levels of autonomic arousal. This use of biofeedback should be distinguished, however, from techniques involving the direct feedback of patients' blood pressure, as discussed below.

The various treatments listed above are not always clearly distinguishable in appli-cation, and each involves, to a differing extent, two basic components: voluntary mus-cle relaxation and a focusing of attention. It is argued that either or both of these com-ponents elicit a ''hypometabolic'' state (Benson, Greenwood, & Klemchuk, 1975) characterized by reductions in blood pressure, heart rate, oxygen consumption, respira-tion rate, and blood lactate, that is, a generalized lowering of sympathetic nervous sys-tem activity. The evidence of reduced sympathetic arousal via relaxation and meditation exercises, however, remains inconclusive (Jacob, 1984).

In the case of direct blood-pressure biofeedback, patients are provided exact infor-mation about their systolic or diastolic blood pressure, in either analogue or digital form. On occasion, feedback of other hemodynamic parameters that are known to be correlated with blood pressure, such as the velocity of pulse transmission between two arterial sites, is provided. These techniques represent an extension of previous experimental studies demonstrating that healthy individuals can achieve some voluntary modification of blood pressure when presented repeated feedback of current blood-pressure levels.

Initial studies of the efficacy of relaxation and meditation in the control of hyper-tension showed moderate to large reductions in blood pressure following treatment. In reviewing these early investigations, Agras and Jacob (1979) noted that mean blood-pressure reductions of up to 10 mm Hg were obtained in several studies involving treat-ment by either relaxation or meditation alone; even larger effects were seen when inter-ventions combining meditation and relaxation techniques were used. Yet other investi-gations found little, if any, benefit associated with the use of these interventions. Initial clinical studies of blood pressure biofeedback produced results similar to those reported for relaxation: large treatment effects in some studies, but only modest or minimal blood pressure changes in others. It should also be noted that interpreting the results of these early studies is made difficult by a variety of methodological deficiencies, including a lack of appropriate control conditions, inadequate follow-up, and potentially confounding in-fluences of antihypertensive medications and concurrent life-style changes (e.g., modifi-cations in diet or exercise).

More recent data derived from better-controlled studies of behavioral interventions for hypertension have continued to demonstrate variable effects. For example, some researchers have found blood pressure reductions following relaxation (Brauer, Horlick, Nelson, Farquhar, & Agras 1979), biofeedback (Blanchard, Miller, Abel, Haynes, & Wicker, 1979; Shoemaker & Tasto, 1975; Surwit, Shapiro, & Good, 1978), or both (Haf-ner, 1982) to be no greater than those seen among patients who were told simply to re-lax, who were provided psychotherapy, or who were given no treatment at all. On the other hand, other investigators have shown relaxation and/or biofeedback to produce reductions in blood pressure that significantly exceeded those observed among patients receiving control treatments, such as blood pressure monitoring or nonspecific psychotherapy. In one study, blood pressure reductions achieved through the use of relaxation were found to be maintained over a 15-month follow-up and to generalize to measurements taken in a nonclinical setting (i.e., at the work site) (Agras, Southam, & Taylor, 1983; Southam, Agras, Taylor, & Kraemer, 1982). Substantial reductions in blood pressure were also reported by Glasgow, Gaarder, and Engel (1982), using a treatment package involving sequential presentation of relaxation and blood pressure biofeedback. Mean decreases of 12–14/10 mm Hg were achieved, and here, too, there was some evidence of generalization and maintenance of treatment effects. For a more detailed discussion of these investigations, the reader is referred to recent reviews by Johnston (1982), Shapiro and Jacob (1983), and Wadden, Luborsky, Greer, and Crits-Christoph (1984).

In general, it appears that behavioral treatments are more effective than blood pressure monitoring, rest, and some forms of nonspecific psychotherapy (Taylor, Farquhar, Nelson, & Agras, 1977; Wadden et al., 1984). Studies comparing relaxation to biofeedback procedures show these interventions to be equally effective (Wadden et al., 1984), although some added benefit may be derived from combining the two techniques (Glasgow et al., 1982). A failure to observe substantial reductions in blood pressure in some controlled studies may also be due, in part, to the great variability that is typically observed in patients' responses to behavioral interventions. Given the heterogeneity of essential hypertension itself, this variability is not surprising. Indeed, insofar as behavioral therapies would be expected to lower blood pressure through effects on autonomic arousal, it is reasonable to hypothesize that appreciable treatment effects will be obtained only in patients whose hypertension is maintained via autonomic mechanisms (Cottier, Shapiro, & Julius, 1984). To date, however, little attention has been paid to such individual differences, and there are few identified predictors of a favorable response to the behavioral treatment of hypertension (Wadden et al., 1984).

Several limitations of studies of behavioral interventions in hypertension should be noted as well. For example, the effects of relaxation and biofeedback on blood pressure are often of insufficient magnitude to have clinical meaning or are not found consistently for both systolic and diastolic blood pressure. Because of the many behavioral adjustments that may be needed to achieve daily practice of these techniques, it is likely that such interventions are accompanied by the same compliance problems that characterize drug therapies. It has been found also that relaxation training is significantly less effective than pharmacological treatment (Luborsky, Crits-Christoph, Brady, Kron, Weiss, Cohen, & Levy, 1982), and the extent to which behavioral approaches can usefully supplement antihypertensive medications remains unclear. Thus, behavioral treatments are not, at present, viable alternatives to medication in the control of high blood pressure. Because some individuals do appear to be responsive to relaxation and biofeedback approaches, however, these interventions may be considered in the mildly hypertensive patient before recourse to antihypertensive medication.

Finally, few investigators have examined whether behavioral treatments can modify the behavioral correlates and the long-term health risks related to hypertension. One exception was reported by Goldman et al. (1975), who observed that reduction of blood pressure in hypertensive patients through the use of biofeedback was associated with improved performance on neuropsychological testing. Although a reduction in cardiovascular morbidity and mortality would also be expected were blood pressure to be effectively lowered through behavioral treatments, such effects have not yet been demonstrated (Johnston, 1982) and very likely await interventions having more significant and protracted influences on blood-pressure control.

We should also point out a few practical considerations germane to the treatment of hypertensive patients. The psychologist typically becomes involved in the management of a hypertensive individual when the patient is referred by his or her physician. Such referrals are most likely to involve young, borderline hypertensives, whom physicians may be reluctant to begin treating pharmacologically, or patients with established hypertension who are interested in behavioral therapies as an adjunct to antihypertensive medications. In either event, it is important that the psychologist accept for treatment only physician-referred hypertensive patients and do so only after the patient has received a thorough medical examination. The psychologist should also view her or his contributions as part of a comprehensive treatment plan and, therefore, should maintain active and ongoing communication with the patient's physician. This will enable both the psychologist and the physician to appropriately adjust their treatments in response to any changes in the patient's blood pressure, compliance, or reported side effects. If the psychologist is involved in enhancing adherence to a program of weight loss, exercise, and dietary changes, knowledge of the prescribed diet or exercise regimen is, of course, essential. Because in most instances the psychologist will be providing some form of behavioral treatment designed to lower blood pressure (e.g., relaxation or biofeedback), we note below a few points relevant specifically to the implementation of such interventions.

As several investigators have observed significant effects of daily self-monitoring on blood pressure, it is recommended that the first phase of treatment involve an extended baseline period lasting 2 weeks at minimum. For purposes of the baseline phase, patients can be taught to measure their own blood pressures at home using an inexpensive manual or automated blood-pressure monitor. These measurements should be obtained at least twice daily and should include one reading taken immediately on awakening; this reading may provide a best index of the patient's basal blood pressure (Laughlin, 1981). Assessment of blood pressure in other settings, including the physician's or psychologist's office, may also lead to the detection of so-called office reactors and may provide information regarding the variability of the blood pressure. If such assessments reveal that a patient is particularly reactive to the measurement situation and that readings obtained in a clinic setting are not representative of his or her typical blood pressure, this information should be provided to the physician as an aid in determining whether the patient should be treated.

Following the period of baseline monitoring (and if reduction of blood pressure has not occurred during this interval), initiation of the simplest and most cost-effective treatment is recommended. This will most likely involve relaxation training, either progressive muscle relaxation, autogenic relaxation, or meditation. In general, training in these techniques should be conducted on an individual basis, so that the pace of training and adjustments in the exercises may be tailored to individual needs and preferences. Once the patient has learned the technique, it should be practiced for periods of 15 to 20 min at least once daily, and twice daily if possible. When the relaxation training has been completed and a routine of daily practice has been established, the patient may then be encouraged to incorporate more frequent (but shorter) relaxation periods into her or his daily activities in order to enhance generalization of the relaxation effects. Brief relaxation periods may be used on a time-contingent basis (e.g., every hour) or in response to situations and stimuli that have been identified as "arousing." If the training is successful, its effects on blood pressure levels may be observed within a month of treatment, although 3 to 6 months may be required for some patients or for maximal effects (Jacob, 1984). If the desired reductions in blood pressure have not occurred after 6 months of regular practice of relaxation, however, the psychologist may consider introducing biofeedback—such as frontalis electromyography (EMG) or heart-rate feedback—as an aid to relaxation, or feedback of the blood pressure itself. As in standard relaxation training, frequent home practice and the integration of such practice into daily activities is important in achieving a generalization of biofeedback effects. Home practice may include measurement of the feedback-targeted physiological variable (e.g., EMG or blood pressure) if feasible or may simply involve practice of the strategy used to achieve relaxation in the laboratory sessions.

Many of the problems associated with pharmacological therapies apply as well to behavioral treatments of hypertension. As noted previously, compliance difficulties may be expected in many patients because of the considerable time and effort required to maintain daily practice of these techniques. Also, as with antihypertensive medications, behavioral treatments may need to be applied on a continuing basis to achieve long-term blood pressure control. Although in some patients the concomitant benefits of relaxation (e.g., anxiety reduction) may facilitate continued practice, for others it may be necessary to implement "booster sessions" or to follow patients up at infrequent intervals to prevent treatment dropouts. Finally, as indicated earlier, it can be expected that many individuals will not respond adequately to behavioral interventions, even after considerable training, and that these patients may require more intensive medical management. Although determining when it is appropriate to discontinue behavioral treatment is a judgment that can be made only case by case, some of the guidelines mentioned above may be helpful in arriving at such decisions.

REFERENCES

Agras, S., & Jacob, R. (1979). Hypertension. In O. Pomerleau & J. P. Brady (Eds.), *Behavioral medicine: Theory and practice*. Baltimore: Williams & Wilkins.

Agras, W. S., Southam, M. A., & Taylor, B. C. (1983). Long-term persistence of relaxation-induced blood pressure lowering during the working day. *Journal of Consulting and Clinical Psychology, 5*, 792–794.

Alexander, F. (1939). Emotional factors in essential hypertension: Presentation of a tentative hypothesis. *Psychosomatic Medicine, 1*, 173–179.

Bant, W. P. (1978). Antihypertensive drugs and depression: A reappraisal. *Psychological Medicine, 8*, 275–283.

Benson, H., Greenwood, M. M., & Klemchuck, H. (1975). The relaxation response: Psychophysiologic aspects and clinical applications. *International Journal of Psychiatry in Medicine, 6*, 87–97.

Berkow, R. (Ed.). (1982). *The Merck Manual* (14th ed.). Rahway, NJ: Merck, Sharp & Dome Research Laboratories.

Blanchard, E. B., Miller, S. T., Abel, G. G., Haynes, M. R., & Wicker, R. (1979). Evaluation of biofeedback in the treatment of borderline essential hypertension. *Journal of Applied Behavior Analysis, 11*, 99–109.

Boller, F., Vrtunski, P. B., Mack, J. L., & Kim, Y. (1977). Neuropsychological correlates of hypertension. *Archives of Neurology, 34*, 701–705.

Brauer, A. P., Horlick, L., Nelson, E., Farquhar, J. W., & Agras, W. S. (1979). Relaxation therapy for essential hypertension: A Veterans Administration outpatient study. *Journal of Behavioral Medicine, 2,* 21–29.

Bulpitt, C. J., & Dollery, C. T. (1973). Side effects of hypertensive agents evaluated by a self-administered questionnaire. *British Medical Journal, 3,* 485–490.

Burch, E. A. (1983). Primary care management of the depressed hypertensive patient. *Psychosomatics, 24,* 389–394.

Cochrane, R. (1979). Neuroticism and the discovery of high blood pressure. *Journal of Psychosomatic Research, 13,* 21–25.

Cottier, C., Shapiro, K., & Julius, S. (1984). Treatment of mild hypertension with progressive muscle relaxation. *Archives of Internal Medicine, 144,* 1954–1958.

DeMuth, G. W., & Ackerman, S. H. (1983). Alpha-methyldopa and depression: A clinical study and review of the literature. *American Journal of Psychiatry, 140,* 534–538.

Dustan, H. P. (1983). Personal views on the mechanisms of hypertension. In J. Genest, O. Kuchel, P. Hamet, & M. Cantin (Eds.), *Hypertension: Pathophysiology and treatment* (2nd ed.). New York: McGraw-Hill.

Epstein, M., & Oster, J. R. (1984). *Hypertension: A practical approach.* Philadelphia: W. B. Saunders.

Esler, M., Julius, S., Zweifler, A., Randall, O., Harburg, E., Gardiner, H., & DeQuattro, V. (1977). Mild high-renin essential hypertension: Neurogenic human hypertension? *New England Journal of Medicine, 296,* 405–411.

Ferrario, C. M., & Takishita, S. (1983). Baroreceptor reflexes and hypertension. In J. Genest, O. Kuchel, P. Hamet, & M. Cantin (Eds.), *Hypertension: Pathophysiology and treatment* (2nd ed.). New York: McGraw-Hill.

Foster, G. D., & Bell, S. T. (1983). Relation of state and trait anxiety to essential hypertension. *Psychological Reports, 52,* 355–358.

Franeschi, M., Tancredi, O., Smirne, S., Mercinelli, A., & Canal, N. (1982). Cognitive processes in hypertension. *Hypertension, 4,* 226–229.

Friedman, M. J., & Bennett, P. L (1977). Depression and hypertension. *Psychosomatic Medicine, 39,* 139–142.

Gentry, W. D., Chesney, M. A., Gary, H. E., Hall, R. P., & Harburg, E. (1982). Habitual anger-coping styles: I. Effect on mean blood pressure and risk for hypertension. *Psychosomatic Medicine, 44,* 195–202.

Glasgow, M. S., Gaarder, K. R., & Engel, B. T. (1982). Behavioral treatment of high blood pressure: II. Acute and sustained effects of relaxation and systolic blood pressure feedback. *Psychosomatic Medicine, 44,* 155–170.

Goldman, H., Kleinman, K. M., Snow, M. Y., Bidus, D. R., & Korol, B. (1975). Relationship between essential hypertension and cognitive functioning: Effects of biofeedback. *Psychophysiology, 12,* 569–573.

Goldstein, D. (1983). Plasma catecholamines and essential hypertension. *Hypertension, 5,* 86–99.

Gressel, G. E., Shobe, F. O., Saslow, G., DuBois, M., & Schroeder, H. A. (1949). Personality factors in essential hypertension. *Journal of American Medical Association, 140,* 265–272.

Guyton, A. C. (1977). Personal views on mechanisms of hypertension. In J. Genest, E. Koiw, & O. Kuchel (Eds.), *Hypertension: Physiopathology and treatment.* New York: McGraw-Hill.

Hafner, R. J. (1982). Psychological treatment of essential hypertension: A controlled comparison of meditation and meditation plus biofeedback. *Biofeedback and Self-Regulation, 7,* 305–317.

Harburg, E., Erfurt, J. C., Hauenstein, L. S., Chape, C., Shcull, W. J., & Schork, M. A. (1973). Socioecological stress, suppressed hostility, skin color, and black–white male blood pressure: Detroit. *Psychosomatic Medicine, 35,* 276–296.

Harburg, E., Blakelock, E. H., & Roeper, P. J. (1979). Resentful and reflective coping with arbitrary authority and blood pressure: Detroit. *Psychosomatic Medicine, 41,* 189–202.

Harris, R. E., Sokolow, M., Carpenter, L. G., Freedman, M., & Hunt, S. P. (1953). Response to psychologic stress in persons who are potentially hypertensive. *Circulation, 7,* 572–578.

Haynes, R. B. (1974). A critical review of the "determinants" of patient compliance with therapeutic regimens. In D. L. Sackett & R. B. Haynes (Eds.), *Compliance with therapeutic regimens.* Baltimore: Johns Hopkins University Press.

Haynes, R. B., Taylor, D. W., & Sackett, D. L. (1983). Hypertension in the real world. In J. Genest, O.

Kuchel, P. Hamet, & M. Cantin (Eds.), *Hypertension: Pathophysiology and treatment* (2nd ed.). New York: McGraw-Hill.

Hoffman, O., Kolar, M., Reisenauer, R., & Matousek, V. (1973). Significance of the differences in the prevalence of the subjective complaints between normotensive and hypertensive subjects. *Acta Universitatis Carolinae Medica, 19,* 601-616.

Huapaya, L., & Ananth, J. (1980). Depression associated with hypertension: A review. *Psychiatric Journal of the University of Ottawa, 5,* 58-62.

Hypertension Detection and Follow-up Program Cooperation Group. (1979). Five year findings of the hypertension detection and follow-up program: I. Reduction of mortality in persons with high blood pressure, including mild hypertension. *Journal of the American Medical Association, 242,* 2562-2571.

Jacob, R. (1984). Modifying neurogenic components of hypertension: Relaxation and biofeedback therapy. *Maryland State Medical Journal, 33,* 209-214.

Jacob, R. G., & Rapport, M. D. (1984). Panic disorder: Medical and psychological parameters. In S. M. Turner (Ed.), *Behavioral theories and treatment of anxiety.* New York: Plenum Press.

Johnston, D. W. (1982). Behavioural treatment in the reduction of coronary risk factors: Type A behaviour and blood pressure. *British Journal of Clinical Psychology, 21,* 281-294.

Julius, S. (1977). Borderline hypertension: Epidemiologic and clinical implications. In J. Genest, E. Koiw, & O. Kuchel (Eds.), *Hypertension: Physiopathology and treatment.* New York, McGraw-Hill.

Julius, S., & Esler, M. (1975). Autonomic nervous cardiovascular regulation in borderline hypertension. *American Journal of Cardiology, 36,* 685-696.

Julius, S., & Hansson, L. (1983). Classification of hypertension. In J. Genest, O. Kuchel, P. Hamet, & M. Cantin (Eds.), *Hypertension: Pathophysiology and treatment* (2nd ed.). New York: McGraw-Hill.

Julius, S., Weder, A. B., & Egan, B. M. (1983). Pathophysiology of early hypertension: Implications for epidemiological research. In F. Gross & T. Strasser (Eds.), *Mild hypertension: Recent advances.* New York: Raven Press.

Kahn, H. A., Medalie, J. H., Neufeld, H. N., Riss, E., & Goldbourt, U. (1972). The incidence of hypertension and associated factors: The Israel ischemic heart disease study. *American Heart Journal, 84,* 171-182.

Kaplan, N. M. (1980). The control of hypertension: A therapeutic breakthrough. *American Scientist, 68,* 537-545.

Kaplan, N. M. (1982). *Clinical hypertension* (3rd ed.). Baltimore: Williams & Wilkins.

Kottke, T. E., Tuomilehto, J., Puska, P., & Salonen, J. T. (1979). The relationship of symptoms and blood pressure in a population sample. *International Journal of Epidemiology, 8,* 355-359.

Krantz, D. S., & Manuck, S. B. (1984). Acute psychophysiologic reactivity and risk of cardiovascular disease: A review and methodologic critique. *Psychological Bulletin, 96,* 435-464.

Kuchel, O. (1977). Autonomic nervous system in hypertension: Clinical aspects. In J. Genest, E. Koiw, & O. Kuchel (Eds.), *Hypertension: Physiopathology and treatment.* New York: McGraw-Hill.

Laragh, J. H. (1983). Personal views on the mechanisms of hypertension. In J. Genest, O. Kuchel, P. Hamet, & M. Cantin (Eds.), *Hypertension: Pathophysiology and treatment* (2nd ed.). New York : McGraw-Hill.

Laughlin, K. D. (1981). Enhancing the effectiveness of behavioral treatments of essential hypertension. *Physiology and Behavior, 26,* 907-913.

Levitan, H. (1983). Suicidal trends in patients with asthma and hypertension. *Psychotherapy and Psychosomatics, 39,* 165-170.

Lew, E. A. (1973). High blood pressure, other risk factors, and longevity: The insurance viewpoint. *The American Journal of Medicine, 55,* 281-294.

Light, K. C. (1980a). Antihypertensive drugs and behavioral performance. In M. F. Elias & D. H. Streeten (Eds.), *Hypertension and cognitive processes.* Mt. Desert, ME: Beech Hill.

Light, K. C. (1980b). Hypertension and response slowing. In M. F. Elias & D. H. Streeten (Eds.), *Hypertension and cognitive processes.* Mt. Desert, ME: Beech Hill.

Light, K. C., & Obrist, P. A. (1983). Task difficulty, heart rate reactivity, and cardiovascular responses to an appetitive reaction time task. *Psychophysiology, 20,* 301-312.

Luborsky, L., Crits-Christoph, P., Brady, J. P., Kron, R. E., Weiss, T., Cohen, M., & Levy, L. (1982). Behavioral versus pharmacological treatments for essential hypertension—A needed comparison. *Psychosomatic Medicine, 41,* 203-213.

Mann, A. H. (1984). Hypertension: Psychological aspects and diagnostic impact in a clinical trial. *Psychological Medicine (Suppl. 5)*, 1–35.

Manuck, S. B., Morrison, R. L., Bellack, A. S., & Polefrone, J. M. (1985). Behavioral factors in hypertension: Cardiovascular responsivity, anger and social competence. In M. A. Chesney & R. H. Rosenman (Eds.), *Anger and hostility in cardiovascular and behavioral disorders.* Washington, DC: Hemisphere.

Matthews, K. A., & Rakaczky, C. J. (1986). Familial aspects of the Type A behavior pattern and physiologic reactivity to stress. In T. Dembroski & T. Schmidt (Eds.), *Biological and psychological factors in cardiovascular disease.* Heidelberg: Springer-Verlag.

McClelland, D. C. (1979). Inhibited power motivation and high blood pressure in men. *Journal of Abnormal Psychology, 88,* 182–190.

McMahon, F. G. (1978). *Management of essential hypertension.* Mt. Kisco, NY: Futura.

Miller, R. E., Shapiro, A. P., King, H. E., Ginchereau, E. H., & Hosutt, J. A. (1984). Effect of antihypertensive treatment on the behavioral consequences of elevated blood pressure. *Hypertension, 6,* 202–208.

Morganti, A., Pickering, T. G., Lopez-Ouejero, J. A., & Laragh, J. H. (1980). High and low renin subgroups of essential hypertension: Differences and similarities in their renin and sympathetic responses to neural and nonneural stimuli. *The American Journal of Cardiology, 46,* 306–312.

Morrison, R. L., Bellack, A. S., & Manuck, S. B. (1985). The role of social competence in essential hypertension. *Journal of Consulting and Clinical Psychology, 53,* 248–255.

Page, L. B. (1983). Epidemiology of hypertension. In J. Genest, O. Kuchel, P. Hamet, & M. Cantin (Eds.), *Hypertension: Pathophysiology and treatment* (2nd ed.). New York: McGraw-Hill.

Perini, C., Amann, F. W., Bolli, P., & Buhler, F. R. (1982). Personality and adrenergic factors in essential hypertension. *Contributions to Nephrology, 30,* 64–69.

Pottash, A. L., Black, H. R., & Gold, M. S. (1981). Psychiatric complications of antihypertensive medications: *Journal of Nervous and Mental Disorders, 169,* 430–438.

Prichard, B. N. C., & Owens, C. W. I. (1983). Drug treatment of hypertension. In J. Genest, O. Kuchel, P. Hamet, & M. Cantin (Eds.), *Hypertension: Pathophysiology and treatment* (2nd ed.). New York: McGraw-Hill.

Quetsch, R. M., Achor, R. W. P., Litin, E. M., & Faucett, R. L. (1959). Depressive reactions in hypertensive patients: A comparison of those treated with Rauwolfia and those receiving no specific antihypertensive treatment. *Circulation, 19,* 366–375.

Rabkin, J. G., Charles, E., & Kass, F. (1983). Hypertension and DSM-III depression in psychiatric outpatients. *American Journal of Psychiatry, 140,* 1072–1074.

Reichgott, M. J. (1979). Problems of sexual function in patients with hypertension. *Cardiovascular Medicine, 4,* 149–156.

Rowland, M., & Roberts, J. (1982). *Blood pressure levels and hypertension in persons ages 6–74 years: United States, 1976–1980.* (Vital and Health Statistics Report No. 84). Washington, DC: National Center for Health Statistics.

Sandok, B. A., & Whisnant, J. P. (1983). Hypertension and the brain: Clinical aspects. In J. Genest, O. Kuchel, P. Hamet, & M. Cantin (Eds.), *Hypertension: Pathophysiology and treatment* (2nd ed.). New York: McGraw-Hill.

Schultz, N. R., & Elias, M. F. (1980). The effects of hypertension on WAIS performance. In M. F. Elias & D. H. Streeten (Eds.), *Hypertension and cognitive processes.* Mt. Desert, ME: Beech Hill.

Seedat, Y. K. (1980). Trial of atenolol and chlorthalidone for hypertension in black South Africans. *British Medical Journal, 281,* 1241–1243.

Shapiro, A. P. (in press). Clinical relevance of the pharmacological characteristics of beta-adrenergic blocking agents in the treatment of hypertension. In J. I. M. Drayer & M. A. Weber (Eds.), *Drug therapy in hypertension.*

Shapiro, A. P., & Jacob, R. G. (1983). Nonpharmacologic approaches to the treatment of hypertension. In L. Breslow, J. E. Fielding, & L. B. Lave (Eds.), *Annual review of public health* (Vol. 4). Palo Alto; CA: Annual Reviews.

Shapiro, A. P., Miller, R. E., King, H. E., Ginchereau, E. H., & Fitzgibbon, K. (1982). Behavioral consequences of mild hypertension. *Hypertension, 4,* 355–360.

Shoemaker, J. E., & Tasto, D. L. (1975). The effects of muscle relaxation on the blood pressure of essential hypertensives. *Behaviour Research and Therapy, 13,* 29–44.

Sokolow, M., & McIlroy, M. B. (1981). *Clinical cardiology.* Los Altos, CA: Lange Medical Publications.

Solomon, S., Hotchkiss, E., Saraway, S. M., Bayer, C., Ramsey, P., & Blum, R. S. (1983). Impariment of memory function by antihypertensive medication. *Archives of General Psychiatry, 40,* 1109–1112.

Southam, M. A., Agras, W. S., Taylor, B. C., & Kraemer, H. C. (1982). Relaxation training: Blood pressure lowering during the working day. *Archives of General Psychiatry, 39,* 715–717.

Stamler, J., Stamler, R., Riedlinger, W. F., Algra, G., & Roberts, R. (1976). Hypertension screening of 1 million Americans: Community Hypertension Evaluation Clinic (CHEC) Program, 1973–1975. *Journal of American Medical Association, 235,* 2299–2306.

Steptoe, A., Melville, D., & Ross, A. (1982). Essential hypertension and psychological functioning: A study of factory workers. *British Journal of Clinical Psychology, 21,* 303–311.

Surwit, R. W., Shapiro, D., & Good, M. I. (1978). Comparison of cardiovascular biofeedback, neuromuscular biofeedback, and meditation in the treatment of borderline essential hypertension. *Journal of Consulting and Clinical Psychology, 46,* 252–263.

Taylor, B. C., Farquhar, J. W., Nelson, E., & Agras, W. S. (1977). Relaxation therapy and high blood pressure. *Archives of General Psychiatry, 34,* 339–342.

Van Reek, J. Dierderiks, J., Philipsen, H., van Zutphen, W., & Seelen, T. (1982). Subjective complaints and blood pressure. *Journal of Psychosomatic Research, 26,* 155–165.

Wadden, T. A., Luborsky, L., Greer, S., & Crits-Christoph, P. (1984). The behavioral treatment of essential hypertension: An update and comparison with pharmacological treatment. *Clinical Psychology Review, 4,* 403–429.

Watts, R. J. (1981). Sexual functioning, health beliefs, and compliance with high blood pressure medications. *Nursing Research, 31,* 278–283.

Weber, M. A., Priest, R. T., Ricci, B. A. Eltora, M. I., & Brewer, D. D. (1980). Low-dose diuretic and beta adrenoceptor blockers in essential hypertension. *Clinical Pharmacology and Therapeutics, 28,* 149–158.

Weiner, H. (1979). *Psychobiology of essential hypertension.* New York: Elsevier.

Wheatley, D., Balter, M., Levine, J., Lipman, R., Bauer, M. L., & Bonato, R. (1975). Psychiatric aspects of hypertension. *British Journal of Psychiatry, 117,* 327–336.

Wilkie, F. L., & Eisdorfer, C. (1980). Hypertension and tests of memory. In M. F. Elias & D. H. Streeten (Eds.), *Hypertension and cognitive processes.* Mt. Desert, ME: Beech Hill.

Wood, D. L., Sheps, S. G., Elveback, L. R., & Schirger, A. (1984). Cold pressor test as a predictor of hypertension. *Hypertension, 6,* 301–306.

Wood, W. G., & Elias, M. F. (1980). Essential hypertension and neuropsychological test performance. In M. F. Elias & D. H. Streeten (Eds.), *Hypertension and Cognitive Processes.* Mt. Desert, ME: Beech Hill.

Wood, W. G., Elias, M. F., Schultz, N. R., & Pentz, C. A. (1979). Anxiety and depression in young and middle aged hypertensive and normotensive subjects. *Experimental Aging Research, 5,* 15–30.

10

Neurological Disorders

PERRY C. GOLDSTEIN

AND

DOUGLAS F. LEVINSON

This chapter is concerned with the presentation and management of specific psychological and psychiatric problems related to structural brain impairment. Particular attention is devoted to the chronic psychiatric sequelae associated with cerebral damage, because patients with such problems are most frequently referred to mental health clinicians after their acute illnesses have been treated by inpatient neurology and neurosurgery services. We review here some basic principles of brain–behavior relationships and then describe common psychiatric problems associated with head injury, epilepsy, stroke, brain tumor, and multiple sclerosis, as well as approaches to the treatment of the psychiatric aspects of these disorders.

We emphasize here that an understanding of the person with a neurological disorder, regardless of the nature of the pathology, requires appreciation of the specific functions that are impaired, as well as the strengths that remain. In general, neurological patients with psychiatric difficulties also have cognitive (neuropsychological) deficits. It is often difficult to determine whether the psychiatric symptoms are a direct result of the brain lesion, secondary to the individual's response to cognitive deficits in particular and serious illness in general, or independent (i.e., preexisting or provoked in a nonspecific way by the stress of illness and impairment).

Neurological patients are frequently described as having acute or chronic *brain syndromes* (*organicity*). For the initial identification of patients in need of further evaluation, the clinician will find it useful to be familiar with these syndromes, currently called *delirium* and *dementia*. Delirium is a transient, reversible syndrome seen in many brain and systemic illnesses; it may include disorientation, incoherence, fluctuating state, distractibility or confusion, impaired memory for new information, disturbance of the sleep–wake cycle, agitation, and perceptual distortions. Dementia is loss (usually irreversible) of cognitive functions because of a variety of static or progressive brain diseases, including Huntington's chorea and senile dementia of the Alzheimer's type (SDAT). It is never appropriate to accept "brain syndrome," delirium, or dementia as a final diagnosis. These are nonspecific syndromes whose identification calls for complete evaluation of underlying disease states and impairments.

PERRY C. GOLDSTEIN • Department of Rehabilitation Psychology, University of Miami, Jackson Medical Center, Miami, FL 33179.   DOUGLAS F. LEVINSON • The Medical College of Pennsylvania at EPPI, Philadelphia, PA 19129.

MODERATING VARIABLES

Psychiatric and neuropsychological complications of focal or multifocal neurological injury may be related to a variety of factors, including (1) the size of the damaged area; (2) the location and hemisphericity of the lesions; (3) the cause or etiology of the damage; (4) the age at which the damage occurs; (5) the progression or rate of neuronal loss; and (6) the premorbid behavioral and intellectual competencies of the patient. Specific types of lesions or brain dysfunction may lead to characteristic problems (e.g., personality disorder in temporal lobe epilepsy), but there is great variability across individual cases, which is due to moderating variables.

Lashley (1938) reported a high correlation (-0.9) between the actual size of the lesion and the extent of behavorial and learning impairments and the potential for recovery of function in expressive aphasia (see also Kertesz, 1985). It is now clear that lesion location is a key determinant of the qualitative aspects of the behavioral and cognitive changes associated with brain impairment. It has also become clear that brain functions generally require the interaction and integration of many brain structures and pathways (Hecaen & Albert, 1978).

A better prognosis is statistically associated with smaller, nonprogressive vascular lesions, left hemisphere sites, younger age, good social support systems, and higher premorbid intellectual ability; increased cognitive and behavioral complications are found with diffuse or bilateral, progressive diseases, right-hemisphere sites, older age, poor premorbid coping skills, and inadequate social skills and supports (Smith, 1981). These factors appear to contribute independently and additively to the behavorial concomitants of brain dysfunction.

Deficits, Disorganization, and Disinhibition

The types of brain lesions or dysfunction we shall discuss may result in three distinct and different effects upon behavior: (1) decline or loss of functions; (2) disorganized social, cognitive, or perceptual abilities; or (3) a release or disinhibition of behaviors (Kolb & Whishaw, 1985).

Although loss of motor and sensory functions is usually obvious, there may also be more subtle impairments involving perception of language, emotional cues, or visual-spatial information, deficits that may be misinterpreted as psychiatric disorder. This is common with more circumscribed and limited damage in brain regions known as tertiary association cortex, impairing the capacity to integrate sensory input with motor functions in meaningful ways. Damage to association areas may be distant from the primary motor and sensory areas, without evidence of "hard" sensory or motor signs of brain damage.

Disorganized behavior or cognitive function is also a common result of brain injury. Individual components of well-learned behavioral sequences may be preserved, while the sequence itself may be impossible for the patient to perform. For example, a 60-year-old woman who experienced a small stroke in her left parietal lobe was able to dial a phone and pick up the phone receiver as individual behaviors. The same patient was unable to correctly use a phone book to find a phone number, dial it correctly and return the phone receiver correctly on its platform.

Behavioral disinhibition or "release phenomena" refer to either an increase in frequency or duration of behaviors present prior to injury or the occurrence of new behaviors not present in the premorbid repertoire. Examples include labile and sudden mood swings which occur without environmental precipitants, inappropriate sexual behaviors, tremor and other unusual motor behaviors. In general, these behaviors are more reflexive than intentional in nature. They tend to occur when inhibitory pathways are damaged or destroyed, regardless of the cause of damage (Kolb & Whishaw, 1985).

Finally, a common effect of any structural biochemical, infectious, or vascular brain dysfunction is slowness. Increased inefficiency, lethargy, and problems in maintaining arousal or concentration are often reported as initial symptoms in many brain disorders. However, such symptoms are also hallmarks of depression. In some cases, depression with cognitive and neurovegetative signs may be related to brain dysfunction, suggesting the need for specific antidepressant treatment, in addition to traditional psychotherapeutic approaches.

Specialization of Function

Brain Stem, Subcortex, and Cortex. The brain may be divided into cortical, subcortical, and brain stem regions. Brain stem structures arise just above the spinal cord. The lowest portion of the brain stem is the medulla oblongata, followed by the midbrain and the ascending reticular formation, which are directly below the pons and the cerebellum. Most of these regions mediate general arousal and automatic, regulatory functions, such as control of respiration, involuntary motor functions, and direct sensory input. Damage to any of these regions may result in severe, generalized diffuse neurological impairments or death. A number of pathways known to be involved in the regulation of mood, sleep, and appetite (including those using dopamine, norepinephrine, and serotonin as neurotransmitters) also originate in parts of the brain stem. The diencephalon (thalamus and hypothalamus) is usually considered the first set of structures in the brain where integration or transformation of raw sensory input occurs. Although these structures lie in the more "primitive" area of the brain, asymmetrical higher cognitive impairments (e.g., language disturbances) have been demonstrated with specific, unilateral lesions in the thalamus (Riklan & Cooper, 1977). Specialization of functions in the thalamus follows lateralized patterns similar to those described below for the cortex (e.g., language functions typically on the left). These structures have also been related to memory and attention functions (Fedio & Van Buren, 1975). Of all brain-stem structures, the diencephalon is of most interest to mental health professionals, because damage to these structures has also been reported to result in emotional flattening and unusual behavioral syndromes (Watson & Heilman, 1979). The thalamus, in particular, is thought to be responsible for the activation of cortical regions in both cerebral hemispheres (Heilman, Watson & Valenstein, 1985).

The cerebellum, lying behind the brain stem and below the posterior cortex, is known to have sensory and motor functions; cerebellar lesions typically cause disturbances of gait and coordination. It has been suggested that cerebellar lesions may also be responsible for psychiatric symptoms (Hamilton, Frick, Takahasi, & Hopping, 1983).

The cerebrum, lying above the diencephalon, is divided into left and right hemispheres. At the base of each hemisphere, there are identical sets of dense structures, composed of neuronal cell bodies (gray matter). These structures are referred to as *ganglia,* or *nuclei,* and represent the subcortical structures within the cerebrum. The largest subcortical mass is a set of nuclei known as the *basal ganglia.* Basal ganglia lesions can result in a variety of movement disorders, including Parkinsonism, choreiform movements, and other resting or intentional tremors. Depending on the extent of the lesion, damage to this region may also result in impairment of memory and of new learning abilities because of the disruption of pathways to other subcortical and cortical regions.

Another large nuclear mass is the amygdala. Together with the septal nucleus, this structure aids in the regulation and initiation of automatic behaviors related to survival, such as the flight-or-fight response (including rage), chewing, licking, and other behaviors associated with feeding. Damage to this region usually results in an apathetic and flat personality style with little self-initiated behavior, similar to a frontal lobe syndrome.

The limbic system, composed of the hippocampal formation, the mamillary bodies, the fornix, the cingulate gyrus, and projections to the thalamus, is a series of nuclei, gray matter areas, and white matter (axon) tracts also found deep within each hemisphere (including portions of the temporal lobes as well as subcortical structures). Behavioral functions related to learning, memory consolidation, emotional regulation, anticipatory attention, and integration of information are generally associated with this system. Damage to this region often results in marked recent-memory impairments and amnesia; disinhibited behavior, sometimes accompanied by suspiciousness and hallucinations; disorientation; and general problems in appropriately interacting with the natural environment (Lezak, 1983).

The cerebral cortex is the most recently evolved portion of the cerebrum. The most complex integration and interpretation of stimulation and formulation of responses are generally attributed to the cortex. The two hemispheres of the cerebrum have been shown to be anatomically dissimilar, with corresponding differences in the qualitative aspects of behavior connected with each.

Left and Right Hemispheres. Recent studies suggest that the left and right cerebral hemispheres are specialized for sequential versus patterned or simultaneous processing, rather than for verbal versus visual-spatial functions as has traditionally been believed. Left-hemisphere damage may cause impairments of time sequencing, temporal ordering, and other sequential or serial processing and response impairments, whether related to language, spatial, musical, or tactile stimuli. Aphasia, or language impairment, is a common problem seen with left-hemisphere lesions. Correct sequencing in the production or reception of words or series of individual phonemes are disturbed in these patients, as is the production or interpretation of reading and writing. Other sequencing problems seen with left-hemisphere lesions include apraxias. Apraxia represents a difficulty in correctly sequencing a series of movements or commands. The woman who could not use the telephone but was able to perform each individual component of the series of behaviors offers an example of idiomotor apraxia. In many cases, patients with demonstrable, focal left-hemisphere lesions report problems with "mixed-up" thoughts and may appear to demonstrate illogical and loose speech, which is often mistaken for schizophrenic thought disorder. However, thinking disturbance may also be observed in psychiatric patients without a demonstrable focal left-hemisphere lesion.

Prior studies have also suggested a predisposition for depressive and anxiety reactions ("catastrophic" or poorly modulated responses of fear and frustration) following left-hemisphere damage (Gainotti, 1972). Evidence for and against an association of left-hemisphere strokes with depression is presented later. It is unclear whether this association is related to anger and frustration brought on by an awareness of language impairment, or to an inherent biological characteristic of the left hemisphere (Heilman, Watson, & Bowers, 1983).

Right-hemisphere dysfunction typically impairs the capacity to respond rapidly to complex situations in ways that require simultaneous, global, or gestalt (pattern-oriented) integration of stimuli. This may be true of social, verbal, or visual-spatial processes. The belief that the left hemisphere is specialized for "verbal" functions may result from the reliance on sequential processing for many expressive and receptive verbal functions. There are other aspects of language that involve the control of rhythm, melody, intonation, and accompanying physical or "emotional" gestures to permit full communicative expression. These components of language are called *prosody*. On the basis of deficits found in patients with various right-hemisphere lesions, it has been suggested that certain right-hemisphere centers are responsible for prosodic comprehension and expression, anatomically symmetrical with the left-hemisphere centers for these aspects of semantic language (Ross, 1981). Patients with such lesions (e.g., after strokes) may be unable to grasp the emotional meaning of others' intonations and gestures, and/or to convey such meanings themselves (aprosodia). Prosodic comprehension deficits may make it impossible for the patient to grasp social subtleties and cues, or to appreciate their own emotional state, whereas expressive aprosodia may include flat affect with outbursts of inappropriate affect. Either may be mistaken for functional psychiatric disturbance.

Patients with right-hemisphere damage may ignore or neglect visual, auditory, or tactile stimuli occurring toward the left side. Lesions to an area of the nondominant (right) parietal lobe or its inputs produce deficits ranging from subtle misperception of left-sided cues to completely ignoring anything that occurs on the left. Vision may not be impaired by this lesion. This area appears to integrate a series of inputs related to sensory, arousal, and motivational (limbic) information to create a "map" of the motivational significance of objects in the entire visual space. After a right-sided lesion, the left hemisphere can compensate for only the right half of space, so the patient behaves as if stimuli on the left are unimportant (Mesulam, 1981). Similar mechanisms presumably underlie neglect of other types of stimuli. Extinction phenomena may also be seen with right-hemisphere lesions. If one touches the right and left hand simultaneously, for example, such patients may report perceiving only one of the stimuli (typically the right), although they can accurately perceive a touch on either hand alone. Neglect and extinction phenomena have recently been reviewed by Heilman, *et al.* (1985). Such patients' risk of injuries and burns to the left side may be reduced through cognitive and attention-retraining programs (Burns, Halper, & Mogil, 1985; Trexler, 1982). Indifferent or euphoric affect may be accompanied by anosognosia, or failure to recognize one's own illness, leading to unrealistic activities and plans. Extinction and neglect phenomena are uncommon with left-hemisphere lesions. In general, behavioral functions appear to be more diffusely represented within the right hemisphere, and the result is a wider range of heterogeneous impairments following focal brain lesions (Witelson, 1977).

In addition to left–right differences, there are general functional differences between anterior and posterior cerebral regions (roughly demarcated by the central sulcus, also known as the Rolandic fissure) Anterior brain regions are most involved in expressive (response-oriented) behaviors, such as speech output, locomotion, and active planning or anticipation of future needs and behavior. Posterior regions generally are associated with sensory-integrative, receptive functions.

Frontal, Temporal, Parietal, and Occipital Lobes. More specific differences in function can be attributed to the four lobes of the cerebrum. The frontal lobes lie anterior to the central sulcus or fissure and superior to the Sylvian fissures (deep horizontal ridges found on either side of the brain). The precentral gyrus or ridge (just anterior to the central sulcus) contains most of the primary motor areas, with specific locations in each hemisphere controlling specific muscle groups on the opposite side of the body. Lesions produce weakness or paralysis of the arm, the leg, the face, or some combination. The left frontal lobe also contains Broca's speech area, lesions to which cause deficits in producing correct spoken words (expressive aphasia). Motor and speech impairments are common after strokes in this region.

The anterior or "prefrontal" portions of the frontal lobes receive input from posterior cortex and limbic system. Lesions produce impairments in planning ability, initiation of new behavior, problem solving, abstraction, concept formation, and other functions related to complex interaction with the environment. The results are behavioral rigidity, "concreteness," perseveration (tendency to repeat previous actions inappropriately), and loss of initiative. There may be "pathological inertia," in which the patient accurately describes the correct response but does not initiate or perform it (Lezak, 1983). Right frontal damage, in particular, may lead to lack of awareness of behavior, deficient monitoring and evaluation of the social appropriateness of behavior, and impaired initiation and cessation of behavior, along with affective changes resembling hypomania. Apathetic flattening and/or "disinhibited" aggressive or sexual behavior may be misdiagnosed as primary psychiatric disorder. Subtle frontal deficits are generally more difficult to diagnose than "hard" neurological signs, such as weakness or aphasia.

The temporal lobes and the insular regions, located just below the Sylvian fissures, have functions related to hearing, auditory memory, and perceptual organization; the deep temporal regions contain the limbic system. Lesions to Wernicke's area in the posterior left temporal lobe result in disturbed comprehension of written and spoken language (receptive aphasia). The patient may produce a normal quantity of grammatically correct speech that is lacking in meaning, containing instead jargon and nonsensical phrases (fluent aphasia) (Lezak, 1983), which may be mistaken for psychiatric disorder. Involvement of the hippocampus, the mammillary bodies, and other limbic regions may produce anterograde (for events after the lesion) amnesia and impaired verbal memory. Right temporal lesions may impair a recall of complex visual and auditory patterns (Lezak, 1983; Milner, 1970). Behavioral changes associated with epilepsy due to temporal-lobe seizure foci are discussed below.

The parietal lobes lie posterior to the central sulcus and superior to the Sylvian fissures. The postcentral gyrus (just behind the central sulcus) contains most of the primary area for tactile sensation, with lesions producing impairment on the opposite side. The posterior parietal association areas are related to the complex interpretation of sensory input and the organization of responses. Right parietal lesions may produce neglect syndromes and visual-spatial and constructional disorders with indifferent affect, whereas left parietal lesions usually result in apraxia and impaired sequencing of information. Damage to either side may produce contralateral astereognosis (the inability to identify objects by touch alone).

The occipital lobes are the most posterior cortical regions; there is no specific demarcation between the parietal and the occipital lobes. Damage to primary visual areas results in blind spots within the visual field. Damage to visual association areas produces visual agnosia, or impaired recognition of the global aspects of visual stimuli (although the recognition of individual features is preserved). Prosopagnosia (impaired facial recognition) may result from damage to the association cortex close to the temporal and parietal lobes. Bilateral occipital damage occasionally produces visual anosognosia, in which the patient is blind but attempts to act sighted, inventing elaborate explanations for his or her inability to get around or to handle objects (Heilman & Valenstein, 1985; Lezak, 1983).

Cerebral Networks. Most current knowledge about the localization of brain function comes from the study of patients with localized brain damage. This type of study leads to the assumption that a specific area of the brain "contains" a specific function. Before leaving the topic of localization, it should be pointed out that this is an unfortunate oversimplification. Although simple sensory and motor functions can be completely destroyed by damage to critical cells, complex behavioral and cognitive functions cannot be understood in this way. It is currently believed that many more complex functions are served by networks of interrelated brain regions that send projections to specific integrative centers (Geschwind, 1972, 1979). A network for the directing of visual attention to motivationally relevant stimuli has been particularly well studied (Mesulam, 1981).

CLOSED-HEAD INJURY

Incidence

Head trauma represents one of the most frequent reasons for neurological and neurosurgical consultation in the United States. Annual incidence estimates range from 750,000 to 3 million cases requiring hospitalization (Caveness, 1979). An additional 60,000 to 70,000 mild closed-head injuries or concussions occur yearly, without acute complications, but with chronic, residual disabilities primarily involving cognitive and psychiatric problems (Dikman & Reitan, 1977).

Pathophysiology

The most common type of head injury involves acceleration and deceleration of the head in automobile accidents, when a passenger is hurled at a stationary object and the momentum of the head and body are stopped abruptly. These injuries generally produce two types of brain damage: (1) focal, structural damage due to contusion (bruising of brain tissue), intracranial hematoma (collection of blood), or brain laceration (tearing of blood vessels); and (2) generalized or diffuse stretching, tearing, and shearing of nerve fibers throughout the brain (Adams, 1975). There are also pure acceleration injuries (e.g., from a blunt object striking the head) and penetrating wounds (e.g., from gunshots).

Focal lesions in acceleration–deceleration injuries occur in regions where brain tissue is connected or comes in contact with the sharper aspects of the skull. Maximal shearing, twisting, and tearing of nerve fibers also occur in the same regions because of rotational forces; maximal damage typically occurs at the anterior frontal and temporal poles. Focal lesions are easily visualized on CAT or magnetic resonance imaging (MRI) and often produce focal EEG findings. However, diffuse shearing and rotational damage may also occur at a microscopic level in white matter (with normal imaging tests.) In general, focal damage is uncommon in milder injuries, with less than 1-h loss of consciousness (Jennett & Teasdale, 1981; Strich, 1969).

The severity of the initial injuries may range from severe prolonged coma to no apparent impairment. The severity of brain damage and the eventual prognosis are usually correlated with (1) the duration and depth of the coma, and (2) the severity of the posttraumatic amnesia (Jennett & Teasdale, 1981).

Minor Head Injury

The term *concussion* is often used to describe minor head injuries with a duration of unconsciousness 1 h or less (Alexander, 1982). Clinicians are frequently asked to treat patients suffering from postconcussion syndrome (PCS) following mild head trauma (Kay, Derr, & Lassman, 1971). The cluster of symptoms associated with PCS includes headache, dizziness, memory impairment, difficulty concentrating, fatigue, anxiety, depression, irritability, and personality changes (Lindvall, 1974). Unlike severe injuries, PCS does not appear to be correlated with the severity of the posttraumatic amnesia (Rutherford, Merrett, & McDonald, 1977). The symptoms of PCS may be present at the moment of injury or may emerge weeks later. The common sequence of events is decreased arousal following a blow to the head, with rapid return to full alertness. On becoming more alert, patients may vomit, complain of imbalance, and report some difficulty in motor coordination. These symptoms generally disappear over a span of hours (Alexander, 1982). The symptoms of PCS then emerge over the following days or weeks.

Prior approaches to the treatment of PCS emphasized psychogenic and psychodynamic factors presumed to be released by the stress of the event, as implied by the diagnosis of "accident neurosis" (Miller, 1961). Recent studies of PCS confirm the presence of consistent but subtle impairments of attention, concentration, and memory independent of emotional impairment (Dikman, Reitan, & Temkin, 1983; Gronwall & Wrightson, 1975), with little evidence to suggest that postconcussion syndrome represents an exaggeration of symptoms or primary psychopathology (Alexander, 1982; Sisler, 1978). Measures of slowed information-processing in PCS have been shown to improve over time and have been used as a measure of readiness to return to work (Gronwall & Wrightson, 1974). In addition, autopsy findings demonstrate significant neuronal loss in the cases of persons suffering only a single concussion (Oppenheimer, 1968). Recent investigations have also demonstrated physiological damage to cochlear and vestibular structures of the auditory system, which has been related to the delayed onset of hearing loss and unsteadiness in both mild and severe head injuries.

Assuming no other psychosocial complications, PCS usually lasts from 5 to 10 weeks, although certain patients may experience symptoms for a longer period with more severe injuries (Gronwall & Wrightson, 1974). If the symptoms persist, a request for a neurological consultation is appropriate.

In many cases, patients suffering from PCS become frustrated, anxious, and depressed as a result of premature attempts to return to work. A rapid return to work or school usually highlights the patient's decreased cognitive efficiency, as previously performed tasks may appear complex and difficult (Oddy, Humphrey, & Uttley, 1978b). It is often helpful to have patients delay their return to work or school until the frequency and severity of the symptoms subside. In this respect, baseline and repeated neuropsychological measures may aid in plotting behavioral recovery and in determining when maximal cognitive recovery has occurred (Gronwall & Wrightson, 1974). Behavioral management techniques may also be helpful, emphasizing the maintenance of a daily diary and the establishment of a standard daily schedule to improve memory through repetition. In general, an emphasis on shaping, learning, and reinforcement techniques is usually most successful. Involvement of family members or caretakers through support or training groups is often beneficial through increasing an understanding of the behavioral concomitants of PCS. Caretakers frequently feel that they have caused personality changes in the patients by doing something upsetting (Oddy, Humphrey, & Uttley, 1978a). There is limited data on the efficacy of relaxation and biofeedback techniques for PCS, although these procedures may be useful in selected cases for symptomatic relief (Olton & Noonberg, 1980).

Moderate and Severe Head Injury

Moderate and serious injuries typically include those resulting in more than a 24-h impairment in, or loss of, consciousness. More severe injuries are associated with a higher incidence of focal brain lesions and a greater likelihood of persistent focal neurological impairments, including hemiparesis, cranial nerve palsies, aphasia, and visuospatial impairments (Gilroy & Meyer, 1979). However, the most severe, persistent, and disabling neuropsychological impairments are reflected in memory disturbance, concreteness, loss of abstract planning abilities, and problems in maintaining concentration or attention without becoming distracted (Gronwall & Wrightson, 1981; Levin & Grossman, 1978; Levin, Grossman, Rose, & Teasdale, 1979).

These deficits may persist for years following the initial injury, even in the face of good motor and sensory recovery. Clinicians are often misled to believe that ''good'' recovery has occurred because of average motor and sensory abilities in such patients after discharge from rehabilitation hospitals. This is usually not the case (Levin, Benton, & Grossman, 1982).

The typical amnesia that results from closed-head injury (CHI) is an anterograde memory impairment in which new learning of events following the accident is greatly impaired. With focal brain-stem or subcortical lesions, there may also be a retrograde amnesia causing loss of memories before the injury (Lishman, 1973). It is also not uncommon for additional neurobehavioral impairments to arise months or years following an injury. The presence of novel impairments may suggest the presence of a posttraumatic seizure disorder, as 25% of all cases develop late seizure disorders (Alexander, 1982). Complex partial seizures, resulting from temporal lobe damage, are most common (Jennett, 1969). The symptoms of these seizures are discussed below; they may include sensory, repetitive motor, or personality symptoms without frank convulsions. If any such symptoms appear suddenly in CHI patients, neurological consultation should be considered.

Depression is also quite common in the months following mild, moderate, or severe head injury (Levin & Grossman, 1978). The most common factor in reactive types of depression is the patient's increasing awareness of the degree and severity of neuropsychological impairments and their impact on future psychosocial functioning, with feelings of loss, hopelessness, and worthlessness. Such reactions to awareness of impairment parallel reactions to the loss or death of a loved one. The long-term outcome may be improved by helping the patient, the family, and the caretakers to recognize the loss and to verbalize and experience the stages of recovery suggested by Kubler-Ross (1969) for working with dying patients. Some studies have suggested a higher incidence of suicide among depressed head-trauma patients (Kwentus, Hart, Peck, & Kornstein, 1985), although the rates are not compared to those of other groups with neurological or physical illness.

Localized brain damage, especially in the frontal lobe, is a common cause of organic affective syndromes. There is some evidence to suggest that proximity to the frontal pole is associated with increased severity of depression because of damage of norepinephrine projections from subcortical structures (Robinson & Szetela, 1981). Yet, there are few studies examining the efficacy of antidepressant medications in the treatment of major depression following CHI.

A major problem in evaluating depression in CHI is that focal lesions tend to alter or mask the presentation of affective symptoms. In other cases, the effects of brain damage alone may be mistaken for depression. In the case of frontal lobe lesions, a slowed, apathetic, and indifferent personality style may evolve in the absence of self-perceived or self-reported depression. Conversely, frontal lesions may also result in behavorial disinhibition, silliness, hypersexuality, aggressiveness, and hypomanic behavior. Lithium carbonate has been successful in selected cases of disinhibited behavior following CHI (Young, Taylor, & Holmstrom, 1977). Antidepressant medications and electroconvulsive therapy (ECT) have been suggested in more severe posttraumatic depression (Kwentus et al., 1985). Patients suffering CHI may have difficulty in inhibiting most emotional responses, whether they be crying, laughing, sexually laden expressions, or reactions to frustration. Structured daily schedules, diaries, and multidisciplinary, cognitive-behavioral rehabilitation programs emphasizing increased functional independence and family or caretaker involvement should be part of any therapeutic endeavor with these patients (Rosenthal, Griffith, Bond, & Miller, 1983; Trexler, 1982; Wilson & Moffat, 1984). In addition, recent evidence suggests that premorbid personality styles play a major role in behavioral changes following CHI (Fordyce, Romeche, & Prigatono, 1983; Thomsen, 1984).

SEIZURE DISORDERS

Incidence

The cumulative incidence rate of epilepsy, with increasing age, is 0.7% of the population by age 10, 1.1% by age 20, 1.7% by age 40, and 3.2% by age 80. The percentage of combined risk for all types of seizures (single or recurrent) is 4.1% of the population. As the figures indicate, the risk for seizures increases with age and the likelihood of brain dysfunction. It is estimated that approximately 0.5% of the population is under medical care for epilepsy at any one time (Hauser, Annegers, & Anderson, 1983).

Pathophysiology

Seizure disorders represent the end result of various forms of brain dysfunction. In general, seizures usually result from the irritation of brain tissue due to head injuries, tumors, strokes, vascular malformations, infections, or high temperatures. The presence of a seizure disorder, especially one that begins in adulthood, should always raise the question of new or progressive brain disease or brain trauma.

Defining Seizures and Epilepsy

Seizures are the clinical manifestation of an abnormal electrical discharge of a set of neurons in the brain. *Epilepsy* is usually defined as the repeated occurrence of seizures in the absence of an acute, precipitating brain injury. Hence, a child experiencing a single, isolated seizure or an alcoholic who has several seizures during detoxification would not receive a diagnosis of epilepsy. Because there are many types of seizures, with varying behavioral and electrical characteristics, most researchers regard this entity as the group of epilepsies, rather than as a homogeneous disease or syndrome (Dodrill, 1981).

Seizure activity may be observed on the electroencephalogram (EEG) in the form of "epileptiform discharges," which appear as "spikes" on paper tracings. When a history of clinical seizures is present with evidence of epileptiform activity on an EEG, the diagnosis of seizure disorder may be established with a high degree of confidence. Some patients have clear clinical seizures despite a normal EEG, making diagnosis more difficult. Seizure activity from deep brain structures may be absent or distorted on an EEG tracing from electrodes on the scalp. Seizure activity is sometimes elicited during an EEG by "activation" procedures, such as hyperventilation, presentation of strobe lights or rapid sequences of patterned visual stimuli, and sleep (especially following a night of sleep deprivation). When the EEG is normal but seizures are strongly suspected clinically, prolonged (8- or 24-h) scalp recordings may be completed, with direct or videotaped observation to permit correlation with behavior. The most sensitive and reliable procedure for detecting electrical foci is the neurosurgical implantation of small electrodes near the suspected areas. Deep electrodes often demonstrate the localization of seizure activity, which contradicts prior scalp EEG recordings, as when a patient with a right temporal focus on scalp EEG shows initiation of the seizure from a left temporal focus based on direct deep recordings. Depth electrodes are usually reserved for intractable disorders when surgical intervention is being considered and localization is essential.

Classification of Seizure Disorders

Seizures may be characterized along two dimensions: (1) clinical and EEG characteristics, or (2) etiology. The clinical or symptomatic classification of seizures has been standardized by the International League against Epilepsy (Gastaut, 1970). The major categories are as follows:

1. *Partial seizures with elementary symptoms* do not involve generalized seizure activity of the brain or complete loss of consciousness. Focal motor ("Jacksonian") seizures involve localized, slow, repetitive movements (e.g., of the finger or arm), followed by faster movements that may spread on one side (contralateral to the seizure focus in the brain), with gradual cessation, typically over minutes. The individual is awake and alert but cannot control the movements. Focal sensory seizures may present in a similar fashion, with disturbances in *one* sensory modality (tactile, visual, or auditory) and with gradual spread of the perceived changes. Autonomic seizures usually affect muscles of the gastrointestinal system, sometimes causing urinary or fecal incontinence.

2. *Partial seizures with complex symptoms* (psychomotor seizures) are usually due to focal, lateralized temporal-limbic brain pathology. Patients exhibit repetitive behaviors such as lip smacking, chewing, body rocking, and rubbing or patting movements of the hands, with relatively flat or nonreactive affect. It may also be possible to perform more complex, well-learned behaviors, such as brushing the teeth, dressing and undressing, or even driving a car, during these 1- to 4- min episodes of confusion. Patients may appear to be awake but have impaired consciousness and memory and are unable to perform any behaviors requiring new learning, socially responsible actions, judgments, ongoing decisions, or *active* interaction with the environment. The variety of unusual and peculiar behaviors possible during these seizures may lead to an erroneous diagnosis of psychiatric disorder or, during some episodes, intoxication. In many cases, patients report a premonitory "aura" before their seizures. Auras often involve 1 to 2 min of unusual sensory experiences (e.g., strange odors or nausea) or a sense of impending doom and fear.

3. *Generalized seizures* involve both cerebral hemispheres and always result in loss of conscious awareness. They may occur in patients with focal brain pathology (including those producing partial seizures that may generalize on some occasions), or in patients with no known pathology. Grand mal (major motor) and petit mal (minor motor) seizure types are included in this category.

Major motor seizures may or may not include an aura, followed by a sudden loss of consciousness, an initial tonic phase with strong contraction of muscles and rigidity in the limbs, trunk, and neck for about 1 min, followed by brief tremors and a clonic stage that includes bilateral muscle jerks alternating with brief periods of relaxation. A deep coma (loss of consciousness) follows this seizure and can last for as long as 10 min. A period of as much as 12 h of sleep may be required before the individual can function at his or her preseizure level (Eliasson, Prensky, & Hardin, 1978).

Minor motor seizures may occur without awareness of the affected individual. Patients briefly appear slightly dazed and report a momentary loss of awareness, but they may continue with behavior initiated before the seizure with no postictal confusion or memory loss. There is usually a characteristic, repetitive eye-blinking at a rate of 3 times per second, which corresponds with 3-cycle-per-second spike-wave complexes seen on EEG tracings. This disorder usually occurs in children and is seldom seen in patients over 18 years of age.

Other generalized seizures, which are less commonly seen, include infantile spasms and akinetic seizures, which are often associated with severe brain dysfunction in early childhood. Myoclonic seizures involve small muscle groups and may occur alone or in conjunction with major motor attacks. These are not considered dangerous and may occur in normal individuals as they fall asleep, without loss of consciousness.

Etiology has been used as an additional criterion in describing seizure disorders. The usual dichotomy involves idiopathic versus symptomatic seizures. Patients with epilepsy in the absence of any prior neurological disease or trauma are categorized as idiopathic. Conversely, symptomatic epilepsy includes any seizure disorder that can be attributed to a known predisposing factor, including head trauma, stroke, tumor, encephalopathy, or other physical disease. Clinical experience suggests that many persons originally diagnosed as having idiopathic epilepsy will eventually be found to have some form of causal brain lesion or dysfunction.

Neuropsychological Findings

Although there is no unitary neuropsychological profile for the many types of epilepsy, some findings are consistently reported across types. The most common is psychomotor slowing. This may be demonstrated on simple tests of motor speed, the Digit Symbol Substitution Test of the WAIS-R, and simple or complex reaction time tasks. It often represents an interaction between seizure frequency, excessive blood levels of anticonvulsants (Dodrill, 1981), chronicity of the disorder, and seizure type. The greatest impairment is generally seen with generalized major motor seizures (grand mal), probably because of repeated loss of neurons during each seizure over a chronic course.

Reduced attention, concentration, and speed are often accompanied by impairments in recent memory and new learning. Memory deficits are most severe in patients with primary epileptic foci in the temporal lobes, presumably because of the disruption of function within limbic system structures such as the hippocampus, the amygdala, and the mammillary bodies, necessary for the consolidation and storage of new information. An important consideration in the neuropsychological assessment of all seizure patients is consideration of time since the last seizure. To prevent the effects of postictal confusion and state-related deficits, patients should be assessed no sooner than 6 h following a confirmed seizure.

A comprehensive evaluation of neuropsychological abilities in epileptics should include measures of sustained attention and concentration, recent memory of verbal and visual-spatial material, general cognitive abilities, psychomotor functions, and psychosocial or personality measures. Dodrill (1981) compiled a useful battery for epilepsy, and Milner and associates developed techniques for assessing specific memory impairments in patients with partial complex (temporal lobe) seizures (described in Kolb & Whishaw, 1985). In addition to providing localization and baseline data, neuropsychological assessments provide useful information for educational or occupational planning.

Psychosis and Behavior Change in Epilepsy

Schizophrenialike psychoses and unusual personality characteristics are often reported among temporal lobe epileptics (TLE). The unique feature of these behavioral changes is their chronic and persistent nature; they may be present both during and between seizure episodes for long periods of time. Hence, they are not usually attributed to confusion or acute changes in mental status alone.

A deepening of awareness, increased emotional intensity, and concern with philosophical or religious issues represent a cluster of behaviors often considered pathognomonic of the "viscous" epileptic personality. Many patients demonstrate an overly concerned and evaluative approach when relating to others; many events, objects, or behaviors may be ascribed some unknown significance that the patient may attempt to discover through unusual means. Although this behavior may sometimes be described as paranoia, the cognitive style exhibited by such patients is qualitatively different from paranoia associated with functional psychiatric disorders. The viscosity or "stickiness" of these patients may also be exhibited in their difficulty in terminating discussions or conversations. The TLE patient often finds one more important point that needs to be stated or a related issue that may have been neglected. In many cases, these additional "points" are circumstantial or unrelated to the actual conversation, but the patient may phone repeatedly or send quickly scribbled notes to make her or his point (Rodin, 1975).

The tendency to keep detailed, daily diaries and to write extensively is referred to as *hypergraphia.* Many temporal lobe epileptics have been known to record even the most mundane events on paper, or to write lengthy poetry. The content of hypergraphic productions usually involves sexual, religious, or philosophical issues.

Changes in sexual behavior are also commonly associated with TLE. Specifically, striking decreases in sexual activity or desires are often documented. Changes in sexual preferences are sometimes noted, with increased reports of homosexuality or bisexuality (Blumer, 1975).

Episodic mood changes, including irritability, euphoria, and positive symptoms of schizophrenia (e.g., paranoid delusions, thought disorder, and hallucinations), have also been noted at higher frequencies among temporal lobe epileptics than among normal controls (Pincus & Tucker, 1978). These changes have been noted in interictal periods, or immediately preceding, during, and following partial complex seizures. Some reports have suggested an antagonism between seizure activity and interictal personality changes; the occurrence of seizure activity is believed to be related to dopamine antagonism and the relief of unusual psychosis-like symptoms. Although there are no controlled studies demonstrating the specific antagonistic effect of the patient's seizures on interictal personality changes, some clinicians have used ECT and psychotropic medications known to lower seizure thresholds as treatment modalities for TLE behavior changes (Blumer, 1975; Trimble, 1982).

There is voluminous literature describing the psychiatric sequelae of epilepsy. However, a comprehensive review by Hermann and Whitman (1984) highlights serious methodological difficulties that limit conclusions regarding the specificity of these findings to epilepsy or to temporal lobe epilepsy in particular. The major problem with all prior studies has been the absence of chronic-illness control groups matched on demographic, educational, chronicity, and neuropsychological variables. There is some suggestion that the severity of the brain impairment, reflected in overall neuropsychological impairment ratings, is significantly related to the degree of the psychiatric and psychosocial complications in epilepsy (Camfield, Gates, Ronen, Camfield, Ferouson, & McDonald, 1984; Dodrill, 1983; Hermann, 1981). Groups with other chronic medical disorders have also shown similar forms of psychiatric disturbance, a finding suggesting nonspecific psychopathology related to TLE (Mungas, 1982). In addition, the assessment methods used to describe these behavioral changes have been quite variable and nonstandardized. Few or no personality differences between TLE and well-matched patient groups are typically reported when standard measures such as the MMPI are administered (Lachar, Lewis, & Kupke, 1979). However, some have argued that standard psychiatric rating scales may be insensitive to specific changes related to TLE. This is an area that warrants further investigation. Control for multiple seizure types, seizure frequency, anticonvulsant blood levels, medication compliance, and premorbid or family psychosocial adjustment are also lacking in psychological studies of TLE.

Hence, although a variety of unusual personality and behavioral changes are frequently noted among epileptics, the relative contributions of the factors noted above remains unclear. Hermann and Whitman (1984) divided epileptic behavior changes into three categories: (1) brain-related, (2) non-brain-related, and (3) treatment-related. This model allows for more specific hypotheses regarding the etiological significance of specific sets of behaviors or symptoms. This approach is promising in its potential for identifying specific behavioral syndromes suggestive of specific remediative approaches. Such an approach also eliminates the need to dichotomize behaviors into "organic" versus "functional" categories. As with most other neurological diseases, the psychiatric sequelae of epilepsy represent an interaction between brain and psychosocial factors. It may be unwise to attempt to account for *all* behavioral changes on the basis of brain dysfunction alone.

Epilepsy and Aggression

A number of earlier reports suggested that patients suffering psychomotor (complex partial, temporal lobe) seizures were specifically predisposed to exhibit antisocial, aggressive, and violent behavior toward others (Mark & Ervin, 1970). More recently, there have been continuing reports of violent automatisms, howling, and striking-out behavior associated with actual seizure occurrence (ictal behavior) and periods following (postictal behavior) seizure termination Daly, 1975; Devinsky & Bear, 1984.

Evaluation of this literatuare is difficult because of the varying definitions of "violence" and the failure to use standard behavioral evaluations, matched control groups, and prospective designs (Kligman & Goldberg, 1975). In addition, there is much evidence to suggest that disinhibition and violence are associated with brain dysfunction of all types, lowered intellectual abilities, and long-standing psychosocial or environmental deprivation (Goldstein, 1974; Mungas, 1983). Two studies have attempted to document aggressive acts of temporal lobe epileptics through the videotaping of temporal lobe seizures (Delgado-Escueta, Mattson, King, Goldensohn, Spiegel, Madsen, Crandall, Dreifuss, & Porter, 1981; Rodin, 1973). In most cases, few violent or aggressive acts were directed at other persons. There were frequent attempts at removing constraining objects (such as EEG recording leads) and less frequent uncontrolled "aggressive" behavior, usually precipitated by fear or attempts at constraint, and characterized by automatic, repetitive kicking, flailing, or other "fight–flight" defensive motions, often directed at inanimate objects. The use of epilepsy as a legal defense for violent crimes, as in the case of Jack Ruby (Rodin, 1973), is generally implausible because complex, goal-directed activity is not observed during seizures. When patients commit directed violent acts between seizure episodes, there is very likely an interaction of predisposing psychosocial factors and brain pathology.

Psychological Treatments to Reduce Seizure Frequency

A variety of psychological treatments have been found to be useful in reducing seizure frequency in some patients. Anticonvulsant medication is necessary in treating all confirmed seizure disorders; the techniques discussed below should be viewed as adjunctive to medication.

A 12–14 cycles/sec sensorimotor EEG rhythm (SMR) has been associated with motor inhibition (Sterman, Goodman, & Kovalesky, 1978; Sterman & Wyrwicka, 1967) and decreased seizure frequency after the creation of epileptogenic foci in animals. Biofeedback training has been used in efforts to train epileptics to increase their SMR and to diminish the slower EEG frequencies. Reduction of seizure frequency during treatment periods of up to 6 months has been reported (Sterman, 1977). Other EEG operant-conditioning paradigms have also been used with some success in seizure frequency reduction, although they emphasized the reinforcement of different, faster frequencies of brain activity (Kuhlman, 1978; Wyler, Robbins, & Dodrill, 1979). A number of critiques suggest that relaxation and desensitization procedures may account for most of the reported gains, as habituation sessions are often incorporated within the context of EEG biofeedback training (Cott, Pavloski, & Black, 1979; Kaplan, 1975). There are numerous reports of relaxation training, desensitization, and skills training leading to clinical improvement, decreased seizure frequency, and better medication compliance among epileptic patients (Cabral & Scott, 1976; Feldman & Paul, 1976). A relationship between increased anxiety or autonomic arousal and seizure initiation has also been documented (Friis & Lund, 1974; Mattson, Lerner, & Dix, 1974). There are also patients whose seizures are provoked by repetitive blinking, sensory stimulation, reading, or writing (Forster, 1977; Ramani, 1983; Terzano, Parrino, Manzoni, & Mancia, 1983). These are easily treated through behavioral techniques that extinguish and replace responses that initiate seizure activity, even in severely retarded individuals (Adams, 1976).

In general, clinical experience suggests that education of the patient and family about the causes and management of seizures can also decrease anxiety; this process may or may not reduce seizure frequency. Behavioral approaches may decrease the *initiation* of seizure activity. Once a seizure has begun, it is not possible to alter its course by these methods. The extensive literature on medication and surgical treatments for epilepsy will not be reviewed here.

Conversion Seizures

It has been estimated that 10% of seizure patients have conversion or hysterical seizures (Ramani & Gumnit, 1982). They may be seen in patients with or without true seizure disorders. Hysterical seizures are usually bizarre, uncoordinated, excessively long, and lacking in the typical stereotyped rhythm and progression of true seizures. Incontinence, tongue biting, or physical injury from loss of consciousness are seldom seen. Such seizures often appear to serve the function of attracting attention and care. Some evidence suggests that hysterical seizures represent symptoms of more severe psychopathology, such as major affective disorders and character pathology (Stewart, Lovitt, & Stewart, 1982). Diagnosis may be aided by videotelemetry and by the use of suggestion techniques to initiate attacks when the EEG remains normal (Cohen & Suter, 1982).

There is some evidence suggesting the usefulness of behavior therapy for conversion seizures. Ramani and Gumnit (1982) described a procedure for helping such patients to distinguish between ictal and conversion seizures, with recording of emotional events just before conversion seizures, and the learning of coping and relaxation techniques. Seven of eight patients had no seizures at 4-year follow-up, although all remained under the continuing care of neurologists. An excellent review of behavioral approaches in conversion disorders was presented by Walen, Hauserman, and Lavin (1977). Face-saving maneuvers for the patient with conversion seizures and the involvement of family members are crucial factors in replacing these behaviors with more adaptive responses. Deception or trickery should be avoided.

Seizures that present with unusual sensory symptoms, aphasia, vomiting, abdominal pains, and abnormal perceptions or hallucinations may be mistaken for conversion phenomena or other psychiatric disorders (Holtzman & Goldensohn, 1977; Mitchell, Greenwood, & Messenheimer, 1983; Racy, Osborn, Vern, & Molinari, 1980). Any stereotyped set of symptoms that are recurrent and that are associated with recent behavioral or cognitive changes should be evaluated for seizure activity by EEG monitoring before a definitive psychological diagnosis is made. The variety and bizarre nature of seizure presentations cannot be overemphasized.

Psychosocial Complications

Epilepsy often results in loss of employment, loss of friends, and feelings of loss of control and helplessness because of its unpredictable nature. Complex partial seizures present additional difficulties because of frequent bizarre and unusual sensory experiences, anmesia, and feelings of unreality (Rodin, 1975; Ziegler, 1981). For these reasons, a multidisciplinary treatment team including physicians, psychologists, social workers, nurses, and vocational counselors is necessary to enhance overall treatment outcome. An emphasis on objective, standard evaluations of psychosocial and adjustment difficulties secondary to epilepsy also aids in more specific treatment approaches (Dodrill, 1983).

STROKE

Incidence and Pathophysiology

An estimated 0.5 million people suffer strokes annually, and about 40% of these are fatal. Over 5% of people ultimately will have a stroke, 80% of them occurring after age 65. It has been estimated that 1.6 million Americans have stroke-related deficits at any given time, with 40% of these requiring some services and 10% requiring total care (Wolf, Dawber, Thomas, Colton, & Kannel, 1977). Between 1960 and 1975, however, the incidence of stroke declined 34% to 71% (depending on sex and race), probably because of improved treatment of hypertension (Soltero, Liu, Cooper, Stamler, & Garside, 1978).

A stroke is a sudden interruption of blood flow to the brain, leading to the death of neurons. There are three types of strokes:

1. *Thrombotic strokes* are due to blood clots (thrombi) that form in cerebral vessels, usually because of atherosclerosis (fatty deposits in blood vessels).

2. *Embolic strokes* are due to blood clots (usually from the heart) or fatty deposits (usually from large vessels in the neck) that become dislodged and then flow to and block vessels in the brain.

3. *Hemorrhagic strokes* are due to the rupture of arteries, either within the brain (intracerebral hemorrhage) or at its outer lining (subarachnoid hemorrhage). These are most common with chronic hypertension, or they may be due to congenital aneurysms (malformations and weaknesses of vessel walls) that burst.

The specific deficits caused by stroke depend on the affected brain areas as discussed earlier. Common neurobehavioral syndromes, related to the anatomy of cerebral vasculature, are described in neurology and neuropsychology texts. Extensive review of outcome following stroke indicated that 40% of patients were alive, independent, and walking after 18 months and 40% to 70% required no assistance in activities of daily living (Fieigen-sen, McDowell, Meese, McCarthy, & Greenberg, 1977). About half of stroke survivors have motor weakness or paralysis (Gresham, Phillips, Wolf, McNamara, Kannel, & Daw-ber, 1979). Most recovery of specific functions apparently occurs within 6 months, and virtually all within 1 year of the stroke. Studies to date fail to show an advantage for in-tensive rehabilitation programs, although these may be critical for selected individuals.

Behavioral Changes

Stroke patients often fail to resume previous activities, even when physical rehabili-tation has apparently been successful (Labi, Phillips, & Gresham, 1980), although in many stroke patients, other illnesses may contribute to functional decline (Gresham *et al.* 1979). In self-ratings, 77% of 2-year stroke survivors showed deterioration in their quality of life. This rating correlated with reduced capacity for activities of daily living (ADL), but anxiety and depression during the acute stage of stroke treatment also predicted worse quality of life at 2 years (Ahlsio, Britton, Murray, & Theorell, 1984). Feibel and Springer (1982) found that 26% of 91 stroke patients were depressed (by nurses' ratings) at 6 months.

These studies are typical in reporting depression as the most common psychiatric problem following stroke. The multiple stresses and losses that these patients experience are clearly factors, but there is evidence that stroke patients have a higher incidence of depression than other groups of patients with multiple physical and emotional stresses, and that poststroke depression may be related to the site of the lesion, a finding suggest-ing a direct neurobiologic factor as well. Folstein, Maiberger, and McHugh (1977) found a depressive syndrome in 45% of 20 otherwise healty poststroke patients and in 10% of an orthopedic comparison group. They also found a syndrome of "irritability" in 35% of the stroke patients (including 70% of those with right-hemisphere lesions, and none with left) and none of the orthopedic patients. Both syndromes would probably be related to major depression by DSM-III criteria. Finkelstein, Benowitz, Baldessarini, Arana, Le-vine, Woo, Bear, Moya, and Stoll (1982) found abnormal dexamethasone suppression tests (DSTs) in 52% of poststroke patients versus 8% of nonstroke patients. The DST assesses cortisol production after the administration of a synthetic steroid drug, reported to be increased in depressed patients (Carroll, Feinberg, Greden, Tarika, & Albala, 1981). In the stroke patients, abnormal DST was associated with depressed mood and appetite or sleep disturbance. Robinson, Starr, and Price (1984) found DSM-III major depressive disorder in 26% of 50 stroke patients initially and in 34% at 6 months, and dysthymic disorder was found in an additional 18% and 26% at the two time points. Depression tended to persist or worsen. Depressive syndromes were more common with left-hemisphere lesions and euphoric affect with right-hemisphere lesions. This study con-tradicts Folstein *et al.*'s findings. Robinson and Coyle (1980) reported that focal brain lesions can cause asymmetrical depletion of catecholamines in rats and suggested that a similar process may occur following stroke and may lead to depression.

The relationship between depression and aphasia cannot be considered resolved. Robinson and Benson (1981) did find a relationship between depression and nonfluent aphasia (inability to find correct words, without meaningless verbosity), but Robinson, Kubos, Starr, Rao, and Price (1983) did not; few aphasics were included in the latter study, however. Gainotti (1972) found "catastrophic" behaviors and particularly sudden bursts of tears to be common in aphasics, but he did not consider these equivalent to depressive syndromes. Most of the depressed stroke patients reported in the studies cited here had not had aphasia. Nevertheless, aphasia (particularly expressive aphasia) can be an excruciatingly frustrating disorder. It would not be surprising if the incidence of major depression in aphasics did prove to be high for both anatomic and psychological reasons.

Behavioral changes associated with "neglect" phenomena may be equally striking to clinicians and family members. Patients with right frontoparietotemporal infarcts may also show inattention to visual stimuli (as discussed above) and auditory stimuli, impaired recognition of faces, and denial of their illness, particularly denial of (inattention to) deficits on the left side of the body (Hier, Mondlock, & Caplan, 1983; Willanger, Danielsen, & Ankerhus, 1981). Hier et al. (1983) found that 90% of 41 patients with unilateral right-hemisphere strokes showed recovery of impaired face-naming and denial of illness within 20 weeks. About 75% of patients recovered from unilateral visual neglect and spatial inattention during figure drawing, but deficits present at 20 weeks were still present at 60 weeks.

The aprosodic deficits described earlier in this chapter are also common after stroke in the right hemisphere. In patients with expressive aprosodia, emotional flatness may be erroneously interpreted as depression, or actual depression with vegetative symptoms may be missed because of lack of appropriate expressions. Ross and Rush (1981) described several patients; some had a prior history of depression, and antidepressants were effective. Such patients may also show inappropriate emotional outbursts at times. Patients with receptive aprosodia (impaired comprehension) may exhibit unusual behavior because of their lack of awareness of the emotional content of others' communications, and they may deny dysphoria (even when depressive behavior and symptoms are obviously present). Ross and Rush (1981) suggested that, in stroke patients, a diagnosis of depression be considered on the basis of (1) clinical deterioration from a previously stable neurological state; (2) a history of prior depression obtained from patient and family members; (3) pathological laughing and crying in the absence of pseudobulbar palsy (a neurological syndrome related to lesions of specific neuronal tracts in the brain stem); and (4) depressed statements in patients with aprosodia and flat affect.

Changes in sexual functioning are also common following stroke (Renshaw, 1978). Bray, DeFrank, and Wolfe (1981) reported that most stroke patients (88% of men and 73% of women) continued to feel sexual desire, but most experienced some degree of sexual dysfunction. For example, of 24 men studied, the number experiencing erection decreased from 18 (75%) to 11 (46%) after stroke, and the number experiencing ejaculation declined from 21 (88%) to 7 (29%). Among 11 women, 5 (45%) had experienced orgasm before stroke, and only 1 (9%) afterward. Sjogren and Fugl-Meyer (1982) also found that 75% of patients reported having less frequent or no intercourse following stroke, with the greatest reduction found in those who were also dependent on others for ADL. There have not yet been careful studies of the relationship of decreased sexual function to physiological, interpersonal, and psychological factors, including depression.

Mania, hypomania, inappropriate cheerfulness, and disinhibition of sexual and aggressive behavior have been reported to be most common in patients with right-hemisphere lesions (Jampala & Abrams, 1983). However, these latter authors reported two cases of classical manic episodes, one associated with right-hemisphere (frontotemporoparietal) and the other with left-hemisphere (temporoparietal) stroke lesions. Yudofsky and Silver (1985) suggested that the "episodic dyscontrol syndrome" defined in the DSM-III is related to organic illness, including stroke, but empirical studies are lacking.

"Psychiatric" manifestations are also often seen in patients with stroke-related memory deficits. Clinically, it may be difficult to differentiate between primary affective changes and frustration related to memory deficit.

Psychotic symptoms may be seen after stroke, but they are apparently uncommon. None of the large follow-up studies reported above mention any significant incidence of schizophrenialike psychosis. Paranoid feelings and ideas are common in many brain disorders. When these are seen, it should be determined whether they are related to depression (i.e., feeling that one will be harmed because one is bad or repulsive).

Treatment

Stroke patients with behavioral disorders should ideally be treated in an integrated, multidisciplinary fashion combining education, ventilation, and support for the patient, the family, and other caregivers; careful evaluation of psychiatric, neurological, and neuropsychological disturbance to guide treatment; physical rehabilitation; counseling to facilitate social and sexual rehabilitation wherever possible; and psychotropic medication and/or appropriate formal psychotherapeutic treatment when indicated. In practice, patients often receive somewhat fragmented or abbreviated care. The mental health clinician may be pivotal in attending to multiple aspects of rehabilitation, by providing necessary interventions and recognizing the need for referrals to other professionals.

Psychotropic medication should be considered when stroke patients have behavioral syndromes known to respond to specific drugs. Lipsey, Robinson, Pearlson, Rao, and Price (1984) found that treatment with nortriptyline, a tricyclic antidepressant, was effective in poststroke patients with major depressive disorder, in a double-blind, placebo-controlled study. Monoamine oxidase inhibitor antidepressants are also effective and have fewer anticholinergic and cardiac effects. ECT has been used successfully for depression after stroke (Karliner, 1978) and may be preferable to drug treatment when patients have multiple illnesses and medications. Both antidepressant drugs and ECT are most likely to be effective in patients with a depression-related loss of subjective pleasure with vegetative symptoms (changes in appetite, sleep, energy, and concentration). Indications for lithium, antipsychotics, and other drugs are discussed below.

Goodstein (1983) reviewed literature on the psychological aspects of stroke rehabilitation (including the valuable personal accounts that have been published by clinicians who suffered strokes). Patients and family often need assistance in verbalizing and expressing feelings about loss of control, specific fears (of death, insanity, disfigurement, and loss of physical and sexual function), loss of dignity, changes in relationships due to the stroke, lack of recovery of function, deficits that are particularly troubling or confusing, and personal meanings that the individual may attach to the stroke. Interventions should include active anticipation of concerns and education, as well as careful listening to concerns. Denial should not be opposed too rapidly or forcefully but should be "titrated" to permit adjustment. Attention should be given to the stroke as narcissistic injury, necessitating mourning for part of the self. Information should be provided to the patient and the family through direct teaching, personal feedback concerning all gains made in rehabilitation, and use of educational, support, and therapy groups where available (Goodstein, 1983). Patients with sexual dysfunction may require special rehabilitation techniques (Renshaw, 1978).

TUMORS

Incidence and Pathophysiology

Older statistics documented brain tumors in 1.8% of people at autopsy, with 15% of these metastatic from other cancers, but more recent data show that there are many more metastatic tumors (identified in 85,000 deaths yearly) than primary tumors (8,000 deaths yearly) of the brain (Adams & Victor, 1981).

About half of primary brain tumors are reported to be gliomas (arising from the supportive tissue [glial cells] of the brain), including the highly malignant glioblastoma multiforme, the slower-growing but usually fatal astrocytoma, and mixtures of the two. About 12% are meningiomas, nonmalignant tumors arising from the outer lining tissue of the brain and spinal cord that can displace and damage other tissue. There are a variety of other tumors, including congenital, pituitary, blood vessel, and spinal cord tumors, and a number of less common types. Brain tumors occur at all ages, with a peak incidence in the 40s. They may create acute psychiatric disturbance, or long-term psychiatric problems may result from the tumor and/or its treatment.

Brain tumors create behavioral effects by impairing or destroying neuronal functioning via (1) the effects of increased pressure; (2) edema (swelling); (3) direct invasion of surrounding tissue; (4) seizure activity; (5) hemorrhage; (6) abnormal hormonal secretion caused by pituitary tumors; and (7) pain or abnormal sensations (particularly in spinal cord tumors) that are misinterpreted as anxiety or conversion symptoms. In addition, surgical and radiation treatments, psychological reactions to illness, and effects of the drugs used to treat tumors or swelling may lead to psychiatric disturbance.

Problems of Differential Diagnosis

Most brain tumors are discovered after the onset of seizures, changes in consciousness, signs of increased intracranial pressure (vomiting, increased blood pressure, headache, or damage to the cranial nerves), or specific motor or sensory symptoms. Early in the course, patients may experience cognitive symptoms. These have been described by Adams as "psychomotor asthenia," which he defined as reduction and slowing of thought, action, persistence, spontaneity, insight, and judgment, with increased forgetfulness, irritability, and socially inappropriate behavior (Adams & Victor, 1981). There are no recent studies of the frequency with which such symptoms are the initial signs of brain tumor. In two older large series, "mental symptoms" were reported to be early symptoms in 15% and 18% of cases of primary brain tumor (reviewed in Davison & Bagley, 1969). It is not known how often cognitive or psychiatric changes are the first signs of metastatic tumors.

A number of older studies suggested that cerebral tumors were relatively common in psychiatric patients (reviewed by Davison & Bagley, 1969). However, more recent data suggest that they are now uncommon (Wells & Duncan, 1980; Hall, Gardner, Stickney, Le Cann, & Popkin, 1980). It is likely that psychiatric patients now receive improved medical evaluations, aided by the routine availability of computerized axial tomography (CAT) and electroencephalography (EEG). Also, outpatient mental-health clinicians or nonpsychiatric physicians now initially manage the kinds of "depressed," irritable outpatients who may prove ultimately to develop neurological signs suggesting brain tumor. In the acute patient, delayed recognition of a brain tumor may have tragic results.

Lesions such as brain tumors are most likely to be found in psychiatric patients who have acute disorders of recent onset and signs suggesting an atypical mixture of psychiatric and cognitive symptoms. However, psychiatric syndromes can occasionally be due to non-malignant or very slowly growing lesions. Therefore, we believe that all patients with acute, psychotic, atypical, or severely disabling disorders should have a brain-imaging test at an early point in their course.

Behavioral Changes in Patients with Brain Tumors

Unlike stroke patients, brain tumor patients have not been extensively studied for behavioral abnormalities with the use of modern assessment and diagnostic methods. However, it is likely that a large proportion of patients with brain tumors (primary or metastatic) suffer cognitive or behavioral-emotional changes because of the tumor or its treatment. There is a need for closer scientific study and for more specific clinical approaches in this area.

Evidence of the frequency of mental changes in tumor patients comes largely from older studies that did not assess these changes in detail. These studies reported a high incidence of "personality" and/or intellectual changes in patients with frontal and temporal tumors and to a lesser extent, with parietal tumors (evidence reviewed by Davison & Bagley, 1969). These changes include the nonspecific slowing and irritability described by Adams, as well as the more site-specific changes described earlier in this chapter. Many of these site-specific changes were identified in studies that did not separate tumors from other disorders.

Certain types of brain tumors are known to cause a high rate of behavioral symptoms. Malamud (1967) described 18 cases of tumors found in limbic system sites (temporal lobe, cingulate gyri, and third ventricle) in patients who exhibited striking affective and/or psychotic symptoms. As the cases were all obtained from psychiatric hospital sources, the tumors may have been coincidental. However, a causal relationship between tumor and psychiatric difficulties could not be excluded. Davison and Bagley (1969) reviewed reported cases of brain tumors with psychotic symptoms. They found increased schizophrenialike symptoms in cases of temporal lobe (particularly left-hemisphere) and pituitary tumors. Tumors of the corpus callosum, the major tracts connecting the two cerebral hemispheres, have often been noted to cause psychiatric symptoms (reviewed by Nasrallah & McChesney, 1981). The latter authors compared 5 patients with these tumors to 8 patients with noncallosal tumors. The former showed significantly more symptoms of DSM-III disorders, primarily related to depression but, in two cases, also delusions or hallucinations. In addition, these tumors often result in unusual split-brain syndromes in which information is prevented from crossing between the cerebral hemispheres. Split-brain patients are unable to read material presented in the left visual field and may have difficulty controlling the motor output of their nondominant (left) side. Callosal apraxia and "alien" body parts are also reported; patients may experience nondominant body parts as not belonging to them (Heilman & Valenstein, 1985). Epstein, Epstein, and Postel (1971) described 4 patients with spinal cord tumors whose pain and, in some cases, irritability were initially considered neurotic symptoms.

Although no modern empirical studies exist, behavioral changes are often noted in frontal, temporal, and pituitary tumors. Adenomas (tumors of the secretory cells) of the pituitary gland comprise 6% to 8% of primary brain tumors. Pituitary tumors are classified according to the hormones they secrete. Pituitary tumors may compress (because of hydrocephalus, increased fluid pressure) nearby structures, including the limbic structures around the third cerebral ventricle (fluid-containing space) and the deep portions of the frontal lobe, locations that account for the frequency of behavioral symptoms; the optic nerves are also usually affected, the result being visual symptoms. Tumors that affect the hypothalamus may cause excessive sleepiness and obesity as well as personality changes. Clinically, depression is often seen in patients with prolactinomas and may be reduced by the suppression of prolactin secretion by drugs, although empirical studies are lacking. Excess steroid hormones can lead to depressive or manic syndromes. Also found in the pituitary region are craniopharyngiomas, which may invade limbic or frontal structures.

Tumors in the posterior fossa (cerebellum and brain stem) were found to be less likely to cause cognitive and behavioral changes in the older studies cited above. However, patients with lesions of the cerebellum may have schizophrenic, manic or depressive symptoms (Hamilton et al., 1983; Lishman, 1978; Yadalam, Jain, & Simpson, 1985), and unusual movement disorders.

Cognitive changes in tumor patients have received some recent study. Hom and Reitan (1984) found that rapidly growing brain tumors caused greater neuropsychological impairment than slowly growing tumors, in addition to the effects of tumor site on specific deficits. Hochberg and Slotnick (1980) demonstrated generalized neuropsychological impairments, without clear localization, in 13 astrocytoma survivors who had received whole-head radiation therapy, had not had a recurrence of the tumor, yet had failed to return to previous functional levels. Tumor location, age, and cognitive and behavioral deficits were quite variable. It is suggested that the radiation therapy may have accounted for some of the impairments, in the absence of more specific pathological factors following treatment. A significant incidence of neuropsychological impairments has been documented in children who received radiation treatment for brain neoplasm and who were studied with psychometric tests or clinical observation, but not in all studies (reviewed by Eiser, 1981). In patients with large or widespread lesions (such as diffuse metastases), gross cognitive changes and the syndrome of delirium are common.

Treatment

There has been no recent empirical study of the management of the psychiatric aspects of care for patients with primary and metastatic brain tumors. Individual patients may present with combinations of cognitive and behavioral-emotional symptoms, depending on the location and extent of the lesions. Depressive, manic, or psychotic syndromes or severe anxiety may be treated pharmacologically. Treatment of pain may be important for psychological management. Effective psychological intervention follows principles similar to those described for stroke patients and their families, with attention to education about the illness, the deficits and their treatment, individual feelings and conflicts, and family relationships. In addition, brain tumor patients have a low survival rate (currently under 25%), so that issues related to dying may be central.

MULTIPLE SCLEROSIS

Multiple sclerosis (MS) is another relatively common, chronic neurological disorder that is associated with a significant incidence of psychiatric and cognitive impairments. Because of space limitations, a complete discussion of MS is not attempted here. Briefly, MS is the most common demyelinating disorder (i.e., involving deterioration of the myelin sheaths that surround and "insulate" the long nerve fibers). Incidence reaches 50–60/100,000 in some areas (highest in colder climates, for unknown reasons), with a peak incidence at ages 30 to 35. Demyelinated "plaques" occur in multiple sites in the brain and the spinal cord, leading typically to symptoms such as double vision or other visual disturbances, slurred speech, tremor while reaching for objects (intention tremor), gait instability (ataxia), inability to walk because of weakness and spasticity of the legs, urinary incontinence, and loss of perception of body position and of vibration. Symptoms classically appear, remit, and then reappear over many years. Early symptoms may be vague and transient, leading to misdiagnosis as "hysterical" or other problems. Neurological deterioration is usually gradual (over 10–30 years) but is rapid in some cases. Further description of the disorder may be found in neurological texts (Gilroy & Meyer, 1979). Confavreaux, Aimard, and Devic (1980) have discussed current diagnostic criteria.

Affective and cognitive disturbances can be seen in MS patients. Classically, MS patients have been described as being prone to inappropriately euphoric affect. However, modern empirical studies have cast doubt on whether this occurs more frequently in MS than in other chronic disorders, such as muscular dystrophy. The appearance of euphoria in individual patients is now assumed to be directly due to neuropathology (Trimble & Grant, 1982). A significant number of MS patients have depressive symptoms, which may be related to the chronicity of the illness, acute exacerbations, and the presence of plaques in the cerebral cortex (Dalos, Rabins, Brooks, & O'Donnell, 1983).

The neuropsychological concomitants of the disorder are varied. A series of early studies with the Halstead–Reitan Neuropsychological Test Battery (HRB) demonstrated deficits on time-based speeded tasks, simple and complex motor tests, perceptual problem-solving tests, and measures of abstracting ability, with relative preservations of verbal functions. The pattern of impairments in MS patients was often "spotty" or multifocal (Goldstein & Shelly, 1974; Reitan, Reed, & Dyken, 1971). Rao, Hammeke, McQuillen, Khatri, and Lloyd (1984) identified three separate clusters of neuropsychological findings among 44 MS patients. One group (20%) of patients had marked memory impairments, severe global cognitive impairments, and psychosislike profiles on the MMPI, with a high incidence of psychotic behavior. A second group (43%) had only mild memory disturbance, little cognitive impairment, and a relatively high prevalence of self-reported depressive symptoms and use of psychotropic medications. Finally, a third group (37%) performed in the normal range on memory tests with no apparent psychological distress.

Neuropsychological assessment can be quite valuable in treatment planning for MS patients, to identify those patients with deficits that may interfere with rehabilitation efforts (Staples & Lincoln, 1979). Igbal, Goldstein, and Tocco (1982) noted that the severity of the neuropsychological impairments was positively correlated with duration of inpatient treatment, degree of euphoria, and frustration among the rehabilitation staff treating MS patients. Counseling and education of patient and family are important in this chronic disorder, and psychiatric consultation may be needed for depression or other psychiatric presentations. There are no controlled studies of the use of antidepressant medications in MS patients, although they are commonly used when needed.

Psychopharmacological Treatment in Neurological Disorders

Although many patients with neurological disorders receive psychotropic drugs, there has been little empirical research on their use in such patients. The potential for adverse (unwanted) effects must always be assessed when psychotropic drugs are given to patients with existing cognitive-behavioral problems. There is some overlap in the adverse effects of the major classes of psychotropics. Hypotension, drug-induced Parkinsonism, abnormal cardiac rhythms, and sedation may be of great concern in neurological patients. Anticholinergic effects can cause or worsen memory impairment and, in extreme cases, delirium. All of these effects may be compunded by the drug accumulation that may occur over days or weeks because of the relatively long time required for the elimination of many psychotropic drugs from the bloodstream, particularly in elderly people. Adverse effects such as hypotension, sedation, anticholinergic effects, or Parkinsonism may be mistaken for cognitive decline or depression. Careful attention to the behavioral effects of all medications is therefore necessary.

The psychotropic drugs commonly used with these disorders include antidepressants, antipsychotics, sedative-hypnotics, lithium, and miscellaneous other drugs, such as propranolol and anticonvulsants. Electroconvulsive therapy will also be considered here.

Antidepressants

These drugs have the most well-established uses in neurological disorders. There is good evidence that patients with the signs and symptoms defined as major depressive disorder in the DSM-III classification are likely to benefit from antidepressant drug therapy (Nelson & Charney, 1981), regardless of the apparent "cause" of the depression. It is currently believed that this syndrome is the "final common pathway" for numerous etiologies, and that it signifies the involvement of neurotransmitter systems amenable to change by currently available drugs. Antidepressants have received the most careful study in poststroke patients (as discussed above), but clinical experience suggests that they are also of use with other neurological patients with the depressive syndrome. The reader is referred to Chapter 2 by Simpson and Pi, on psychotropic drugs for a discussion of tricyclic and monoamine oxidase inhibitor antidepressants and their adverse effects.

ECT is an effective treatment for severe depression, and it also causes the fewest serious adverse effects (Avery & Winokur, 1976). Karliner (1978) reviewed its effectiveness in patients with depression associated with stroke, multiple sclerosis, head trauma, and other disorders. It is sometimes effective for mania as well as for depression. However, patients with increased intracranial pressure should not receive ECT, which causes transient increases in blood pressure and thus in intracranial pressure as well; for this reason, serious complications and death have sometimes resulted from the use of ECT on patients with brain tumors.

Lithium

Patients with neurological disorders commonly have typical or atypical forms of mania. Patients receiving steroids may also become manic. Lithium is apparently often effective regardless of whether the patient has a prior history of mania or not. Lithium has also been recommended for the treatment of aggression. It can sometimes be effective in brain-lesioned patients with agitation accompanied by excited mood states and increased motor activity and speech. However, it has been noted clinically that brain-injured patients may be more prone to lithium toxicity, so that lithium blood levels must be increased cautiously.

Propranolol

Propranolol (Inderal) is a drug used for the treatment of hypertension and other cardiac illness. It has been reported to be useful in the management of rage and violence in patients with neurological disorders (Yudofsky & Silver, 1985). It is sometimes combined with lithium. Although low doses, such as might be used for hypertension, have sometimes been reported as effective, much higher doses have been necessary in some cases. Because of the potential for inducing hypotension and slowed heart rate, this drug must be used carefully in patients with medical contraindications. Its effects have not received careful study in this area.

Sedative-Hypnotics

Drugs used for nonspecific sedation and sleep are frequently prescribed. Most are of the benzodiazepine class, although milder sedative (chloral hydrate and antihistamines) and barbiturates are also sometimes used. A major problem with benzodiazepine drugs is that most of them such as diazepam (Valium), are eliminated over periods of many hours or days, so that accumulation of drug levels and of sedative effects is common and at times dangerous, particularly in the elderly. The shortest-acting benzodiazepines are triazolam (Halcion), which is usually eliminated overnight, and lorazepam (Ativan). Although generally safe and often quite useful, the benzodiazepines have other problems, such as excessive sedation, cognitive disturbance at higher doses, disinhibition of aggression in some patients, lowering of the pain threshold, and the possibility of seizures when large doses are discontinued abruptly. For this reason, they should not be used without clear indications and should be used in the lowest effective dose for the shortest possible time, except where chronic, generalized anxiety is unresponsive to other therapy.

Anticonvulsants

In some, but not all, patients with temporal lobe seizures, carbamazepine (Tegretol) may bring about behavioral improvement; carbamazepine and valproic acid (Depakene) have been reported to be useful in some patients with manic syndromes and aggressive behavior (Ballenger & Post, 1980). It is not yet clear which patients are most likely to respond. Hydantoin (Dilantin) is generally considered of limited value in the treatment of behavioral disturbances, except for the beneficial effects of seizure control.

Antipsychotics

Antipsychotic drugs are frequently prescribed for patients with diverse brain disorders who have behavioral abnormalities such as agitation, aggression or overt violence, paranoia, or psychotic symptoms such as hallucinations and delusions. Yet, this type of use has not received careful empirical study. Because antipsychotics have both immediate adverse effects (Parkinsonism, sedation, hypotension, and anticholinergic effects) and long-term risks (tardive dyskinesia), their indiscriminate use must be condemned. However, there are many patients whose symptoms cannot be suppressed and whose behavior cannot be controlled with any other available treatment.

Because of the long-term risks of antipsychotics, consideration should always be given to the possibility that safer drugs may be useful. In the presence of neurological disorders, great skill may be required to detect depressive or manic symptoms in the presence of other behavioral cognitive and motor impairments. Patients with cognitive dysfunction may become agitated because of changes in their life circumstances or environment; psychological management of such reactions may prove useful without resort to antipsychotics. Propranolol and/or lithium may be useful in the violent nondepressed patient.

When antipsychotic drugs must be used for nonschizophrenic neurological patients, they should generally be initiated at the lowest possible dose and increased cautiously. No antipsychotic has been shown to be most effective in this or any other specific clinical context, so the choice of drug depends entirely on anticipation of adverse effects. Where sedation is desirable, chlorpromazine (Thorazine) or thioridazine (Mellaril) may be used; the latter is more anticholinergic, is less likely to cause Parkinsonism, is hypotensive but less so than the former, and is more likely to cause weight gain, particularly in children. Otherwise, low doses of high-potency antipsychotics are generally used. Haloperidol (Haldol) is the least anticholinergic; fluphenazine (Prolixin) is similar in dosage and effectiveness. Dosages as low as 1 mg daily may be useful with some patients. However, in patients with severe psychotic syndromes, dosages of 300 m to 2000 mg daily of chlorpromazine (equivalent to 5–40 mg or more of haloperidol) are generally required. Antipsychotics may be combined with lithium, propranolol, or anticonvulsants to achieve better behavioral control in some patients.

GENERAL APPROACH TO BEHAVIORAL TREATMENT IN NEUROLOGICAL DISORDERS

A complete discussion of the psychosocial treatment of patients with these disorders will not be attempted here. We would like to emphasize certain principles of intervention with such patients. To an extent, psychiatric problems such as major depression or psychological conflicts concerning a marriage are treated with appropriate psychotherapy, guidance, and/or medication whether or not the patient has a neurological disorder.

However, the presence of brain impairment necessitates awareness of a number of special issues.

We have attempted to emphasize the importance of defining the specific nature of the patient's neuropsychological impairments. It makes a difference whether or not the patient has difficulty with auditory sequential memory, word finding, recognition of facial expressions, fine motor movements, tactile sensation, or any other of the many specific impairments that may result from brain illness. It is not useful to think of the patient as suffering from "organic brain syndrome" or "brain damage," because this tells the clinician little about the particular functional abilities and disabilities that will determine the effectiveness of any intervention. Misconceptions about the nature of these impairments are common among professionals, as well as among patients and families.

Psychological interventions should always include an attempt to educate the patient and the family (and any caretakers) about the nature and course of the illness and of recovery from it, and about the patient's specific impairments. This education will occasionally prove difficult or even inadvisable because of intellectual or emotional limitations. In the vast majority of cases, however, both patient and family benefit from this education, and from specific guidance in ways of coping with each impairment. Although it might be ideal for such guidance to come from professionals equally well trained in neurology, rehabilitation, and psychotherapy, in reality many patients receive little useful information from any source. To be effective with such patients, the mental health clinician must become familiar with their illness and with the problems associated with their impairments and must either help the patient and the family to find a source of information or must provide it directly.

Patients and families may resist practical help with these issues for any of the reasons familiar to psychotherapists (e.g., guilt, anxiety, anger, or specific emotional or family conflicts exacerbated by the illness). However, there may also be resistance if the patient and/or the family members have not reached a sufficient state of acceptance of the illness and its impairments. Eager and energetic therapists may attempt extensive educative and psychotherapeutic interventions, or even state-of-the-art behavioral programs, with patients who are not psychologically ready to use them. Kubler-Ross's model (1969) of the stages of grief is applicable to the loss experienced by these patients. For example, initial denial of impairment may lead to repeated attempts to obtain second opinions or to seek magical cures. This is often, at least in part, a healthy reaction, but it indicates a lack of readiness for specific intervention. The second phase of recovery may include anger at family members, projection of blame for the disability, emotional distance from others, emotional overreactions, and irritability at minor events. Patients often have difficulty accepting that they and not someone else have acquired an illness and disability. These reactions usually occur acutely after injury or just after a conclusive diagnosis has been established.

After some time has passed, patients may attempt to bargain with caretakers or professionals. There may be guilt and anxiety over the uncertain future, as well as attempts to gain support and praise: "If I try to shave, will you help me get outside?" These negotiations may represent an initial attempt at reconciling oneself to losses of function. It is helpful to encourage patients at this point to do as much for themselves as possible, within their limitations. Overprotectiveness by family or caretakers may lead to decreased self-esteem and independence, with exacerbation of the depression and despair experienced by most patients as the final phase in their recovery and their acceptance of their condition. This sequence is most applicable to those with mild or moderate impairments, whereas more severely impaired patients may be unaware or disoriented. Family and caretakers usually benefit from being told about these stages and about recommended responses to the patient's reactions and behaviors during this process. In some cases, clinicians may be able to facilitate this process to the point where the patient and/or the relative does become accessible to interventions relevant to specific impairments or psychiatric complications.

We would emphasize, again, that nonspecific, nondirective psychological interventions are seldom the most appropriate approach to this group of patients and families. It is usually a mistake to focus solely on a psychological conflict or a behavioral symptom, without an assessment of the patient's neuropsychological impairments. Functional problems may be directly related to these deficits, to ineffective mechanisms for coping with these deficits, or to deficiencies in treatment, such as ineffective seizure-medication regimens.

There has also been increasing interest in "cognitive" or computer-based retraining programs for brain-injured patients (Trexler, 1982; Wilson & Moffat, 1984). The terms *remediation* and *retraining* are somewhat misleading, as they imply a recovery of lost skills. Some degree of functional recovery does occur following brain injury, independent of treatment, although the mechanisms remain unclear (Finger, 1978; Kolb & Whishaw, 1985). There is usually greater recovery of complex, multicomponent skills relative to specific individual skills, a finding suggesting that recovery involves the development of compensatory alternative strategies using preserved skills (Kolb & Whishaw, 1985; Luria, 1980) rather than neuronal regeneration as proposed by others. Clinically, participation in microcomputer retraining programs often provides patients an opportunity to achieve new goals, to increase perceptions of self-efficacy and control, and to enhance motivation for participation in rehabilitation. However, because of the dearth of treatment outcome studies on brain-injured populations, little is known about the relative efficacy, generalization, and interactions of behavioral, cognitive, educative, pharmacological, and physical rehabilitation. These will be major areas of investigation over the next decade.

REFERENCES

Adams, J. H. (1975). The neuropathology of head injuries. In P. J. Vinken & G. E. Bryn, (Eds.), *Handbook of clinical neurology: Vol. 23. Injuries of the brain and skull* (Part I). Amsterdam: Elsevier Press.

Adams, K. M. (1976). Behavioral treatment of reflex or sensory evoked seizures. *Journal of Behavior Therapy and Experimental Psychiatry, 7*, 123–127.

Adams, R. D., & Victor, M. (1981). *Principles of neurology*. New York: McGraw-Hill.

Ahlsio, B., Britton, M., Murrary, V., & Theorell, T. (1984). Disablement and quality of life after stroke. *Stroke, 15*, 886–890.

Alexander, M. P. (1982). Traumatic brain injury. In D. F. Benson & D. Blumer (Eds.), *Psychiatric aspects of neurologic disease* (Vol. 2). New York: Grune & Stratton.

Avery, D., & Winokur, G. (1976). Mortality in depressed patients treated with electroconvulsive therapy and antidepressants. *Archives of General Psychiatry, 33*, 1029–1037.

Ballenger, J. C. & Post, R. M. (1980). Carbamazepine in manic-depressive illness: A new treatment. *American Journal of Psychiatry, 137*, 782–790.

Blumer, D. (1975). Temporal lobe epilepsy and its psychiatric significance. In D. F. Benson & D. Blumer (Eds.), *Psychiatric aspects of neurological disease* (Vol. 1). New York: Grune & Stratton.

Bray, G. P., DeFrank, R. S., & Wolfe, T. L. (1981). Sexual functioning in stroke survivors. *Archive Physical Medicine Rehabilitation, 62*, 286–288.

Burns, M. S., Halper, A. A., & Mogil, S. I. (1985). *Clinical management of right hemisphere dysfunction.* Rockville, MD: Aspen.

Cabral, R. J., & Scott, F. (1976). Effects of two desensitization techniques, biofeedback and relaxation on intractable epilepsy: Follow-up study. *Journal of Neurology, Neurosurgery, and Psychiatry, 39*, 504–507.

Camfield, P. R., Gates, R., Ronen, G., Camfield, C., Ferguson, A., & Mcdonald, G. W. (1984). Comparison of cognitive ability, personality profile, and school success in epileptic children with right versus left temporal lobe EEG foci. *Annals of Neurology, 15*, 122–126.

Carroll, B. J., Feinberg, M., Greden, J. F. Tarika, J., & Albala, A. A. (1981). A specific laboratory test for the diagnosis of melancholia. *Archives of General Psychiatry, 38*, 15–22.

Caveness, W. F. (1979). Incidence of craniocerebral trauma in the United States in 1976 and trends from 1970–1975. In R. A. Thompson & J. R. Green (Eds.), *Advances in neurology* (Vol. 22). New York: Raven Press.

Cohen, R. J., & Suter, C. (1982). Hysterical seizures: Suggestion as a provactive EEG test. *Annals of Neurology, 11*, 391–395.

Confavreaux, C., Aimard, G., & Devic, M. (1980). Course and prognosis of multiple sclerosis assessed by the computerized data processing of 349 patients. *Brain, 103*, 281–300.

Cott, A., Pavloski, R. P., & Black, A. H. (1979). Reducing epileptic seizures through operant conditioning of central nervous system activity: Procedural variables. *Science, 203*, 73–75.

Dalos, N. P., Rabins, P. V., Brooks, B. R., & O'Donnell, P. (1983). Disease activity and emotional state in multiple sclerosis. *Annals of Neurology, 13*, 573–577.

Daly, D. D. (1975). Ictal clinical manifestations of complex partial seizures. *Advances in Neurology, 11*, 85–112.

Davison, K., & Bagley, C. R. (1969). Schizophrenic-like psychoses associated with organic disorders of the central nervous system: A review of the literature. In R. N. Herrington (Ed.), *Current problems in neuropsychiatry.* (*British Journal of Psychiatry* Special publication). United Kingdom: Headley Bros.

Delgado-Escueta, A. V., Mattson, R. H., King, L., Goldensohn, E. S., Spiegel, H., Madsen, J., Crandall, P., Dreifuss, F., & Porter, R. J. (1981). Special Report: The nature of aggression during epileptic seizures. *New England Journal of Medicine, 305*, 711–716.

Devinsky, O., & Bear, D. (1984). Varieties of aggressive behavior in temporal lobe epilepsy. *American Journal of Psychiatry, 141*, 651–656.

Dikman, S., & Reitan, R. M. (1977). Emotional sequelae of head injury. *Annals of Neurology, 2*, 492–494.

Dikman, S., Reitan, R. M., & Temkin, N. R. (1983). Neuropsychological recovery in head injury. *Archives of Neurology, 40*, 333–338.

Dodrill, C. B. (1981). Neuropsychology of epilepsy. In S. Filskov & T. Boll (Eds.), *Handbook of clinical neuropsychology.* New York: Wiley.

Dodrill, C. B. (1983). Psychosocial characteristics of epileptic patients. In A. A. Ward, Jr. & J. K. Penry (Eds.), *Epilepsy* (Research Publications: Association for Research in Nervous and Mental Disease, Vol. 61). New York: Raven Press.

Eiser, C. (1981). Psychological sequelae of brain tumours in childhood: A retrospective study. *British Journal of Clinical Psychology, 20*, 35–38.

Eliasson, S. G., Prensky, A. L., & Hardin, W. B., Jr. (1978). *Neurological pathophysiology.* New York: Oxford University Press.

Epstein, B. S., Epstein, J. A., & Postel, D. M. (1971). Tumors of spinal cord simulating psychiatric disorders. *Diseases of the Nervous System, 32*, 741–743.

Fedio, P., & Van Buren, J. M. (1975). Memory and perceptual deficits during electrical stimulation in the left and right thalamus and parietal subcortex. *Brain and Language, 2*, 78–100.

Feibel, J. H., & Springer, C. J. (1982). Depression and failure to resume social activities after stroke. *Archive Physical Medicine Rehabilitation, 63*, 276–278.

Feldman, B. G., & Paul, N. G. (1976). Identity of emotional triggers in epilepsy. *Journal of Nervous and Mental Disease, 162*, 345–352.

Fieigensen, J. S., McDowell, F. H., Meese, P., McCarthy, L., & Greenberg, S. (1977). Factors influencing outcome and length of stay in a stroke rehabilitation unit. *Stroke, 8*, 651–656.

Finger, S. (Ed.). (1978). *Recovery from brain damage.* New York: Plenum Press.

Finklestein, S., Benowitz, L. I., Baldessarini, R. J., Arana, G. W., Levine, D., Woo, E., Bear, D., Moya, K., & Stoll, A. L. (1982). Mood, vegetative disturbance, and dexamethasone suppression test after stroke. *Annals of Neurology, 12*, 463–468.

Folstein, M. F., Maiberger, R., & McHugh, P. R. (1977). Mood disorder as a specific complication of stroke. *Journal of Neurology, Neurosurgery, and Psychiatry, 40*, 1018–1020.

Fordyce, D. J., Romeche, J. R., & Prigatano, G. P. (1983). Enhanced emotional reactions in chronic head trauma patients. *Journal of Neurology, Neurosurgery, and Psychiatry, 46*, 620–624.

Forster, F. M. (1977). *Reflex epilepsy, behavioral therapy and conditional reflexes.* Springfield, IL: Charles C Thomas.

Friis, M. L., & Lund, M. (1974). Stress convulsions. *Archives of Neurology, 31*, 155–159.

Gainotti, G. (1972). Emotional behavior and hemispheric side of the lesion. *Cortex, 8*, 41–55.

Gastaut, H. (1970). Clinical and electroencephalographical classification of epileptic seizures. *Epilepsia, 11*, 102–113.

Geschwind, N. (1972). Language and the brain. *Scientific American, 226*, 76–83.

Greschwind, N. (1979). Specializations of the human brain. *Scientific American, 241*, 180–199.

Gilroy, J., & Meyer, J. S. (1979). *Medical Neurology* (3rd ed.). New York: Macmillan.

Goldstein, G., & Shelly, C. H. (1974). Neuropsychological diagnosis of multiple sclerosis in neuropsychiatric setting. *Journal of Nervous and Mental Disease, 158*, 280–290.

Goldstein, M. (1974). Brain research and violent behavior. *Archives of Neurology, 30*, 1–35.

Goodstein, R. K. (1983). Overview: cerebrovascular accident and the hospitalized elderly—A multidimensional clinical problem. *The American Journal of Psychiatry, 140*, 141–147.

Gresham, G. E., Phillips, T. F., Wolf, P. A., McNamara, P. M., Kannel, W. B., & Dawber, T. R. (1979). Epidemiologic profile of long-term stroke disability: The Framingham study. *Archive Physical Medicine Rehabilitation, 60*, 487–491.

Gronwall, D., & Wrightson, P. (1974). Delayed recovery of intellectual function after minor head injury. *Lancet 2*, 506–509.

Gronwall, D., & Wrightson, P. (1975). Cumulative effect of concussion. *Lancet, 1*, 995–997.

Gronwall, D., & Wrightson, P. (1981). Memory and information processing capacity after closed head injury. *Journal of Neurology, Neurosurgery, and Psychiatry, 44*, 889–895.

Hall, R. C. W., Gardner, E. R., Stickney, S. K., Le Cann, A. F., & Popkin, M. K. (1980). Physical illness manifesting as psychiatric disease: II. Analysis of a state hospital inpatient population. *Archives of General Psychiatry, 37*, 989–995.

Hamilton, N. G., Frick, R. B., Takahasi, T., & Hopping, M. W. (1983). Psychiatric symptoms and cerebellar pathology. *American Journal of Psychiatry, 140*, 1322–1326.

Hauser, W. A., Annegers, J. F., & Anderson, E. (1983). Epidemiology and genetics of epilepsy. In A. A. Ward, Jr., J. K. Penry, & D. Purpura (Eds.), *Epilepsy* (Research Publication: Association for Research in Nervous and Mental Disease, Vol. 61). New York: Raven Press.

Hecaen, H., & Albert, M. (1978). Conclusions: Cerebral localization of function. In H. Hecaen & M. Albert (Eds.), *Human neuropsychology.* New York: Wiley.

Heilman, K. M., & Valenstein, E. (Eds.). (1985). *Clinical neuropsychology* (2nd ed.). New York: Oxford University Press.

Heilman, K. M., Watson, R. T., & Bowers, D. (1983). Affective disorders with hemispheric disease. In K. M. Heilman, & P. Satz (Eds.), *Neuropsychology of human emotion.* New York: Guilford Press.

Heilman, K. M., Watson, R. T., & Valenstein, E. (1985). Neglect and related disorders. In K. M. Heilman & E. Valenstein (Eds.), *Clinical neuropsychology* (2nd ed.). New York: Oxford University Press.

Herman, B. P. (1981). Deficits in neuropsychological functioning and psychopathology in epilepsy: A rejected hypothesis revisited. *Epilepsia, 22*, 161–167.

Herman, B. P., & Whitman, S. (1984). Behavioral and personality correlates of epilepsy: A review, methodological critique and conceptual model. *Psychological Bulletin, 95*, 451–497.

Hier, D. B., Mondlock, J., & Caplan, L. (1983). Recovery of behavioral abnormalities after right hemisphere stroke. *Neurology, 33*, 345–350.

Hochberg, F. H., & Slotnick, B. (1980). Neuropsychologic impairment in astrocytoma survivors. *Neurology, 30,* 172–177.

Holtzman, R. N., & Goldensohn, E. S. (1977). Sensations of ocular movement in seizures originating in occipital lobe. *Neurology, 27,* 554–556.

Hom, J., & Reitan, R. M. (1984). Neuropsychological correlates of rapidly vs. slowly growing intrinsic cerebral neoplasms. *Journal of Clinical Neuropsychology, 6,* 309–324.

Igbal, S. N., Goldstein, P. C., & Tocco, S. (1982). Neuropsychological deficits in multiple sclerosis: Impact on patient treatment. *Archives of Physical Medicine and Rehabilitation, 63,* 521–522.

Jampala, V. C., & Abrams, R. Mania secondary to left and right hemisphere damage. (1983). *American Journal of Psychiatry, 140,* 1197–1199.

Jennett, B. (1969). Early traumatic epilepsy. *Lancet, 1,* 1023–1025.

Jennett, B., & Teasdale, G. (1981). *Management of head injuries.* Philadelphia: F. A. Davis.

Kaplan, B. J. (1975). Biofeedback in epileptics: Equivocal relationship of reinforced EEG frequency to seizure reduction. *Epilepsia, 16,* 477–485.

Karliner, W. (1978). ECT for patients with CNS Disease. *Psychosomatics, 19,* 781–783.

Kay, D. W. K., Derr, T. A., & Lassman, L. P. (1971). Brain trauma and the postconcussion syndrome. *Lancet, 2,* 1052–1055.

Kertesz, A. (1985). Recovery of function. In K. M. Heilman & E. Valenstein (Eds.), *Clinical neuropsychology* (2nd ed.). New York: Wiley.

Kligman, D., & Goldberg, D. A. (1975). Temporal lobe epilepsy and aggression. *Journal of Nervous and Mental Disease, 160,* 324–341.

Kolb, B., & Whishaw, I. Q. (1985). Techniques, problems, and models. In B. Kolb & I. Q. Whishaw (Eds.), *Fundamentals of human neuropsychology.* New York: W. H. Freeman.

Kubler-Ross, E. (1969). *On death and dying.* New York: Macmillan.

Kuhlman, W. N. (1978). EEG feedback training of epileptic patients: Clinical and electroencephalographic analysis. *Electroencephalography and Clinical Neurophysiology, 45,* 699–715.

Kwentus, J. A., Hart, R. P., Peck, E. T., & Kornstein, S. (1985). Psychiatric complications of closed head trauma. *Psychosomatics, 26,* 8–17.

Labi, M. L. C., Phillips, T. F., & Gresham, G. E. (1980). Psychosocial disability in physically restored long-term stroke survivors. *Archive Physical Medicine Rehabilitation, 61,* 561–565.

Lachar, D., Lewis, R., & Kupe, T. (1979). MMPI in differentiation of temporal lobe and non-temporal lobe epilepsy: Investigation of three levels of test performance. *Journal of Consulting and Clinical Psychology, 47,* 186–188.

Lashley, K. S. (1938). Factors limiting recovery after central nervous lesions. *Journal of Nervous and Mental Diseases, 88,* 733–755.

Levin, H. S., & Grossman, R. G. (1978). Behavioral sequelae of closed head injury. *Archives of Neurology, 35,* 720–727.

Levin, H. S., Grossman, R. G., Rose, J. E., & Teasdale, G. (1979). Long-term neuropsychological outcome of closed head injury. *Journal of Neurosurgery, 50,* 412–422.

Levin, H. S., Benton, A. L., & Grossman, R. G. (1982). *Neurobehavioral cosequences of closed head injury.* New York: Oxford University Press.

Lezak, M. D. (1983). *Neuropsychological assessment* (2nd ed.). New York: Oxford University Press.

Lindvall, F. (1974). Causes of post concussional syndrome. *Acta Neurologica Scandinavica, 56* (Supplementum), 1–145.

Lipsey, J. R., Robinson, R. G., Pearlson, G. D., Rao, K., & Price, T. R. (1984). Nortriptyline treatment of post-stroke depression: A double-blind study. *Lancet, 1,* 297–300.

Lishman, W. A. (1973). The psychiatric sequelae of head injury: A review. *Psychological Medicine, 3,* 304–318.

Lishman, W. A. (1978). *Organic psychiatry: The psychological consequences of cerebral disorder.* London: Blackwell Scientific.

Luria, A. R. (1980). *Higher cortical functions in man* (2nd ed.). New York: Basic Books.

Malamud, N. (1967). Psychiatric disorder with intracranial tumors of limbic system. *Archives of Neurology, 17,* 113–123.

Mark, V., & Ervin, F. (1970). *Violence and the brain.* New York: Harper & Row.

Mattson, R. H., Lerner, E., & Dix, G. (1974). Precipitating and inhibiting factors in epilepsy: A statistical study. *Epilepsia, 15,* 217–272.

Mesulam, M. (1981). A cortical network for directed attention and unilateral neglect. *Annuals of Neurology, 10,* 309.

Miller, H. (1961). Accident neurosis. *British Medical Journal, 1,* 919–925.

Milner, B. (1970). Memory and the medial temporal regions of the brain. In K. H. Pribram & D. E. Broadbent (Eds.), *Biology of memory.* New York: Academic Press.

Mitchell, W. G., Greenwood, R. S., & Messenheimer, J. A. (1983). Abdominal epilepsy. *Archives of Neurology, 40,* 251–252.

Mungas, D. (1982). Interictal behavior abnormality in temporal lobe epilepsy: A specific syndrome or nonspecific psychopathology? *Archives of General Psychiatry, 39,* 108–111.

Mungas, D. (1983). An empirical analysis of specific syndromes of violent behavior. *Journal of Nervous and Mental Disease, 171,* 354–361.

Nasrallah, H. A., & McChesney, C. M. (1981). Psychopathology of corpus callosum tumors. *Biological Psychiatry, 16,* 663–669.

Nelson, J. C., & Charney, D. S.(1981). The symptoms of major depressive illness. *American Journal of Psychiatry, 138,* 1–13.

Oddy, M., Humphrey, M., & Uttley, D. (1978a). Stresses upon the relatives of head-injured patients. *British Journal of Psychiatry, 133,* 507–513.

Oddy, M., Humphrey, M., & Uttley, D. (1978b). Subjective impairment and social recovery after closed head injury. *Journal of Neurology, Neurosurgery, and Psychiatry, 41,* 611–616.

Olton, D. S., & Noonberg, A. R. (1980). *Biofeedback: Clinical applications in behavioral medicine.* Englewood Cliffs, NJ: Prentice-Hall.

Oppenheimer, D. R. (1968). Microscopie lesions in the brain following head injury. *Journal of Neurology, Neurosurgery, and Psychiatry, 31,* 299–306.

Pincus, J. H., & Tucker, G. J. (1978). *Behavioral neurology.* New York: Oxford University Press.

Racy, A., Osborn, M. A., Vern, B. A., & Molinari, G. F. (1980). Epileptic aphasia. *Archives of Neurology, 37,* 419–422.

Ramani, V. (1983). Primary reading epilepsy. *Archives of Neurology, 40,* 39–41.

Ramani, V., & Gumnit, R. J. (1982). Management of hysterical seizures in epileptic patients. *Archives of Neurology, 39,* 78–81.

Rao, S. M., Hammeke, T. A., McQuillen, M. P., Khatri, B. O., & Lloyd, D. (1984). Memory disturbance in chronic progressive multiple sclerosis. *Archives of Neurology, 41,* 625–631.

Reitan, R. M., Reed, T. C., & Dyken, M. L. (1971). Cognitive psychomotor and motor correlates of multiple sclerosis. *Journal of Nervous and Mental Disease, 153,* 218–224.

Renshaw, D. C. (1978). Stroke and sex. In A. Comfort (Ed.), *Sexual consequences of disability.* Philadelphia: Stickley.

Riklan, M., & Cooper, I. S. (1977). Thalamic lateralization of psychological functions: Psychometric studies. In S. Harnad, R. W. Doty, L. Goldstein, J. Jaynes, & G. Krauthamer (Eds.), *Lateralization in the nervous system.* New York: Academic Press.

Robinson, R. B., & Benson, D. F. (1981). Depression in aphasia patients: frequency, severity, and clinical pathology correlations. *Brain and Language, 14,* 282–291.

Robinson, R. G., & Coyle, J. T. (1980). The differential effect of right versus left hemispheric cerebral infraction on catecholamines and behavior in the rat. *Brain Research, 188,* 63–78.

Robinson, R. G., & Szetela, B. (1981). Mood change following left hemisphere brain injury. *Annals of Neurology, 9,* 447–453.

Robinson, R. G., Kubos, K. L., Starr, K. R., Rao, K., & Price, T. R. (1983). Mood changes in stroke patients: Relationship to lesion location. *Comprehensive Psychiatry, 24,* 555–566.

Robinson, R. G., Starr, L. B., & Price, T. R. (1984). A two year longitudinal study of mood disorders following stroke: Prevalence and duration at six months follow-up. *British Journal of Psychiatry, 144,* 256–262.

Rodin, E. A. (1973). Psychomotor epilepsy and aggressive behavior. *Archives of General Psychiatry, 28,* 210–213.

Rodin, E. A. (1975). Psychosocial management of patients with complex partial seizures. *Advances in Neu-*

rology, 11, 383–414.

Rosenthal, M., Griffith, E., Bond, M. R., & Miller, J. D. (1983). *Rehabilitation of the head injured adult.* Philadelphia: F. A. Davis.

Ross, E. D. (1981). The aprosodias: Functional-anatomical organization of the effective components of language in the right hemisphere. *Archives of Neurology, 38*, 561–569.

Ross, E. D., & Rush, A. J. (1981). Diagnosis and neuroanatomical correlates of depression in brain-damaged patients. *Archives of General Psychiatry, 38*, 1344–1354.

Rutherford, W. H., Merrett, J. D., & McDonald, J. R. (1977). Sequelae of concussion caused by minor head injury. *Lancet, 1*, 1–4.

Sisler, G. (1978). Psychiatric disorder associated with head injury. *Psychiatric Clinics of North America, 1*, 137–152.

Sjogren, K., & Fugl-Meyer, A. R. (1982). Adjustment to life after stroke with special reference to sexual intercourse and leisure. *Journal of Psychosomatic Research, 4*, 409–417.

Smith, A. (1981). Principles underlying human brain functions in neuropsychological sequelae of different neuropathological processes. In S. B. Filskov & T. J. Boll (Eds.), *Handbook of clinical neuropsychology.* New York: Wiley.

Soltero, I., Liu, K., Cooper, R., Stamler, J., & Garside, D. (1978). Trends in mortality from cerebrovascular diseases in the United States, 1960 to 1975. *Stroke, 9*, 549–555.

Staples, D., & Lincoln, N. B. (1979). Intellectual impairment in multiple sclerosis and its relation to functional abilities. *Rheumatology and Rehabilitation, 18*, 153–160.

Sterman, M. B. (1977). Effects of sensorimotor EEG feedback training on sleep and clinical manifestations of epilepsy. In J. Beatty & H. Legewice (Eds.), *Biofeedback and behavior.* New York: Plenum Press.

Sterman, M. B., & Wyrwicka, W. A. (1967). EEG correlates of sleep: Evidence for separate forebrain structures. *Brain Research, 6*, 143–153.

Sterman, M. B., Goodman, S. J., & Kovalesky, R. (1978). Effects of sensorimotor EEG feedback training on seizure susceptibility in the rhesus monkey. *Experimental Neurology, 62*, 735–747.

Stewart, R. S., Lovitt, R., & Stewart, M. (1982). Are hysterical seizures more than hysteria? A research diagnostic criteria, DSM-II and psychometric analysis. *American Journal of Psychiatry, 139*, 926–929.

Strich, S. J. (1969). The pathology of brain damage due to blunt head injuries. In A. E. Walker, W. F. Caveness, & M. Critchley (Eds.), *The late effects of head injury.* Springfield, IL: Charles C Thomas.

Terzano, M., Parrino, L., Manzoni, G. C., & Mancia, D. (1983). Seizures triggered by blinking when beginning to speak. *Archives of Neurology, 40*, 103–106.

Thomsen, I. V. (1984). Late outcome of very severe blunt head trauma: A 10–15 year second follow-up. *Journal of Neurology, Neurosurgery, and Psychiatry, 47*, 260–268.

Trexler, L. E. (1982). *Cognitive rehabilitation.* New York: Plenum Press.

Trimble, M. R. (1982). The interictal psychoses of epilepsy. In D. F. Benson & D. Blumer (Eds.), *Psychiatric aspects of neurologic disease* (Vol. 2). New York: Grune & Stratton.

Trimble, M. R., & Grant, I. (1982). Psychiatric aspects of multiple sclerosis. In D. F. Benson & D. Blumer (Eds.), *Psychiatric aspects of neurologic disease* (Vol. 2). New York: Grune & Stratton.

Walen, S., Hauserman, N. M., & Lavin, P. J. (Eds.). (1977). *Clinical guide to behavior therapy.* Baltimore: Williams & Wilkens.

Watson, R. T., & Heilman, K. M. (1979). Thalmic neglect. *Neurology, 29*, 690–694.

Wells, C. E., & Duncan, G. W. (1980). *Neurology for psychiatrists.* Philadelphia: F. A. Davis.

Whitlock, F. A. (1978). Suicide, cancer and depression. *British Journal of Psychiatry, 132*, 269–275.

Willanger, R., Danielsen, U. T., & Ankerhus, J. (1981). Denial and neglect of hemiparesis in right-handed apoplectic lesions. *Acta Neurologia Scandinavia, 64*, 310–326.

Wilson, B. A., & Moffat, N. (1984). *Clinical management of memory problems.* Rockville, MD: Aspen.

Witelson, S. F. (1977). Early hemispheric specialization and interhemispheric plasticity, an empirical and theoretical review. In S. J. Segalowitz & F. F. Gruber (Eds.), *Language development and neurological theory.* New York: Academic Press.

Wolf, P. A., Dawber, T. R., Thomas, H. E., Colton, T., & Kannel, W. B. (1977). Epidemiology of stroke. *Advances in Neurology, 16*, 5–19.

Wyler, A. R., Robbins, C. A., & Dodrill, C. B. (1979). EEG operant conditioning for control of epilepsy. *Epilepsia, 20*, 279–286.

Yadalam, K. G., Jain, A. K., & Simpson, S. G. (1985). Mania in two sisters with similar cerebellar disturbance. *American Journal of Psychiatry, 142,* 1067–1069.

Young, L. D., Taylor, I., & Holmstrom, V. (1977). Lithium treatment of patients with affective illness associated with organic brain syndromes. *American Journal of Psychiatry, 134,* 1405–1407.

Yudofsky, S., & Silver, J. M. (1985). Psychiatric aspects of brain injury: Trauma, stroke and tumor. In R.
E. Hales & A. J. Frances (Eds.), *American Psychiatric Association annual review* (Vol. 4). Washington,
DC: American Psychiatric Press.

Ziegler, R. G. (1981). Impairments of control and competence in epileptic children and their families. *Epilepsia, 22,* 339–346.

11

Psychosomatic Medicine

BARBARA J. DORIAN AND C. BARR TAYLOR

There is no doubt that psychosocial and biological aspects of diseases are inseparable and interdependent. However, few researchers in psychosomatic medicine now believe, as did the early researchers in this field, that psychological factors are the primary cause of most of the diseases once classified as psychosomatic. Rather psychosocial, social, and biological phenomena interplay in complicated ways to determine the developing course and outcome of the disease. This being the case, the term *psychosomatic disorders* is falling out of favor and has been replaced, as we discuss later, with a new nomenclature.

In this chapter, we discuss the history of psychosomatic medicine; describe the biopsychosocial model of disease; provide examples of the interplay of genetic, physiological, behavioral, cognitive, affective, and cultural factors with the initiation, exacerbation, and maintenance of disease; and conclude with an overview of psychotherapeutic procedures useful in psychosomatic medicine.

HISTORICAL PERSPECTIVE

Although the fact that psychological factors affect disease has been observed and commented on from the beginning of recorded medicine, it was not until the 1940s in America that psychosomatic medicine became a subject of major research. Psychosomatic research can be broken down into three overlapping periods: the 1940s and 1950s, dominated by the intensive single-subject case investigations of specificity models; the 1960s and 1970s, dominated by neurobiology, psychoneuroendocrinology, developmental psychophysiology, autonomic conditioning, and the nonspecific model; and the rise of the biopsychosocial model in the 1970s and 1980s, which continued the trends of the 1960s and 1970s but placed greater emphasis on developing interventions to alter the course of the disease and saw the rise of behavioral medicine and health psychology.

It was during the first period of psychosomatic medicine that the notion of a psychosomatic disorder (from *psyche*, "mind"; *soma*, "body") was defined to apply to (1) disease of unknown origin, in which (2) personality, stress, or some other largely psychological factors were deemed to play a prominent role. Two types of evidence were used to set these diseases apart from other illnesses. First, a series of observations (e.g., Cannon, 1929; Cobb, 1976; Wolff, 1953) established the fact that the diseased organ can be

BARBARA J. DORIAN • Department of Psychiatry, Toronto General Hospital, 101 College Street, Toronto, Ontario, Canada M5J 1L7.   C. BARR TAYLOR • Department of Psychiatry, Stanford University Medical Center, Stanford, CA 94305.

affected by strong emotions and assuaged by security and relaxation. Second, careful analyses of the biographies of patients with these diseases revealed an inordinately high incidence of frustrating or disturbing events, resentment and hostility, conflicts about dependence or independence, suppressed emotionality, inability to communicate personal issues and emotional concerns, or lack of clarity in the differentiation between reality and fantasy. Diseases for which such evidence was reported include peptic ulcer disease, mucous colitis, ulcerative colitis, Crohn's disease, bronchial asthma, atopical dermatitis, urticaria, angioneurotic edema, hay fever, Raynaud's disease, hypertension, hyperthyroidism, amenorrhea and other disturbances of menstruation, enuresis, dysuria, rheumatoid and other forms of arthritis, headache, syncope, and even epilepsy.

During the first period, two models were most intensively investigated: the specificity model and the individual response-specificity model. The specificity model grew from the work of Alexander, French, and Pollack (1968). Alexander and his associates focused on seven diseases: bronchial asthma, arthritis, ulcerative colitis, essential hypertension, peptic ulcer, neurodermatitis, and thyroiditis. These became known as the classic psychosomatic or psychophysiological disorders. In the course of intensive psychological study of patients with these illnesses, Alexander hypothesized that characteristic constellations of unresolved psychological conflicts and the associated chronic suppressed affect led to specific disease states via sympathetic or parasympathetic nervous system hyperactivity. He postulated, for example, that the individual with duodenal ulcer has an unconscious wish to be cared for (fed) of which he or she is ashamed and therefore becomes excessively independent. The patient with essential hypertension has a fear of her or his aggressiveness, which she or he represses because of expectation of retaliation. Alexander felt that such dynamic constellations were specific to each disease, but that patients with psychosomatic illnesses were similar to one another in an underlying psychological dependency within interpersonal relationships.

A related specificity model was proposed by Wolff (1953). He observed that pathology could be induced in the mucosa of the gastrointestinal and respiratory systems by chronic hyperfunction or hypofunction of the vascular bed and secretory cells. He theorized that physiological responses to stress affected particularly vulnerable organic systems within each individual, thereby producing disease. Wolff believed that the reactions of organic systems were adaptive and defensive, and that they reflected aspects of personality functioning. Genetic factors and prior learning also determined which organs were particularly vulnerable and whether the individual would react to stress with hypofunctioning or hyperfunctioning. He postulated, for example, that a dependent individual, when stressed by the loss of someone who has been a major source of support, may adopt a defense of withdrawal. This defense is associated with parasympathetic hyperactivity that may affect the stomach (producing peptic ulcer), the colon (producing colitis), or the lungs (producing asthma). If the dependent person adopts a defense of pseudoindependence, sympathetic hyperactivity ensues and may affect the vascular bed (producing hypertension or migraine).

These models fell into disfavor for several reasons. First, despite numerous investigations, it was never clearly demonstrated that specific personalities developed the predicted disease or that individuals with the disease shared predicted personality characteristics. Second, studies failed to demonstrate that physiological changes during laboratory assessments produced sustained pathophysiological states.

In the 1950s and 1960s, other models were proposed. The individual response-specificity model was first elucidated by Lacey, Kagan, Lacey, and Moss (1963). They showed that individuals exhibit characteristic and consistent patterns of autonomic-nervous-system (ANS) activity in association with emotional arousal. One individual may exhibit increased blood pressure and galvanic skin responses, but no heart-rate change, to a particular stimulus. Another individual may show marked heart-rate changes, but no changes in blood pressure or galvanic skin responses, to the same stimulus. According to this model, these characteristic autonomic patterns give rise to disease when the individual is subjected to prolonged stress. However, again, this prediction has not been demonstrated empirically.

The final model of this period, the nonspecific model, was proposed by Hans Selye (1974), who is considered the father of our modern concepts of stress. To Selye, stress is the "nonspecific response of the body to any demand made upon it." A stressful stimulus or situation must be sufficiently intense to require the organism to readjust or adapt; stress, according to Selye, is the organism's response to readjustment or adaptation. Selye derived his concept from studies extending over many years. He initially wished to understand why many different diseases or types of bodily trauma produced similar symptoms. He found that restraining rats, injecting them with different toxic substances, or subjecting them to noxious stimuli, such as heat, cold, radiation, burns, or infection, produced a similar clinical picture and the same morphological syndrome. This syndrome included (1) an enlarged adrenal cortex; (2) shrunken thymus, spleen, lymph nodes, and other lymphatic structures; and (3) deep bleeding ulcers in the stomach and the upper intestine.

Selye called this syndrome the "general adaptation syndrome" (GAS) and characterized three separate stages. The first stage involves a defensive alarm reaction consisting of catecholamine and adrenocortical steroid production with the release of vasopressin and increased ANS discharge. These reactions were felt to counteract the tissue catabolism, hyperkalemia, hypothermia, hypotension, hemoconcentration, increased membrane permeability, and gastric erosion produced by the external stressor. If the organism survives, the mobilization of hormones and the ANS lead to a resistance reaction in which the adrenal cortex becomes rich in granulation particles; hemodilution, hyperchloremia, and catabolism occur; and body weight returns to normal. If exposure to the noxious agent continues, however, the organism could become exhausted and die. According to Selye, the GAS is mediated by the hypothalamic-pituitary-adrenocortical axis. For Selye, stress was a normal part of life, and distress began only with the failure of an organism to adapt to life stressors. During stress, the body produces massive amounts of corticosteroids, and in later writings, Selye (1974) became concerned with the deleterious rather than the defensive effects of these hormones. This shift presaged the development of confusion and controversy regarding the operational definition of stress in much of the literature that followed Selye's initial description. The term *stress* has subsequently been used to refer to both the environmental situation and the subjective inner experience of distress.

The nonspecific model of Selye is consistent with many animal data, especially those pertaining to physical rather than psychological or behavioral stressors. However, it does not explain the individual response patterns observed by Lacey *et al.* (1963). Increasing awareness of individual differences stemming from genetic predisposition, sex, age, diet, and prior exposure to drugs and hormones, along with advances in such fields as neurobiology, psychoneuroendocrinology, developmental psychophysiology, and autonomic conditioning, have challenged the simple classifications of psychosomatic illness based on early specific and nonspecific models.

This evolution has led to the development of a more general psychobiology of health and disease, in which the confluence of biologic, constitutional, psychological, social, and behavioral factors is felt to influence the predisposition to, the initiation of, and the course of all disease processes. In its simplest form, this model is called the *biopsychosocial model* and is represented by three interlocking circles representing the domains of biological, psychological, and social factors interacting and interdependent, one upon the other. Each of these domains is, in turn, highly complex, as can be seen by taking the example of essential hypertension. First, the elevation of blood pressure that is used to define essential hypertension is the end result of complicated interactions among many physiological and biological systems (see Chapter 9). Surprisingly, the diagnosis of essential hypertension is made on the basis of the *absence* of defined causes of illness, although a differential diagnosis is required to eliminate the 5% to 10% of diseases that can present with elevated blood pressure. Table 1 represents the diseases that are associated with essential hypertension.

The psychological domain of essential hypertension is equally complicated. Psychological factors that have been shown to influence blood pressure levels include the state of tension-relaxation at the time of measurement, the rate and type of conversation, the attitude toward the individual obtaining the measurement, irritability, diet, exercise, medications taken, and other behaviors.

Social context factors have also been demonstrated to influence blood pressure. These factors include age, sex, race, culture, and living arrangements.

As we shall discuss, the biopsychosocial model has implications for our understanding of the role of a variety of factors that can impinge on different disease states. Also, examination of the interactive role of various factors results in a number of considerations regarding treatment. Generally, the biopsychosocial model suggests a general systems perspective and therefore emphasizes the potential importance of nonsomatic treatment factors.

DIAGNOSIS

The diagnostic nomenclature of the American Psychiatric Association has changed to reflect the development of the biopsychosocial model of psychosomatic medicine. In the second edition of the *Diagnostic and Statistical Manual of Mental Disorders* (DSM-II; APA, 1968), psychosomatic disorders were labeled "Psychophysiological Disorders" and were defined as follows:

> This group of disorders is characterized by physical symptoms that are caused by emotional factors and involve a single organ system, usually under autonomic nervous system innervation. The physiological changes involved are those that normally accompany certain emotional states, but in these disorders the changes are more intense and sustained. The individual may not be consciously aware of his emotional state. (p. 46)

Table 1. Classification of Arterial Hypertension

I. Systolic hypertension with wide pulse pressure
  A. Decreased compliance of aorta (arteriosclerosis)
  B. Decreased stroke volume
    1. Arteriovenous fistula
    2. Thyrotoxicosis
    3. Hyperkinetic heart disease
    4. Fever
    5. Psychogenic factors
    6. Aortic regurgitation
    7. Patent ductus arteriosus

II. Systolic and diastolic hypertension (increased peripheral vascular resistance)
  A. Renal (2%–5% of all cases of hypertension)
    Examples
    1. Chronic pyelonephritis
    2. Acute and chronic glomerulonephritis
    3. Renin-producing tumors
  B. Endocrine (2%–5% of all cases of hypertension in general population)
    Examples
    1. Oral contraceptives
    2. Adrenocortical hyperfunction
    3. Pheochromocytoma
    4. Hypothyroidism
    5. Acromegaly
  C. Neurogenic
    Examples
    1. Diencephalic syndrome
    2. Familial dysautonomia
    3. Poliomyelitis (bulbar)
  D. Miscellaneous
    1. Coarctation of aorta
    2. Increased vascular volume
    3. Polyarteritis nodosa
    4. Hypercalcemia
    5. Toxemia of pregnancy
    6. Acute intermittent porphyria
    7. Essential hypertension (90% of all cases of hypertension)
    8. Unknown etiology

As stated, subsequent research has failed to confirm the hypothesis embedded in the DSM-II definition: intense and sustained emotional states, with their physiological concomitants, do not appear to be necessary or sufficient causes of psychophysiological disorders. In the current (third-edition) *Diagnostic and Statistical Manual* (DSM-III; APA, 1980), the category "Psychophysiological Disorders" is replaced by a broader category: "Psychological Factors Affecting Physical Condition." This diagnosis follows the model that views all disease as having a psychological component, whether in etiology or effect. The psychological factors that contribute to the onset or exacerbation of a disease may be designated in a qualifying phrase attached to the diagnostic label (e.g., rheumatoid arthritis precipitated by death of a spouse—316.10).

Disease processes may frequently occur as the consequence of the dynamic interaction of an overlapping constellation of risk factors and, in this sense, illness may also be considered a failure of adaptation. For example, the experience of bereavement in a biologically vulnerable individual may lead to affective states of helplessness, hopelessness, giving up and given up, and disease may ensue. However, if adequate social support or other environmental circumstances promote active and effective coping strategies, then adaptation may occur and disease may be prevented.

One problem of the current DSM-III definition is that it may be overly inclusive. Within this diagnostic system there are no such things as psychosomatic disorders or psychophysiologic disorders; the diseases traditionally defined as such could not be considered different from any other disease. Differential diagnosis of the disease proceeds by considering the various "medical causes" of the disease (as in Table 1 for essential hypertension) with the final diagnosis being made on the basis of the consistency of the signs, symptoms, physical findings, and laboratory findings with a medical disease or syndrome with subsequent consideration being given to the contribution of psychosocial issues as previously noted.

In the final section of this chapter we will highlight the principles of psychosomatic medicine most relevant to psychologists. In the next section we review what is known about the predisposing, initiating, and exacerbating factors which apply to such disorders as peptic ulcer, anorexia nervosa, essential hypertension, and coronary heart disease. For brevity and convenience in the remainder of this chapter, we retain the term *psychosomatic disorders*, but we thereby imply a full acknowledgment of the biopsychosocial model and current trends in nomenclature.

THE MULTIPLE PREDISPOSITIONS TO DISEASE

Inherited Traits

Much of the work on predisposing factors has come from longitudinal studies of populations at risk. Classical studies by Weiner, Thaler, Reiser, and Mirsky (1957) on peptic duodenal ulcer revealed the contribution of pepsinogen hypersecretion and also provided formulations regarding the specific constellations of psychological factors and social stressors that may be involved in the initiation of actual disease. Sixty percent of patients have elevations of pepsinogen I isoenzyme, which is inherited as an autosomal dominant trait. Mirsky (1958) posited that the genetic constitutional predisposition to pepsinogen hypersecretion produced excessive needs for feeding in the infant, which then evoked particular parental responses of either frustration or gratification. The parental responses were then, in turn, responded to by the infant in a way that represented both the consequence of the underlying biological predisposition and the secondary psychological and physical effects of the initial parental environment. This sequence of events thus set the stage for the development of specific conflicts and patterns of psychosocial stressors. These stressors may in later life exacerbate the conflict and become a focus for the initiation of illness. From this model, it can be seen that an inherited biological trait may become the basis for the evolution of a complex, dynamic matrix of other psychological, physical, and social forces which may ultimately relate to the development of a particular illness in a particular individual at a given moment in time. In further studies on the development of duodenal ulcer during induction to military training. Mirsky (1958) was able to identify 70% of the pepsinogen hypersecretors on the basis of psychological test data and to reliably predict which individuals would develop ulcers from a combination of significant psychological conflict and increased pepsinogen levels. However, the heterogeneity of illness was also demonstrated in these studies, because not everyone with the identified psychological profile and pepsinogen hypersecretion developed an ulcer and a number of individuals with no known predisposing factors did become ill. As well, it is known that some people may develop duodenal ulcers in situations without obvious psychosocial stress or intrapsychic conflict. Subsequent authors have documented an association between peptic ulcer and blood type O, but not A, B, or AB, and alterations in hydrochloric acid secretion, parietal cell mass, and gastric regulation or acid secretion in other subgroups of patients with duodenal ulcer. These conditions may be determined genetically or by some interaction between physiological factors and the early environment which influences the development of personality, psychological conflicts, and neurobiological regulatory systems thus producing a constitutional vulnerability.

Underlying genetic and biological predispositions are relevant in many other disease states. Turner's syndrome, a specific chromosomal anomaly (XO), is a risk factor in approximately 10% of patients with primary anorexia nervosa. The presence of a twin and the phenomenon of early pubertal maturation have also been suggested as risk factors for the development of anorexia (Garfinkel & Garner, 1982).

Different forms of essential hypertension exist, depending on the precise pattern of circulatory disturbance (i.e., increased cardiac output versus increased peripheral resistance) and on the alterations of renin, angiotensin, and aldosterone production and metabolism (Henry & Cassel, 1969). The etiologic factors leading to these metabolic and regulatory disturbances are not precisely known. However, normotensive children of hypertensive parents demonstrate enhanced cardiovascular reactivity to challenging tasks, a response that has been linked to a predisposition to both hypertension and coronary artery disease (Dembroski & MacDougall, 1984; Price, 1982).

Pre- to Postnatal Environment and Genetics

Cardiovascular reactivity may be genetically determined; however, there is also evidence that pre- and postnatal environmental influences may interact with innate biological variables to influence the ultimate regulation of heart rate and blood pressure. Certain behavioral and temperamental variables in children that are evident from birth have been associated with impairments in growth and development and, frequently, negative parent–child interactions. Children on the extreme of the temperamental spectrum, with marked irregularity in biological functions, withdrawal responses to new stimuli, slow adaptability to change, and intense negative mood expressions, have been found to be at particular risk (Thomas & Chess, 1977). An association between these temperamental variables and alterations in heart-rate regulation when confronting unfamiliar circumstances has been observed by the age of 2 (Kagan, 1982). It is possible that poor fit between constitutional givens and environmental capacities may lead to deficits in the neurobiological regulation of emotional experience and its physiological accompaniments. This deficit in regulation may be reflected in later life in enhanced cardiovascular reactivity or in one of the other patterns of circulatory disturbance related to hypertension. Highly sophisticated and innovative recent work in animals by Hofer and colleagues (Hofer & Shair, 1982; Hofer & Weiner, 1975) has compellingly demonstrated that the development of normal cardiovascular neural regulatory responses depends on subtle biological regulators contained within aspects of the mother–infant relationship, and that maternal separation leads to changes in cardiac and vasoconstrictor autonomic activity. These regulators, which include such things as body warmth, tactile responses, milk output, and regularity of feeding, also influence the regulation of activity, sucking, oxygen consumption, sleep, and levels of neurotransmitters within the central nervous system. Maternal separations early in life produce disturbances in the regulation of functions such as sleep and temperature control, which may be unmasked or elicited only later in life, when the animal is under stress. This work provides further evidence that early life experience and environmental interactions may influence physiological processes in ways relevant to later illness onset if the individual is subsequently exposed to specific provoking or initiating conditions.

Immunological Factors

Immunological factors play an important role in the predisposition to allergic, infectious, autoimmune, and malignant diseases. The capacity to form immunoglobulin E (IqE) antibodies is an inherited condition necessary but not sufficient for the development of atopic dermatitis, allergic rhinitis, and bronchial asthma. Bronchial asthma in particular requires the presence of bronchial hyperreactivity and a number of other inciting conditions often including viruses. Without the tendency to bronchoconstriction, asthma cannot occur despite the presence of other immunological, psychological, or familial factors commonly associated with asthma attacks. The capacity to form autoimmune antibodies is in part inherited and is an important determinant of such diseases as juvenile diabetes mellitus, systemic lupus erythematosus, rheumatoid arthritis, ulcerative colitis, Grave's disease, and other forms of thyroiditis. The capacity to form such antibodies may be etiologic in these diseases as well as pathogenic manifestations of them. This is demonstrated by the finding of antibody levels in healthy siblings of patients with rheumatoid arthritis (Moos & Solomon, 1965).

Physiological Risk and Behavior

Behavior combined with other risks may predispose to disease, as illustrated by the Type A behavior pattern. The Type A behavior pattern (TABP) is considered a major risk factor for the development of coronary artery disease and for increased morbidity and mortality from that disease (Dorian & Taylor, 1984). Type A is a style of overt behavior dedicated to performance, maintenance of control, and mastery over the environment, especially when this is perceived as challenging or threatening. It is characterized by aggressive achievement striving, impatience, sense of time urgency, rapid and emphatic speech, irritability, and free-floating hostility. Antecedents of Type A behavior itself include social, cultural, and religious beliefs, economic factors, urbanization, educational systems, and familial expectations and interactions. It is believed that contingencies within all of these areas positively reward and reinforce aggressive individualism, competitiveness, industry, and the virtue of continually striving to attain higher levels of financial and vocational success or status (Price, 1982).

There is little evidence that the TABP is inherited. However, there are suggestions from animal studies and research on sex differences that components of Type A such as aggressiveness and high activity levels may have a genetic basis. Type A individuals respond to challenging tasks which stimulate competition with enhanced systolic blood pressure and heart rate (Dembroski & MacDougall, 1984). It is unclear at present whether this demonstrates a genetically determined sensitivity to challenge or a general reactivity to environmental events which therefore predisposes to Type A behavior; or whether the reactivity is the consequence of the interaction between other constitutional variables and the environmental contingencies which produce the behavioral style.

A number of other biological risk factors for coronary artery disease are found in association with the TABP. These include elevated cholesterol and triglyceride levels, enhanced platelet aggregation, reduced clotting time, and excess catecholamine secretion during working hours and under challenge (Dorian & Taylor, 1984). These physiological correlates may represent either antecedents or consequences of the Type A pattern. As well, Type A is predictive of other lifestyle and behavioral traits such as smoking, high fat diet, low exercise, excess alcohol intake, work overload and high levels of environmental stressors which in themselves may be associated with a greater predisposition to coronary heart disease. Psychosocial risk factors may act in a multiplicative fashion with whatever background constitutional risk is already present and through behavioral or metabolic pathways increase the risk of disease expression.

Cognitive and Affective Disturbances

As well as personality and behavioral traits, certain cognitive and affective disturbances may be associated with a predisposition to physical illness. Alexithymia is a disorder characterized by a defective communication style, diminished capacities for fantasizing, dreaming, and symbolic thinking, and deficits in recognizing and describing feelings and in discriminating between emotional states and bodily sensations (Taylor, 1974). This disturbance was described initially in association with the classical psychosomatic disorders. However, more recently it has been reported in many other physical and psychological illnesses. It is a frequent accompaniment to the TABP. Alexithymia itself may be the consequence of a number of overlapping genetic, constitutional, neurophysiological, developmental, and psychological conditions.

Family

The role of family relationships in initiating, sustaining, or exacerbating psychophysiological illness has been the focus of much recent study. Two groups, including that of Selvini Palazolli (1974) and Minuchin (Minuchin, Rosman, & Baker, 1978) have evolved a systems model for understanding the interdependent forces within family interaction which predispose to psychosomatic illness.

Minuchin's work began with juvenile onset diabetes mellitus and gradually expanded to include other disorders such as anorexia nervosa and asthma. Based on his clinical studies, Minuchin concluded that certain kinds of family organizations are closely related to the development and maintenance of psychosomatic syndromes in children, and that the child's illness, in turn, plays an important role in maintaining homeostasis in the family's role relations. He has elaborated the transactional characteristics of families which facilitate the development of psychosomatic disorders. These include enmeshment, an extreme form of proximity and intrusion with lack of defined boundaries between members, overprotectiveness, rigidity or commitment to the maintenance of the status quo, lack of conflict resolution, and involvement of the child in parental conflict by covert coalitions with parents or displacement of the conflict onto the child's symptomatology.

The Palazolli group has also described the child as the arbitrator, mediator, or secret ally of the mother or father and identified the theme of extreme intrusiveness and lack of privacy within the family system. The transactional patterns in these families are felt to impair the child's development of autonomy, competence, and mastery and involvement outside the family home. Families may also act as culture bearers and magnify particular societal ideals and expectations which then become a predisposition to illness. Familial ideals for slimness, perfection, and performance may antedate anorexia nervosa, while rewards for escalating levels of accomplishment and rapid pace may stimulate Type A behavior. Societal modeling of hard driving, achievement-oriented behavior, as well as excessive criticism and severe punishment, are parental attributes which may also contribute to the development of the TABP.

Culture

Sociocultural factors may also be linked with predispositions to various illnesses. An increased cultural pressure to diet and be slim and the current idealized body form for women of bony thinness has been linked to the increasing prevalence of anorexia nervosa. Previously, anorexia was a disease preponderantly observed in the upper social classes, however, presently it is more equally distributed through all social classes. Garfinkel and Garner (1982) documented the shift in the ideal standard of Playboy centerfold and Miss America pageant contestants toward a thinner size and more androgynous body form over the past 10 years. This has occurred while the average woman of similar age has been getting heavier due to improved nutrition over the past 20 years. These authors feel that these findings demonstrate the tension between biological forces determining weight and the cultural ideal. They link this conflict to the pervasiveness of dieting among women and facilitation of the development of anorexia nervosa.

A recent focus of study has also been the role of North American culture in the etiology of coronary artery disease. Americans have the world's second highest mortality rate from this disease, and people from other cultures who become absorbed into American society begin to experience the same rate of heart disease as Americans in general. For example, Bruhn and colleagues (Bruhn, Chandler, Miller, Wolf, & Lynn, 1966) found that people living in the almost exclusively Italian town of Rosetto, Pennsylvania, had a myocardial infarction death rate that was less than half that of neighboring communities. This reduced death rate was not accounted for by differences in traditional cardiovascular risk factors, such as obesity, hypercholesterolemia, and smoking. A genetic explanation was ruled out by the fact that relatives of Rosetto residents living elsewhere did not have a mycardial infarction rate lower than that of the general population. Bruhn attributed the relative cardiovascular health of Rosetto residents to the integrated structure and cohesiveness of their community.

The results of a second study implicated American culture in the predisposition to disease (Trulson, Clancy, Jessop, Childers, & Stare, 1964). The findings indicated that death rates from coronary artery disease were higher for Irish people who emigrated to the United States than for their relatives who remained in Ireland. The immigrants exhibited a higher prevalence of risk factors that seem related to habits of North American society. They were heavier and fatter, smoked more, exercised less, and had higher blood pressure and higher serum cholesterol levels than their Irish relatives.

In a third study, Marmot and Syme (1976) classified 3,809 Japanese-Americans in California according to the degree to which they retained Japanese traditions. The most traditional group of Japanese-Americans had a coronary artery disease prevalence as low as that observed in Japan; the most acculturated group had a three- to fivefold increase in disease prevalence that was not accounted for by differences in coronary risk factors. Because this was not a prospective controlled trial, the more acculturated Japanese may have differed from the traditional group in ways not measured. However, the present evidence suggests a role for cultural factors in the etiology of coronary heart disease.

Summary

A wide variety of factors can affect an individual predisposition to illness. These factors include intraindividual somatic and psychological variables, as well as extraindividual factors, including familial and cultural-societal influences. The interaction of these variables is complex. Weiner (1977) posited four points as overview conclusions about the interplay of predispositional factors:

1. Illness often results from an interplay of predisposing forces acting on an individual.
2. Of many people with the predisposition to an illness, only some actually develop it.
3. For individuals with a disease, the exact interaction of predisposing forces varies.
4. The same predisposing forces may actually develop in different people in different ways.

FACTORS INITIATING ILLNESS

The factors that initiate an episode of illness may be distinguished from those that predispose to it. Factors that affect the predisposition to a particular illness, however, may be independent of factors involved in the pathogenesis of that disorder.

Life Events

There is a large body of research linking the onset of illness and the occurrence within the individual's life of events that are perceived as challenging or threatening (e.g., Dohrenwend & Dohrenwend, 1974; Rabkin & Shuvening, 1976). Those circumstances that require a change in the individual's ongoing life pattern and those circumstances in which the person perceives himself to have inadequate resources to meet the demand for adaptation may be the most common precipitants of illness. It is the perception of the severity of the impact of the event, the failure to mobilize adequate coping repertoires, and the associated psychological distress that are the potent mediators of the relationship between life events and illness onset. The impact of life event stress is presumed to be additive, the assumption being that a greater number of events are expected to produce greater effects. Most investigators working in this field adopted in original or modified form a recent life-change checklist developed by Holmes and Rahe (1967) or developed substantively similar itemized measures for quantifying the magnitude of recent life change. Subsequently, ratings have been assigned to assess the impact of the events and the necessary degree of adjustment required to accommodate to a life event. For example, death of a spouse has been assigned a score of 100, marriage 50, retirement 45, and so on.

The types of demands which may overwhelm the individual's adaptive capacities and result in the onset of illness may be highly varied and include such things as infections, toxins, injuries, conflict, losses of all kinds, threats to self-esteem, and bereavement. Onset of psychiatric illness, as well as physical disorders and accidents, have been studied in both prospective and retrospective designs within the life-events framework. Modest but statistically significant relationships have been found between mounting life change and the occurrence or onset of sudden cardiac death, myocardial infarction, accidents, athletic injuries, tuberculosis, leukemia, multiple sclerosis, diabetes, influenza, pneumonia, asthma, ulcerative colitis, rheumatoid arthritis, as well as the whole gamut of minor medical complaints. Neurosis, acute episodes of schizophrenia, and suicide attempts all show positive correlations with the accumulation of life-event stress.

A subset of the population with high levels of life change have a higher likelihood of developing disease than persons without such changes. However, the correlations between the numbers of recent events and the onset of clinical disease ranges between only 0.16 and 0.56. Even the highest of these correlations is relatively modest, suggesting that recent life changes alone do not exert a strong primary effect on illness onset.

The effects of stressors are influenced or mediated by individual vulnerabilities and adaptive capacities as evidenced by the person's perception of the event, his or her psychological defenses, social supports, ongoing coping capabilities, and illness behavior characteristics. A critical factor in evaluating the impact of stressful events is the individual's perception of the immediate event and the personal characteristics which determine the likelihood of appraising events as potentially harmful, challenging, or threatening. It is the cognitive process, which determines the nature of the stress reaction and subsequent coping activities. Personal factors may include such things as biological and psychological threshold sensitivities, intelligence, verbal skills, morale, personality type, past experience, and a general sense of mastery over one's fate. Demographic characteristics such as age, education, income, and occupation may also contribute to the individual's evaluation of the stressful conditions and his response to them (Valliant, 1976).

Mitigating Factors

In evaluating the process of disease initiation, the contribution of mitigating factors such as social support must be considered as potential modifiers of the dynamic interplay of multiple predispositions and immediate risks. There is evidence that supportive relationships may act as a moderator of life stress and serve as a protection, buffering the individual from the physiological or pathological consequences of exposure to life change. *Social support* has been defined by Cobb (1976) as information leading a person to believe that he or she is loved, cared for, esteemed, and a member of a network of mutual obligations. In contrast, it is the context of major personal loss, separation, or bereavement that may be the most potent initiator of disease (Jacobs & Ostfeld, 1977; Parkes & Brown, 1972). There is evidence from human studies and from observations of the consequences of premature separation in animals that relationships are essential for the development and maintenance of multiple neurobiological regulatory systems and for the preservation of physical and psychological health (Hofer, 1984; Hofer & Shair, 1982; Hofer & Weiner, 1975). In both animals and humans the response to separation can be divided into an early phase of protest and a longer-lasting phase of chronic disturbance or despair. Each of these phases is associated with discernible alterations in heart-rate regulation, sleep, body weight, metabolism, hormone pattern, and immunological function. Analysis of the effects of separation in infants indicates that it is not a global experience, but that each behavioral and physiological system is regulated by a specific mother–infant interaction. Premature separation interrupts all of these inputs, simultaneously producing the complex pattern of physiological changes associated with grief.

Loss and Affective States

Clinical studies have consistently demonstrated increased morbidity and mortality in bereaved persons. Parkes and Brown (1972) demonstrated that the health of 76% of widows declines within 1 year of bereavement, and that psychiatric morbidity increases. Young, Benjamin, & Wallis (1963) found that mortality among widowers over 55 years of age is 40% greater than that of married men of the same age. Real or threatened separation or bereavement has been linked to the onset of malignancies, autoimmune disease, diabetes mellitus, ulcers, infections, and manifestations of ischemic heart disease. Individuals who have been sensitized by separations or losses early in life may be at greatest risk for the pathological consequences of bereavement, including illness onset. Losses that alter the usual pattern of relationships or of individual functioning, such as losses of capabilities, skills, intelligence, youth, strength, beauty, valued attributes, or physical well-being, may also precipitate physiological changes. In our current society, the loss of work frequently produces a grief reaction, and studies have demonstrated increased duodenal ulcer and depressive illness with unemployment (Engel, 1967, 1968; Schmale, 1958; Weiner, 1975).

A number of authors have delineated specific emotional constellations which may occur in the context of loss or acutely stressful situations and which are highly correlated with disease onset. These include feelings of helplessness and hopelessness and the "giving-up, given-up" complex (Engel, 1967, 1968; Schmale, 1958). This complex is characterized by a sense of inadequacy and inability to adapt or to cope, a sense of futility, a diminished orientation to the future, and a preoccupation with the misfortunes of the past. Individuals predisposed by the experience of previous losses or similar events in which resolution was not possible may be most vulnerable to this state and are at the greatest risk for the development of illness. Other biological factors such as developmental and age-related changes in endocrine function, immunocompetence, brain and neurological function, and the regulation of the periodic rhythmicity of most biological systems, also contribute to the timing of disease onset in the context of separation and bereavement.

FACTORS SUSTAINING DISEASE PROCESSES

Once a disease has become established and in particular if it has long-term adverse health consequence, not only do the original psychological, physiological, and environmental forces giving rise to illness contribute to its maintenance, but also secondary psychological, social, and physical consequences of the disability may perpetuate both the physical manifestations of illness and behaviors related to the patient role. Loss of employment, financial difficulties, familial conflicts over changing roles and expectations, marital dissatisfaction, loss of self-esteem, anxiety, depression, conflicts about accepting care, fears of helplessness or invalidism, anger, and frustration, are but a few of the many psychological and social consequences of illness which may exacerbate or maintain the original condition. Physiological consequences of treatments such as pain, sleep disturbance, depression, and impotence may also contribute to ongoing disability.

The syndrome of anorexia nervosa convincingly illustrates the complexity of interactive factors which may serve to maintain illness. Psychological issues related to low self-esteem, sense of ineffectiveness, expression of family conflicts, maturity fears, and acceptance of cultural ideals for thinness may initiate dieting. However, severe caloric restriction and weight loss produces a physiologically based starvation syndrome which in itself is associated with depression, lethargy, food preoccupation, low self-esteem, social withdrawal, increased obsessiveness, pressures to overeat, and a sense of loss of control. The anorexic patient responds to these symptoms by attempting to gain control through increased dieting behavior. The consequent weight loss then perpetuates the starvation syndrome and triggers a further vicious circle of dieting, thus accounting for the progressive downward spiral of illness in some patients whenever a crucial minimum weight is attained.

Individuals with the Type A behavior pattern and investment in rapid aggressive achievement striving are particularly prone to the effects of work overload and often experience stress from excessive and conflicting demands, deadline pressures, competition, fatigue, and increased supervisory responsibility. It has been shown that Type A individuals will also ignore, suppress, or deny psychological and physical symptoms while working toward self-imposed goals. Thus, these individuals may respond to the sense of not coping with occupational demands by reacting with greater impatience and hostility and by actually increasing their work time and occupational burden. This behavior further perpetuates the salient features of the TABP and carries the risk of psychic exhaustion and emotional drain, which have been shown to predispose people to myocardial infarction and sudden death, especially in the context of underlying atherosclerotic disease.

PHYSIOLOGICAL MECHANISMS OF PSYCHOSOCIAL CONTRIBUTIONS TO DISEASE

The predominant explantion for psychosocial influences on disease processes has been the mechanism of hypothalamic-pituitary-adrenal-hormonal stimulation and alterations of sympathetic and parasympathetic limbs of the autonomic nervous system (Barchas, Akil, Elliot, Holman, & Watson, 1978; Henry, Kross, Stephens, & Watson, 1976; Mason, 1975; Rose, 1980). The stress responsiveness of ACTH, corticosteroids, catecholamines, growth hormone, and prolactin has been extensively documented in humans. Stress-induced alterations in thyroid hormones, testosterone, insulin, aldosterone, and the peptide endorphins and enkephalins have also been demonstrated (Borysenko & Borysenko, 1982).

Affective states such as sadness and fear have been shown to produce differential patterns of secretion of cortisol, prolactin, and growth hormone. In attempts to demonstrate connections between stressful life events, affective distress, and the onset of illness, there has been great recent interest in the connections between the central nervous system and the immune system (Ader, 1980; Rogers, Duby, & Reich, 1979). The immune system plays a major role in the maintenance of homeostatis and health and provides the first line of defense against infections and malignant disease. It is comprised of two major limbs: the humoral (B-cells and antibodies) and the cellular (T-cells and lymphokines).

A number of recent studies have demonstrated stress-induced alterations of the cellular immune system, primarily in the direction of immunosuppression (Locke, 1982). These paradigms include such stressors as sleep deprivation, space flight, examination and academic stress, bereavement, loneliness, major depression, and other psychiatric disturbances (Stein & Schliefer, 1984).

The immune system may be both influenced and regulated by active circulating factors such as the stress-responsive hormones, insulin, histamine, E-prostaglandins, acetylcholine, and endorphins, as mature lymphocytes have receptors for many of these factors and a number are crucial for the maturation of functionally active cellular subsets. The autonomic nervous system may also have direct effects on immune reactivity, as adrenergic nerve endings are present in the spleen and the thymus (immunologically active organs), and lymphocytes have alpha- and beta-adrenergic receptors. Thus, there is evidence that subpopulations of lymphocytes involved in different stages of the immune response may be characterized by different sets of receptors, thereby leading to subtle hormonal and autonomic regulatory effects that may be influenced directly by experimental processes or by accompanying changes in behavior that influence sleep, circadian rhythms, nutritional state, or level of exercise (Ader, 1981; Borysenko & Borysenko, 1982; Moore-Ede, Sulzman, & Fuller, 1982).

Finally, there is the possibility of a separate mechanism of action suggestive of a direct link between the immune response and the brain. In animals, destructive lesions in the dorsal hypothalamus lead to suppression of primary immunological responses and provide protection against lethal anaphylaxis. Electrical activity in the ventromedial hypothalamus occurs immediately after antigen–antibody interaction and prior to any hormonal changes indicating a flow of information from the activated immune system to the hypothalamus and suggesting that the brain is involved in the immune response. In humans, hypnosis has been found to alter the clinical manifestations of delayed hypersensitivity. A series of studies in animals that demonstrated behaviorally conditioned immunosuppression provided further evidence that central nervous system processes are directly capable of influencing immune responses (Ader, 1981).

This brief overview of the importance of biological, psychological, and social factors in producing, maintaining, and exacerbating disease demonstrates the importance of viewing the patient and his or her illness from a general systems standpoint. The treatment of illness is best accomplished by taking into account psychological and social factors influencing the patient and the disease.

Forms of Treatment

Psychotherapy

The most common psychological treatment of the psychological factors affecting medical illness is individual psychotherapy. The principles and techniques of psychotherapy applied in treating psychological factors affecting medical illness are the same as those applied in treating other nonpsychotic disorders. The therapist explores the patient's illness experiences, work stresses, family problems, and other interpersonal conflicts, as well as historical contributions to the patient's present state and the patient's adaptive capacities. No specific psychotherapeutic approach has been demonstrated to be more effective than another in helping to manage these factors, but evidence for the effectiveness of several approaches has been found.

Group Therapy

The focus of group therapy may be on the patient's intrapsychic conflicts, methods of handling stress, or style of interacting as revealed through his participation in the group. The therapeutic techniques used in groups for patients with illnesses affected by predisposing factors are the same as those used in other therapy groups (Yalom, 1985). Group therapy has been used successfully to help treat patients with asthma, rheumatoid arthritis, peptic ulcers, and obesity. Groups can also be helpful in the treatment of patients with chronic disorders such as renal failure, diabetes, and coronary artery disease.

Family Therapy

Family therapy may be either supportive and educational or change-oriented. Educative and supportive therapies aim at improving the family's ability to understand and cope with the patient's illness, and to better enable them to participate in the treatment process. Change-oriented therapies seek to modify patterns of communication, roles, and power relations in the family. Formal outcome studies of these approaches are rare. Nevertheless, the importance of including a patient's family in his medical therapy is obvious, and several studies have shown that family involvement can facilitate treatment. Recent monographs on the use of change-oriented approaches, particularly with anorexia, present ideas that promise to have wider application.

Hypnosis

Hypnotic techniques have long been useful in the management of predisposing factors affecting medical disorders (Peterfy, 1977). The hypnotic state may be used as a mode of therapy or may allow other therapies to be employed. When the hypnotic state is itself used as therapy, studies suggest its effectiveness is related to physiological changes characteristic of relaxation and meditation. When the hypnotic state provides a backdrop for other therapeutic techniques, suggestion, persuasion, and imagery are used to uncover and explore interactions between conflicts, emotions, early learning experiences, and current symptoms. Hypnotized patients can experience asthmatic attacks, wheals, hypertension, or other symptoms. Several controlled studies have demonstrated that hypnosis helps a substantial proportion of patients. Uncontrolled case reports offer additional suggestive evidence.

Behavior Therapy

Behavior therapies are based on learning theory concepts such as stimulus, response, reward, extinction, and conditioning. The list of behavior therapies is long and growing. Techniques that have been found effective for these disorders include several based on operant conditioning (i.e., token economies), several based on classical conditioning (e.g., extinction and aversive techniques), systematic desensitization, relaxation training, and biofeedback.

Operant conditioning programs have been used to change symptoms and behaviors that seem to be reinforced by the environment. The most extensive work has been done with anorexia nervosa. Behavior modification programs that shape and reinforce eating, weight gain, or even bite-counting, increase weight. Operant conditioning has also been used to increase activity in chronic pain patients and to decrease complaints by patients with other problems. Classical conditioning procedures have been used to change pain report, eating, and many other behaviors.

Relaxation and related techniques use instruction to help the patient achieve mental and physical relaxation. These techniques all involve encouraging the patient to assume a relaxed, comfortable position in a quiet environment; assume a passive frame of mind; repeat a phrase or word; and, breathe deeply and regularly. Relaxation appears to be useful as an adjunct to the treatment of hypertension, insomnia, and tension headaches. The specific usefulness of relaxation has not been demonstrated in other conditons, but many case studies suggest effectiveness in treating asthma, pain, and other psychophysiological conditions (Taylor, 1978).

Biofeedback

Biofeedback involves providing the patient with auditory, visual, or other information about the state of a physiological function. Every psychophysiological variable studied to date has exhibited modest change with biofeedback, but controlled studies have not demonstrated that biofeedback is superior to relaxation and related techniques for treating medical illnesses. This is disappointing, because the idea of altering abnormal functions by painless and noninvasive self-control is appealing. Practitioners should avoid overselling biofeedback while remaining alert for evidence of its usefulness.

Psychopharmacology

Both antianxiety and antidepressant agents are often useful to treat the emotional concomitants of medical illness.

Other Treatments

Several other procedures have been used to treat these disorders. Autogenic therapy, a popular treatment in Europe, has a long history of clinical application. The technique seems to act in much the same way as hypnosis and relaxation. Morita's therapy, popular in Japan, begins with enforced bed rest and progresses to work therapy, all in a therapeutic milieu.

CONCLUSION: MANAGEMENT ISSUES RELEVANT TO PSYCHOLOGISTS

Medical illnesses once thought to result from the overactivity of physiological systems (particularly the ANS), are now viewed as resulting from interactions among biological, psychological, and social systems. Explanations drawn from only one of these systems rarely suffice for the planning of maximally effective treatment interventions. The systems view has promoted the exploration of new treatments to these often disabling disorders. Individual, group, and family therapy, as well as behaviorally based treatments have been added to the traditional medical treatments for these disorders. The indications for each of these treatments and their relative effectiveness is still being evaluated, but preliminary studies suggest these new treatments will become standard additions to the therapeutic armamentarium. In coming decades, primary care physicians will find it increasingly valuable to master techniques of psychological and social intervention to help their patients enhance health and minimize disability.

Most of the illnesses discussed in this chapter are chronic and require long-term if not lifelong care. More so than in most disorders treated by psychologists or psychiatrists, the patient's medical care is a major factor in the management of the patient. For too many years, psychologists and psychiatrists have acted independently of the patient's primary medical care provider; the separation has lessened with the advent of behavioral medicine, the renewed interest in health psychology, and the greater role and access psychologists have achieved in medical centers, but the problem remains.

Effective communication between the psychologist or psychiatrist and the primary health care provider is important for a variety of reasons. First, the diagnosis of an illness meeting the DSM-III criteria of "psychological factors affecting medical illness" is one of exclusion. However, correctable medical factors may have been overlooked or were not yet sufficiently evident early in the course of illness to be diagnosed. For instance, about 5% to 10% of cases diagnosed as having essential hypertension have a concomitant illness that, upon proper treatment, will cause the blood pressure to "normalize." Psychologists and psychiatrists should never assume that referral from a physician means that the patient has been adequately evaluated; they should look for evidence that some other disease has been overlooked or a complication from the disease or its treatment has occurred. Second, these diseases often produce psychological symptoms (conversely, many psychological disorders present as medical problems) which improve as the illness improves. Third, the medical treatment of the disease often produces psychological side effects. For instance, medications used to lower blood pressure commonly produce fatigue, depression, dizziness, impotence, sleep disturbance, and other symptoms. Effective communication between the patient's primary health care provider and his or her psychologist or psychiatrist can help each understand how medical management issues affect the patient's psychological responses and, conversely, how the psychological issues affect the course of illness.

Finally, the patient's acceptance of psychological treatment may hinge on how it is presented. The primary care provider can facilitate the ongoing psychological treatment by stressing its value for the patient and for the primary physician. In working with medical patients referred for psychiatric consultation, Pasnau (1985) gave this advice to psychiatric consultants as well as to psychologists: (1) before meeting the patient find out what the referring physician really wants; (2) do not procrastinate in seeing the patient; (3) do not obfuscate; (4) make concrete recommendations; (5) involve the family in recommendations; (6) discuss your findings with the physician; (7) follow up on your recommendations; and (8) do not preach to physicians.

REFERENCES

Ader, R. (1980). Psychosomatic and psychoimmunologic research. *Psychiatric Medicine, 42,* 307–321.

Ader, R. (Ed.). (1981). *Psychoneuroimmunology.* New York: Academic Press.

Alexander, F., French, T., Pollack, G. H. (1968). *Psychosomatic specificity.* Chicago: University of Chicago Press.

American Psychiatric Association. (1968). *Diagnostic and statistical manual of mental disorders* (2nd ed.). Washington, DC: Author.

American Psychiatric Association. (1980). *Diagnostic and statistical manual of mental disorders* (3rd ed.). Washington, DC: Author.

Barchas. J. D., Akil, H., Elliot, G. R., Holman. R. B., & Watson, S. J. (1978). Behavioral neurochemistry: Neuroregulators and behavioral states. *Science, 200,* 964–973.

Borysenko, M., & Borysenko, J. (1982). Stress, behavior and immunity: Animal models and mediating mechanisms. *General Hospital Psychiatry, 4,* 59–67.

Bruhn, J. G., Chandler, B., Miller, M. C., Wolf, S., & Lynn, T. N. (1966). Social aspects of coronary heart disease in two adjacent, ethically different communities. *American Journal of Public Health, 56,* 1493–1506.

Cannon, W. (1929). *Bodily changes in pain, hunger, fear and range.* New York: Appleton-Century-Crofts.

Cobb, S. (1976). Social support as a moderator of life stress. *Psychological Medicine, 38,* 300–314.

Dembroski, T. M., & MacDougall, J. M. (1984). Psychosocial factors and coronary heart disease: A biochemical model. In U. Stocksmeier (Ed.), *Advances in stress research.* Berlin: Springer-Verlag.

Dohrenwend, B. S., & Dohrenwend, B. P. (1974). *Stressful life events: Their nature and effects.* New York: Wiley.

Dorian, B., & Taylor, C. B. (1984). Stress factors in the development of coronary artery disease. *Journal of Occupational Medicine, 26,* 747–756.

Engel, G. L. (1967). A psychological setting of somatic disease: The "giving-up–given-up" complex. *Proceedings of the Royal Society of Medicine, 60,* 553–555.

Engel, G. L. (1968). A life setting conducive to illness: The giving up, given-up complex. *Archives of Internal Medicine, 69,* 293–300.

Garfinkel, P. E., & Garner, D. M. (1982). *Anorexia nervosa: A multidimensional perspective.* New York: Brunner/Mazel.

Henry, J. P., & Cassel, J. C. (1969). Psychosocial factors in essential hypertension. Recent epidemiological and animal experimental evidence. *American of Epidemiology, 90,* 171–193.

Henry, J. P., Kross, M. E., Stephens, P. M., & Watson, F. M. C. (1976). Evidence that differing pyschosocial stimuli lead to adrenal cortical simulation by autonomic or endocrine pathways. In E. Usdin, R. Kvetnarksy, & I. J. Kopin (Eds.), *Catecholamines and stress.* Oxford: Pergamon Press.

Hofer, M. A., & Shair, H. (1982). Control of sleep wake states in the infant rat by features of the mother–infant relationship. *Developmental Psychology, 15,* 229–244.

Hofer, M. A., & Weiner, H. (1975). Psychological mechanisms for cardiac control by nutritional intake after early maternal separation in the young rat. *Psychiatric Medicine, 37,* 8–24.

Holmes, T., & Rahe, R. (1967). Social readjustment scale. *Journal of Psychosomatic Illness, 11,* 213.

Jacobs, S., & Ostfeld, A. (1977). An epidemiological review of the mortality of bereavement. *Psychological Medicine, 39,* 344–357.

Kagar, J. (1982). *Psychological research on the human infant: An evaluative summary.* New York: William T. Grant Foundation.

Lacey, J. I., Kagan, J., Lacey, B. C., & Moss, H. L. (1963). The visceral level: Situational determinants and behavioral correlates of autonomic response patterns. In P. H. Knapp (Ed.), *Expression of the emotions in man.* New York: International Universities Press.

Locke, S. E. (1982). Stress, adaptation, and immunity: Studies in humans. *General Hospital Psychiatry, 4,* 49–58.

Marmot, M. G., & Syme, S. L. (1976). Acculturation and coronary heart disease in Japanese-Americans. *American Journal of Epidemiology, 104,* 225–247.

Mason, J. W. (1975). Emotion as reflected in patterns of endocrine integration. In L. Levi (Ed.), *Emotions: Their parameters and measurement.* New York: Raven Press.

Minuchin, S., Rosmar, B. L., & Baker, L. (1978). Psychosomatic families: Anorexia nervosa in context. Cambridge: Harvard University Press.

Mirsky, I. A. (1958). Physiologic, psychologic and social determinants in the etiology of duodenal ulcer. *American Journal of Digestive Diseases, 3,* 285–314.

Moore-Ede, M. C., Sulzman, F. M., & Fuller, C. A. (1982). *The clocks that time us.* Cambridge: Harvard University Press.

Moos, R. H., & Solomon, G. F. (1965). Psychological comparisons between women with rheumatoid arthritis and their non-arthritic sisters. *Psychosomatic Medicine, 27,* 135–150.

Parkes, C. M., & Brown, R. J. (1972). Health after bereavement. *Psychosomatic Medicine, 34,* 449–461.

Pasnau, R. O. (1985). Ten commandments of medical etiquette for psychiatrists. *Psychosomatics, 26,* 128–132.

Peterfy, D. (1977). Hypnosis. In E. D. Wittkower & H. Warnes (Eds.), *Psychosomatic medicine.* New York: Harper & Row.

Price, V. A. (1982). *Type A behavior pattern: A model for research and practice.* New York: Academic Press.

Rabkin, J. G., & Struvening, E. L. (1976). Life events, stress and illness. *Science, 194,* 1013–1020.

Rogers, M. P., Dubey, H. D., & Rich, P. (1979). The influence of the psyche and brain on immunity and disease susceptibility: A critical review. *Psychosomatic Medicine, 41,* 147–164.

Rose, R. M. (1980). Endocrine responses to stressful psychological events. *Psychiatric Clinics of North America, 3,* 251–276.

Schmale, A. H. Jr. (1958). Relation of separation and depression to disease: I. A report on a hospitalized medi-medical population. *Psychosomatic Medicine, 20,* 259–277.

Selvini Palazolli, M. (1974). *Self-starvation.* London: Chaucer Publishing.

Selye, H. (1974). *Stress without distress.* Philadelphia: Lippincott.

Stein, M., & Schliefer, S. J. (1984). Frontiers of stress research: Stress and immunity. In M. D. Zales (Ed.), *Stress in health and disease.* New York: Brunner/Mazel.

Taylor, C. B. (1978). Relaxation training and related techniques. In W. S. Agras (Ed.), *Behavior modification: Principles and clinical applications.* Boston: Little, Brown.

Taylor, G. J. (1974). Alexithymia: Concept, measurement and implications for treatment. *American Journal of Psychiatry, 141*(6), 725–731.

Thomas, A., & Chess, S. (1977). *Temperament and development.* New York: Brunner/Mazel.

Trueson, M. F., Clancy, R. E., Jessop, W. J. E., Childers, R. W., & Stare, F. J. (1964). Comparisons of siblings in Boston and Ireland. *Journal of the American Dietetic Association, 45,* 225–236.

Valliant, G. E. (1976). Natural history of male psychological health: The relation of choice of ego mechanisms of defense to adult adjustment. *Archives of General Psychiatry, 33,* 535–545.

Weiner, H. (1975). Autonomic psychophysiology: Peripheral autonomic mechanisms and their central control. In M. Reiser (Ed.), *American handbook of psychiatry.* New York: Basic Books.

Weiner, H. (1977). *Psychobiology and human disease.* New York: Elsevier/North Holland.

Weiner, H., Thaler, M., Reiser, M. F., & Mirsky, T. A. (1957). Etiology of duodenal ulcer: I. Relation of specific psychological characteristics to rate of gastric secretion (serum pepsinogen). *Psychosomatic Medicine, 19*(1), 1–10.

Wolff, H. G. (1953). *Stress and disease.* Springfield, IL: Charles C Thomas.

Yalom, I. (1985). *Theory and practice of group psychotherapy* (3rd ed.). New York: Basic Books.

Young, M., Benjamin, B., & Wallis, C. (1963). The mortality of widowers. *The Lancet, 2,* 454–456.

12

Life-Threatening Disease
Biopsychosocial Dimensions of Cancer Care

MICHAEL A. ANDRYKOWSKI AND WILLIAM H. REDD

The twentieth century has witnessed significant changes in life expectancy and in the major causes of death in the United States. Two related trends are often cited. First, people are living longer. Mean life expectancy at birth rose from 49.2 years for 1900–1902 to 73.7 years in 1979 (U.S. Department of Health and Human Services, 1984). This dramatic increase has been attributed to the control of acute infectious diseases. In 1900, approximately 36% of all deaths resulted from infectious or infection-related diseases such as measles, tuberculosis, diphtheria, influenza, or pneumonia. The corresponding figure for 1980 was 6% (Matarazzo, 1982). Increased longevity, however, has been associated with increased vulnerability to chronic diseases. Deaths related to chronic diseases rose from approximately 20% in 1900 to 70% in 1980 (Matarazzo, 1982). Indeed, today the three leading causes of death in the United States (heart disease, cancer, and cerebrovascular disease) are chronic conditions. Together, they account for 68.3% of all deaths (U.S. Department of Health and Human Services, 1984).

Underlying these trends has been the major advancement of medical knowledge and technology. Many diseases that were previously life-threatening have been essentially controlled or eliminated. More visible, however, have been recent developments in the capacity to sustain and prolong life. Quite simply, pharmacological and technological advances have allowed many individuals to live for weeks, months, or even years beyond the point where death would have been likely or even certain in a previous era.

The increase in life-threatening chronic disease has had a major impact on health care. After they become aware of the critical nature of their condition, patients enter what Pattison (1978) referred to as the "living–dying interval." This interval culminates with either the individual's death or the certain knowledge that his or her medical status is no longer life-threatening. With chronic diseases, this living–dying interval may span months or years. Because in most cases physical and psychosocial functioning are impaired, patterns of daily living are likely to be disrupted. Thus, patients and their families must make significant adjustments in their plans and routines. Because of the broad impact of such illness, professional intervention on many fronts (i.e., medical, social, and psychological) is typically required.

MICHAEL A. ANDRYKOWSKI • Department of Behavioral Science, University of Kentucky, College of Medicine, Lexington, KY 40536-0086.   **WILLIAM H. REDD** • Memorial Sloan-Kettering Cancer Center, 1275 York Avenue, New York, NY 10021.

CHAPTER FOCUS AND OUTLINE

The purpose of this chapter is to identify the contribution that psychosocially oriented clinicians can make to the care of the individual with life-threatening disease. Such providers have traditionally been afforded a role in helping patients and their families cope with the psychological and existential crises aroused by the possibility of death. However, recent advances in health psychology and behavioral medicine have made it clear that psychological expertise can be important in many aspects of care. It is our aim to highlight some of the new challenges and opportunities available to mental health specialists interested in the care of patients with chronic life-threatening disease.

Although *life-threatening disease* is a generic term that encompasses many separate medical conditions, such as cancer, cardiovascular and renal disease, or diabetes, this chapter focuses on the psychosocial clinician's role in the care of the individual with cancer. Readers interested in the psychosocial aspects of care for other serious life-threatening diseases are encouraged to refer to other reviews of psychological and behavioral factors in chronic disease (e.g., Burish & Bradley, 1983; Doehrman, 1977; Hamburg, Lipsett, Inoff, & Drash, 1980; Mossman, 1980; Razin, 1982; Stonnington, 1980).

We chose to focus our discussion on cancer for a number of reasons. First, cancer is extremely prevalent. Recent estimates indicate that approximately 700,000 new diagnoses of cancer are made annually in the United States (American Cancer Society, 1978). Despite advances in early detection, diagnosis, and treatment, which have yielded increasing numbers of cures and extended remissions, cancer continues to be a serious threat to life. In 1979, malignant neoplasms were the second leading cause of death in the United States, implicated in 21.1% of all deaths (U.S. Department of Health and Human Services, 1984). Even for those forms of cancer that are essentially curable, fear of recurrence is likely to have a major negative impact on the individual's psychological adjustment. Second, cancer perhaps more than any other disease, often requires intense psychosocial intervention during all its stages. Moreover, we feel that many of the psychosocial issues encountered when working with cancer patients and their families are also relevant to the care of patients with other chronic, life-threatening diseases.

Another reason for selecting cancer is the existence of a large and rapidly expanding literature on the psychosocial aspects of cancer and its treatment (e.g., Burish & Lyles, 1983; Cullen, Fox, & Isom, 1976; Goldberg & Tull, 1983; Meyerowitz, Heinrich, & Schag, 1983; Redd & Hendler, 1983). This literature suggests the emergence of an innovative perspective on the psychosocial needs and requisite care of the individual with cancer. No longer is interest limited to the identification and treatment of the affective disequilibrium (i.e., depression and anxiety) that is presumed to accompany the diagnosis of cancer. Rather, there is increasing recognition that cancer has a major impact on many aspects of the patient's life. Consequently, the potential for psychosocial intervention extends beyond the provision of supportive emotional care. New possibilities exist for enabling patients to manage the numerous problems in daily living posed by the disease and its treatment (e.g., Burish & Lyles, 1983; Meyerowitz *et al.*, 1983; Redd, 1982a).

This chapter is divided into two major topics: cancer-related problems and methods of intervention. In the first section, we identify the physical, psychological, and social conditions associated with cancer. It is our contention that these conditions are often interrelated and hence cannot be viewed in isolation. For this reason, psychosocial intervention with the cancer patient demands an understanding of how the patient is embedded within an interactive biopsychosocial system (H. J. Sobel, 1981). According to this viewpoint, the patient's behavior and physical symptoms are related to a variety of factors, including (1) the disease process itself; (2) the treatment modalities used, (3) the patient's interpersonal milieu, and (4) the environment in which medical care is received. Hence, our discussion emphasizes the identification of potential functional relationships between the elements of this model and the specific conditions presented by the individual with cancer.

In the second section, the focus shifts to the intervention approaches suitable for use with this population of patients. We begin with an examination of the traditional intervention approaches and then describe the emerging behavioral perspective. We believe that behavioral conceptualizations of the biopsychosocial impact of cancer and its treatment provide useful insights into the nature of the problems presented by the oncology patient as well as suggestions about how to intervene. As a result, the domain and potential contribution of psychosocial oncology is greatly expanded.

PROBLEM CONDITIONS ASSOCIATED WITH CANCER

Cancer encompasses a variety of disease entities and poses a wide variety of problems for the patient (e.g., Freidenbergs, Gordon, Hibbard, Levine, Wolf, & Diller, 1981–1982; Gordon, Friedenbergs, Diller, Hibbard, Wolf, Levine, Lipkins, Ezrachi, & Lucido, 1980; Lehman, DeLisa, Warren, deLateur, Bryant, & Nicholson, 1978; Wellisch, Landsverk, Guidera, Pasnau, & Fawzy, 1983). For example, in a study of the problems experienced by 570 homebound cancer patients, Wellish *et al.* (1983) found the following prevalence rates: (1) somatic side effects (83%); (2) mood disturbance (44%); (3) equipment problems (34%); (4) family relationship impairment (32%); (5) cognitive impairment (27%); (6) treatment-compliance difficulties (26%); (7) financial difficulties or worries (20%); (8) role difficulties in the family (17%); and (9) problems with body image (8%). The specific constellation of problems presented by a patient varies as a function of both medical and psychosocial variables. Key medical parameters include the primary diagnosis and disease site, the stage of the disease, the prognosis, and the mode of treatment. Some important psychosocial factors include the age of the patient, the psychological functioning and personal coping resources evidenced by the patient before the diagnosis of cancer, and the patient's social network (e.g., the presence of a spouse or dependent children).

It is our belief that comprehensive cancer care requires the adoption of a biopsychosocial orientation. Hence, in the discussion that follows, the problem conditions associated with cancer are divided into three broad categories: somatic, psychological, and social. Within each category, selected specific problems are examined in detail. Although these categories overlap to some extent (nausea, for example, can have both somatic and psychological dimensions), we believe that they provide a useful heuristic framework for viewing the problems encountered in the treatment of oncology patients.

Somatic Conditions

Somatic symptoms are common in cancer. In a study of homebound cancer patients, Wellisch *et al.* (1983) found that 83% of the patients in their sample experienced somatic symptoms. Pain was the most frequently reported complaint (66%). Even when pain was excluded, 61% of their sample still reported somatic complaints, including weakness, nausea, vomiting, dyspnea, bowel or bladder difficulties, anorexia, or sexual dysfunction.

Physical symptoms may occur as a direct result of the disease itself or as side effects of cancer treatments, most notably radiotherapy or chemotherapy. Medical management of these symptoms is a primary concern of physicians. Recent research suggests, however, that physical symptoms can have important psychosocial dimensions (i.e., they are directly affected by social and psychological factors) and thus are appropriate targets for psychosocial intervention (Fordyce, 1976; Redd, 1982a; Redd, Burish, & Andrykowski, 1985). To date, the most fruitful areas for research and clinical intervention have been the nausea and vomiting associated with chemotherapy, pain, sexual dysfunction, and anorexia.

Nausea and Vomiting. Many cancer patients experience some degree of nausea and vomiting during the course of their disease. These symptoms can be a direct result of the disease process (e.g., in brain metastases, bowel obstruction, gall bladder disease, or metabolic derangements) or the iatrogenic effects of chemotherapy or radiotherapy. Nausea and vomiting can occur together or alone. Some patients report feeling nauseated continuously, and others experience intermittent nausea. Bouts of nausea and vomiting may be brief or protracted. Patients are nearly uniform in reporting that these symptoms are extremely unpleasant and disrupt their daily activities. Indeed, many patients are bedridden during prolonged bouts of nausea and vomiting and are left weak, dehydrated, and nutritionally depleted when these bouts end.

Chemotherapy-related nausea and vomiting have been a major focus of psychosocially oriented research for several reasons. First, chemotherapy is the most common form of cancer treatment, and most chemotherapy patients experience some degree of nausea and vomiting. Second, the occurrence, or the anticipated occurrence, of these symptoms may produce anxiety and depression (Stoudemire, Cotanch, & Laszlo, 1984) and, in severe instances, may cause patients to refuse to initiate or to continue a potentially beneficial course of chemotherapy treatment (Seigel & Longo, 1981; Weddington, 1982; Whitehead, 1975). Finally, evidence suggests that psychosocial factors can contribute to both the development and the treatment of chemotherapy-related nausea and vomiting (Burish, Redd, & Carey, 1985; Redd *et al.*, 1985).

Cancer chemotherapy involves the administration of any of a wide variety of cytotoxic drugs. These drugs are toxic to cancerous tissue but may also have a variety of adverse effects on normal tissue (e.g., Burish & Lyles, 1983; Golden, 1985). For most patients, nausea and vomiting are the most prominent and unpleasant of these side effects. Posttreatment nausea and vomiting begin some time after drug infusion or ingestion and are presumed to be pharmacological in nature. Whether or not a patient experiences these symptoms will, in large measure, be a function of the particular drug and of the antiemetic regimens they receive. Chemotherapy agents vary in their emetic potential. Some drugs, such as cisplatin and Adriamycin, invariably produce some degree of nausea and vomiting. Others, such as Fluorouracil and vincristine, seldom produce these symptoms. A wide variety of drugs have been evaluated for their antiemetic effectiveness (Penta,

Poster, & Bruno, 1983). At present, no available regimen is completely effective. Rather, different antiemetic regimens may be more or less effective for different chemotherapeutic agents (Penta *et al.*, 1983). In addition, the importance of patient compliance with a prescribed antiemetic regimen is a serious problem that has been largely overlooked. Indeed, even an antiemetic regimen with clinically demonstrated efficacy is of little use when patients fail to comply with their prescribed regimen. Antiemetic compliance is primarily an issue for outpatients who are typically entrusted with the responsibility for medicating themselves.

The duration and severity of posttreatment nausea and vomiting varies across patients (Morrow, 1984). Some patients may report mild nausea and vomiting for 24 to 72 h following treatment, and others may experience severe nausea and vomiting but of a limited duration. Pharmacological factors, such as the specific drug and antiemetic regimens involved, account for a large portion of variance in the course of posttreatment nausea. Nevertheless, considerable variance is evident even among patients receiving identical drug and antiemetic regimens (Fetting, Grochow, Folstein, Ettinger, & Colvin, 1982). Other disease-related or psychosocial variables, such as anxiety or coping responses, may be important, but their specific impact is still poorly understood.

In addition to posttreatment nausea and vomiting, some patients experience nausea and vomiting before their chemotherapy infusions. Patients may become nauseated or may vomit when thinking about their chemotherapy treatment the day before a scheduled infusion, while traveling to the clinic, on arrival at the clinic, or as the nurse begins the infusion. Such anticipatory nausea appears to develop as a result of respondent conditioning processes (Andrykowski, Redd, & Hatfield, 1985; Redd & Andrykowski, 1982). According to this formulation, the infusion of cytotoxic drugs functions as an unconditioned stimulus producing nausea and vomiting, the unconditioned response(s). Through repeated association with treatment, environmental stimuli (e.g., the smell of the nurse's cologne, the sound of the doctor's voice, or the sight of the clinic) acquire the ability to elicit nausea and vomiting; that is, they function as conditioned stimuli. This learning is automatic and is clearly beyond the patient's control.

Approximately 25% to 50% of all chemotherapy patients ultimately develop anticipatory nausea, and a smaller percentage develop anticipatory vomiting (Redd & Andrykowski, 1982). A variety of patient- and treatment-related variables have characterized patients who develop anticipatory symptoms. In general, these patients (1) are younger (Andrykowski *et al.*, 1985; Ingle, Burish, & Wallston, 1984; Morrow, 1982); (2) have received a greater number of chemotherapy treatments (Fetting, Wilcox, Iwata, Criswell, Bosmajian, & Sheidler, 1983); (3) report elevated levels of state anxiety (Andrykowski *et al.*, 1985; Ingle *et al.*, 1984) or "emotional distress" (Nerenz, Leventhal, & Love, 1982); and (4) experience more severe posttreatment nausea and vomiting (Andrykowski *et al.*, 1985; Fetting *et al.*, 1983; Ingle *et al.*, 1984; Morrow, 1982; Wilcox, Fetting, Nettesheim, & Abeloff, 1982). The latter factor (i.e., greater severity of posttreatment side effects) appears to be the most significant predictor of the likelihood of developing anticipatory nausea and vomiting. Quite simply, a patient does not develop these anticipatory symptoms unless she or he has previously experienced some degree of posttreatment nausea and vomiting.

It is important to note that neither personality nor psychosocial adjustment factors have been shown to influence the development of conditioned anticipatory side effects. They *do not* represent psychopathology or psychological weakness. Unfortunately, many patients believe that they are somehow responsible and feel embarrassed by these symptoms. We once heard one of our patients chastising another, saying "It's crazy, you're not even getting the drugs and you're getting sick. It's all in your head." (As it turned out, 2 months later, the patient who had given this criticism began experiencing the same sensations in the waiting room. His symptoms were even worse: in addition to anticipatory nausea, he experienced uncontrolled vomiting whenever the nurse cleaned his arm in preparation for his infusion.) Such attributions only compound the patient's problems and may prevent the patient's seeking effective intervention. Our strategy is to instruct nurses to explain the role of conditioning processes in the acquisition of anticipatory side effects and to stress that they represent a natural and quite expected result of invasive treatment.

Although chemotherapy is regarded by most patients as the most aversive part of comprehensive cancer treatment and as producing the most side effects, radiation therapy can also be extremely unpleasant for patients. A typical course of external-beam radiotherapy involves a series of daily doses of radiation for a period of one to several weeks. Depending on the dosage and the area of the body that is irradiated, nausea and vomiting can result. Nausea and vomiting are most likely when radiation is administered to the abdomen or over a large body area. (For example, Welch, 1980, found that 79% of patients sampled experienced emesis with external-beam radiation to the trunk area.) When radiation is administered daily, nausea and vomiting may be experienced continuously throughout the course of treatment. The occurrence of anticipatory nausea in patients receiving radiation therapy has also been reported (Peck & Boland, 1977). However, whether this constitutes true "conditioned" nausea or whether such pretreatment nausea is simply chronic radiation-induced nausea is difficult to determine.

Pain. Cancer is commonly viewed as a painful disease, and hence, pain is one of the major concerns of cancer patients (Turk & Rennert, 1981; Twycross & Lack, 1983). Although no large-scale epidemiological studies are available, a number of smaller surveys of cancer-pain prevalence are available (see, e.g., Twycross & Lack, 1983). The evidence suggests that the prevalence of pain depends in part on the site of the neoplasm. For example, leukemia and lymphoma are least likely to be associated with pain (5% and 20% of patients, respectively), whereas bone, cervical, and oral cancers result in pain in over 80% of patients (Bonica, 1980; Foley, 1979b). The prevalence of pain also increases with disease progression (Foley, 1985). Pain occurs in approximately 15% of patients with nonmetastatic cancer (Daut & Cleeland, 1982), whereas 60% to 90% of patients with advanced disease report significant pain (Cleeland, 1984; Foley, 1979a).

Two different types of pain may be presented by cancer patients (Foley, 1985). Acute pain is characterized by a well-defined temporal pattern of pain onset. Hyperactivity of the autonomic nervous system is present along with objective physical signs of pain, such as bone or tissue destruction. Chronic pain, on the other hand, is pain of greater than 6 months duration. Adaptation of the autonomic system occurs, and the objective, physical signs common to acute pain are lacking. However, chronic pain is often associated with a series of psychological and physiological symptoms, such as sleep or appetite disturbances, irritability, and impaired concentration (Foley, 1985). The distinction between acute and chronic pain is a significant one. It is likely that these two types of pain differ with respect to the types of factors that cause and contribute to the experience of pain in cancer patients.

The pain that cancer patients experience can stem from a number of causes. The malignant process itself can produce a variety of physiological bases for the experience of pain. These include bone or luminal destruction, nerve compression or infiltration, and distension or infiltration of the integument or organ capsules (Foley, 1985; Turk & Rennert, 1981). Pain may also occur following surgery or during the course of chemotherapy or radiotherapy. For example, pain may result from the occurrence of reflex sympathetic dystrophy following radiation treatments.

Extensive experimental research suggests, however, that physiological factors alone are insufficient to account for the experience of pain in cancer patients (e.g., Chapman, 1979; Weisenberg, 1977). For example, many cancer patients do not report pain during the terminal stage of their disease even though autopsy reveals no physiological differences between these patients and those who reported severe pain (Bonica, 1979). The lack of an isomorphic relationship between pain and tissue pathology suggests the importance of conceptualizing pain as a multidimensional phenomenon (Melzack & Casey, 1968; Melzack & Wall, 1965; Turk & Rennert, 1981; Twycross & Lack, 1983). Melzack and Casey (1968), for instance, suggested that pain has three components: (1) sensory, (2) affective, and (3) cognitive. The sensory component is the physiological basis for pain, that is, the nature and extent of tissue damage or painful sensory stimulation. The affective component is an individual's emotional response to pain. The actual or anticipated presence of pain can produce anxiety or depression, which can exacerbate the experience of pain. Finally, the cognitive component is an individual's appraisal of pain sensations and his or her ability to cope with pain. For example, a belief that pain is intractable or that one is unable to cope with pain may exacerbate pain complaints and may increase the patient's suffering.

In general, this multidimensional model suggests that the experience of pain is based on a combination of physiological and psychological factors. Foley (1985) suggested that acute pain and chronic pain differ in the relative contribution of each of these two factors. Psychological factors may play an especially prominent role in chronic pain. Because chronic pain is often associated with advanced disease, depression and fear of death may contribute to the intensity of the pain experienced. In addition, the sense of hopelessness, intractability, and lack of control may increase suffering and distress. The role of psychological factors in acute pain, though perhaps less prominent, should nevertheless not be overlooked. For example, for some patients, acute pain may have been a major symptom leading to the diagnosis of cancer. Subsequent recurrence of pain may imply recurrent disease. Hence, the meaning that patients ascribe to pain may engender an affective response (in this case, anxiety) that serves to exacerbate the pain experience. Psychological factors can function to mitigate pain as well. For instance, acute pain secondary to cancer therapies such as surgery or chemotherapy may be better tolerated because pain is perceived as being predictable and time-limited, and as being in the service of securing a successful therapeutic response (Foley, 1985).

Recognition of the role of both physiological and psychological factors in the experience of pain has obvious implications for the clinical management of cancer-related pain. The therapeutic approaches to pain control used with this population include the use of narcotic and nonnarcotic drugs, neurosurgical and anesthetic procedures, and behavioral methods. (Detailed discussions of these procedures can be found in Bonica & Ventafridda, 1979; Foley, 1979b, 1985; Turk & Rennert, 1981; and Twycross & Lack, 1983.) Behavioral approaches, such as relaxation training, biofeedback, hypnosis, and cognitive training, may be indicated when pain has a large psychological component. Although at present it is impossible to explain the exact mechanisms involved, it is possible that at least part of the effectiveness of these approaches lies in their ability to increase a patient's sense of control and to reduce the hopelessness and demoralization associated with chronic pain. It has also been suggested that behavioral methods may also ameliorate pain by providing a calming diversion of attention (Foley, 1985), which may serve to disrupt the pain–anxiety–tension cycle.

In addition to being a significant concern in itself, pain may also be related to the occurrence of other problem conditions. For example, pain may seriously weaken patients' morale and reduce their "will to live." As a result, patients may refuse to initiate or to continue potentially life-extending treatment programs. Second, medical interventions to control pain may result in a variety of unpleasant or dangerous side effects. Narcotic analgesics (e.g., morphine) may produce sedation, constipation, respiratory depression, and nausea and vomiting (Black, 1979). Complications of spinothalamic tractotomy, a neurosurgical procedure, may include loss of bowel and bladder control, lower extremity weakness, and loss of sexual function (Murphy, 1973). Finally, inadequately controlled pain may cause the cancer patient to emit a variety of "pain behaviors," such as moaning, crying, complaining, or yelling (Fordyce, 1973, 1976). Initially, medical staff and family are likely to respond to these behaviors with sympathy, companionship, and rapid accommodation of the patient's needs. As a result, these pain behaviors are likely to continue or intensify even though the intensity of the pain experience itself may remain constant or may even diminish. Family and staff may, in time, find such pain behaviors overly aversive and may begin to withdraw from the patient (Redd, 1982b).

Sexual Dysfunction. Impaired sexual functioning may also be a significant problem for the individual with cancer (Andersen & Hacker, 1983b; Derogatis & Kourlesis, 1981; Fisher, 1983; Schain, 1982). Discussion of sexual dysfunction in the context of the somatic problems associated with cancer does not imply that sexual dysfunction is strictly a physiological problem. Both organic and psychological factors can be involved in either the etiology or the manifestations of sexual dysfunction. However, because the disease process itself underlies both organic and psychological reactions, we have chosen to discuss sexual dysfunction in the context of the somatic problems of cancer patients.

Cancer-related sexual dysfunctions may be evidenced by a variety of specific problems. No general epidemiological study of the prevalence of sexual dysfunction among cancer patients exists, however. Rather, research in this area has focused on the occurrence of sexual dysfunction among specific diagnostic groups, such as patients with testicular (Bracken & Johnson, 1976), breast (Silberfarb, Maurer, & Crouthamel, 1980), or cervical (Vincent, Vincent, Greiss, & Linton, 1975) cancer, or among patients who have undergone specific cancer treatments, such as pelvic exenteration (Andersen & Hacker, 1983a) or mastectomy (Jamison, Wellisch, & Pasnau, 1978).

In general, research indicates that sexual dysfunction is fairly common among cancer patients and is not limited to patients with genital cancers. Because a wide range of sexual dysfunction is possible, exhaustive discussion of the sexual problems typically associated with specific treatments and disease sites is beyond the scope of this chapter. Rather, a general discussion of the major sources of sexual dysfunction in cancer patients is presented. Readers interested in a more detailed discussion of specific sexual dysfunctions associated with cancer may consult other sources, including Andersen and Hacker (1983b), Burish and Lyles (1983), and Schain (1982).

Cancer-related sexual dysfunction may stem from several sources. First, the physical impact of the disease and its treatment may produce functional or structural damage that directly affects the individual's sexual functioning. For example, radiation treatments for carcinoma of the cervix may produce vaginal atrophy and stenosis (Abitpol & Davenport, 1974). The resulting dyspareunia is likely to limit the frequency and enjoyment of coitus. Similarly, erectile dysfunction is highly likely in males who have undergone a radical prostatectomy (Jewett, 1975).

A second potential cause of sexual dysfunction in the cancer patient is the general debilitation and dysphoria likely to result from the disease and its treatment. Chronic or intermittent experience of fatigue, weakness, pain, nausea, anxiety, or depression is likely to limit the individual's desire for sexual activity. Even when sexual desire is intact, pain or weakness may pose an obstacle to the physical performance of sexual activities.

A third cause of sexual dysfunction is the cancer patient's psychological reaction to her or his disease. Such reactions may take a variety of forms. Sexual activity may be curtailed, particularly when cancers of the genitalia are involved, because of unfounded fears of transmitting cancer (Krant, 1981). Marked changes in the individual's self-concept may also occur. In particular, alteration of the cancer patient's body image has been noted. This may be especially acute when cosmetic changes are present. For example, Bronner-Huszar (1971) noted that, following mastectomy, many women "feel worthless, ugly, defeminized, socially and sexually unacceptable" (p. 134). Clearly, a patient who feels unattractive or repulsive is likely to have difficulty in functioning effectively in a sexual relationship. Fears of rejection or undesirability may motivate avoidance of sexual activities. Anxiety generated by fears of abandonment may interfere with sexual functioning by reducing libido or hampering communication with the partner (Fisher, 1979; Lamont, DePetrillo, & Sargeant, 1978). Although the impact of mastectomy has received the most attention (e.g., Holland & Mastrovito, 1980; Jamison et al., 1978; Meyerowitz, 1980; Polivy, 1977), patients with cancers of the head, neck, and genitalia are also at significant risk for developing body-image disturbances (e.g., Andersen & Hacker, 1983b; Sewell & Edwards, 1980).

A fourth factor that may contribute to the occurrence of sexual dysfunction is the reaction of the cancer patient's partner. The partner may withdraw from sexual activity because of feelings of repulsion or a fear of hurting the patient. In a study of spouses of mastectomy patients, Wellisch, Jamison, and Pasnau (1978) reported that 20% of the sample had never seen their wives unclothed following surgery. In some instances, such a pattern of nonviewing was attributable to the husband's reluctance to view his wife's surgical site rather than shame and embarrassment on her part. In either case, the authors suggested that such avoidant behavior was associated with an impaired sexual relationship following the mastectomy.

Cancer-related sexual dysfunction can have obvious emotional and psychological ramifications. For many individuals, healthy sexual functioning is a significant source of personal identity, satisfaction, and self-esteem. Hence, sexual dysfunction can result in depression and a subjectively poorer quality of life. Sexual dysfunction can strain relationships, particularly if sexual activity has been an integral aspect. Of course, alienation from his or her partner is likely to increase the degree of isolation that the cancer patient may experience.

The presence of sexual dysfunction may also affect a patient's willingness to continue receiving treatment for his or her disease. As indicated previously, poor sexual dysfunctioning may contribute to a correspondingly poor quality of life. The patient's perception of the latter is likely to influence his or her will to live. To the extent that a person feels that the present quality of life falls below a certain level of acceptability, the less likely he or she is to feel that further treatment is desirable. Similarly, the fear of sexual dysfunction may influence a patient's decision to inititate a course of potentially life-extending therapy. Some patients may prefer the risks associated with either a less aggressive treatment or no treatment at all to living with impaired sexual functioning and a consequently unacceptable quality of life.

Nutritional Problems. Nutritional problems are widespread in neoplastic disease and may occur in all types of cancer or at any stage of disease. Cachexia is the most common nutrition-related complication of cancer. This syndrome is characterized primarily by weight loss, protein–calorie malnutrition, and tissue wasting. Cachexia results from disease-related disruption of the normal food-intake regulatory process. Although complex and incompletely understood, regulation is aimed at matching food intake with metabolic needs. Weight loss is evidence of a negative caloric balance caused by nutrient intake that is insufficient to match energy expenditures.

The causes of negative caloric balance in the cancer patient are complex. Although food consumption is typically depressed, caloric balance may be negative even when consumption is normal. For example, impaired absorption of nutrients from the alimentary tract may occur because of tumor location in this region or because of the iatrogenic effects of chemotherapy or radiation (DeWys, 1979). Alternatively, patients may be hypermetabolic, so that caloric expenditures are elevated relative to activity level and typical nutrient intake (Knox, Crosby, Feurer, Buzby, Miller, & Mullen, 1983). Finally, caloric deficit may result from parasitization of available nutrients by the tumor (Costa, 1977).

The most apparent basis for cancer-related weight loss, however, is a decrease in food consumption. The factors leading to decreased food consumption may be organized into three groups: (1) localized disease-related effects, (2) systemic disease-related effects, and (3) treatment-related effects (DeWys, 1980). These categories are not mutually exclusive, as a number of consumption-reducing factors, such as pain, nausea, or alterations in taste, may arise from several sources. In addition to their etiology, it is also helpful to view consumption-reducing factors in terms of their specific impact on food consumption. Some conditions may lead to a reduced desire to eat (i.e., anorexia), whereas other conditions may compromise the ability to eat while leaving the desire to eat intact.

A reduced desire to eat may result from inappropriate signals of satiety from the gastrointestinal tract. Early satiety is frequently reported by cancer patients. Patients may be hungry in the morning but may feel sated for the duration of the day following an initial meal. This symptom has been attributed to a slowing of the digestive process because of decreased gastrointestinal secretions, mucosal atrophy of the small intestine, or atrophy of the stomach muscle wall (DeWys, 1979). A sense of "chronic fullness" may also be reported. This condition has been attributed to cancer's systemic effects on the normal metabolism of protein, fats, and carbohydrates (DeWys, 1979) or the suppression of appetite via the effect of tumor metabolites on feeding-control centers in the hypothalamus (Theologides, 1972).

A reduced desire to eat may also result from a decrease in the excitatory aspects of food consumption. The taste, smell, temperature, and consistency of food contribute to the hedonic value of consumption. They also trigger various physiological reflexes necessary for digestion, such as salivary flow, gastric secretion, and the swallowing reflex. Cancer patients often experience disruption or alteration of these gustatory sensations. Taste abnormalities have been the most frequently reported (Carson & Gormican, 1977; DeWys & Walters, 1975). Patients may report that "food tastes blah." In extreme instances, particularly when radiation to the head or neck is involved, taste may be completely absent (Donaldson & Lenon, 1979). Some chemotherapy drugs may leave the patient with an unpleasant taste (e.g., metallic) in the mouth, which may contribute to reduced oral intake (Knox, 1983). Finally, patients may develop aversions to the taste or smell of various foods. Aversions may range from mild to severe and are frequently reported in association with nausea-producing radiation or chemotherapy treatments (Bernstein, Wallace, Bernstein, Bleyer, Chard, & Hartmann, 1979; Nielsen, Theologides, & Vickers, 1980). Obviously, nutritional status can be seriously compromised if aversions develop to common or preferred dietary items.

Even when the desire to eat is intact, certain conditions may make it difficult for the individual to maintain adequate food intake. Tumor involvement in or near the gastrointestinal tract, the head, or the neck may interfere with swallowing or chewing food. As a consequence, gagging or pain may accompany attempts to chew or swallow. Bowel obstruction may trigger abdominal pains shortly after eating. Mucositis, causing painful mouth ulceration, is a common side effect of chemotherapy and may serve to reduce oral intake.

Eating may produce discomfort even after the primary physical limitation (e.g., bowel obstruction or mucositis) has been resolved (DeWys & Herbst, 1977). For example, our own clinical work (Redd, 1980a) suggests how a conditioned aversive response may develop through repeated association of eating with disease symptoms. The patient was a 53-year-old woman who had initially sought medical treatment when she began experiencing unusual throat sensations and gagging whenever she ate. Medical examination revealed carcinoma of the esophagus and the upper stomach, and radiation was prescribed. Treatment successfully shrank the tumor, and she became symptom-free. Unfortunately, 5 months later, her symptoms reappeared: immediately after eating, she would begin gagging and then regurgitate what she had just consumed. At this time, surgery was performed, and the tumor was removed. However, her symptoms persisted, and she became convinced that the cancer was still present. She was depressed and refused to eat; whenever food was presented, she became visibly agitated. Because no physical basis for her problem could be identified, it was hypothesized that her symptoms constituted a phobic reaction to solid foods. This conceptualization was based on recognition that, during two separate periods over the course of her disease, the patient had experienced repeated pairings of the unusual throat sensation, solid foods, and regurgitation. As a result, stimuli associated with "eating while experiencing unusual throat sensations" became conditioned stimuli capable of eliciting regurgitation.

A behavioral treatment program was implemented involving (1) pairing of deep-muscle relaxation training with consumption of small amounts of selected foods and

(2) alteration of the manner in which the nursing staff responded to her eating problem (i.e., rather than focusing on her refusal to eat, they focused on her trying to keep down small bites of food). After 2 1/2 weeks of *in vivo* desensitization and social reinforcement from medical staff, her eating problems were reduced. Within 3 weeks, she was able to retain solid foods and continued to improve until her discharge 2 weeks later. Follow-up evaluations at 3, 6, and 12 months revealed no recurrence of her eating problems or any other behavioral or psychological disorders.

In addition to specific eating disorders, the general activity level and performance status of the cancer patient may preclude adequate food intake. Chronic weakness and fatigue may hamper a patient's ability to shop for, prepare, or eat meals. Pain, nausea, or other disabilities may also limit these activities. Food consumption may also be reduced through the effects of the above conditions on the quality of the available meals. Less effort devoted to meal preparation is likely to result in less attractive meals and hence less eating, especially when taste or olfactory acuity has been reduced.

In addition to its impact on the patient's quality of life, nutritional status is also a significant factor in the treatment of cancer. Poor nutritional status may preclude the use of surgical procedures, chemotherapy, and radiation regimens. In patients who are receiving some form of antitumor therapy, improved nutritional status may increase the likelihood of response to treatment or the patient's ability to tolerate the toxic side effects of therapy. In turn, the patient's tolerance may allow the use of more aggressive—and hence, potentially more beneficial—therapeutic regimens.

Psychological Conditions

Few diseases have as great a psychological impact as cancer. Even before the formal diagnosis has been made, the possibility of cancer arouses anxiety. Indeed, patients often delay seeking medical attention because of the fear that the diagnosis will be cancer. Following the diagnosis and throughout the subsequent course of the disease, the likelihood of psychological and emotional disruption is high (Derogatis, Morrow, Fetting, Penman, Piasetsky, Schmale, Henrichs, & Carnicke, 1983; Meyerowitz, 1980; Silberfarb & Greer, 1982). Anxiety and depression are common. Derogatis *et al.* (1983), for instance, reported that 40% of a random sample of 215 cancer patients received DSM-III diagnoses for conditions in which depression, anxiety, or both were the prominent features. Cognitive impairments such as confusion, disorientation, forgetfulness, and unresponsiveness may also be evidenced. In a study of the psychosocial problems of homebound cancer patients, Wellisch *et al.* (1983) found such symptoms in 27% of their sample.

*Depression.*The incidence of depression in cancer patients has been the focus of a number of empirical studies (e.g., Bukberg, Penman, & Holland, 1984; Craig & Abeloff, 1974; Derogatis *et al.*, 1983; Levine, Silberfarb, & Lipowski, 1978; Plumb & Holland, 1977). Prevalence rates have varied considerably across this research. Plumb and Holland (1977), for example, reported a prevalence rate of 23%, whereas Levine *et al.* (1978) reported a rate of 56% (compared with prevalence rates in the 12%–to 30% range for general medical populations—Derogatis *et al.,* 1983). Variance in prevalence rates is very likely attributable to the variety of research methodologies used. For example, data collection methods have included patient interviews, retrospective examination of patient records, and paper-and-pencil measures. Patient characteristics have also varied across studies. Both inpatient and outpatient samples have been used, as well as groups of patients referred for psychiatric consultation. In perhaps the most comprehensive study to date, Derogatis *et al.* (1983) assessed 215 randomly selected inpatient and outpatient admissions to three different cancer centers. Information was obtained via a formal psychiatric interview as well as several symptom and psychiatric rating scales. Using DSM-III criteria, the authors reported that 6% of their sample evidenced a major affective disorder, 12% displayed an adjustment disorder with depressed mood, and 13% displayed an adjustment disorder with mixed anxious and depressed features.

The above studies all attempted to estimate the prevalence of depression in a sample of patients at a single point in time. Hence, they probably underestimated the occurrence of depression. Clinical observation suggests that nearly all cancer patients exhibit depressive symptoms at some time during the course of their disease. Depression may be evidenced by a range of affective, cognitive, and somatic symptoms, including dysphoric mood; tearfulness; guilt; impaired concentration; suicidal ideation; feelings of worthlessness, hopelessness, and helplessness; decreased libido, energy, or appetite; and sleep disturbance (Silberfarb, 1984). The specific constellation of symptoms observed varies across individuals, as does the temporal course of their expression. The symptoms may be chronic. Patients may exhibit lengthy periods of depression, frequently coinciding with initial diagnosis, recurrence, or entrance into a terminal phase of palliative care. On the other hand, the symptoms may be transitory, coinciding with the patients' temporary successes or failures in coping with the stresses imposed by their disease.

Although the experience of cancer is psychologically stressful for most patients, alterations in mood, thought, or behavior do not necessarily reflect a psychological reaction (Goldberg & Tull, 1983). Both medical and psychosocial factors may underlie the appearance of depressive symptoms. The potential medical origins of depressive symptoms in cancer patients involve both disease-related and iatrogenic factors. Examples of the former include (1) hypercalcemia (Segaloff, 1981; Weizman, Eldar, Shoenfeld, Hirschoro, Wijsenbeck, & Pinkhas, 1979); (2) liver failure (Schafer & Jones, 1982); (3) endocrine imbalances (Segaloff, 1981); (4) tumor-produced psychoactive hormonal substances (Brown & Paraskevas, 1982; Sachar, 1975); (5) decreased blood oxygen levels (Goldberg & Tull, 1983); and (6) central nervous system tumors or metastases (Nasrallah & McChesney, 1981; Posner, 1971). Depressive symptoms may also result from iatrogenic factors, including medications used to control pain and nausea, as well as a variety of chemotherapeutic agents. Examples of the latter include L-asparaginase, vinblastine, vincristine, and prednisone (Goldberg & Tull, 1983; Massie & Holland, 1984; Peterson & Popkin, 1980).

The potential psychosocial origins of depression in the individual with cancer are obvious and need not be elaborated in detail. Sadness, remorse, and guilt are experienced by many patients as they confront their own mortality. Feelings of helplessness and hopelessness are often experienced by patients during the long and often aversive course of treatment. Finally, sexual, social, occupational, and recreational activities are likely to be restricted or altered as a result of progressive disease or the impact of surgery, chemotherapy, or radiotherapy. Lethargy and sadness may be the consequence of such losses.

In summary, although depressive symptoms are common in cancer patients, only infrequently are these symptoms indicative of a major affective disorder. Rather, they are more likely to constitute a relatively transient response to the multiple psychosocial stresses associated with cancer (i.e., adjustment reaction) or to be attributable to the secondary effects of the disease and its treatment (i.e., secondary depression). Paradoxically, our experience suggests that medical staff are apt to attribute depressive symptomatology to psychosocial factors. The belief that "anyone would be depressed if she or he had cancer" often precludes careful evaluation of the potential medical causes of depressive symptoms. Although often difficult, correct attribution of depressive symptoms to either medical or psychosocial origins provides the foundation for effective therapeutic intervention. In general, medical factors should be considered first when evaluating a cancer patient who displays depressive symptoms (Goldberg & Tull, 1983). Frequently, the symptoms can be quickly alleviated by addressing the underlying medical cause. In addition, time-consuming and labor-intensive counseling or behaviorally oriented interventions (W. K. Sobel, 1981) are most suitable for depressions of psychosocial origin and may be largely ineffective when the symptoms stem from medical factors.

In general, major affective disorders and secondary depressions are distinguishable from adjustment reactions by the relative absence in the latter of prominent neurovegetative symptoms such as lethargy, anorexia, or sleep disturbance (Endicott, 1984; Peteet, 1979; Petty & Noyes, 1981). On the other hand, when more cognitively oriented symptoms, such as expressions of guilt, helplessness, or hopelessness, are prominent, depression of psychosocial origin is likely. Another clue to differential diagnosis is the relative chronicity of symptoms. Intermittent symptomatology with retention of the ability to display relatively normal or even cheerful mood suggests a depression that is psychosocial in origin (Endicott, 1984). The differential diagnosis of major affective disorders and secondary depressions may be the most difficult. A previous or family history of major affective disorder is significant. In its absence, it is likely that the depressive symptoms are secondary to some disease-related or iatrogenic factor. If a major affective disorder is involved, treatment with tricyclic antidepressants is indicated (Massie & Holland, 1984). As antidepressant effects are not immediately apparent, 1 or 2 weeks may be necessary to evaluate treatment success or failure (Goldberg & Tull, 1983).

Anxiety. It is frequently stated that cancer is the most dreaded disease of our time. Certainly, there are few diseases that arouse more anxiety (Greer & Silberfarb, 1982). In research similar to that on depression, a number of studies have attempted to assess the prevalence of anxiety in cancer patients (e.g., Craig & Abeloff, 1974; Derogatis *et al.*, 1983; Lee & Maguire, 1975; Morris, Greer, & White, 1977). Unfortunately, it is difficult to estimate the prevalence of anxiety in this population because the research methodologies and the sample characteristics have generally varied quite dramatically across these investigations. Nevertheless, it is probably fair to conclude that, although anxiety is a common experience for cancer patients, a minority of patients exhibit conditions that would merit formal DSM-III diagnosis. For example, in a study of psychiatric disorders among a random sample of cancer patients, Derogatis *et al.* (1983) reported that only 21% received DSM-III diagnoses with anxiety as a prominent symptom. Over 90% of these anxiety-related diagnoses were reactive in nature (i.e., adjustment disorders with anxious mood or mixed emotional features).

A number of specific fears and anxieties commonly associated with cancer have been identified (Pattison, 1978). These include a fear of death and the unknown, as well as fears of suffering and pain, loss of self-control, and loneliness. In addition to these general issues, a more specialized set of concerns may be uniquely associated with various disease sites. For example, much has been written about the psychological sequelae of mastectomy (Meyerowitz, 1980), including fears of loss of sexual identity, disfigurement, and abandonment. Similar concerns are common among patients with head and neck, gynecological, or genitourinary cancers. Cancers of the latter two sites may also arouse fears of impaired sexual performance and loss of fertility.

Anxiety may also vary as a function of the stage of the disease. Throughout the course of their disease, patients must cope with considerable uncertainty. Because uncertainty is likely to breed anxiety, periods of high uncertainty are also likely to be highly stressful. For example, Hughes (1982) found anxiety to be elevated in patients awaiting biopsy results. Interestingly, the anxiety associated with uncertainty may be greater than that associated with confirmation of the diagnosis (although in the latter case, denial or psychological "numbing" may mitigate the immediate experience and expression of anxiety). Uncertainty also underlies the fears of disease recurrence experienced by patients who are no longer receiving active treatment. During this time, patients who are "cured" or in remission may vigilantly monitor their physical status. Any new or different ache, pain, or physical sensation may trigger anxiety if it is perceived as signaling recurrence (Quint, 1963). The fear of recurrence may also underlie the somewhat paradoxical observation that many patients experience anxiety and depression at the conclusion of a course of chemotherapy or radiotherapy (Gorzynski & Holland, 1979; Krant, 1981). Even if the therapy has been an aversive one, there may be a certain comfort in the knowledge that some active measures are being taken to combat the disease. Of course, when and if recurrence occurs, significant anxiety is likely to be experienced. In a study of breast cancer patients, Silberfarb, Maurer, and Crouthamel (1980) reported more anxiety associated with the time of first recurrence than with the period of time postmastectomy or at the time that a final treatment course was initiated in patients for whom all other therapeutic options had been exhausted.

Certain medical procedures used in the treatment of cancer may also be a significant source of anxiety for the patient (Redd & Hendler, 1983). Patients may come to fear aversive procedures such as bone marrow aspirations or lumbar punctures (Katz, Kellerman, & Siegel, 1980). Chemotherapy (Redd et al., 1985) and radiation treatments (Peck & Boland, 1977) may also trigger anxiety reactions, particularly when they produce relatively immediate aversive side effects, such as nausea and vomiting. The repetitive nature of these procedures provides the patient ample opportunity to display anxiety in anticipating them. In extreme cases, patients may report being preoccupied and overwhelmed by fear and anxiety for several days before a scheduled procedure.

In addition to the inherent aversiveness to the patient, the presence of significant levels of anxiety may make it more difficult for medical staff to complete the required treatment procedures. For example, anxiety may initially make it difficult for staff to find a "good vein" when inserting an intravenous line. Anxiety may escalate even further during repeated unsuccessful needle sticks, making insertion even more difficult.

State anxiety has also been linked to the development of anticipatory nausea in cancer chemotherapy (Andrykowski et al., 1985; Redd & Andrykowski, 1982). In a prospective study of the development of anticipatory nausea, Andrykowski et al. (1985) found that patients who subsequently developed anticipatory nausea evidenced higher levels of anxiety (than patients who did not develop anticipatory nausea) in conjunction with their initial two chemotherapy infusions. The exact process by which anxiety contributes to the development of anticipatory nausea is unclear, however. Anxiety may directly facilitate the acquisition of classically conditioned responses (Spence, 1964). Alternatively, anxiety may indirectly facilitate the development of anticipatory nausea by increasing the magnitude of posttreatment nausea or the length of time required for drug infusion. These latter two factors were also found to characterize patients who developed anticipatory nausea (Andrykowski et al., 1985).

Finally, procedure-related anxiety reactions may motivate a patient to refuse certain forms of treatment. A patient may elect to forego treatment entirely or to switch to a less effective form of treatment in order to avoid a particular dreaded procedure. For example, patients may elect to "take their chances" with a clinically less effective oral chemotherapy regimen rather than undergo the frequent needle sticks associated with a potentially more effective intravenous regimen.

Cognitive Impairment. Mental status changes are frequently observed in cancer patients and may be evidenced by a wide range of specific symptoms. Memory, concentration, reasoning, and judgment may be adversely affected. Confusion and disorientation may be present. Behavioral symptoms may be prominent, including disruption of normal sleep patterns, irritability, inappropriate or "out-of-character" behavior, or alteration in psychomotor activity levels ranging from excitement to apathy and stupor. Two basic syndromes are often distinguished: delirium and dementia (Fetting, 1982). Delirium is characterized by frequent transitory symptoms of disorientation, impaired recall and recent memory, poor attention span, and, in extreme cases, delusions and hallucinations. The onset is typically acute. Dementia is characterized by memory loss and personality changes, such as apathy and withdrawal. The onset is insidious. Both delirium and dementia are associated with organic brain syndromes, and research suggests that the incidence of such disorders may be relatively high in cancer patients. For example, Levine, et al. (1978) reported that 40% of their sample of cancer patients referred for psychiatric consultation were diagnosed as having an organic brain syndrome, and Derogatis et al. (1983) reported a prevalence rate of 8% in their random sample of cancer patients.

The presence of impaired cognitive functioning in cancer patients is significant in several respects. First, evidence suggests that such impairments are associated with a poor prognosis (Rabins & Folstein, 1982). Second, even when mild, such symptoms are distressing to both the patient and the family, as the patient's ability to perform routine vocational and social roles may be compromised. Finally, impaired mental status may diminish patients' ability to participate and cooperate in their treatment program (e.g., to provide informed consent).

Despite their frequency and importance, symptoms of cognitive impairment are often overlooked. Recognition may be difficult because the symptoms may be mild or transitory. Even when their presence is noted, they are likely to be misdiagnosed. In particular, mental status changes are often mistaken for reactive (i.e., psychosocial) depression (Levine et al., 1978). Unfortunately, the attribution of such symptoms to a patient's emotional reaction to cancer limits the possibilities for modifying or reversing these symptoms. A variety of physiological factors can produce changes in mental status. Often, appropriate treatment simply involves recognition and correction (if possible) of the underlying medical condition.

Mental status changes may be systemic or iatrogenic in origin. Foremost among the systemic factors is tumor or metastatic involvement of the CNS (Levine et al., 1978; Posner, 1971). For example, clouding of consciousness is present in about 80% of patients with cerebral neoplasms (Levine *et al.*, 1978). Other potential systemic sources of mental status changes include (1) tumor-produced CNS toxins, such as parathormone or vasopressin (Bartuska, 1975); (2) metabolic disorders such as hypocalcemia (Weizman *et al.*, 1979), hyponatremia (Gehi, Rosenthal, Fizette, Crowe, & Webb, 1981), or hypomagnesemia (Webb & Gehi, 1981); (3) liver failure (Schafer & Jones, 1982); (4) low blood oxygen levels (Goldberg & Tull, 1983); and, (5) nonbacterial thrombotic endocarditis (Reagan & Okazaki, 1974).

Iatrogenic factors may also underlie the cognitive impairments associated with cancer. The effects of cytotoxic chemotherapy on cognitive functioning have often been cited (Peterson & Popkin, 1980; Silberfarb, 1983; Silberfarb, Philibert, & Levine, 1980; Young & Posner, 1980). Certain types of drugs are associated with a higher risk of such symptoms, including prednisone, procarbazine, 5-fluorouracil, vincristine, L-asparaginase, methotrexate, and doxorubicin (Goldberg & Tull, 1983; Peterson & Popkin, 1980; Young & Posner, 1980). The majority of symptoms are acute and appear shortly after drug administration. However, symptoms may initially appear after a substantial time lag and thus may be incorrectly attributed to other more temporally contiguous sources. Fortunately, most chemotherapy-induced cognitive impairments are dose-related and reversible (Peterson & Popkin, 1980).

Relative to chemotherapy, the impact of radiation therapy on cognitive functioning in cancer patients has received less attention. The major focus has been the neuropsychological impact of prophylactic brain irradiation on children and adolescents receiving treatment for acute lymphoblastic leukemia. Although some studies have not discovered any neuropsychological deficits after cranial irradiation (Soni, Marten, Pitner, Duenas, & Powazek, 1975; Verzosa, Aur, Simone, Hustu, & Pinkel, 1976), the majority of studies have found some deficits in academic achievement, overall intellectual functioning, short-term memory, and attention and concentration (Gluck, Baron, Brallier, Fink & Leiken, 1980; Ivnik, Colligan, Obetz, & Smithson, 1981; McIntosh, Klatskin, O'Brien, Aspnes, Kammerer, Snead, Kalavsky, and Pearson, 1976; Meadows, Gordon Massari, Littman, Fergusson, & Moss, 1981; Moss, Nannis, & Poplack, 1981). Unfortunately, it is difficult to attribute these impairments solely to the impact of cranial irradiation because the latter is often used in combination with systemic chemotherapy or intrathecal methotrexate. In addition, the observed impairments may be attributable to the disruptive psychosocial effects of the diagnosis of cancer and the prolonged and intensive course of treatment that is required. Anxiety, missed school, and disrupted peer relationships may contribute to subsequently impaired cognitive functioning (Tamaroff, Miller, Murphy, Salwen, Ghavimi, & Nir, 1982).

Finally, mental status changes may be produced by the drugs used to control other symptoms frequently associated with cancer. For example, hypnosedatives for insomnia, benzodiazepines for anxiety, and narcotic analgesics for pain may all product symptoms associated with cognitive impairment (Silberfarb, 1984). Again, such symptoms are reversible and may disappear after appropriate drug or dosage modification.

Social Conditions

The primary contribution of the biopsychosocial model is its emphasis on the multiple forces that shape the experience and behavior of the cancer patient. This model stresses that patients do not exist in a social vacuum. Rather, they are embedded in a network of relationships involving their immediate family, relatives, friends, and medical staff. The impact of medical staff and of the social and physical environment within which medical care occurs is particularly salient for the patient who is hospitalized or otherwise placed in a long-term care facility (e.g., a nursing home).

Two social conditions frequently encountered during the course of cancer are isolation and loss of control. In some instances, these conditions may be clinically significant, requiring direct intervention themselves. In other instances, their importance lies in the recognition of their role in the etiology of other maladaptive responses (e.g., psychosomatic symptomatology and anger) associated with this population of patients (Redd, 1982a; Redd & Hendler, 1983).

Loss of Control. Retaining a sense of personal control is important for most individuals. Control may be a particularly salient issue for the individual with cancer (Cassileth, Zupkis, Sutton-Smith, & March, 1980; Trillin, 1981), as there is little that the individual can do to significantly affect the course of the disease. Nearly complete reliance on the physician and other members of the medical team is often required. Apart from perhaps minor dietary adjustments, the patient is asked simply to undergo treatment—and wait (Burish & Lyles, 1983; Silberfarb, 1984). Indeed, the appeal of many current unconventional modes of cancer therapy (such as special diets, exercise programs, or visual imaging) may reflect the patient's desire to experience some degree of personal control over the course of his or her disease (Burish & Lyles, 1983; Silberfarb, 1984).

The lack of control can have a variety of consequences. Most notable is the anxiety and depression that may be linked to the experience of helplessness (Abramson, Seligman, & Teasdale, 1978; Averill, 1973). In addition, the unacceptable (from the perspective of the medical staff) behavior of the so-called problem patient may be usefully construed in terms of the concept of control. Frequently, patients who complain, ask "too many" questions, or are otherwise unusually demanding of medical staff are identified as problem patients. Similar behavior may be directed toward family members. Patients may become angry and agitated when their requests are ignored and their opinions appear not to be valued. The more the patient feels that his or her questions are not taken seriously, the more the patient may attempt to exert control (Kastenbaum, 1978). Indeed, a negative spiral may develop, with staff and family writing off the patient as difficult and the patient reacting by being more difficult and demanding, all because he or she is trying to gain control over, or at least to influence, what is happening. In some instances, family members may respond by reducing the frequency of visits. Staff, on the other hand, often react by rigidly refusing to accede to the patient's demands in order to avoid being "inappropriately" controlled by the patient. Either response may actually serve to exacerbate the problem by legitimizing the patient's beliefs that his or her actions have no impact on the course of treatment.

The desire for control is not evident in all patients. It may be hypothesized, however, that patients who have experienced a high degree of control in their life before the diagnosis of cancer are most likely to feel the impact of its loss. Family and medical staff should be cognizant of the legitimacy and subjective importance of a patient's desire for control. This desire may be adaptively satisfied through generous provision of information to patients about their disease and treatment. Aversive expressions of the desire for control may also be reduced by allowing patients the opportunity for exercising behavioral options and choices (Kastenbaum, 1978).

Isolation. During the protracted course of cancer treatment, patients often must tolerate repeated hospitalizations and lengthy periods of homebound recuperation. Routine life activities that provide structure, purpose, and enjoyment are disrupted and, for some patients, never return. For cancer patients, the form and length of isolation are often extreme. Because of reduced immunocompetence, many cancer patients must be placed in reverse isolation. During these periods, the patient is restricted to a single hospital room, and all visitors must wear gowns, masks, and gloves. Physical contact, even between family members, is forbidden. In extreme instances, the patient is placed in a "germ-free" environment (i.e., a plastic bubble) in which he or she is separated from visitors by a glass screen.

Needless to say, such circumstances reduce social interaction and contribute to a pateint's feeling of isolation. One effect of reverse isolation is a reduction in the absolute number of visitors. Because of the extra time needed to complete scrubbing and gowning procedures, medical staff are discouraged from making casual, social visits. Moreover, visits by family and friends often decrease because of the need to reduce the patient's exposure to colds or flu. Additionally, some people may avoid the patient because of their own anxiety associated with terminal disease. Patients frequently report that friends "don't know what to say" and make excuses for cutting their visits short. One of our patients found that her relationship with her fiancé had changed during her hospitalizations; in her words, "He treats me like a patient; he is overly nice, obliging, almost condescending." Rather than providing her comfort and support, he inadvertently made her feel isolated and deviant. Similar feelings may occur when family and friends communicate the misguided belief that they can catch the disease or, when the patient is receiving radiation treatments, that the patient is radioactive (Burish & Lyles, 1983; Rotman, Rogow, DeLeon, & Heskel, 1977).

A major thrust of work for those responsible for the psychosocial care of cancer patients should be helping patients understand the reactions of family and friends. In some cases, the patient is able to discuss these issues with the individuals involved, but unfortunately, this is the exception rather than the rule. It is this emotional isolation from family and friends that some patients experience that often underlies their development of strong bonds with individual staff members ?with whom they are able to communicate more openly.

In addition to these emotional reactions, some patients develop significant behavior problems as a result of restrictive isolation. Two especially clear examples were provided by Redd (1980a,b) in his clinical research on the role of social factors in the occurrence of medical symptoms. While a consultant to the UCLA surgical oncology service, he observed that the symptom behaviors (e.g., coughing, retching, and complaining of pain) of some patients varied as a function of social-environmental conditions. The pattern was similar to what Fordyce (1973, 1976) identified in chronic pain patients: in some cases, complaining, pressing the nurses' call button, and so on, appeared to be controlled by the social consequences (i.e., staff attention) they produced. This relationship was especially clear in two leukemia patients (one male, one female) in reverse isolation following bone marrow transplantation. Redd (1980b) observed that behavioral symptoms such as coughing, retching, or choking tended to worsen when house staff were present. After careful analysis, he found that the symptoms occurred significantly more often when nurses entered the room. In fact, the nurses appeared to evoke the patients' symptoms. As soon as a nurse entered the room, the frequency of the symptoms increased. This increase, in turn, resulted in the nurses's spending extra time checking on the patient's condition and trying to make him or her more comfortable. The nurse's care apparently served to reinforce the occurrence of the symptoms. When individual nurses were taught simple behavioral techniques, such as extinction (i.e., ignoring the symptoms after checking the patient's condition and verifying the absence of any physical cause or irritation) and differential positive reinforcement (i.e., providing extra attention and praise whenever the patient did not emit the symptom behavior), the symptoms decreased in frequency during those times when the nurse was present. In the presence of other staff or family, the symptoms continued. When all nurses and staff implemented the behavioral intervention, the symptoms ceased and did not reappear.

Psychosomatic symptoms and excessive complaints of distress may also develop independently of social contingencies. Isolation can cause patients to become increasingly sensitized to bodily sensations. As a result, they may attend to sensations that might otherwise have gone unnoticed. Reporting of these insignificant sensations to medical staff is encouraged by the patient's well-intentioned desire to provide information that may facilitate treatment as well as by the care and attention they elicit from staff (Redd, 1982a).

Psychosocial Intervention in Cancer Care

Although not an exhaustive discussion, the preceding section illustrates the wide range of problems that may be presented by the individual with cancer. Consistent with a biopsychosocial framework, biological, social, and psychological factors may be involved in the etiology, the expression, or the maintenance of many problem conditions. Even such apparently physiological conditions as pain, nausea, or nutritional problems may have psychosocial components. Thus, comprehensive care of the cancer patient requires an appropriate combination of medical and psychosocial intervention. This section focuses on the contribution of the psychosocially oriented clinician to the comprehensive care of the cancer patient. We begin by discussing the traditional psychiatric-psychological approach to intervention with this population. This discussion is followed by an examination of relatively recent problem-oriented approaches to intervention. The section concludes with a detailed presentation of the emerging behavioral approach to management of the biopsychosocial problems presented by cancer patients.

Traditional Psychosocial Intervention Approaches

The range of psychosocial interventions considered suitable for use with cancer patients is constrained to a large degree by conceptions of the predominant psychosocial needs of this population. Cancer has always been associated with death. In part, this association is evidenced by the common lay perception of the diagnosis of cancer as being akin to a "death sentence." This perception, in turn, has fostered the belief that the primary psychosocial needs of the cancer patient revolve around "death and dying" issues. Most clinicians presume that cancer is emotionally traumatic, and indeed, research provides ample documentation of the emotional disequilibrium associated with cancer (Derogatis et al., 1983; Meyerowitz, 1980; Silberfarb & Greer, 1982). As a result, the traditional goal of psychosocial intervention has been the provision of emotional support for coping with the awareness of impending death.

In order to accomplish this goal, traditional counseling or psychotherapeutic modes of intervention have been used. Within this framework, the specific techniques, goals, and focal issues have varied (e.g., Cassem & Stewart, 1975; Feigenberg & Shneidman, 1979; Kastenbaum & Aisenberg, 1972; Shneidman, 1978; Weisman, 1972). McKitrick (1981–1982), for instance, identified a number of distinct therapeutic viewpoints, including psychoanalytic (Eissler, 1955), patient-centered (Feigenberg, 1975), self-actualization (Bowers, Jackson, Knight, & LeShan, 1964), insight (Rosenthal, 1957), and stage (Kubler-Ross, 1969, 1970). (Although all of these authors have identified their strategies as suitable for all dying patients, their recommendations have been based on their experience with cancer patients.) Such supportive psychotherapy is typically offered on an individual basis; however, group (Spiegel, 1979; Yalom & Greaves, 1977) and combinations of group and individual approaches have also been used (Ferlic, Goldman, & Kennedy, 1979). Data on the impact of this type of intervention are quite limited, although empirical evaluations have become more common in recent years (e.g., Ferlic et al., 1979; Linn, Linn, & Harris, 1982; Spiegel, Bloom, & Yalom, 1981). In general, however, the results of this research are equivocal, partly, perhaps, because of the methodological inadequacies that characterize the majority of studies in this area. Common methodological problems include a failure to precisely describe the characteristics of the sample of cancer patients examined or the type of support program offered; the absence of an appropriate control group; the lack of an objective, impartial evaluation of the therapeutic outcome; and a failure to report statistical analyses or attrition rates (Watson, 1983).

In addition to a lack of convincing evidence of its effectiveness, the traditional approach to the psychosocial care of the cancer patient raises several conceptual issues as well. Unresolved are questions concerning the appropriate target population for this type of intervention, as well as its appropriate goals. Each of these issues is examined here in turn.

Because cancer can produce emotional trauma, the assumption is often made that all cancer patients need and want a supportive, emotion-focused therapeutic intervention. In our view, this is an inaccurate assumption. Insofar as need is concerned, Weisman (1979) found that many patients require little or no professional assistance. Clinical experience reveals a number of patients who appear to be psychologically healthy and well adjusted throughout the course of their disease. Although denial may be involved, its presence is impossible to document unequivocally. Rather, these patients may experience a significant amount of stress, yet cope well on their own because of their ability to draw on personal or environmental resources such as religious beliefs, social supports, or feelings of self-efficacy. Even when a need for appropriate therapy exists, the patient may not desire professional assistance (Liss-Levinson, 1982a,b; Worden & Weisman, 1980). This situation may arise from several circumstances. Need is a subjectively defined phenomenon. Hence, patients may reject therapy because they do not perceive the need for assistance. Alternatively, a patient may reject professional assistance because of a desire to "tough it out" alone. Finally, professional assistance may be rejected because the patient's needs and values are inconsistent with the type of assistance offered. Some patients may view traditional, emotion-focused interventions as foolish, useless, threatening, or disconcerting. Patients may also resist psychological assistance in order to avoid the implication that they are "crazy."

Another issue raised by the traditional approach to the psychosocial care of the cancer patient concerns the appropriate goal of intervention. It is often not clear what providing emotional support and assistance is expected to achieve. Some specific (although still quite general) goals have been identified, such as provision of hope (Eissler, 1955); assistance in coping with fear and guilt (Rosenthal, 1957); self-actualization (Bowers *et al.*, 1964); or psychological comfort (Shneidman, 1978). Frequently, the goal is described as enabling the patient to achieve a "good" or "appropriate" death (Weisman, 1970). Of course, what constitutes a good or appropriate death is subject to considerable debate because it is likely to be heavily influenced by a therapist's personal values and perceptions of what the patient "needs." Weisman (1970) suggested, however, that the criteria for an appropriate death are patient-specific. That is, a death is appropriate when the patient views death and lives out his or her dying in a fashion consistent with the patient's own pattern of coping, own definition of the meaning of death, and own life context. Far too frequently, however, we find that this pluralistic concept of an "appropriate" death is confused with a more proscribed concept of an "ideal" death.

In our experience, the definition of what constitutes an "ideal" death has been heavily influenced by Kubler-Ross's model (1969) of the process of dying. According to Kubler-Ross, patients pass through a series of five distinct stages between the diagnosis of a terminal illness and their ultimate death. The specific stages are denial, anger, bargaining, depression, and acceptance. The final stage of acceptance is characterized by an absence of negative emotions such as depression, anger, or envy of the living. The person no longer struggles against death and lives out her or his remaining days quietly and peacefully. It is Kubler-Ross's concept of this final stage of acceptance that has become specifically associated with the notion of an "ideal" death.

Although Kubler-Ross's work has attained wide acceptance among both professionals and laypeople, it is not without its critics. The existence of the various stages of dying identified by Kubler-Ross has been questioned (Pattison, 1976; Schulz & Aderman, 1974). It has been suggested that, rather than progressing through stages, patients tend to adopt a particular pattern of emotional response that they then maintain until death. For example, some patients may initially react with denial to the diagnosis of cancer and many continue to evidence denial throughout the course of the disease. Other patients, perhaps after an initial period of denial, may evidence a consistent pattern of anger or depression. Even if the sequence of stages were found to have some clear, objective existence, the issue remains whether these stages constitute a naturally occurring phenomenon. Charmaz (1980) suggested that the stages of dying are "real" but are a consequence of how illness and dying are handled in Western society. Rather than being a natural process of adjustment to death, the various stages are the products of a subtle process of socialization initiated by family and medical staff. For example, denial in cancer patients may not stem from the coping needs of the patient alone but may be cued by the patient's awareness of the denial that is evidenced by family or staff.

A final criticism centers on the use of Kubler-Ross's model of the process of dying as a guide for the provision of psychosocial care. According to Kubler-Ross (1969, 1970) the role of the therapist is to facilitate movement of the patient through the various stages until the ultimate goal of acceptance of death has been attained. In our view, however, the notion that all patients must be assisted toward a final stage of peaceful acceptance of death can result in the therapist's imposition of a set of inappropriate expectations on the patient. There is the very real risk that such preconceptions may make the therapist less sensitive to the patient's own needs and wishes than he or she would otherwise be. Indeed, patients who never evidence a peaceful acceptance of death are likely to be labeled as neurotic or pathological. From the patient's perspective, there is no reason to believe that dying in a stage of acceptance is inherently more adaptive than dying in a stage of anger, depression, or denial. Medical staff, however, have a clear preference for patients who evidence acceptance of their impending death. Such calm and quiescent patients are less stressful to work with because they pose fewer management problems.

In defense of Kubler-Ross, we must acknowledge that she herself has been disturbed by many practitioners' rigid adherence to her model. Careful reading of her work (Kubler-Ross, 1969) reveals her presentation of a number of counterexamples and exceptions to her stage theory. It is indeed unfortunate that her ideas have been oversold to the health professions and the general public. Rather than constituting a rich and insightful description of the many psychological nuances evident while human beings cope with death, her stage theory has become a prescription for death. Rather than fitting patients into the procrustean bed that Kubler-Ross's stages have become, we embrace the concept of a plurality of dying. There are as many ways of dying as there are ways of living, and practitioners may need to become less concerned about how patients should die and more attuned to how patients would prefer to die. In most instances, this will be in a fashion consistent with their self-concept and the manner in which they have faced life (Liss-Levinson, 1982b; Shneidman, 1978).

Problem-Oriented Intervention Approaches

The increased life expectancy of cancer patients has had a significant impact on the psychosocial care of this population. For many patients, coping with death is no longer of primary concern, and increased recognition is now being given to helping patients live with the disease and the problems it raises in everyday living (e.g., Meyerowitz et al., 1983; Wellisch, et al., 1983). As our discussion has indicated, social, vocational, somatic, sexual, and cosmetic, as well as emotional concerns need to be addressed. As a result, programs of psychosocial support of the cancer patient have undergone expansion. Less frequently are "death and dying" issues the primary focus. Increasingly, intervention is directed toward assisting the cancer patient in confronting a broad spectrum of day-to-day disease-related difficulties (e.g., Gordon et al., 1980).

Reports of a number of different interventions of this more problem-oriented nature have appeared in the literature (e.g., Capone, Good, Weste, & Jacobson, 1980; Gordon et al., 1980; Jacobs, Ross, Walker, & Stockdale, 1983; Maguire, Brooke, Tait, Thomas, & Sellwood, 1983; Pfefferbaum, Pasnau, Jamison, & Wellisch, 1977–1978; Winick & Robbins, 1976). The specific form of these intervention programs varies widely. Some provide psychosocial care on an individual basis (e.g., Gordon et al., 1980), whereas others involve a group format (e.g., Capone et al., 1980; Jacobs et al., 1983). Some programs are designed to incorporate a variety of cancer patients, and others provide assistance to specific subgroups of patients. For example, programs have been offered for particular diagnostic groups, such as those with genital malignancies (Capone et al.,

1980) or Hodgkin's disease (Jacobs *et al.*, 1983). Alternatively, intervention has been directed at patients undergoing particular treatment procedures, such as mastectomy (Maguire *et al.*, 1983; Pfefferbaum *et al.*, 1977–1978; Winick & Robbins, 1976).

Generally speaking, the problem-oriented approach to psychosocial intervention focuses on the provision of emotional support as well as education. Patients are provided information regarding particular practical, everyday difficulties. In addition, information is provided on specific coping techniques and rehabilitative resources available in the community. The systematic inclusion of this latter informational component is what distinguishes this class of problem-oriented interventions from the traditional, emotion-focused approach to the psychosocial care of the cancer patient.

Behavioral Intervention in Cancer Care

Remediation of the immediate, practical (as opposed to existential) issues surrounding cancer and its treatment has received even greater attention since the advent of behavioral medicine. In recent years, behaviorally oriented clinicians have made great strides in developing techniques for reducing treatment side effects and psychosomatic symptoms in adults and children (e.g., Burish *et al.*, 1985; Morrow & Morrel, 1982; Redd, 1982a; Redd, Andresen, & Minagawa, 1982). Indeed, before 1981, the notion of behavioral medicine within comprehensive cancer care had not even been mentioned in the literature. Yet, today, "behavioral-psychosocial oncology" merits discussion in professional journals in a variety of disciplines (i.e., medicine, psychology, nursing, social work, rehabilitation, and pastoral counseling). This new application of behavioral psychology is not introduced as a replacement for traditional, one-to-one supportive psychotherapy and counseling. Rather, behavioral procedures are proposed as an adjunct to more traditional psychosocial intervention methods in order to treat problems heretofore unaddressed (Redd & Hendler, 1983).

The primary goal of behavioral intervention is the relatively direct modification of maladaptive behavior rather than the uncovering of deep-seated psychological conflicts and defenses. In almost all instances, intervention is (1) focused on the remediation of immediate (i.e., concrete) symptoms; (2) individualized in accordance with the patient's experience and preferences; (3) time-limited; (4) evaluated in terms of objectively observable changes in patient behavior; and (5) discarded, altered, or maintained, depending on the patient's response.

In general, we have encountered widespread acceptance and endorsement of this approach among oncologists and health-care staff familiar with behavioral conceptualizations and interventions. We believe that there are at least five reasons:

1. As will be shown in the subsequent discussion, behavioral techniques have been shown to be effective in reducing concrete problems that disrupt medical treatment and that are often refractory to traditional medical interventions.

2. The intervention strategies used in behavioral medicine (i.e., time-limited intervention, reliance on the direct assessment of treatment impact, and continuous monitoring of patient progress) are consistent with those used in medical oncology. In a very real sense, the behavioral clinician and the oncologist share a common strategy for assessing the impact of treatment and deciding what to do next. Although the behavioral clinician certainly uses clinical judgment and practices an "art," his or her orientation can be characterized as empirical rather than theoretical. That is, the techniques used are generally

derived from empirical research and observation, rather than from psychological or psychiatric theory.

3. The criteria used to evaluate the outcome of intervention are observable. Thus, all individuals involved in the case (including the patient) are able to "see for themselves" whether the behavioral intervention is having the desired effect. A "trained eye," able to detect subtle changes in function, is not required. If it works, everyone can see the results.

4. Patients are generally open to behavioral intervention because they do not believe that its use implies that they are "crazy," weak, or otherwise maladjusted (as many believe is implied by a psychiatric consultation and intervention) (Hendler & Redd, 1985). Indeed, in our clinical work, we rarely encounter patients who refuse behavioral intervention, and a growing number of patients actually request such assistance on their own (the most frequent self-referral is for anxiety and symptom reduction).

5. Behavioral intervention and its successful remediation of practical problems of medical treatment do not represent a challenge to the competence of the other members of the health-care team. Before the advent of behavioral medicine in oncology, no one saw "behavioral problems" as his or her responsibility. Indeed, in most cases, behavioral problems were not even addressed. If they were recognized, they were seen as unavoidable or as reason for psychiatric referral. At the present time, at least, the use of behavioral methods within medical oncology does not arouse any professional "turf" issues.

It is also worth adding that we have not encountered ethical or religious objections to our use of behavioral interventions. Despite H. J. Sobel's warnings (1981) that some may find the notion of applying behavioral methods in the context of fatal illness repugnant and inhumane, we have not found this to be the case. Neither patients nor staff have expressed reservations regarding behavioral intervention. Although some patients may report an initial fear of hypnosis, such misgivings are more related to the use of the term *hypnosis* itself rather than to the actual behavioral procedures used (Hendler & Redd, 1985). In over 8 years of participation in research and patient care in both university and private inpatient and outpatient oncology units, we have never had a patient terminate ongoing behavior therapy.

It must be stressed that this area of behavioral-psychosocial oncology is relatively new (less than 8 years have passed since the publication of the first report of the successful application of behavioral principles with cancer patients). Hence, current research and clinical practice are embryonic and primitive in many ways. As indicated earlier in this chapter, behavioral interventions have been used with adults to treat psychosomatic symptoms (Redd, 1980b, 1982b) and phobic reactions (Redd, 1980a). However, the research in these areas has not progressed beyond the use of case-study methodologies. Greater and more systematic attention has been devoted to the behavioral analysis and control of the posttreatment and conditioned side effects of chemotherapy in both adolescents and adults (Burish *et al.*, 1985), and to the use of behavioral intervention to reduce pain and anxiety in children undergoing bone marrow aspirations and lumbar punctures (Jay & Elliott, 1984). The discussion that follows focuses on these two areas of application because the intervention procedures used clearly demonstrate the application of behavioral methodology in the treatment of chronic, life-threatening disease.

Aversion Reactions to Chemotherapy. In addition to severe nausea and emesis following chemotherapy infusions, at least 25% of chemotherapy patients develop anticipatory side effects. That is, they become nauseated and/or vomit *before* treatments. Nausea or emesis may occur as they approach the hospital for treatment, when they see the oncology nurses, or as the nurse prepares for the infusion. Some patients report that even talking about chemotherapy makes them nauseated; others state that they are nauseated the entire day before treatment.

Anticipatory nausea or emesis is the result of respondent conditioning (Andrykowski, Redd, & Hatfield, 1985). Through repeated association with chemotherapy and its aversive aftereffects, previously neutral stimuli (e.g., the sights, sounds, and smells of the treatment environment) acquire nausea- or emesis-eliciting properties. It should also be noted that such conditioned aversion reactions can be cognitively mediated. As was pointed out earlier, some patients report becoming nauseated while merely thinking about treatment.

The behavioral interventions that have been devised to control the anticipatory side effects of chemotherapy clearly demonstrate the general strategy of behavioral intervention: (1) a focus on observable and concrete problems; (2) individualized treatment; (3) adjustments during the course of treatment to meet patient needs; (4) time-limited intervention; and (5) an evaluation of treatment outcome in terms of readily observable changes in patient behavior. A variety of behavioral procedures have been successfully used to control anticipatory side effects, and they share important characteristics.

Using an individual-analysis, multiple-baseline design, Redd et al. (1982) employed therapist-directed passive muscle-relaxation with guided imagery (a hypnosislike procedure) to control anticipatory nausea or vomiting in women undergoing adjuvant chemotherapy for breast cancer. The patients were first seen by a therapist who taught them a self-relaxation technique. With the patient seated in a comfortable chair located in a quiet room, the therapist began by asking her to stare at a point on the wall or to close her eyes. He then instructed the patient to focus her attention on the sensations present in different muscle groups. The therapist then systematically progressed across the body, describing feelings of relaxation and comfort in various muscle groups, such as the arms, the legs, the neck, the back, or the lower torso. The procedure was quite similar to a visual fixation induction that might be used in traditional hypnosis. After the patient was quiet and still, the therapist described several relaxing images, and the patient was asked to focus her attention on them. Images that most patients find comforting, like a quiet beach on a warm day or a grassy field in the springtime, were typically used. If the patient had a particular scene that was personally relaxing, then its use was encouraged. For example, for one patient who enjoyed thinking about a cozy den with plush carpeting, overstuffed furniture, and a fireplace, the induction was individualized. She learned to relax by concentrating on sinking into the cushions of a chair while looking at the various colors of the fire. Detailed descriptions of relevant colors, scents, textures, and sounds added to the patient's involvement in the image.

After two training sessions, the therapist directed the patient through these relaxation procedures before and during regular chemotherapy infusions. If, during a chemotherapy infusion, it appeared that the patient was likely to start gagging and retching, the therapists elaborated the imagery by providing greater detail (e.g., "You're at the beach—feel the sand under your toes while the cool water rolls over your feet"). The basic strategy then involved careful monitoring the patient's behavior to obtain feedback on how well the procedure was working and when to adjust it.

Immediate decreases in nausea before and during chemotherapy were reported by all patients whenever the relaxation and imagery intervention was used. Moreover, anticipatory vomiting was eliminated in all patients when this procedure was used. The results were reversed (i.e., anticipatory nausea or emesis returned) when three patients chose to undergo chemotherapy treatment without the therapist present to direct the relaxation and distraction intervention. Anticipatory vomiting was again eliminated for these three patients when relaxation and imagery were reintroduced during subsequent chemotherapy sessions (Redd *et al.*, 1982).

Zeltzer and her associates (Zeltzer, Kellerman, Ellenberg, & Dash, 1983; Zeltzer, LeBaron, & Zeltzer, 1982) used similar procedures to reduce postchemotherapy nausea and vomiting in eight adolescent patients. The patients received one to three training sessions using an eye fixation induction and guided imagery. They were then instructed to use these techniques on their own during and after subsequent chemotherapy treatments. Analysis of these patients' self-reports of posttreatment nausea and vomiting revealed a significant reduction in the frequency and intensity (but not the duration) of vomiting following training in self-relaxation techniques.

A series of studies concerning the use of progressive-muscle-relaxation training in conjunction with guided imagery has been completed by Burish and his colleagues (Burish & Lyles, 1979, 1981; Lyles, Burish, Krozely, & Oldham, 1982). The methods they used have been similar across their research. Adult patients with anticipatory nausea were studied across 5 to 10 consecutive chemotherapy treatments divided into baseline, treatment and follow-up phases. Measures of pulse rate, blood pressure, anxiety, and depression were obtained before and after all chemotherapy sessions. Patient and nurse ratings of nausea during chemotherapy infusions, as well as nurses' observations of emesis, were obtained after each chemotherapy session. After a no-treatment baseline phase, the therapist directed patients in progressive muscle relaxation and guided-relaxation imagery both before and during chemotherapy injections. During the follow-up phase, the therapist was withdrawn, and the patients were instructed to use the relaxation and imagery intervention on their own before and during chemotherapy. In the group-comparison research (Burish & Lyles, 1981; Lyles *et al.*, 1982), no-treatment and therapist-contact control groups were added in order to assess the contribution of nonspecific factors to treatment outcomes.

The results were consistent across the research. Therapist-directed progressive muscle relaxation with guided imagery resulted in reductions in pulse rate and blood pressure as well as in self-reported anxiety and nausea. The patients in the control conditions did not evidence these reductions. The follow-up results were less impressive, however. When the therapist was no longer present to direct the relaxation intervention, the patients in the treatment groups did not display as large a reduction in nausea and physiological arousal.

Multiple-muscle-site EMG biofeedback in conjunction with relaxation training and imagery was also used in one case study with an adult (Burish, Shartner, & Lyles, 1981). The intervention strategy and the assessment methods closely followed those of Burish's previous research. Biofeedback was used to augment the relaxation training during drug infusions. The results replicated the earlier findings: Distress and nausea were reduced.

Finally, systematic desensitization was used to control anticipatory nausea and emesis (Morrow & Morrell, 1982). In this study, adult chemotherapy patients were assigned to one of three groups: systematic desensitization, standard counseling (involving a supportive and problem-solving approach), or a no-treatment control group. All patients in the desensitization and counseling groups participated in two 1-hour treatment sessions between their fourth and fifth chemotherapy treatments. In the desensitization group, hierarchies were individualized somewhat for each patient but typically began with scenes describing the patient entering the waiting room for treatment. Patient ratings of the frequency, severity, and duration of anticipatory nausea and vomiting were obtained for two follow-up chemotherapy treatments. The authors reported that systematic desensitization was superior to both the counseling and the no-treatment control with respect to reducing the anticipatory nausea and vomiting that occurred outside the immediate clinic setting. No data were collected on the patients' experiences during the chemotherapy injection.

Fear of Medical Procedures. In addition to developing aversions to chemotherapy, some patients come to fear painful procedures and routine injections. As discussed earlier, these fear responses may become severe and debilitating, as some patients report becoming preoccupied by their fear and overwhelmed by anxiety for 2 or 3 days before a scheduled procedure. Fear reactions are especially common in young children. For example, a leukemic child who must undergo repeated bone-marrow aspirations and lumbar punctures may actively resist these procedures, rendering treatment extremely difficult. Routine pain- and anxiety-control medications have generally proved ineffective for such procedures, and the staff is required to physically restrain some children while the physician or nurse clinician completes the procedures. Needless to say, the situation is extremely stressful for the patient as well as for the parents and the staff.

A comprehensive intervention package devised by Jay and her colleagues (Jay & Elliott, 1984; Jay, Elliott, Ozolins, & Olson, 1983; Jay, Ozolins, Elliott, & Caldwell, 1983) has been shown to yield significant reductions in patient distress and, like the procedures used to control chemotherapy side effects, exemplifies behavioral intervention principles. The intervention package they used consists of five distinct components: (1) filmed modeling, (2) reinforcement, (3) breathing exercises, (4) emotive imagery, and (5) behavioral rehearsal. The child is first shown a short film (selected from a series of films individualized for children of different ages and sexes) of a child undergoing a bone marrow aspiration and lumbar puncture (i.e., a spinal tap). The film is designed to show how a child of the patient's age goes through the procedure. In order to alleviate the child's fears of being punished or tortured, the film emphasizes that the doctors and nurses are the patient's friends. Specific coping strategies involving deep, slow-paced breathing and focusing attention on distracting imagery (i.e., emotive imagery) are also introduced. In order to help the child visualize and perform the breathing exercises, the child is told to pretend to be a big tire with air being pumped in and and then slowly let out. During the actual procedure, the therapist or nurse describes how "Superman" or "Wonder Woman" (or whatever storybook character the child chooses) deals with an important adventure with the child's assistance. These heroes presumably endow the child with special powers that make the medical procedures less painful.

After the above four components of the treatment package are described, the procedure is behaviorally rehearsed three times. The patient practices administering the procedure to a doll first and then to the therapist. The child reminds the doll to lie still and to practice the appropriate breathing exercises, and the therapist models coping statements. Finally, the child goes through a rehearsal of the procedure as the patient while the psychologist pretends to be the doctor. The behavioral rehearsal helps the patient to identify with the physician, to become desensitized to the actual treatment, and to practice his or her new coping techniques.

Clinical Issues. As the preceding discussion has pointed out, behavioral intervention procedures can produce immediate benefits for the patient. What is more, their use can often have important side effects. One clear benefit of behavioral techniques is that they are usually less intrusive than the medical and surgical alternatives. For example, in the case reported earlier in the chapter of a female patient who was unable to retain solid foods following gastrointestinal surgery, the alternative to *in vivo* desensitization was the insertion of a permanent feeding tube through her nose (Redd, 1980a). In another clinical case treated by the junior author, relaxation training to control prechemotherapy nausea and anxiety was used instead of the installation of a catheter for the administration of chemotherapy. These methods can also be directly applied to reduce other symptoms (especially pain). Through relaxation and distraction, it appears that patients can reduce much of the distress, pain, and anxiety associated with invasive medical treatment. In addition to these "medical"-physical benefits, patients often report that using behavioral procedures has given them a greater sense of personal control. This awareness is significant for patients suffering from a disease over which they may feel that they have little or no control (Thompson, 1981).

Behavioral intervention is an interpersonal event; both clinician and patient are active participants. The use of behavioral intervention techniques in no way negates the significance of important aspects of traditional psychosocial interventions. The effect of the development of rapport and trust cannot be underestimated. There is a positive snowballing effect; rapport is enhanced through the use of behavioral techniques and facilitates the development of a therapeutic relationship. Patients feel comfortable disclosing emotional concerns to a clinician whom they come to know in a nonthreatening context. The behavioral treatment allows the patient to request psychological, supportive counseling without formally seeking psychotherapy for a "psychiatric disorder." For example, we have had patients bring up interpersonal conflicts with family members, issues of self-esteem, and existential concerns after they felt at ease with us. This process of deepening rapport in the context of behavioral intervention highlights the fact that the behavioral clinician is indeed a *clinician*, rather than a technician.

SUMMARY

Cancer represents one of the most dreaded diseases of our time. It is often associated with disfigurement, pain, nausea, fatigue, and, for nearly half of cancer patients, eventual death. In addition to the emotional and existential problems associated with the disease, patients typically experience significant aversive side effects from treatment. Indeed, for some patients, the treatment is worse than the disease itself. For these reasons, comprehensive care of the cancer patient requires the use of a multitude of medical and psychosocial resources.

An examination of the somatic, psychological, and social conditions associated with the diagnosis and treatment of cancer reveals numerous factors and environmental contingencies that may facilitate the development of existential, psychological, and behavioral problems. An otherwise normal, healthy individual suddenly receives a diagnosis that he or she most likely views as a death sentence and is then thrust into a treatment regimen that disrupts almost every aspect of his or her life. In a probable state of significant depression and anxiety, patients may (1) have to drastically alter their work schedule and responsibilities, which hitherto have provided structure and purpose to their life; (2) reside for extended periods of time in a hospital oncology unit, where privacy is limited, the adoption of a role of passive recipient of treatment is implicitly encouraged, and many hours are spent with nothing to do; (3) receive treatment that makes them sick, weak, and disfigured; and (4) assume a new and typically dependent role with family and friends. In light of the degree of personal pain and suffering that are caused by the disease and its treatment, it is surprising that the incidence of severe psychopathology is not greater.

With the advent of behavioral medicine and the broadening domain of behavioral psychology (i.e., behavior modification and behavior therapy), the modes of treatment available to the psychosocial clinician have expanded considerably. Three distinct intervention approaches currently in use in psychosocial oncology can be identified: (1) traditional, (2) problem-oriented, and (3) behavioral. The traditional approach to psychosocial intervention focuses on the psychological and existential concerns of the patient who is confronted with the possibility of imminent death. The primary mode of intervention is supportive counseling following the guidelines formulated by Kubler-Ross (1969, 1970). The problem-oriented approach is more practical in focus, dealing primarily with issues of daily living. The specific form of intervention varies widely. Some programs use an individual format, and others use group methods. Some focus on patients with a particular form of cancer (e.g., head and neck, breast, or Hodgkin's disease), and other intervention programs group patients by type of treatment (e.g., mastectomy or pelvic exenteration). Most problem-oriented approaches rely heavily on teaching and the importance of peer counseling and support. The behavioral approach is the most recent to appear and is even more concrete in its focus than the problem-oriented approach. Based on clinical observation and research that suggests that behavioral symptoms can result from inadvertent-respondent and operant-conditioning processes, behavioral methods have been used to deal with specific treatment symptoms, and behavioral techniques (e.g., relaxation training, hypnosis, biofeedback, and operant reinforcement) have been used to reduce the severity of these symptoms. The behavioral approach is compatible with the practice of medical oncology with respect to problem diagnosis and treatment evaluation. Like medical oncology, behavioral intervention (1) focuses on concrete, objectively measurable problems; (2) individualizes treatment operations in accordance with changes in patient behavior; and (3) is empirical, rather than theoretical, in its orientation.

To date, the major contribution of behavioral psychosocial oncology has been the development of a series of intervention procedures that effectively control aversion reactions to chemotherapy, as well as of methods of reducing distress during invasive medical procedures. The techniques that have been used to control chemotherapy aversions include active and passive relaxation in conjunction with guided imagery, biofeedback with imagery, and systematic desensitization. With children, techniques have included positive reinforcement, *in vivo* desensitization, and various relaxation and attentional distraction tasks. Independent research conducted in separate medical settings has consistently demonstrated clinically significant benefits following the use of these procedures.

The application of behavioral techniques to the care and treatment of individuals with life-threatening chronic disease is burgeoning. The significant characteristics of these diseases, including the lengthy time course involved as well as the highly aversive treatment procedures used to treat them, provide ample opportunity for the development of significant behavioral problems. Indeed, one is often puzzled about why all patients undergoing such treatment do not develop such problems. The nature of the methods used to treat life-threatening chronic disease permits careful behavioral analysis and intervention. Those interested in behavioral methods are to be encouraged; these methods have a great deal to offer to both patients and their families, and the intellectual and emotional benefits for the clinician-researcher are many.

REFERENCES

Abitpol, M. M., & Davenport, J. H. (1974). Sexual dysfunction after therapy for cervical carcinoma. *American Journal of Obstetrics and Gynecology, 119,* 181–189.

Abramson, L. Y., Seligman, M. E. P., & Teasdale, J. D. (1978). Learned helplessness in humans: Critique and reformulation. *Journal of Abnormal Psychology, 87,* 49–74.

American Cancer Society. (1978). *Cancer facts and figures.* New York: Author.

Andersen, B. L., & Hacker, N. F. (1983a). Psychosexual adjustment following pelvic exenteration. *Obstetrics and Gynecology, 61,* 331–338.

Andersen, B. L., & Hacker, N. F. (1983b). Treatment for gynecologic cancer: A review of the effects on female sexuality. *Health Psychology, 2,* 203–221.

Andrykowski, M. A., Redd, W. H., & Hatfield, A. K. (1985). The development of anticipatory nausea: A prospective analysis. *Journal of Consulting and Clinical Psychology, 53,* 447–454.

Averill, J. R. (1973). Personal control over aversive stimuli and its relationship to stress. *Psychological Bulletin, 80,* 286–303.

Bartuska, D. G. (1975). Humoral manifestations of neoplasms. *Seminars in Oncology, 2,* 405–409.

Bernstein, I. L., Wallace, M. J., Bernstein, I. D., Bleyer, W. A., Chard, R. L., & Hartmann, J. R. (1979). Learned food aversions as a consequence of cancer treatment. In J. van Eys, M. S. Seelig, & B. L. Nichols, Jr. (Eds.), *Nutrition and cancer.* New York: SP Medical and Scientific Books.

Black, P. (1979). Management of cancer pain: An overview. *Neurosurgery, 5,* 507–518.

Bonica, J. (1979). Importance of the problem. In J. Bonica & V. Ventafridda (Eds.), *Advances in pain research and therapy* (Vol. 2). New York: Raven Press.

Bonica, J. (1980). Cancer pain. In J. Bonica (Ed.), *Pain.* New York: Raven Press.

Bonica, J., & Ventafridda, V. (Eds.). (1979). *Advances in pain research and therapy* (Vol. 2). New York: Raven Press.

Bowers, M., Jackson, E., Knight, J., & LeShan, L. (1964). *Counseling the dying.* New York: Nelson.

Bracken, R. B., & Johnson, D. E. (1976). Sexual function and fecundity after treatment for testicular tumors. *Urology, 7,* 35–38.

Bronner-Huszar, J. (1971). The psychological aspects of cancer in man. *Psychosomatics, 12,* 133–138.

Brown, H. J., & Paraskevas, F. (1982). Cancer and depression. Cancer presenting with depressive illness: An autoimmune disease. *British Journal of Psychiatry, 141,* 227–232.

Bukberg, J., Penman, D., & Holland, J. C. (1984). Depression in hospitalized cancer patients. *Psychosomatic Medicine, 46,* 199–212.

Burish, T. G., & Bradley, L. A. (Eds.). (1983). *Coping with chronic disease.* New York: Academic Press.

Burish, T. G., & Lyles, J. N. (1979). Effectiveness of relaxation training in reducing the aversiveness of chemotherapy in the treatment of cancer. *Behavior Therapy and Experimental Psychiatry, 10,* 357–361.

Burish, T. G., & Lyles, J. N. (1981). Effectiveness of relaxation training in reducing adverse reactions to cancer chemotherapy. *Journal of Behavioral Medicine, 4,* 65–78.

Burish, T. G., & Lyles, J. N. (1983). Coping with the adverse effects of cancer treatments. In T. G. Burish & J. N. Lyles (Eds.), *Coping with chronic disease.* New York: Academic Press.

Burish, T. G., Shartner, C. D., & Lyles, J. N. (1981). Effectiveness of multiple muscle-site EMG biofeedback and relaxation training in reducing the aversiveness of cancer chemotherapy. *Biofeedback and Self-Regulation, 6,* 523–535.

Burish, T. G., Redd, W. H., & Carey, M. P. (1985). Conditioned nausea and vomiting in cancer chemotherapy: Treatment approaches. In T. G. Burish, S. M. Levy, & B. E. Meyerowitz (Eds.), *Nutrition, taste aversion, and cancer: A biobehavioral perspective.* Hillsdale, NJ: Erlbaum.

Capone, M. A., Good, R. S., Westle, K. S., & Jacobson, A. F. (1980). Psychosocial rehabilitation of gynecologic oncology patients. *Archives of Physical Medicine and Rehabilitation, 61,* 128–132.

Carson, J. A. S., & Gormican, A. (1977). Taste acuity and food attitudes of selected patients with cancer. *Journal of the American Dietetic Association, 70,* 361–365.

Cassem, N. H., & Stewart, R. S. (1975). Management and care of the dying patient. *International Journal of Psychiatry in Medicine, 8,* 235–241.

Cassileth, B. R., Zupkis, R. V., Sutton-Smith, K. & March, V. (1980). Information and participation preferences among cancer patients. *Annals of Internal Medicine, 92,* 832–836.

Chapman, C. (1979). Psychologic and behavioral aspects of pain. In J. Bonica & V. Ventafridda (Eds.), *Advances in pain research and therapy* (Vol. 2). New York: Raven Press.

Charmaz, K. (1980). *The social reality of death.* Reading, MA: Addison-Wesley.

Cleeland, C. S. (1984). The impact of pain on patients with cancer. *Cancer, 54* (Suppl. 11), 2635–2641.

Costa, G. (1977). Cachexia: The metabolic component of neoplastic diseases. *Cancer Research, 37,* 2327–2335.

Craig, T. J., & Abeloff, M. D. (1974). Psychiatric symptomatology among hospitalized cancer patients. *American Journal of Psychiatry, 141,* 1323–1327.

Cullen, J. W., Fox, B. H., & Isom, R. N. (1976). *Cancer: The behavioral dimensions.* New York: Raven Press.

Daut, R. L., & Cleeland, C. S. (1982). The prevalence and severity of pain in cancer. *Cancer, 50,* 1913–1918.

Derogatis, L. R., & Kourlesis, S. M. (1981). An approach to evaluation of sexual problems in the cancer patient. *CA-A Cancer Journal for Clinicians, 31,* 46–50.

Derogatis, L. R., Morrow, G. R., Fetting, J., Penman, D., Piasetsky, S., Schmale, A. M., Henrichs, M., & Carnicke, C. L., Jr. (1983). The prevalence of psychiatric disorders among cancer patients. *The Journal of the American Medical Association, 249,* 751–757.

DeWys, W. D. (1979). Anorexia as a general effect of cancer. *Cancer, 43,* 2013–2019.

DeWys, W. D. (1980). Nutritional care of the cancer patient. *Journal of the American Medical Association, 244,* 374–376.

DeWys, W. D., & Herbst, S. H. (1977). Oral feeding in the nutritional management of the cancer patient. *Cancer Research, 37,* 2429–2431.

DeWys, W. D., & Walters, K. (1975). Abnormalities of taste sensation in cancer patients. *Cancer, 36,* 1888–1896.

Doehrman, S. R. (1977). Psycho-social aspects of recovery from coronary heart disease: A review. *Social Science and Medicine, 11,* 199–218.

Donaldson, S. S., & Lenon, R. A. (1979). Alterations of nutritional status: Impact of chemotherapy and radiation therapy. *Cancer, 43,* 2036–2052.

Eissler, K. (1955). *The psychiatrist and the dying patient.* New York: International Universities Press.

Endicott, J. (1984). Measurement of depression in patients with cancer. *Cancer, 53*(Pt. 3, Suppl.), 2243–2248.

Feigenberg, L. (1975). Care and understanding of the dying: A patient centered approach. *Omega, 6,* 81–95.

Feigenberg, L., & Shneidman, E. S. (1979). Clinical thanatology and psychotherapy: Some reflections on caring for the dying person. *Omega, 10,* 1–9.

Ferlic, M., Goldman, A., & Kennedy, B. J. (1979). Group counseling in adult patients with advanced cancer. *Cancer, 43,* 760–766.

Fetting, J. H. (1982). Identifying and treating psychiatric disorders in cancer patients. *Geriatrics, 37,* 95–105.

Fetting, J. H., Grochow, L. B., Folstein, J. F., Ettinger, D. S., & Colvin, M. (1982). The course of nausea and vomiting after high-dose cyclophosphamide. *Cancer Treatment Reports, 66,* 1487–1493.

Fetting, J. H., Wilcox, P. M., Iwata, B. A., Criswell, E. L., Bosmajian, L. S., & Sheidler, V. R. (1983). Anticipatory nausea and vomiting in an ambulatory oncology population. *Cancer Treatment Reports, 67,* 1093–1098.

Fisher, S. G. (1979). Psychosexual adjustments following total pelvic exenteration. *Cancer Nursing, 2,* 219–225.

Fisher, S. G. (1983). The psychosexual effects of cancer and cancer treatment. *Oncology Nursing Forum, 10,* 63–68.

Foley, K. M. (1979a). The management of pain of malignant origin. In H. R. Tyler & D. M. Dawson (Eds.), *Current neurology*. Boston: Houghton Mifflin.

Foley, K. M. (1979b). Pain syndromes in patients with cancer. In J. Bonica & V. Ventafridda (Eds.), *Advances in pain research and therapy* (Vol. 2). New York: Raven Press.

Foley, K. M. (1985). The treatment of chronic pain. *The New England Journal of Medicine, 313,* 84–95.

Fordyce, W. E. (1973). An operant conditioning method for managing chronic pain. *Postgraduate Medicine, 53,* 123–134.

Fordyce, W. E. (1976). *Behavior methods for chronic pain in illness*. St. Louis: Moseby.

Freidenbergs, I., Gordon, W., Hibbard, M., Levine, L., Wolf, C., & Diller, L. (1981–1982). Psychosocial aspects of living with cancer: A review of the literature. *International Journal of Psychiatry and Medicine, 11,* 303–329.

Gehi, M. M., Rosenthal, R. H., Fizette, N. B., Crowe, L. R., & Webb, W. L. (1981). Psychiatric manifestations of hyponatremia. *Psychosomatics, 22,* 739–743.

Gluck, R. S., Baron, J. S., Brallier, D. R., Fink, N., & Leiken, S. C. (1980). Follow-up of central nervous system prophylaxis in acute lymphocytic leukemia. *Pediatric Research, 14,* 434.

Goldberg, R., & Tull, R. M. (1983). *The psychosocial dimensions of cancer*. New York: Free Press.

Golden, S. (1975). Cancer chemotherapy and management of patient problems. *Nursing Forum, 12,* 279–303.

Gordon, W. A., Freidenbergs, I., Diller, L., Hibbard, M., Wolf, C., Levine, L., Lipkins, R., Ezrachi, O., & Lucido, D. (1980). Efficacy of psychosocial intervention with cancer patients. *Journal of Consulting and Clinical Psychology, 48,* 743–759.

Gorzynski, J. G., & Holland, J. C. (1979). Psychological aspects of testicular cancer. *Seminars in Oncology, 6,* 125–129.

Greer, S., & Silberfarb, P. M. (1982). Psychological concomitants of cancer: Current state of research. *Psychological Medicine, 12,* 563–573.

Hamburg, B. A., Lipsett, L. F., Inoff, G. E., & Drash, A. L. (Eds.). (1980). *Behavioral and psychosocial aspects of diabetes: Proceedings of a national conference* (NIH Publication No. 80-1993). Washington, DC: U.S. Government Printing Office.

Hendler, C. S., & Redd, W. H. (1985). Fear of hypnosis: The role of labeling in patients' acceptance of behavioral interventions. *Behavior Therapy, 17,* 2–13.

Holland, J. C., & Mastrovito, R. (1980). Psychologic adaptation to breast cancer. *Cancer, 46,* 1045–1052.

Hughes, J. (1982). Emotional reactions to the diagnosis and treatment of early breast cancer. *Journal of Psychosomatic Research, 26,* 277–283.

Ingle, R. J., Burish, T. G., & Wallston, K. A. (1984). Conditionability of cancer chemotherapy patients. *Oncology Nursing Forum, 11,* 97–102.

Ivnik, R. J., Colligan, R. C., Obetz, S. W., & Smithson, W. A. (1981). Neuropsychologic performance among children in remission from acute lymphocytic leukemia. *Journal of Developmental and Behavioral Pediatrics, 2,* 29–34.

Jacobs, C., Ross, R. D., Walker, I. M., & Stockdale, F. E. (1983). Behavior of cancer patients: A randomized study of the effects of education and peer support groups. *American Journal of Clinical Oncology, 6,* 347–353.

Jamison, K. R., Wellisch, D. K., & Pasnau, R. O. (1978). Psychosocial aspects of mastectomy: I. The woman's perspective. *American Journal of Psychiatry, 135,* 432–436.

Jay, S. M., & Elliott, C. H. (1984). Psychological intervention for pain in pediatric cancer patients. In G. B. Humphrey, G. B. Grindey, L. P., Dehner, R. T. Acton, & T. J. Pysher (Eds.), *Adrenal and endocrine tumors in children*. Boston: Martinus Nijhoff.

Jay, S. M., Elliott, C. H., Ozolins, M., & Olson, R. A. (1983, September). *Behavioral management of children's distress during painful medical procedures*. Paper presented at the meeting of the International Society of Pediatric Oncology, York, United Kingdom.

Jay, S. M., Ozolins, M., Elliott, C. H., & Caldwell, S. (1983). Assessment of children's distress during painful medical procedures. *Health Psychology, 2,* 133–147.

Jewett, H. J. (1975). The present status of radical prostatectomy for stages A and B prostatic cancer. *Urology Clinics of North America, 2,* 105–124.

Kastenbaum, R. (1978). In control. In C. A. Garfield (Ed.), *Psychosocial care of the dying patient*. New York: McGraw-Hill.

Kastenbaum, R., & Aisenberg, R. (1972). *The psychology of death*. New York: Springer.

Katz, E. R., Kellerman, J., & Siegel, S. E. (1980). Behavioral distress in children with cancer undergoing medical procedures: Developmental considerations. *Journal of Consulting and Clinical Psychology, 48,* 356-365.

Knox, L. S. (1983). Nutrition and cancer. *Nursing Clinics of North America, 18,* 97-109.

Knox, L. S., Crosby, L. O., Feurer, I. D., Buzby, G. P., Miller, C. L., & Mullen, J. L. (1983). Energy expenditure in malnourished cancer patients. *Annals of Surgery, 197,* 152-162.

Krant, M. J. (1981). Psychosocial impact of gynecologic cancer. *Cancer, 48,* 608-612.

Kubler-Ross, E. (1969). *On death and dying.* New York: Macmillan.

Kubler-Ross, E. (1970). Psychotherapy for the dying patient. *Current Psychiatric Therapies, 10,* 110-117.

Lamont, J. A., DePetrillo, A. D., & Sargeant, E. J. (1978). Psychosexual rehabilitation and exenterative surgery. *Gynecological Oncology, 6,* 236-242.

Lee, E. C., & Maguire, G. P. (1975). Emotional distress in patients attending a breast clinic. *British Journal of Surgery, 62,* 162.

Lehman, J. F., DeLisa, J. H., Warren, C. G., deLateur, B. J., Bryant, P. L., & Nicholson, C. G. (1978). Cancer rehabilitation: Assessment of need, development, and evaluation of a model of care. *Archives of Psychical Medicine and Rehabilitation, 59,* 410-419.

Levine, P. M., Silberfarb, P. M., & Lipowski, Z. J. (1978). Mental disorders in cancer patients. *Cancer, 42,* 1385-1391.

Linn, M. W., Linn, B. S., & Harris, R. (1982). Effects of counseling for late stage cancer patients. *Cancer, 49,* 1048-1055.

Liss-Levinson, W. S. (1982a). Clinical observations on the emotional responses of males to cancer. *Psychotherapy: Theory, Research, and Practice, 19,* 325-330.

Liss-Levinson, W. S. (1982b). Reality perspectives for psychological services in a hospice program. *American Psychologist, 37,* 1266-1270.

Lyles, J. N., Burish, T. G., Krozely, M. G., & Oldham, R. K. (1982). Efficacy of relaxation training and guided imagery in reducing the aversiveness of cancer chemotherapy. *Journal of Consulting and Clinical Psychology, 50,* 509-524.

Maguire, P., Brooke, M., Tait, A., Thomas, C., & Sellwood, R. (1983). The effect of counseling on physical disability and social recovery after mastectomy. *Clinical Oncology, 9,* 319-324.

Massie, M. J., & Holland, J. C. (1984). Diagnosis and treatment of depression in the cancer patient. *Journal of Clinical Psychiatry, 45(3* Pt. 2), 25-29.

Matarazzo, J. D. (1982). Behavioral health's challenge to academic, scientific, and professional psychology. *American Psychologist, 37,* 1-14.

McIntosh, S., Klatskin, E. H., O'Brien, R. T., Aspnes, G. T., Kammerer, B. L., Snead, C., Kalavsky, S. M., & Pearson, H. A. (1976). Chronic neurologic disturbance in childhood leukemia. *Cancer, 37,* 853-857.

McKitrick, D. (1981-1982). Counseling dying clients. *Omega, 12,* 165-187.

Meadows, A. T., Gordon, J., Massari, D. J., Littman, P., Fergusson, J., & Moss, K. (1981). Declines in IQ scores and cognitive dysfunction in children with acute lymphocytic leukaemia treated with cranial irradiation. *Lancet, 2,* 1015-1018.

Melzack, R., & Casey, K. (1968). Sensory, motivational, and central control determinants of pain: A new conceptual model. In D. Kenshalo (Ed.), *The skin senses.* Springfield, IL: Charles C Thomas.

Melzack, R., & Wall, P. (1965). Pain mechanisms: A new theory. *Science, 150,* 971-979.

Meyerowitz, B. E. (1980). Psychosocial correlates of breast cancer and its treatments. *Psychological Bulletin, 87,* 108-131.

Meyerowitz, B. E., Heinrich, R. L., & Schag, C. C. (1983). A competency-based approach to coping with cancer. In T. G. Burish & L. A. Bradley (Eds.), *Coping with chronic disease: Research and applications.* New York: Academic Press.

Morris, T., Greer, H. S., & White, P. (1977). Psychological and social adjustment to mastectomy: A two-year follow-up study. *Cancer, 40,* 2381-2387.

Morrow, G. R. (1982). Prevalence and correlates of anticipatory nausea and vomiting in chemotherapy patients. *Journal of the National Cancer Institute, 68,* 484-488.

Morrow, G. R. (1984). The assessment of nausea and vomiting: Past problems, current issues, and suggestions for future research. *Cancer, 53(Pt. 3,* Suppl.), 2267-2278.

Morrow, G. R., & Morrell, B. S. (1982). Behavioral treatment for the anticipatory nausea and vomiting induced by cancer chemotherapy. *New England Journal of Medicine, 307,* 1476-1480.

Moss, H. A., Nannis, E. D., & Poplack, D. G. (1981). The effects of prophylactic treatment of the central nervous system on the intellectual functioning of children with acute lymphocytic leukemia. *American Journal of Medicine, 71,* 47–52.

Mossman, P. L. (1980). *A problem oriented approach to stroke rehabilitation.* Springfield, IL: Charles C Thomas.

Murphy, T. (1973). Cancer pain. *Postgraduate Medicine, 53,* 187–194.

Nasrallah, H. A., & McChesney, C. M. (1981). Psychopathology of corpus callosum tumors. *Biological Psychiatry, 16,* 663–669.

Nerenz, D. R., Leventhal, H., & Love, R. R. (1982). Factors contributing to emotional distress during cancer chemotherapy. *Cancer, 50,* 1020–1027.

Nielson, S. S., Theologides, A., & Vickers, Z. M. (1980). Influence of food odors on food aversions and preferences in patients with cancer. *American Journal of Clinical Nutrition, 33,* 2253–2261.

Pattison, E. M. (1976). *The experience of dying.* Englewood Cliffs, NJ: Prentice-Hall.

Pattison, E. M. (1978). The living–dying process. In C. A. Garfield (Ed.), *Psychosocial care of the dying patient.* New York: McGraw-Hill.

Peck, A., & Boland, J. (1977). Emotional reactions to radiation treatment. *Cancer, 40,* 180–184.

Penta, J., Poster, D., & Bruno, S. (1983). The pharmacologic treatment of nausea and vomiting caused by cancer chemotherapy: A review. In J. Laszlo (Ed.), *Antiemetics and cancer chemotherapy.* Baltimore: Williams & Wilkins.

Peteet, J. R. (1979). Depression in cancer patients: An approach to differential diagnosis and treatment. *Journal of the American Medical Association, 241,* 1487–1489.

Peterson, L., & Popkin, M. (1980). Neuropsychiatric effects of chemotherapeutic agents for cancer. *Psychosomatics, 21,* 141–153.

Petty, F., & Noyes, R., Jr. (1981). Depression secondary to cancer. *Biological Psychiatry, 16,* 1203–1220.

Pfefferbaum, B., Pasnau, R. O., Jamison, K., & Wellisch, A. (1977–1978). Comprehensive program of psychosocial care for mastectomy patients. *International Journal of Psychiatry in Medicine, 8,* 63–72.

Plumb, M. M., & Holland, J. (1977). Comparative studies of psychological functions in patients with advanced cancer: I. Self-reported depressive symptoms. *Psychosomatic Medicine, 39,* 264–276.

Polivy, J. (1977). Psychological effects of mastectomy on a woman's feminine self-concept. *Journal of Nervous and Mental Disease, 164,* 77–87.

Posner, J. (1971). Neurological complications of systemic cancer. *Medical Clinics of North America, 55,* 625–646.

Quint, J. C. (1963). The impact of mastectomy. *American Journal of Nursing, 63,* 88–92.

Rabins, P. V., & Folstein, M. F. (1982). Delirium and dementia: Diagnostic criteria and fatality rates. *British Journal of Psychiatry, 140,* 149–153.

Razin, A. M. (1982). Psychosocial intervention in coronary artery disease: A review. *Psychosomatic Medicine, 44,* 363–388.

Reagan, T. J., & Okazaki, H. (1974). The thrombotic syndrome associated with carcinoma. *Archives of Neurology, 31,* 390–395.

Redd, W. H. (1980a). In vivo desensitization in the treatment of chronic emesis following gastrointestinal surgery. *Behavior Therapy, 11,* 421–427.

Redd, W. H. (1980b). Stimulus control and extinction of psychosomatic symptoms in cancer patients in protective isolation. *Journal of Consulting and Clinical Psychology, 48,* 448–455.

Redd, W. H. (1982a). Behavioral analysis and control of psychosomatic symptoms of patients receiving intensive cancer treatment. *British Journal of Clinical Psychology, 21,* 351–358.

Redd, W. H. (1982b). Treatment of excessive crying in a terminal cancer patient: A time-series analysis. *Journal of Behavioral Medicine, 5,* 225–236.

Redd, W. H., & Andrykowski, M. A. (1982). Behavioral intervention in cancer treatment: Controlling aversion reactions to chemotherapy. *Journal of Consulting and Clinical Psychology, 50,* 1018–1029.

Redd, W. H., & Hendler, C. S. (1983). Behavioral medicine in comprehensive cancer treatment. *Journal of Psychosocial Oncology, 1,* 3 17.

Redd, W. H., Andresen, G. V., & Minagawa, R. Y. (1982). Hypnotic control of anticipatory emesis in patients receiving cancer chemotherapy. *Journal of Consulting and Clinical Psychology, 50,* 14–19.

Redd, W. H., Burish, T. G., & Andrykowski, M. A. (1985). Aversive conditioning and cancer chemotherapy. In T. G. Burish, S. M. Levy, & B. E. Meyerowitz (Eds.), *Nutrition, taste aversion, and cancer: A biobehavioral perspective.* Hillsdale, NJ: Erlbaum.

Rosenthal, H. (1957). Psychotherapy for the dying. *American Journal of Psychotherapy, 11,* 626–633.

Rotman, M., Rogow, L., DeLeon, G., & Heskel, N. (1977). Supportive therapy in radiation oncology. *Cancer, 39,* 744–750.

Sachar, E. (1975). Evaluating depression in the medical patient. In J. Strain & S. Grossman (Eds.), *Psychological care of the medically ill.* New York: Appleton-Century-Crofts.

Schafer, D. F., & Jones, E. A. (1982). Hepatic encephalopathy and the y-aminobutyric-acid neurotransmitter system. *Lancet, 1*(8162), 18–20.

Schain, W. S. (1982). Sexual problems of patients with cancer. In V. T. DeVita, S. Hellman, & S. A. Rosenberg (Eds.), *Cancer: Principles and practice of oncology.* Philadelphia: J. B. Lippincott.

Schulz, R., & Aderman, D. (1974). Clinical research and the stages of dying. *Omega, 5,* 137–143.

Segaloff, A. (1981). Managing endocrine and metabolic problems in the patient with advanced cancer. *Journal of the American Medical Association, 245,* 177–179.

Seigel, L. J., & Longo, D. L. (1981). The control of chemotherapy-induced emesis. *Annals of Internal Medicine, 95,* 352–359.

Sewell, H. H., & Edwards, D. W. (1980). Pelvic genital cancer: Body image and sexuality. In J. M. Vaeth (Ed.), *Frontiers of Radiation Therapy and Oncology, 14,* 35–41.

Shneidman, E. S. (1978). Some aspects of psychotherapy with dying persons. In C. A. Garfield (Ed.), *Psychosocial care of the dying patient.* New York: McGraw-Hill.

Silberfarb, P. M. (1983). Chemotherapy and cognitive defects in cancer patients. *Annual Review of Medicine, 34,* 35–46.

Silberfarb, P. M. (1984). Psychiatric problems in breast cancer. *Cancer, 53*(Suppl. 3), 820–824.

Silberfarb, P. M., & Greer, S. (1982). Psychological concomitants of cancer: Clinical aspects. *American Journal of Psychotherapy, 36,* 470–478.

Silberfarb, P. M., Maurer, L. H., & Crouthamel, C. S. (1980). Psychosocial aspects of neoplastic disease: I. Functional status of breast cancer patients during different treatment regimens. *American Journal of Psychiatry, 137,* 450–455.

Silberfarb, P. M., Philibert, D., & Levine, P. M. (1980). Psychosocial aspects of neoplastic disease: II. Affective and cognitive effects of chemotherapy in cancer patients. *American Journal of Psychiatry, 137,* 597–601.

Sobel, H. J. (1981). Toward a behavioral thanatology in clinical care. In H. J. Sobel (Ed.), *Behavior therapy in terminal care: A humanistic approach.* Cambridge, MA: Ballinger Publishing.

Sobel, W. K. (1981). Behavioral treatment of depression in the dying patient. In H. J. Sobel (Ed.), *Behavior therapy in terminal care: A humanistic approach.* Cambridge, MA: Ballinger Publishing.

Soni, S. S., Marten, G. W., Pitner, S. E., Duenas, D. A., & Powazek, M. (1975). Effects of central-nervous-system irradiation on neuropsychologic functioning of children with acute lymphocytic leukemia. *The New England Journal of Medicine, 293,* 113–118.

Spence, K. W. (1964). Anxiety (drive) level and performance in eyelid conditioning. *Psychological Bulletin, 61,* 129–139.

Spiegel, D. (1979). Psychological support for women with metastatic carcinoma. *Psychosomatics, 20,* 780–785.

Spiegel, D., Bloom, J. R., & Yalom, I. (1981). Group support for patients with metastatic cancer. *Archives of General Psychiatry, 38,* 527–533.

Stonnington, H. H. (1980). Rehabilitation in cerebrovascular diseases. *Primary Care, 7,* 87–106.

Stoudemire, A., Cotanch, P., & Laszlo, J. (1984). Recent advances in the pharmacologic and behavioral management of chemotherapy-induced emesis. *Archives of Internal Medicine, 144,* 1029–1033.

Tamaroff, M., Miller, D. R., Murphy, M. L., Salwen, M. A., Ghavimi, F., & Nir, Y. (1982). Immediate and long-term posttherapy neuropsychologic performance in children with acute lymphoblastic leukemia treated without central nervous system radiation. *The Journal of Pediatrics, 101,* 524–529.

Theologides, A. (1972). Pathogenesis of cachexia in cancer. *Cancer, 29,* 484–488.

Thompson, S. C. (1981). Will it hurt less if I can control it? A complex answer to a simple question. *Psychological Bulletin, 90,* 89–101.

Trillin, A. S. (1981). Of dragons and garden peas: A cancer patient talks to doctors. *New England Journal of Medicine, 304,* 699–701.

Turk, D. C., & Rennert, K. (1981). Pain and the terminally ill cancer patient: A cognitive-social learning perspective. In H. J. Sobel (Ed.), *Behavior therapy in terminal care: A humanistic approach.* Cambridge, MA: Ballinger Publishing.

Twycross, R. G., & Lack, S. A. (1983). *Symptom control in far advanced cancer: Pain relief.* London: Pitman.

U.S. Department of Health and Human Services. (1984). *Vital statistics of the United States: 1979* (Vol. 2, Part A; DHHS Publication No. PHS 84-1101). Washington, DC: U.S. Government Printing Office.

Verzosa, M. S., Aur, R. J. A., Simone, J. V., Hustu, H. O., & Pinkel, D. P. (1976). Five years after central nervous system irradiation of children with leukemia. *International Journal of Radiation Oncology Biology and Physics, 1,* 209–215.

Vincent, C. E., Vincent, B., Greiss, F. C., & Linton, E. G. (1975). Some marital-sexual concomitants of carcinoma of the cervix. *Southern Medical Journal, 68,* 552–558.

Watson, M. (1983). Psychosocial intervention with cancer patients: A review. *Psychological Medicine, 13,* 839–846.

Webb, W. L., & Gehi, M. (1981). Electrolyte and fluid imbalance: Neuropsychiatric manifestations. *Psychosomatics, 22,* 199–203.

Weddington, W. W. (1982). Psychogenic nausea and vomiting associated with termination of cancer chemotherapy. *Psychotherapy and Psychosomatics, 37,* 129–136.

Weisenberg, M. (1977). Pain and pain control. *Psychological Bulletin, 84,* 1008–1044.

Weisman, A. D. (1970). Misgivings and misconceptions in the psychiatric care of the terminal patient. *Psychiatry, 33,* 67–81.

Weisman, A. D. (1972). Psychosocial considerations in terminal care. In B. Schoenberg, A. C., Carr, D. Peretz, & A. H. Kutscher (Eds.), *Psychosocial aspects of terminal care.* New York: Columbia University Press.

Weisman, A. D. (1979). *Coping with cancer.* New York: McGraw-Hill.

Weizman, A., Eldar, M., Shoenfeld, Y., Hirschoro, M., Wijsenbeck, H., & Pinkhas, J. (1979). Hypercalcaemia-induced psychopathology in malignant disease. *British Journal of Psychiatry, 135,* 363–366.

Welch, D. A. (1980). Assessment of nausea and vomiting in cancer patients undergoing external beam radiotherapy. *Cancer Nursing, 3,* 365–371.

Wellisch, D. K., Jamison, K. R., & Pasnau, R. O. (1978). Psychosocial aspects of mastectomy: II. The man's perspective. *American Journal of Psychiatry, 135,* 543–546.

Wellisch, D., Landsverk, J., Guidera, K., Pasnau, R. O., & Fawzy, F. (1983). Evaluation of the psychosocial problems of the homebound cancer patient: I. Methodology and problem frequencies. *Psychosomatic Medicine, 45,* 11–21.

Whitehead, V. M. (1975). Cancer treatment needs better antiemetics. *New England Journal of Medicine, 293,* 199–200.

Wilcox, P. M., Fetting, J. H., Nettesheim, K. M., & Abeloff, M. D. (1982). Anticipatory vomiting in women receiving Cyclophosphamide, Methotrexate, and 5-FU (CMF) adjuvant chemotherapy for breast carcinoma. *Cancer Treatment Reports, 66,* 1601–1604.

Winick, L., & Robbins, G. F. (1976). The post mastectomy rehabilitation group. *American Journal of Surgery, 132,* 599–602.

Worden, J. W., & Weisman, A. D. (1980). Do cancer patients really want counseling? *General Hospital Psychiatry, 2,* 100–103.

Yalom, I. D., & Greaves, C. (1977). Group therapy with the terminally ill. *American Journal of Psychiatry, 134,* 396.

Young, D. F., & Posner, J. B. (1980). Nervous system toxicity of the chemotherapeutic agents. In P. J. Vinken & G. W. Bruyn (Eds.), *Handbook of chemical neurology: 39. Neurological manifestations of systemic disease.* New York: Elsevier North-Holland.

Zeltzer, L., LeBaron, S., & Zeltzer, P. (1982). Children on chemotherapy: Reduction of nausea and vomiting with behavioral intervention. *Clinical Research, 30,* 138A.

Zeltzer, L., Kellerman, J., Ellenberg, L., & Dash, J. (1983). Hypnosis for reduction of vomiting associated with chemotherapy and disease in adolescents with cancer. *Journal of Adolescent Health Care, 4,* 77–84.

13

Headache

FRANK ANDRASIK

AND

STEVEN BASKIN

INTRODUCTION

Surveys of health care providers reveal that headache is a frequent presenting complaint. For example, headache was the chief complaint of 6% of patients seeking emergency medical care at Bronx Municipal Hospital, 7% of individuals seeking outpatient care (fourth most common mentioned complaint) at Toronto General Hospital, and 8% of patients (or the third most common complaint) at a prepaid medical clinic in California. Data collected during a review of symptoms with new patients revealed that headache was present in a considerably larger number of individuals. Here, estimates range from 35% to 90%. Population or community surveys mirror the prevalence rates obtained during this review of symptoms (see Leviton, 1978).

Headache may not be as dramatic as many of the other disorders addressed in this volume in terms of severity, but it does exact a direct toll on the individual sufferer and an indirect toll on society at large. Hurley (1969) estimated that approximately 10% to 12% of people experiencing headache actually seek medical treatment; this estimate is consistent with findings from the outpatient medical studies mentioned earlier. Hurley reported that the 6.1 million patients treated for headache in a 1 year period in the late 1960s sustained 5.3 million days of restricted activity. In children, headache is a leading cause of school absences (see Andrasik, Blake, & McCarran, 1986). The typical patient seeking psychological treatment at the State University of New York (SUNY) at Albany reported having spent approximately $500 per year of each of the past 2 years for headache care. This sum reflects the "maintenance cost" of chronic headache, as the typical patient seen at SUNY—Albany had been experiencing headaches for 15 years when first seen; yearly expenses for new cases would probably be much higher.

The high prevalence of headache and an increased awareness of the impact of psychological factors in the genesis, exacerbation, and maintenance of headache, combined with the development of viable nondrug treatments for headache (most notably biofeed-

FRANK ANDRASIK • Pain Therapy Centers, Greenville Hospital System, 100 Mallard Street, Greenville, SC 29601.   STEVEN BASKIN • New England Center for Headache, 40 East Putnam Avenue, Cos Cob, CT 06807.   Preparation of this chapter was supported by Research Career Development Award 1 K04 NS00818 from the National Institute of Neurological and Communicative Disorders and Stroke.

back and relaxation therapies), have led medical psychologists to become increasingly involved with these patients. This chapter reviews headache classification and diagnosis, the pathophysiology of headaches, and the medical treatment implications, complications, and contraindications for medical psychologists who plan to work with headache patients.

ISSUES IN CLASSIFICATION AND DIAGNOSIS OF HEADACHE

Although headache has plagued humankind for centuries, little attention has been devoted to developing and refining a classification scheme for it. The first (and only) formal attempt grew out of a 6-member study group of headache experts who delineated 15 distinct headache types on the basis of pain mechanism (Ad Hoc Committee on Classification of Headache, 1962; see Table 1). The committee acknowledged certain limitations in the proposed typology but hoped it would serve as a useful framework in subsequent research. To date, no classification system has surfaced as a viable replacement, so it will be instructive to examine this typology in greater depth.

A useful classificatory dimension for the purposes of this text concerns whether the headache can be attributed to a permanent structural defect or a diagnosable physical condition other than a primary headache disorder. An affirmative answer takes the headache outside the province of the medical psychologist, for the moment. We say, "for the moment," because once the physician has instituted the treatment of choice, individuals experiencing psychoadjustive difficulties as a result of the medical problem may find psychotherapy a useful adjunct. Thus, neurological examination and indicated follow-up laboratory evaluations are seen as essential components of the initial workup of the head-

Table 1. Classification of Headache [a]

---

1. Vascular headache of migraine type
   A. "Classic" migraine
   B. "Common" migraine
   C. "Cluster" headache
   D. "Hemiplegic" and "ophthalmoplegic" migraine
   E. "Lower-Half" Headache
2. Muscle-contraction
3. Combined headache: Vascular and muscle-contraction
4. Headache of nasal vasomotor reaction
5. Headache of delusional, conversion, or hypochondriacal states
6. Nonmigrainous vascular headaches
7. Traction headache
8. Headache due to overt cranial inflammation
9. Headache due to disease of ocular structures
10. Headache due to disease of aural structures
11. Headache due to disease of nasal and sinusal structures
12. Headache due to disease of dental structures
13. Headache due to disease of other cranial or neck structures
14. Cranial neuritides
15. Cranial neuralgias

---

[a] Adapted from a report of the Ad Hoc Committee on Classification of Headache (1962).

ache patient and should be arranged before the pursuit of psychological treatment. In certain cases, it will be necessary for the medical psychologist to maintain a close collaboration with a physician throughout the treatment of the headache patient. Even after arranging a medical evaluation, the medical psychologist must be continually alert for evidence of an underlying physical problem. Table 2 contains a list of "danger signs" that may suggest a need for immediate referral to a physician.

The absence of specific neurological findings indicates the headache must fall within one of the four remaining categories (migraine, cluster, muscle-contraction, combined migraine and muscle-contraction, and conversion), and hence into the domain of the medical psychologist. These headache types, although they represent a minority of the 15 total categories, appear to encompass the majority of all headache patients. For example, 94% of patients seeking treatment at a well-known headache clinic received one of these diagnoses (Lance, Curran, & Anthony, 1965). Clinical features of these four headache types are detailed below.

Clinical Features of Headache

Migraine. Migraine is an age-old condition, yet our knowledge of this disorder is far from complete. Although most experts believe that over 70% of migraine patients have a first-degree relative with migraine and that it should be considered a familial disorder (Dalessio, 1980; Diamond & Dalessio, 1982), one review concluded that the better designed the family incidence study, the lower the obtained concordance rate (Bakal,

Table 2. "Danger Signs" in Headache Patients That May Suggest the Need for Immediate Referral to Physician[a]

1. Headache is a new symptom for the individual in the past three months or the nature of the headache has changed markedly in the past three months.
2. Presence of any sensory or motor deficits preceding or accompanying headache other than the typical visual prodromata of classic migraine. Examples include weakness or numbness in an extremity, twitching of the hands or feet, aphasia, or slurred speech.
3. Headache is one-sided and has always been on the same side of the head.
4. Headache is due to trauma, especially if it follows a period of unconsciousness (even if only momentary).
5. Headache is constant and unremitting.
6. For a patient reporting muscle-contraction headachelike symptoms:
   a. Pain intensity has been steadily increasing over a period of weeks to months with little or no relief.
   b. Headache is worse in the morning and becomes less severe during the day.
   c. Headache is accompanied by vomiting.
7. Patient has been treated for any kind of cancer and now has a complaint of headache.
8. Patient or significant other reports a noticeable change in personality or behavior or a notable decrease in memory or other intellectual functioning.
9. The patient is over 60 years of age and the headache is a relatively new complaint.
10. Pain onset is sudden and occurs during conditions of exertion (such as lifting heavy objects), sexual intercourse, or "heated" interpersonal situations.
11. Patient's family has a history of cerebral aneurysm, other vascular anomalies, or polycystic kidneys.

[a]List developed in consultation with Lawrence D. Rodichok, M. D., Department of Neurology, Albany Medical College, Albany, New York.

1982). Ziegler's review (1977) revealed concordance rates ranging from a low of 15% to a high of 90%, with most of the studies being judged to have serious methodological flaws. We mention this here because a positive family history of migraine is one of the diagnostic criteria used by clinicians.

Migraine often begins in childhood, at 6 to 8 years of age in boys, and typically after menarche in girls. It may occur at any time from early childhood to late in life, however. In children, attacks of cyclic vomiting or motion sickness may be precursors to this disorder or migraine equivalents. The male:female ratio for migraine patients is approximately 1:1 in children; the disorder becomes progressively more frequent in women postmenarche. In women, there is frequently a relationship between menstrual periods and attacks of migraine. Many women report being free of migraine attacks after the first trimester of pregnancy, a report suggesting a hormonal relationship in the disorder (Diamond & Dalessio, 1982).

For a headache to be called migraine, it must be paroxysmal or episodic. Lance (1973) believes that the paroxysmal nature of the disorder is the critical defining feature. The frequency of migraine is rarely more than one per week, and the typical patient reports one or two attacks per month. Most experts would agree that an individual who presents with a headache diagnosed as migraine typically has some gastrointestinal symptoms, most notably nausea, as an essential feature of the episode (Olesen, 1978). During most of the migraine episodes, the pain is of considerable severity, often necessitating that the patient lie down or at least dramatically decrease his or her functional capacity. The patient often hibernates during the attack, getting into bed in a darkened room, and being especially careful to avoid sounds and lights. The headache presents unilaterally in 60% to 80% of the cases, although many migraine patients report bilateral pain. The headache is reported as a throbbing, pulsating, deep pain, which is most often located temporally, retro-orbitally, or generalized throughout the cranium. It usually lasts about 8 h on the average but can range between 2 h and several days in duration. Associated features may include nausea (which is most common), vomiting, anorexia, pallor, diarrhea, dizziness, sensitivity to sound, sensitivity to light, cold in the extremities, parasthesia, and fatigue.

In classic migraine, there is a distinct prodromal episode, which lasts from 20 to 30 min, consisting primarily of a visual aura. The visual phenomena are characteristically scintillating scotomata or disturbances in the peripheral field of vision (occasionally the central visual field), with sensations that resemble flickering lights. Some headaches are preceded by zigzag lines, termed *fortification spectra*. The headache phase usually begins as the prodromal symptoms fade. Classic migraine occurs in approximately 10% of the patients with migraine (Diamond & Dalessio, 1982).

Common migraine is the most frequent type of migraine, occurring in from 80% to 90% of migraine sufferers. There is no visual aura, and if a prodrome exists, it is usually vague and may precede the attack by several hours to several days. Prodromal symptoms may include psychological changes, fatigue, nausea, and water retention. However, many patients experience the headache without any apparent prodromal symptoms.

The Ad Hoc Committee on Classification of Headache (1962) made reference to menstrual headache as being a variant of common migraine. The term *menstrual migraine* is used when speaking of a migrainous headache occurring during menses or within 3 days before or after cessation of flow (Solbach, Sargent, & Coyne, 1984). *Hormonal mi-*

graine, in contradistinction, refers to headache resulting from *extrinsic* estrogrens, most notably oral contraceptives or estrogen-replacement therapy. Many women begin having migraine only after starting birth control pills, and a sizable portion of these women do not have a positive family history for the disorder (Kudrow, 1976a).

It is important for the medical psychologist to rule out menstrual migraine, as recent findings suggest that this migraine variant is highly resilient to psychological treatment. Solbach *et al.* (1984) carefully followed 83 women experiencing menstrual migraine for a period of 36 weeks. Patients were randomly assigned at inception to one of four experimental conditions: autogenic-type relaxation, electromyographic biofeedback, thermal biofeedback augmented by autogenic-type relaxation, or no-treatment control. Each of the patients assigned to the three active treatment conditions participated in a total of 22 sessions. None of the behavioral treatments led to improvement that exceeded the control condition. Solbach *et al.* argued on the basis of these and other findings (Nattero, 1982), that menstrual migraine merits recognition as a distinct clinical entity, and that its treatment should be restricted to medical procedures. Until our psychological technologies improve, the medical psychologist is advised to rule out menstrual migraine and to refer these patients to a physician for planning the first line of treatment. The medical psychologist, however, may be able to fulfill an adjunctive role by helping the patient to cope better with headache-related distress, and possibly by administering relaxation or biofeedback as a palliative procedure.

Cluster. Cluster headache is a type of vascular headache, so named because it appears in "clusters" of one to three attacks per day, with these bouts lasting typically from 4 to 6 weeks (although they may last as long as 12 weeks). Remission periods are variable but have an average duration of 12 months. The attacks often begin at the same time each year, predominantly in the fall and occasionally in the spring. Each headache lasts approximately 30 to 90 min and is always unilateral and periorbital in location. The pain may radiate over one side of the head or into the cheek or mastoid area and is described as excruciating in severity, boring and nonthrobbing in character as though a "hot poker is being thrust through the eye." The associated symptoms are also unilateral and consist of ipsilateral (on the same side) reddening and tearing of the eye, ptosis (drooping of the upper eyelid), miosis (contraction of the pupil), and stuffiness and/or rhinorrhea (nasal discharge) of the ipsilateral nostril. Patients in a cluster period are very sensitive to alcohol, which often induces a cluster attack immediately after ingestion. Attacks occur most often during sleep and awaken the patient, most commonly 90 min after falling asleep, which is coincident with the onset of the first period of rapid-eye-movement (REM) sleep. Attacks often occur as well on awakening from a nap in the afternoon.

A distinguishing characteristic of the cluster headache is the behavior of the patient during the attack. The patient is typically unable to lie still and must pace or keep in motion. There is no other primary headache disorder in which this type of behavior is an associated feature.

Cluster headache predominates in men (in approximately a male:female ratio of 9:1), who appear to have identifiable physical characteristics: ruddy complexions, deep skin furrows, a "leonine" appearance, and "orange peel" thick skin (Graham, 1969; Kudrow, 1980). These patients are generally tall and trim and are rarely obese, and 38% of them have hazel eye color, which is a significantly greater percentage than that in the general population. They also tend to be heavy smokers and to use alcohol moderately to excessively when not in cluster. They also have a higher incidence of ulcer and coronary artery disease (Kudrow, 1976c). Most cluster headache is *episodic* and remits completely between cluster periods. A small percentage of people with cluster headache, however, develop either primary or secondary *chronic* cluster headache, defined by the absence of a remission period. *Primary chronic cluster* refers to those individuals in whom remission periods have never occurred. Cluster headaches that formerly remitted but are now chronic are termed *secondary chronic cluster headaches*.

Cluster headache also appears to be minimally responsive to psychological treatments. Although a couple small-scale uncontrolled case studies have reported significant improvement following biofeedback (Adler & Adler, 1975; Fritz & Fehmi, 1983), a more carefully conducted study, with a sample size equaling that of the two uncontrolled investigations combined, found only minimal effects for similar treatment procedures. In this latter investigation, 11 patients with episodic cluster headaches were begun on a 14-week psychological treatment regimen consisting of 10 sessions of relaxation training and 12 sessions of thermal biofeedback (Blanchard, Andrasik, Jurish, & Teders, 1982). Four patients were early dropouts. Of the 7 completing treatment, only 3 reported any improvement when their next cluster bout occurred, and these improvements were slight. No patient reported marked improvement, and one actually deteriorated during treatment. The medical psychologist is advised to proceed cautiously and to remain in close contact with a physician when attempting to treat cluster headache patients.

The remaining forms of this disorder—hemiplegic, ophthalmoplegic, and basilar artery migraine—are extremely rare and are unlikely to be encountered by the medical psychologist. Hemiplegic migraine is common migraine with a concurrent hemiparesis (a slight paralysis affecting one side only); the neurological phenomena often persist for a while after the headache has ceased. Ophthalmoplegic migraine usually presents in a young adult with a third-nerve palsy on the side of the headache. Ptosis, pupillary dilation, and double vision are often evident, and the headache has a prodromal phase. Basilar artery migraine predominates in adolescent girls and presents with symptoms of basilar artery insufficiencies, such as aphasia, vertigo, dizziness, sweating, unsteady gait, and possible loss of consciousness.

Muscle-Contraction Headache. Scalp muscle-contraction headache, in its varied forms, is probably the most common headache. Most people experience acute scalp muscle-contraction headache under conditions of acute emotional, physical, or mental stress. The headache is described as mild to moderate in intensity, nonthrobbing, bilateral, often frontal, bitemporal, occipital, or generalized in location; it is experienced as a steady squeezing or pressing ache. Individuals having this type of headache rarely seek medical treatment; it is usually successfully self-treated with relaxation or over-the-counter analgesics.

Chronic scalp muscle-contraction headache is experienced as a constant dull to moderate pain. It is described as bilateral, fronto-occipital, generalized, or bandlike and is almost always accompanied by neck tension. Associated symptoms often include depression, anxiety, and sleep disorder. Patients often report awakening with headache every morning, and although the headache may wax and wane throughout the day, it rarely disappears.

Depression and headache have a strong association, particularly in the case of muscle-contraction headache. Not only are chronic headache sufferers frequently depressed, but headache is the most frequent somatic symptom of depression, occurring in over 50%

of depressed patients (Davis, Wetzel, Kashiwagi, & McClure, 1976; Diamond, 1983; Kudrow, 1976b; Martin, 1978; Ziegler, Rhodes, & Hassanein, 1978). One assessment task for the medical psychologist is to determine whether the depression preceded the headache and thus may be causing or increasing the patient's vulnerability to headache (Luborsky, Docherty, & Penick, 1973) or is more a result of living with chronic pain. This determination is often difficult to make because several of the vegetative signs of depression (anorexia, sleep disturbance, lack of energy, and somatic complaints) may be attributable to headache. We routinely conduct a mental status exam with headache patients to rule out preexisting psychopathology, chiefly depression, which may compromise direct psychological treatment of headache, and we delay or adjust the treatment approach as necessary. The presence of even low levels of depressive symptoms is associated with a poor response to psychological treatment (Blanchard, Andrasik, Neff, Arena, Ahles, Jurish, Pallmeyer, Saunders, Teders, Barron, & Rodichok, 1982; Jacob, Turner, Szekely, & Eidelman, 1983). Preliminary evidence suggests, fortunately, that psychological treatment of headache can lead to concomitant improvements in depression (Cox, Lefebvre, & Hobbs, 1982; Cox & Thomas, 1981).

Combined Migraine and Muscle-Contraction Headache. Many patients have combination headaches (both migraine and chronic scalp muscle-contraction), or what Saper (1982) termed the "chronic mixed headache syndrome." These patients are probably the most "typical" in the clinic specializing in headache treatment. These patients characteristically have had intermittent migraine attacks over the years with a gradual increase in scalp muscle-contraction headaches, as well as concomitant analgesic use. They eventually present to a headache treatment facility with occasional incapacitating headaches, daily or almost daily moderate intensity headaches, and daily or almost daily analgesic use, which is often excessive. Most diagnostic disagreements in headache reliability studies (Blanchard, O'Keefe, Neff, Jurish, & Andrasik, 1981; Weeks, Baskin, Rapoport, & Sheftell, 1984) have to do with these combinations or mixed headache syndrome patients.

Conversion. There is very little we can contribute about this headache disorder because it has rarely served as a focus in headache research. Some (Adams, Brantley, & Thompson, 1982) suspect that a sizable portion of individuals who now are routinely classified as having muscle-contraction headache may be more appropriately categorized as having conversion headache, but data supporting the utility of this alternative classification scheme, agreed-upon criteria for deciding when a diagnosis of conversion headache is warranted, and suggestions for developing treatment strategies for individuals so diagnosed are virtually nonexistent. Kudrow and Sutkus (1979) proposed diagnostic criteria for conversion headache in a study of psychological aspects of patients. The criteria they proposed are quite similar to those for muscle-contraction headache. Thus their differential utility awaits further research. In a recent discussion, Dr. Kudrow (personal communication) informed us that an additional distinguishing feature of conversion headache is the presence of significant occupational and social dysfunction.

Differential Diagnosis of Headache

Accurate diagnosis is the cornerstone of good clinical care of the headache patient. The Ad Hoc Committee on Classification of Headache (1962) carefully delineated the various headache types, but the committee stopped short of providing specific sets of diagnostic criteria. Lacking agreed-upon criteria, clinicians and researchers have been left to devise their own systems. We have found the criteria presented in Table 3 to be most useful in distinguishing types of headache. These criteria were devised from material contained in the report by the Ad Hoc Committee on Classification of Headache (1962), various headache reference texts, and our own experience.

One of the first investigations of contemporary diagnostic practices (Blanchard *et al.*, 1981) used criteria somewhat similar to those presented in Table 3 for the four most common headache types seen by medical psychologists (the criteria were developed by Andrasik, Blanchard, Arena, Teders, Teevan, & Rodichok, 1982). The subtypes "common" and "classic," which are important to distinguish from a medical perspective because of their varied treatment regimens, were not differentiated in this investigation, as this distinction has not thus far proved to be of value in planning or predicting response to behavioral treatment. Neither were subtypes of cluster headache distinguished. Sixty-six patients were interviewed separately by a board-certified neurologist and a doctoral student in clinical psychology, and at the end of the study, the rate of agreement and the reasons for disagreement were determined.

The level of perfect agreement between the diagnosticians was 86%. High agreement was found for individuals possessing pure migraine (84% agreement), pure muscle-contraction headache (96%), and cluster headache (100%). The majority of disagreements occurred for individuals who reported a mixture of migraine and muscle-contraction symptoms. Here the rate of agreement was only 62%. Just over one half of the discrepant diagnoses arose because the patient either gave different information to the two separate assessors or, when presenting the same information, emphasized aspects of it in a different manner. In most cases, the patient actually stated a belief that he or she possessed two separate types of headaches when evaluated by the psychologist but claimed to have only one headache type when seen by the neurologist. Thus, the professional orientation of the interviewer seems to influence what material the patient reports as important. Of the individuals for whom a diagnostic disagreement resulted, 80% had reported a previous history of psychiatric treatment. Previous psychiatric treatment was reported for only 40% of the remaining patients. This finding suggests that assessors need to exercise extra care when obtaining information from a patient with a previous psychiatric history. Use of a semistructured interview format may be helpful in minimizing discrepant self-reports by headache patients (see Blanchard & Andrasik, 1985, for a model).

A subsequent study by these same investigators evaluated the utility of diagnosing headache type from a brief symptom questionnaire (16 items, each rated on a 5-point scale) completed by 129 headache patients (Arena, Blanchard, Andrasik, & Dudek, 1982). With this information, it was possible to correctly classify only 68% of all patients (the consensus diagnosis of the doctoral students and the board-certified neurologist served as the reference for comparison). Correct classification rates for the separate headache types were as follows: 54% for migraine, 65% for combined migraine and muscle-contraction, 73% for cluster, and 77% for muscle-contraction alone. Although these results did not fare very well when compared to the overall agreement achieved by experienced diagnosticians, diagnoses for combined headache sufferers revealed nearly identical rates of agreement across diagnostic methods (62% agreement between experienced diagnosticians vs. 65% agreement between diagnoses derived from the self-report form and the consensus of the experienced diagnosticians).

Table 3. Criteria for Diagnosing Headache

Headache type	Diagnostic criteria
Common migraine	Headache that is paroxysmal, occurs no more frequently than 8 times per month, and displays 4 of the 7 following symptoms: 1. Onset usually unilateral 2. Usually accompanied by GI symptoms, most notably nausea and less commonly vomiting 3. Usually described as throbbing or pulsating 4. Usually accompanied by photophobia or sonophobia 5. One or more first-degree relatives diagnosed as having migraine 6. Ergotamine tartrate effectively relieves pain 7. Pain intensity usually judged to be severe
Classic migraine	Presence of both of the following: 1. Headache meets the diagnostic criteria for common migraine 2. Headache usually preceded, from a few minutes to several hours, by visual changes, hemiparesthesias, transient hemiparesis, or noticeable speech difficulty
Episodic cluster	Presence of both of the following: 1. Headache meets the diagnostic criteria for cluster headache (see below) 2. Remission periods experienced longer than 2 months duration (headache episodes typically last 6–8 weeks)
Chronic cluster	Presence of both of the following: 1. Headache meets the diagnostic criteria for cluster headache (see below) 2. Remission periods absent for at least one year Headache that displays all of the following symptoms: 1. Onset is always unilateral, with an occular or occulotemporal distribution 2. Patient rarely able to lie quietly during an attack 3. Pain intensity judged to be severe 4. Patient is headache-free between attacks 5. Attack frequency is typically 1–3 per day and rarely less than four per week 6. Duration of attacks is usually between 15 and 120 min 7. Usually accompanied by ipsilateral lacrimation, ptosis, reddening of the eyes, and rhinnorhea or nasal congestion
Chronic muscle-contraction	Headache that is rarely absent and displays 3 of the 5 following symptoms: 1. Location is bitemporal, bifrontotemporal, suboccipital, or generalized 2. Usually experienced as a tightness, pressure, band, or cap 3. Rarely accompanied by GI symptoms 4. Aspirin and acetaminophen rarely effective at relieving pain 5. Often described as a continuing dull ache that waxes and wanes in intensity
Combined migraine and muscle-contraction	Presence of both of the following: 1. Patient clearly identifies having two distinct types of headache 2. Patient meets criteria for migraine and for muscle-contraction headache

Turkat, Brantley, Orton, and Adams (1981) conducted a reliability investigation similar to that of Blanchard *et al.* (1981), but with a smaller number of patients ($n = 25$). Overall level of agreement for their separate assessors (three doctoral students in clinical psychology) was 71%, somewhat lower than that obtained by Blanchard *et al.* (1981). Reasons for the disagreement were not provided.

The remaining investigation attempted to assess whether diagnostic practices were at all comparable across settings, a question that is important given the apparent idiosyncratic manner by which headache patients are diagnosed. To accomplish this, Weeks *et al.* (1984) mailed headache patient histories to a large number of headache specialists employed in a variety of clinical settings. The raters were asked to make blind diagnoses for all 50 patient histories sent them, and on completion of this task they were asked to describe the diagnostic system they used and the kind of information they found important in arriving at their decision.

Multiple individuals worked in two of the surveyed settings. This arrangement allowed the investigators to calculate rates of diagnostic agreement for professionals employed within a particular setting, as well. Ratings given by individuals working within the same setting revealed perfect agreement in approximately 85% of all cases, a result that is comparable to the results of Blanchard *et al.* (1981). Comparison *across* settings revealed a mean perfect agreement rate of only 52%. Diagnostic agreement rates for the four different professional disciplines participating in the study (neurologists, R.N.'s, internists, and psychologists) were strikingly similar and ranged from 53% to 58%. The rather poor rate of diagnostic agreement across individuals and settings is viewed as all the more problematic because the majority of raters claimed to be using the same diagnostic system—the one proposed by the Ad Hoc Committee on Classification of Headache!

Findings from these three studies indicate that there is a significant problem with respect to the diagnosis of headache type. These findings also suggest that there may be a serious problem in interpreting the available literature, in that anywhere from 15% to 48% of cases may be questionably diagnosed. As earlier mentioned, the Ad Hoc Committee on Classification of Headache did not articulate precise diagnostic criteria nor a system for combining the various symptoms to arrive at a final diagnosis. The absence of agreed-upon criteria certainly accounts in part for the discrepant diagnoses. Note also that few of the diagnostic criteria are pathognomonic; the result is a heterogeneous array of patients even within a particular diagnostic group. A major source of disagreement noted by Weeks *et al.* concerned evaluators' electing to use the diagnosis of "medication rebound" headache, a headache entity not referenced by the Ad Hoc Committee. Data published after the report of the Ad Hoc Committee on Classification of Headache suggest the importance of being alert to this headache type.

Two types of medication rebound headaches have been identified: analgesic rebound and ergotamine rebound. The term *rebound* refers both to the worsening of the headache as the medication wears off and to the fact that the patient goes through a marked exacerbation after the abrupt discontinuation of the medication (a withdrawal-like phenomenon).

Modal analgesic abusers start out having infrequent but very intense headaches. These patients gradually begin to use over-the-counter or prescription analgesics in increasing amounts. They often note only temporary and partial relief and begin to medicate three to four times per day, as relief wears off quickly. Some start to take medication in anticipation of a severe headache in an effort to prevent expected attacks. Thus, analgesics used symptomatically at first become habitual. This frequent and excessive use of non-narcotic analgesics, such as aspirin and acetaminophen, by chronic scalp muscle-contraction headache sufferers often paradoxically perpetuates and worsens head pain, rather than relieving it. Kudrow (1982) speculated that frequent use of analgesics sustains pain by suppressing the central serotonergic pathways concerned with the regulation of dull pain.

Analgesic abuse can also interfere with standard, usually effective, pharmacological therapy. Kudrow (1982) found a mean improvement rate of only 30% for analgesic-abusing headache patients treated by amitriptyline when they were permitted to continue their unrestricted use of analgesics. The improvement rate more than doubled ($M = 72\%$) for patients who were given amitriptyline *and* were withdrawn from all analgesics. Similar effects would seem likely for psychological treatment, but to our knowledge they have yet to be tested. The study by Kudrow (1982) contained two additional treatment conditions for assessing the effects of restricting analgesic usage alone (in the absence of additional treatment). Discontinuation of analgesics led to 43% symptom improvement by itself; this level of improvement far exceeded the 18% improvement for the patients continuing analgesics in the absence of other treatment (essentially a symptom-monitoring control condition) and slightly exceeded the level of improvement for patients given an effective medication but allowed to continue taking analgesics at abusive levels ($M = 30\%$). This clinical phenomenon was confirmed by Rapoport, Sheftell, Baskin, and Weeks (1984).

Ala-Hurula, Myllyla, and Hokkanen (1982) reported that overuse of the abortive treatment of choice for migraine, ergotamine tartrate, can also serve to maintain headache. These authors reported that ergotamine rebound headache occurred in patients taking dosages as small as 0.5 to 1.0 mg per day. Relatively severe withdrawal symptoms, similar to migraine, occurred on discontinuation of daily use. Saper and Van Meter (1980) reported similar findings.

The above studies indicate the importance of identifying patients who may be experiencing medication rebound headaches and of helping them to reduce, preferrably to eliminate, the medications producing the paradoxical effects on headache. The request to discontinue medication is easily made but is not easily followed. The medication abuser has typically exhausted all other medical treatments and may be reluctant to give up the current medication even though realizing it is not working optimally. The medical psychologist often needs to work hand-in-hand with a physician as the patient attempts to withdraw from an iatrogenic medication regime, and occasionally, a patient may need an inpatient stay to achieve this goal. For analgesics, the washout period typically lasts from 5 to 21 days before the patient begins to improve; some patients need a great deal more time, however.

In practice, a diagnosis is based almost exclusively on information reported by the patient during interviewing. Neurological examination and laboratory evaluation are an important part of the initial workup of the headache patient, but these are conducted essentially to *rule out* a disease process (e.g., tumor, aneurysm, etc.) that the headache may be secondary to and thus would make psychological treatment inappropriate, rather than to *rule in* a diagnosis of, say, migraine or muscle-contraction headache. Some investigators (e.g., Lake, 1981; Thompson, 1982; Turkat *et al.*, 1981) believe that supplementing patient self-report information with behavioral and psychophysiological findings would enhance diagnostic practices. Unfortunately, there have been no studies of the behavioral parameters of headache sufferers, and the voluminous literature on the psychophysiology of headache is equivocal at best (see reviews by Andrasik, Blanchard, Arena, Saunders, & Barron, 1982; Cohen, 1978; Haynes, Cuevas, & Gannon, 1982; Philips, 1978). We suspect that, for some time, careful patient interviewing will continue to serve as the primary basis for making diagnostic decisions.

A more basic diagnostic question is beginning to be raised by some headache researchers: Are migraine and muscle-contraction headaches really etiologically distinct? A vocal minority (e.g., Bakal, 1982; Raskin & Appenzeller, 1980) believe not and conclude that the fundamental pathophysiological mechanisms underlying each headache are the same. The differences in symptomatology between migraine and muscle-contraction headaches are attributed merely to the degree of involvement of the underlying mechanism, and muscle-contraction headache is assumed to be the less severe form. This "severity" or continuum model is quite appealing because of its parsimony; it would certainly simplify the assessment task and facilitate treatment planning. Unfortunately, the relevant data remain equivocal at best. In the absence of definitive data, we believe that it is best to retain the traditional nosological framework.

PATHOPHYSIOLOGY OF HEADACHE

Migraine Headache

The majority of early pathophysiological research was directed toward pinpointing the vascular phenomena underlying migraine. Much of the early work, conducted by Harold Wolff and his associates (see Dalessio, 1980), involved experimentation with drugs that were known to influence the intra- and extracranial vasculature. The classic vascular theory of migraine that was developed from this research concluded that this type of headache was due to a two-phase vascular process. During the first phase of a migraine headache, there is a decrease in the intracranial blood flow, but this is not accompanied by visible changes in angiography in large or medium-sized vessels, so the decrease is probably in the arterioles or the small cerebral blood vessels. This arteriolar narrowing leads to a decreased cerebral blood flow and a resultant brain ischemia. In classic migraine, the ischemia results in an aura, but it is symptomless in common migraine. The visual aura of classic migraine most likely originates in the occipital cortex, initiated by a local vasoconstriction of the calcarine artery, which results in ischemia of the occipital cortex.

The headache phase begins when the accumulation of carbon dioxide is sufficient to produce arteriolar dilation and a resultant increase in cerebral blood flow, which continues beyond the duration of the headache. Blood flow returns only gradually to normal levels, and the vasomotor dysregulation can last days after the pain terminates. The headache is considered extracranial, involving an increased extracranial flow and a decreased cutaneous flow (pallor), as well as multiple local, chemical, and vasoactive substances (catecholamines, serotonin, histamine, prostaglandins, and neurokinins), which, when liberated, lead to changes in the pain threshold, as well as a local inflammatory reaction.

Although the classic vascular theory of migraine has been supported by regional cerebral blood flow (rCBF) studies using a 133-xenon clearance technique, the primacy of vascular events may not be as simple as was originally hypothesized in the classic vascular theory (Edmeads, 1982). Olesen, Lauritzen, Tfelt-Hansen, Henriksen, and Larsen (1982) used extremely sophisticated equipment to measure rCBF and clearly separated classic from common migraine. Their research demonstrated a reduction of cerebral blood flow in all cases of classic migraine studied during the prodrome. In common migraine, cerebral blood flow remained constant focally and globally during the development of the attacks. The changes occurring in classic migraine began as a focal-blood-flow reduction beginning at the posterior pole of the hemisphere (occipitally) and spreading anteriorly at about 2 mm/min, often becoming generalized. Olesen *et al.* stated that this pattern of spread is not what one would expect from a spasm of a major cerebral artery. They hypothesized that the underlying mechanism may actually be a neurogenic event, a spreading depression of cortical activity. Their findings argue against the vasospastic model and suggest that alteration in neuronal function in the blood–brain barrier, or in some other brain process, is more likely to be the primary event in the genesis of migraine. This change may be followed by vascular reactions and ischemia, most likely involving the vasoactive neurotransmitters.

The foregoing indicates that several mechanisms, both neurogenic and vascular, contribute to migraine pathophysiology. It is also believed that many of the symptoms of migraine are due to circulating vasoactive substances. Many of the major biochemical changes in migraine seem to be linked to an abnormality in platelet function (Hanington, 1982). Platelets contain all of the serotonin present in the blood and release it during aggregation. Plasma levels of serotonin rise during the prodrome of migraine and significantly decrease during the headache phase, which parallels the pattern of platelet aggregation during a headache cycle (Anthony, Hinterberger, & Lance, 1969; Hanington, 1982; Rydzewski, 1976). During attack-free intervals migraine patients reveal an increase in platelet activity, as well as a lower threshold for the platelets to undergo a release reaction; this is possibly mediated by high levels of free fatty acids, which flood the circulation with vasoactive substances (Couch & Hassanein, 1977; Gawel & Rose, 1982; Spierings, 1980).

The serotonergic changes produced by platelet aggregation affect other circulating substances, resulting in a lower pain threshold and a vasodilating effect on blood vessels. It seems that the induced platelet aggregation leads to the serotonin release reaction, causing the cerebral-vascular constriction responsible for the prodromal stage of migraine. After the constriction, serotonin is then absorbed into the vessel wall and combines with histamine and kinins to increase the pain sensitivity of the affected arteries (Lance, 1982). Circulating serotonin also induces prostaglandin release from lung tissue, which is, in part, responsible for the extracranial arterial dilation during the headache phase. The fall in blood serotonin levels during the acute migraine attack is accompanied by a fall in plasma norepinephrine, after a prodromal surge (Fox-Moller, Genefke, & Bryndum, 1978). Because both of these substances are potent endogenous vasoconstrictors, the normal humoral restraints on dilator substances, such as histamine, bradykinin, and prostaglandins, are removed, contributing to the sustained, painful period (Friedman, 1982).

Sicuteri (1979, 1982) proposed a central biochemical theory of migraine. The theory suggests that migraine patients have a biochemical lesion in a serotonergic system of the brain, most likely in the brain stem, that is associated with modulating nociception or pain threshold information. This central serotonergic deficiency may lead to a lowered pain threshold with the experience of spontaneous pain as well as anhedonia (i.e., the loss of a sense of well-being) and dysautonomia (nausea, vomiting, and impaired thermal regulation).

Both central and peripheral theories of migraine suggest that serotonin is the naturally occurring substance most likely to play a role in migraine pathophysiology. These two hypotheses may not be mutually exclusive. Serotonin disturbances can manifest themselves simultaneously at a peripheral site, the cranial arteries, as well as in the brain centers.

Cluster Headache

Although neither the pathogenesis nor the etiology of cluster headache is known, some interesting consistencies have emerged. Cluster headache appears to be associated with a dilation of arteries coming off the external carotid system, such as the superficial temporal arteries, and a vasoconstriction of the internal carotid artery and its end branches that emerge from the orbit (supraorbital and frontal arteries). Kudrow (1980, 1985) found an ipsilateral decrease in supraorbital blood flow in 65% to 70% of cluster headache patients, both during and between attacks.

Several reports suggest that histamine release in the affected area is involved in the symptoms of cluster headache. Studies have shown evidence of increased urinary excretion and blood concentration of histamine in cluster patients in comparison to migraine patients (Anthony & Lance, 1971; Kudrow, 1980; Sjaastad & Sjaastad, 1977). An acute cluster attack can often be induced by the administration of histamine and other vasodilator medications, such as nitroglycerin, in cluster patients. Decreases in plasma testosterone have also been found during the cluster period, with values returning to normal during remission (Kudrow, 1976c; Nelson, 1978; Romiti, Martelletti, Gallo, & Giacovazzo, 1983).

The unilateral autonomic symptoms that accompany the disorder are a consistent feature of the cluster headache syndrome. The ipsilateral miosis in the cluster patient, which may be permanent or may occur only during an attack, indicates that the pupillary autonomic system in most likely affected in this disorder (Ekbom, 1970). Sicuteri (1980) used the term *empty neuron* to describe the pupillary sympathetic neuron of cluster patients due to a deficiency of opiate function. Cluster patients seem to have a deficiency in the endogenous opiate system, where their spinal fluid enkephalin levels were found to be particularly low (Anselmi, Baldi, Casacci, & Salmon, 1980). Therefore, a primary central origin of the cluster syndrome is suggested, with a deficiency in the endorphinergic system, which regulates pain perception and autonomic function, proposed as an explanatory mechanism (Fanciullacci, Pietrini, Gatto, Boccuni, & Sicuteri, 1982; Sjaastad, 1978).

Muscle-Contraction Headache

Wolff's experiments (see Dalessio, 1980) demonstrated a link between muscular action, secondary vascular changes, and headache. Rodbard (1970) stated that the head pain in muscle-contraction headache has to do with an accumulation of a toxic catabolite that produces pain that is released during the state of relative ischemia which occurs in the contracting muscle. However, surface-electrode EMG studies exhibit a confusing array of evidence (Andrasik, 1980; Haynes *et al.*, 1982; Philips, 1978). It is possible that scalp muscle-contraction headaches may be several different entities, only some of which are related to scalp muscles and some to central brain mechanisms. The research on the analgesic rebound phenomena within chronic scalp muscle-contraction headache suggests a central nature to that pain, with a possible suppression of a central serotonergic antinociceptive system (Kudrow, 1982).

MEDICAL TREATMENT OF HEADACHE

Information presented in this section is culled in large part from the standard texts of Diamond and Dalessio (1982) and of Raskin and Appenzeller (1980), as well as from the clinical experience of the staff of the New England Center for Headache. This review focuses chiefly on medical treatment, limitations, complications, and contraindications as they may influence the treatment efforts of the medical psychologist. Readers seeking information about psychological treatment procedures and considerations are referred to Andrasik (1986), Bakal (1982), Blanchard and Andrasik (1985), and Holroyd and Andrasik (1982).

Migraine Headache

The array of abortive and preventive pharmacological interventions proposed for migraine is remarkable for its diversity. This review focuses on the more common agents used in the treatment of the acute attack, as well as in prophylactic therapy.

Most patients who present for treatment at multidiscipline clinics have consulted with many professionals and nonprofessionals (family, friends, and so on). They often have many misconceptions about the nature of head pain as well as about the various therapeutic alternatives. In fact, a survey of patients seeking medical care revealed that they were most interested in receiving an explanation of what was causing their headache pain (Packard, 1979). They are often taking many medications, either self- or physician-prescribed, that may paradoxically increase their headache frequency and reduce the effectiveness of other interventions. The most common substance that may worsen their pain is the frequent and excessive use of over-the-counter or prescription analgesics, caffeine, decongestants, estrogens, and ergotamines. Often, these patients report "daily" migraine headaches, which are in actuality rebound headaches secondary to analgesics, decongestants, or caffeine. Although no empirical guidelines exist for what constitutes abuse, the wisest course in most cases would be to eliminate daily analgesics and/or decongestants. Caffeine should be gradually reduced to no more than 150 mg a day. Many patients believe that caffeine has preventive antimigraine effects because it is contained in many abortive migraine medications. It must be explained to them that large amounts of caffeine taken daily will increase the frequency of headache because of caffeine withdrawal. Consumption of caffeine is occasionally helpful in the treatment of the acute attack, however, because of its vasoconstrictive effects.

Because estrogens alter vasomotor stability, many women begin having migraine only after starting birth control pills. The withdrawal of oral contraceptives often leads to a marked reduction in migraine frequency. Women on estrogen-replacement therapy often experience a frequency decrease with a reduction in the daily levels of the estrogen preparation, as well as the use of exogenous estrogens noncyclically, without periodic interruption, thus preventing abrupt estrogen withdrawal (Somerville, 1971, 1972).

Treatment of the Acute Attack. Migraine headaches are usually treated acutely or symptomatically if the headaches occur two times per month or less. The most effective abortive treatments are the ergot preparations, which have been used for over 40 years. Although many ergot compounds are available, ergotamine tartrate is the most frequently used and comes in a variety of forms (oral, suppository, and sublingual).

Ergotamine. Ergotamine tartrate is most likely a partial agonist–antagonist of the alpha receptor, with its action dependent on the amount of sympathetic tone. When there is a situation compatible with vasodilation, ergotamine acts as an alpha agonist to cause the vessels to constrict. On the other hand, when the sympathetic tone is high (in general, in a state of relative vasoconstriction), ergotamine acts as an alpha antagonist to cause the vessels to dilate. The vasoconstrictive action of ergotamine may be augmented by its ability to block the reuptake of norephinephrine; ergotamine may also inhibit the reuptake of serotonin by platelets (Fanchamps, 1975). Caffeine in combination with ergotamine appears to potentiate the vasoconstrictive effect of the ergot, and also to promote faster and more complete absorption of the ergotamine (Scheife & Hills, 1980).

Dosage. Ergotamine tartrate must be given at the first sign of a migraine attack. The recommended oral, sublingual, or rectal dose is 2 mg at the onset of the headache, followed by a repeat dosage in 1 h, if necessary. Manufacturers' recommendations suggest that the total weekly dose should not exceed 10 mg. However, some investigations (Saper & Van Meter, 1980) suggest that ergotamine rebound pain may begin in some patients chronically taking as little as 4 mg of ergotamine tartrate per week. Many patients who have been prescribed ergotamine develop these ergotamine habituation headaches, which almost identically resemble their original migraine headache. They then medicate these headaches with ergotamine, maintaining the rebound effect.

Because nausea and vomiting often occur as part of the migraine syndrome, and as a side effect of ergot alkaloids, it is often helpful for the patient to take antiemetic drugs before the ergotamine administration; 25 to 50 mg of promethazine hydrochloride (Phenergan), given in tablet or suppository form approximately 20 to 30 min before ergot ingestion, is often the most useful antiemetic.

Side Effects. The side effects of ergotamine are numerous. The more frequent side effects include nausea, vomiting, abdominal cramps, muscle pains, and parasthesia of the extremities. Excessive use of ergotamine tartrate may lead to a condition known as *ergotism*, which is characterized by severe muscle cramping, stiffness and weakness of the legs, drowsiness, anorexia, and profound peripheral vasospasm.

Contraindications. Ergotamine preparations are contraindicated during pregnancy as well as in patients with severe peripheral vascular disease, coronary artery disease, and septic states. They are relatively contraindicated when patients have impaired renal or hepatic function and severe hypertension.

Prophylactic Therapy. Typically preventive treatments are used when a patient experiences three or more severe migraines per month. Most pharmaceuticals introduced for the prevention of migraine were first used to treat other disorders.

Methysergide Maleate. Methysergide (Sansert) was the first efficacious agent to be used preventively in migraine. It seems to suppress attacks partially or completely in approximately 60% of patients (Appenzeller, Feldman, & Friedman, 1979). Although it is an ergot derivative, it is indicated for prophylactic treatment only and must be taken on a regular (daily) basis. It is judged to be of no value in the treatment of an acute attack of migraine. Methysergide is a potent peripheral antagonist of serotonin and seems to act by substituting for serotonin at receptor sites. The drug also appears to inhibit histamine release from mast cells and may stabilize platelets against the spontaneous release of serotonin (Fanchamps, 1975).

Side Effects. The major side effects of methysergide, although infrequently reported, can be life-threatening. The most serious of these include retroperitoneal, pleuropulmonary, and cardiac fibrotic changes. Therefore, patients should have chest X-rays, electrocardiographs, and appropriate chemical studies at frequent intervals during drug treatment. Consequently, methysergide use is limited to patients who have severe migraine, which is refractory to other treatments, and who agree to have frequent checkups and to participate in drug holidays every three to four months of treatment. Many patients receiving methysergide therapy experience fewer, more minor side effects. These include gastrointestinal disturbances (nausea, vomiting, diarrhea, and abdominal cramping), vascular insufficiency of the lower limbs and leg cramping, parasthesia of the hands and feet, weight gain, edema, occasional euphoria or hallucinatory experiences, insomnia, ataxia, drowsiness, and dizziness.

Dosage. The typical daily dosage ranges from 4 to 8 mg, which is usually taken at meals. The typical patient starts with 2 mg once per day and will increase every 3 to 4 days, up to 2 mg three times per day. It usually takes 3 or 4 weeks for an adequate trial of the medication. When patients discontinue methysergide, it should be discontinued gradually over a 2- to 3-week period to minimize rebound headaches (Scheife & Hills, 1980).

Contraindications. The contraindications for methysergide are similar to those for the ergotamines (see previous section).

Beta-Adrenergic Blocking Agents. The three most well-known beta blockers used either clinically or experimentally in migraine prophylaxis are propranolol (Inderal), nadolol (Corgard), and timolol (Blocadren). Dalessio (1984) noted that the most effective beta blockers are those that are not cardiac-selective (nonselective beta blockers serve to decrease overall sympathetic activity in the autonomic nervous system). Propranolol is the only one of these medications to have FDA approval for the prophylaxis of common migraine, and thus, it is the model for this section. Depending on the methodological rigor of the outcome study, from 50% to 80% of migraine patients treated with propranolol have reported a decrease of greater than 50% in the frequency of their headaches (Anthony, 1978; Bekes, Matos, Rausch, Torok, 1968; Diamond & Medina, 1976; Forssman, Hendricksson, & Johannsson, 1976; Weber & Reinmuth, 1971, 1972; Wideroe & Vigander, 1974).

In propranolol treatment, only a few patients are rendered headache-free, but many report a decrease in frequency and severity. The beta blockers do not abolish the prodromal symptoms of migraine, and some investigators consider them contraindicated in classic or complicated migraine (Meyer, Dowell, Mathew, & Hardenberg, 1984).

Propranolol blocks beta-noradrenergic receptors in the peripheral sympathetic nervous system and may do so centrally as well. The drug has extensive effects on the cardiovascular system and is used to control angina pectoris, certain cardiac arrhythmias, and hypertension. Although the mechanism of action of propranolol in the prophylaxis of common migraine is not understood, the antimigraine effect may be due to preventing vasodilation, as beta-adrenoreceptors exist in higher density in the external carotid artery, which is considered a major pain site in migraine (Anthony, 1978; Diamond & Medina, 1976). Propranolol also has the ability to block the reuptake of serotonin by platelets, which may possibly prevent the dramatic fall in plasma serotonin just before the headache phase of migraine (Anthony, 1978; Fozard, 1982).

Dosage. Dosage levels of propranolol in the treatment of migraine are very variable. Most patients are started on a fairly low dose (40–80 mg per day taken in divided doses). Patients are typically titrated every 2 or 3 days, or as tolerated, up to 120 to 160 mg per day, which is taken in three or four divided doses each day. Very few patients receive clinical benefit above 160 mg of propranolol per day. When patients are tapered off propranolol, decrements in headache frequency and severity continue for many patients, whereas others need to reinstitute treatment, usually at lower doses (Anthony, 1978; Diamond & Dalessio, 1982; Saper, 1978; Scheife & Hills, 1980).

Side Effects. One of the most striking side effects of propranolol is fatigue. Patients often report feeling tired and lethargic. Other significant side effects include insomnia, depression, diarrhea, abdominal cramping, and impotence. Because propranolol is the most widely prescribed preventive migraine medicine, it is frequently encountered in clinical practice. The medication often increases an existing depression and/or sleep disorder, and these should always be evaluated in a patient taking propranolol.

Contraindications. Propranolol is relatively contraindicated in patients with bronchial asthma, chronic obstructive pulmonary disease, diabetes mellitus, and congestive heart failure. If the drug is to be decreased or discontinued, it should be done very gradually, as a potentially hazardous cardiovascular rebound phenomenon may occur when propranolol is suddenly withdrawn (Scheife & Hills, 1980).

Although combining psychological treatment with propranolol appears to lead to an enhanced outcome relative to either treatment by itself (Mathew, 1981), research suggests that there may be a minor problem with this particular treatment combination for vascular patients. Jay, Renelli, and Mead (1984) found that propranolol impeded the progress of patients undergoing concurrent thermal biofeedback; curiously, this medication appeared to increase physiological variability. Patients were ultimately able to reach the established biofeedback training criteria, but with significantly greater difficulty and increased frustration. Informing biofeedback patients about the potential interference effects of propranolol may help minimize frustration and offset lapses in motivation.

Amitriptyline and Other Tricyclic Compounds. Initial studies suggested amitriptyline was highly effective for migraine prophylaxis (Couch & Hassenien, 1979; Couch, Ziegler, & Hassanein, 1976; Scheife & Hills, 1980). Subsequent results from a multicenter, double-blind trial involving a large number of patients revealed that amitriptyline's effectiveness was limited to patients whose migraines were accompanied by features of muscle-contraction headache as well (Diamond & Medina, 1981).

The tricyclic antidepressants affect the availability of catecholamine and indolamine neurotransmitters. They appear to block the reuptake of norepinephrine and serotonin peripherally and centrally. They also possess anticholingergic and antihistaminic properties. Clinical evidence suggests that the tricyclics that inhibit the reuptake of serotonin (most notably amitriptyline and doxepin) seem to exert the best prophylactic effect. Antidepressants seem to produce similar outcomes whether or not the headache patient has any symptoms of depression (Couch & Hassanein, 1979, a result that lends further support to the notion that the antimigraine effect is most likely due to the alterations in serotonergic activity and metabolism that these drugs induce. Tricyclics are thought to have an analgesic effect as well when used with headache sufferers (Diamond & Dalessio, 1982).

Dosage. Dosage levels of amitriptyline in migraine vary widely. Some patients respond to as little as 20 mg per day, whereas others require antidepressant levels of over 150 mg per day. Common side effects are drowsiness, dry mouth, constipation, weight gain, blurred vision, and urinary retention. Administering the medication at bedtime helps prevent morning drowsiness.

Contraindications. The drug is contraindicated during the acute recovery phase of myocardial infarction and in patients with narrow-angle glaucoma (Bassuk, Schoonover, & Gelenberg, 1983; Scheife & Hills, 1980).

Naproxen Sodium. Naproxen sodium is a potent anti-inflammatory and analgesic agent that is also a potent inhibitor of prostaglandin synthesis, platelet aggregation, and 5 HT release. Two recent studies found that patients treated with 550 mg twice per day exhibited significant reductions in headache frequency and duration as compared to patients treated with placebo (Welch, Ellis, & Keenan, 1984; Ziegler & Ellis, 1985). Sargent *et al.* (1984) reported females treated with naproxen sodium (550 mg twice per day) experienced their greatest decrease in headache severity during the premenstrual period and that the response to naproxen sodium exceeded that of propranolol and placebo. Baskin, Rapoport, Weeks, and Sheftell (1985) studied the effectiveness of 275 mg of naproxen sodium given three times per day as an intermittent prophylactic (perimenstrually only). Females so treated experienced significant reductions in headache frequency, duration, and intensity. The only notable side effect of naproxen sodium is gastrointestinal tract symptoms.

Cyproheptadine Hydrochloride. Cyproheptadine (Periactin) is both an antihistamine and a serotonin antagonist. It is used for migraine prophylaxis, although the clinical efficacy of this drug has not been established. It tends to work better in children, and its major side effects are drowsiness and weight gain. Patients usually require from 2 to 12 mg per day, with the majority of the dosage taken at bedtime.

Cluster Headache

Episodic Cluster. The treatment of intermittent cluster headache is complex. The acute attack, which is very brief in duration, may often be aborted by either an ergotamine preparation or the inhalation of oxygen. Inhalation of 7 to 10 l of oxygen per minute for 5 to 10 min through a loose-fitting mask stops the pain in an acute cluster attack in approximately 70% of patients, 70%–80% of the time (Kudrow, 1979).

The prophylactic treatment of the episodic cluster patient is based on several considerations, including age, duration of disease, and possible drug tolerance, as well as the presence of other disorders that contraindicate some medications. Usually, for the patient under 50, methysergide (6–8 mg per day) or prednisone is the treatment of choice. Prednisone is a glucocorticoid, a synthetic derivative of cortisone. To help prevent cluster attacks in the episodic patient, prednisone is prescribed at 40 to 60 mg per day for 5 days and is then tapered off over a period of 3 weeks. It is contraindicated in ulcer disease, diabetes, hypertension, active infections, and diverticulosis. Outcome data for episodic cluster headaches showed that approximately 77% of patients obtain significant improvement with prednisone, and that 50% of patients achieve a significant response with methysergide (Kudrow, 1978). Ergotamine preparations may also be given before bedtime to prevent the early-morning attack. Beta blockers, such as propranolol do not appear to be effective in cluster headache, although they remain widely prescribed.

Chronic Cluster. In chronic cluster, the most effective results are obtained with lithium carbonate. Lithium is given at from 600 to 1200 mg per day, in divided doses. Besides being the first choice for patients with chronic cluster, it is often given to patients over 45 years of age with episodic cluster. Common side effects include tremor and gastrointestinal symptoms. It is important to avoid lithium toxicity by keeping blood levels below 1.2 mg%. This medication is contraindicated in patients with significant renal or cardiovascular disease. Outcome studies suggest effective results for approximately 60% to 87% of chronic cluster patients (Ekbom, 1977; Kudrow, 1977, 1980).

Preliminary evidence suggests that calcium-channel antagonists may also be helpful in the treatment of chronic and episodic cluster (Meyer & Hardenberg, 1983; Meyer *et al.*, 1984). Calcium antagonists are now in the experimental stages in the treatment of classic and common migraine as well with similar positive results (Solomon, 1985). These medications have been used for years in the treatment of various cardiovascular disorders. It has been proposed that calcium antagonists exert their clinical effects (prevention of vascular headache) by inhibiting smooth muscle contractions of the cerebral vasculature (Meyer *et al.*, 1984). Side effects appear to be minimal, with the most notable being constipation.

Muscle-Contraction Headache

An important therapeutic consideration is the paradoxical effect of daily analgesic ingestion on the frequency of headache, as well as the possibility that analgesics interfere with the effectivenes of amitriptyline treatment. It appears that approximately 70% to 80% of chronic scalp muscle-contraction headache patients obtain significant reductions in headache frequency with amitriptyline treatment without daily analgesics (Diamond & Baltes, 1971; Kudrow, 1982; Lance & Curran, 1964). Most clinicians in the field believe amitriptyline to be the first-choice tricyclic and doxepin the second. The effective dosage is much lower than the levels required for an antidepressant effect. It is helpful to start patients at the smallest possible dosage, usually given at bedtime, and gradually to increase the dosage every 3 to 7 days, up to a total of approximately 50 mg per day. The majority of patients show a favorable response to 50 mg per day of amitriptyline (Kudrow, 1982).

Jay *et al.*'s study (1984) of adverse effects of psychological and medical treatment combinations found that amitriptyline complicated concurrent training in electromyographic biofeedback for muscle-contraction patients. Patients need to be forewarned of this possibility.

Combined Migraine and Muscle-Contraction Headache

For combination or mixed headache patients, most clinicians usually begin treatment preventively with either amitriptyline or propranolol and observe the results. Depending on the outcome, they may then add the other medication.

SUMMARY

This chapter was written to help familiarize psychologists with diagnostic issues that may arise when evaluating headache patients, to acquaint them with a basic understanding of the pathophysiology of headache, and to review the advantages and disadvantages of the medical treatments commonly used to manage headache. The diagnostic issues of greatest importance concern (1) ruling out and continually monitoring for the presence of an identifiable lesion as a physical cause for the headache; (2) recognizing migraine patients who are experiencing cluster or menstrual headache, as these subtypes respond questionably to psychological interventions; (3) assessing the possibility that medication serves inadvertently to exacerbate or maintain headache and, if so, taking steps to have the patient reduce or eliminate these medications; and (4) determining if depression or other psychological factors may pose a significant barrier to the direct psychological treatment of headache.

A review of the available pathophysiological literature indicates that headache is a complex disorder. For example, migraine has been variously viewed as a peripheral vascular disorder, a biochemical disorder, and a central nervous system disorder. Multiple pathophysiological accounts have been advanced for muscle-contraction headache as well.

The medical treatments available to the headache patient are diverse, and evidence is available to support the effectiveness of most. Unfortunately, no medication reviewed is free of untoward effects, and the side effects of a few warrant their use in only special cases. There is some evidence that patients who are being maintained on a course of propranolol or amitriptyline may encounter difficulties when biofeedback training is begun with them.

REFERENCES

Ad Hoc Committee on Classification of Headache. (1962). Classification of headache. *Journal of American Medical Association, 179,* 717–718.

Adams, H. E., Brantley, P. J., & Thompson, K. (1982). Biofeedback and headache: Methodological issues. In L. White & B. Tursky (Eds.), *Clinical biofeedback: Efficacy and mechanisms.* New York: Guilford Press.

Adler, C. S., & Adler, S. M. (1975). Biofeedback-psychotherapy for the treatment of headaches: A 5-year follow-up. *Headache, 16,* 189–191.

Ala-Hurula, V., Myllyla, V., & Hokkanen, E. (1982). Ergotamine abuse: Results of ergotamine discontinuation, with special reference to the plasma concentration. *Cephalalgia, 2,* 189–195.

Andrasik, F. (1986). Relaxation and biofeedback for chronic headaches. In A. D. Holzman & D. C. Turk (Eds.), *Pain management: A handbook of psychological treatment approaches.* New York: Pergamon Press.

Andrasik, F., Blanchard, E. B., Arena, J. G., Saunders, N. L., & Barron, K. D. (1982). Psychophysiology of recurrent headache: Methodological issues and new empirical findings. *Behavior Therapy, 13,* 407–429.

Andrasik, F., Blanchard, E. B., Arena, J. G., Teders, S. J., Teevan, R. C., & Rodichok, L. D. (1982). Psychological functioning in headache sufferers. *Psychosomatic Medicine, 44,* 171–182.

Andrasik, F., Blake, D. D., & McCarran, M. S. (1986). A biobehavioral analysis of pediatric headache. In N. A. Krasnegor, J. D. Arasteh, & M. F. Cataldo (Eds.), *Child health behavior: A behavioral pediatrics perspective.* New York: Wiley.

Anselmi, B., Baldi, E., Casacci, F., & Salmon, S. (1980). Endogenous opioids in cerebral spinal fluid and blood in idiopathic headache sufferers. *Headache, 20,* 294–299.

Anthony, M. (1978). Beta-blockers in migraine prophylaxis. *Drugs, 15,* 249–250.

Anthony, M., & Lance, J. (1971). Histamine and serotonin in cluster headache. *Archives of Neurology, 25,* 225–231.

Anthony, M., Hinterberger, H., & Lance, J. (1969). The possible relationship of serotonin to the migraine syndrome. In A. Friedman (Ed.), *Research and clinical studies in headache*. Basel: Karger.

Appenzeller, O., Feldman, R. G., & Friedman, A. P. (1979). Migraine headache and related conditions. *Archives of Neurology, 36,* 784–805.

Arena, J. G., Blanchard, E. B., Andrasik, F., & Dudek, B. C. (1982). The Headache Symptom Questionnaire: Discriminant classificatory ability and headache syndromes suggested by a factor analysis. *Journal of Behavioral Assessment, 4,* 55–69.

Bakal, D. A. (1982). *The psychobiology of chronic headache*. New York: Springer.

Baskin, S. M., Rapoport, A. R., Weeks, R. E., & Sheftell, F. D. (1985). *The effect of naproxen sodium on menstrual migraine*. Paper presented at the 27th meeting of the American Association for the Study of Headache, New York.

Bassuk, E. L., Schoonover, S. C., & Gelenberg,A. J. (Eds.). (1983). *The practitioner's guide to psychoactive drugs*. New York: Plenum Press.

Bekes, M., Matos, L., Rausch, J., & Torok, E. (1968). Treatment of migraine with propranolol. *Lancet, 2,* 1355–1356.

Blanchard, E. B., & Andrasik, F. (1985). *Management of chronic headaches: A psychological approach*. New York: Pergamon Press.

Blanchard, E. B., Andrasik, F., Jurish, S. E., & Teders, S. J. (1982). The treatment of cluster headache with relaxation and thermal biofeedback. *Biofeedback and Self-Regulation, 7,* 185–191.

Blanchard, E. B., O'Keefe, D., Neff, D., Jurish, S., & Andrasik, F. (1981). Interdisciplinary agreement in the diagnosis of headache types. *Journal of Behavioral Assessment, 3,* 5–9.

Blanchard, E. B., Andrasik, F., Neff, D. F., Arena, J. G., Ahles, T. A., Jurish, S. E., Pallmeyer, T. P., Saunders, N. L., Teders, S. J., Barron, K. D., & Rodichok, L. D. (1982). Biofeedback and relaxation training with three kinds of headache: Treatment effects and their prediction. *Journal of Consulting and Clinical Psychology, 50,* 562–575.

Cohen, M. J. (1978). Psychophysiological studies of headache: Is there similarity between migraine and muscle-contraction headaches? *Headache, 18,* 189–196.

Couch, J. R., & Hassanein, R. S. (1977). Platelet aggregability in migraine. *Neurology, 27,* 843–848.

Couch, J. R., & Hassanein, R. S. (1979). Amitriptyline in migraine prophylaxis. *Archives of Neurology, 36,* 659–699.

Couch, J. R., Ziegler, D. K., & Hassanein, R. S. (1976). Amitriptyline in the prophylaxis of migraine. *Neurology, 26,* 121–127.

Cox, D. J., & Thomas, D. (1981). Relationship between headaches and depression. *Headache, 21,* 261–263.

Cox, D. J., Lefebvre, R. C., & Hobbs, W. R. (1982). Ancillary symptoms in the biofeedback treatment of headaches. *Headache, 22,* 213–215.

Dalessio, D. J. (Ed.). (1980). *Wolff's headache and other head pain* (4th ed.). New York: Oxford University Press.

Dalessio, D. J. (1984). Beta-blockers and migraine (Editorial). *Journal of the American Medical Association, 252,* 2614.

Davis, R. A., Wetzel, R. D., Kashiwagi, M. D., & McClure, J. N. (1976). Personality, depression and headache. *Headache, 16,* 246–251.

Diamond, S. (1983). Depression and headache. *Headache, 23,* 123–126.

Diamond, S., & Baltes, B. J. (1971). Chronic tension headache treated with amitriptyline: Double-blind study. *Headache, 11,* 110–116.

Diamond, S., & Dalessio, D. J. (1982). *The practicing physician's approach to headache* (3rd ed.). Baltimore: Williams & Wilkins.

Diamond, S., & Medina, J. (1976). Double-blind study of propranolol for migraine prophylaxis. *Headache, 16,* 24–27.

Diamond, S., & Medina, J. L (1981). Pharmacological treatment of migraine. In R. J. Mathew (Ed.), *Treatment of migraine: Pharmacological and biofeedback considerations*. New York: SP Medical and Scientific Books.

Edmeads, J. (1982). Migraine as a model of neurogenic ischemia. *Headache, 22,* 277–288.

Ekbom, K. (1970). A clinical comparison of cluster headache and migraine. *Acta Neurologica Scandinavica,* *46,* 1–48.

Ekbom, K. (1977). Lithium in the treatment of chronic cluster headache. *Headache, 17,* 39–42.

Fanchamps, A. (1975). Pharmacodynamic principles of anti-migraine therapy. *Headache, 15,* 79–90.

Fanciullacci, M., Pietrini, U., Gatto, G., Boccuni, M., & Sicuteri, F. (1982). Latent dysautonomic pupillary lateralization in cluster headache: A pupillometric study. *Cephalalgia, 2,* 135–144.

Forssman, B., Hendricksson, K. G., & Johannsson, V. (1976). Propranolol for migraine prophylaxis. *Headache, 16,* 238–245.

Fox-Moller, F., Genefke, I., & Bryndum, B. (1978). Changes in concentration of catecholamines in blood during spontaneous migraine attacks and reserpine-induced attacks. In R. Greene (Ed.), *Current concepts in migraine research.* New York: Raven Press.

Fozard, J. R. (1982). Basic mechanisms of anti-migraine drugs. In M. Critchley, A. Friedman, S. Gorini, & F. Sicuteri (Eds.), *Headache: Physiopathological and clinical concepts (Advances in Neurology,* Vol. 33). New York: Raven Press.

Friedman, A. P. (1982). Overview of migraine. In M. Critchley, A. Friedman, S. Gorini, & F. Sicuteri (Eds.), *Headache: Physiopathological and clinical concepts.* New York: Raven Press.

Fritz, G., & Fehmi, L. (1983). Cluster headaches: A cerebrovascular disorder treated with biofeedback-assisted attention training. In *Proceedings of the 14th Annual Meeting of the Biofeedback Society of America,* pp. 82–83.

Gawel, M., & Rose, F. C. (1982). Platelet function in migraineurs. In M. Critchley, A. Friedman, S. Gorini, F. Sicuteri (Eds.), *Headache: Physiopathological and clinical concepts (Advances in Neurology,* Vol. 33). New York: Raven Press.

Graham, J. (1969, October). *Cluster headache.* Paper presented at the International Symposium on Headache, Chicago.

Hanington, E. (1982). Migraine as a blood disorder: Preliminary studies. In E. Critchley, A. Friedman, S. Gorini, & F. Sicuteri (Eds.), *Headache: Physiopathological and clinical concepts (Advances in Neurology,* Vol. 33). New York: Raven Press.

Haynes, S. N., Cuevas, J., & Gannon, L. R. (1982). The psychophysiological etiology of muscle-contraction headache. *Headache, 22,* 122–132.

Holroyd, K. A., & Andrasik, F. (1982). A cognitive-behavioral approach to recurrent tension and migraine headache. In P. C. Kendall (Ed.), *Advances in cognitive-behavioral research and therapy* (Vol. 1). New York: Academic Press.

Hurley, F. E. (1969, March). *Practical management of headache in office practice.* Paper presented at the meeting of the Chicago Medical Society, Chicago.

Jacob, R. G., Turner, S. M., Szekely, B. C., & Eidelman, B. H. (1983). Predicting outcome of relaxation therapy in headaches: The role of "depression." *Behavior Therapy, 14,* 457–465.

Jay, G. W., Renelli, D., & Mead, T. (1984). The effects of propranolol and amitriptyline on vascular and EMG biofeedback training. *Headache, 24,* 59–69.

Kudrow, L. (1976a). Hormones, pregnancy and migraine. In O. Appenzeller (Ed.), *Pathogenesis and treatment of headache.* New York: Spectrum.

Kudrow, L. (1976b). Tension headache (scalp muscle-contraction headache). In O. Appenzeller (Ed.), *Pathogenesis and treatment of headache.* New York: Spectrum.

Kudrow, L. (1976c). Prevalence of migraine, peptic ulcer, coronary heart disease, and hypertension in cluster headache. *Headache, 16,* 66–69.

Kudrow, L. (1977). Lithium prophylaxis for chronic cluster headache. *Headache, 17,* 15–18.

Kudrow, L. (1978). Comparative results of prednisone, methysergide, and lithium therapy in cluster headache. In R. Green (Ed.), *Current concepts in migraine research.* New York: Raven Press.

Kudrow, L. (1979). Cluster headache: Diagnosis and management. *Headache, 19,* 142–150.

Kudrow, L. (1980). *Cluster headache: Mechanisms and management.* New York: Oxford University Press.

Kudrow, L. (1982). Paradoxical effects of frequent analgesic use. In M. Critchley, A. Friedman, S. Gorini, & F. Sicuteri (Eds.), *Headache: Physiopathological and clinical concepts (Advances in Neurology,* Vol. 33). New York: Raven Press.

Kudrow, L. (1985). A distinctive facial thermographic pattern in cluster headache—The "Chai" sign. *Headache, 25,* 33–36.

Kudrow, L., & Sutkus, B. J. (1979). MMPI pattern specificity in primary headache disorders. *Headache, 19,*

18–24.

Lake, A. E. (1981). Behavioral assessment considerations in the management of headache. *Headache, 21,* 170–178.

Lance, J. W. (1973). *Mechanisms and management of headache* (2nd ed.). London: Butterworth.

Lance, J. W. (1982). What is migraine? In M. Critchley, A. Friedman, S. Gorini, & F. Sicuteri (Eds.), *Headache: Physiopathological and clinical concepts (Advances in Neurology,* Vol. 33). New York: Raven Press.

Lance, J. W., & Curran, D. A. (1964). Treatment of chronic tension headache. *Lancet, 1,* 1236–1239.

Lance, J. W., Curran, D. A., & Anthony, M. (1965). Investigations into the mechanism and treatment of chronic headache. *Medical Journal of Australia, 2,* 909–914.

Leviton, A. (1978). Epidemiology of headache. In V. S. Schoenberg (Ed.), *Advances in neurology* (Vol. 19). New York: Raven Press.

Luborsky, L., Docherty, J. P., & Penick, S. (1973). Onset conditions for psychosomatic symptoms: A comparative review of immediate observation with retrospective research. *Psychosomatic Medicine, 35,* 187–204.

Martin, J. J. (1978). Psychogenic factors in headache. *Medical Clinics of North America, 62,* 559–570.

Mathew, N. T. (1981). Prohylaxis of migraine and mixed headache: A randomized controlled study. *Headache, 21,* 105–109.

Meyer, J. S., & Hardenberg, J. (1983). Clinical effectiveness of calcium entry blockers in prophylactic treatment of migraine and cluster headaches. *Headache, 23,* 266–277.

Meyer, J. S., Dowell, R., Mathew, N., & Hardenberg, J. (1984). Clinical and hemodynamic effects during treatment of vascular headaches with Verapamil. *Headache, 24,* 313–321.

Nattero, G. (1982). Menstrual headache. In M. Critchley, A. Friedman, S. Gorini, & F. Sicuteri (Eds.), *Headache: Physiopathological and clinical concepts (Advances in Neurology,* Vol. 33). New York: Raven Press.

Nelson, R. (1978). Testosterone levels in cluster and non-cluster migrainous headache patients. *Headache, 18,* 265–267.

Olesen, J. (1978). Some clinical features of the acute migraine attack: An analysis of 750 patients. *Headache, 18,* 268–271.

Olesen, J., Lauritzen, M., Tfelt-Hansen, P., Henriksen, L., & Larsen, B. (1982). Spreading cerebral oligemia in classical and normal cerebral blood flow in common migraine. *Headache, 22,* 242–248.

Packard, R. C. (1979). What does the headache patient want? *Headache, 19,* 370–374.

Philips, H. C. (1978). Tension headache: Theoretical problems. *Behaviour Research and Therapy, 16,* 249–261.

Rapaport, A., Sheftell, F., Baskin, S., & Weeks, R. (1984, September). *Analgesic rebound headache.* Paper presented at the meeting of the Migraine Trust, London.

Raskin, N. H., & Appenzeller, O. (1980). *Headache.* Philadelphia: Saunders.

Rodbard, S. (1970). Pain associated with muscle contraction. *Headache, 10,* 105–115.

Romiti, A., Martelletti, P., Gallo, M. F., & Giacovazzo, M. (1983). Low testosterone levels in cluster headache. *Cephalalgia, 3,* 41–44.

Rydzewski, W. (1976). Serotonin (5H.T.) in migraine: Levels in whole blood in and between attacks. *Headache, 16,* 16–19.

Saper, J. R. (1978). Migraine. *Journal of American Medical Association, 239,* 2380–2382, 2480–2484.

Saper, J. (1982). The mixed headache syndrome: A new perspective. *Headache, 22,* 284–286.

Saper, J., & Van Meter, M. J. (1980, June). *Ergotamine habituation: An analysis and profile.* Paper presented at the 22nd meeting of the American Association for the Study of Headache, San Francisco.

Sargent, J., Solbach, P., Damasio, H., Baumel, B., Corbett, J., Eisner, L., Jessen, B., Kudrow, L., Mathew, N., Medina, J., Saper, J., Vijayan, N., Watson, C., & Alger, J. (1985). A comparison of naproxen sodium to propranolol hydrochloride and a placebo control for the prophylaxis of migraine headache. *Headache, 25,* 320–324.

Scheife, R. T., & Hills, J. R. (1980). Migraine headache: Signs and symptoms, biochemistry, and current therapy. *American Journal of Hospital Pharmacy, 37,* 65–74.

Sicuteri, F. (1979). Headache as the most common disease of the antinociceptive system: Analogies with morphine abstinence. In J. Bonica & V. Ventafridda (Eds.), *Advances in pain research and therapy* (Vol. 2). New York: Raven Press.

Sicuteri, F. (1980). Empty neuron theory as a research prospective of diseases of the nociceptive system. *Journal of Drug Research, 5,* 73–78.

Sicuteri, F. (1982). Natural opioids in migraine. In M. Critchley, A. Friedman, S. Gorini, & F. Sicuteri (Eds.), *Headache: Physiopathological and clinical concepts (Advances in Neurology,* Vol. 33). New York: Raven Press.

Sjaastad, O. (1978). Pathogenesis of the cluster headache syndrome. *Research and Clinical Study of Headache, 6,* 53–64.

Sjaatad, O., & Sjaastad, O. V. (1977). Histamine metabolism in cluster headache and migraine. *Journal of Neurology, 216,* 105–117.

Solbach, P., Sargent, J., & Coyne, L. (1984). Menstrual migraine headache: Results of a controlled, experimental, outcome study of non-drug treatments. *Headache, 24,* 75–78.

Solomon, G. D. (1985). Comparative efficacy of calcium antagonist drugs in the prophylaxis of migraine. *Headache, 25,* 368–371.

Somerville, B. W. (1971). The role of progesterone in menstrual migraine. *Neurology, 21,* 853–859.

Somerville, B. W. (1972). The role of estradiol withdrawal in the etiology of menstrual migraine. *Neurology, 22,* 355–365.

Spierings, E. L. H. (1980). *The pathophysiology of the migraine attack.* Stafleu's Wetenschappelijke Uitgeversmaatschappij BV, Alphen aan den Rijn, the Netherlands.

Thompson, J. K. (1982). Diagnosis of head pain: An idiographic approach to assessment and classification. *Headache, 22,* 221–232.

Turkat, I. D., Brantley, P. J., Orton, K., & Adams, H. E. (1981). Reliability of headache diagnosis. *Journal of Behavioral Assessment, 3,* 1–4.

Weber, R. B., & Reinmuth, O. M. (1971). The treatment of migraine with propranolol. *Neurology, 21,* 404–405.

Weber, R. B., & Reinmuth, O. M. (1972). The treatment of migraine with propranolol. *Neurology, 22,* 366–369.

Weeks, R., Baskin, S., Rapoport, A., & Sheftell, F. (1984, June). *Reliability of headache diagnosis: A valid assumption or convenient fiction?* Paper presented at the 26th meeting of the American Association for the Study of Headache, San Francisco.

Welch, K. M. A., Ellis, D., & Keenan, P. A. (1984). Naproxen sodium in migraine prophylaxis. *Neurology* (NY, Suppl. 1), *34,* 246.

Wideroe, T., & Vigander, T. (1974). Propranolol in the treatment of migraine. *Bristish Medical Journal, 2,* 699–701.

Ziegler, D. K. (1977). Genetics of migraine. *Headache, 16,* 330–331.

Ziegler, D. K., & Ellis, D. J. (1985). Naproxen in prophylaxis of migraine. *Archives of Neurology, 42,* 582–584.

Ziegler, D. K., Rhodes, R. J., & Hassanein, R. S. (1978). Association of psychological measurements of anxiety and depression with headache history in a nonclinical population. M. E. Granger (Eds.), *Research Clinical Studies in Headache (Vol. 5).* Basel: Karger.

14

Eating Disorders

DONALD A. WILLIAMSON, C. J. DAVIS,

AND LAURIE RUGGIERO

Anorexia nervosa, bulimia, and obesity are the most common eating disorders seen in medical and mental health settings. In recent years, these disorders have received increasing attention from researchers in the fields of psychology, psychiatry, and medicine. Earlier efforts to identify specific physical or neurological causes of these disorders were generally unsuccessful. However, more recent models that have integrated biological and psychological factors have produced more encouraging results (Rosen & Leitenberg, 1982; Stunkard, 1980). These more integrated models have led researchers to begin the development of more innovative and comprehensive treatment approaches (Brownell, 1982). One of the implications of these more integrated treatment approaches is that psychologists, in particular, must become familiar with the medical consequences of these eating disorders so that proper assessment of these medical problems can be accomplished and appropriate referrals for medical treatment can be made. The purposes of this chapter are to describe the common physical problems that accompany anorexia nervosa, bulimia, and obesity, and to point out the implications of these problems for treatment planning.

ANOREXIA NERVOSA

Diagnosis

Clinical Description. "Nervosa atrophy" was first described in 1689 by Morton (1720), who reported that sadness and anxiety accounted for the emaciation of his 18-year-old patient. Approximately 300 years later, the term *anorexia nervosa* was introduced. According to current diagnostic standards, it is an eating disorder characterized by the criteria in Table 1.

Anorexia occurs predominantly in female adolescents and young adults, the age of onset typically being between 12 and 25 (Halmi, 1974, 1980a). The emaciation of anorexics, which is the cardinal characteristic of the disorder, is attained through various methods, including rigorous exercise programs and drastic reduction of food intake; carbohydrate and fat-containing foods are especially avoided. Even though the anorexic is well below the standard weight for her height (at least 25% below), fear of weight gain

DONALD A. WILLIAMSON, C. J. DAVIS AND LAURIE RUGGIERO • Department of Psychology, Louisiana State University, Baton Rouge, LA 70803-5501.

Table 1. Diagnostic Criteria for Anorexia Nervosa

Diagnostic criteria

1. Intense fear of obesity which does not diminish as weight loss progresses.
2. Distorted body image, that is, perception of body as fat despite low body weight.
3. Weight status of at least 25% underweight. (New criteria for DSM III-R have been proposed to be at least 15% underweight.)
4. Refusal to maintain normal body weight.

ensures that these severe weight-control methods will continue to be used. Body image dysfunction, or "feeling fat," even when very slim, may also explain this dietary regimen. Studies of body image distortion have consistently shown that anorexics overestimate the size of their bodies and wish to be exceedingly thin (Casper, Halmi, Goldberg, Eckert, & Davis, 1979; Crisp & Kalucy, 1974; Garner, Garfinkel, Stancer, & Moldofsky, 1976; Slade & Russell, 1973).

Preoccupation with weight is not abnormal within the adolescent and young-adult female population. However, an early warning sign of anorexia is a singular obsession with dieting and weight (Bruch, 1977). This preoccupation may lead to the unusual eating habits sometimes displayed by anorexics. Continuous thoughts of food, eccentric diets (sometimes consisting of very selective foods, e.g., only cheese and crackers), the hiding of food (Baruch, 1973, 1977; Halmi, 1980a), and anxiety while eating in the presence of others (Bruch, 1977; Casper *et al.*, 1979) have all been noted in the literature describing anorexia.

Differential Diagnosis. A diagnosis of anorexia nervosa is sometimes difficult to make, as patients with this disorder are often secretive, denying both the symptomatology and the seriousness of their disorder. Therefore, information from significant others (e.g., parents, friends, or teachers, if the patient is an adolescent) is helpful. In particular, these persons can often provide important information regarding the patient's dieting, the first signs of weight loss, and the patient's weight history.

It is important that the anorexic patient have a thorough physical and neurological examination before the final diagnosis. In some cases, brain tumors have been found to be the cause of anorexia (Halmi, 1980). Also, any medical problems that may account for the severe weight loss must be ruled out before the diagnosis of anorexia can be made (DSM-III, APA, 1980).

Symptoms of anorexia (weight loss, vomiting, and ritualistic or bizarre eating patterns) can also occur in several psychiatric disorders. Depressive disorders and anorexia are similar in that weight loss, depressed affect, obsessive thoughts, and suicidal ideation have been noted in both (Halmi, 1980a). Typically, the depressed patient does not experience the severity of weight loss that the anorexic does. The obsession with weight, exercise, food, and food preparation evident in anorexics is not present in the patient who is depressed.

A second disorder that must be differentiated from anorexia is the somatization disorder. Amenorrhea and weight loss sometimes occur in both. Amenorrhea in a female with a somatization disorder rarely lasts beyond 3 months, however. Also, the weight loss experienced by a patient with a somatization disorder is usually not as severe as that in anorexia. On rare occasions, a patient will meet the diagnostic criteria of both of these disorders, and so both diagnoses should be made.

Occasionally, anorexia must be differentiated from schizophrenia. Delusions regarding food and weight are rarely concerned with calories and fear of weight gain. Also, anorexics are alert and oriented, characteristics that may distinguish them from some schizophrenics (Halmi, 1980a).

The major diagnostic criterion that separates anorexia from bulimia is binge eating (Ben-Tovim, Marilov, & Crisp, 1979; Casper, Eckert, Halmi, Goldberg, & Davis, 1980; Garfinkel, Moldofsky, & Garner, 1980). Bulimics exhibit a pattern of the consumption of large quantities of food within a short period of time (usually 2 hours or less), which is often followed by depression, self-deprecating thoughts, and purging (vomiting or the use of laxatives and/or diuretics). Bulimics are typically of normal to above-normal weight, which is quite different from the weight of anorexics (Fairburn, 1981; Halmi & Falk, & Schwartz, 1981). Also, amenorrhea is not found as consistently in bulimic patients (Schlesier-Stropp, 1984).

Therefore, before a diagnostic of anorexia nervosa can be made, a thorough medical and psychological examination should be conducted. Any physiological problems that can account for or are maintaining severe weight loss should be identified. Also, depressive disorders, somatization disorders, schizophrenia, and bulimia should be ruled out before the diagnosis of anorexia is made.

Medical Problems

Mortality. A review of the literature indicates that mortality among anorexics ranges from 0% to 21.5% (Cantwell, Sturzenberger, Burroughs, Salkin, & Green, 1977; Garfinkel, Garner, & Moldofsky, 1977; Hsu, 1980; Pertschuk, 1977). The mean mortality rate for anorexics is approximately 5% (Hsu, 1980). Primary causes of death include inanition (exhaustion from lack of food), suicide, infection, and hypothermia. However, a decrease in the death rate among anorexics has been noted in recent years. This decline may be attributed to earlier recognition of the disorder and increased referrals to those with experience in treating anorexia (Halmi, 1980a; Pierloot, Wellins, & Horiben, 1975). Therefore, anorexia is a serious disorder that is potentially life-threatening because of the serious medical problems associated with the diagnosis, as well as the risk of suicide.

Endocrine Problems. ''The most obvious endocrine aberration in anorexia nervosa is amenorrhea'' (Halmi, 1983). Amenorrhea is present in over 70% of anorexics (Bruch, 1973; Nillius, 1983; Theander, 1970). Lowered secretion of luteinizing hormone (LH) from the anterior hypophysis explains this phenomenon (Nillius, 1983). Secretion of a second gonadotropic hormone, follicle-stimulating hormone (FSH), is normal, except in those women who are critically underweight. This pattern of secretion of LH and FSH is similar to that of prepubescent girls who have not yet attained the critical fat storage for menstruation. Frisch and McArthur (1974) stated that 17% fat to body weight is needed for the onset of menstruation, and 22% fat to body weight is necessary for maintenance. When a women's weight falls significantly below its optimal value for her height, her menses can be expected to cease. However, other factors may be involved, as amenorrhea sometimes precedes weight loss and may persist after weight has been regained (Gold, Poltash, Martin, Extein, & Howard 1981–1982; Morgan & Russell, 1975).

Recent studies of thyroid function in anorexics have shown that serum triiodothyronine (T_3) levels are low (Burman, Vigersky, & Loriaux, 1977; Croxson & Ibbertson, 1977). Triiodothyronine exerts the same biological effects as thyroxin but is more potent and has a more rapid onset of effect. This thyroid hormone is thought to affect protein synthesis in the body. The same phenomenon of T_3 deprivation found in anorexics is also found in patients with protein–calorie malnutrition, as well as in obese patients on no-carbohydrate hypocaloric diets (Chopra, Chopra, & Smith, 1975; Vagenakias, Burger, & Portney, 1975). In light of these findings, it appears that the presence of protein and carbohydrates is important in facilitating the production of T_3 (Hsu, 1980). Thus, the low levels of T_3 observed in anorexics are likely to be the result of a diet low in protein and carbohydrate.

Another common endocrine aberration seen in anorexics is the abnormal secretion of growth hormone. Anorexics have been shown to have a pattern of secretion different from that of normals (Kalucy, Crisp, Chard, T., McNeilly, Chen, & Lacey, 1976), but similar to that of a group of malnourished, sleep-deprived patients (Wolff & Money, 1973). The pattern of low nocturnal and high-resting diurnal levels of growth hormone can be remediated after the restoration of weight to normal levels. In addition to the problems noted earlier, other endocrine problems have been identified in those diagnosed as anorexic. They include hyperinsulinism, insulin resistance, and increased cortisol production (Halmi, 1983; Kalucy *et al.*, 1976; Weiner, 1982).

Thus, anorexia nervosa is a disorder that may cause a variety of endocrine aberrations. The most common abnormalities are an abnormal pattern of gonadotropic hormone secretion, low serum triiodothyronine levels, abnormal secretion of growth hormone, excessive secretion of insulin, and increased cortisol production.

Hematological Problems. Anemia and immunological system problems are two of the most common problems associated with anorexia. These conditions result from the starvation state of the anorexic.

As early as 1959, abnormalities in hematopoiesis (the process of the formation and development of the various types of blood cells) were noted in anorexics (Carryer, Berkman, & Mason, 1959). Severe leukopenia (a condition in which the total number of white blood cells in the blood is lower than normal) and lymphocytosis (an abnormally large number of white blood cells, as observed in acute infections) were evident in severely emaciated patients. Since that time, it has also been shown that bone marrow abnormalities can occur in anorexics, adversely affecting the normal development of blood cells (Mant & Fargher, 1972), which may lead to severe anemia, as well as immunological problems. Several studies have shown that some anorexics have a reduced capacity to fight infections, which is caused by a lowered white-blood-cell count (Palmblad, Fohlin, & Lundstrom, 1977). However, with weight gain, it has been shown that both the anemia and the increased risk of infection experienced by anorexics can be remediated.

Metabolic Problems. Studies investigating metabolism changes resulting from starvation and semistarvation suggest that several adaptive changes occur. Studies on both animal and human subjects indicate that food is used more efficiently after a period of starvation (Boyle, Storlein, & Keesey, 1978; Keys, Brozek, Hanschel, Mickelson, & Taylor, 1950; Walker, Roberts, & Halmi, 1979). One study of anorexics showed that those with the greatest weight loss needed the fewest calories to gain 1 kg of weight when recovery occurred (Walker *et al.*, 1979). Another metabolic consequence of fasting is a reduction in the body's dependence on gluconeogenesis (formation of glycogen from noncarbohydrates), which spares the breakdown of body protein (Cahill, Herrera, Morgan, Sueldmer, Steinker, Levy, Richard, & Kipnis, 1966). This economization allows essential body functions to continue much longer than normal.

Stordy, Marks, Kalucy, and Crisp (1977) found that anorexics had a basal metabolic rate 24% below that off a normal eater of the same age, height, and target weight. It was predicted from this study that this "hypometabolic" population would have future problems maintaining an average weight (that is, not gaining excess weight) because of the observed lowered metabolism. However, other research has shown that providing a totally fasted individual with glucose can reverse the metabolic alterations that have occurred with the starvation (Aoki, Muller, & Brennan, 1975). Therefore, the long-term metabolic effects of anorexia are still unknown.

Other Medical Problems. It has been shown that cardiovascular problems can develop in patients with anorexia. Abnormalities of cardiac rate and conduction have been reported, including bradycardia, tachycardia, sinus arrests, and ectopic atrial rhythm (Fohlin, 1977; Mitchell & Gillum, 1980; Palossy & Oo, 1977; Thurston & Marks, 1974).

Other medical complications associated with anorexia are hypocarotenemia, impaired water diuresis, hypothermia, and hypotension. High levels of serum cholesterol in anorexics has been the subject of several studies (Crisp, Blendis, & Palwan, 1968; Klinefelter, 1965; Nestel, 1974). However, the results of these studies are mixed with findings ranging from high to normal levels of serum cholesterol in anorexics. Impaired water diuresis, hypothermia, and hypotension have been noted primarily in severely emaciated anorexics (Aperia, Broberger, & Fohlin, 1978; Halmi, 1980a; Russell & Bruce, 1966). These conditions all seem to result from severely reduced caloric intake.

Cardiovascular problems (bradycardia, tachycardia, sinus arrests, ectopic atrial rhythm, and hypotension), hypothermia, and impaired water diuresis are all medical problems associated with anorexia. All have been reported to remediate after weight recovery is attained. However, few studies have investigated the etiology of these problems. Further research is needed to clarify the complications associated with these problems.

Treatment Implications

Beneficial Effects of Weight Gain. Many of the physiological problems experienced by anorexics can be remediated with weight gain. Endocrine functions (increase production of T_3 hormone, normal pattern of growth hormone secretions, and decreased cortisol and insulin levels) return to normal, with the exception of the problem of amenorrhea. After treatment, the onset of menses may lag behind the return to normal weight. In a review of 16 studies of treatment outcome, Hsu (1980) found that only 50% to 75% of anorexics were menstruating at follow-up. It was noted that women experiencing menstrual irregularities had significantly more symptoms of anorexia (behaviors and cognitions), and that the return of menses was correlated with psychological improvement (Morgan & Russell, 1975). Cardiovascular and hematological problems (arrhythmias, normal production of blood cells, and remediation in bone marrow abnormalities) also improved, most often returning to premorbid levels (Fohlin, 1977; Mant & Fargher, 1972; Mitchell & Gillum, 1980).

Problems That May Accompany Weight Gain. Medically, the goal of treatment in anorexia is to assist the patient in reaching a normal state of nutrition (Halmi, 1980a). Behavioral strategies to increase eating and thus produce weight gain have been found to be quite effective (Bellack & Williamson, 1982). A typical behavioral treatment program for anorexia may involve hospitalization and reinforcement of eating and weight gain (Azerrand & Stafford, 1969; Clark & Munford, 1980; Erwin, 1977; Garfinkel, Kline, & Stancer, 1973). However, with refeeding, several considerations regarding the management of the anorexic patient must be noted.

Because of possible impaired water diuresis, fluid intake and urine output should be recorded daily. Any constipation resulting from electrolyte imbalance should be relieved with weight gain. Laxatives should not be given if at all possible because of possible laxative abuse.

With refeeding, care should be taken in choosing the initial level of calories to be consumed by the patient, because of possible circulatory overload and stomach dilation. Five hundred calories over the number needed to maintain the patient's current weight is an advisable level at which to begin, with gradual increases in the number of calories consumed (Halmi, 1980a).

Because of the suggested relationship between anorexia and the affective disorders (Cantwell *et al.*, 1977), some physicians have treated anorexics with tricyclic antidepressants. In fact, some success has been effected through the use of tricyclics with anorexics (Moore, 1977; White & Schnaultz, 1977). However these drugs may cause cardiac complications, and therefore, caution should be exercised when anorexics are prescribed tricyclic antidepressants (Mitchell & Gillum, 1980).

A final word of caution is necessary regarding the process of treatment of those diagnosed as anorexic. Death in anorexics is often very sudden and does not appear to be necessarily related to the severity of the disorder (Bruch, 1971). During treatment, electrolyte, creatinine, and blood gas levels should be monitored (Warren & Steinberg, 1979), as well as heart function. Because of the physiological problems associated with anorexia nervosa, the patient with anorexia must be very closely monitored to ensure that, with weight gain, any existing medical problems will be remediated.

Change to the Bulimic Syndrome. In a sample of 30 bulimics, Russell (1979) found that 17 of these subjects had been anorexic before becoming bulimic. Our clinical experience indicates that many anorexics find that their emaciation is the object of extreme concern from their family, friends, and therapists. Because of the pressure to gain weight exerted on the anorexic, many with this disorder begin the binge–purge pattern of eating exhibited by bulimics. The anorexic who previously abstained from eating may begin eating again, which decreases the concern of the significant others in her life, but may secretively purge in order to continue a disordered eating pattern. Some weight is usually gained with this new pattern of eating. Bulimia is not as noticeable as anorexia because of the emaciation experienced in anorexia is usually not a problem with bulimia, and the binge–purge cycle is secretive. Therefore, this new "weight-control technique" is adopted by many anorexics. The overconcern of friends and family regarding the anorexic's eating behavior is then no longer a problem. Therefore, many anorexics become bulimic in order to decrease the concern of significant others in their lives, and to still ensure weight control. However, as noted in the next section, this method of weight control leads to many additional medical problems and is as serious medically as is anorexia.

Summary

Anorexia nervosa is an eating disorder characterized by fear of weight gain, body image dysfunction, weight loss of at least 25%, and refusal to maintain a normal body weight. Many medical problems may result from this dysfunction, including endocrine problems (amenorrhea and low thyroid hormone levels); hematological problems (anemia, immunological problems, and changes in metabolism); and cardiovascular problems. Although many of the medical abnormalities caused by anorexia are remediated with weight gain, caution should be exercised when the anorexic patient begins to gain weight. Circulatory overload and stomach dilation may occur if refeeding is too rapid. Also, some anorexics adopt the binge–purge syndrome associated with bulimia in order to continue to control their weight. The use of bulimia as a weight-control technique also involves many medical complications, which will be discussed in the next section.

BULIMIA

Diagnosis

Clinical Description. Bulimia, once believed to be a subclass of anorexia nervosa, has recently been recognized as a separate and independent eating disorder (APA, 1980). According to the *Diagnostic and Statistical Manual of Mental Disorders* (DSM-III, APA, 1980), five major criteria are necessary for a diagnosis of bulimia (see Table 2). Generally, bulimia involves recurrent uncontrollable binge-eating episodes followed by guilt and self-denigration. These binges are recognized as abnormal by the bulimic and are often conducted in secret. Binges may involve the consumption of "forbidden foods" (i.e., particular foods that the individual believes will produce rapid weight gain regardless of the amount eaten, for example, fats and carbohydrates) or large quantities of food. In an attempt to compensate for the expected or experienced weight gain, bulimics often use various maladaptive weight-control techniques. These practices may include fasting or restrictive dieting, compulsive exercise, self-induced vomiting, laxative use, and/or diuretic use. Although these weight-control practices do not need to be present according to the DSM-III criteria, the binge-eating pattern of many bulimics is often accompanied by one or more of these practices (e.g., binge–diet; binge–vomit; binge–vomit and/or laxative use).

Differential Diagnosis. Before deciding on the diagnosis of bulimia, a number of alternative explanations of the individual's abnormal eating behavior must be ruled out, es-

Table 2. Diagnostic Criteria for Bulimia

Diagnostic criteria

1. Frequent episodes of binge eating.
2. At least three of the following:
   a. Binge foods tend to be characterized as high-caloric and easily ingested
   b. Secretiveness while binging
   c. Termination of binges by abdominal pain, sleep, social interruption, or self-induced vomiting
   d. Repeated attempts to lose weight by very restrictive diets, self-induced vomiting, or use of laxatives and/or diuretics
   e. Frequent weight fluctuations of more than 10 pounds due to alternating binges and fasts
3. Awareness that the eating pattern is abnormal and fear of not being in control of eating.
4. Depressed mood following binges.

---

pecially anorexia nervosa (Table 1). The differentiation of bulimia from anorexia is often a difficult task. Although the primary features of anorexia nervosa (i.e., intense preoccupation with extreme weight loss) and bulimia (i.e., recurrent uncontrollable binge-eating episodes) are distinct, there is much overlap in the associated symptoms of these disorders (e.g., fear of fatness, distorted body image, and the types of weight-loss methods used).

In addition to considering the presenting weight level, clinicians and researchers often attempt to differentiate these two disorders on the basis of the major weight-control approach used (i.e., starvation or purging). Differentiation based primarily on weight-control methods is very difficult because, although fasting or restrictive dieting is often the major manifestation of anorexia nervosa, these individuals may additionally engage in vomiting or purging to lose weight (e.g., Garfinkel *et al.*, 1980). To make the task of differential diagnosis even more difficult, bulimics may also engage in either restrictive dieting or purging in an attempt to compensate for their binge-eating episodes (e.g., Boskind-Lodahl & White, 1978; Russell, 1979). Because anorexia nervosa must be ruled out as the primary diagnosis before the diagnosis of bulimia can be made, the major differentiating criterion that can be objectively measured is the degree of weight loss. Whereas a 25% reduction is necessary for a diagnosis of anorexia nervosa, bulimics usually experience less marked weight losses or may even be obese. However, if a bulimic's weight drops to 25% or less of original body weight, the diagnosis of anorexia nervosa must be seriously considered. Although for the researcher the careful differentiation of these two disorders is very important in determining group membership, the focus of the clinician should be on the careful differentiation and thorough evaluation of the specific weight-loss methods used by individuals for the purpose of further assessment (e.g., medical examination and lab tests) and treatment planning.

Furthermore, as previously mentioned, a number of bulimic individuals may be obese. This subgroup of bulimics include those individuals who experience uncontrollable binge-eating episodes but either do not use weight-loss practices or are unsuccessful in their weight-loss attempts (e.g., self-induced vomiting and dieting). It is important to differentiate obese bulimics from other individuals who are obese but who do not engage in bulimic behaviors. The differentiation of these groups is discussed in the section on obesity.

In addition to differentiating bulimia from other psychological disorders (i.e., anorexia nervosa and schizophrenia), extreme care must be taken to rule out medical explanations as the primary cause of an individual's bulimic behavior. This can best be accomplished by referring an individual for a thorough medical workup before beginning any psychological intervention. This medical examination should especially rule out the neurological disorders (e.g., Klüver-Bucy syndrome or Klein-Levin syndrome) that may involve abnormal eating patterns, as well as endocrinological disorders (e.g., diabetes mellitus or thyroid disorders) that may involve bulimic symptoms (e.g., rapid weight changes and polyphagia). Therefore, before beginning psychological treatment with bulimics, it is very important to rule out other possible explanations of the individual's abnormal eating habits and to carefully identify the specific bulimic behaviors in which the person engages.

Medical Problems

Mortality. In contrast to the wealth of literature on the mortality rate of anorexia ($m=5\%$; Hsu, 1980), to date no research has been conducted on the mortality rate of bulimics. It may be postulated that bulimics who are of near anorexic weight may experience a mortality rate similar to that of anorexics. Additionally, bulimics of any weight may experience increased mortality associated with the medical complications of the weight-control methods they use (i.e., self-induced vomiting, use of diuretics or laxatives, or fasting). The remainder of this section highlights the potential medical complications associated with bulimia.

Endocrine Problems. Although most bulimics are in the low normal to obese weight range, a few may present with near-anorexic body weights. A number of endocrinological abnormalities have been documented in association with the malnourished state and low weight of anorexics that should be considered with this subgroup of bulimics. These include abnormalities in the following hormonal secretions: growth hormone (GH), triiodothyromine (thyroid hormone T_3), estrogen, and luteinizing hormone (Halmi, 1983; Kalucy et al., 1976). The common endocrinological complaints that a clinician may encounter with individuals of very low weight include amenorrhea and infertility.

The research on bulimics in a normal weight range is very limited and involves small sample sizes. Although this research is inconclusive at best, it suggests that normal-weight bulimics may experience abnormalities in GH (Gwirtsman, Roy-Byrne, Yager & Gerner, 1983), cortisol suppression (Gwirtsman et al., Hudson, Laffer, & Pope, 1982), and thyroid-stimulating hormone (TSH) (Mitchell & Bantle, 1983). The most common endocrinological symptom of bulimia is irregular menses. Therefore, it is important to include questions concerning menstrual abnormalities when assessing bulimics in order to determine if this is a problem area that may require further medical tests or treatment.

Electrolyte, Fluid, and Acid–Base Disturbances. In order to remain healthy, the body must maintain homeostasis. It is especially important to maintain normal fluid volume and to maintain balances in electrolytes and acid–base concentrations. Homeostasis of these substances is maintained by a balance in intake and losses. These substances are obtained through the individual's daily intake of food and fluids. Normal daily losses of these substances occur in breathing, tears, urine, perspiration, and feces. Additionally, these substances may be lost through other bodily processes, including vomiting and diarrhea. It follows from this discussion that bulimics who purge through self-induced vomiting, laxative use, and/or diuretic use are particularly apt to develop problems in maintaining balance in fluid volume, electrolytes, and acid–base concentrations. The literature in this area indicates that this is indeed the case.

Each of the primary weight-control practices of bulimics (i.e., restrictive dieting, self-induced vomiting, laxative use, and diuretic use) may contribute to disturbances in fluid, electrolyte, and acid–base balances. A recent investigation evaluated these abnormalities in 168 bulimics in the low-normal to obese weight range who used at least one other weight-control method in addition to restrictive dieting (Mitchell, Pyle, Eckert, Hatsukami, & Lentz, 1983). The results indicated that 48.8% of these individuals had some type of electrolyte abnormality. The most common abnormality (27.4%) was increased bicarbonate, which is indicative of metabolic alkalosis (increased pH of the blood). Other common abnormalities included decreased chloride levels (hypochloremia) and decreased potassium levels (hypokalemia). Each of the weight control tecnhiques employed by bulimics has been independently associated with disturbances in the fluid, electrolyte, and acid–base balance, and the use of multiple methods may compound the risk of these disturbances.

Eating-disorder individuals who use self-induced vomiting (Halmi & Falk, 1981; Mitchell et al., 1983), laxatives, and/or diuretics (Harris, 1983; Oster, Materson, &

Rogers, 1980) are apt to develop metabolic alkalosis. This may result from excessive loss of fluids (hypovolemia), hydrogen and chloride ions, and potassium, with a compensatory increase in bicarbonate ions. Although there are no specific symptoms of metabolic alkalosis, eating-disorder individuals may complain of symptoms related to hypokalemia and dehydration. The clinical manifestations of hypokalemia include muscle weakness or cramps, easy fatigability, palpitations, abnormal pain, polydipsia, and polyuria. The most frequent clinical manifestations of dehydration include thirst, nausea, lightheadedness, and weakness. Severe, long-standing acid–base or electrolyte disturbances may result in a number of serious medical complications involving the heart, the muscles, the kidneys, and/or the gastrointestinal tract (Wyngarden, 1979). Because the weight control practices of bulimics increase their susceptibility to electrolyte, acid–base, or fluid disturbances, it is important to assess them for the symptoms of these problems and to refer them to a physician if these symptoms are present.

Metabolic Problems. Although no investigations have yet been conducted on the metabolic rate of bulimics, some useful information may be extrapolated from the available literature on the effects of caloric intake on metabolism. Research has indicated that the rate of weight loss experienced by a dieting individual is not constant; instead, it decreases across time (e.g., Stordy *et al.,* 1977). Furthermore, the decreased rate of weight loss across time may be related to a decrease in resting metablolic rate (i.e., increased efficiency of energy use) associated with dieting (Donahoe, Lin, Kirschenbaum, & Kessey, 1984). Additionally, an investigation of normal-weight individuals placed on increased or decreased caloric diets for 15 days indicated that those on the restrictive diet experienced a decrease in metabolic rate and that those who overate experienced an increase (Apfelbaum, Bostsarron, & Lacatis, 1971). These findings suggest that bulimics may experience changes in their metabolic rate associated with the different phases of their eating pattern (i.e., binge eating or dieting), and that these changes may, in turn, influence the rate, degree, and direction of weight fluctuations experienced. Further research is needed to investigate metabolic changes in bulimia and their relationship to eating patterns and weight changes.

Other Problems. In addition to the aforementioned disorders, a bulimic eating pattern of fasting followed by binge eating may result in gastric dilation (Mitchell, Pyle, & Miner, 1982). This problem is manifested by abdominal pain and bloating. Additionally, although rare, gastric dilation may result in gastric rupture, which has an 80% mortality rate (Evans, 1968). A number of cases of unexplained benign parotid (salivary) gland enlargement have been identified in bulimic individuals who binge-eat and vomit (Levin, Falko, Dixon, Gallup, & Saunders, 1980). Further complications of self-induced vomiting may include sore throats, dental problems, bruised knuckles, lacerations or contusions of the pharnyx, exophagitis (inflamed and painful esophagus), and, although rare, aspiration pneumonia (e.g., Harris, 1983; Russell, 1979). Frequent laxative abusers may additionally experience cathartic colon, which involves the cessation of normal peristaltic functioning of the colon without the aid of laxatives (Oster *et al.,* 1980) and frequently results in the paradoxical complaint of constipation by laxative abusers.

Treatment Implications

Because bulimia has only recently been recognized as an independent eating disorder, there is a paucity of literature on the treatment of this disorder. Therefore, this section is based primarily on information extrapolated from other areas and from clinical experience.

Beneficial Effects of Successful Treatment. Although no treatment studies have evaluated changes in bulimia-related physical abnormalities following the treatment of this disorder, it is generally believed that most of these abnormalities can be corrected with the establishment of normal eating habits (e.g., nutritionally sound meals) and the discontinuation of the maladaptive weight-control practices (e.g., laxative use and vomiting). Specifically, the elimination of the bulimic eating pattern (e.g., binge–fast and binge–vomit) and the establishment of regular, balanced eating habits may aid in the correction of many of the experienced physical problems, especially endocrine abnormalities and electrolyte–fluid imbalances. Furthermore, the elimination of the purging behaviors is necessary to correct current abnormalities and to prevent further complications due to prolonged electrolyte, fluid, and/or acid–base disturbances (e.g., renal or cardiovascular complications). Therefore, successful treatment of the bulimic behaviors by a psychologist in cooperation with a physician may correct most of the medical problems experienced by bulimics.

Problems Associated with the Return to Normal Eating Habits and the Associated Weight Gain. The primary goals of treatment for bulimic individuals are the establishment of normal eating habits and the replacement of their maladaptive weight-control methods (e.g., vomiting and fasting) with more appropriate ones (e.g., exercise and balanced diet). Some bulimics may primarily use a binge–fast eating pattern and may present with low body weights when they seek treatment. These bulimics, like anorexics, may be treated with rapid refeeding techniques to provide nutritional rehabilitation and rapid weight gain. However, caution is necessary when using rapid refeeding because a number of serious medical complications may result. The complications associated with the sudden ingestion of large intakes after chronic dietary restrictions may involve acute pancreatitis, which is associated with a 10% mortality rate; gastric dilation, which may result in rupture (80% mortality); and edema, which may lead to heart failure (see Halmi & Falk, 1981; Harris, 1983).

In addition to these potential medical complications, treatment that involves a rapid return to normal eating habits that may be accompanied by weight gain is replete with problems. First, the initiation of bulimics' maladaptive weight-control practices typically occurs in response to their fears of fatness. Therefore, any treatment that involves a rapid gain in weight may elicit further anxiety associated with becoming obese. Additionally, a treatment program that leads to rapid weight gain may result in poor treatment acceptability and high attrition. Therefore, to avoid many of the problems associated with rapid returns to normal eating habits and the associated weight gains, a more appropriate treatment program would involve a gradual return to normal eating habits and weight levels. In addition, it is beneficial to introduce alternative, appropriate weight-control techniques (e.g., moderate exercise) early in the treatment to counteract the concerns about continued weight gain associated with treatment.

The decreased resting metabolic rate associated with dieting and weight loss may result in an initial rapid increase in weight even with a gradual return to normal eating. This effect may initially influence treatment acceptability. However, the clinician may be able to maintain bulimics' confidence in treatment by prewarning them about this effect and explaining that their weight will not continue to increase at the same rate and that their resting metabolic rate should increase (Apfelbaum *et al.*, 1971).

Adjunctive Pharmacological Treatment. Before any medication is prescribed for eating-disorder individuals, it is important to consider its potential effects on weight. For example, tricyclic antidepressants are sometimes prescribed for the treatment of depression in bulimics, and these medications may include weight gains as side effects. These weight changes related to adjunctive pharmacological therapy may have detrimental effects on the treatment of the bulimic behavior pattern. That is, an experienced weight gain may exacerbate the bulimic's concern about becoming obese and may therefore further complicate treatment endeavors. Thus, it is important to consider the potential effects of adjunctive pharmacological treatments on weight before including them in a comprehensive program for the treatment of bulimia.

Summary

Bulimia is an eating disorder characterized by recurrent uncontrollable binge-eating episodes, often followed by compensatory weight-control practices, especially self-induced vomiting, fasting, and laxative use. When assigning the diagnosis of bulimia to an individual, it is important to rule out other psychological and medical disorders that may involve eating behaviors similar to those of bulimia.

Furthermore, a number of physical problems (e.g., endocrinological abnormalities, electrolyte disturbances, and dental problems) may occur secondary to the weight-control practices used by bulimics. Therefore, it is important for the clinician to be aware of the potential physical problems associated with bulimia and to assess the physical symptoms of bulimic individuals. When physical symptoms are reported, the clinician should refer the bulimic for a medical examination and collaborate with the physician on treatment if necessary. Lastly, successful treatment of bulimia involving the establishment of regular, nutritionally balanced eating habits and the discontinuation of maladaptive weight-control practices (e.g., vomiting, fasting, laxative use) should usually be accompanied by improvements in the physical complications of this eating disorder.

OBESITY

Diagnosis

Clinical Description. Obesity is derived from the Latin words *ob* ("over") and *edere* ("to eat") (Brownell & Stunkard, 1980). Thus, implicit in our commonsensical notions about obesity is that it is primarily determined by overeating. Research over the years has demonstrated that this conception of obesity is much too simplistic. In the final analysis, the primary symptom of obesity is excessive adipose (fat) tissue (Bellack & Williamson, 1982). Excessive adiposity is generally the result of a positive energy balance (i.e., consuming more calories than are expended). In most cases, this condition of positive energy balance is the result of excessive eating, inadequate exercise, or both. Research evidence suggests that, on the average, the obesity of most adults, as well as children, is due to low levels of activity or insufficient exercising (Brownell & Stunkard, 1980). However, endocrine abnormalities and certain genetic disorders (e.g., Prader–Willi syndrome) can cause obesity and must be ruled out with proper medical examination. Thus, the most common clinical description of an obese person is a person who consistently either eats too much or engages in very little exercise. Overeating may range from eating too much at meals, to excessive snacking, to planned binges. Most obese persons lead very sedentary lives. It is well established that as body weight increases, activity decreases (Chirico & Stunkard, 1960), thus complicating remediation of the resulting problem of obesity.

Differential Diagnosis. The commonly used weight criterion for a diagnosis of obesity is 20% above ideal weight as defined by actuarial tables. However, because a person weighs 20% more than normal does not necessarily mean that a diagnosis of obesity is most appropriate. In particular, other medical disorders (e.g., endocrine abnormalities or genetic diseases) that cause obesity must be ruled out as the primary diagnosis (Bray & Teague, 1980). If this is accomplished, the next diffferential-diagnostic step is to rule out bulimia. In particular, bulimics who binge-eat but do not purge and bulimics who use laxatives as a purgative method often present with excessive weight. Therefore, careful assessment of binge-eating patterns, weight-control methods (e.g., frequent restrictive dieting and laxative use), and negative affect after binge eating is important in making this distinction. Current findings from our clinic suggest that great similarities exist among cases of binge-eating bulimics and traditional cases of obesity. Therefore, this diagnostic distinction is often very difficult. Binge eating is the key symptom of bulimia. The binge eating of bulimics is generally secretive and involves the consumption of large amounts of food and/or foods high in calories, carbohydrates, or fats. In comparison, obese patients tend to binge less frequently and less secretively. Also, their self-defined "binges" are often large meals or snacks. In general, bulimics show stronger negative affect to their eating habits and express a greater degree of concern about their inability to control their eating. These considerations are often helpful in differentially diagnosing these two groups.

Medical Problems

Mortality. Increased mortality has been clearly associated with obesity. Increased risk of death begins when an individual is 30% overweight and increases logarithmically with further increases in obesity (Bray, 1976). This increased mortality rate is primarily due to the effects of obesity on endocrine and cardiovascular functioning.

Endocrine Problems. It is well established that obesity is associated with problems of glucose intolerance and increased risk of developing diabetes mellitus (Bray & Teague, 1980; Brownell & Stunkard, 1980). For example, Bray and Teague (1980) found abnormalities of glucose tolerance in 24% of their obese patients. Recent research in animals has shown that obesity increases the risk of developing glucose intolerance, and that developing problems of glucose tolerance, in turn, increases the probability of gaining further weight (Cunningham, Calles, Eisikovitz, Zawalich, & Felig, 1983). These data suggest that once obesity is developed in persons prone to diabetes, the probability of both conditions' worsening is increased, making treatment of both disorders even more complicated. In addition to problems related to diabetes, obesity is also associated with other endocrine abnormalities, such as menstrual irregularity and thyroid abnormalities (Bray & Teague, 1980; Moore, Mehrishi, Howard, & Mills, 1982).

Cardiovascular Problems. It is well established that obesity is associated with elevated blood pressure (Bray & Teague, 1980; Shapiro & Goldstein, 1982). Because hypertension is one of the primary risk factors for coronary heart disease, obesity is a significant precursor of cardiovascular illness. A recent study (Raison, Achimastos, Boutheir, London, & Sofar, 1983) has shown that this elevation of blood pressure in obese hypertensives is caused by increased water cell content, which increases the pressure on cell membranes. Obesity is also implicated in other abnormalities associated with cardiovascular illness. Serum lipids (fats) have been found to be elevated in many cases of obesity (Bray & Teague, 1980; Brownell & Stunkard, 1980) and is a special problem in cases of extreme obesity (Weltman, 1983). High-density lipoprotein, which is considered the "good" cholesterol because it is negatively correlated with heart disease (Miller & Miller, 1975), has also been found to be negatively correlated with obesity (Brownell & Stunkard, 1980).

Metabolic Problems. Attempts to establish lowered basal metabolism as the primary cause of obesity have generally failed to find this relationship (Blaza & Garrow, 1983). However, studies that have examined the effects of obesity on the metabolic responses to eating have generally shown that the obese have a significantly reduced metabolic response in comparison to normals (Bessard, Schutz, & Jequier, 1983; Danforth, 1980). Also, a recent clinical study documented that one effect of dieting is a reduction in resting metabolic rate (Dohahoe *et al.*, 1984). These studies suggest that one correlate of efforts to correct obesity through caloric restriction may be reduced metabolic rate, which has the effect of making weight loss difficult and weight gain very easy.

Other Problems. Obesity has been associated with increased incidence of gall bladder disease (Bray & Teague, 1980). Also, obesity complicates the medical management of other problems; for example, surgical risks are increased, and obstetrical complications often result from obesity. Increased maternal and fetal morbidity and mortality have been associated with maternal obesity (Cohen & Gabbe, 1980).

Treatment Implications

Beneficial Effects of Weight Loss. In general, most of the medical consequences of obesity can be reversed by losing weight. There is substantial evidence that blood pressure can be reduced if the obese patient loses weight (Brownell & Stunkard, 1981; Epstein & Martin, 1977; Lewis, Hasskell, Wood, Manoogian, Bailey, & Pereira, 1976; Reisin *et al.*, 1983). Studies investigating the physiological mechanisms underlying this improvement of hypertension with weight loss have suggested that it may be due to reduction of body fluid (Raison *et al.*, 1983) and/or reduction of plasma norepinephrine (Sowers, Nyby, Stern, Beck, Baron, Catania, & Vlachis, 1982). Fagerberg, Anderson, Isaksson, and Bjöintorp (1984) have shown that this reduction of blood pressure in obese hypertensives via weight loss is independent of restriction of sodium intake and is more likely the result of reduced norepinephrine secretion.

Weight loss also reduces other cardiovascular risk factors. Cholesterol levels are generally lowered with weight reduction (Brownell & Stunkard, 1980). In particular, the ratio of high-density lipoproteins to low-density lipoproteins is increased, and this increase reduces cardiovascular risk. Brownell and Stunkard (1981) found this effect to be most significant in middle-aged men, the group most vulnerable to heart disease.

Weight loss has also been found to improve glucose tolerance in the obese (Björtorp, DeJounge, Krotkiewiski, Sullivan, Sjöström, & Stenberg, 1973). Berglund, Ljungman, Hartford, Wilhelmsen, and Bjorntorp (1982) established that glucose intolerance is directly associated with fat cell size, a finding that suggests that a primary goal of treatment for obese diabetics should be weight loss.

Effects of Dieting and Exercise on Metabolism. As mentioned earlier, resting metabolism is reduced as a function of restricting caloric intake. This reduction is generally about 15% to 30%. This reduced metabolism is best regarded as the body's adaptation to reduced energy consumption, because it is also associated with lowered activity levels (Keesey, 1980). Of particular importance to persons attempting to lose weight is Garrow's finding (1974) that resting metabolism is reduced further with each successive diet that the obese individual initiates. This evidence suggests that dieting as a treatment for obesity is complicated by alterations in metabolism that make long-term weight loss very difficult. Furthermore, Garrow's research suggests that chronic dieters may literally be making their problem of obesity more difficult to control with each successive diet. There is, however, one possible solution to this dilemma. Donahoe *et al.* (1984) demonstrated that exercise can reverse the adverse metabolic effects of dieting. According to these data, long-term exercise may be essential as one component of treatment for obesity.

Limitations of Obesity on Exercise. Unfortunately, strenuous exercise (e.g., jogging and tennis) often produces joint and muscle injuries in the obese because of the extra stress of excessive weight on joints, ligaments, and tendons. Therefore, it is advisable that obese patients who are not in good physical condition begin with walking or a light exercise program (Brownell & Stunkard, 1980). Walking is an especially good form of exercise for the obese because it produces many of the physical benefits of jogging without the danger of injury (Leon, Conrad, Hunninghake, & Serfass, 1979).

Managing the Diabetic. Dietary management of the obese diabetic is especially difficult because it is difficult to eat a nutritionally balanced diet below 1000 calories per day (Munves, 1980). Fitz, Sperling, and Fein (1983) showed that a low-calorie, high-protein diet can be safely used with these patients. This diet allowed them to wean their parents off insulin in a very short period of time. This process required hospitalization and should be conducted only under close medical supervision.

Managing the Massively Obese. One of the implications of the evidence concerning the medical consequences of obesity is that, for the massively obese, permanent weight loss is important for health as well as cosmetic purposes. This conclusion is reinforced by recent findings showing that the total number of adipose (fat) cells is increased each time the patient diets and then regains the weight that was lost (Sjöstrom, 1980). Therefore, it is essential that the seriously overweight individual lose weight and keep it off. The approach used by many individuals is severe fasting or starvation. Van Itallie (1980) reported that this approach to dieting has been found to deplete body protein and has resulted in many deaths due to ventricular arrhythmia. Therefore, sensible, nutritionally sound diets plus modest exercise must be the first form of treatment used with the massively obese patient. If this approach fails, then more intensive medical efforts (e.g., gastric bypass surgery) should be considered, especially if the patient has already developed other serious medical problems that can be reversed only by weight loss (Bray, 1976; Halmi, 1980b).

Summary

Obesity is a very common disorder with the primary symptoms of excess adipose (fat) tissue. It is now well documented that obesity is associated with increased mortality and that this increased death rate is primarily due to the cardiovascular and endocrine problems caused by obesity or faulty eating habits. Fortunately, many of these medical problems can be reversed with successful weight loss. However, given recent evidence that regaining weight has the effect of creating new adipose tissue, it is very important that weight loss be accompanied by lifelong weight maintenance.

CONCLUSION

Eating disorders have been found to have very serious medical consequences. The medical problems associated with anorexia nervosa, bulimia, and obesity differ. The medical consequences of anorexia are primarily the result of fasting and an extremely low weight level. With bulimia, the medical problems are caused by frequent binge-eating and/or purging. The medical problems of obesity are usually due to excessive weight, poor dietary habits, or low levels of exercise. For each of these disorders, successful treatment usually reverses most of the medical consequences of the disorder. However, careful assessment of these medical problems throughout the treatment process is very important for the comprehensive care of these patients.

REFERENCES

American Psychiatric Association. (1980). *Diagnostic and statistical manual of mental disorders* (3rd ed.). Washington, DC: Author.

Aoki, T. T., Muller, W. A., & Brennan, M. F. (1975). Metabolic effects of glucose in a brief and prolonged fasted man. *American Journal of Clinical Nutrition, 28,* 507–510.

Aperia, A., Broberger, O., & Fohlin, L. (1978). Renal function in anorexia nervosa. *Acta Paediatrica Scandinavia, 67,* 219–220.

Apfelbaum, M., Bostsarron, J., & Lacatis, D. (1971). Effect of caloric restriction and excessive caloric intake on energy expenditure. *American Journal of Clinical Nutrition, 24,* 1405–1409.

Azerrand, J., & Stafford, R. (1969). Restoration of eating behavior in an anorexic through operant conditioning and environmental manipulation. *Behaviour Research and Therapy, 7,* 165–171.

Bellack, A. S., & Williamson, D. A. (1982). Obesity and anorexia nervosa. In D. M. Doleys, R. L. Meredith, & A. R. Ciminero (Eds.), *Behavioral medicine.* New York: Plenum Press.

Ben-Tovim, D. I., Marilov, V., & Crisp, A. H. (1979). Personality and mental state within anorexia nervosa. *Journal of Psychosomatic Research, 23,* 321–325.

Berglund, G., Ljungman, S., Hartford, J., Wilhelmsen, L., & Björntorp, P. (1982). Type of obesity and blood pressure. *Hypertension, 4,* 692–696.

Bessard, T., Schutz, Y., & Jequier, E. (1983). Energy and expenditure postprandial thermogenesis in obese women before and after weight loss. *American Journal of Clinical Nutrition, 38,* 825–834.

Björntorp, P., DeJounge, K., Krotkiewski, M., Sullivan, L., Sjöstrom, L., & Stenberg, J. (1973). Physical training in human obesity: III. Effects of long-term physical training on body composition, *Metabolism, 22,* 1467–1475.

Blaza, S., & Garrow, J. S. (1983). Thermogenic response to temperature, exercise, and food stimuli in lean and obese women, studied by 24th direct calorimetry. *British Journal of Nutrition, 49,* 171–180.

Boskind-Lodahl, M., & White, W. C. (1978). The definition and treatment of bulimarexia in college women—A pilot study. *Journal of American College Health Association, 27,* 84–86, 97.

Boyle, P. C., Storlein, L. H., & Keesey, R. E. (1978). Increased efficiency of food utilization following weight loss. *Physiology of Behavior, 21,* 261–263.

Bray, G. A. (1976). *The obese patient.* Philadelphia: W. B. Saunders.

Bray, G. A., & Teague, R. J. (1980). An algorithm for the medical evaluation of obese patients. In A. J. Stunkard (Ed.), *Obesity*. Philadelphia: W. B. Saunders.

Brownell, K. D. (1982). Obesity: Understanding and treating a serious prevalent, and refractory disorder. *Journal of Consulting and Clinical Psychology, 50,* 820–840.

Brownell, K. D., Stunkard, A. J. (1980). Physical activity in the development and control of obesity. In A. J. Stunkard (Ed.), *Obesity*. Philadelphia: W. B. Saunders.

Brownell, K. D., & Stunkard, A. J. (1981). Differential changes in plasma high-density lipoprotein-cholesterol levels in obese men and women during weight reduction. *Archives of Internal Medicine, 141,* 1142–1146.

Bruch, H. (1971). Death in anorexia nervosa. *Psychosomatic Medicine, 33,* 135–144.

Bruch, H. (1973). *Eating disorders: Obesity, anorexia nervosa and the person within.* New York: Basic Books.

Bruch, H. (1977). Anorexia nervosa and its treatment. *Journal of Pediatric Psychology, 2,* 110–112.

Burman, K. D., Vigersky, R. A., & Loriaux, D. L. (1977). Investigations concerning thyroxin deiodination pathways in patients with anorexia nervosa. In R. A. Vigersky (Ed.), *Anorexia nervosa*. New York: Raven Press.

Cahill, G. F., Herrera, M. G., Morgan, A. P., Sueldmer, J. S., Steinker, J., Levy, P. L., Richard, G. A., & Kipnis, D. M. (1966). Hormone–fuel interrelationships during fasting. *Journal of Clinical Investigations, 45,* 1751–1754.

Cantwell, J. P., Sturzenberger, S., Burroughs, J., Salkin, B., & Green, J. (1977). Anorexia nervosa: An affective disorder? *Archives of General Psychiatry, 34,* 1087–1093.

Carryer, H. J., Berkman, J. M., & Mason, H. L. (1959). Relative lymphocytosis in anorexia nervosa. *Staff Meeting of Mayo Clinic, 34,* 426–432.

Casper, R. C., Halmi, K. A., Goldberg, S. C., Eckert, E. D., & Davis, J. M. (1979). Disturbances in body image atriation as related to other characteristics and otucome in anorexia nervosa. *British Journal of Psychiatry, 134,* 71–78.

Casper, R. C., Eckert, E. D., Halmi, K. A., Goldberg, S. C., & Davis, J. M. (1980). Bulimia: Its incidence and clinical importance in patients with anorexia nervosa. *Archives of General Psychiatry, 37,* 1030–1035.

Chirico, A. M., & Stunkard, A. J. (1960). Physical activity and human obesity. *New England Journal of Medicine, 263,* 935–940.

Chopra, I. J., Chopra, V., & Smith, S. R. (1975). Reciprocal changes in serum concentration of 3, 3′, 5′-triiodothyronine (reversed T3) and 3, 3′, 5′-triiodothyronine (T3) in systemic illnesses. *Journal of Clinical Endocrinology and Metabolism, 41,* 1043–1049.

Clark, D. B., & Munford, P. R. (1980). Behavioral consulation to pediatrics. *Child Behavior Theory, 2,* 25–33.

Cohen, A. W., & Gabbe, S. C. (1980). Obstetrical problems in the obese patient. In A. J. Stunkard (Ed.), *Obesity*. Philadelphia: W. B. Saunders.

Crisp, A. H., & Kalucy, R. S. (1974). Aspects of the perceptual disorder is anorexia nervosa. *British Journal of Medical Psychology, 47,* 349–361.

Crisp, A. H., Blendis, L. M. & Palwan, G. L. (1968). Aspects of fat metabolism in anorexia nervosa. *Metabolism, 17,* 1109–1112.

Croxson, M. S., & Ibbertson, H. K. (1977). Low serum triiodothyronine (T3) and hypothyroidism in anorexia nervosa. *Journal of Clinical Endocrinology and Metabolism, 44,* 174–176.

Cunningham, J., Calles, J., Eisikowitz, L., Zawalich, W., & Felig, P. (1983). Increased efficiency of weight gain and altered cellularity of brown adipose tissue in rats with impaired glucose tolerance during diet-induced overfeeding. *Diabetes, 32,* 1023–1027.

Danforth, E. (1980). Nutritionally induced alterations in metabolism. In J. M. Kinney (Ed.), *Assessment of energy metabolism in health and disease.* Columbus: Ross Laboratories.

Donahoe, C. P., Lin, D. H., Kirschenbaum, D. S., & Kessey, R. E. (1984). Metabolic consequences of dieting and exercise in the treatment of obesity. *Journal of Consulting and Clinical Psychology, 52,* 827–836.

Epstein, L. H., & Martin, J. E. (1977). Compliance and side effects of weight regulation groups. *Behavior Modification, 1,* 551–558.

Erwin, W. J. (1977). A 16-year follow-up of a case of severe anorexia nervosa. *Journal of Behavioral Therapy and Experimental Psychiatry, 8,* 157–160.

Evans, D. S. (1968). Acute dilatation and spontaneous rupture of the stomach. *British Journal of Surgery, 55,* 940–942.

Fagerberg, B., Anderson, O. K., Isaksson, B., & Björntorp, P. (1984). Blood pressure control during weight reduction in obese hypertensive men: Separate effects of sodium and energy restriction. *British Medical Journal, 228,* 11–14.

Fairburn, C. G. (1981). Self-induced vomiting. *Journal of Psychosomatic Research, 24,* 193–197.

Fitz, J. D., Sperling, E. M., & Fein, H. G. (1983). A hypocaloric high-protein diet as primary therapy for adults with obesity-related diabetes: Effective long-term use in a community hospital. *Diabetes Care, 6,* 328–333.

Fohlin, L. (1977). Body composition, cardiovascular and renal function in adolescent patients with anorexia nervosa. *Acta Paediatrica Scandinavia, 268* (Supplementum).

Frisch, R. E., & McArthur, J. W. (1974). Menstrual cycles: Fatness as a determinant of minimum weight for height necessary for their maintenance or onset. *Science, 185,* 949.

Garfinkel, P. E., Kline, S. A., & Stancer, H. C. (1973). Treatment of anorexia nervosa using operant conditioning techniques. *Journal of Nervous and Mental Disease, 157,* 428–433.

Garfinkel, P. E., Garner, D. M., & Moldofsky, H. (1977). The role of behavior modification in the treatment of anorexia nervosa. *Journal of Pediatric Psychology, 2,* 113–122.

Garfinkel, P. E., Moldofsky, H., & Garner, D. M. (1980). The heterogeneity of anorexia nervosa. *Archives of General Psychiatry, 37,* 1036–1040.

Garner, D. M. Garfinkel, P. E., Stancer, H. C., & Moldofsky, H. (1976). Body image disturbances in anorexia nervosa and obesity. *Psychosomatic Medicine, 38,* 337–347.

Garrow, J. (1974). *Energy balance and obesity in man.* New York: Elsevier.

Gold, M. S., Poltash, A. C., Martin, D., Extein, I., & Howard, E. (1981–1982). *International Journal of Psychiatry in Medicine, 11,* 245–250.

Gwirtsman, H. E., Roy-Byrne, P., Yager, J., & Gerner, R. H. (1983). Neuroendocrine abnormalities in bulimia. *American Journal of Psychiatry, 140,* 559–563.

Halmi, K. A. (1974). Anorexia nervosa: Demographic and clinical factors in 94 cases. *Psychosomatic Medicine, 36,* 18–25.

Halmi, K. A. (1980a). Anorexia nervosa. In H. I. Kaplan, A. M. Freedman & B. J. Sadock (Eds.), *Comprehensive textbook of psychiatry* (Vol. 3). Baltimore: Williams & Wilkins.

Halmi, K. A. (1980b). Gastric Bypass for Massive Obesity. In A. J. Stunkard (Ed.), *Obesity.* Philadelphia: W. B. Saunders.

Halmi, K. A. (1983). Anorexia nervosa and bulimia. *Psychosomatics, 24,* 111–129.

Halmi, K. A., & Falk, J. R. (1981). Common physiological changes in anorexia nervosa. *International Journal of Eating Disorders, 1,* 16–27.

Halmi, K. A., Falk, J. R., & Schwartz, E. (1981). Binge-eating and vomiting: A survey of a college population. *Psychological Medicine, 11,* 697–706.

Harris, R. T. (1983). Bulimarexia and related serious eating disorders with medical complications. *Annals of Internal Medicine, 99,* (800–807.

Hsu, L. K. G. (1980). Outcome of anorexia nervosa. *Archives of General Psychiatry, 37,* 1041–1046.

Hudson, J. I., Laffer, P. S. & Pope, H. G. (1982). Bulimia related to affective disorder by family history and response to the dexamethasone suppression test. *American Journal of Psychiatry, 139,* 685–687.

Kalucy, R. S., Crisp, A. H., Chard, T., McNeilly, A., Chen, C. N., & Lacey, J. H. (1976). Nocturnal hormonal profiles in massive obesity, anorexia nervosa and normal females. *Journal of Psychosomatic Research, 20,* 595–604.

Keesey, R. E. (1980). A set-point analysis of the regulation of body weight. In A. J. Stunkard (Ed.), *Obesity.* Philadelphia: W. B. Saunders.

Keys, A. Brozek, J., Hanschel, A., Mickelson, O., & Taylor, H. L. (1950). *The biology of human starvation.* Minneapolis: University of Minnesota Press.

Klinefelter, H. F. (1965). Hypercholesterolemia in anorexia nervosa. *Journal of Clinical Endocrinology and Metabolism, 25,* 1520.

Leon, A. S., Conrad, J., Hunninghake, D. B., & Serfass, R. (1979). Effects of a vigorous walking program on body composition and carbohydrate and lipid metabolism of obese young men. *American Journal of Clinical Nutrition, 32,* 1776–1787.

Levin, P. A., Falko, J. M., Dixon, K., Gallup, E. M., & Saunders, W. (1980). Benign parotid enlargement in bulimia. *Annals of Internal Medicine, 93,* 827–829.

Lewis, S., Haskell, W. L., Wood, P. D., Manoogian, N., Bailey, J. E., & Pereira, M. B. (1976). Effects of physical activity on weight reduction in obese middle-aged women. *The American Journal of Clinical Nutrition, 29,* 151–156.

Mant, M. J., & Fargher, B. S. (1972). The hematology of anorexia nervosa. *British Journal of Haematology, 27,* 737–749.

Miller, G. J., & Miller, N. E. (1975). Plasma high-density lipoprotein concentration and the development of ischaemic heart disease. In A. J. Stunkard (Ed.), *Obesity.* Philadelphia: W. B. Saunders.

Mitchell, J. E., & Bantle, J. P. (1983). Metabolic and endocrine investigations in women of normal weight with the bulimia syndrome. *Biological Psychiatry, 18,* 355–365.

Mitchell, J. E., & Gillum, R. (1980). Weight-dependent arrhythmia in a patient with anorexia nervosa. *American Journal of Psychiatry, 137,* 377–378.

Mitchell, J. E., Pyle, R. L., & Miner, R. A. (1982). Gastric dilatation as a complication of bulimia. *Psychosomatics, 23,* 96–97.

Mitchell, J. E., Pyle, R. L., Eckert, E. D., Hatsukami, D., & Lentz, R. (1983). Electrolyte and other physiological abnormalities in patients with bulimia. *Psychological Medicine, 13,* 273–278.

Moore, D. C. (1977). Amitriptyline therapy in anorexia nervosa. *American Journal of Psychiatry, 134,* 1303–1304.

Moore, R., Mehrishi, J. N., Howard, A. N., & Mills, I. H. (1982). Lymphocyte thyroid hormone receptors in obesity. *International Journal of Obesity, 6,* 541–548.

Morgan, H. G., & Russell, G. F. (1975). Value of family background and clinical features as predictors of long-term outcome in anorexia nervosa. *Psychological Medicine, 5,* 355–371.

Morton, R. (1720). *Phthisiologia or a treatise of consumption* (2nd ed.). Smith: London.

Munves, E. (1980). Managing the diet. In A. J. Stunkard (Ed.), *Obesity.* Philadelphia: W. B. Saunders.

Nestel, P. J. (1974). Cholesterol metabolism in anorexia nervosa and hypercholesterolemia. *Journal of Clinical Endocrinology and Metabolism, 38,* 325–328.

Nillius, S. J. (1983). Weight and the menstrual cycle. In *Understanding Anorexia Nervosa and Bulimia: Report of the Fourth Ross Conference on Medical Research.* Columbus: Ross Laboratories.

Oster, J. R., Materson, B. J., & Rogers, A. I. (1980). Laxative abuse syndrome. *American Journal of Gastroenterology, 74,* 451–458.

Palmblad, J., Fohlin, L., & Lundstrom, M. (1977). Anorexia nervosa and polymorphonuclear (PMN) granulocyte reactions. *Scandanavian Journal of Haematology, 19,* 334–342.

Palossy, B. & Oo, M. (1977). ECG alterations in anorexia nervosa. *Advances in Cardiology, 19,* 280–282.

Pertschuk, M. J. (1977). Behavior therapy: Extended follow-up. In R. A. Vigersky (Ed.), *Anorexia nervosa.* New York: Raven Press.

Pierloot, R., Wellins, W., & Horiben, M. (1975). Elements of resistance to a controlled medical and psychotherapeutic program in anorexia nervosa. *Psychotherapy and Psychosomatics, 26,* 101–117.

Raison, J., Achimastos, A., Boutheir, J., London, G., & Safar, M. (1983). Intravascular volume, extracellular fluid volume, and total body water in obese and nonobese hypertensive patients. *American Journal of Cardiology, 51,* 165–170.

Reisin, E., Frohlich, E. D., Messerli, F. H., Dreslinski, G. R., Dunn, F. G., Jones, M. M., & Batson, H. M. (1983). Cardiovascular changes after weight reduction in obesity hypertension. *Annals of Internal Medicine, 98,* 315–319.

Rosen, J. C., & Leitenberg, H. (1982). Bulimia nervosa: Treatment with exposure and response prevention. *Behavior Therapy, 13,* 117–124.

Russell, G. (1979). Bulimia nervosa: An ominous variant of anorexia nervosa. *Psychological Medicine, 9,* 429–448.

Russell, G. F., & Bruce, J. T. (1966). Impaired water diuresis in patients with anorexia nervosa. *American Journal of Medicine, 40,* 38–40.

Schlesier-Stropp, B. (1984). Bulimia: A review of the literature. *Psychological Bulletin, 95,* 247–257.

Shapiro, D., & Goldstein, I. B. (1982). Biobehavioral perspectives on hypertension. *Journal of Consulting and Clinical Psychology, 50,* 804–819.

Sjöstrom, L. (1980). Fat cells and body weight. In A. J. Stunkard (Ed.), *Obesity.* Philadelphia: W. B. Saunders.

Slade, P. D., & Russell, G. F. (1973). Awareness of body dimensions in anorexia nervosa: Cross-sectional and longitudinal studies. *Psychological Medicine, 3,* 188–193.

Sowers, J. R., Nyby, M., Stern, N., Beck, F., Baron, S., Catania, R., & Vlachis, N. (1982). Blood pressure and hormone changes associated with weight reduction in the obese. *Hypertension, 4,* 686–691.

Stordy, B. J., Marks, V, Kalucy, R. S., & Crisp, A. H. (1977). Weight gain, thermic effect of glucose and resting metabolic rate during recovery from anorexia nervosa. *American Journal of Clinical Nutrition, 30,* 138–146.

Stunkard, A. J. (1980). *Obesity.* Philadelphia: W. B. Saunders.

Theander, S. (1970). Anorexia nervosa: A psychiatric investigation of 94 female patients. *Psychosomatic Medicine, 24,* 551–558.

Thurston, J., & Marks, P. (1974). Electrocardiographic abnormalities in patients with anorexia nervosa. *British Heart Journal, 36,* 719–723.

Vagenakias, A. G., Burger, A., & Portney, G. I. (1975). Division of peripheral thyroxin metabolism from activating to inactivating pathways during complete fasting. *Journal of Clinical Endocrinology and Metabolism, 41,* 191–194.

Van Itallie, T. B. (1980). Dietary approaches to the treatment of obesity. In A. J. Stunkard (Ed.), *Obesity.* Philadelphia: W. B. Saunders.

Walker, J., Roberts, S. L., & Halmi, K. A. (1979). Caloric requirements for weight gain in anorexia nervosa. *American Journal of Clinical Nutrition, 32,* 1396.

Warren, S. E., & Steinberg, S. M. (1979). Acid–base and electrolyte disturbances in anorexia nervosa. *American Journal of Psychiatry, 136,* 415–418.

Weiner, H. (1982). Abiding problems in the psychoendocrinology of anorexia nervosa. In *Understanding Anorexia Nervosa and Bulimia: Report of the Fourth Ross Conference in Medical Research.* Columbus: Ross Laboratories.

Weltman, A. (1983). Unfavorable serum lipid profiles in extremely overfat women. *International Journal of Obesity, 7,* 109–114.

White, J. H., & Schnaultz, N. C. (1977). Successful treatment of anorexia nervosa with impiramine. *Diseases of the Nervous System, 38,* 567–568.

Wolff, G., & Money, J. (1973). Late puberty, retarded growth and reversible hyposomatotropinism. In G. J. Williams & J. Money (Eds.), *Traumatic abuse and neglect of children at home.* Baltimore: Johns Hopkins Press.

Wyngaarden, J. B. (1979). Diseases of metabolism. In B. P. Beeson, W. McDermott, & J. B. Wyngaarden (Eds.), *Cecil textbook of medicine* (15th ed.). Philadelphia: W. B. Saunders.

Index